HTML Publishing Bible, Windows 95 Edition

Alan Simpson

IDG Books Worldwide, Inc.
An International Data Group Company

Foster City, CA ◆ Chicago, IL ◆ Indianapolis, IN ◆ Southlake, TX

HTML Publishing Bible, Windows 95 Edition

Published by
IDG Books Worldwide, Inc.
An International Data Group Company
919 E. Hillsdale Blvd.
Suite 400
Foster City, CA 94404

Library of Congress Catalog Card No.: 96-76235

ISBN: 0-7645-3009-7

Printed in the United States of America

10 9 8 7 6 5 4 3 2 1

1E/QY/QX/ZW/IN

Distributed in the United States by IDG Books Worldwide, Inc.

Distributed by Macmillan Canada for Canada; by Contemporanea de Ediciones for Venezuela; by Distribuidora Cuspide for Argentina; by CITEC for Brazil; by Ediciones ZETA S.C.R. Ltda. for Peru; by Editorial Limusa SA for Mexico; by Transworld Publishers Limited in the United Kingdom and Europe; by Academic Bookshop for Egypt; by Levant Distributors S.A.R.L. for Lebanon; by Al Jassim for Saudi Arabia; by Simron Pty. Ltd. for South Africa; by Pustak Mahal for India; by The Computer Bookshop for India; by Toppan Company Ltd. for Japan; by Addison Wesley Publishing Company for Korea; by Longman Singapore Publishers Ltd. for Singapore, Malaysia, Thailand, and Indonesia; by Unalis Corporation for Taiwan; by WS Computer Publishing Company, Inc. for the Philippines; by WoodsLane Pty. Ltd. for Australia; by WoodsLane Enterprises Ltd. for New Zealand. Authorized Sales Agent: Anthony Rudkin Associates for the Middle East and North Africa.

For general information on IDG Books Worldwide's books in the U.S., please call our Consumer Customer Service department at 800-762-2974. For reseller information, including discounts and premium sales, please call our Reseller Customer Service department at 800-434-3422.

For information on where to purchase IDG Books Worldwide's books outside the U.S., contact IDG Books Worldwide's International Sales department at 415-655-3078 or fax 415-655-3281.

For information on foreign language translations, contact IDG Books Worldwide's Foreign & Subsidiary Rights department at 415-655-3018 or fax 415-655-3281.

For sales inquiries and special prices for bulk quantities, contact IDG Books Worldwide's Sales department at 415-655-3200 or write to the address above.

For information on using IDG Books Worldwide's books in the classroom or for ordering examination copies, contact IDG Books Worldwide's Educational Sales department at 800-434-2086 or fax 817-251-8174.

For authorization to photocopy items for corporate, personal, or educational use, please contact Copyright Clearance Center, 222 Rosewood Drive, Danvers, MA 01923, or fax 508-750-4470.

About the Author

Alan Simpson is a free-lance computer guru and veteran author of *digilit* (digital literature, a phrase that he coined). Before writing this book, Alan penned the best selling *Windows 95 Uncut* and dozens of other titles on a wide rage of PC topics including databases, word processing, programming, and other operating systems. These books have been published throughout the world in over a dozen languages, and they've sold millions of copies

For the past 15 months, Alan's focus has been on World Wide Web publishing, and he is the author/publisher of the popular coolnerds Web site (`http://www.coolnerds.com`). Alan lives and works at home in San Diego, California, with his wife, Susan; their two young children; numerous pets; and a hefty collection of computers, printers, modems, and other high-tech gadgets.

ABOUT IDG BOOKS WORLDWIDE

Welcome to the world of IDG Books Worldwide.

IDG Books Worldwide, Inc., is a subsidiary of International Data Group, the world's largest publisher of computer-related information and the leading global provider of information services on information technology. IDG was founded more than 25 years ago and now employs more than 7,700 people worldwide. IDG publishes more than 250 computer publications in 67 countries (see listing below). More than 70 million people read one or more IDG publications each month.

Launched in 1990, IDG Books Worldwide is today the #1 publisher of best-selling computer books in the United States. We are proud to have received 8 awards from the Computer Press Association in recognition of editorial excellence and three from Computer Currents' First Annual Readers' Choice Awards, and our best-selling *...For Dummies®* series has more than 19 million copies in print with translations in 28 languages. IDG Books Worldwide, through a joint venture with IDG's Hi-Tech Beijing, became the first U.S. publisher to publish a computer book in the People's Republic of China. In record time, IDG Books Worldwide has become the first choice for millions of readers around the world who want to learn how to better manage their businesses.

WINNER
Eighth Annual Computer Press Awards 1992

Our mission is simple: Every one of our books is designed to bring extra value and skill-building instructions to the reader. Our books are written by experts who understand and care about our readers. The knowledge base of our editorial staff comes from years of experience in publishing, education, and journalism — experience which we use to produce books for the '90s. In short, we care about books, so we attract the best people. We devote special attention to details such as audience, interior design, use of icons, and illustrations. And because we use an efficient process of authoring, editing, and desktop publishing our books electronically, we can spend more time ensuring superior content and spend less time on the technicalities of making books.

You can count on our commitment to deliver high-quality books at competitive prices on topics you want to read about. At IDG Books Worldwide, we continue in the IDG tradition of delivering quality for more than 25 years. You'll find no better book on a subject than one from IDG Books Worldwide.

John Kilcullen
President and CEO
IDG Books Worldwide, Inc.

WINNER
Ninth Annual Computer Press Awards 1993

IDG Books Worldwide, Inc., is a subsidiary of International Data Group, the world's largest publisher of computer-related information and the leading global provider of information services on information technology. International Data Group publishes over 250 computer publications in 67 countries. Seventy million people read one or more International Data Group publications each month. International Data Group's publications include: **ARGENTINA:** Computerworld Argentina, GamePro, Infoworld, PC World Argentina; **AUSTRALIA:** Australian Macworld, Client/Server Journal, Computer Living, Computerworld, Digital News, Network World, PC World, Publishing Essentials, Reseller; **AUSTRIA:** Computerwelt, PC TEST; **BELARUS:** PC World Belarus; **BELGIUM:** Data News; **BRAZIL:** Annuário de Informática, Computerworld Brazil, Connections, Super Game Power, Macworld, PC World Brazil, Publish Brazil, SUPERGAME; **BULGARIA:** Computerworld Bulgaria, Networkworld/Bulgaria, PC & MacWorld Bulgaria; **CANADA:** CIO Canada, ComputerWorld Canada, InfoCanada, Network World Canada, Reseller World; **CHILE:** Computerworld Chile, GamePro, PC World Chile; **COLUMBIA:** Computerworld Colombia, GamePro, PC World Colombia; **COSTA RICA:** PC World Costa Rica/Nicaragua; **THE CZECH AND SLOVAK REPUBLICS:** Computerworld Czechoslovakia, Elektronika Czechoslovakia, PC World Czechoslovakia; **DENMARK:** Communications World, Computerworld Danmark, Macworld Danmark, PC World Danmark, PC World Danmark Supplements, TECH World; **DOMINICAN REPUBLIC:** PC World Republica Dominicana; **ECUADOR:** PC World Ecuador, GamePro; **EGYPT:** Computerworld Middle East, PC World Middle East; **EL SALVADOR:** PC World Centro America; **FINLAND:** MikroPC, Tietoverkko, Tietoviikko; **FRANCE:** Distributique, Golden, Info PC, Le Guide du Monde Informatique, Le Monde Informatique, Reseaux & Telecoms; **GERMANY:** Computer Business, Computerwoche, Computerwoche Extra, Computerwoche Focus, Electronic Entertainment, GamePro, I/M Information Management, Macwelt, PC Welt; **GREECE:** GamePro, Macworld & Publish; **GUATEMALA:** PC World Centro America; **HONDURAS:** PC World Centro America; **HONG KONG:** Computerworld Hong Kong, PCWorld Hong Kong, Publish in Asia; **HUNGARY:** ABCD CD-ROM, Computerworld Szamitastechnika, PC & Mac World Hungary, PC-X Magazine; **INDIA:** Computerworld India, PC World India, Publish in Asia; **INDONESIA:** InfoKomputer PC World, Komputek Computerworld, Publish in Asia; **IRELAND:** ComputerScope, PC Live!; **ISRAEL:** PC World 32 BIT, People & Computers; **ITALY:** Computerworld Italia, Computerworld Italia Special Editions, Lotus Italia, Macworld Italia, Networking Italia, PC Shopping, PC World Italia, PC World/Walt Disney; **JAPAN:** Macworld Japan, Nikkei Personal Computing, SunWorld Japan, Windows World Japan; **KENYA:** East African Computer News; **KOREA:** Hi-Tech Information/Computerworld, Macworld Korea, PC World Korea; **MACEDONIA:** PC World Macedonia; **MALAYSIA:** Computerworld Malaysia, PC World Malaysia, Publish in Asia; **MEXICO:** Computerworld Mexico, GamePro, Macworld, PC World Mexico; **MYANMAR:** PC World Myanmar; **NETHERLANDS:** Computable, Computer! Totaal, LAN Magazine, Macworld, Net Magazine; **NEW ZEALAND:** Computer Buyer, Computerworld New Zealand, MTB, Network World, PC World New Zealand; **NICARAGUA:** PC World Costa Rica/Nicaragua; **NIGERIA:** PC World Africa; **NORWAY:** Computerworld Norge, Computerworld Privat, CW Rapport Klient/Tjener, CW Rapport Nettverk & Telecom, CW Rapport Offentlig Sektor, IDG's KURSGUIDE, Macworld Norge, Multimedia World, PC World Ekspress, PC World Nettverk, PC World Norge, PC World's Produktguide, Windows Spesial; **PAKISTAN:** Computerworld Pakistan, PC World Pakistan; **PANAMA:** GamePro, PC World Panama; **PARAGUAY:** PC World Paraguay; **P. R. OF CHINA:** China Computerworld, China Infoworld, Computer & Communication, Electronic Product World, Electronics Today, Game Camp, PC World China, Popular Computer Week, Software World, Telecom Product World; **PERU:** Computerworld Peru, GamePro, PC World Profesional Peru, PC World Peru; **POLAND:** Computerworld Poland, Computerworld Special Report, Macworld, Networld, PC World Komputer; **PHILIPPINES:** Computerworld Philippines, PC Digest, Publish in Asia; **PORTUGAL:** Cerebro/PC World, Correio Informático/Computerworld, Mac•In/PC•In Portugal; **PUERTO RICO:** PC World Puerto Rico; **ROMANIA:** Computerworld Romania, PC World Romania, Telecom Romania; **RUSSIA:** Computerworld Rossiya, Network World Russia, PC World Russia; **SINGAPORE:** Computerworld Singapore, PC World Singapore, Publish in Asia; **SLOVENIA:** MONITOR; **SOUTH AFRICA:** Computing S.A., Network World S.A., Software World; **SPAIN:** Computerworld España, COMUNICACIONES WORLD, Dealer World, Macworld España, PC World España; **SWEDEN:** CAP&Design, Computer Sweden, Corporate Computing, MacWorld, Maxi Data, MikroDatorn, Nätverk & Kommunikation, PC/Aktiv, PC World, Windows World; **SWITZERLAND:** Computerworld Schweiz, Macworld Schweiz, PCtip; **TAIWAN:** Computerworld Taiwan, Macworld Taiwan, PC World Taiwan, Publish Taiwan, Windows World; **THAILAND:** Thai Computerworld, Publish in Asia; **TURKEY:** Computerworld Monitör, MACWORLD Turkiye, PC WORLD Turkiye; **UKRAINE:** Computerworld Kiev, Computers & Software Magazine, PC World Ukraine; **UNITED KINGDOM:** Acorn User, Amiga Action, Amiga Computing, Amiga, Appletalk, CD Powerplay, CD-ROM Now, Computing, Connexion, GamePro, Lotus Magazine, Macaction, Macworld, Open Computing, Parents and Computers, PC Home, PC Works, The WEB; **UNITED STATES:** Cable in the Classroom, CD Review, CIO Magazine, Computerworld, Computerworld Client/Server Journal, Digital Video Magazine, DOS World, Electronic, InfoWorld, I-Way, Macworld, Maximize, MULTIMEDIA WORLD, Network World, PC World, PUBLISH, SWATPro Magazine, Video Event, WebMaster; **URUGUAY:** PC World Uruguay; **VENEZUELA:** Computerworld Venezuela, GamePro, PC World Venezuela; and **VIETNAM:** PC World Vietnam. 10/17/95b

Dedication

To Susan, Ashley, and Alec.

Credits

Senior Vice President and Group Publisher
Brenda McLaughlin

Acquisitions Manager
Gregory Croy

Acquisitions Editor
Ellen Camm

Software Acquisitions Editor
Tracy Lehman Cramer

Brand Manager
Melisa M. Duffy

Managing Editor
Andy Cummings

Administrative Assistant
Laura J. Moss

Editorial Assistant
Timothy Borek

Production Director
Beth Jenkins

Production Assistant
Jacalyn L. Pennywell

Supervisor of Project Coordination
Cindy L. Phipps

Supervisor of Page Layout
Kathie S. Schnorr

Supervisor of Graphics and Design
Shelley Lea

Reprint/Blueline Coordination
Tony Augsburger
Patricia R. Reynolds
Theresa Sánchez-Baker

Senior Development Editor
Erik Dafforn

Editor
Kerrie Klein

Technical Reviewer
Dennis Cox

Media Archive Coordination
Leslie Popplewell
Melissa Stauffer
Jason Marcuson

Project Coordinator
Sherry Gomoll

Graphics Coordination
Gina Scott
Angela F. Hunckler

Production Page Layout
E. Shawn Aylsworth
Cameron Booker
Linda M. Boyer
Mark Owens
Anna Rohrer

Proofreaders
Sandra Profant
Dwight Ramsey
Robert Springer
Carrie Voorhis
Ethel Winslow

Indexer
Steve Rath

Cover Design

Acknowledgments

Every book is a team effort, and this one is no exception. Much credit, and my sincerest thanks, are due the following people who contributed to the creation of this book:

To the folks at IDG who produced and published this book. In particular, Greg Croy, Erik Dafforn, Kerrie Klein, Melisa Duffy, Dennis Cox, and the terrific layout and proofreading staff.

To Elizabeth Olson, who actually wrote most of Part VI and Appendix B.

To the fine people at Webs R Us, who actually got my first Web site up-and-running, and helped me tremendously during the early stages of a fairly long and confusing learning curve.

To the gang at Waterside Productions, my literary agency, for bringing me this (and many other) opportunities. And for taking care of all the business details so I can focus on the part I like – the creative stuff.

And last but certainly not least, many thanks to Susan, Ashley, and Alec for their patience and support through yet another long and attention-consuming Daddy project.

(The publisher would like to give special thanks to Patrick J. McGovern, who made this book possible.)

Contents at a Glance

Table of Contents

Chapter 19: Tweaking HTML Tags 303

Part IV: Even Cooler Web Pages 311

Chapter 20: Coolsite: Instant Web Site 313

Chapter 21: Charts, Word Art, and More 341

Chapter 22: Improving Your Image(s) 361

Introduction

Hello, and welcome to *HTML Publishing Bible*. The premise of this book is fairly simple. I want to take you from wherever you are in your Web expertise right now and provide you with the knowledge, tools, and skills required to become a world-class, Web publishing guru. Part of the trick to achieving that goal is ensuring that I start at wherever you happen to be in your Web experience at the moment. After all, learning only occurs on the fringes of what we already know, so here I assume two things:

- ✦ You know that a thing called the World Wide Web exists, and you want to be a part of it
- ✦ You know the basics of how to work a PC with Windows 95

Despite the fact that this is a large book, I do want to help you accomplish that goal with a certain efficiency. Those of you who have read my earlier books know that I'm not one to fill pages with long, boring discourses on "theoretical" issues, history, and old technologies. This book is no exception. As in all my books, the focus here is on how to get the job done, with minimal fuss and confusion.

I don't expect everyone to read the book cover to cover. A book this size has to work as a reference as well as a tutorial. I've broken down the material into sections, small chapters, and even smaller sections within chapters, so you should have no problem looking up information on an as-needed basis. But for those of you with the patience to read through it, I have come up with an overall strategy for helping you achieve Web publishing guruhood . . .

The Strategy of This Book

The idea here is to get you from point A (wherever you are right now) to point Z (guruhood) fairly quickly. The book is structured in such a way as to take you through all the "need-to-know" information in the order in which you need to learn it:

Part I: Touring Cyberspace — Windows Style

Knowing that the World Wide Web exists isn't quite a sufficient starting point for publishing in the Web. You need to get in there and experience it for yourself, first-hand, as a "consumer" or "reader." Part I shows you how to do that, in case you haven't gotten that far yet.

Part II: How to Establish Your Own Web Site

Next, you need to find a place to publish your Web site. You need to put Web pages on a computer that has a full-time, high-speed connection to the Internet. This process can take weeks (much of it spent waiting), especially if you want a custom domain name (that is, `www.`*`yournamehere`*`.com`). Part II presents all the options and techniques for getting that squared away while you're building your site on your own PC.

Part III: Authoring Cool Web Pages with Word Internet Assistant

With all the details of getting connected to the Web and finding a place to publish your pages out of the way, you can begin creating your Web site. This task you'll do on your own PC, using tools that you're (hopefully) somewhat familiar with already. In this book, I've chosen Microsoft's Word Internet Assistant (Word IA) as the authoring tool. I discuss why I chose Word IA a little later in this Introduction.

The goals of Part III are to teach you all the basics of creating Web pages, from basic text formatting and graphics to hyperlinks, tables, and interactive forms. By the time you finish this part of the book, you'll be able to create a Web site that's as good as most of the sites currently out there on the Web. But in keeping with the tradition of my previous book (*Windows 95 Uncut*), we want to go beyond "as good as" to a higher level of expertise.

Part IV: Even Cooler Web Pages

Part IV takes you into more sophisticated Web authoring techniques, including using a database to manage lists; adding charts, equations, and Word Art; creating and modifying your own Web graphics; adding multimedia to your site; creating clickable image maps; and designing sites that use Netscape-style frames.

Part V: Hyper-Interactivity with JavaScript

For the truly hardcore, Part V teaches you all about JavaScript — a relatively easy programming language that can add new levels of interactivity (what I call "hyper-interactivity") to your site. I've included tons of sample code on the CD-ROM, most of which you can just cut and paste from my pages right into your own.

Part VI: Potpourri

Part VI is sort of a "catch-all" area for topics that didn't quite fit in with the main flow of the book. Here I talk about using Netscape Navigator for browsing the Web and creating Web pages. Also, the important issues of security, "doing money" on the Net, and promotion — getting people to visit your site — are covered here. And finally, I briefly cover those non-World Wide Web features of the Internet — e-mail, FTP, and newsgroups — especially those aspects that are of interest to Web publishers.

Reference Guides

Appendixes B and C provide quick reference to HTML and JavaScript for when you just need to look up some little, technical detail. And I've also pointed out places on the Web where you can get some great electronic reference guides for free.

Icons in the book

The book does have some margin icons, so I guess I'd better explain what those are about.

This icon signifies your basic tip: a trick, technique, or other tidbit that's worth calling special attention to just so you don't miss it.

Struggling with Web publishing can be confusing and puzzling. The "Puzzled?" icon is an attempt to predict where you may get that Rubik's Cube feeling and an attempt to bring you to the "A-ha!" experience a little sooner.

This icon refers to a source of additional information on a topic (just in case I didn't already tell you enough to bore you to tears).

If there is a way to undo a mistake, fix a problem, or get out of a jam, this icon points the way.

This icon points out a technique that you really need to think about before you act. Tread carefully, because if you make mistake, it'll be difficult — or impossible — to undo the mistake.

About the CD-ROM

The CD-ROM that comes with this book includes lots of tools, examples, and gizmos that will be valuable to both aspiring and accomplished Web publishers:

- **Microsoft Internet Explorer 2.0:** In case you don't already have a Web browser, here's one you can install right from the CD-ROM for free.
- **Microsoft Word Internet Assistant for Windows 95:** A must-have tool for all Web authors and publishers. Lets you create dazzling Web pages without the nit-picky headaches of manually typing in HTML tags.
- **Coolsite:** An exclusive shareware app that lets you create commonly-used lists (Frequently Asked Questions, news items, tips, and links to other sites) in a simple, fill-in-the-blanks format. With a push of a button, Coolsite then produces HTML documents ready for publication on the Web.
- **Paint Shop Pro:** This new, 32-bit Windows 95 version of Paint Shop Pro offers full graphics capabilities and supports Internet GIF and JPEG formats, including transparent-background GIFs. Another must-have for Web publishers.
- **Map This!:** A terrific tool for creating state-of-the-art, client-side clickable image maps with Windows 95 ease.
- **WinZip for Windows 95:** This new Windows 95 version of the classic zip-and-unzip utility supports the Internet TAR format.
- **Web Art:** Some ready-to-use clip-art images, including backgrounds, bullets, buttons, lines, and sound clips, that you can cut and paste right into your own Web pages.
- **Examples:** Sample video clips, forms, entire Web sites (with Frames!), and a ton of pre-written, ready-to-use JavaScript code!

Complete instructions for using the CD-ROM are in Appendix A.

HTML Publishing Bible Web Site

The World Wide Web is constantly evolving. No printed book can keep up with all the changes. But a Web site can. I've set aside a special area in my own Web site just for *HTML Publishing Bible* readers. There you can catch up on all the latest tools and techniques, ask questions, and find *tons* of more great stuff that you can add to your Web publishing arsenal, free of charge! Just point your Web browser to `http://www.coolnerds.com` at any time.

About the Products I've Chosen

As you probably know, the Internet is a *multi-platform* environment. Which is to say, it's not just for PCs, or Macs, or Unix machines. Anyone can hook up. Sometimes, that fact can cause a lot of confusion. For example, you might be reading some book on the Internet, feeling totally lost, only to realize that the author is talking about everything from a Unix standpoint. And you don't have Unix.

Well, as it turns out, even though the Internet is multi-platform, *creating* a Web site is *not* a multi-platform endeavor. You author Web pages in exactly the same way you author word-processing documents, spreadsheets, databases, graphics — whatever, by sitting at your own PC and using the programs that you have available to you. When you present those published pages on the World Wide Web, the Internet itself takes care of presenting those pages to all members of the Internet.

Given all of these facts, I chose Windows 95 as the platform for this book for one very simple reason: It's what I use for my own work. Given Windows 95 as my authoring environment, it then became a matter of choosing authoring tools that work best in that environment. Word Internet Assistant got about a zillion points in that category because it essentially lets you use *all* of Microsoft Office as your authoring weapon, without learning HTML first. This means you can leverage whatever knowledge you have of the (quite formidable) Microsoft Office suite of applications into creating Web pages, without learning much of anything new. This is good if your goal is to be productive.

Granted, there are tons of great authoring tools out there, and I could have chosen any one of them. Choosing Word IA is in no way an attempt to discredit any of the other fine products out there. But I had to pick *something* to work with. Word IA works well for me, and I trust it will do the same for you.

You might also notice that I display many of my sample Web pages in Microsoft's Internet Explorer Web browser. This is not because I'm some kind of Microsoft bigot. I'm well aware of the fact that there are many fine Web browsers out there. And in fact, I'm quite a Netscape Navigator fan. But I often use Internet Explorer as the sample Web browser in this book because the tight integration between Windows 95, Microsoft Office, Word Internet Assistant, and Internet Explorer makes for a smooth, clean environment in which to author and in which to learn.

In later chapters, I do get into features that (at the time of this writing) are supported only by Netscape Navigator 2.0 — namely *frames* and *JavaScript.* But before you get into that more advanced stuff, you really need to understand the basics of creating Web pages. And I think you'll find the Word IA/Internet Explorer combination to be a quick and efficient environment in which to learn those basics.

Enough Ado

So now, without any further proverbial ado, let's get down to the business of making you into a Web publishing guru. Just one more thing: I want you to know that I'm well aware of the fact that there are zillions of books on Web publishing out there. I thank you for choosing this book and trusting me to help you achieve your goals. I hope I live up to your expectations. As always, I'm wide open to suggestions on how to improve this book for future editions. If you have a suggestion or a question or just want to say hi, you can reach me at any of the following addresses:

Alan Simpson
P.O. Box 630
Rancho Santa Fe, CA 92067
Fax: 619-756-0159
Web: `http://www.coolnerds.com`
E-mail: `alan@coolnerds.com`
AOL: coolnerds
MSN: coolnerds
CIS: 72420,2236 (or coolnerds, once they get those addresses working)

Touring Cyberspace — Windows Style

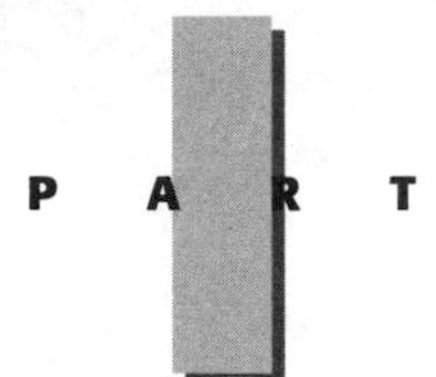

✦ ✦ ✦ ✦

In This Part

✦ ✦ ✦ ✦

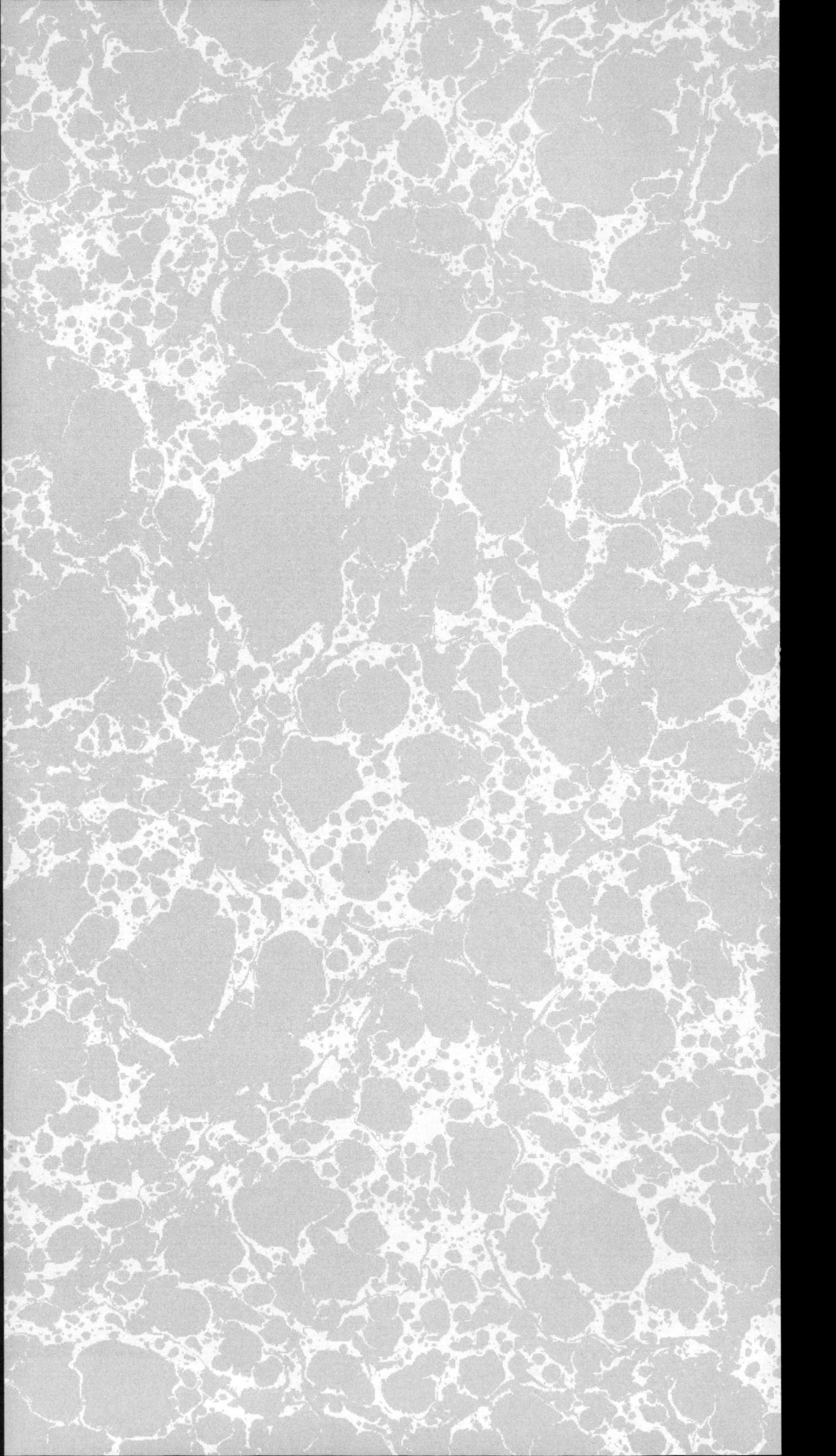

CHAPTER 1

Get Your Modem Working

In This Chapter

Checking your modem

Purchasing a modem

Installing a modem

Testing and troubleshooting a modem

Some of you reading this book undoubtedly are experienced Web cruisers. You can hop on the Web and browse around anytime you feel like it. If you are such a person, you probably can just skip this chapter and browse lightly over Chapters 2 and 3.

Others of you reading this book may not have experienced the World Wide Web first-hand yet. You know that the Internet and World Wide Web are hot new opportunities for doing business. You know that you want to have a presence on the Web and get your shingle or virtual storefront out there. You just don't know how to go about doing that.

These first four chapters are for you folks. In these chapters, I want to get you connected to the World Wide Web as a *consumer,* so that you can experience the Web from the viewpoint of your potential customers. It's not absolutely *necessary* that you go through this process. You could, for instance, just hand over your company brochure (and a check) to an Internet Presence Provider and have the people there construct and host your Web site. I discuss how you do that in Chapter 7.

But if you plan to do any publishing or business on the Web, you really should have a feel for what the Web is all about — even if you only spend a couple of hours a month checking out the sites. Also throughout this book, I occasionally refer to useful stuff that you can download from the Internet for free. And I may also mention some sites worth seeing on the Web. You won't be able to do any of these things, however, if you can't browse the Web from your own PC.

In these first four chapters, I show you a quick and easy way to get connected to the Internet and how to browse the World Wide Web by using Microsoft's Internet Explorer. I also use The Microsoft Network (MSN) as your connection to the Internet. I'm not doing this to sell you on Microsoft — you can connect to the Internet in dozens of different ways without using any Microsoft products. The only reason I'm using Microsoft products in these chapters is that connecting to the Internet in this fashion is quick, easy, and not terribly expensive. I discuss alternative connections in Part II.

Puzzled? If you are a member of a LAN in a large company or university and your organization is already connected to the Internet, you probably won't need a modem. Instead, you need to talk to the Network Administrator about getting access to the Internet via the LAN from your own PC.

The very first item that you need in order to get connected to the Internet is a modem that's properly installed and ready to go. If you already have a modem installed and working, you can skip this chapter. But if you do not have a modem or if you haven't used your modem yet, read on.

Is Your Modem Ready to Go?

If you are not sure whether there is a working modem connected to your PC, here's an easy way to find out (assuming that you are using Windows 95):

1. Click the Start button, and choose Settings⇨Control Panel.
2. Double-click the Modems icon.
3. If you see at least one modem listed in the Modems Properties dialog box, as shown in Figure 1-1, your modem is installed and ready to go. Click OK, close the Control Panel dialog box, and skip down to the "Testing and Troubleshooting the Modem" section later in this chapter.

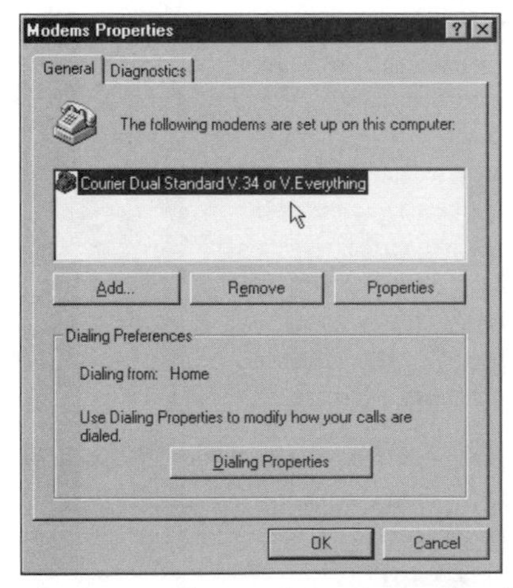

Figure 1-1: The Modems Properties dialog box tells me that a "Courier Dual Standard V.34 or V.Everything" modem is already set up and ready for use on this computer.

4. If no modem is listed in the Modems Properties dialog box or if the system takes you directly to the Install New Modem Wizard shown in Figure 1-2, then a modem has not been set up on this computer.

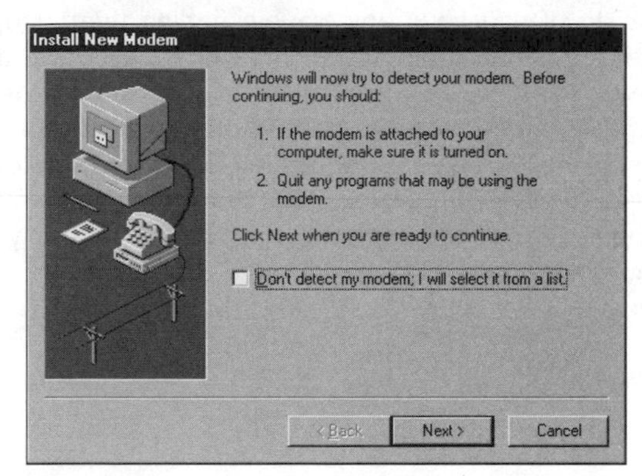

Figure 1-2: The Install New Modem Wizard may appear if you have never installed a modem on this PC.

If, in Step 4, you discovered that no modem is set up on this PC, your next steps should be to purchase a modem, physically attach it to your computer, and set it up on the computer, as discussed in the next two sections. For now, however, you can click the Cancel button (if one appears), close any open windows, and proceed with the next section.

Buying a Modem

If you don't already have a modem, you'll need to go to a computer store and buy one. There are three main factors to consider when purchasing a modem:

- **Speed.** You want to buy the fastest modem you can afford. Preferably 28.8 Kbps, although 14.4 Kbps will work (it will just be painfully slow).
- **Ease-Of-Installation.** If you purchase a modem that is Windows 95 Plug-and-Play compatible, the modem will be easier to install and configure.
- **Style.** You can choose an internal modem, an external modem, or if you use a portable computer with a PC Card slot (also called a PCMCIA slot), you can use a PC Card modem.

If you are not sure which "style" of modem is best for you, be aware that any style of modem will work. A modem is a modem regardless of how you have to install it. But each style has some advantages and disadvantages that can help you make your decision.

ISDN modem and connection

As an alternative to using a regular modem to connect to the Internet, you can get a special ISDN account, which also requires a special modem. The advantage of ISDN is that it's about twice as fast as a 28.8K "regular" modem. Establishing an ISDN account is somewhat complicated and can take several weeks. Step 1 is to contact your Internet Service Provider to determine if ISDN is possible. Then let it guide you through setting up an account with your local telephone company and purchasing an appropriate ISDN modem.

As a Windows 95 user, you'll also have to get a copy of the ISDN drivers from Windows 95. If you have any trouble finding them, stop by the Windows 95 area of my Web site at `http://www.coolnerds.com` and look for information on ISDN. Or send me a fax at 619-756-0159 requesting the latest news on ISDN connections. Be sure to include your e-mail address or fax number so I can reply.

An internal modem has several advantages over an external modem. For one, an internal modem does not take up any desk space because it goes inside your PC. Also, an internal modem doesn't need external power or a cable connecting it to another cable. As a result, it eliminates the need for two outside cables and the need to plug yet another device into the wall socket. The only disadvantage to an internal modem, for some people at least, is that you have to take the PC apart (a little) to install the modem. This task is easy to do, but some people are very skittish about taking the case off a PC and messing with its insides. In that case, an internal modem might be a little unnerving to install!

An external modem resides outside your PC. Its main advantage is that you don't need to take the PC apart to install the modem. Also, it is possible to share one external modem among several computers that are hooked together in a local area network (LAN). External modems have some disadvantages, however. For one, you will probably need to plug the modem into the wall socket. You also will need to plug the modem into a serial port on the back of your PC.

The advantage to a PC Card modem is that it is small enough to be portable (not much larger than a credit card). But, of course, you can only use it with a PC that has a PCMCIA slot into which you can plug the modem. Typically, only portable computers have a PCMCIA slot.

Hot Stuff

PC Card modems also come in two flavors — regular modems for regular phone lines and cellular modems for cellular phones. The latter requires that you already have a cellular phone with an appropriate jack for connecting a modem. Also, the folks who sold you the cellular phone may need to tweak the phone's sensitivity in order to get the phone to work with the modem.

Hooking Up the Modem

Once you have a modem in hand, you need to physically connect it to your PC and to a standard phone jack on the wall. You should follow the modem manufacturer's instructions to do this. *But if the manufacturer's instructions include steps for installing DOS drivers or Windows 3.x drivers, you should ignore those instructions!* You'll want to use the 32-bit Windows 95 drivers for your modem rather than the old, 16-bit drivers designed for DOS and Windows 95. The basic installation procedure will go something like this:

- ✦ Turn off everything (system unit, monitor, and so on).
- ✦ Plug the modem into the PC. (With an internal modem, you plug into a slot inside the system unit. With an external modem, you plug into a serial port on the back of the PC. With a PC Card modem, you plug the entire modem into the PCMCIA slot.)
- ✦ Plug the *Line* or *Telco* jack on the modem into the phone jack on the wall, using a standard phone-line type of cable.
- ✦ Optionally, if you'll be using the same phone number for regular voice calls, you can plug a regular telephone into the phone jack on the modem, again using standard phone-line cables.

Puzzled? Most PCMCIA modems do not provide a jack for a connection to the telephone. If your laptop computer has a built-in speaker phone and sound system, however, you can use those capabilities for regular voice telephone calls.

- ✦ If you installed an external modem, you then need to plug the modem into a wall outlet and turn on the modem.

At this point, the manufacturer's instructions may tell you how to install the DOS and Windows 3.*x* drivers for the modem. Once again, ignore those instructions, and follow the instructions under "Installing a Modem" section instead.

Figure 1-3 shows how everything will be wired up if you install an external modem. Remember, though, that the connection between the modem and the telephone is optional; the modem requires it only if you need to use the same phone number for voice calls.

Figure 1-4 shows how an internal modem will connect. There's just one cable running from the modem to the wall jack. Optionally, if you need to use the same phone number for voice calls, you can also connect a telephone to the phone jack on the modem.

The connection to a PC Card modem is usually pretty simple. The modem slides into the PCMCIA slot in the laptop computer. Then a cable connects the modem to the phone jack on the wall (see Figure 1-5). Or, in the case of a cellular modem, the cable connects the modem to a cellular phone.

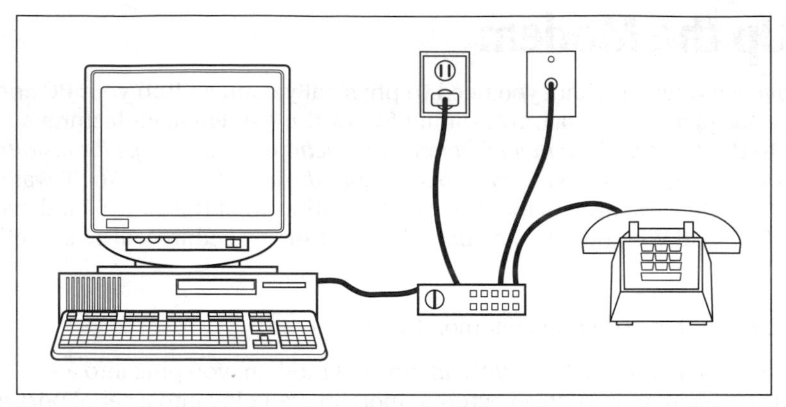

Figure 1-3: An external modem all hooked up and ready to install the software.

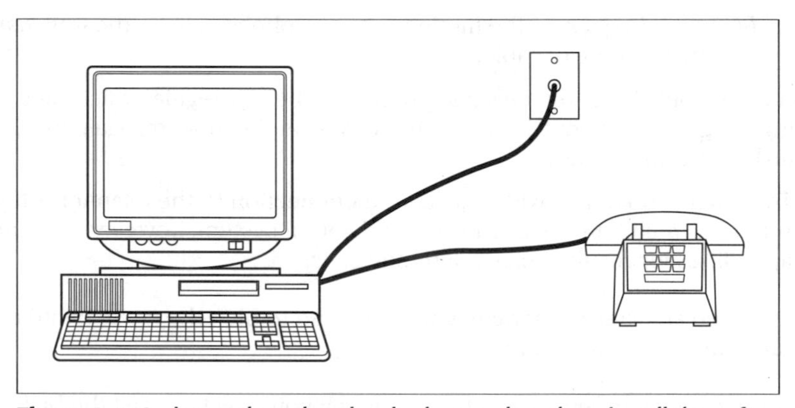

Figure 1-4: An internal modem hooked up and ready to install the software.

Figure 1-5: A PC Card modem slides into the PCMCIA slot on a portable computer and then connects to the phone jack on the wall, or to a cellular phone.

Installing the Modem Software

After you have physically connected the modem to the PC and telephone lines, you need to tell Windows 95 that the modem is there. This is called *installing the modem* and is the step where the 32-bit Windows 95 drivers for the modem (rather than the old 16-bit drivers) will be installed. Follow these steps:

1. Gather up your original Windows 95 floppy disks or CD-ROM (you may be prompted for them during the installation).
2. Start up your PC and Windows 95 as you normally would.
3. Windows 95 may detect your modem automatically and install the appropriate drivers. If that occurs, just follow any instructions that appear on the screen until you get to the normal Windows 95 desktop. Then skip to "Testing and Troubleshooting the Modem" later in this chapter.
4. If Windows 95 doesn't automatically detect your modem at startup, click the Start button and choose Settings⇨Control Panel.
5. Double-click the Modems icon. The system may take you to the Install New Modem Wizard, as was shown in Figure 1-2. If so, skip to Step 7 now.
6. In the Modems Properties dialog box that appears, click the Add button. The system will take you to the Install New Modem Wizard.
7. Follow the Wizard's instructions and answer all its questions to complete the installation of your modem.

After you've finished with the modem installation and you're sure that the modem is connected to the phone jack on the wall, you should test the modem to make sure that you can get a dial tone, as described in the next section.

Testing and Troubleshooting the Modem

Once your modem is installed, you'll want to make sure that it is working properly before you actually try to get onto the Internet. Here's a simple way to test the modem to make sure that it can get a dial tone and dial out:

1. Click the Start button and point to Programs.
2. Point to Accessories and click Phone Dialer to open that program (Figure 1-6).

Puzzled? If Phone Dialer isn't available in the Accessories menu, you just haven't yet installed it. You can just skip this little test or install Phone Dialer now. To do the latter, click the Start button and choose Settings⇨Control Panel. Double-click Add/Remove Programs, click the Windows Setup tab, click Communications, and then click the Details button. Choose Phone Dialer (so that a check mark appears next to it), click the OK button twice, and follow the instructions on the screen.

Figure 1-6: The phone Dialer that comes with Windows 95 is a quick and easy way to check your modem connection.

3. Enter a phone number (such as your own or the number you dial to get the local time/weather) by clicking the buttons in the Phone Dialer dialog box or by typing the number at the keyboard.
4. Click the Dial button.

If all is well, you'll see a message like one shown in Figure 1-7. You may also hear the sound of the dial tone and the modem dialing the number you entered. You can click Hang Up now, because the sole purpose of this test was to make sure that you could get a dial tone and dial out. You can now move on to Chapter 2.

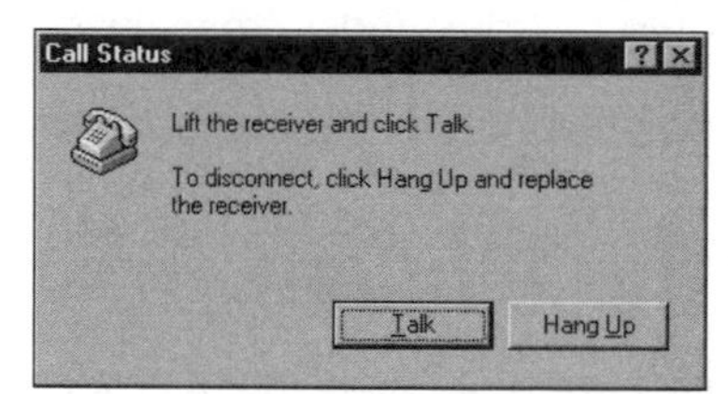

Figure 1-7: Phone Dialer successfully dialed the number you specified.

If your modem can't dial out and you see an error message on the screen when you try to dial out, you'll need to resolve the problem now, before you try to use your modem to get online. I know from experience that the most common modem problem is wrong cabling, so I suggest you follow these troubleshooting steps first.

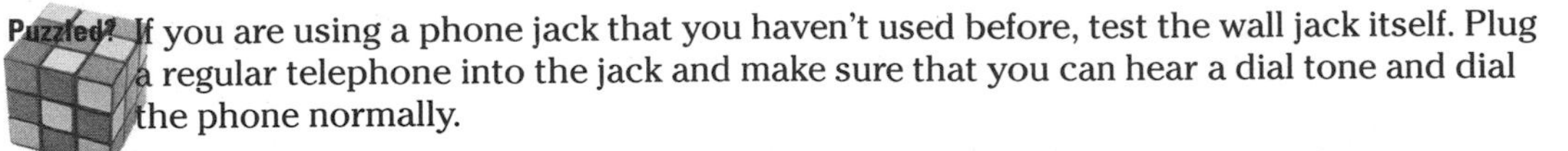

If you are using a phone jack that you haven't used before, test the wall jack itself. Plug a regular telephone into the jack and make sure that you can hear a dial tone and dial the phone normally.

1. Go to where the modem is plugged into the phone jack in the wall.
2. Carefully follow the cable to the modem and make sure that cable is plugged into the socket labeled Line or Jack or Telco on the modem, NOT the jack labeled Phone.
3. If you are using an external modem, make sure that you have plugged it into the wall and turned it on. Most external modems have an indicator light that tells you whether the modem is on or off.

If you discover any problems during those steps, just rectify the problem and try using Phone Dialer to dial out again. If problems persist, I suggest that you try the Troubleshooter built into Windows 95. Follow these steps:

1. Click the Start button, and then click Help.
2. Click the Contents tab, and then double-click the Troubleshooting book.
3. Double-click "If you have trouble using your modem" (Figure 1-8).

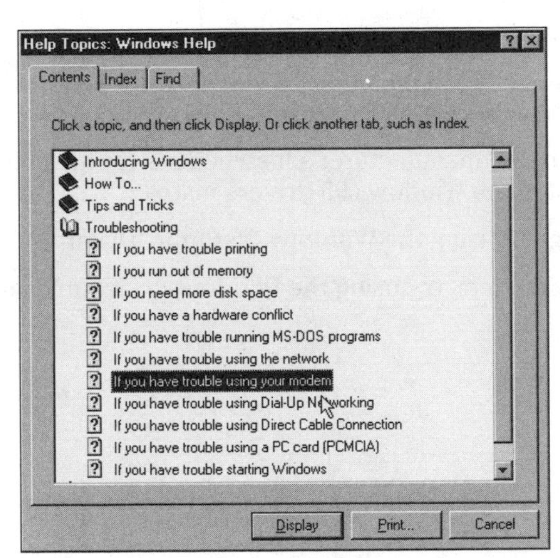

Figure 1-8: Use the built-in troubleshooters to help resolve modem problems.

4. Choose "Dialing doesn't work correctly," and then follow the instructions presented by the Troubleshooter.

If you still can't get the modem to work after trying a couple of other troubleshooters, you can try these tricks:

✦ If you're having problems with an internal or external modem, try the Device Conflict Troubleshooter (Start⇨Help⇨Contents⇨Troubleshooting⇨"If you have a hardware conflict").

✦ If you're having problems with a PCMCIA modem, try the PC Card Troubleshooter (Start⇨Help⇨Contents⇨Troubleshooting⇨"If you have trouble using a PC card (PCMCIA)").

If you *still* can't get the modem to dial out, then you'll probably need to install the manufacturer's DOS and Windows drivers, as per the manufacturer's instructions that came with the modem. Also check the Troubleshooting section of the modem's manual for other techniques that you can try to resolve any problems.

Summary

Here's a quick recap of what you learned in this chapter:

✦ You need a modem to connect to the Internet.

✦ The modem connects your computer to the phone jack on the wall.

✦ You only need to connect the modem to a telephone if you'll be using the same phone number for both data (modem) and voice calls.

✦ When installing a modem, ignore the manufacturer's instructions for installing DOS/Windows 3.*x* software. Install the Windows 95 drivers instead.

✦ To test your modem, try dialing out using the Windows 95 Phone Dialer.

✦ If you have problems with your modem, try using the Windows 95 troubleshooters to correct any problems.

✦ ✦ ✦

CHAPTER 2

A Quick and Easy Internet On-Ramp

In This Chapter

Getting an account with an Internet Service Provider

Keeping your expenses to a minimum

Setting up an Internet account via The Microsoft Network (MSN)

Connecting to the Internet via MSN

Downloading the latest Internet Explorer and Virtual Explorer

Once you have your modem working, the second step to getting on the World Wide Web is to get an Internet Service Provider (ISP). If you can already "surf the Net" from your PC, you can skip this chapter. Also, if you already have an account with America Online, CompuServe, Prodigy, or one of the other large commercial services, you can probably hop onto the Internet from that service. Just log on to your service as you usually do and look around for information about connecting to the Internet. In that case, you can also skip this chapter.

If you currently have no access to the Internet or to any other online service, you can follow the simple instructions in this chapter to get onto the Internet via The Microsoft Network (MSN). Keep in mind, however, that MSN is not the only way to get onto the Internet — not by a longshot. There are hundreds of Internet Service Providers to choose from. I use MSN as a practical example because as a Windows 95 user, you probably have everything you need to set up an account.

Signing up with MSN is not a lifelong commitment, so don't be afraid to give it a try. After you've gained some experience using the Web and are ready to "open up shop" on the Web, then you may want to find a different Internet Service Provider. No problem. You can either keep your MSN/Internet account or just cancel it. No big deal either way.

What It Will Cost You

You may have heard that the Internet is free. That statement is only half true. Before you can use the Internet, you need to get an account with an Internet Service Provider, and that is going to cost some money. How *much* it costs depends on many factors, which I'll discuss in future chapters. But if you don't work for a large organization that already has an Internet account, the bottom line is that you have to pay the ISP yourself.

When people say that the Internet is free, they are referring to the fact that the phone company is not involved in any long-distance transactions. For example, whether you read a Web page from halfway around the block or halfway around the world, the cost is the same — nothing. Whether you send an e-mail to your neighbor or someone in Japan or Sweden, the cost is the same — nothing. You only pay for the connection between your PC and your Internet Service Provider.

Internet Service Provider charges

If you use MSN as your Internet Service Provider, you can choose from several subscription plans, as shown in Table 2-1. You should note, however, that any dollar figures I give you in this book are ballpark figures. Prices constantly change in the competitive PC industry, so always double-check with the vendor before you assume that the price estimates I have provided here are still accurate.

Table 2-1
Approximate Costs of MSN Membership Plans within the United States

Plan	*Fee*	*Hours per Month*	*Each Additional Hour*
Charter (until 3/31/96)	$39.95 annual	3	$2.50
Standard	$4.95 monthly	3	$2.50
Frequent User	$19.95 monthly	20	$2.00

Phone company charges

Whether your Internet connect time shows up on your phone bill depends on the type of service you have from your local phone company and the prefix of the number you dial to connect to the Internet. For example, here in my home, I have a typical, residential *flat rate* service with Pacific Bell. I can dial local numbers within a radius of approximately 16 miles for free. I can dial nearby numbers for a little more.

To determine exactly where you can call for free, open your local telephone directory (the White Pages) and turn to the Local and Nearby Calling section of the Customer Guide. The guide should show you which prefixes you can dial for free (if any) and which carry a toll. If you can find an ISP that offers a phone number within your toll-free calling area, then you can keep Ma Bell out of the picture altogether. The only charges that you will incur are those that come from the ISP.

If you cannot find a toll-free number to an Internet Service Provider, then you will chalk up some additional phone charges when you call it. Your call to the ISP will be treated like, and billed as, any normal voice call. For example, if it costs a penny a minute to talk on the phone to that number and you stay on the Internet for an hour, 60 cents will be tacked onto your phone bill for that call.

Most ISPs try to offer several different phone numbers that you can use to dial in so that you can find the cheapest route from your particular phone. Whether or not you can find a toll-free number for dialing MSN depends on what type of deal you have with your phone company and the sheer luck of the draw as to whether an appropriate phone number exists for your locale.

Remember that the phone company is involved *only* in the connection between your modem and your Internet Service Provider. From that point, the Internet handles all traffic and the phone company has no involvement.

Hot Stuff

Some ISPs offer an 800 number that you can dial into, which is particularly handy if you are on the road a great deal and need to dial in to the ISP from all over the country. The ISP typically charges more for 800 access. But it does keep the connection off of your phone bill.

As I mentioned earlier, all we are trying to do in this chapter is get you connected to the Internet as a spectator, not as a publisher or "shopkeeper." When you do start setting up your own Web site, you will probably need to set up a different (and most likely, more expensive) Internet account. But that process can take weeks, even months, to accomplish. In the meantime, you may as well experience the Web from a simple connection through MSN.

Establishing Your MSN/Internet Account

To explore the Web via MSN and Microsoft's Internet Explorer, you need two pieces of software:

- The Microsoft Network version 1.05 (or later)
- Microsoft's Internet Explorer and Internet Jumpstart Kit

If you bought a PC with Windows 95 preinstalled, chances are that all the software you need is already installed on your PC. If you upgraded from Windows 3.*x*, you can purchase the Microsoft Plus! package or Microsoft's Internet Connection Kit from any computer store. Both packages come with all the stuff you need to get online to the Internet via MSN.

To actually connect your PC to the Internet, follow these steps:

1. Gather up your original Windows 95 CD-ROM or floppies and a credit card.
   - If you are installing from the Microsoft Plus! package, install Plus! as per the instructions that came with your Plus! package.
   - If your computer came with The Microsoft Network and Internet Jumpstart Kit preinstalled, run the Internet Jumpstart program by double-clicking its icon.

Puzzled? If you cannot find an icon for the Internet Jumpstart Kit on your PC, check the manuals that came with that PC for information on connecting to the Internet. Or, use Find on the Start menu to locate and start Inetwiz.exe. Or, install Microsoft Internet Explorer 2.0 from the *Web Publishing Uncut* CD-ROM (Appendix A) and let it help you get your Internet account going.

2. Once you get the Jumpstart Kit going, follow the instructions that appear on the screen.

A Wizard appears on your screen to take you through the complete process of signing up for a combination MSN and Internet account. The Wizard is pretty good at figuring out what you need in relation to what you already have. For example, if you already have an MSN account, the Wizard helps you add only the Internet Explorer to that account. If you don't have an MSN account, the Wizard helps you set up one. If you follow the instructions that appear on the screen, you shouldn't have any problems installing the software and getting connected.

Connecting to the Internet via MSN

After you have finished signing up for your Internet account, you should see an icon titled The Internet on your Windows 95 desktop. Whenever you want to connect to the Internet, just follow these simple steps:

1. Double-click the The Internet icon. Your screen will look something like the one shown in Figure 2-1.

2. Type your Member ID (if it isn't already typed in) and password (if you don't see the **** symbols that represent your password) in the appropriate fields, and then click the Connect button.

Danger Zone If you select the Remember my password check box on the Sign In screen, you won't have to type your password each time you log on. But if you share this PC with others and don't want them logging in under your account name, you should leave the Remember my password check box cleared.

3. Wait a minute or so until the connection is made. Once you are online, the Sign In box will disappear, and you will (probably) be at Microsoft's Home Page, which looks something like Figure 2-2.

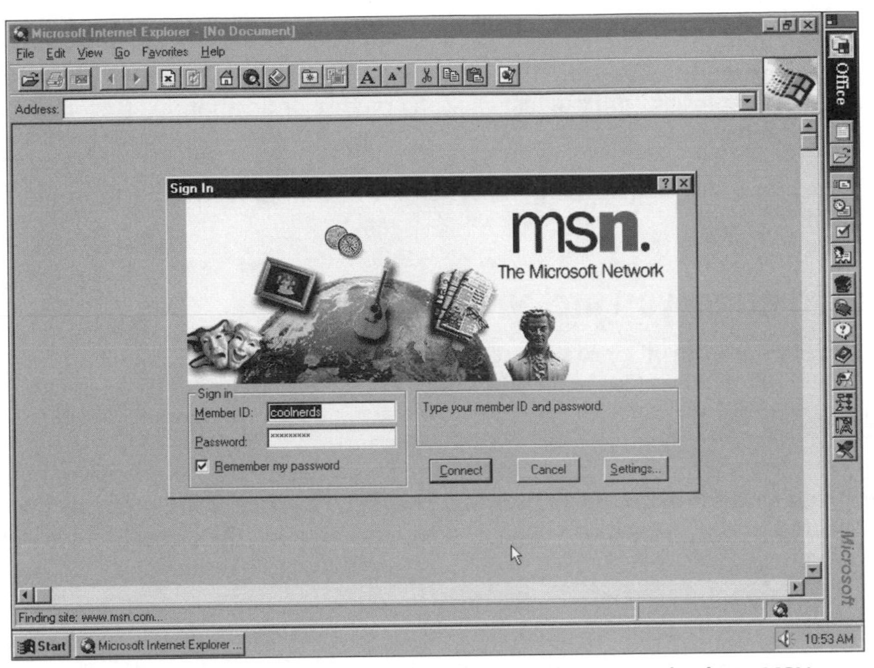

Figure 2-1: Internet Explorer on the screen, waiting for you to sign in to MSN.

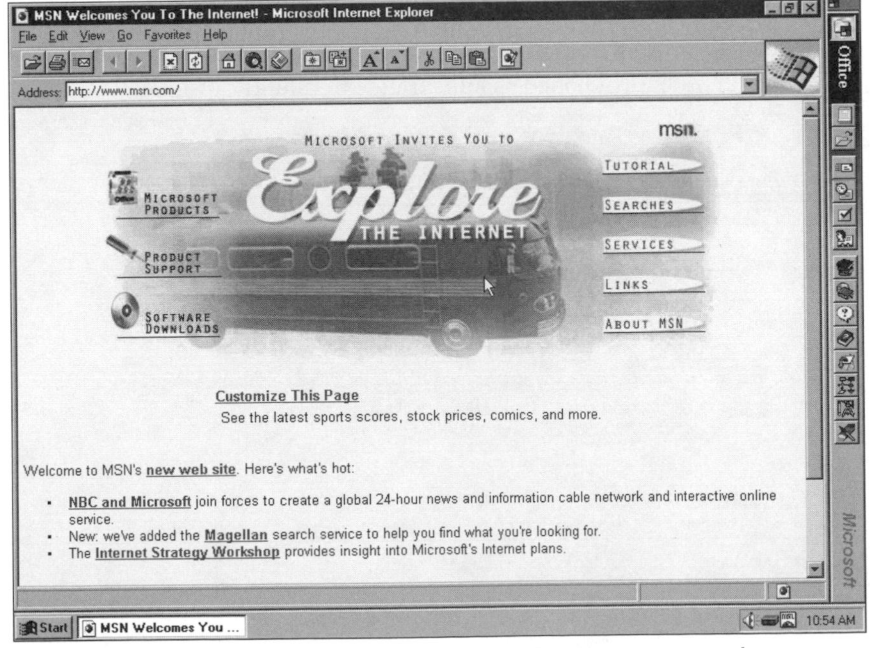

Figure 2-2: You are (most likely) taken to Microsoft's Home Page on the World Wide Web once you have successfully connected to the Internet.

Congratulations! You are now connected to the Internet, along with millions of other people, and have access to the vast resources that the Internet offers. At this particular moment, you are hooked into the most popular Internet service, the World Wide Web. To start exploring, you can just click any picture or any hot text (text that's colored or underlined).

When the mouse pointer is resting on a clickable hot spot, the pointer turns into a little pointing hand.

How to know you are online

No great fireworks go off once you are connected to the Internet. Chances are, however, that you are paying for that connection. As a result, you want to be able to tell, at a glance, whether you are — or are not — online at any given moment. There are a couple of easy, though subtle, ways to know for sure:

✦ If you're in the Internet Explorer window (Figure 2-3), you are probably connected to the Internet (though if you lose your connection, the Internet Explorer won't necessarily leave your screen).

✦ If you point to the MSN indicator in the taskbar and see the words `Connected to The Microsoft Network` (see Figure 2-3), you are definitely online.

Exactly what appears *inside* your Internet Explorer window depends on whose site you happen to be visiting on the World Wide Web at the moment. Figure 2-3 shows Microsoft's home page as it looked in early 1996. By the time you read this book, that page may look completely different. Try not to let appearance changes confuse you; change is the essence of the Internet and World Wide Web. When you publish your own site, you will probably change its appearance frequently, too!

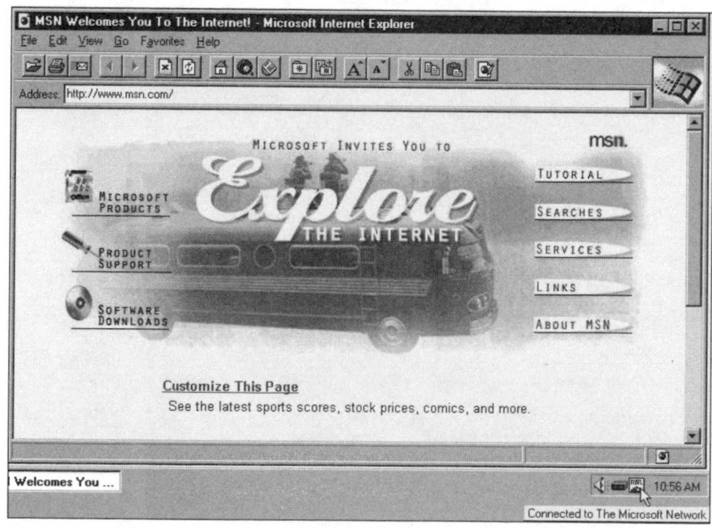

Figure 2-3: Internet Explorer open and pointing to Microsoft's home page. The MSN indicator in the taskbar shows that I am online with MSN.

Disconnecting from the Internet/MSN

After you have finished exploring the Web for the time being, you can disconnect and sign off. Doing so will free up the phone line and stop your connect-time charges (if you have any). You can use either of these simple methods to sign off:

✦ Choose File➪Exit from Internet Explorer's menu bar.

✦ Alternatively, you can right-click the MSN indicator in the taskbar and choose Sign Out from the shortcut menu that appears.

MSN gives you a chance to change your mind (see Figure 2-4). If you are sure that you want to disconnect now, just click the Yes button. The Internet Explorer window closes, and the MSN indicator disappears from the taskbar, indicating that you are no longer online.

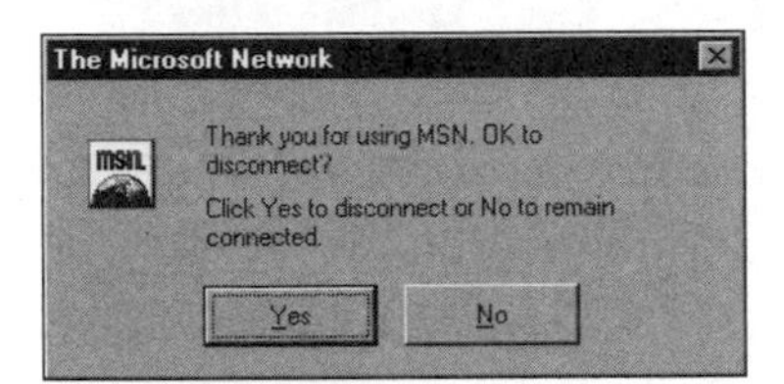

Figure 2-4: Last chance to change your mind before going offline.

Downloading the Latest Internet Explorer

Since releasing Windows 95 and Microsoft Plus! in 1995, Microsoft has released several upgrades to its Internet Explorer. In Chapters 3 and 4 (and to some extent, throughout this book), I refer to Microsoft Internet Explorer version 2.0. You would do well to check which version you currently are using and, if necessary, upgrade to version 2.0. This upgrade is easy to do:

1. If you've disconnected from the Internet, go ahead and get back on (double-click The Internet icon on your desktop).
2. When the Internet Explorer window opens, choose Help➪About Internet Explorer from the menu bar. An information window (Figure 2-5) appears.
3. If you are already using version 2.0 (or later), you can skip the rest of the steps. If you want to download the Virtual Explorer now, skip to Step 2 under the heading "Downloading Virtual Explorer."
4. Look around on your screen for a link to Internet Products or Internet Explorer 2.0 and then click that link.

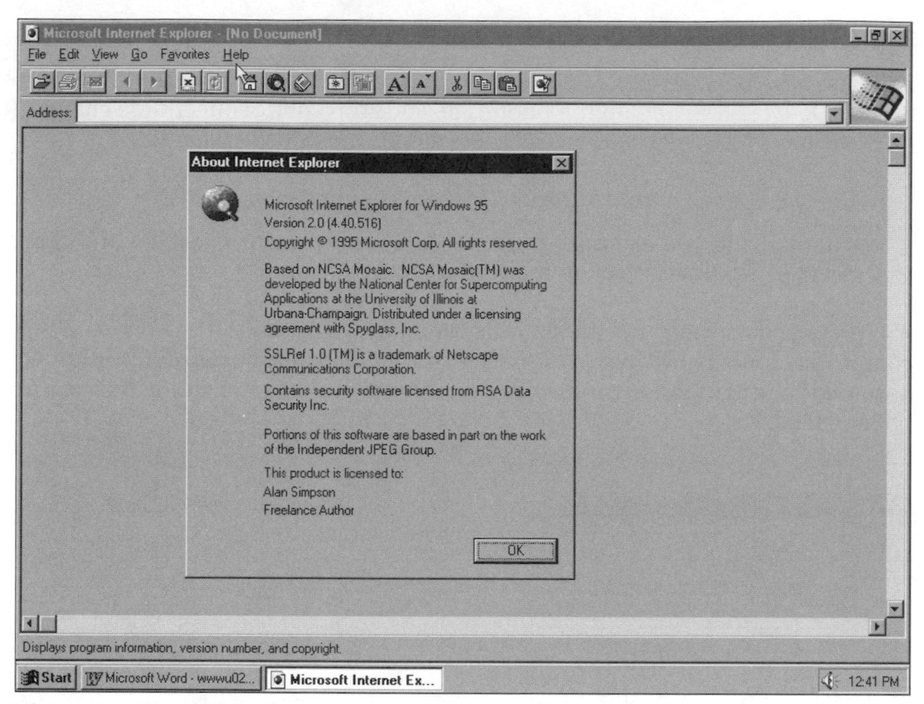

Figure 2-5: Use Help➪About Internet Explorer to determine which version you're using.

Hot Stuff

After you're connected to MSN, you can search around for information on ISDN if you're interested in setting up a quicker phone connection to MSN.

You should be able to find an option to download both Internet Explorer 2.0 and Virtual Explorer, looking something like Figure 2-6. Just follow the instructions that appear on your screen to download the software and update your current version of Internet Explorer.

Life Saver

You also can download the latest version of Internet Explorer from America Online (keyword WINNEWS), CompuServe (GO WINNEWS), MSN (Categories➪Internet Center), and Prodigy (Jump WINNEWS).

Life Saver

If Microsoft's home page still looks like the one shown back in Figure 2-3, you can click Software Downloads and then Internet Explorer to get to the screen shown in Figure 2-6. If you have trouble finding *any* of the downloadable files discussed in this book, point your Web browser (Internet Explorer) to my Web site (`http://www.coolnerds.com`), and I'll try to get you to the correct place from there.

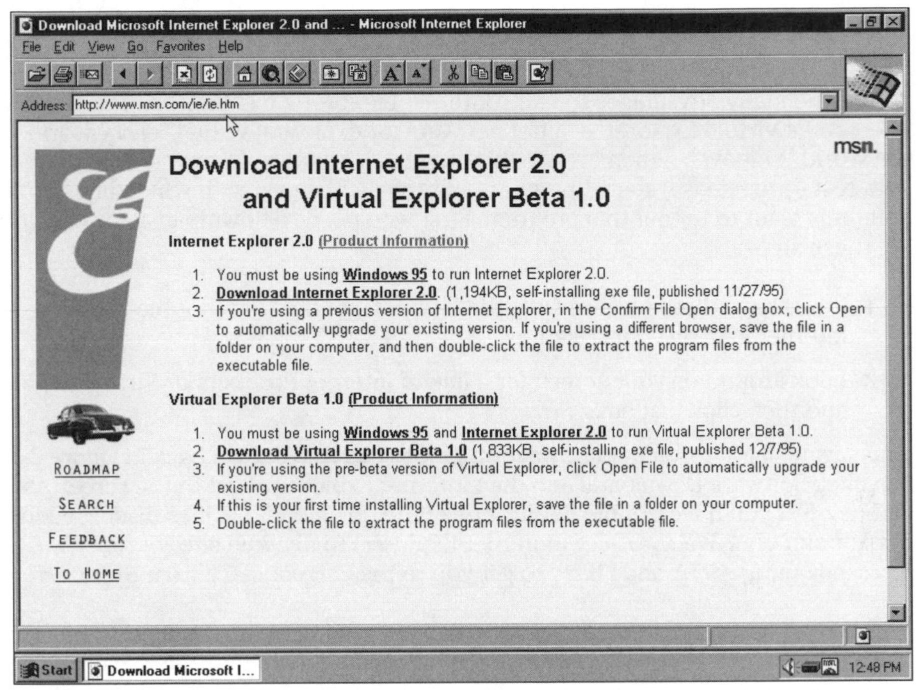

Figure 2-6: The home page for downloading Internet Explorer 2.0 and Virtual Explorer.

Point my Web browser? Huh?

As you are reading stuff about the Internet, you'll often see an instruction telling you to "point your Web browser to . . . (some site)." This may sound like a strange request, but it is actually easy to do. While you're connected to the World Wide Web with Internet Explorer (or with any other browser, for that matter), you just type the specified address into the Address: or Open: line that appears near the top of your screen. Then press Enter. For more information, see "Going to a Specific Site" in Chapter 3.

Downloading the Virtual Explorer

One of the many advantages to using Internet Explorer 2.0 is that you can also use Microsoft's Virtual Explorer — a hot new tool for exploring virtual reality worlds on the World Wide Web. When I wrote this chapter, Virtual Explorer was still in the beta test (pre-release) stage but was readily available for free downloading. You'll definitely want to try out this program. First, you need to download a copy by following these steps:

1. If you have disconnected from the Internet, get back on (double-click The Internet icon on your desktop).
2. Look around on your screen for a link to Internet Products or Virtual Explorer and then click that link.

Life Saver

Once again, if Microsoft's home page still looks like that shown back in Figure 2-3, you can click Software Downloads and then Internet Explorer to get to the screen shown in Figure 2-6. If you have trouble finding *any* of the downloadable files discussed in this book, point your Web browser (Internet Explorer) to my Web site (`http://www.coolnerds.com`), and I'll try to get you to the correct place from there.

3. When you get to the right spot (which looks something like Figure 2-6), follow the instructions on the screen to download and install Virtual Explorer.

In Step 3, you can print any download and installation instructions that appear on the screen by choosing File⇨Print from Internet Explorer's menu bar. Be sure to follow all instructions that appear on the screen to fully install the Virtual Explorer after you have downloaded it.

You Are Online

I don't know what kind of Internet connection you had, if any, before you started reading this chapter, but if you made it this far without a hitch, you can easily hop on the Internet at any time. Just double-click the desktop icon titled The Internet to do so. This takes you straight to the World Wide Web, where Microsoft's home page is the first page to greet you.

By the way, if you are not planning to go to Chapter 3 right now, you may want to check to see if you're still online. Remember, if you're not actually using the Internet, there's no sense in being logged on to it. You can sign out by choosing File⇨Exit from Internet Explorer's menu bar or by right-clicking that MSN indicator in the taskbar and choosing Sign Out.

Summary

Now you have your modem and your connection to the Internet. Let's take a moment to review the pertinent facts before you start browsing the World Wide Web in depth:

- ✦ To use the Internet, you first need to set up an account with an Internet Service Provider.
- ✦ If you have an account with one of the big commercial services, such as America Online, CompuServe, or Prodigy, you can use that service as your Internet Service Provider.
- ✦ You also can use The Microsoft Network (MSN) as your Internet Service Provider. The software you need to set up an MSN account is built right into Windows 95.
- ✦ You can use the Internet Jumpstart Kit, which comes preinstalled with Microsoft Plus! on some new PCs, to set up a joint MSN/Internet account.
- ✦ The program you use to browse the World Wide Web and other Internet services is called a *Web browser*. There are hundreds of Web browsers that you can choose from. In this book, I use Microsoft's Internet Explorer version 2.0 as the sample Web browser.
- ✦ To download the latest version on Internet Explorer and Virtual Explorer, go to Microsoft's home page and check out the Software Downloads area.

✦ ✦ ✦

Browsing the World Wide Web

In This Chapter

Going to a specific address on the World Wide Web

Navigating through pages on the World Wide Web

Keeping track of favorite places

Finding stuff on the World Wide Web

Printing and saving Web pages

It's difficult to describe the World Wide Web to someone who has never been there. The Web is kind of like the biggest library in the world, except that rather than being organized into books, the Web is organized into millions and millions of pages. The Web is a single huge book, so to speak. You don't have to walk around or use card catalogs to find stuff. Instead, you can just click your way from one page to the next. It doesn't matter that one page is on a computer in Hoboken, New Jersey, and the next one is on a computer in France; each page is just a mouse click and a few seconds away. No long-distance charges are associated with skipping about the Web, so the page's location makes no difference cost-wise, either.

The Web offers more than just pages of information. It also has art galleries, museums, shopping malls, virtual worlds, and other kinds of stuff to explore. You also can get up-to-the-minute information and technical support for all kinds of products.

To top that off, once you display a Web page on your screen, it is essentially in your computer. You can save any text or pictures that you find right to your computer with just a couple of mouse clicks. Often, you can find great programs to download to your own computer, free of charge, with just a couple of clicks.

Perhaps the best part of all is that the entire World Wide Web is accessible from one simple, easy-to-use program called a *Web browser.* I know that this all sounds too good to be true, but it is. And the hour (or so) of time you invest in learning to use a Web browser will undoubtedly be time extremely well spent. This one tiny chapter contains all the information you need to master your Web browser and take full advantage of the vast resources of the World Wide Web.

Web browsers

In this book, I use Microsoft's Internet Explorer version 2.0 as the Web browser. Thousands of Web browsers are available, however, for all kinds of computers. All browsers work in a similar manner, so you shouldn't have any problems learning to use another Windows 95-oriented Web browser from this chapter.

There is one small but mention-worthy advantage to using Internet Explorer. When *creating* your Web pages (not just browsing the Web), the tight integration between Windows 95, Microsoft Office, Word Internet Assistant, and Internet Explorer makes for an especially nice authoring environment. So even if you are a Navigator fan, consider downloading the free Internet Explorer, as discussed in Chapter 2, or installing it from my CD-ROM (Appendix A) to simplify your Web authoring efforts a little. Switching to some other Web browser later won't be a problem. Browsers are so similar that the learning curve for switching from one browser to another consists of just a few minutes of "getting adjusted" — sort of like switching from your regular car to a new car or a rental car.

Getting Around the World Wide Web

When you first connect to the Internet by using a Web browser, you'll be taken to someone's home page. This first page is sometimes called the *start page* or the *default home page*. For example, when you hook into the Internet by using MSN and Internet Explorer, you are automatically taken to Microsoft's home page. It really doesn't matter where you start, though, because once you are on the Web, the millions of other pages around the world are just a few clicks — or a little typing — away.

Every page on the Web has a unique address called a *URL* (Universal Resource Locator). You have probably noticed these addresses popping up in ads, on billboards, and so on. Most addresses look something like this:

```
http://www.someplace.com
```

The `http` stands for HyperText Transfer Protocol, and the `www` part stands for World Wide Web. Most Web addresses start with those same letters. Many addresses, such as the example shown, end with `.com`, which stands for *commercial*. This part indicates the type of organization sponsoring the Web page. Other suffixes are out there, however, including `.gov` (government) and `.edu` (educational institution), just to name a couple.

Some addresses are very long. You never need to memorize a page's address, though, because there are many different ways to get from one page to the next. In this section, I talk about the various ways you can get around the Web by using Internet Explorer as the sample Web browser.

More Info

If you'd like to learn these basic browsing skills for using the ever-popular Netscape Navigator, refer to Chapter 33.

Going to a specific site

If you know the URL (address) of the site that you want to go to, you can just follow these steps to go to that site:

1. Click in the Address (or Open) line of your Web browser. Or, if you only want to change part of the address currently shown in the Address line, select the part you want to change by dragging the mouse through it, as shown in Figure 3-1.

Figure 3-1: Here I've selected the part of the address that I want to change.

2. Type in the new address or the part that needs to be changed. For example, in Figure 3-2, I changed `msn.com` to `whitehouse.gov`.

Figure 3-2: Here I've changed `http://www.msn.com` to `http://www.whitehouse.gov` by replacing `msn.com`.

3. Press Enter and wait.

Hot Stuff

When typing an address into Internet Explorer, you can omit the `http://`. For example, if you just type `www.whitehouse.gov`, Internet Explorer will automatically change that to `http://www.whitehouse.gov`.

While your browser finds and downloads the site's home page, you see some activity near the upper-right corner of your browser. For example, in Internet Explorer, the clouds behind the Windows logo move through the picture (to indicate that you are "going somewhere"). When the journey is complete, you see the requested site's *home page* (the first page of that site). For example, Figure 3-3 shows the home page of the White House site (`http://www.whitehouse.gov`). If you want to practice typing URLs and do a little "site-seeing" along the way, try visiting some of the sites listed in Table 3-1.

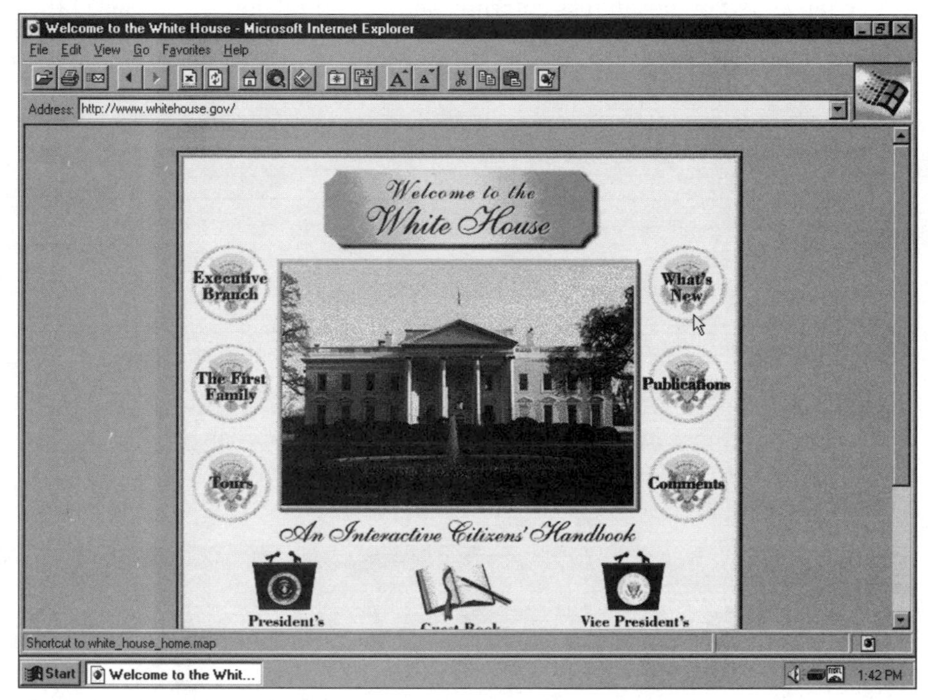

Figure 3-3: Now I'm at the home page for `http://www.whitehouse.gov`.

Puzzled? Remember, when someone tells you to "point your Web browser to (some URL)," they want you to type that URL into the Address box on your Web browser. For example, in Steps 1 through 3 from earlier, I pointed my Web browser to `http://www.whitehouse.gov`.

Table 3-1
Practice URL Sites

Theme	Site	URL (Address)
Art	Le Louvre	http://www.emf.net/louvre
Business	Big Dreams	http://vanbc.wimsey.com/~duncans
Classified Ads	Ad Web	http://ourworld.compuserve.com/homepage/cybernet/adhome.html
Computers	Internet Safari	http://www.bloomfield.k12.mi.us/CompCntr/safari/1net.html
Fun	Letterman's Top Ten	http://www.cbs.lateshow/ttlist.html
Government	White House	http://www.whitehouse.gov
Questions	coolnerds	http://www.coolnerds.com
Shopping	1 World Plaza	http://www2.clever.net/1world/plaza/shop.html
Sports	AllSports.com	http://allsports.questtech.com/nfl/nfl.html
Time Waste	Most Annoying	http://www.cs.vassar.edu/~anschorr/annoying.html
Yellow Pages	NYNEX Interactive	http://www.nyip.com

Danger Zone

The Internet is based on Unix, which uses forward slashes (/), whereas DOS uses backslashes (\). When typing a URL or navigating through directories on the Internet, be sure to use the forward slashes. Backslashes won't work.

Hot-clicking to another site

Many Web sites contain *hypertext* and graphic *hot spots* that you can click to go to a related site without typing in its address. Hot text (called a *hypertext link,* or *hyperlink* for short) is usually colored, underlined, or both. You also can determine whether text or a graphic image is a hot spot just by moving the mouse pointer to it. If the mouse pointer turns into a little pointing hand, then the spot is hot. Just click the spot to go wherever the spot offers to take you.

Hot Stuff

When the mouse pointer is on a hot spot, the lower-left corner of the screen shows information about the hotspot, such as "Shortcut to . . . (wherever)."

Some pages are larger than what your screen can show. But as in any word processing program, you can scroll up and down through a page by using the scroll bar to the right of Internet Explorer.

Up, down, back, forward, stop, home

You also can move around the Web in relation to whatever page you currently happen to be on by using buttons in the Internet Explorer toolbar. If you're not sure which button is which, you can easily discover the name of the button. Move your mouse pointer so that it touches the toolbar button and wait for the little tooltip to appear, as in Figure 3-4.

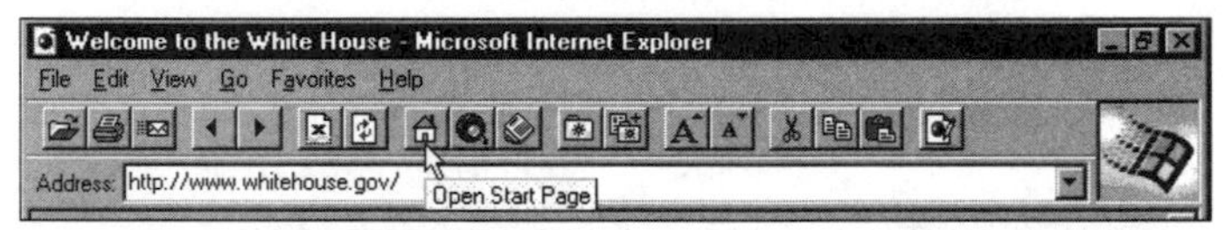

Figure 3-4: The Internet Explorer toolbar, with the tooltip for the Open Start Page button displayed.

The Back and Forward buttons in the toolbar take you forward and backward through pages you have visited during this session. For example, if you go to a new page and then want to go back to the page you just left, click the Back button.

If you don't see the toolbar in Internet Explorer, choose View➪Toolbar from the menus.

The Address box where you type a URL also keeps track of the sites you have visited recently. If you want to return to a recent site, just click the drop-down list button at the right edge of the Address box and choose the address of the site to which you want to return (see Figure 3-5).

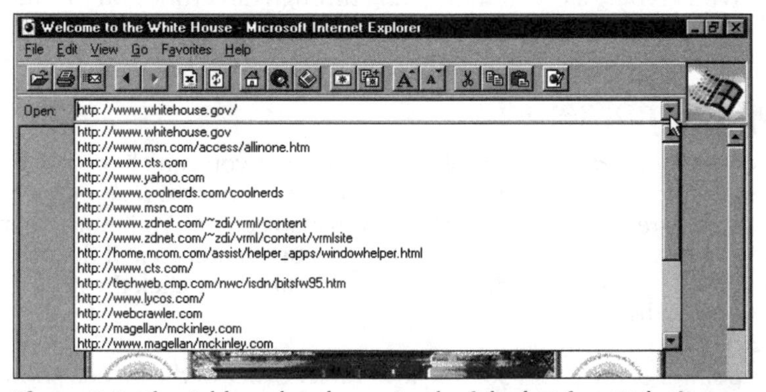

Figure 3-5: The Address box keeps track of the last few Web sites you have visited.

If you want to see a *really* complete list of the sites that you have visited, open the Internet Explorer History folder (choose File➪More History from the menu bar). You come to the History folder shown in Figure 3-6. To go to a site that is listed in the history folder, double-click its icon.

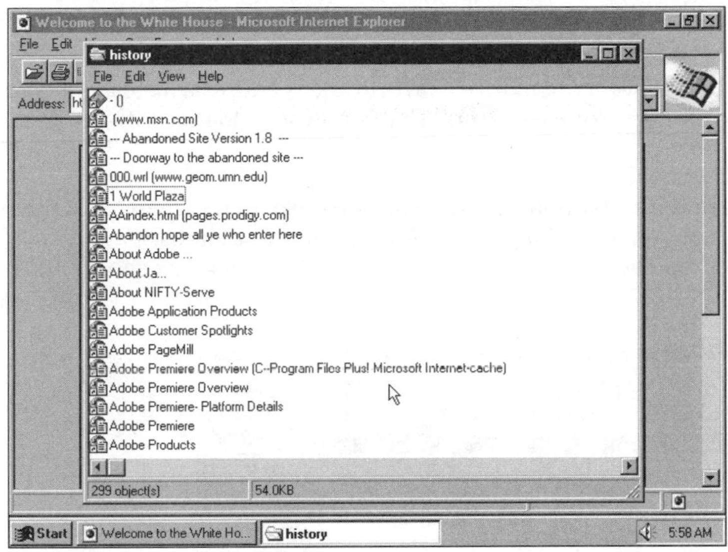

Figure 3-6: The History folder keeps track of the last 300 sites that you have visited.

If you get completely lost and want to go all the way back to the page you were on when you first connected to the Web, click the Open Start Page button.

More Info

For a quick reminder on just about anything you learn in this chapter, refer to Internet Explorer's built-in Help (press F1, or choose Help➪Help Topics from the Internet Explorer menu bar).

If you try to go to another site and getting there seems to be taking *way* too long, just click the Stop button in the toolbar to stop the process.

Zooming in

If the text on a page is too small to read, click the Use Larger Font button until the text is a comfortable size. Likewise, you can click the Use Smaller Font button to shrink the text size. As an alternative to using the toolbar buttons, you can choose View➪Fonts from the Internet Explorer menu bar.

Note that both techniques change only the size of the font used to display text. Graphic images are unaffected.

Keeping Track of Favorite Sites

It is darn near impossible to remember a bunch of URLs, especially those big, honkin', long ones like

```
http://www.someplace.elsewhere.com/homepage/~somenet/
    spareme.html.
```

Fortunately, you don't have to memorize a favorite site's address. Instead, *bookmark* the site while you are there for easy return. Here's how you do that with Internet Explorer:

1. While you are at a site (or page) you think you'd like to return to, click the Add To Favorites button in the Internet Explorer toolbar (or choose Favorites⇨Add to Favorites from the menu bar). You'll come to the dialog box shown in Figure 3-7.

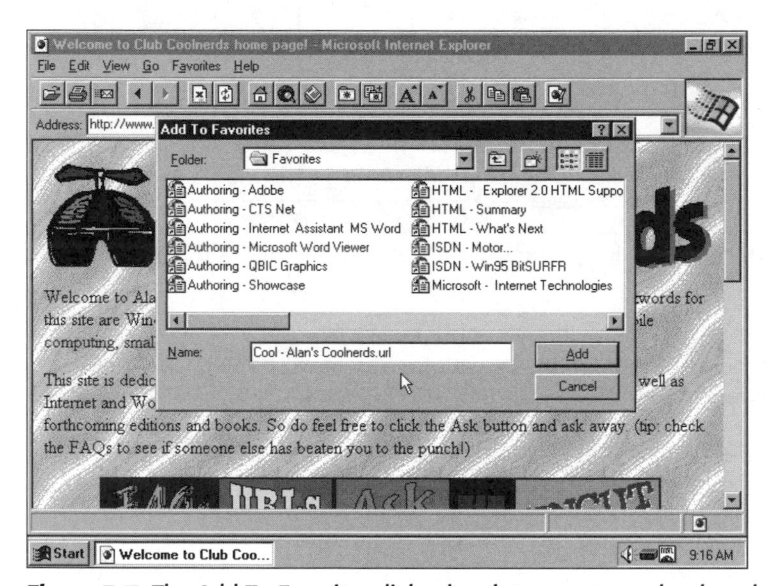

Figure 3-7: The Add To Favorites dialog box lets you store a bookmark.

2. If you don't like the suggested name that appears in the Name box, type a new one. Do, however, add the `.url` extension to whatever name you provide.

Hot Stuff

When naming a favorite place, consider giving it a general category name first, followed by a specific name. For example, `Art - Louvre.url` or `Windows 95 - Tips.url`. That way, when you later open your Favorites folder, your shortcut icons will be neatly categorized into groups.

3. Choose Add.

That's all there is to it. Whenever you want to return to that site in the future, just choose Favorites from the Internet Explorer menu bar and click the name of the site to which you want to go. Or, to review the entire list, click the Open Favorites button in the Internet Explorer toolbar or choose Favorites⇨Open Favorites from the menu bar. You end up at the Favorites window shown in Figure 3-8.

Figure 3-8: The Internet Explorer Favorites window.

As with any Windows 95 browsing window, you can view large icons, small icons, a list, or details, simply by choosing an option from the View menu or the toolbar. In Details view, you can alphabetize the names (by clicking on the Name column heading) or put them into order by the date created (by clicking on the Modified column heading). To open a site, double-click its icon.

Each of the icons in the Favorites window is actually a shortcut. You can do everything with these Internet shortcuts that you can do with any other shortcut:

✦ To rename a shortcut, right-click it and choose Rename.

✦ To delete a shortcut, right-click it and choose Delete.

✦ To copy a shortcut to the desktop, right-drag it onto the desktop, release the right mouse button, and choose Create Shortcut(s) Here from the menu.

✦ To e-mail a shortcut to someone on MSN, drag the shortcut icon into your e-mail message.

Knowing about e-mail is not absolutely necessary if you just want to browse the Web. But e-mail is a very useful Internet service. You can learn about e-mail at your leisure in Chapter 38.

✦ To change a shortcut's icon, right-click the icon, choose Properties, click the Internet Shortcut tab, and then click the Change Icon button.

If your Favorites folder gets too crowded, consider categorizing it into folders. To create a folder while you're in Favorites, choose File⇨New⇨Folder and give the folder a name. For example, you could create a folder named Art and then move all your art-related shortcut icons into that folder by dragging them there.

Searching the Web

Random site-seeing and clicking from one place to the next are fun ways to explore the Web. There are times, however, when you'll want to go looking for specific information. Is there an index to this massive, multimillion-page virtual book that we call the Web, so that you can look up stuff easily? Yes and no. Several indexes exist, not just one — each of which has its own particular strengths. The sites that provide an index to the World Wide Web are called *search engines*. Here are two ways to get to, and use, those search engines:

✦ In Internet Explorer, click on the Search the Internet button in the toolbar.

✦ Go to any one of the addresses listed in Table 3-2.

Table 3-2
Popular Internet Search Engines

Search Site	*Address*
Excite	`http://www.excite.com`
Infoseek	`http://www.infoseek.com`
Lycos	`http://www.lycos.com`
Magellan	`http://magellan/mckinley.com`
Microsoft All In One	`http://www.msn.com/access/allinone.htm`
Open Text	`http://www.opentext.com`
Web Crawler	`http://webcrawler.com`
Yahoo!	`http://www.yahoo.com`

If you chose the first option, you end up at the site shown in Figure 3-9, Microsoft's All In One search page. This page lets you type a search word or phrase right into a small text box that's on your screen. It then passes that word or phrase to the search engine directly, so you don't need to type the site's URL yourself. Here's how to use the All In One search page.

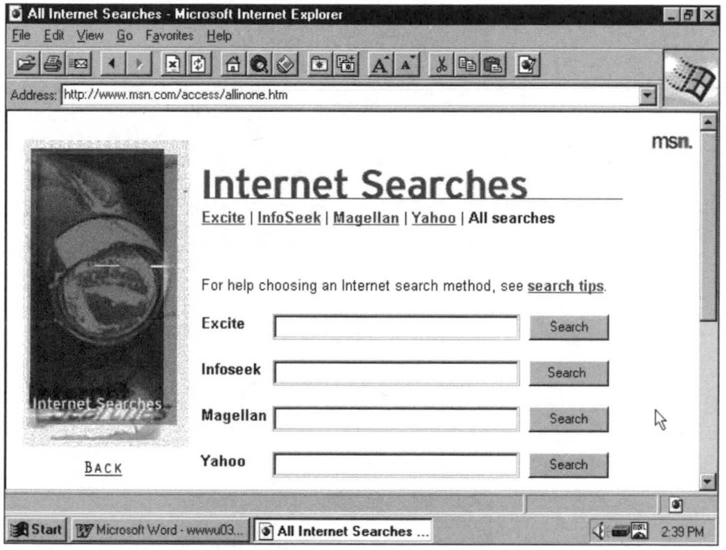

Figure 3-9: Microsoft's All In One search page provides quick access to several Web search engines.

1. Type the word you're looking for into any box.
2. Click the Search button.
3. A list of Web Sites about, or containing references to, that word will appear. Click any site name to jump straight to it.

You'll probably see additional instructions on your screen for using whichever search engine you selected. Keep in mind that each search engine uses a slightly different technique for locating references to your selected word. So if you want to thoroughly track down a particular topic, try using several different search engines.

Hot Stuff

Some search engines also offer options for performing complex searches using "and" and "or" logic. When you are in a site that offers searching, look around for information on search options or query options.

Categorical searching

Another handy way to search the Internet is to start with some broad category, such as Art or Business, and then narrow down from there. Yahoo! is a great service for that type of searching. To get there, point your browser to `http://www.yahoo.com`. You arrive at a page that looks something like Figure 3-10.

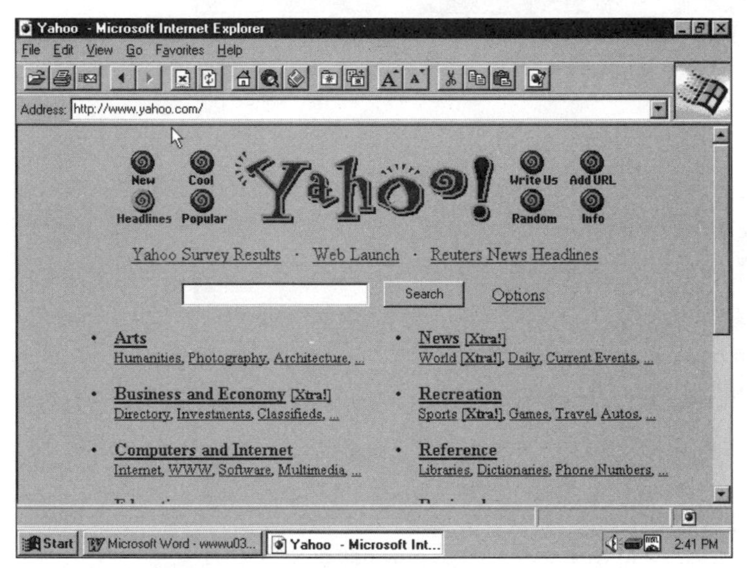

Figure 3-10: The first page of Yahoo! offers a categorical approach to searching, as well as specific-word searching.

Once you get to the Yahoo! page, you can click on any broad category to see the subcategories within it. Keep drilling down through the categories and their branches to get more specific information.

Searching the current page

Once you are in a page, you can search that page for a particular word or phrase. The technique is identical to using Find in most word-processing programs.

1. Choose Edit⇨Find from the Internet Explorer menu bar.
2. Type the text that you want to find.
3. Change either of the options provided — *Start from top of page* and *Match case* — as appropriate for your needs at the moment.
4. Click the Find Next button.

If Internet Explorer finds a match but the Find dialog box is covering it, move the Find dialog box out of the way (by dragging its title bar). Or, if you find what you're looking for on the first try, click the Cancel or Close button on the Find dialog box to move it out of the way.

Printing and Saving Web Material

If you're accustomed to cruising bulletin boards or commercial online services with your modem, you may think that when you view a page on the World Wide Web, you're viewing it from afar. But actually, it doesn't work that way on the Web. The Web is part of the Internet, and the Internet is based on the client-server concept of computing.

So what does this mean? It means that when you point your browser to an address, a *server* computer at that address responds to your request. It responds by sending a copy of the requested page to your computer, the client. Your computer, in turn, takes responsibility for formatting that document and displaying it on your screen.

Why is this fact important? Because it means that whatever page you are currently viewing on the screen is actually a document that is "in your computer." The fact that the page is "in your computer" means that you can use everyday Windows cut-and-paste techniques to take whatever you see on the screen and save it to your local hard disk for future use.

Printing Web pages

Let's start with the simplest form of saving something from the Web. Suppose that you want to print (not save) a copy of whatever document you are viewing at the moment. No problem — just print it as you would a document you created yourself: Choose File⇨Print from the Internet Explorer menu bar, press Ctrl+P, or click the Print button in the toolbar. You'll be taken to a standard Print dialog box where you can choose a printer, page range, and number of copies. Choose OK from that dialog box to start printing.

Saving text from a Web page

If you want to save some text from a Web page, perhaps to read later or to put in a file somewhere, you can use the standard Windows cut-and-paste techniques. Here are the exact steps to follow:

1. In Internet Explorer, select the text that you want to save (by dragging the mouse pointer through it). Or, if you want to save the entire page, choose Edit⇨Select All or press Ctrl+A. For example, in Figure 3-11, I have selected some instructions that I want to save for future reference.

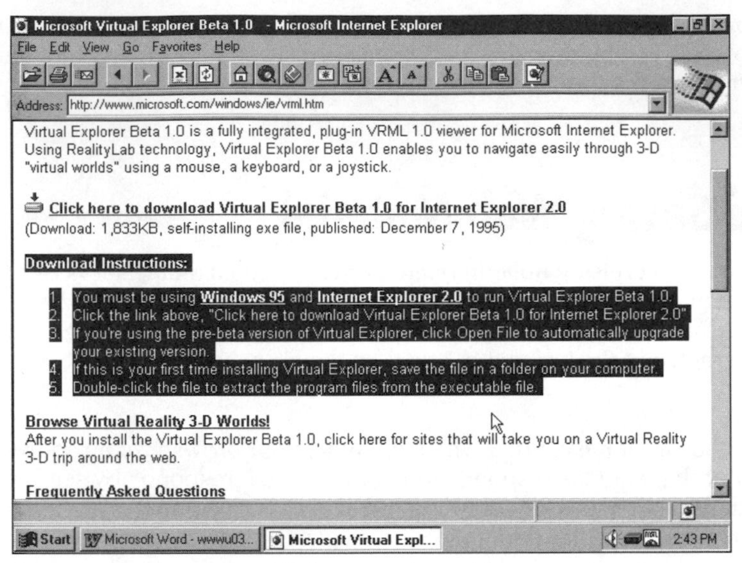

Figure 3-11: Text from a Web page selected for cut and paste.

2. Choose Edit➪Copy from the menu bar, click the Copy button on the toolbar, or press Ctrl+C. A copy of the selection is placed in the (invisible) Windows Clipboard.
3. Open your favorite word processor, such as Microsoft Word. Optionally, you can open a simple text editor, such as Notepad.
4. Click within the document window of the word processor or text editor and press Ctrl+V (or choose Edit➪Paste from the word processor's menu bar, or click the Paste button in the word processor's toolbar).

In Figure 3-12, I opened Microsoft Word for Windows with a new blank document. Then I pasted in the selected text and used some basic editing methods to format the pasted text a little. I can now choose File➪Save from the Word menu bar to save that copied text as a standard Word document on my PC.

Saving a graphic from a Web page

When you cut and paste text from a Web page, the graphics are excluded. The reason is that text and graphics are stored in separate files for Web pages (I discuss that fact in more detail in Part III of this book). For now, just be aware that if you want to copy a graphic image from a Web page to a file on your own PC, you have to use this slightly different technique:

1. When you see the graphic image that you want to copy, right-click it and choose Save Picture As.

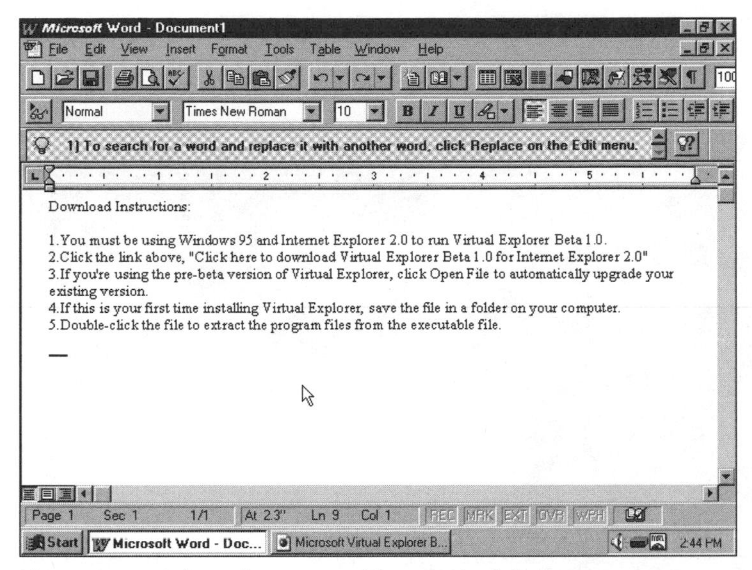

Figure 3-12: Selected text pasted into a Word document.

2. In the Save As dialog box that appears, choose a location for the file and enter a filename. For example, in Figure 3-13, I'm saving a copy of the globe image to a file named GLOBE.GIF in a folder named SWIPED PICS on my PC.
3. Choose OK.

Danger Zone

Although you technically can swipe *any* graphic image off of any Web page, it is not always ethical to do so. Company logos and trademarks, clip art that people sell, original art that a site paid for, and the like are not good candidates for swiping and placing into your own site!

Most of the images that you copy from a Web page will be in GIF or JPEG format. Not all graphics programs will let you edit that type of image, and not all word processors will allow you to import that type of image. But I have included on the *Web Publishing Uncut* CD-ROM a program named Paint Shop Pro, which is an excellent GIF/JPEG editor. Word Internet Assistant (Word IA), which we'll use for "word processing" Web pages later in the book, can easily handle GIF and JPEG pictures.

Hot Stuff

To see the properties of an object displayed on your screen, right-click that object and choose Properties from the shortcut menu that appears.

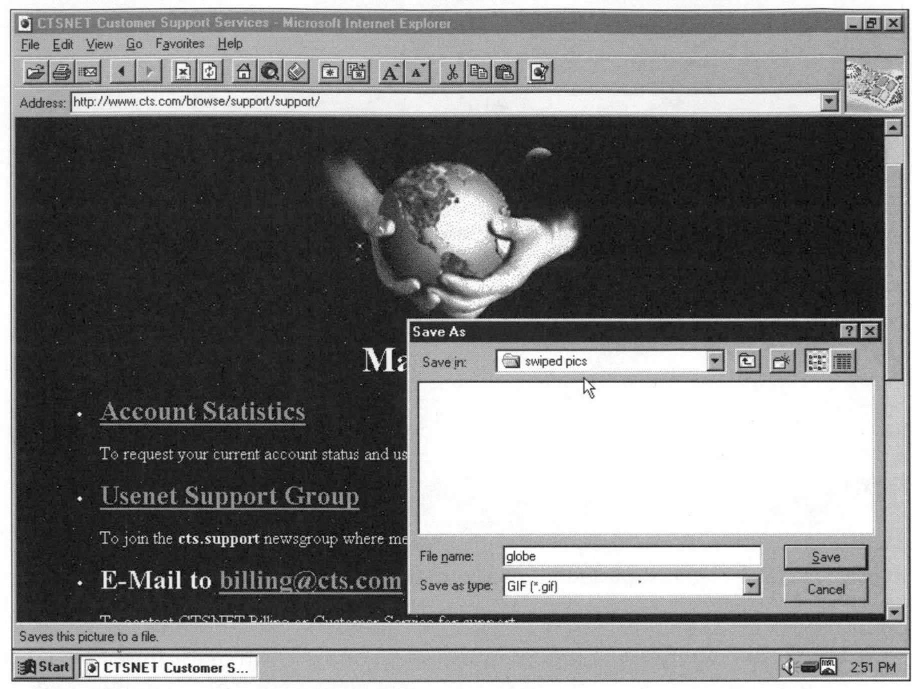

Figure 3-13: Saving a graphic image from a Web page to a file on my own PC.

Saving a background image from a Web page

Many Web sites also use background textures and images, such as the stars that appear in CTSNET's page in Figure 3-13. You can easily swipe a Web page's background image and store it as a file on your own PC. To do so, follow these steps:

1. Right-click anywhere on the background image that you want to save and choose Save Background As from the shortcut menu.
2. Choose a location and filename for the saved image and then choose Save.

The saved image will be stored as a GIF or JPEG graphic. Typically, a background image is just a small square that is "tiled" onto your screen, so the image won't take up a lot of space on your disk. As mentioned earlier, Parts III and IV will show you how to manipulate GIF and JPEG images. There you also learn how to define background textures for the Web documents that you author.

Troubleshooting

If you try to go to a site and see a message like the one shown in Figure 3-14, or you see an Error 404 message, your browser cannot get to the site that you have requested. The three most likely reasons for this problem, and their solutions, are listed here:

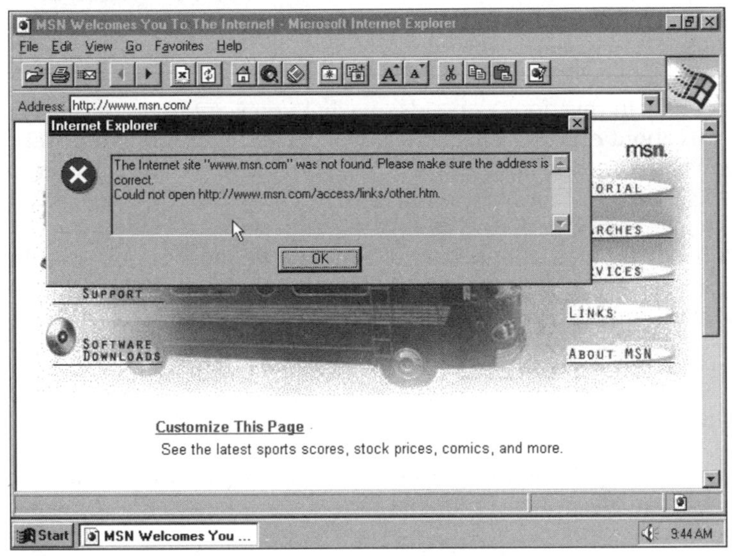

Figure 3-14: An error trying to get to an inaccessible site.

- ✦ You mistyped the site's URL. Check it carefully and make any necessary corrections.
- ✦ The site is temporarily offline or has moved to a new address. Try again later, or try using a search engine to find the site's new address.
- ✦ You are not online. You just need to get back online and try again.

If you look closely at the screen in Figure 3-14, you can easily see the problem. Neither the MSN nor modem indicator appear in the taskbar. Thus, I'm not online, and therefore Internet Explorer cannot find the requested site. The solution here simply is to reconnect to the Internet and try again.

You may be able to visit some sites that you have visited in the past even when you're not online. You have this capability because Internet Explorer automatically saves copies of recently visited sites to your hard disk. When you re-visit such a site, Internet Explorer just reloads the site from your local hard disk (a folder named cache) rather than retrieving the document from the remote server again. The advantage here is that you save a great deal of time. And, some sites will appear to be available even when you're not online!

More Info

For information on customizing Internet Explorer, please refer to Chapter 37.

You Are a Webbie

Congratulations! You are now an official Web-cruising guru. The techniques you learned in this chapter will take you to any of the millions of Web pages scattered throughout the world. The best thing you can do right now is set aside this book and practice cruising the World Wide Web. You may feel a little strange at first, having such quick and easy access to so many documents from all over the world. But practice makes perfect, and nothing explains the many wonders of the Web better than a little hands-on experience.

Where you go from here in this book depends on what you want to do next. In the next chapter, I briefly talk about cruising Virtual Reality sites on the World Wide Web. Then in Part II, you learn about setting up your own Web site that other Web cruisers can visit.

If you're not quite ready for all that and want to learn a little more about other Internet services, such as e-mail, FTP, newsgroups, and so on, that's fine, too. Just skip to Chapter 38 for a quick, get-your-feet-wet introduction.

Summary

In this chapter, you learned all the skills necessary to browse the World Wide Web like a pro. To summarize, you learned the following:

- When you first connect to the Internet through a Web browser, such as Internet Explorer, you are taken to a specific start page.
- No matter what page you start at, you can get to any other page on the World Wide Web simply by entering the page's URL (address) in the Address box.
- You can use the Back and Forward buttons on the toolbar to navigate through pages that you have already visited.
- You can use various search engines to locate pages based on some topic or category.
- To make it easy to return to a specific page in the future, you can add the page to your list of Favorites.
- When a Web page is displayed on your screen, you can choose File⇨Print to print that page.
- You can also save whatever is on your screen. To save text, select the text and use standard Windows cut-and-paste techniques.
- To save a graphic from a Web page, right-click the graphic image and choose Save Picture As.

✦ ✦ ✦

CHAPTER 4

Multimedia and Virtual Worlds

✦ ✦ ✦ ✦

In This Chapter

Exploring multimedia sites

Exploring virtual worlds

Downloading the Virtual Explorer software

Navigating virtual worlds with the keyboard, mouse, and joystick

✦ ✦ ✦ ✦

Most of the Web pages you visit will have text and pictures. But you also can find sites that offer sound and video, including spoken voice, sound effects, music, motion, animation, and live video. Unlike many older browsers, Internet Explorer doesn't need additional helper applications to play sound and video. To cruise virtual worlds, however, you will need to get a copy of Virtual Explorer. This chapter discusses all of these topics in detail.

Multimedia Site Browsing

Most Web pages offer text and pictures. *Multimedia pages* add sound, motion, and live video to that. Microsoft's Internet Explorer comes with the built-in capabilities to play multimedia files automatically when you encounter them, as well as provides the more traditional method of double-clicking an icon when you want to hear a sound or watch a video.

A couple of words of caution here: First, multimedia files can be *huge,* so it can take a while to download and actually play one on your PC (especially if you are using a 14.4 Kbps modem). Second, some browsers require that you add *helper apps* or *plug-ins* to play multimedia files. To simplify things, I suggest you try this chapter using Internet Explorer, which you can set up to auto-play multimedia files, without requiring additional software and with little or no tweaking.

Activating sound and video auto-play

You can only play sound if your PC has a sound card installed. You may want to check your sound system before you even try exploring multimedia Web sites. You can do this right from the Windows 95 desktop — you do not need to be online.

To test you sound system, you can use Find to locate a wave file (search for *wav*). Then double-click any file of the type Wave Sound. The Sound Recorder applet should appear on your screen, and the requested sound file will play. If you get Sound Recorder but no sound, check the volume setting on your screen (click the speaker indicator in the taskbar) and on the speakers. If those settings both seem to be okay, check your mixer as well (click the Start button and choose Programs⇨Accessories⇨Multimedia⇨Volume Control).

If you don't even get Sound Recorder to appear on your screen, your sound card may not be installed correctly. First, check to see if you have a hardware conflict (click the Start button⇨Help⇨Contents⇨Troubleshooting⇨If you have a hardware conflict . . .). If the troubleshooter doesn't help, you'll need to refer to the sound card manufacturer's instruction manual for troubleshooting tips.

Next, make sure that sound and animation are activated in Internet Explorer:

1. Open Internet Explorer (you don't need to go online right away).
2. Choose View⇨Options from Internet Explorer's menu bar.
3. Click the Appearance tab.
4. Make sure that the Play sounds and Show animations check boxes are both checked, as shown in Figure 4-1.

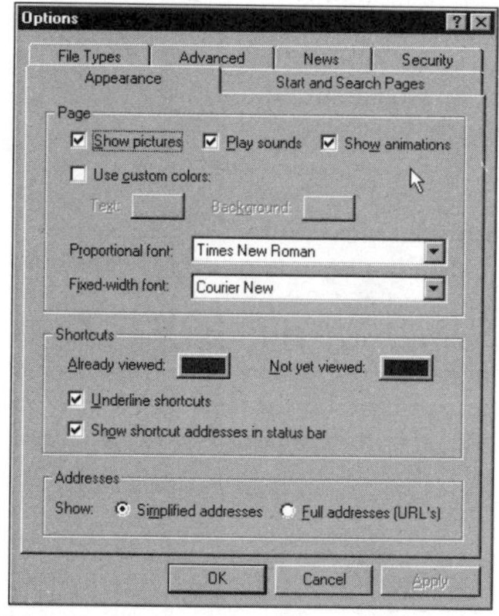

Figure 4-1: The Appearance tab in Internet Explorer options.

5. Click OK.

Now you can go online. (An easy way to do this would be to exit and then restart Internet Explorer.)

Check out some multimedia sites

To show off the multimedia features of Internet Explorer, Microsoft has put up a Web page for a hypothetical coffee company. This is a good site for testing your multimedia browsing capabilities. To get to the site, point Internet Explorer to

```
http://www.microsoft.com/windows/ie/iedemo.htm
```

When you get to the site, sit tight for a minute and give it a chance to download all the files. You should hear a drumbeat sound automatically and also see an animated coffee cup spinning near the center of the screen (see Figure 4-2).

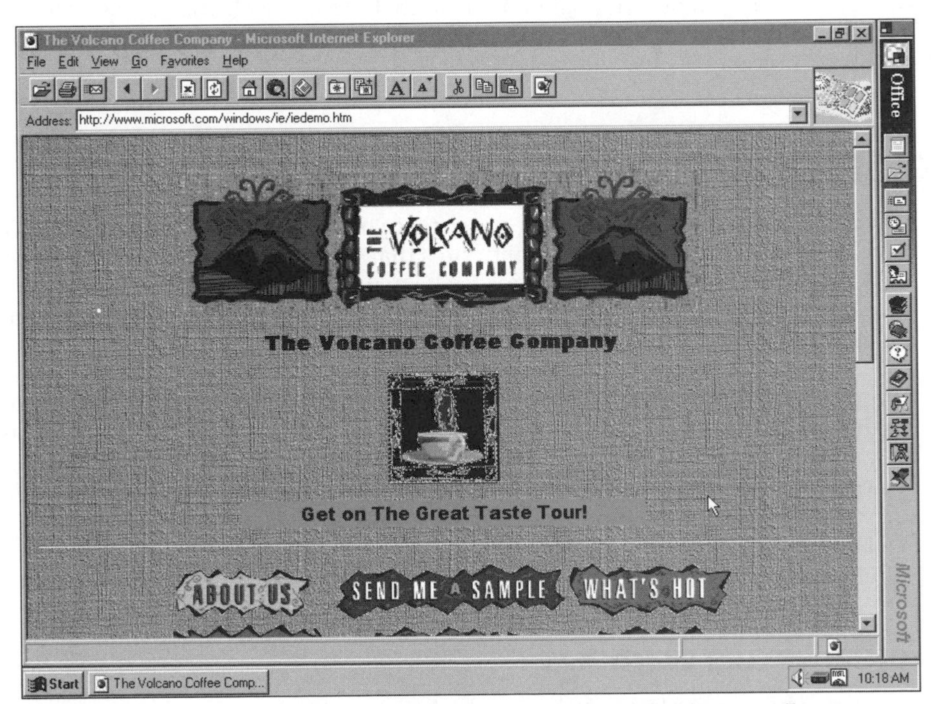

Figure 4-2: For motion and video, check out the hypothetical Volcano Coffee Company site.

As I write this chapter, I know of dozens of new multimedia sites that are currently "under construction" but have no permanent address yet. If you want to try out some other multimedia sites, just hop on over to coolnerds (`http://www.coolnerds.com`) and check out the Multimedia section under Site-Seeing.

Speeding up your browsing

The downside to allowing Internet Explorer to play sounds and animations automatically is this: Web browsing can become extremely s-l-o-o-o-o-o-o-w. To speed things up, you can skip the sounds, animations, and even graphics. Use any combination of the following techniques:

✦ Go back to View➪Options➪Appearance, and turn off the Show pictures, Play sounds, or Show animations options. These objects will then appear as icons in the new pages you explore. To see a picture or animation, right-click its icon and choose Show Picture. To play a sound file, double-click its icon.

✦ To interrupt a sound or animation while it is playing, click the Stop button or press Escape.

Puzzled?

You may not be able to play every sound and multimedia file you come across on the Web. Don't worry about that right now, though. Here in Part I, you just need to learn what is available on the Web and how to get around. You'll learn all the technical details of multimedia files in Chapter 23.

Exploring Virtual Worlds

In addition to the millions of regular pages that you can visit on the World Wide Web, there are also some cool Virtual Reality sites that you can move around in. You need a VRML browser to do so (VRML stands for Virtual Reality Modeling Language). If you have downloaded Virtual Explorer from Microsoft's Web site, then you already have the appropriate browser installed and you are ready to go.

If you have not downloaded Internet Explorer 2.0 and Virtual Explorer, see "Downloading the Latest Internet Explorer" and "Downloading the Virtual Explorer" in Chapter 2 for instructions on how to do so. If you're using Netscape Navigator or some other browser, you can download Virtual Reality Modeling Language (VRML) plug-ins from several sites. Use your favorite search engine to look up *VRML* and see what is available, or check out the following sites: `http://www.paperinc.com`, `http://www.chaco.com/vrscout`, or `http://www.intervista.com/worldview.html`.

A few virtual warnings

Before you begin your journey into a virtual world, let me give you a couple of brief warnings. First, you are bound to feel like a total klutz when you first start navigating around a 3-D virtual world. It takes some practice. If you end up out in space (in a blue sky), click the Return to Starting Point button in the VR controls or right-click the VR image and choose Viewpoints➪Starting Point to return to the virtual world's starting point.

If you get a weird angle but don't want to go all the way back to the starting point, click the Straighten button.

Also, if you get to a virtual world and it starts spinning all over the place, the most likely reason is that your joystick is not properly calibrated. See "Navigating with a Joystick" later in this chapter.

Finally, be aware that in spite of all the hype and hoopla, a virtual world is usually more like a "virtual closet" (or small room). I have yet to see any sites that would qualify as a "world," or even a country, state, or city for that matter. Nonetheless, it can be fun to play around in 3-D virtuality, so here's how you do it.

Finding virtual worlds

After you install a VRML browser, it becomes a seamless part of your current Web browser. All you need to do is point your Web browser to a site that offers Virtual Reality, and the VRML browser kicks in automatically. There is nothing special about a virtual world's address — most use the typical `http://www` prefix. To start exploring virtual worlds, try Microsoft's Cool 3-D Virtual Worlds site shown in Figure 4-3. To get there, follow these steps:

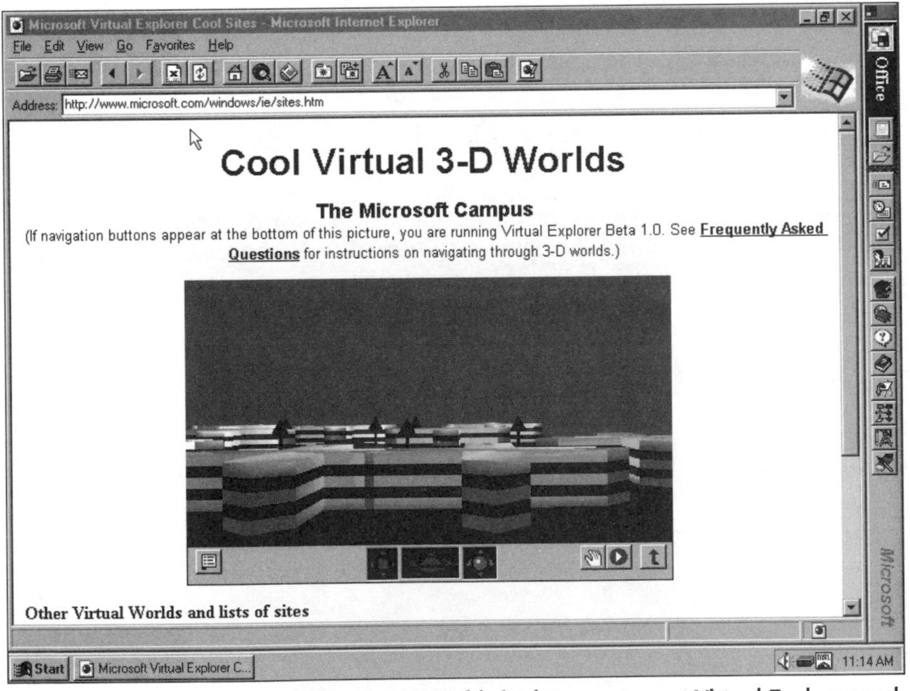

Figure 4-3: Microsoft's Cool Virtual 3-D World site lets you try out Virtual Explorer and includes links to other Virtual Reality sites.

1. If you haven't already done so, start Internet Explorer (or your favorite Web browser) and get onto the Internet.
2. In the Address box, type `http:www.microsoft.com/windows/ie/sites.htm`.
3. Press Enter.

Hot Stuff

For an up-to-date list of Virtual Reality sites, check out the Virtual Reality category under Site-Seeing in my coolnerds site (`http://www.coolnerds.com`).

Notice that the graphic image in Figure 4-3 has controls along the bottom. These controls indicate that the graphic image is a virtual world, and you can move around within that image by using your keyboard, mouse, or a joystick. To see a brief description of a control, move your mouse pointer to the control and wait a moment for the tooltip to appear, as shown in Figure 4-4.

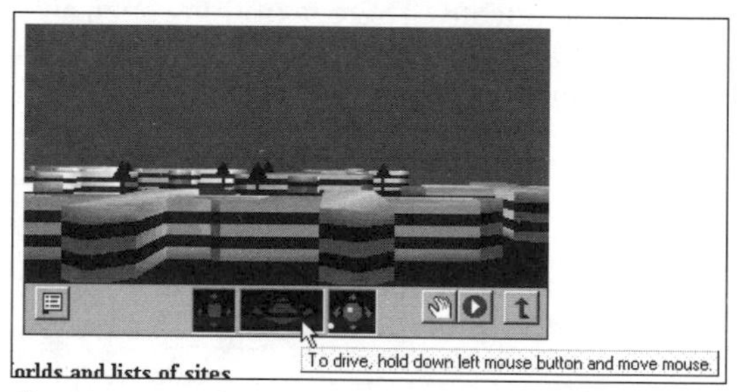
To drive, hold down left mouse button and move mouse.

Figure 4-4: Point to any control to see a tooltip.

For more detailed instructions on navigating in a 3-D world, click on the Frequently Asked Questions link shown in Figure 4-3. Or, read on for specific instruction on navigating with the mouse, keyboard, or a joystick.

Navigating with the Keyboard

Once you are at a Web site that shows a virtual world, click anywhere within the world. Then use the keys listed in Table 4-1 to move, turn, slide, and tilt.

Table 4-1
Navigating a Virtual World with the Keyboard

Direction	*Key*
Move forward	Up arrow
Move backward	Down arrow
Turn left	Left arrow
Turn right	Right arrow
Slide	Hold down Ctrl while pressing Up-, Down-, Left-, or Right-arrow key
Tilt	Hold down Shift while pressing Up-, Down-, Left-, or Right-arrow key

Navigating with the Mouse

To navigate with your mouse, first click within the virtual world. Then follow these steps:

1. Click on one of the directional controls along the bottom of the virtual world.
2. Hold down the left mouse button and move the mouse in the direction you want to go.

Optionally, you can click on any portion of the virtual world to start moving to that spot. When you want to stop, click a second time.

Navigating with a Joystick

You also can get around a virtual world by using your joystick. But first, if you have not yet done so, you'll need to purchase and install the joystick as per the manufacturer's instructions. Then you'll need to calibrate the joystick.

Calibrating your joystick

You first need to calibrate your joystick (if you've never done so) by following these steps:

1. Click the Start button and choose Settings⇨Control Panel.
2. Double-click the Joystick icon to get to the Joystick Properties dialog box shown in Figure 4-5.

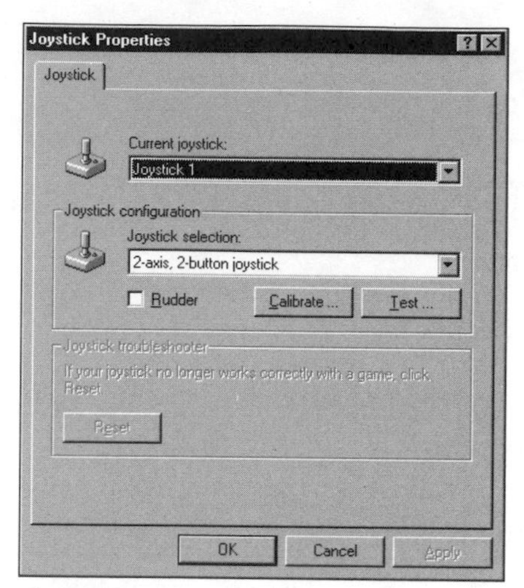

Figure 4-5: The Joystick Properties dialog box.

3. Click the Calibrate button and follow the instructions presented by the Wizard to calibrate your stick.

Maneuvering with your joystick

When your joystick is ready to go, just click within the virtual world picture. If the world starts moving on its own, adjust your joystick's calibration buttons until the motion stops. (You may need to click the Return to starting viewpoint a few times to come in from outer space.) Finally, how you use your joystick depends on whether your stick has a POV hat (an extra control that is available on joysticks that are geared toward flight-simulation packages):

- ✦ If your joystick has a POV hat, then the joystick works similarly to the joystick in an airplane: The forward/back axis tilts you up and down. The left/right axis turns you left and right. The POV hat controls forward, backward, left, and right movement.
- ✦ If your joystick does not have a POV hat, then the forward/back axis moves you forward and backward. The left/right axis turns you left and right.

Examining 3-D Objects

You also can examine objects — sort of twirl them around on the screen. Just click the Examine button (so that it is pushed in) and then use the keyboard, mouse, or joystick to adjust your point of view. To return to normal navigation, click the Examine button a second time so that it is no longer pushed in.

Colliding with Walls

Unlike the real world, virtual worlds typically let you move through walls and objects. If you want to make the virtual world behave more like the real world, right-click the virtual world and choose Prevent Collisions. Or, click on the Menu button and choose Prevent Collisions.

If you can't move at all in a virtual world, chances are you are just in a world that doesn't support collision detection. Clear the Prevent Collisions selection and try again

Speeding Up Virtual Worlds

Virtual Reality over a modem can be very slow. If you want to speed things up, you can disable textures and inlines:

1. Right-click the virtual world and choose Options.
2. Clear the Load Inlines and Load Textures options.

If the site you are exploring uses inlines and textures, Virtual Explorer will not download them anymore, thus giving you faster play and faster action — though less detail on the objects within the world.

Hopping to Another World

Sometimes, as you move through a virtual world, the mouse pointer will change to a pointing hand. This change is usually an indication that clicking on the spot will take you to a different virtual world. Ziff-Davis's Terminal Reality has such links. To try it out, point your Web browser to `http://www.zdnet.com/vrml/content/vrmlsite/outside.wrl`. It takes several minutes to download all the components of that site — wait for the `Copying file...` messages in the status bar to subside before you try cruising that world.

Summary

And that, my friend, is all there is to navigating virtual worlds on the Web. Now, not only are you a Web cruiser, you're also an explorer of virtual worlds. You have total control over the World Wide Web. The next chapter begins Part II, which gets into the *real* meat of this book: creating your own Web site. The more salient points from this chapter are as follows:

- Internet Explorer version 2.0 comes with built-in multimedia viewing capabilities.
- If you're using Internet Explorer 2.0 as your Web browser, you can download and install Virtual Explorer from Microsoft's Web site.
- Once you have installed Virtual Explorer, you automatically see Virtual Explorer's navigation buttons at the bottom of a graphic image that contains a virtual world.
- To navigate with the keyboard, press the arrow keys to indicate the direction in which you want to go. To slide, hold down the Ctrl key while pressing an arrow key. To tilt, hold down Shift while pressing an arrow key.
- To navigate with a mouse, click the appropriate direction control at the bottom of the virtual world (Slide, Drive, or Tilt), then hold down the left mouse button, and move the mouse in the direction that you want to go.
- To navigate with a joystick, move the stick in the direction you want to go. If your joystick has a POV hat, then the joystick behaves like the joystick in an airplane.

✦ ✦ ✦

How to Establish Your Own Web Site

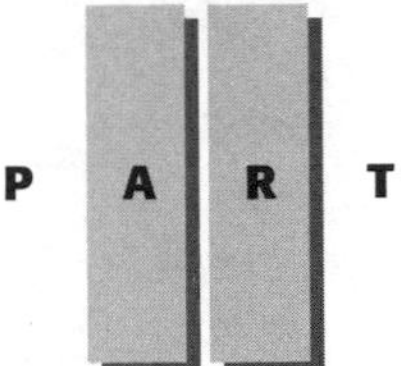

✦ ✦ ✦ ✦

In This Part

✦ ✦ ✦ ✦

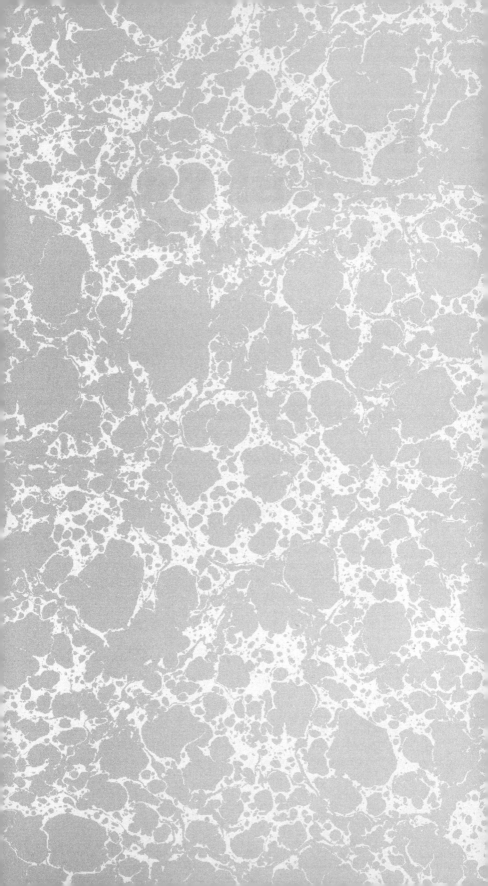

CHAPTER 5

How It All Works

In This Chapter

How the Internet and World Wide Web work

What is a Web site?

What are Web pages?

How do I create Web pages?

Setting a site name (`www.yournamehere.com`)

Shopping for a site

By the time you reach this chapter, hopefully you have been on the World Wide Web and have seen some Web pages on your own. If you know the address (URL) of a particular Web site, you just need to type that address into your Web browser to see the site. Your Web browser then sends a message to that address, via the Internet, saying "send me your Web document." A server machine on the Internet gets the message, says "OK," and sends the Web document back over the Internet to your PC. Your Web browser then grabs the document on its way into your computer and displays it on your screen so that you can read the document, print it, save stuff from it, and so on.

At this point, you may have lots of questions floating around in your mind, such as "Where are those Web pages coming from?" and "How did the authors of those pages create those pages in the first place?" and "How did those authors get those pages to wherever it is that they are?" This chapter looks a little deeper into how all that works. I discuss what is really going on behind the scenes so you can start thinking of ways to get your own pages on the Web.

Just so you know that I'm not totally naïve, let me say this: I know that for many of you, the big question is "Can I make any money off all this?" That question is kind of a tough one. But I give you some opinions (for what they are worth) on that matter near the end of this chapter. For now, though, let's start with the simple facts about how the World Wide Web works.

What Is the Internet?

The World Wide Web is one of several services that the Internet offers. So, what is the Internet? Basically, it consists of a whole bunch of cables connecting a whole bunch of computers. If you could go up into space, look down at the United States, and see the cables that make up the Internet, it might look something like Figure 5-1.

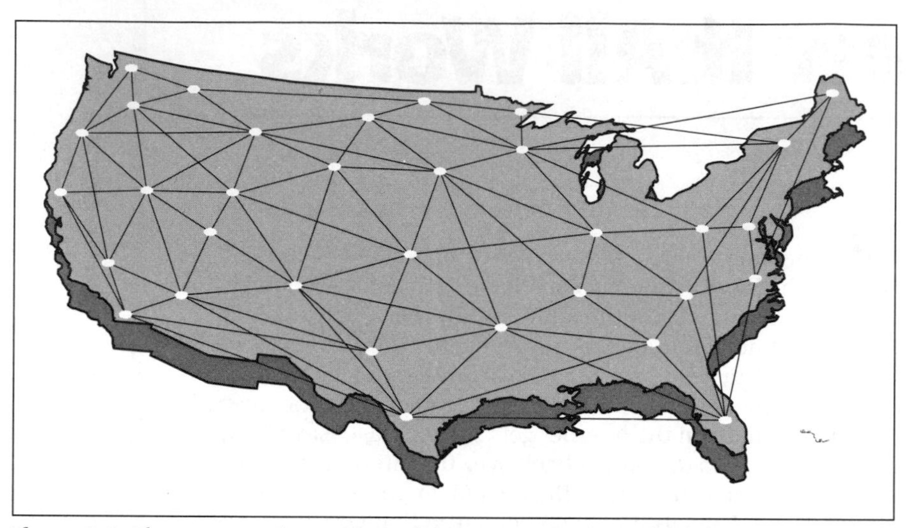

Figure 5-1: The astronaut's-eye view of the Internet in the United States.

Although Figure 5-1 shows only the U.S., the Internet actually extends all the way around the world. And the "web" of cables that exists is a much finer mesh than I can show. Millions, not just a few dozen, of computers are linked together by those cables.

Once you have a bunch of computers linked together with cables, you can do a great deal with those cables and computers. For example, e-mail is one of the most widely used services of the Internet. With e-mail, you type a message on your own computer screen and send it to someone else's e-mail address. The Internet takes your message, locates the destination computer, and stores your message on that computer. When the recipient checks his or her e-mail, your message is there, waiting to be read.

In this respect, the Internet is like the phone company. When you dial a phone number, the appropriate phone rings. Then someone (or an answering machine) answers the phone. As long as you dial the number correctly, you get the right person (or answering machine) because no two phones have the same phone number. Likewise, no two people on the Internet have the same e-mail address.

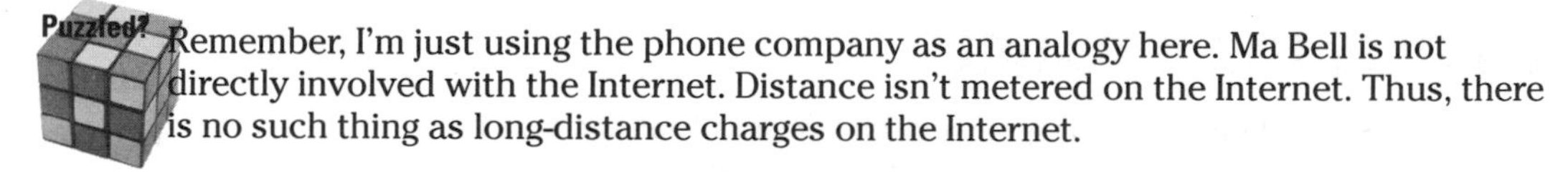

Remember, I'm just using the phone company as an analogy here. Ma Bell is not directly involved with the Internet. Distance isn't metered on the Internet. Thus, there is no such thing as long-distance charges on the Internet.

But like I said, there are lots of things that you can do once you have a bunch of computers hooked up with cables as with the Internet. E-mail is just one service offered by the Internet. In *HTML Publishing Bible,* the service that we are most interested in is the World Wide Web.

What Is the World Wide Web?

Now that we have established what the Internet is and that the World Wide Web is just one of many services offered on the Internet, we need to answer this question: "Well, just what *is* the World Wide Web?" I think that question is best answered by first describing what the Web is *not*. Let's go back to the telephone analogy for a minute.

When you dial a phone number, the phone at the other end of that number rings. Then a person or machine answers that phone. E-mail works in a similar fashion. You send a message out to an e-mail address. The message gets stored at that address. And the person who "lives at" that address sees your message when he or she checks e-mail.

The World Wide Web is different in a couple of major ways:

- The *message* is one or more Web pages, which are basically documents with text, pictures, and maybe some fancier stuff such as sound or video.
- You don't send the Web documents to anyone in particular. Instead, you just put the documents out there for all to see. Anyone who is interested is welcome to come and browse through your pages.

Another way to look at the Web is as an alternative to traditional publishing. In traditional publishing, someone (like me) writes a book (or magazine article, newspaper article, or whatever). Then a publisher prints a zillion copies of it, sends them out all over the world, and hopes that people will buy the publication. The publisher and the bookstores act as the middlemen between the author and the reader.

On the Web, there are no middlemen. No printing is involved, no trucks to distribute the printed books, and no bookstores to carry the books. The Web itself is the middleman. A Web document just sits there on the Web, like a book just sits there on a shelf in the bookstore. But when users want to browse through a document that is sitting there on the Web, they don't need to go anywhere. They can sit at their PCs and type in the document's Web site address — the Internet takes care of the rest.

What Is a Web Site?

This brings us to the next question: So, what is a Web site? In a nutshell, a Web site is a folder (directory) on a disk on a computer connected to the Internet. That folder has its own unique address (URL). When someone types a URL into his or her Web browser, the Internet points the person to that particular folder on that particular computer.

In order for all this to work, the Web site folder needs to contain documents for the browser to read. Every Web site has a *home page*. That page is the one automatically sent to the browser when the browser calls up the site's address. For example, back in

Chapter 3, I pointed my browser to the White House's Web site, whose address is `http://www.whitehouse.gov`. In response, that Web site sent me its home page, which looks something like Figure 5-2.

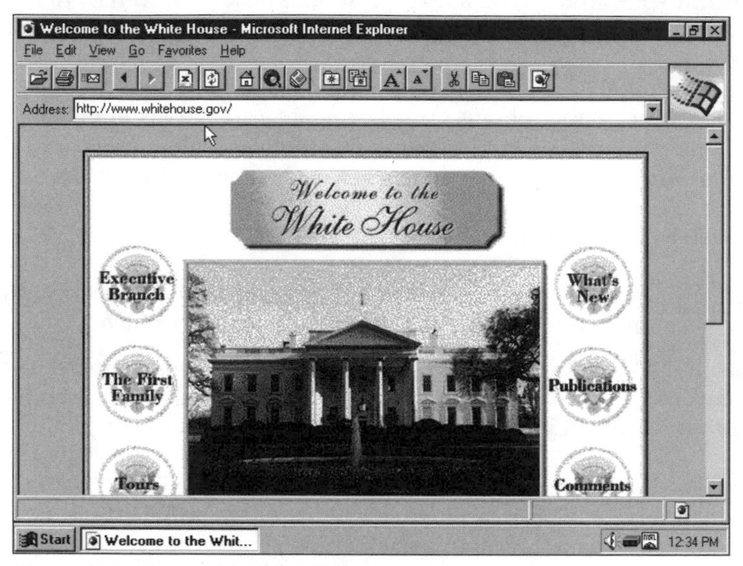

Figure 5-2: The White House's home page.

Although the home page is the only page that the White House's Web site automatically sends me, this page is not the only one that the site has to offer. By looking at its home page, I see that several other pages are available for my viewing pleasure, such as Executive Branch, The First Family, Tours, What's New, Publications, and Comments.

To see one of those pages, I click the appropriate link (hot spot) on the home page. For example, I may click The First Family. That click then sends a message to the White House's Web site, saying "Hey, send me the pages about the First Family." Those pages are sent through the Internet and appear on my screen, as in Figure 5-3.

The whole concept is so practical, so elegant, and so simple that it just boggles the mind. The potential of this kind of communication medium is so far reaching that one can hardly imagine the new opportunities it will present. And you, my friend, are right at the ground floor of this medium's popularity. When combined with preparation, this spells O-P-P-O-R-T-U-N-I-T-Y in a big, big way.

But let's get back to the technical stuff. We have determined that a Web site is a folder (directory) on a hard disk, similar to the folders on your own hard disk, such as My Documents, Windows, and all those other folders that appear in Windows Explorer and My Computer. The only difference is that the Web site's folder resides on a computer that is connected to the Internet at all times. The Web site folder also has an address (URL) that gives it a unique identity on the Internet (just as your phone number gives your telephone a unique identity in the phone system).

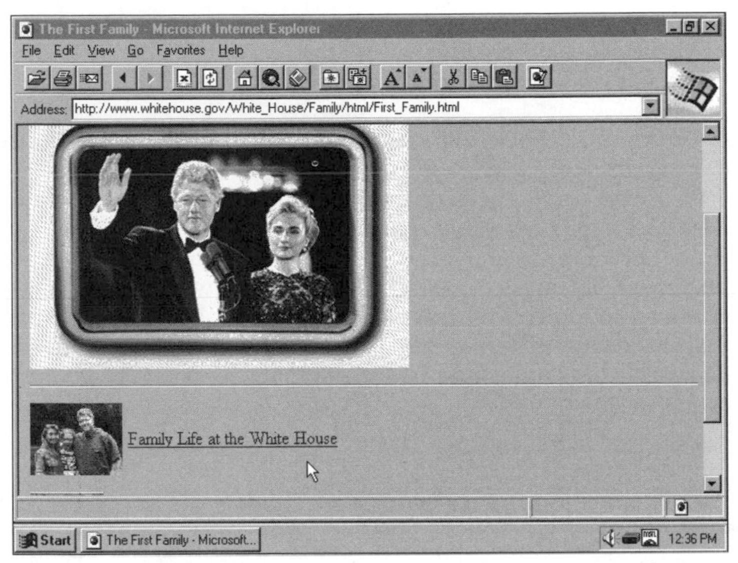

Figure 5-3: The First Family page from the White House's Web site.

What Are Web Pages?

Now we need to examine the question "So, just what kind of documents are in those Web site folders?" Actually, you may be surprised to learn that those documents are not much different from the standard word-processing documents that many of you have created numerous times. In fact, you can use familiar word processors, such as Microsoft Word or WordPerfect, to create Web documents.

The biggest difference between an everyday, run-of-the-mill, word-processing document and a document designed for the Web is the use of *hypertext links,* also called *hyperlinks* for short. Hypertext links are those little hot spots that you can click on to go from one document to the next. As you learn to author your own pages in Part III of this book, you also learn how to add hyperlinks to those pages (in Chapter 16). But for now, let's look at why the links are important.

It takes time to send a Web document over the Internet. If you put, say, 20 pages on your Web site, you don't want to download all of them at once to your readers. Why? Because it would take too long for the entire 20-page document to get there. Your potential reader may get tired of waiting, click the Stop button, and move on to some other site that responds more quickly. (Also, if everyone downloaded 20-page Web documents, those transactions would create a great deal of Internet traffic, which would slow the Internet's response time for everyone!)

Instead, just send them a small home page that contains links to other documents. That way, the home page can get there quickly and the reader can choose to download only those documents in which he or she is interested.

Virtually all Web sites are organized in this manner. For example, the White House's Web site probably contains seven documents. The home page (shown back in Figure 5-2) is one document, then a separate document probably exists for each hot spot on the home page. Figure 5-4 shows what that setup might look like.

As a potential Web publisher, you need to start thinking about what kinds of information you want to put into your own site, as well as how you could create a simple home page that makes it easy for the reader to pick-and-choose what he or she wants to read. See the sidebar text for some food for thought on what you may want to publish in your own Web site.

Makin' money on the Web

You are probably not the person running the White House Web site. Chances are that you are more interested in the Web as a sales and promotional tool for your business. If that is the case, you may be interested in putting the following kinds of documents into your Web site:

Information about your business: Let people know what your business is all about. Promote yourself!

Products and services offered: Publish your product catalog or descriptions of the services your offer, for all the world to see.

Order forms: Enable people to fill in an order form and submit it to you with the click of a button. Makes it oh-so-easy for them to buy!

Frequently asked questions: Post the answers to common questions on the Web so that you don't have to answer them all by phone, mail, and fax.

News items: Keep customers informed of new products and services, upcoming sales, or recent accomplishments.

Talent samples: If you are a creative professional, show off your work on the Web so that potential clients or employers can see your talent right away. Multimedia lets you publish writing, art, photography, video, music, and animation.

Resume: If you are hunting for a job, post your resume on the Web so that potential employers can see it right away.

Links to other sites: Share similar interests with other people. Point your customers to other sites they might find interesting.

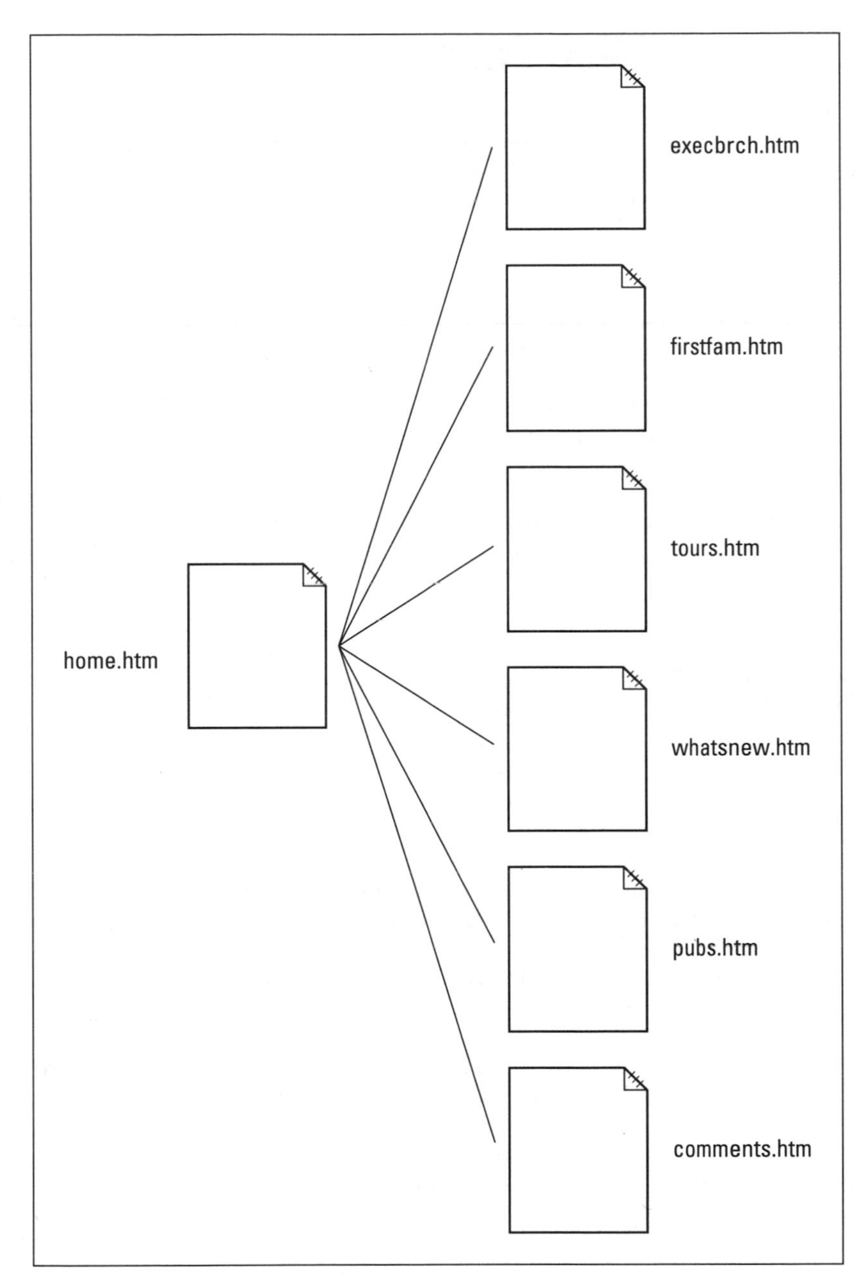

Figure 5-4: How the White House's Web documents might be organized.

How Do I Create Web Pages?

You can create Web pages on your own PC by using standard word-processing techniques. In this book, I focus on Microsoft's Word Internet Assistant (Word IA for short) as the tool for creating Web documents, but *not* because it is the only tool available and not because I'm kissing up to Microsoft. Rather, I talk about this tool because (1) most Windows 95 users probably own a copy of Microsoft Word and have some experience with it, (2) the Internet Assistant is free and you can easily download it from Microsoft's Web site, and (3) if you do know how to use Word, this tool will probably be the easiest and most efficient one available to you. I discuss how to use Word Internet Assistant in Part III of this book.

Dozens, even hundreds of products are available for authoring Web documents — feel free to use whatever authoring tools you like. Or, for that matter, don't use any tools at all. Just gather up your company brochure, or jot down some notes, and hand it all over to an Internet Presence Provider. Let the people there change your raw material into Web documents. This method will cost you more money, but it will also take up a great deal less of your time. I discuss this "hands-off" approach to creating your Web documents in Chapter 7.

How Do I Get Those Pages on the Web?

Authoring Web documents is actually the easy part of getting your Web pages on the Web. Getting a Web site to put them on the Web can be a bit more complicated. Not that this task is inherently difficult to do; rather, the reason is because there are so many ways you can go about getting, or creating, a Web site.

At one extreme, there is the simple, inexpensive "instant" home page (which I discuss in detail in Chapter 6). At the other extreme lies the complex and expensive approach of actually creating a Web server and hooking it directly to the Internet. You'll have to decide which method works best for you based on what I cover in the next few chapters.

Once you make a decision and take action, it may take your Web site service provider a few days, maybe even weeks, to get your site squared away and ready to hold your documents. For that reason, I'm going to help you find a Web site before you start creating Web documents. Once you have ordered your Web site, you can create your Web documents while the service provider is setting up your site.

Domain Names: `www.`*`yournamehere`*`.com`

One last pesky detail to consider early in the process is whether you want your own custom domain name. That is, if you are XYZ Incorporated, do you want your Web site address to be `www.xyz.com`? Or, will you be content to use someone else's domain name with your name "tacked on," as in `www.WebbeWebs.com/~xyz`? I ask this question for three reasons:

- ✦ A custom domain name costs money (about $100 up front plus anywhere from $10 to $100 per month).
- ✦ Only about half of the service providers that provide Web sites can give you a custom domain name. If you want a custom domain name, you'll need to shop for a service that can give you one.
- ✦ Setting up a domain takes several days, if not weeks, so you need to get started on that task as soon as possible.

The value of a custom domain name is that it can be easy to remember. For example, a shopping mall named University Towne Center is located near my home, but everyone calls it UTC. The mall has a billboard out on the freeway that says you can visit them on the Web at

```
http://www.shoputc.com
```

Here's another example. One of my local TV stations, KGTV, has a Web site. Occasionally, it runs a little spot that provides information about the station, which shows the station's Web site address:

```
http://www.kgtv.com
```

The value of these custom domain names is that they are easy to remember. Like most URLs, both start with `http://www.` and end with `.com`. If I want to make a mental note of these sites, I just need to remember *shoputc* or *kgtv,* both of which are easy to remember. If these sites had addresses like

```
http://www.klog.nix.edu/~shoputc
```

or

```
http://myplace.compuserve.com/homepage/psychonet/kgtv.htm
```

there is no way that I'd be able to memorize the names. Hence, I'd be much less likely to just stop by and take a peek at these sites the next time I'm sitting at my PC.

The "clean URL" also has something of a professional air about it. It presents a good image (even if the business behind the name is run from your garage!). The clean name looks impressive when printed on your business card and stationery.

On the other hand, if you won't be advertising your domain name out in the real world, the expense of getting a customized domain name may not be worthwhile. For example, if you are selling flowers and a hotlink to your site appears when people search Yahoo! or Magellan (or one of the other search engines) for the word *flowers*, then who cares how your domain name reads? The user may not even see your domain name — all he or she will see is your business name as a hot spot on the screen of the search engine. To get to your site, the reader simply clicks on that hot spot.

The bottom line is this: Deciding whether or not a clean, easily-memorized domain name is worth the expense to you is a decision that you have to make on your own. But you should make your decision as early as possible, and even think of several possible alternative names if you decide that a custom name is the way you want to go. Many domain names are already taken. Of course, you'll also want to find a service provider who can give you that custom domain name at a reasonable price.

Shopping for a Web Site

Allrighty then. At this point, you should understand that setting up shop on the Web is going to require two major steps: (1) finding someplace on the Internet to store your Web pages (that is, a Web site) and (2) creating some Web pages to put on that site. Because putting together a Web site can take some time, I help you do that task first. We'll explore each of your alternatives in the chapters that follow, but here I summarize the various approaches so that you can skip the chapters that may be totally irrelevant to your needs.

Is my favorite domain name taken?

If you think of a good domain name, you can find out quickly whether or not that name is already taken. First, point your Web browser to InterNIC's Whois server at `http://rs.internic.net/cgi-bin/whois`. You'll come to a query form where you can type the domain name in which you are interested. Type that name (for example, ***coolstuff***), press Enter, and wait a couple of seconds.

You'll see a list of sites (if any) that contain that name. But don't assume that just because some sites appear, the name is taken. For example, your search for *coolstuff* may point you to the entry for *CoolStuff, Inc.* But CoolStuff, Inc.'s *domain name* may be COOLBOY.COM or GOCOOL.COM. In that case, `Coolstuff.com` may still be available as a domain name!

If you don't see the name you want listed specifically as a domain name, then perhaps the domain name is available. It's worth a try!

Keep in mind that Whois only shows you the names of existing sites. You cannot register a new domain name through this site. You can register a new domain name through InterNIC. But typically, you'll want to go through your Internet Service Provider to get a domain name fully registered.

By the way, if you ever need to get back to Whois and can't remember the URL, you can look it up in any search engine. Just go to Microsoft's All In One Search Page or Yahoo! or any other search site and look up the word *InterNIC* or *Whois*.

You may already have a Web site

If you have an account with America Online, CompuServe, or Prodigy, you already have a Web site! A *real* Web site that is accessible to Internet users all over the world — not just members of that same service! Your site is probably empty right now. All you have to do, though, is stick some pages in it.

The kind of sites offered by these services are sometimes called *personal publishing* sites because they have some limitations. For example, you may be able to fit only a few pages and a couple of pictures into your site. Also, you have to use the URL that your provider gives you — you can't get a custom domain name. In addition, a personal publishing site does not really provide enough flexibility to conduct a serious business on the Web.

More Info

By the time you read this, The Microsoft Network (MSN) may also be offering free, or low-cost, Web sites. But I can't make any promises.

The good news is that the site is free! If you are already an America Online, CompuServe, or Prodigy member, you can post your Web pages without any additional expense over your current membership fees. The online services will even help you create your home page using simple, fill-in-the-blank forms. See Chapter 6 for information on taking advantage of this type of Web site.

Throw money at a site

If you are planning to promote a business or conduct business on the Internet, a personal publishing site may not have the capabilities to fit your needs. If you are also way too busy running the business and don't have time to learn all the details of creating Web documents and such, you can still hire an Internet Presence Provider to do all the technical stuff for you. Basically, you just send them your company brochure or handwritten notes — whatever — explaining what you want to put into your Web site. The Internet Presence Provider will make it happen. See Chapter 7 for more information on hiring an Internet Presence Provider to handle your site.

Throw time at a site

If you want something fancier than a personal publishing page but also want to keep expenses down and create your own Web pages, then you may want to sign up with a local Internet Service Provider. Many ISPs can give you all the Web space you want, a custom domain name, and much, much more. But ISPs only give you the basic tools that you need — authoring, maintaining, and promoting your own Web pages are your responsibility.

As a result, although this approach costs less than hiring an Internet Presence Provider, you have to put in more of your own time to get the site going and keep it going. I used this approach to create my coolnerds site (`http://www.coolnerds.com`). For more information on setting up this kind of site, see Chapter 8.

Throw everything at a site

If you have time and money burning holes in your pockets or if you are thinking of *really* going big time on the Web, then you can create your own Web server. The advantage of this approach is that your site can be as large and complex as you want. The disadvantage is that you have to buy the computer ($$), buy and install Web server software ($), get a dedicated line to the Internet ($$$), and create your own Web pages (time cost). This approach makes getting a presence on the Web a pretty hefty endeavor. Chapter 9 describes this approach in more detail.

Summary

Hopefully, you now have a little better feel for how the World Wide Web works and what you need to do to become part of it as a publisher, not just a reader. The following list summarizes the main points:

- The Internet is a network of cables connecting millions of PCs around the world.
- The World Wide Web is one of many services that the Internet offers and also is the service that you are most likely to publish on.
- A Web site is a collection of documents stored somewhere on the Internet that anyone can read by pointing their Web browser to the site's URL.
- The documents that you store on your Web site must be coded with HTML tags. You can either insert the tags yourself or use a Web authoring tool that lets you take a more standard word-processing approach to the job.
- If you are planning to publish on the Web, it is a good idea to start thinking of a domain name (URL) early on.
- There are several approaches you can take to create a Web site, which are discussed in the next three chapters.

✦ ✦ ✦

CHAPTER 6

Your Free AOL, CompuServe, or Prodigy Site

✦ ✦ ✦ ✦

In This Chapter

Setting up your free America Online Web site

Setting up your free CompuServe Web site

Setting up your free Prodigy Web site

✦ ✦ ✦ ✦

I have good news for America Online, CompuServe, and Prodigy members. You already have a Web site! Granted, if you haven't done anything with that site, it is just sitting there empty. But if you have created some Web-publishable documents, all you have to do next is put them in your Web site for all the world to see.

Overview of Freebie Sites

Before I show you some examples of publishing on a "freebie" site, let me point out some general issues that you may encounter while using them. The generalities that follow apply to all of the freebie sites:

- ✦ These sites are geared toward personal publishing — they are not really intended for those who want to conduct business on the Internet.
- ✦ As a member of the service, you get some free publishing space as part of your existing membership fees (see Table 6-1).
- ✦ You can get all of the Web publishing information that you need from the service (see Table 6-1). In this chapter, I provide some examples of publishing on these sites to round out the information you get online.
- ✦ You must use the address (URL) that the service provides. You cannot create your own custom domain name.
- ✦ CompuServe and America Online's My Home Page service even offers its own authoring tools, so you can publish *before* reading Part III (and beyond) in this book.

Table 6-1
Web Publishing Offered by Various Online Services

Service	*Free Space*	*Where to Start*
America Online "My Home Page"	1 MB	Keyword **my home page**
America Online "My Place"	1-2MB	Keyword **my place**
CompuServe	1MB	Go **Internet**
The Microsoft Network (MSN)	TBD	Check Microsoft's home page for availability
Prodigy	1MB	Jump word **Internet**

When I wrote this chapter, Microsoft was not offering free Web publishing, hence the TBD (To Be Determined) rating under "Free Space" in Table 6-1. But I think it's safe to assume that MSN will do so, perhaps even by the time you read this book. If you are an MSN member, keep an eye out for such announcements on Microsoft's home page.

In the sections that follow, I explain each service in some detail and take you through the actual process of publishing your pages. But I cannot get into too much depth on authoring fancy Web pages yet; we don't get into that topic until Part III of this book. I'm also not going to try to repeat all the information readily available to you online. I simply want to give you a feel for what is involved in Web publishing and perhaps help you get your first real home page out there on the Web!

Web Publishing via America Online

If you are an America Online (AOL) member, then you already have two Web sites available to you. One is called *My Home Page,* and the other is called *My Place*. The first, My Home Page, is a small, personal publishing site that you can set up in minutes — even if you know very little about authoring Web documents. Let's take a look at that approach first.

Creating your AOL My Home Page

AOL's My Home Page offers a Web page toolkit that makes it easy to create a simple home page. To get the toolkit, follow these steps:

1. Sign on to America Online in the usual manner. If you have multiple screen names, sign on with whichever name you think will make the best Web Site address.
2. From AOL's menu bar, select Go To➪Keyword, type **home page**, and then click on Go. You'll come to AOL's Personal Publisher, shown in Figure 6-1.

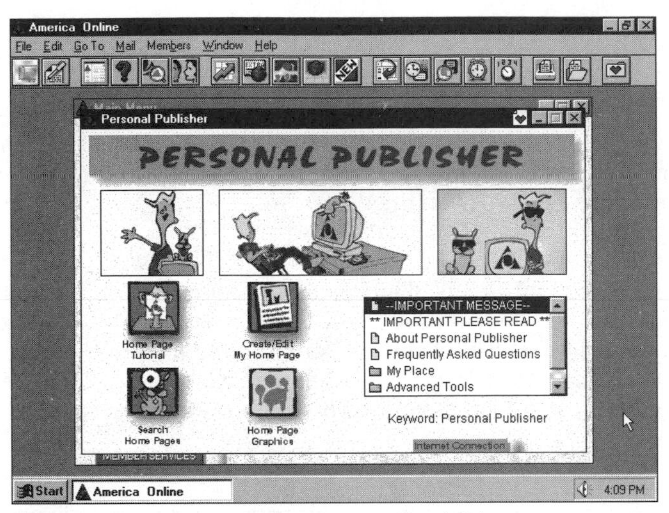

Figure 6-1: America Online's Personal Publisher.

3. If you want to take some lessons on creating a home page, click on the Home Page Tutorial button and follow the instructions on the screen.
4. When you are ready to create your home page, click on Create/Edit My Home Page.
5. Now just follow the instructions as they appear on the screen.

When it asks you who will be allowed to view your page, be sure to choose *AOL and Internet* if you want your home page to be accessible to the entire World Wide Web. After you complete and save your home page, you'll see a message indicating your page's URL, as in Figure 6-2.

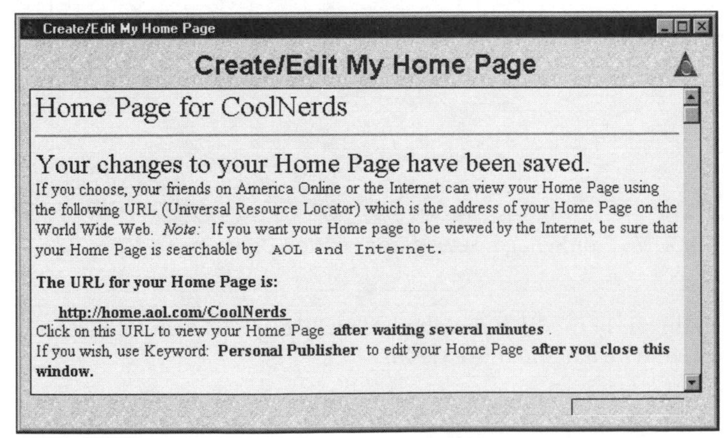

Figure 6-2: AOL shows you your home page's URL after you save that home page.

Viewing your AOL My Home Page

To see your AOL home page as it will look to people on the World Wide Web, you first need to sign out from AOL. Wait a few minutes for your page to get posted. Then start up your Web browser (Internet Explorer in this example) and get connected to the Web. Enter the URL for your new Web site, `http://home.aol.com/CoolNerds` in my case, and you'll see your page as it looks on the Web.

Figure 6-3 shows how I set up my sample *AOL My Home Page.* To view it, I connected to the Internet via my MSN account and used Internet Explorer as my Web browser. Much of the page currently is scrolled off the screen. But you can see the multimedia files I've added, including a photo (GIF file) and a link to a sound file (a WAV file) displayed as the *Simpson Family Alma Mater* link. When you click on that link, the sound plays. If you want to try it out, point your own Web browser to `http://home.aol.com/CoolNerds`.

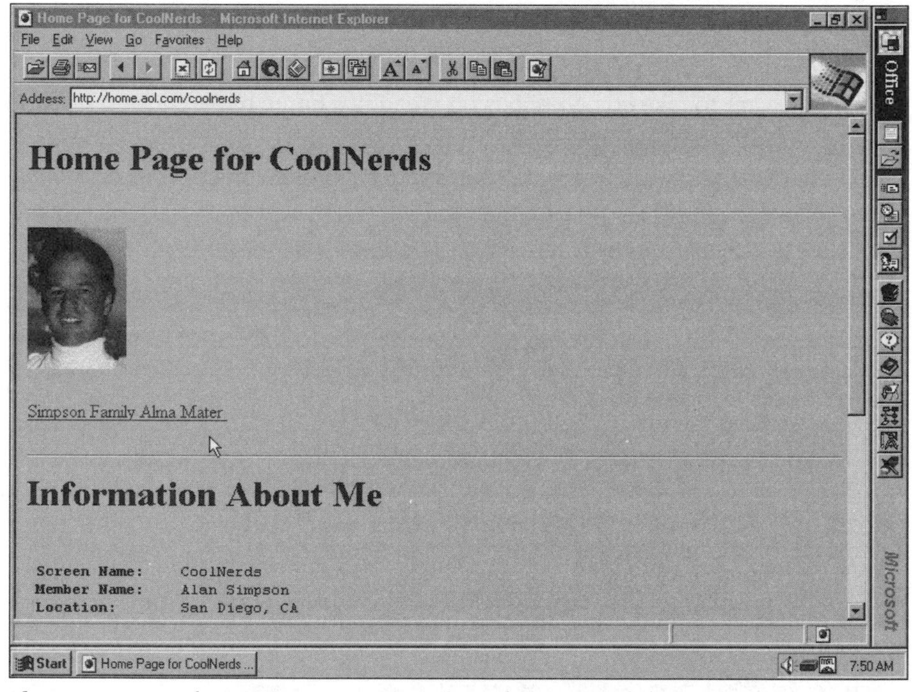

Figure 6-3: Sample AOL My Home Page viewed from a Web browser.

More Info Pictures that you publish on the Web need to be in GIF or JPEG format. Chapters 15 and 22 discuss those file formats in more detail.

AOL's My Home Page doesn't give you a whole lot of leeway in designing your page. The upside of the home page approach, however, is that you can create a page in less than five minutes — even if you don't know a thing about Web publishing. And you can learn everything you need to know right from the on-screen tutorial. If you want to create fancier pages, you can use AOL's My Place rather than its My Home Page.

Fancier pages on AOL's My Place

AOL's My Place is not as easy to use as My Home Page. Instead, it is more like a traditional Web site, where you take full responsibility for creating documents on your own PC and then uploading them to My Place. To read about My Place online, sign into America Online in the usual manner. From AOL's menu bar, choose Go To➪ Keyword and type **my place** as your keyword. Then click on GO or press Enter. You'll come to a small introductory screen like the one in Figure 6-4. You'll definitely want to start off with the Frequently Asked Questions button.

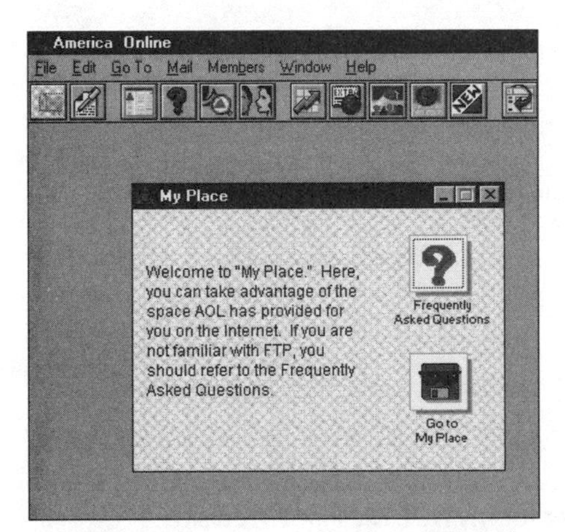

Figure 6-4: America Online's My Place lets you publish more sophisticated Web pages.

My Place provides both WWW (World Wide Web) and FTP (File Transfer Protocol) services. You can use FTP to store the files that you want other people to download. But be careful — this service is free only if you keep the Web pages *and* downloadable files to 2MB or less! Chapter 38 describes what FTP is all about, but it is not necessary to learn about that right now.

Documents for AOL's My Place

As you read about AOL's My Place, you'll discover that, unlike My Home Page, My Place doesn't offer any assistance in authoring Web documents. You have to do that task on your own at your PC. Keep in mind, too, that I'm not going to talk about Web authoring until Part III of this book.

As an example of a completed document, Figure 6-5 shows a sample I created using Microsoft's Word Internet Assistant. I named this document index.htm (a common name to assign to Web home pages). There are two graphic images displayed on the page, one named aolbeany.gif (the beany) and the other named coolaol.gif (the headline aol text). I saved index.htm, aolbeany.gif, and coolaol.gif in one folder so that I can easily find them when it is time to upload them to my AOL site.

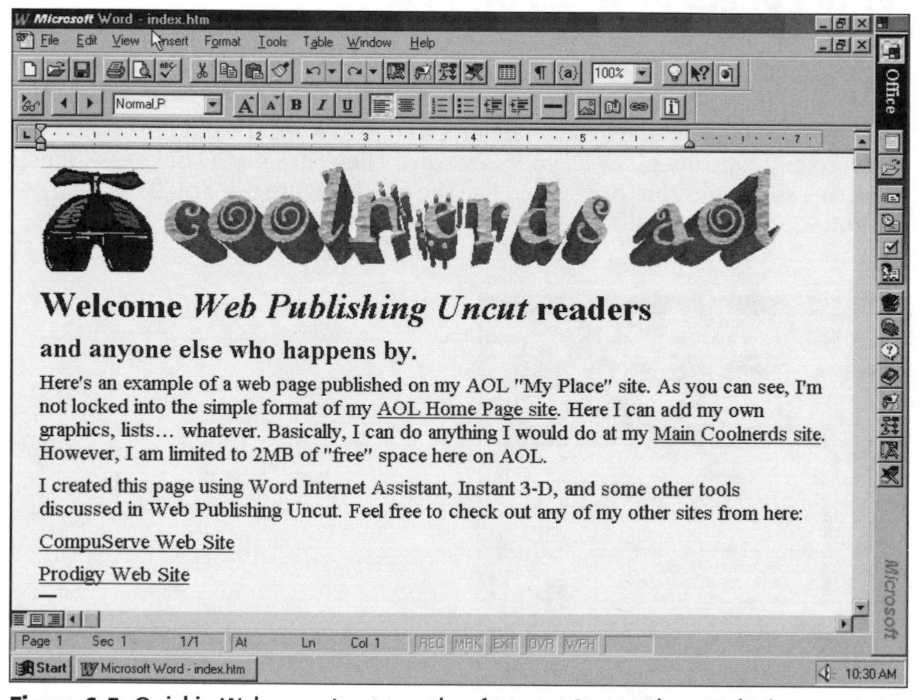

Figure 6-5: Quickie Web page I put together for my AOL My Place Web site.

Danger Zone

Many Internet sites are case-sensitive to filenames, which means *coolaol.gif* would not be considered the same as *CoolAol.gif*. I suggest that you try to get in the habit of always using all lowercase letters for files you plan to publish on the Web, so that you don't get stung by this case-sensitivity thing!

Uploading documents to AOL's My Place

Say that you have created your Web home page, graphics, and whatever else you want to publish. Now you are ready to upload them to your AOL My Place site for all the world to see. Here's how you would proceed:

1. Sign on to America Online in the usual manner.

2. From the menu bar, choose Go To⇨Keyword and enter **personal publishing** as the keyword.
3. In the list box, double-click on the My Place option.
4. Click the Go To My Place button. You'll be connected to your own space in `members.aol.com`.
5. Click on the Upload button. Your screen will look something like Figure 6-6.

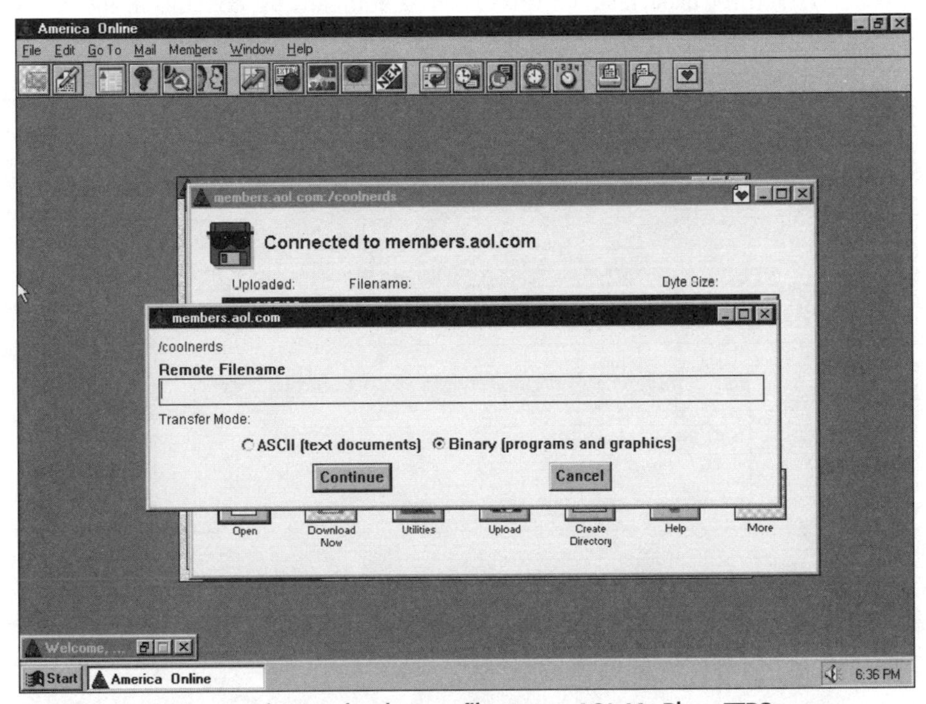

Figure 6-6: Getting ready to upload some files to my AOL My Place FTPSpace.

6. Now you need to upload each file for your site — one file at a time. Enter the name of the file you are about to upload (just the filename, such as coolaol.gif; don't include a drive letter or folder name at this point).
7. If you are uploading a graphic image or any other non-text file, choose Binary. If you are uploading a plain text document, choose ASCII.
8. Click the Continue button.
9. Click the Select File button, and use the Drives, Folders, and File name lists to specify one file to upload (the file you named in Step 8). Then click OK.
10. Click the Send button to upload that one file, and wait for the File Transfer Complete message to appear. Click OK.

11. Repeat Steps 7 through 11 for every file you need to upload.
12. When all of your files have been uploaded, close all open windows until you get back to America Online's Main Menu window.

Before you try to get to your site via the Internet, you may want to double-check to make sure that you have uploaded all the necessary files. To do so, repeat Steps 3 through 5 to take another look at your site. Your list of files should now include all the files that make up your Web site. For example, in Figure 6-7, you can see that I have uploaded the three files I need for this example: aolbeany.gif, coolaol.gif, and index.htm. (The Private folder was already there and need not concern you right now.)

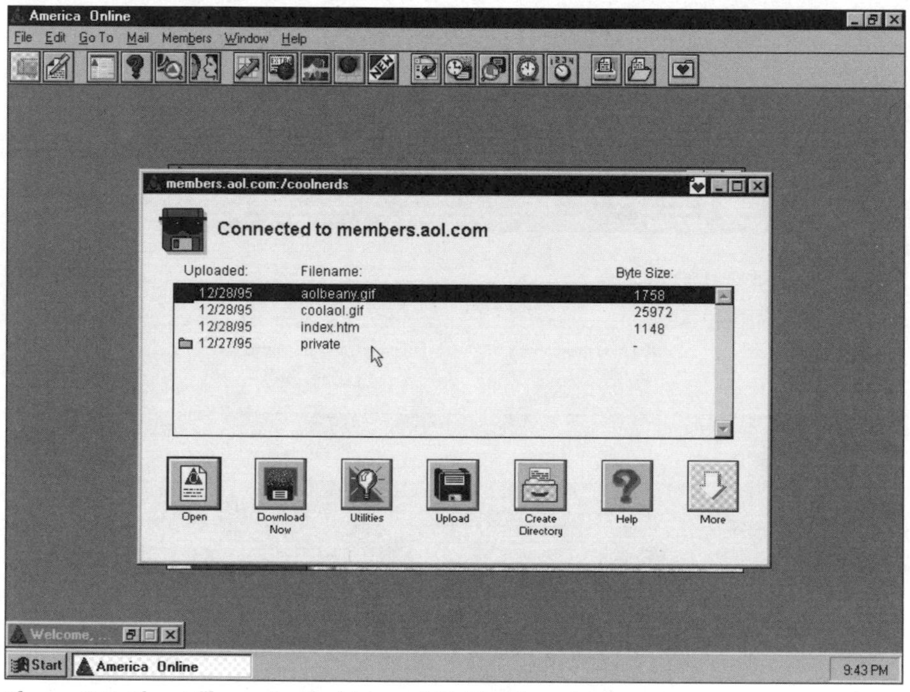

Figure 6-7: Three files uploaded to my AOL My Place FTPSpace.

The URL for your AOL My Page

To view your published pages via the Internet, you need to know the site's URL. For your AOL My page site, the URL will be `http://members.aol.com` followed by a slash and your screen name (*coolnerds* in my example) and then followed by a slash and the name of your home page (the document that opens as soon as the user points to your site). This must be the name of a valid HTML file. In my example, *index.htm* is my home page, so the complete URL for my AOL My Page site is as follows:

```
http://members.aol.com/coolnerds/index.htm
```

After you finish, you can sign out of America Online (choose File⇨Exit and click the Exit Application button). You'll then be returned to the Windows 95 desktop.

Viewing your AOL My Page from the Web

To see how your site will look to most of the people out there on the Web, just point your browser (any Web browser) to your site. For example, in Figure 6-8, I've pointed Internet Explorer to `http://members.aol.com/coolnerds/index.htm`, and my page appears.

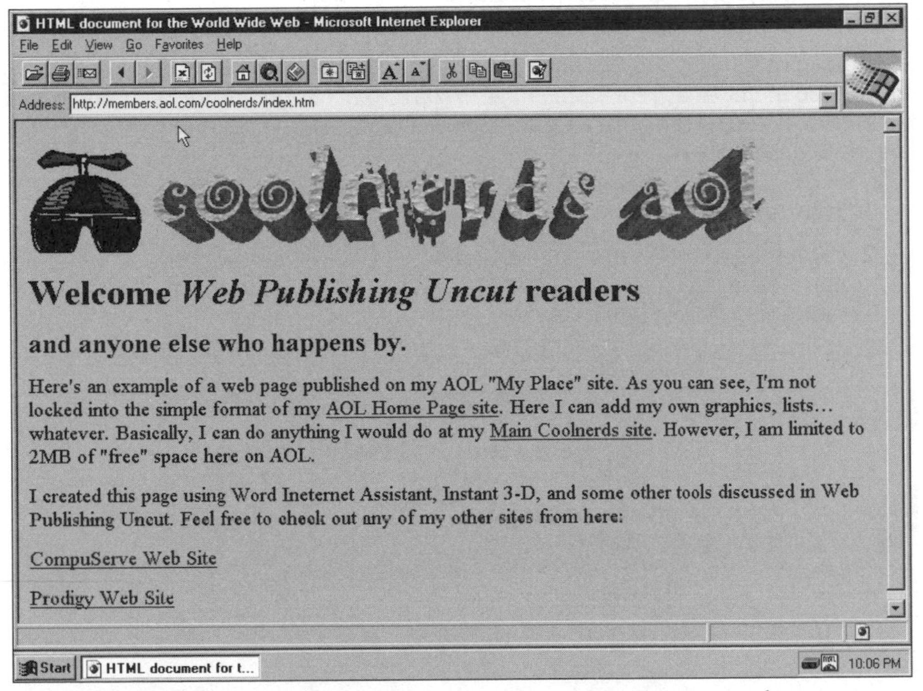

Figure 6-8: My AOL My Place Web documents viewed from Internet Explorer.

Remember that even though you used America Online to *publish* your Web document, the document is available for *viewing* for anyone on the Internet — not just America Online members. So, for example, no matter how you are connected to the Internet, if you have a Web browser, you can point it to `http://members.aol.com/coolnerds/index.htm` and view that page.

If you are an America Online member and are interested in learning more about the My Place service, check out the Web Diner. Sign on to America Online in the usual manner and go to the keyword Web Diner. Also, stop back by AOL's My Place (keyword My Place) and click the Frequently Asked Questions button.

Why so many sites?

You may be wondering why I have so many Web sites spread around. Truth is, creating all of these Web sites was actually just research for this book. One Web site is all a person or company really needs.

Of course, if you happen to have an AOL, CompuServe, and Prodigy account, you *could* hot-link all three sites together and get up to 4MB of free storage that way. Just a thought.

Web Publishing via CompuServe

CompuServe Information Service (CIS) also offers free Web publishing to its members. Its service includes a great Home Page Wizard to help you author Web documents with ease. If you already are a CompuServe member, you can follow these steps to see what CIS has to offer:

1. Start up WinCIM in the usual manner on your PC.
2. Click the Internet button in the Explore Services window and wait a couple of minutes for the login process to complete. You'll come to a page that looks (something) like Figure 6-9.

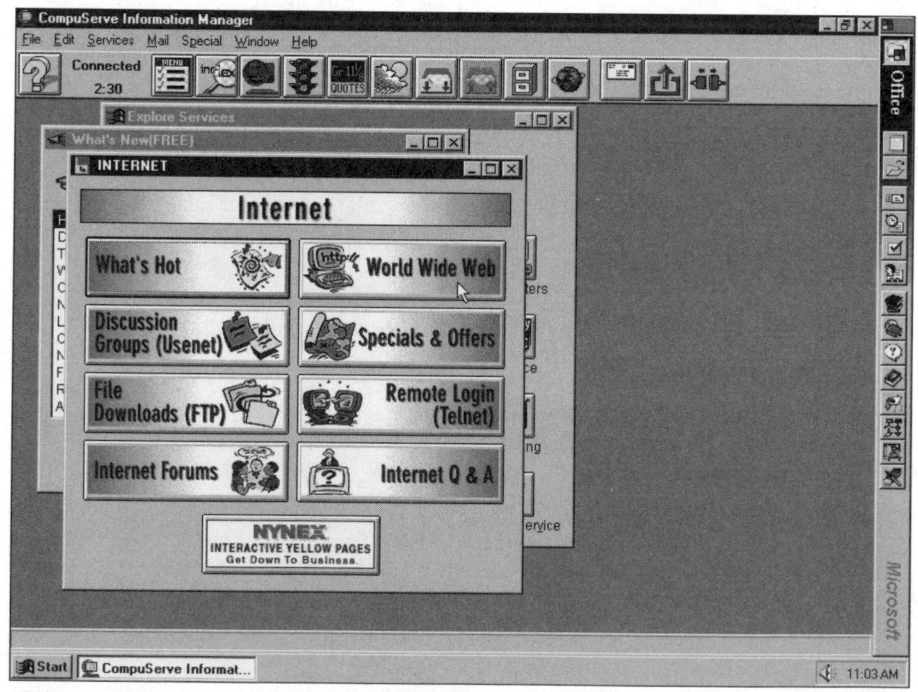

Figure 6-9: CompuServe's Internet offerings.

3. Click the World Wide Web button.

Feel free to look around and see what's available. If you want to get started creating your Web site right away, go to the Home Page Wizard screen. You can do so either by clicking buttons that appear on the screen or — if you want to hop right to it — by choosing Services⇨Go from the menu bar, typing **hpwiz**, and clicking the OK button. You'll come to the window shown in Figure 6-10.

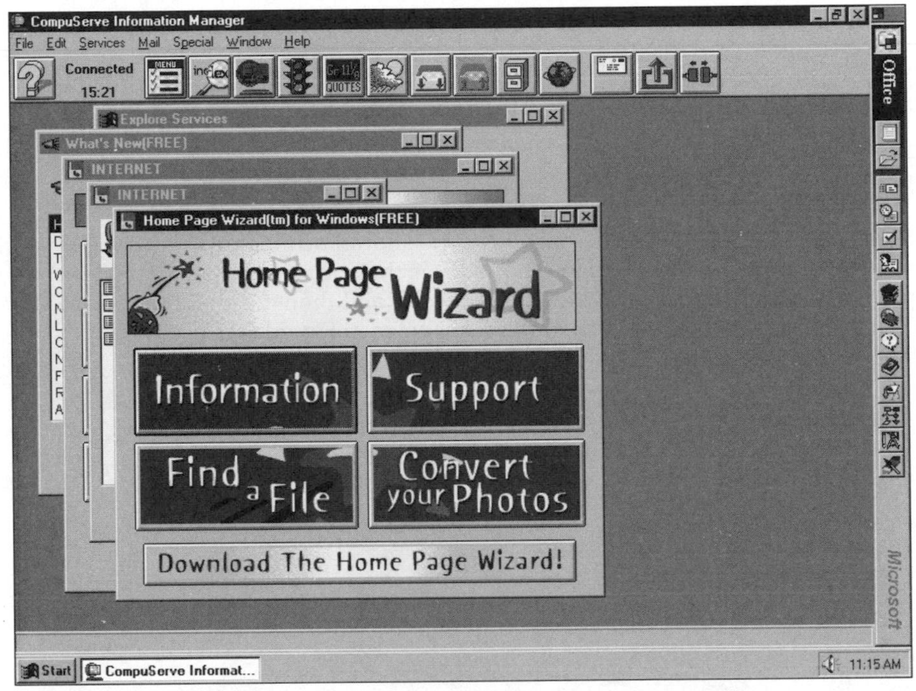

Figure 6-10: CompuServe's Home Page Wizard for Windows.

The Information and Support buttons provide useful information about Web publishing via CIS. You can create your Web pages by using any of the authoring techniques described later in this book. Alternatively, you can take advantage of CIS's free Home Page Wizard, which makes document creation quick and easy. To use the Home Page Wizard, click the Download Home Page Wizard! button and read (and perhaps print) the Downloading/Installation instructions. Then download the HPWIZ.EXE file as per the instructions.

Installing CompuServe's Home Page Wizard

After you have downloaded the HPWIZ.EXE file to your own PC, you can sign off of CompuServe. Then follow these instructions to decompress the HPWIZ.EXE file and install its programs to your hard disk:

1. At the Windows 95 desktop, click the Start button and choose Run.
2. Browse to, or type in, **c:\cserve\download\hpwiz.exe** and then click on OK.
3. Follow the instructions that appear on the screen.

You will be given the opportunity to choose your own folders for storing the Home Page Wizard. Use whatever folders will be easiest for you to remember.

Using CompuServe's Home Page Wizard

After the Home Page Wizard is installed, you should be able to start it as you would any other Windows 95 program. That is, click the Start button, point to Programs, point to the appropriate program group folder, and then click on Home Page Wizard. You'll start off in the New Project window shown in Figure 6-11.

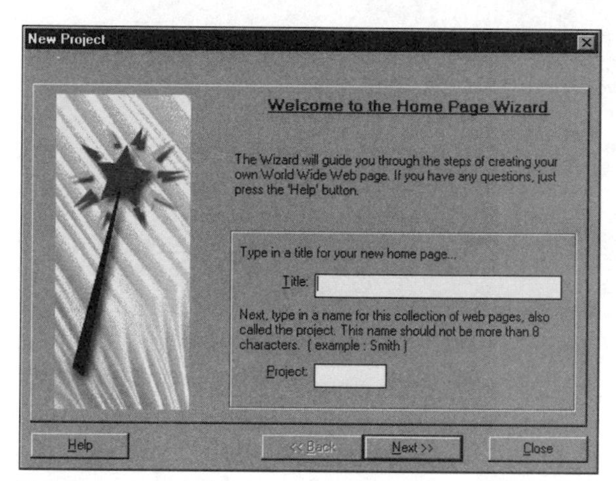

Figure 6-11: The first page of CompuServe's Home Page Wizard.

Follow the instructions that appear on the screen and click the Next button to move to the next Wizard page. After you finish filling in the blanks on the form, you'll be taken to the initial first draft of your home page, which looks something like Figure 6-12. From there, you can use the various buttons and menu items that appear across the top of the window to author the page, by adding text, graphics (images), lines, links, and so on. You also can edit existing text and other elements. Just right-click whatever you want to change, and then choose Edit to change or Delete to remove. You also can move an element just by clicking on it and then dragging it to a new location.

Figure 6-12: First draft of a CIS Wizard-created home page.

Completely revamping the Wizard-generated page is easy. Figure 6-13 shows how I changed my page by deleting most of what was there and replacing it with graphics (GIF files) and text of my own.

Figure 6-13: My Wizard-created home page after a few minutes of hacking it.

Publishing your CIS home page

When you are ready to publish your CompuServe home page, click on the Publish button in the Home Page Wizard's toolbar. Or, choose File⇨Publish Pages from the menu bar. A Wizard pops up (see Figure 6-14), and once again, you follow the instructions that appear on the screen to upload your site's pages.

Figure 6-14: The Wizard for publishing your CompuServe Web pages.

You'll also see a message along the way that shows you the URL of your Web site. For example, my URL is `http://ourworld.compuserve.com/homepages/coolnerds`, as shown in Figure 6-15.

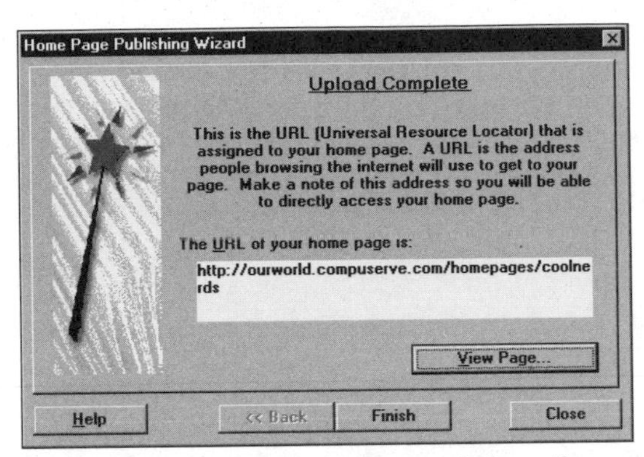

Figure 6-15: CIS's publishing Wizard also tells you your site's URL.

Viewing your CIS home page

After you have successfully uploaded your files to your CompuServe Web site, you (and anyone else in the world) can view your pages with a standard Internet connection and Web browser. The person who wants to view the site need not be a CompuServe member. Figure 6-16 shows my sample CompuServe site after pointing my Web browser (Internet Explorer) to the URL for that site, `http://ourworld.compuserve.com/homepages/coolnerds`.

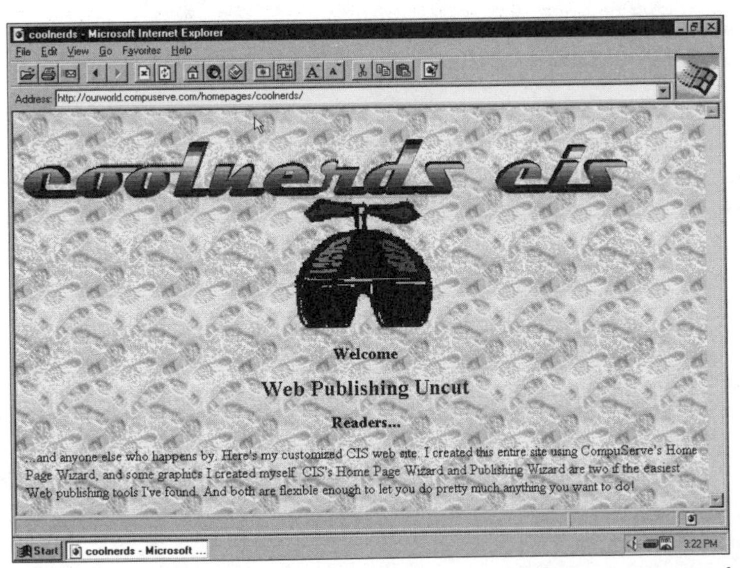

Figure 6-16: Viewing my CompuServe home page from Internet Explorer.

There is lots more to learn about CompuServe's Web publishing services. If you are interested in learning more, I recommend that you read the information CompuServe presents online. That way, you'll know that you are getting up-to-the-minute information on options. Just sign onto CompuServe in the usual manner and check out the general Internet areas and forums (GO INTERNET). You also may want to take a look at the Internet Publishing forum (GO INETPU) and the WebMasters forum (GO INETWE).

Web Publishing via Prodigy

Prodigy members can get free Web site space, too. To use the site, you first need to create your Web pages on your own PC, using any of the authoring techniques described in Part III of this book. You should name the home page (the first page to appear when someone contacts your site) **index.htm** or **index.html**.

For example, to create a home page for my Prodigy example here, I first created a "coolnerds on prodigy" graphic and beany by using Microsoft Word Art, Paint Shop Pro, and the techniques described in Part IV (Chapters 21 and 22) of this book. I saved that image as coolprod.gif. Then I used Word's Internet Assistant to create the actual Web document, index.htm. Figure 6-17 shows the top part of that index.htm document as it looks in Microsoft Word.

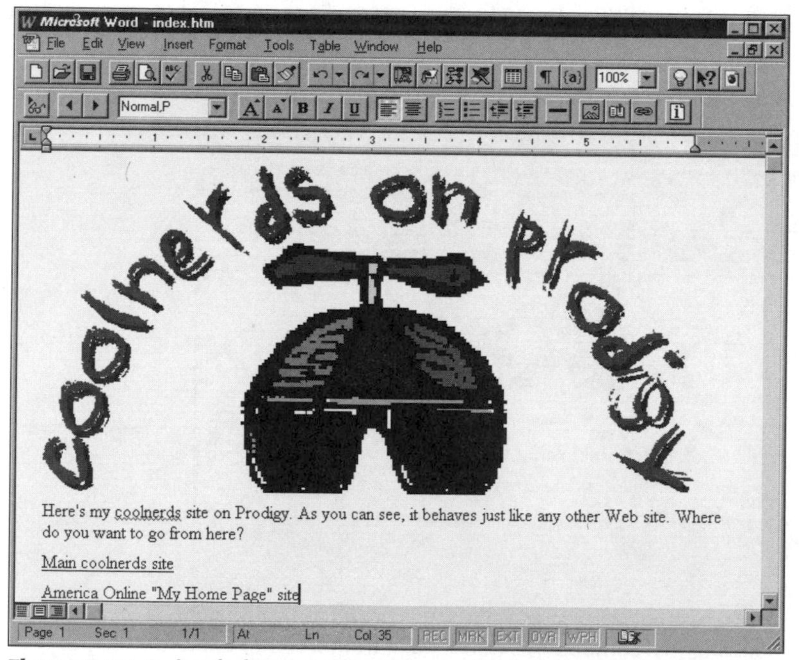

Figure 6-17: A simple home page created with Word's Internet Assistant.

Uploading your Prodigy home page

Now let's say that you have already created a home page and want to upload it to the Web for the entire world to see. The following steps list all that you have to do as a Prodigy member:

1. Connect to Prodigy in the usual manner on your PC.
2. Choose GoTo⇨Jump To and type **personal Web pages** as your jump word.
3. Click the OK button to get to the screen shown in Figure 6-18.

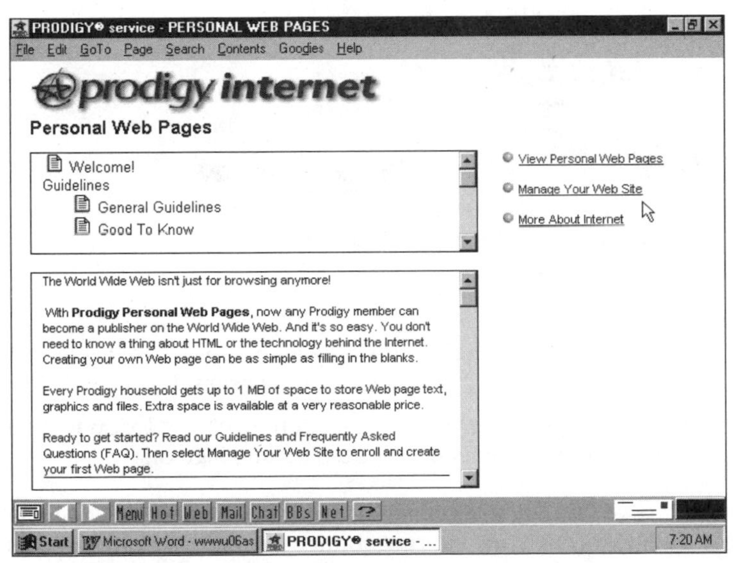

Figure 6-18: Starting point for using Prodigy's Web services.

4. On your first visit, you'll probably want to read about Prodigy's Web offerings. But here I just want to take you through the steps of actually uploading your pages. Click on the *Manage Your Web Site* option.
5. If you have not uploaded Web pages before, you'll need to register your site. Just follow the simple instructions on the screen, using the Help button as needed to get more information.
6. Eventually, you come to a screen like the one shown in Figure 6-19. From there, you can select files needed for your home page and then click the Upload button to copy them to your site. For example, in Figure 6-19, I've uploaded two files named index.htm (the home page) and coolprod.gif (the graphic that appears at the top of the home page).

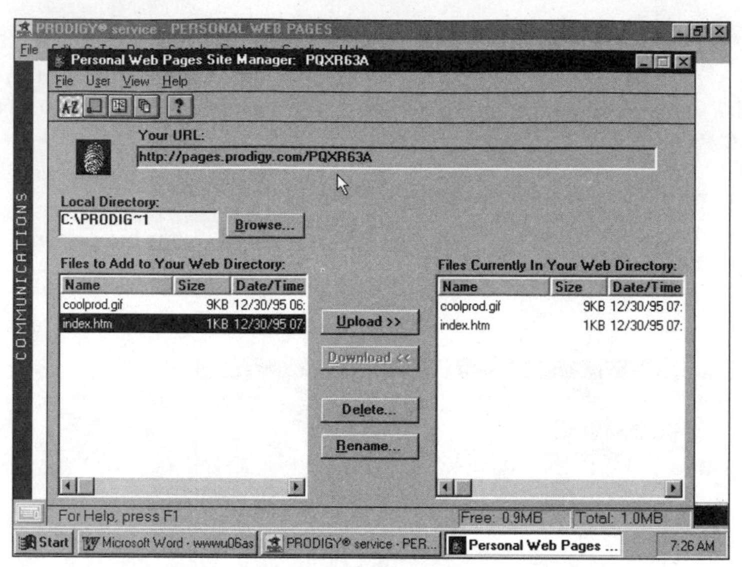

Figure 6-19: Two files uploaded to my Prodigy Web site at `http://pages.prodigy.com/PQXR63A`.

7. You should also jot down the URL of your site, which appears in the same screen (`http://pages.prodigy.com/PQXR63A` in my example).

8. After you have finished uploading your files, just choose File⇨Exit until you get to the final screen where you can end your session and sign off.

That's all there is to it. Give Prodigy a few minutes to get your site in order and on the Web. Then you can view it through any Internet connection and Web browser, as discussed next.

Viewing your Prodigy Web site

Viewing your Prodigy Web site is the same as viewing any other Web site. Just point your Web browser to the appropriate URL. For example, in Figure 6-20, I've logged into the Internet via my MSN account. Then I pointed my Web browser, Internet Explorer, to `http://pages.prodigy.com/PQXR63A`. Lo and behold, my page appears.

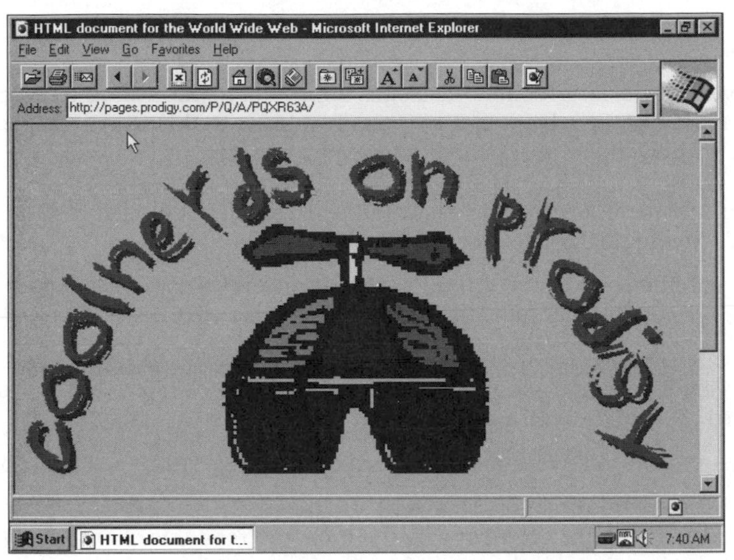

Figure 6-20: My Web page on Prodigy viewed through Internet Explorer.

Summary

So there you have it — the large-commercial-sites approach to publishing Web pages. Let's do a quick review of the advantages and disadvantages to this approach before moving on to an entirely different approach in the next chapter:

- ✦ If you're an AOL member, you can easily publish a small personal-info page using AOL's My Home Page service.
- ✦ As an AOL member, you also can use the My Place service to publish up to 2MB of Web pages and files for other Internet explorers to download to their own PCs.
- ✦ CompuServe members get a megabyte of free storage place plus a handy Home Page Wizard that makes Web authoring a breeze.
- ✦ Prodigy members also receive a megabyte of free storage space on the Web.
- ✦ As of the writing of this chapter, Microsoft still had not put together a home page service. But MSN may have one by the time you read this chapter. Log into MSN and look around under the general topic of Internet Services.
- ✦ All of these services have some limitations. If you are looking to do some major business on the Web, the approaches described in the next three chapters may be more appropriate (albeit more expensive).

✦ ✦ ✦

Throw Money at a Site

CHAPTER 7

In This Chapter

Using an Internet Presence Provider (and some cash) to turn a Web site idea into a reality

Creating a wish list for your Internet Presence Provider

A sample Internet Presence Provider

Finding an Internet Presence Provider

In the preceding chapter, we looked at some inexpensive, do-it-yourself approaches to authoring and publishing Web pages. But for some people, saving a little money isn't nearly as important as saving time! This fact is especially true of self-employed people and small-business owners who have umpteen zillion other responsibilities. There just may not be enough time in the day to set up a Web site, learn how to author Web documents, and then create those documents.

If you are such a person, you may want to consider hiring an *Internet Presence Provider* to handle the job. This method will cost you a little more in dollars, but it will save you a bundle in time. In this chapter, I talk about how this approach works, what you need to ask for, and give you an example using an Internet Presence Provider that I have worked with myself.

Internet Presence Providers

I talked about *Internet Service Providers* (which are also called Internet Access Providers) in earlier chapters. ISPs are companies that let you hook into the Internet via your PC and a modem as a *consumer,* so to speak. An Internet *Presence* Provider gives you more than that. It gives you an actual *presence* on the Internet in the form of a Web site. It not only rents you the space for your virtual storefront, but it also builds, decorates, promotes, and manages that storefront as well.

The basic idea behind working with Internet Presence Providers is that you come to the table with a business to promote or a product to sell and also some ideas about how you want to do that. Any written materials, such as your company brochure, logo, or even hand-written notes, will be helpful. You meet with your Internet Presence Provider or send your materials to it. The presence provider fashions a Web site for you. You review the site — going through a back and forth process until you are happy with the site. It then posts the site on the Web for you, and you obtain your worldwide exposure.

Thus, you get to be the "concept person" — the designer. Other people take care of all the technical details involved in making your idea into a reality. Of course, you have to pay those people, which is why I call this the "Throw Money at a Site" approach. But the costs are usually reasonable because the Internet Presence Provider handles lots of Web sites; hence, it already has the necessary equipment, know-how, and people in place to assist with your Web site.

Figure 7-1 illustrates the relationship between you, your Internet Presence Provider, and the Internet in this type of scenario. The Internet Presence Provider creates and stores your Web pages and then keeps them connected to the Internet 24 hours a day, seven days a week through its expensive, high-speed Internet connection. Technically, you don't even need to be connected to the Internet Presence Provider. (In reality, though, you will probably want to set up some kind of Internet connection for e-mail and so on.)

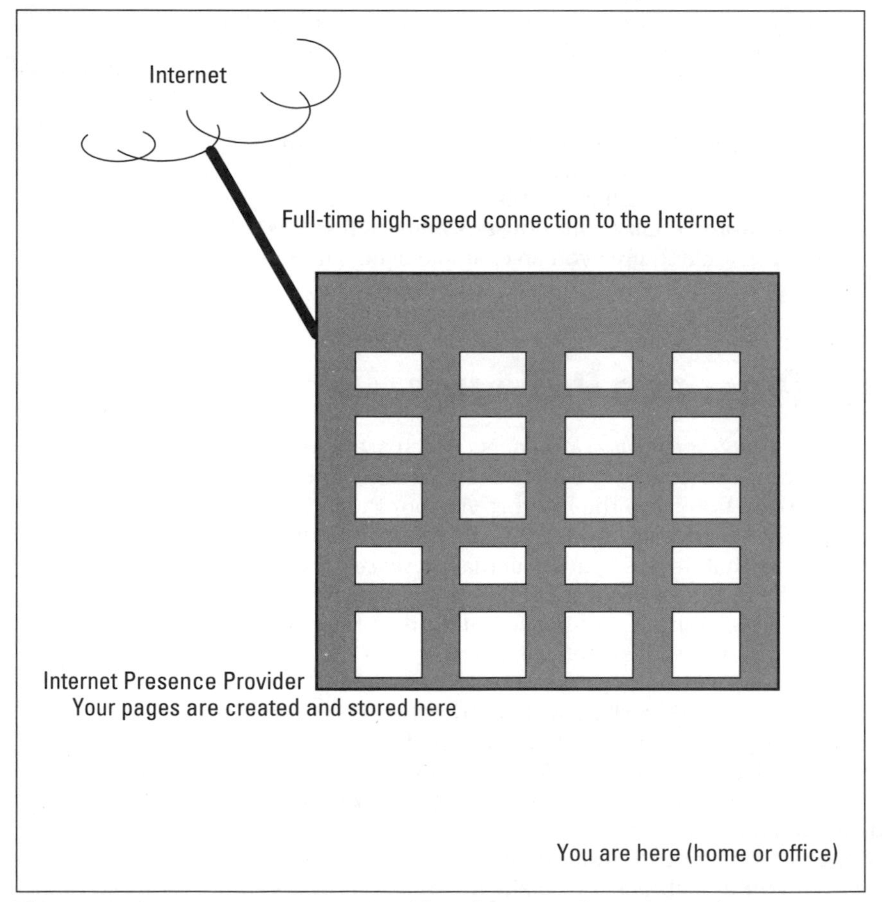

Figure 7-1: An Internet Presence Provider takes care of creating and storing your Web pages.

The Internet often is represented as a cloud in diagrams, and it is not a bad analogy. A cloud is composed of millions of droplets of water. The Internet is composed of millions of small, individual computers.

Defining Your Needs

Not all Internet Presence Providers are equal. Some companies offer more options than others. Therefore, knowing exactly what you want *before* you start shopping around is a good idea. You can use Table 7-1 as a sort of "Things I Want" checklist that you can give to your potential presence providers to see if they can deliver what you want and also to help you determine exactly how much their services are going to cost. I explain each section of the table in more detail in the sections that follow.

Table 7-1
Creating a Wish List for an Internet Presence Provider

Site Elements	*What I Need*
Pages:	
Home page (required)	____
Frequently Asked Questions page	____
Links to Other Sites page	____
News page	____
Feedback/Questions form	____
Order form	____
FTP page for downloading files	____
Other pages I need	____
I will create and supply all Web documents	____
I need someone to create Web documents for me	____
Graphics:	
I already have my own logo/photos	____
I need someone to create a logo and/or other art	____
Domain Name Service:	
I want my WWW address to be:	____________
I want my e-mail address to be:	____________

(continued)

Table 7-1 *(continued)*

Site Elements	*What I Need*
Interactivity:	
I want feedback from customers	_____
I want to present an order form to customers	_____
I want security so that customers can send their credit card info	_____
Promotion:	
I want my Internet Presence Provider to do all site promotion	_____

Web site pages

Many Internet Presence Providers base their charges on the number of pages in your Web site. At the very least, you need a home page. But what other types of information do you want to present to your browsers? A list of FAQs (Frequently Asked Questions) and news on new products, upcoming sales, and special events? An order form for purchasing products over the Web?

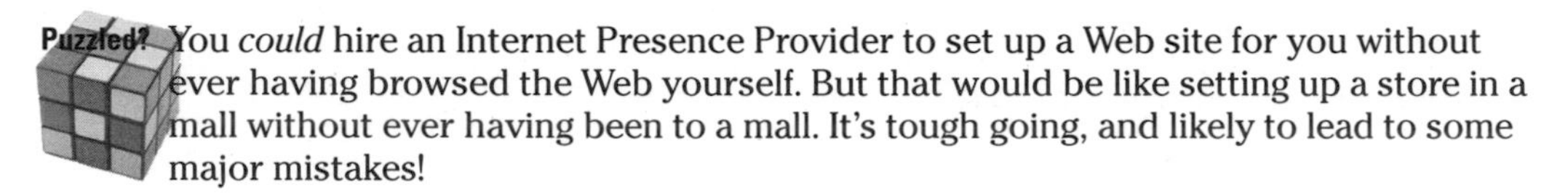

You *could* hire an Internet Presence Provider to set up a Web site for you without ever having browsed the Web yourself. But that would be like setting up a store in a mall without ever having been to a mall. It's tough going, and likely to lead to some major mistakes!

If you are already connected to the Internet, you may want to look around and see what other people are offering. Browsing the Web is a good source for ideas and also a good way to check out the competition. For example, if you are selling flowers, you may want to use Yahoo! or one of the other search engines (see Chapter 3) to look for other sites that use *flowers* as a keyword.

Graphics

Most Internet Presence Providers assume that you are already running a business and that you already have established your logo, brochures, and other standard business stuff. Their setup fees assume that you will provide that information in printed or electronic form. If you only have an idea of what you want rather than something tangible to give to the Internet Presence Provider, then either you or the Internet Presence Provider may need to hire a graphic artist.

You do need to take that added expense into account because creating even a simple logo can cost as much as your entire setup fee! For example, your Internet Presence Provider may charge you $400 to set up your account and Web pages. But a graphic artist may charge $200 or more per item to do the necessary art. So, be very clear about the kinds of graphics you want when you are discussing setup fees with a potential presence provider.

Domain name service

Some Internet Presence Providers can supply you with a *clean URL* (a custom domain name) of your own choosing. Some providers may charge you $10 a month for that service, whereas others may charge $100 a month for the same thing. Many presence providers cannot provide a custom domain name at all. Instead, these providers tack your name onto the end of their own URLs.

InterNIC, the service that doles out custom domain names, charges $50 to set up a new name, plus $50 a year to maintain it. You need to pay for the first two years at startup, so the total cost is $150. (This is a ballpark figure — InterNIC can change its prices at any time.) The InterNIC charges are separate from your Internet Presence Provider charges.

If you know for certain that you want a specific address for your Web site (or for an e-mail address), you should *write down the exact name(s) and submit them to your potential presence provider.* If you do not get this part squared away before finalizing the deal with a presence provider, you may end up spending a great deal more money, after the fact, trying to get your custom domain name. Or, if you end up with a presence provider that cannot give you a custom domain name, then you'll have to waste a great deal of time and money switching to a new presence provider!

Any Internet Presence Provider can register a custom domain name for you, but not all can give you a clean URL with that domain name. Thus, it's important to be very clear on the exact URL of your Web site before you close the deal!

Of course, if the domain name you want is already taken, then nobody can give you that name. Domain names are like social security numbers and phone numbers: only one to a customer. You may do well to come up with at least three possible custom names in case some of your favorites are already taken.

Interactivity

Some businesses post only their addresses, telephone numbers, and fax numbers in their Web sites. Personally, I think this is a very bad idea. If potential customers are shopping around for a product or service you offer and they come across your Web site, chances are they will want to get in touch with you right then and there — from your Web site. They can only do so if your Web site has some kind of form (or forms) that potential customers can fill out on the spot.

The forms you provide can be simple or complex. For example, you may offer a simple feedback and questions form, such as my Ask Alan form (Figure 7-2), where the user just sends you a note. This kind of form lets the potential customer contact you on the spur of the moment and can also help you build a Frequently Asked Questions page for your site. You may want to provide a slightly more complex form where people can enter their complete mailing addresses to get on your mailing list or a membership list.

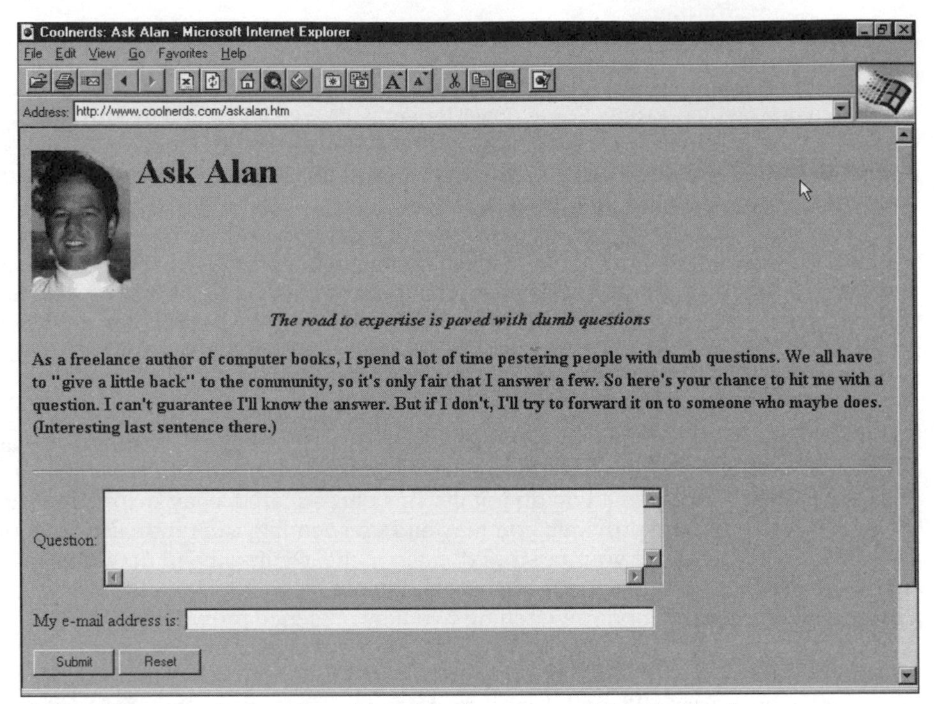

Figure 7-2: A simple form for asking questions or providing feedback.

Some (though certainly not all) Internet Presence Providers can even supply your site with a secure order form, where customers actually order products and supply credit card information for payment right on the spot. Netscape's site (`http://www.netscape.com`), shown in Figure 7-3, offers a General Store where you can look at products and put them in a "shopping basket." When you're ready to check out, the site takes you to a form where you can enter your billing address, shipping address, credit card info, and so on. I can't show you the entire form here because it takes up more than a single screen, but I can show you the bottom of the form (Figure 7-3).

If you do plan to have people send credit card information to you from your Web site, finding an Internet Presence Provider that can provide the appropriate security is important. Customers are (rightfully) leery of sending credit card information over the (very public) Internet without some guarantee that the information won't fall into the wrong hands.

You can do yourself a big favor by sketching out, even just on paper, any forms that you would like your Web site to contain. If you need transaction security, be sure to discuss this with your potential Internet Presence Provider. For a primer on Internet security, see Chapter 35.

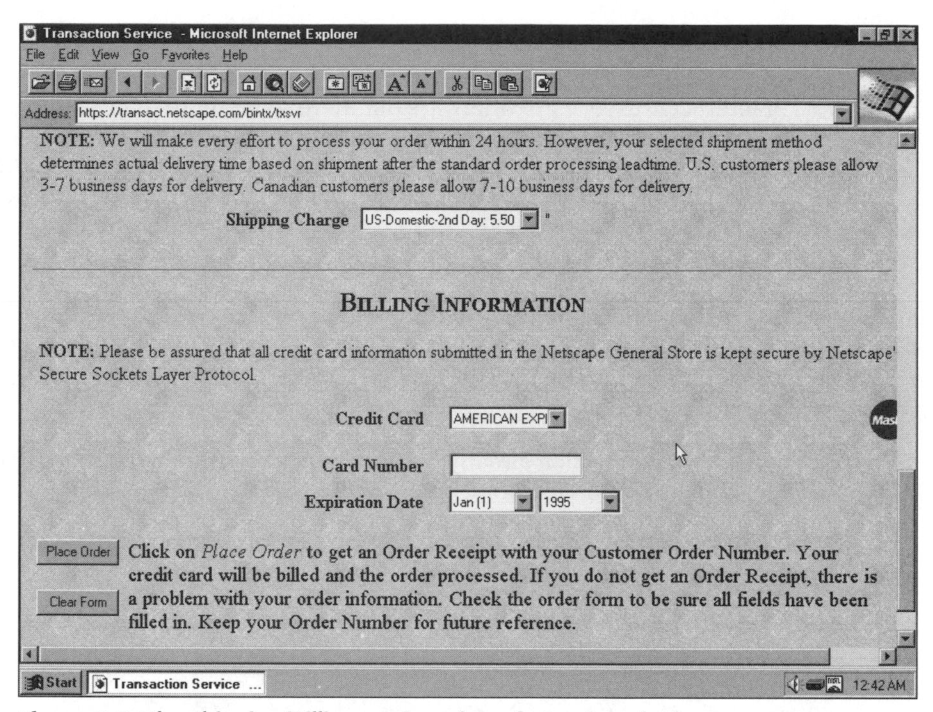

Figure 7-3: The Shipping/Billing portion of an electronic order form.

Promotion

The setup fees charged by an Internet Presence Provider are often surprisingly small. But the monthly charges for maintaining your site are considerably higher than the other alternatives discussed in Chapters 6 and 8. To get your money's worth, ask your potential presence provider what kind of promotion is provided as part of the regular monthly service charge.

Hot Stuff

You can reduce your monthly fees by hiring a firm to just create, not promote, your Web pages. Then have that firm post the completed Web pages on a site that you have acquired through an Internet Service Provider (see Chapter 8).

Remember that there are millions of Web sites out there and thousands more coming online every day. Good promotion is *vital* to the success of any Web site. A good presence provider will have special software that enables it to keep your name and site address in all major search engines. That way, when people on the Web go searching for the products or services you offer, your name appears on their screens. In the long run, the quality of your Internet Presence Provider can really be measured by how well it promotes your site!

An Example: Webs Are Us

Thousands of Internet Presence Providers are out there — far more than I can discuss in this entire book. To give you an example of what an Internet Presence Provider "looks like," I had to sort of pick one out of a hat. I picked Webs Are Us because this provider helped me set up my original Web site when I was too busy to do it myself. I also chose this provider because it happens to be close to my house, which allows for the occasional face-to-face meeting.

Hot Stuff

It really doesn't matter where your Internet Presence Provider is located because you can do most of your business via e-mail and fax. There are some benefits to having your provider nearby, though, such as being able to meet in person when hashing out the details of your site.

If you have an Internet connection already, you can check out the current offerings of Webs Are Us right on the Web. Just point your browser to `http://www.websrus.com` (see Figure 7-4). Webs Are Us offers samples of sites that it has created and currently manages, and describes its services, promotional capabilities, and features right on the site.

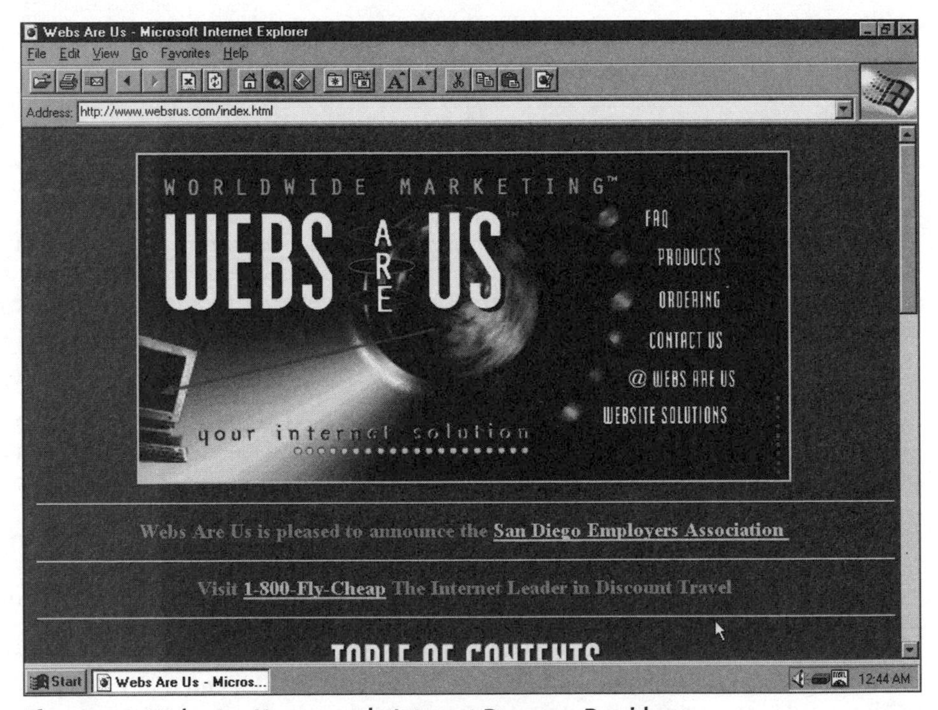

Figure 7-4: Webs Are Us, a sample Internet Presence Provider.

You also can find current pricing at its site. For those of you who have not connected to the Internet yet, here's a summary of charges from Webs Are Us at the time this chapter was written. Prices, of course, are always subject to change, so please use these figures as ballpark estimates and as a comparison point for shopping around. But don't quote me on any of these prices, please!

```
JUMPSTART PRESENCE:
5 PAGE SITE: text and graphics, 1 interactive form included
3 scannable images + unlimited disked images
Design Fee (One Time): $395
Monthly Fee: $115

POWER PRESENCE:
10 PAGE SITE: text and graphics, 1 interactive form included
5 scannable images + unlimited disked images
Design Fee (One Time): $525
Monthly Fee: $195

STELLAR PRESENCE:
15 PAGE SITE: text and graphics, 1 interactive form included
7 scannable images + unlimited disked images
Design Fee (One Time): $675
Monthly Fee: $225

OMNI PRESENCE:
20 PAGE SITE: text and graphics, 2 interactive forms included
10 scannable images + unlimited disked images
Design Fee (One Time): $825
Monthly Fee: $275

OPTIONAL FEATURES available at additional cost include:
*       Customized databases
*       Multilingual Web sites
*       Sound
*       Video
*       Automatic Email response
*       "Do It Yourself" site updates with security password
        accounts
*       Custom site updates
*       Reciprocal link contracts examples
*       On-Site dedicated advertising space
*       Real Audio (permits real time audio for clients)
*       Dynamic Document Updating (animations)
```

Shopping for an Internet Presence Provider

If you like the idea of throwing a little money at a Web site rather than a lot of time, then your next step is to start thinking about what you want your site to look like and do. You also need to start shopping around for an Internet Presence Provider. Like I said earlier, thousands of them are out there doing business. Here are some resources you can use to shop around for your own provider:

- Check your local Yellow Pages under Internet or Computer Networking.
- Check your local computer store for local newsletters and ads.
- If you're hooked into the Internet, search any service (Excite, InfoSeek, Magellan, or Yahoo) for *Internet Presence Providers*.
- For a partial listing organized by city and state, point your browser to `http://www.holonet.com/holonet/consultants.html`.

Trust me. If you try any *one* of the suggestions listed here, you'll probably be overwhelmed by the sheer number of businesses providing Web presences. That is why it is good to write down a wish list for your future site. If you know what you want, you can e-mail or fax your list to a number of providers and do your comparison shopping from their replies.

Summary

Let's do a quick review of the concepts that we have discussed in this chapter:

- An Internet Presence Provider can turn an idea for a Web site into an actual Web site. You just need to supply the inspiration, content, and some cash.
- Before you hire an Internet Presence Provider, make a wish list of all the things you want your site to offer.
- Don't forget that if a clean custom domain name (for example, `http://www.yournamehere.com`) is important to you, make sure that you find an Internet Presence Provider that can supply it.
- To really get your money's worth from an Internet Presence Provider, make sure that it will promote your site on a regular basis.
- Your local telephone directory and computer stores are good sources for finding Internet Presence Providers. The Web itself is also a good source.

✦ ✦ ✦

Throw Time at a Site

✦ ✦ ✦ ✦

In This Chapter

Advantages of a local Internet Service Provider (ISP)

Determining what you need in an ISP account

A sample local ISP

Shopping around for your own local ISP

✦ ✦ ✦ ✦

In Chapter 6, we looked at do-it-yourself techniques for creating a small Web site on a large commercial online service such as America Online, CompuServe, or Prodigy. In Chapter 7, we looked at ways you can create a Web site simply by hiring a firm to take care of everything. In this chapter, we look at an approach where you rent Web space from a local Internet Service Provider (which is fairly inexpensive) and then do all your own authoring and promotion. This approach has the following advantages:

- You won't be limited to 1 or 2 megabytes of storage space.
- You may be able to give your site a clean URL (such as `http://www.yournamehere.com`).
- You will probably have complete control over the contents of your Web site, including how frequently it gets updated.

Although this approach won't cost you as much money, it will eat up some of your time. You'll spend most of this time authoring your Web documents and promoting them. You'll also need a bit of technical expertise to upload pages to your Web site. In general, though, the technicalities of this approach are not too overwhelming.

Danger Zone If you still think of PCs as scary machines with minds of their own, or if all the digital clocks in your house and car flash 12:00 because you haven't yet figured out how to set the time, then this approach to Web publishing may be a bit too techno-nerdy for your current level of digital prowess.

The approaches I discuss here are probably the most widely used in the industry, mainly because they are cost effective. Your initial investment and monthly fees can be kept to a minimum by using these techniques. Having complete editorial control over the contents of your Web site also helps to keep costs down. I use the approach discussed in this chapter to maintain my own Web site at `http://www.coolnerds.com`.

Local Internet Service Provider

A key player in this approach to Web publishing is your local *Internet Service Provider* (ISP; also called an *Internet Access Provider,* or IAP). Unlike an Internet *Presence* Provider, which gives you an actual presence on the Web, an ISP only provides access to the Internet and, optionally, some space for storing your Web pages. The tasks of creating, maintaining, and promoting those pages are entirely up to you.

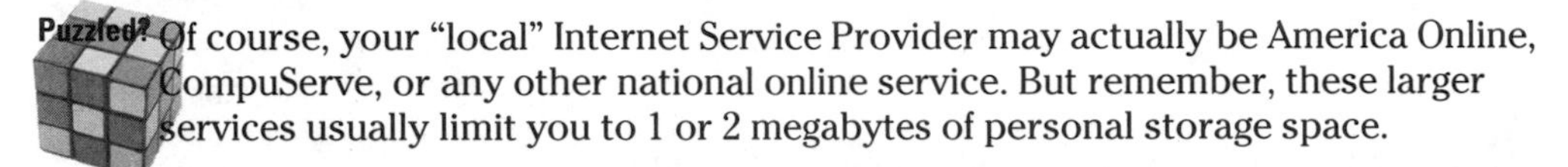

Of course, your "local" Internet Service Provider may actually be America Online, CompuServe, or any other national online service. But remember, these larger services usually limit you to 1 or 2 megabytes of personal storage space.

Figure 8-1 illustrates how the ISP approach works. Your Internet Service Provider has an expensive, high-speed, 24-hours-a-day, 7-days-a-week connection to the Internet (shown as a cloud in the picture). Your Web pages are actually stored on a computer at the ISP's site. But you *create* your pages at your own site. When you are ready to show those pages to the world, you upload them to your Web site via an inexpensive, dial-up telephone account. Typically, this task only takes a few minutes; after you've completed the uploading process, you can disconnect from the Internet again. Your pages are available for all the world to see because they are now on the Internet Service Provider's computer.

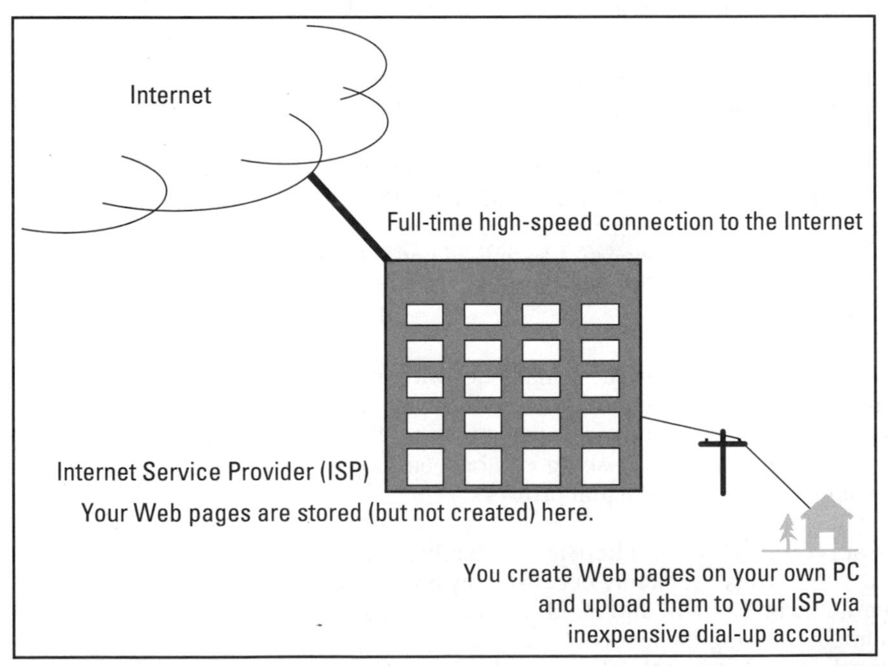

Figure 8-1: An ISP provides worldwide, 24-hour/7-days-a-week access to your Web pages. You just need an inexpensive dial-up account.

Defining Your Needs

Not all ISPs are created equal, so you will need to shop around a bit. Some important points to keep in mind when shopping for an ISP are listed here:

✦ Try to find an ISP that charges a flat, monthly rate for your entire service, including your Web site. You won't want one that charges "per hit" on your Web site.

✦ See if there is a storage limit (such as 2MB) for your Web site, and if so, how charges are applied when you exceed that limit.

✦ Make sure that you'll be free to modify your pages whenever you want, without charges and without having to go through any formalities, such as submitting a change order to the Webmaster.

✦ If you want a clean URL for your site, be sure to find an ISP that can provide one.

✦ If you want to do commerce over the Internet, be sure to find an ISP that can provide transaction security.

✦ If you want people to be able to download files or send files to you, you need an ISP that also can provide you with FTP (File Transfer Protocol) space.

✦ If you plan to use the same Internet Service Provider for your day-to-day Internet stuff (such as e-mail and Web browsing), try to find one that can provide a toll-free number to keep your phone bill to a minimum.

✦ Try to find an ISP with a T1 or T3 connection to the Internet.

The last item centers around the ISP's connection to the Internet (not your connection to the ISP). I don't want to get too deep into telecommunications stuff right now, but let me explain why the ISP's connection to the Internet is important to you as a Web publisher.

Let's look at an extreme example. Say that your Internet Service Provider is connected to the Internet through a standard 28.8K modem, such as your modem. John Doe points his Web browser to your Web site, and your ISP sends information to John Doe at 28.8K. John Doe is happy because he is accustomed to 28.8K modem speeds.

Now, suppose that Jane Deer also points her Web browser and 28.8K modem to your Web site while John Doe is there. Now your ISP has to serve *two* PCs, using its one modem. To do that, it splits its time between Joe and Jane. Now Joe and Jane are each being served at 14.4K, which is half of the speed to which they are accustomed. They both may perceive your Web site as being slow.

Now let's compound the problem. Suppose that a third person, fourth person, fifth person, and so on all point their Web browsers to your site at the same time. The little 28.8K modem serving them is so overworked that each of those readers gets information from your site at a snail's pace. They will soon tire of waiting and move on to some other site. As a result, you lose customers. See the problem?

Why don't I just get a T1 or T3?

Some of you probably just realized "Hey, if I get one of those T1 or T3 connections to the Internet, I can *be* an Internet Service Provider." This is true, but it's not quite that simple. For one thing, you need lots of hardware horsepower and technical expertise to take advantage of a T1 or T3 connection. *Lots* of power and expertise, as in *lots* of money.

Add to those hardware and technical-expertise costs the cost of the connection itself. A T1 connection costs about $1,500 to $2,000 per month. A T3 connection can cost between $65,000 and $80,000 per month. Not cheap!

That example is rather extreme; I don't think anyone who is serving the Web with a 28.8K modem could actually call him- or herself an Internet Service Provider. Your ISP should be serving the Web with at least a *fractional T1* connection — which can easily handle several people browsing your site at the same time. Still better is a full T1 connection because it can handle more traffic than a fractional T1. Best of all (though rare) is a direct T3 connection to the Internet, which can handle hundreds, if not thousands, of people simultaneously viewing your site.

How will you know what kind of connection a given ISP has? You can just ask. In general though, if an ISP has a direct T1 or T3 connection to the Internet, it will probably advertise that fact in any literature it sends you. If an ISP offers unusually low service rates and doesn't mention what type of connection it has, chances are it has a slow connection.

An Example Local ISP

Thousands of local and national ISPs can host your Web site for you. I can't discuss all of them, but I can pick one example to show you what kind of information to look for. Once again, I'll use a local San Diego service, CTSNET, as the example. These are the people who host my main coolnerds site at `http://www.coolnerds.com`. As usual, please consider any prices I give you in this book as ballpark figures. Prices change all the time in the competitive ISP market, so what I quote here may not be accurate by the time you read this book. I tell you what all the different services listed under "Rates" are about in the sections that follow.

```
CTSNET is San Diego's premier Internet service provider. Locally
       owned and operated,
CTSNET delivers the hottest item in business and personal commu-
       nications since the fax machine: The Internet! All you
       need to get started is a computer, modem, and communica-
       tions software.
```

```
Here's what you get with CTSNET:

*    A real Internet Connection with full access
*    Over 11,000 news and discussion groups
*    Access to financial and government resources
*    Online libraries, databases, museums, and stores
*    Real-time teleconferencing and multimedia
*    Free global electronic mail delivery
*    Free software from thousands of archives
*    And more!

Rates

Services              Mo/Rate    Setup     Info
Shell account          $35.00    $25.00    required
PPP / SLIP              $5.00    $10.00    req'd for Windows
Custom domain name     $15.00    $10.00    plus InterNIC charges
WWW publishing         $50.00    $10.00
FTP Dropbox             $0.00    $10.00
```

Shell account and PPP

A shell account is the basic service that brings you e-mail and other Internet services. Windows users require the additional PPP/SLIP option. These two services alone would be sufficient for a person who is just a consumer on the Internet. But as a publisher or businessperson on the Web, you need at least some of the additional services described in the following sections.

WWW publishing

Don't assume that all ISPs can host your Web site. Virtually all service providers can give you access to the World Wide Web as a "browser." Not all ISPs can give you space to act as a publisher on the Web, however. As a Web publisher, you are only interested in services that can host your Web site.

More Info

CTSNET's rates are not the cheapest available, but it does have an actual T3 connection to the Internet. This means that even if a bunch of people browse my site at the same time, they will all get speedy service. This functionality is good for me as a Web publisher.

Don't confuse Web site hosting with Web page design and development. For example, the $10 setup and $50 monthly charge from CTSNET is *solely* for the Web space. They do not offer any service or support for creating Web pages, nor do they go to any great lengths in the promotion department. Authoring the pages and promoting them through search engines and other sites are entirely my responsibility.

I don't have to author all my own Web pages. Plenty of services are out there that will design and create Web pages for me, for a fee. These services will even upload the pages to my site (if I give them the password). If you are interested in finding a firm to create your Web pages (but not to host them), check with your local Internet Service Provider for some leads.

Custom domain name

The tricky domain name part is important. As I mentioned earlier in the book, just about any ISP can register a domain name for you. But relatively few can give you a simple `http://www.yournamehere.com` type of URL. If you have a specific URL in mind, make sure that you get this name squared away with your potential ISP before you sign any agreements. Otherwise, you could end up with one of those `http://www.howdy.doody.yowsa.com/~browse/igor/index.html` kind of URLs that nobody can remember. CTSNET, the sample ISP, was able to provide both my e-mail name, `alan@coolnerds.com`, and my clean Web site URL, `http://www.coolnerds.com`. Note that there is a small additional charge for that service though.

Funky domain names

Meng Weng Wong's "Cool Hostnames" site (`http://homepage.seas.upenn.edu/~mengwong/coolhosts.html`) keeps track of unusual domain names, host names, and e-mail names. Here are some samples:

`me@my.com`

`polka.com (polka dot com)`

`gratuitouslylonghostname.apana.org.au`

`int.ter.net`

`howling@themoon.com`

`drag.net`

`waiting@busstop.com`

`do.not.touch.their.net`

`me@this.net`

`elvis@undead.com`

`up@night.com`

`right.back@you.com`

`command.com`

`geeksrus.com`

`my-hostname-is-longer-than-yours.mit.edu`

`someone@nowhere.com`

`no-sir-I-did-not-see-you-playing-with-your-dolls-again.ai.mit.edu`

`com.com.com`

`i.am.lame.com`

`geeks.org`

FTP dropbox

If you want people to be able to download files from your Web site or to upload files to you, you'll need some kind of FTP dropbox. My CTSNET account has this feature, where I keep sample databases for readers of my database books (see Figure 8-2). Anyone on the Internet can get to my FTP site right from my home page at `http://www.coolnerds.com` or go directly to it at `ftp.cts.com/pub/alan`.

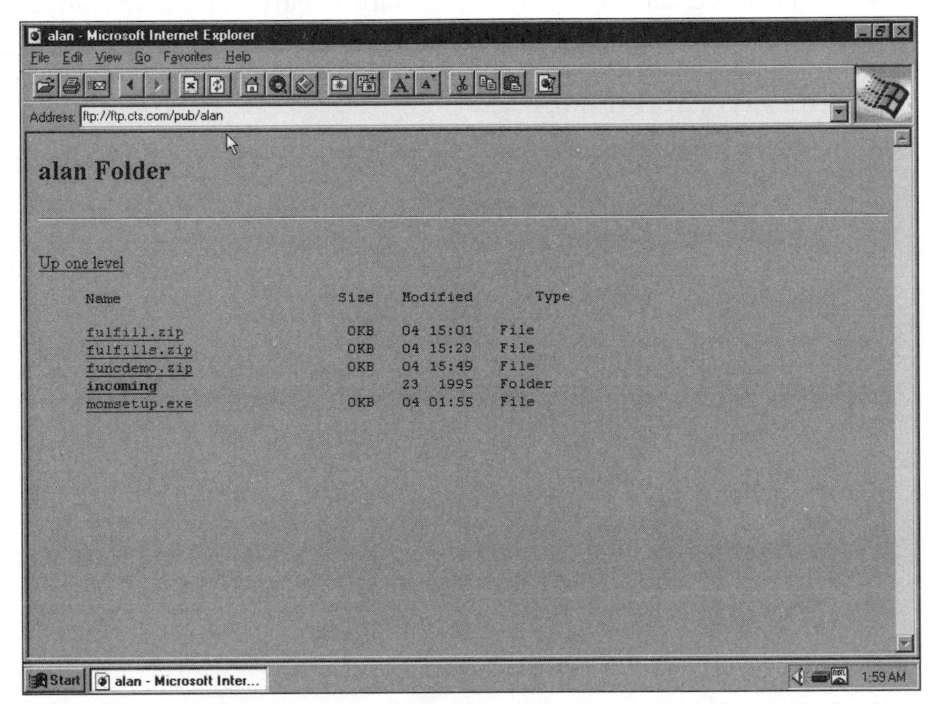

Figure 8-2: My FTP site provides readers of my database books with sample databases.

How to Find a Local ISP

As I mentioned, there are thousands of Internet Service Providers to choose from. Here are some tips that will help you find one suitable for your own Web publishing needs:

- ✦ Check your local Yellow Pages under Internet or Computer Networking.
- ✦ Check out any local computer-oriented circulars in your neighborhood (offered at most computer stores).
- ✦ If you already have an Internet account, search any engine (Yahoo!, Magellan, or others) for *Internet Service Providers*.

Summary

Hiring a local Internet Service Provider to host your Web site and then doing all the authoring and promotion yourself is a very cost-effective way to run a serious Web site. As a Web publisher, you need to consider the following when hiring an ISP:

- You are only interested in ISPs that can host your Web site.
- If you want a clean URL for your site, be sure to find an ISP that can provide that feature.
- If you want people to be able to download files from your Web site, you also need some kind of FTP dropbox.
- The faster your ISP's connection to the Internet, the better your Web customers will be served.

✦ ✦ ✦

CHAPTER 9

Throw Everything at a Site

✦ ✦ ✦ ✦

In This Chapter

Building your own Web server

Choosing Web server hardware

Choosing Web server software

Choosing an Internet connection for your server

✦ ✦ ✦ ✦

Last but certainly not least in possible approaches to publishing and doing business on the Web is to build your own Web server and connect it to the Internet on a full-time basis. Although certainly not cheap, this approach does offer a couple of advantages. For one, all of your Web pages are on a PC located right in your office (or home). You can use Windows NT (or even Windows 95) as your operating system, which takes the Unix confusion out of the picture. And you have total control over every aspect of your Web site.

Puzzled? The Internet was built around the Unix operating system, and most ISPs use Unix as their in-house operating system. You don't need to know a great deal of Unix to publish on the Web, but occasionally you'll be faced with Unix terminology and concepts that may seem totally foreign to you.

There are two major disadvantages to this build-your-own-server approach: (1) it's expensive and (2) it's time consuming. Money-wise, this approach will probably cost you a few thousand dollars just to purchase the hardware and set up an appropriate connection to the Internet. Also, the standard dial-up type of Internet account won't work for this method; you'll need some kind of dedicated connection to the Internet, which will have a considerably higher monthly cost.

Time-wise, you need to invest some time in setting up your Web server hardware and software, as well as in making special arrangements with your Internet Service Provider and perhaps your local phone company as well. Also, there is the ongoing time cost of maintaining the server, which can be nearly a full-time job!

I don't recommend this approach if you are just getting started on the Web. Any of the methods described in the preceding chapters will probably be more than sufficient for getting started. Should your Web site become a smashing success and generate a great deal of income, the flexibility and power you get from owning your own server may then be worth the cost. For right now though, knowing what is involved in setting up your own server is probably sufficient, and that is what I cover in this chapter.

The Web Server Approach

The main differences between the build-your-own-server approach and the approaches discussed in the preceding chapters are as follows:

- Your Web pages are stored on a PC at your own site.
- A simple dial-up account won't do. You'll need a more expensive dedicated connection to an ISP.

Figure 9-1 illustrates this arrangement. In the sections that follow, I discuss some of the unique hardware, software, and Internet connections that this approach requires.

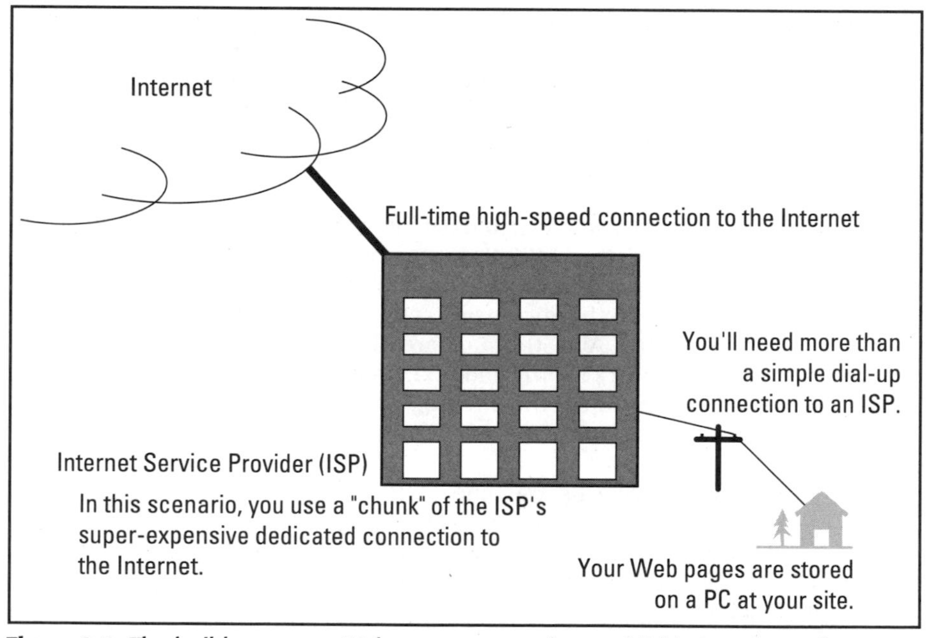

Figure 9-1: The build-your-own Web server approach to publishing on the Web.

Web Server Hardware

Technically, just about any PC can play the role of a Web server. Realistically, however, you're probably looking at Windows NT as your operating system. In that case, you need a PC that can run NT. You also need some extra disk space for your Web files and so forth, so you are probably looking at a PC with *at least* this much hardware horsepower:

✦ 486 DX 4 100, Pentium, or higher processor

✦ 64MB – 128MB RAM

✦ 1GB (or more) disk storage

If you plan to use the same PC to author your Web pages, you'll probably want to throw in a decent CD-ROM drive, some multimedia capabilities, and a good graphics card. As a ballpark estimate, you are looking at about $5,000 to $10,000 for the initial hardware investment (excluding any special modems or routers you may need for your Internet connection).

Web Server Software

The popularity of the World Wide Web has spawned a whole bunch of software products that simplify the process of setting up a PC as a Web server. Table 9-1 lists some of the more popular products for Windows, the operating system that each uses (that is, Windows NT and/or Windows 95), the approximate cost, and a Web address where you can get more information about each product.

Table 9-1
Examples of Web Server Software for Windows

Product	OS	Cost	More Info
EMWAC HTTP	NT	$0.00	`http:/emwac.ed.ac.uk`
Microsoft Internet Information Server	NT Server	$0.00	`http://www.microsoft.com/infoserv`
Netscape Commerce Server	NT	$1,295.00	`http://www.netscape.com`
Netscape Communications Server	NT	$495.00	`http://www.netscape.com`
O'Reilly WebSite	NT / 95	$499.00	`http://www.ora.com`
Quarterdeck WebServer	3.1 or greater	$169.95	`http://www.qdeck.com`

Hot Stuff

For a current list of Windows Web servers, search Yahoo! or any other search engines for *windows web servers*. Many companies will let you download a free trial copy of their server software on the spot.

If you plan to build your own Web server and do business on the Web, then you should focus on server software that supports one or more of the popular Internet security protocols, such as S-HTTP, PCT, and/or Secure Sockets Layer (SSL). These protocols can authenticate and encrypt sensitive information, such as credit card numbers. These servers cost more, but potential customers are much more willing to submit their credit card information to a secure server. Netscape's Commerce Server, Microsoft's Internet Information Server, and a forthcoming WebSite Professional from O'Reilly all support this kind of security.

Web Server Phone Connection

As mentioned, a simple dial-up account to an Internet Service Provider won't work for a Web server. A dial-up PPP account *could* work because when you are connected to your Internet Service Provider through this type of account, your computer is actually a part of the Internet. The only problem is that as soon as you disconnect, your PC *is no longer* part of the Internet. Anyone trying to browse your site at this time would not be able to get through. Alternatively, you could just dial in and never disconnect. If you have any per-minute charges from your local phone company, however, keeping that line open 7 days a week, 24 hours a day is likely to lead to some astronomical phone bills.

You also have the problem of speed. If you try to serve the Web from a 28.8K modem, then everyone browsing your site has to share that modem speed. For example, if two people try to browse your site at the same time, each user will get only half-speed (14.4K) service. If several people try to browse your site at the same time, your site will serve them slower than molasses at the North Pole in the dead of winter. Offering this type of Web site functionality will not win you any popularity contests.

What you really need to do, if you want to set up your own server, is get some kind of dedicated (full-time) connection to the Internet. The typical scenario here is to contact a local Internet Service Provider and tell the people there what your plan is — which is, of course, that you want to publish on the Web using your own Web server rather than the ISP's Web server. If the ISP offers such a service, it can get you a dedicated connection, which will include an IP address and domain name to uniquely identify your PC on the Internet. You will need that IP address and domain name in order to set up your Web server software.

As far as costs and options for dedicated lines go, you will probably want at least a dedicated ISDN line. You should shop around — there are no fixed rates for dedicated lines. To give you some ballpark figures on what to expect, though, Table 9-2 lists the approximate cost of initial setup and monthly fees for various types of connections. The table also shows how many people using 28.8K modems the connections can serve simultaneously without any slowdown. However, do keep in mind that there are many factors that determine how quickly a person will receive your Web pages, so please consider these numbers as being ballpark estimates as well.

Table 9-2
Speeds and Costs of Dedicated Internet Connections for Web Servers

Service	*Speed*	*Simultaneous Browsers*	*Setup $*	*Monthly $*
POTS	28.8K	1	$300	$35
Leased	56K	2	$750	$540
24-hour ISDN	128K	5	$400	$300
Fractional T1	varies	varies	$1,000	varies
T1	1.5M	50	$1,500	$2,000

If you did not recognize a few of the terms in Table 9-2, have no fear. Here's a few points of clarification on Table 9-2:

✦ POTS stands for *Plain Old Telephone System* and refers to the typical modem connection used for day-to-day Internet browsing.

✦ ISDN is available in some major metropolitan areas only. You need to check with your local phone company to see if ISDN is even an option for you. You also need a special ISDN modem for that service.

✦ The Leased and T1 lines require a *router*, a special type of equipment that is likely to increase your initial setup cost.

Summary

This part of the book covered just about every scenario possible for getting your Web pages onto the World Wide Web. You have to decide which approach makes the most sense for what you are trying to accomplish. Let's review the main points from the last four chapters:

- ✦ If you are a member of America Online, CompuServe, Prodigy, or some other online service, you may be able to get some free Web space. Check your service for keywords like *Internet, World Wide Web,* and *home page.*
- ✦ If you are in a hurry and don't have time to learn Web authoring techniques and such, you can hire an Internet Presence Provider to create, publish, and promote your Web site.
- ✦ You can build a substantial Web site by "renting space" on a computer that is connected to the Internet on a full-time basis. You need to find a local Internet Service Provider that offers Web publishing.
- ✦ If you want to get a custom domain name (`http://www/yournamehere.com`, for example), make sure you clarify that with your Internet Presence Provider or Internet Service Provider before you sign up for an account.
- ✦ If you want full control over your Web space and have lots of time and money to invest, you might consider building your own Web server. You'll need a PC, Web server software, and some kind of full-time connection to the Internet.

✦ ✦ ✦

What You Put in Your Site

In This Chapter

What goes into a Web site

The home page, et al

What HTML is all about

Sneaking a peek at other people's HTML tags

Once you determine where you are going to put your Web site, you need to think about *what* you are going to put in it. Understanding exactly what goes into a Web site and how that information is organized helps you in this process. These are the kinds of things discussed in this chapter.

I should mention that if you hire an Internet Presence Provider to create your site, you really do not need to know any of the material in this chapter — at least not right away. The presence provider already knows this information and can get your site going with whatever raw materials you provide (such as the company logo, brochure, and so on). But if you plan to author your own pages, you'll need a good understanding of the concepts discussed in this chapter.

What's in a Web Site?

A Web site is basically a collection of Web pages. Each Web page is a document or file, similar to the types of documents you create with word-processing and spreadsheet programs. The various pages that make up the site are connected by *hyperlinks,* little hot spots that the reader can click to go from one page to the next.

The home page

The first page that the reader sees when connecting to a Web site is called the *home page.* The purpose of the home page is to give the reader an idea as to what the site is about, as well as what it has to offer. The home page typically contains links to other documents in the site.

If you think of a Web site in terms of print publishing, the home page is like a book cover or magazine cover. If you think of a Web site in terms of a business, the home page is sort of like your storefront. Your home page is an important page in your site because readers base their first impressions about your site on your home page.

The home page, like a book cover or storefront, also is the lure that invites people in to view the rest of your site. You can design your home page however you like. In general though, you want your home page to give the reader a quick description and feel for what the site is about. You also may want to put links to the other pages in your site on the home page. To get some food for thought in planning your own home page, take a look at the sampling of home pages in Figures 10-1 to 10-15. If you want to see one of those pages in color on your own screen, just point your Web browser to the URL that appears in the figure's caption.

Hot Stuff

As an alternative to typing in all those lengthy URLs, you can just go to my site at `http://www.coolnerds.com`. Go to the *HTML Publishing Bible* section, where you will find simple one-click links to those sites.

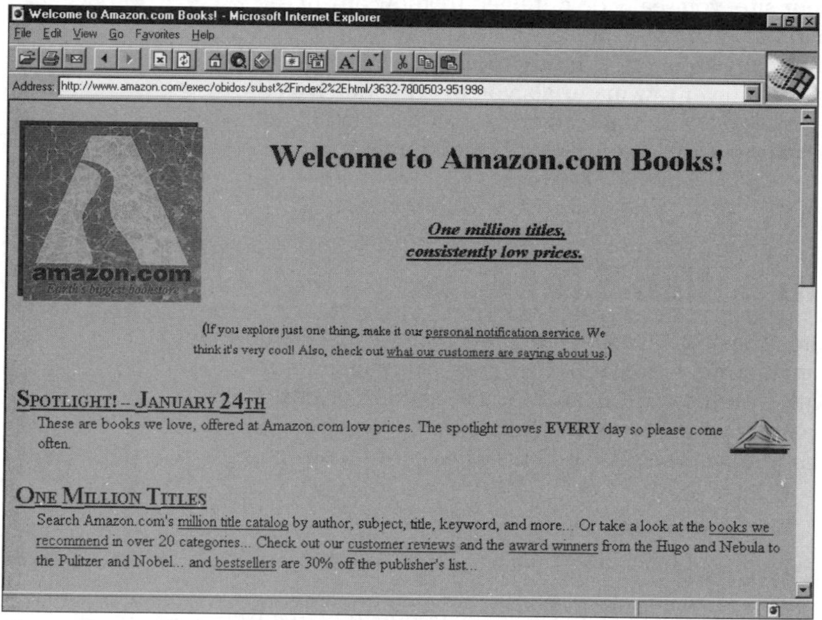

Figure 10-1: Amazon Books (`http://www.amazon.com`).

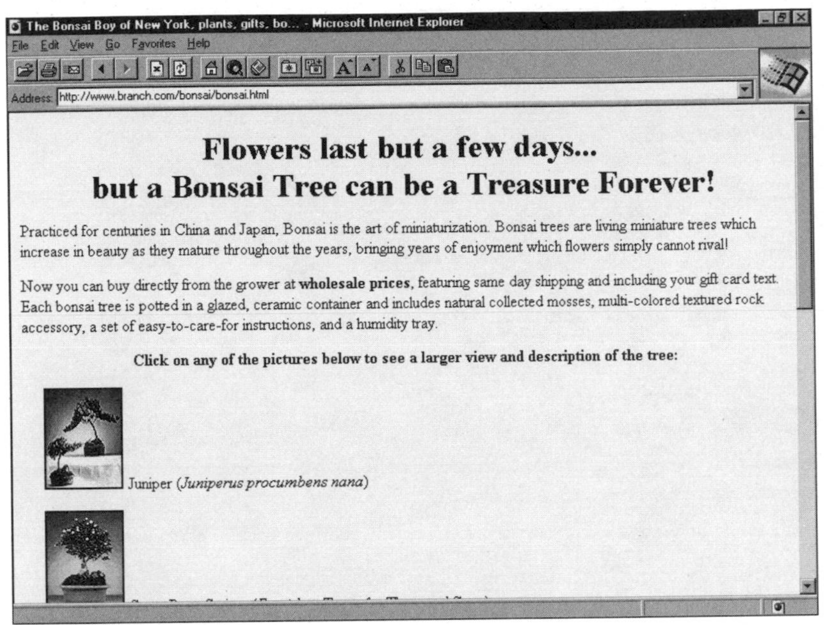

Figure 10-2: The Bonsai on the Web home page (`http://www.branch.com/bonsai/bonsai.html`).

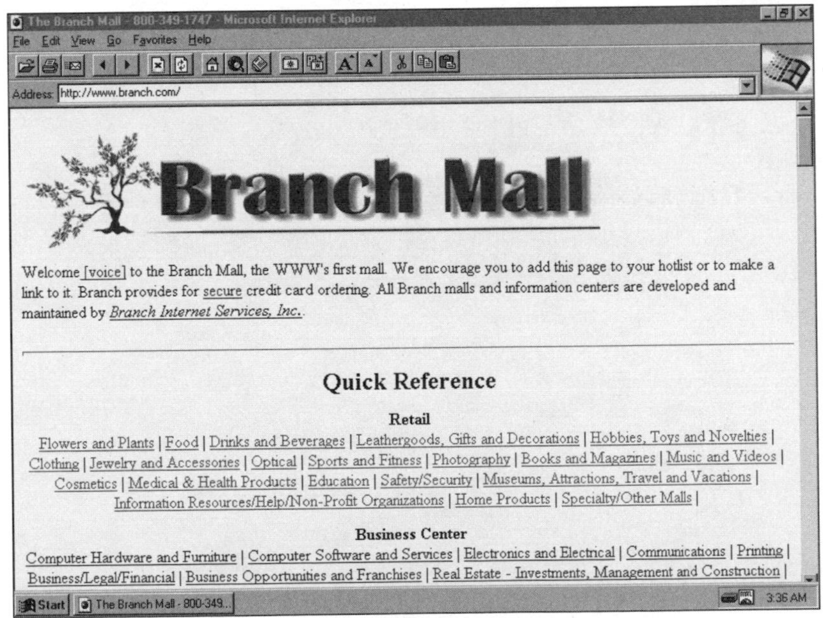

Figure 10-3: The Branch Mall home page (`http://www.branch.com`).

Figure 10-4: Eek — a geek! (`http://www.io.org/~eek`).

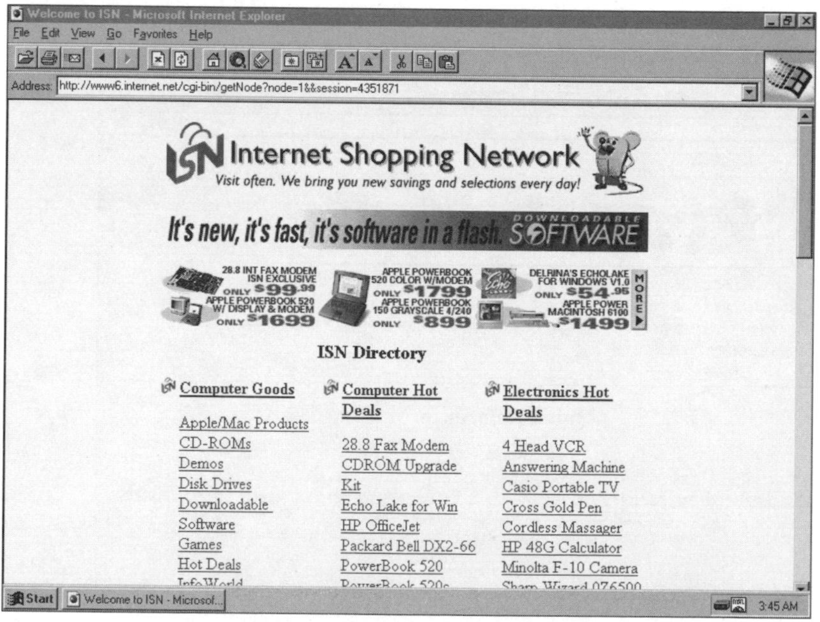

Figure 10-5: The Internet Shopping Network (`http://www.isn.com`).

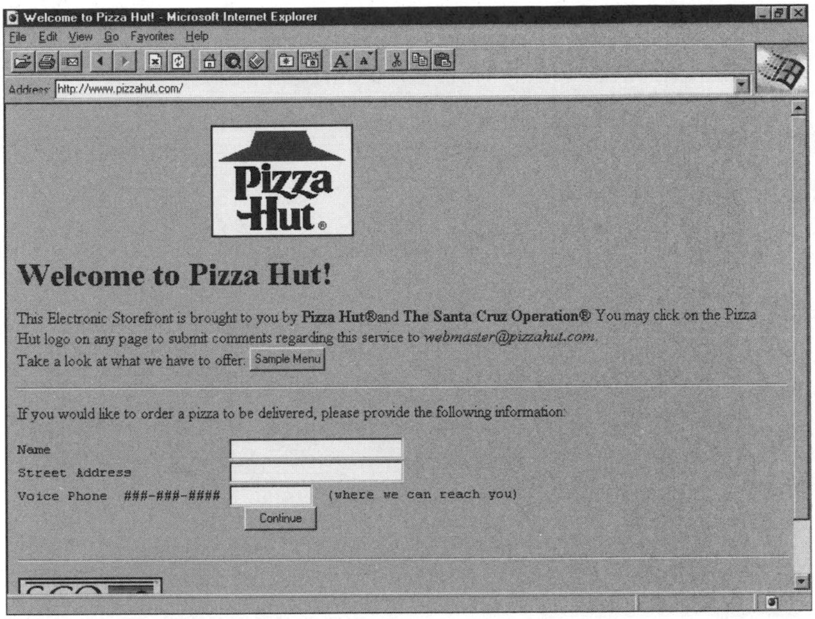

Welcome to Pizza Hut! - Microsoft Internet Explorer
File Edit View Go Favorites Help
Address http://www.pizzahut.com/

Pizza Hut®

Welcome to Pizza Hut!

This Electronic Storefront is brought to you by **Pizza Hut®**and **The Santa Cruz Operation®** You may click on the Pizza Hut logo on any page to submit comments regarding this service to *webmaster@pizzahut.com*.
Take a look at what we have to offer: Sample Menu

If you would like to order a pizza to be delivered, please provide the following information:

Name
Street Address
Voice Phone ###-###-#### (where we can reach you)
Continue

Figure 10-6: Order a pizza (`http://www.pizzahut.com`).

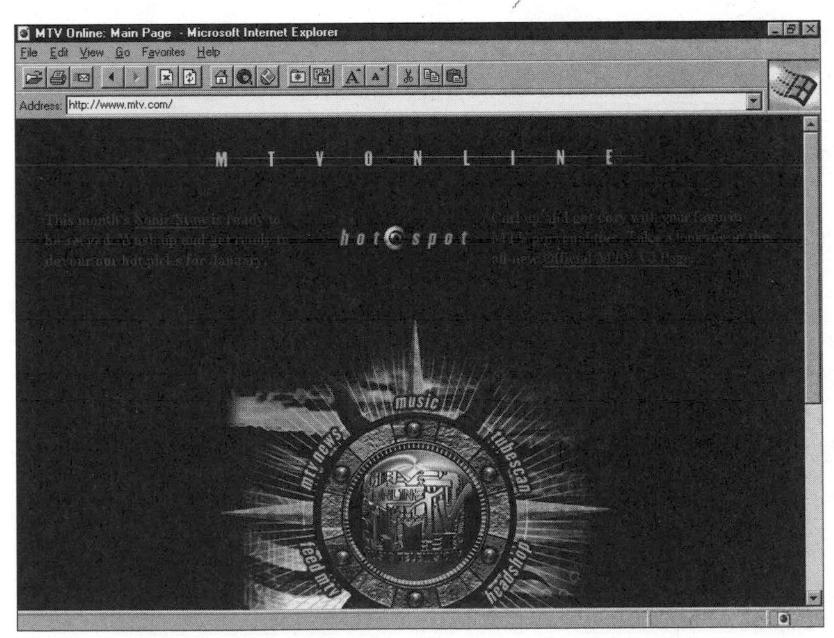

Figure 10-7: MTV Online (`http://www.mtv.com`).

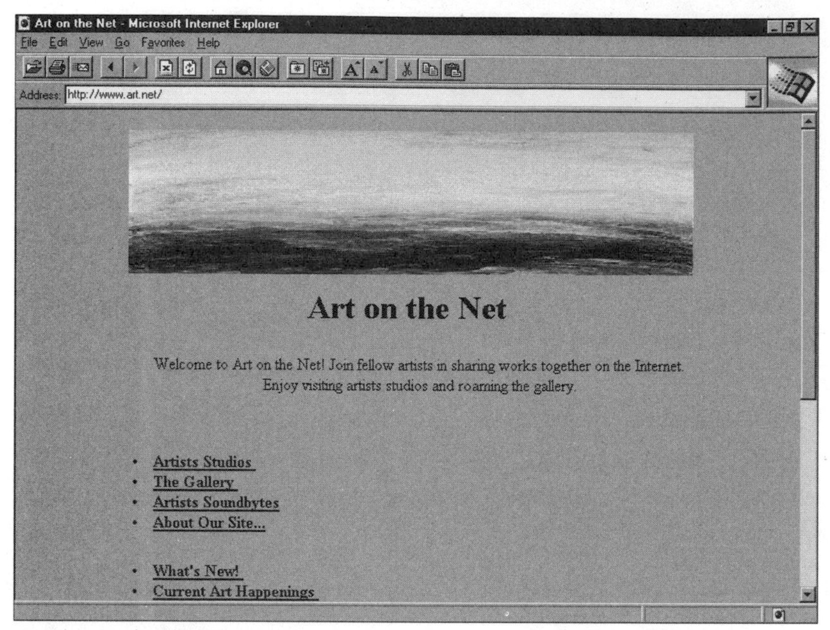

Figure 10-8: Art on the Net (`http://www.art.net`).

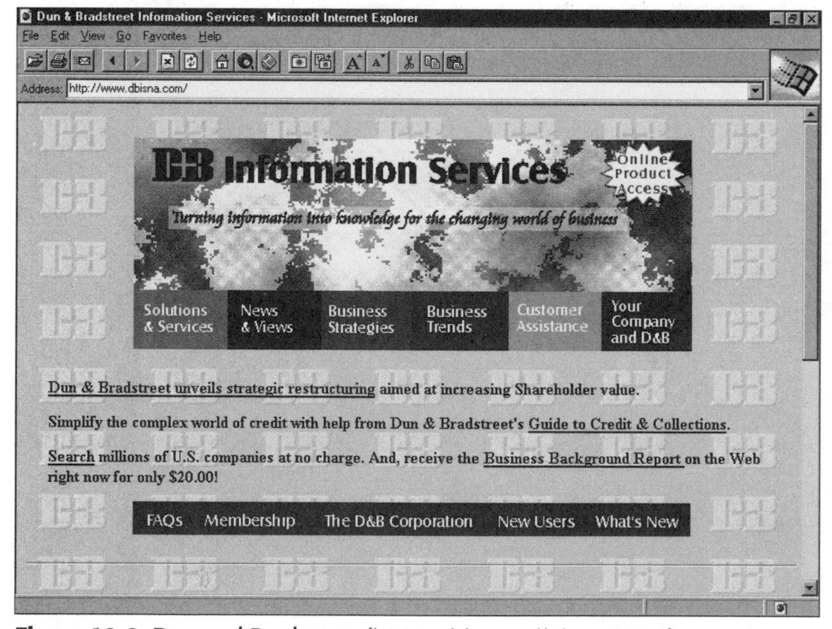

Figure 10-9: Dun and Bradstreet (`http://www.dbisna.com`).

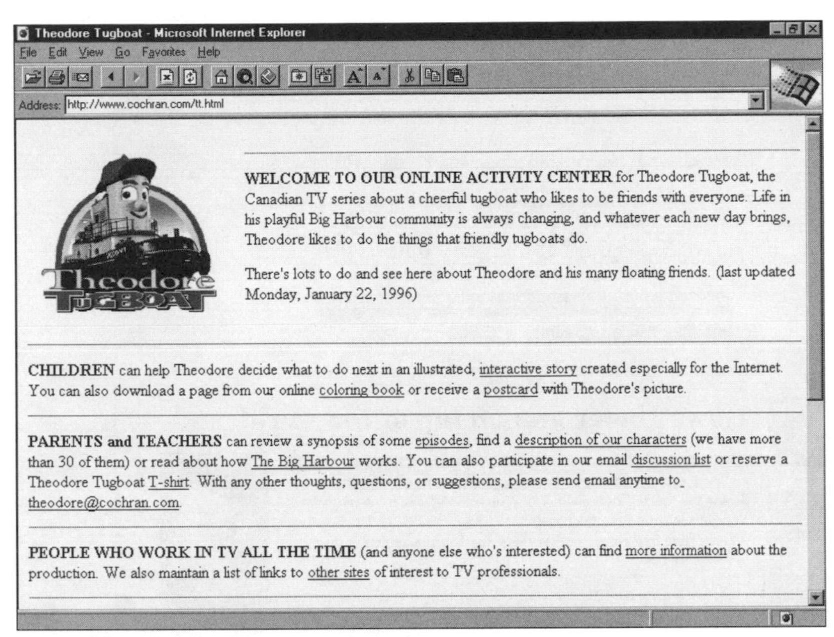

Figure 10-10: Theodore Tugboat (`http://www.cochran.com/tt.html`).

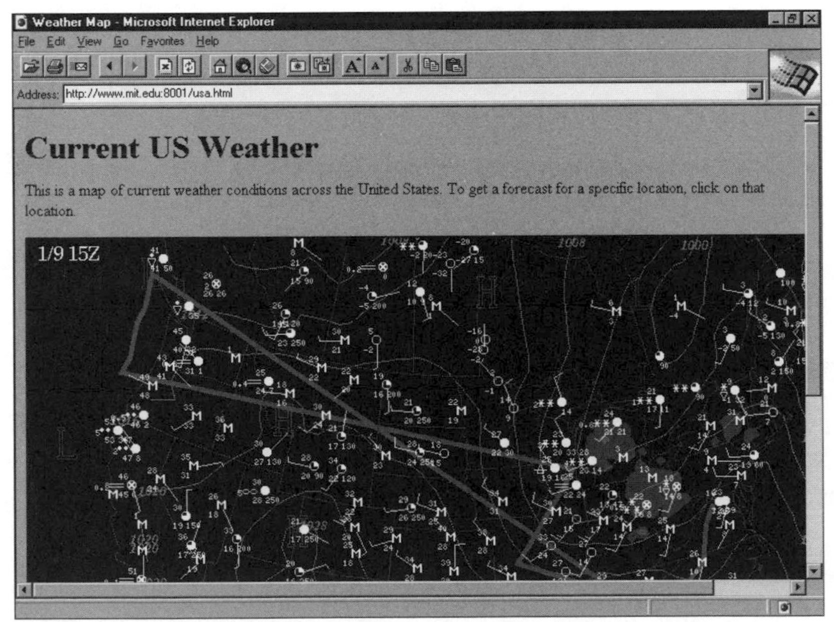

Figure 10-11: Current U.S. Weather (`http://www.mit.edu:8001/usa.html`).

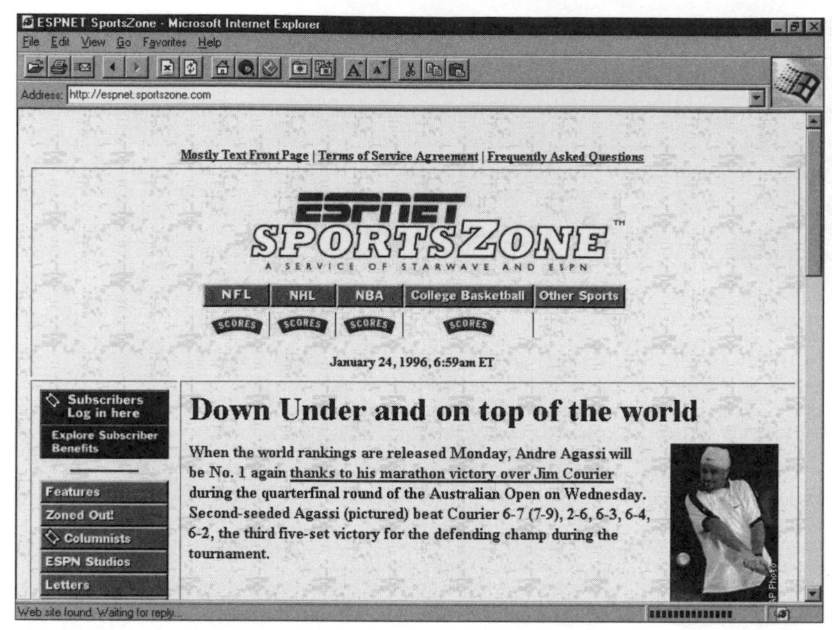

Figure 10-12: ESPNET SportsZone (`http://espnet.sportszone.com`).

Figure 10-13: Jungle Roses (`http://www.jungleroses.com`).

Figure 10-14: Who Shot Mr. Burns? (`http://www.springfield.com`).

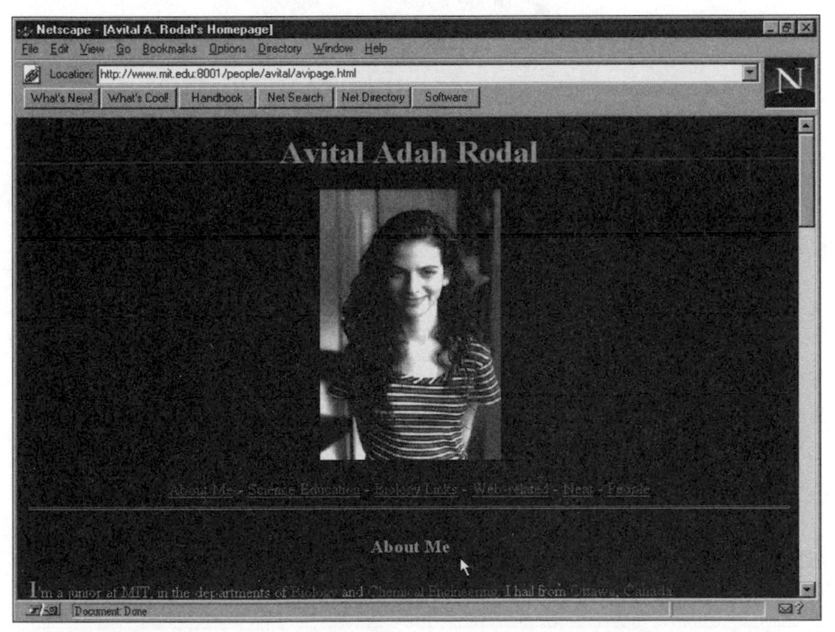

Figure 10-15: A personal site (`http://www.mit.edu:8001/people/avital/avipage.html`).

The rest of the pages

Your Web site can contain as many pages (documents) as you want. You should understand, however, that when a reader requests a page, the entire page is downloaded to the user's PC. The larger a page, the longer the downloading process takes. You'll want to get your pages to the reader as quickly as possible, so that he or she does not get tired of waiting and move on to another site. As a general rule of thumb, then, you want to divide your site's pages into several separate documents and let the reader decide which page(s) he or she wants to view.

Perhaps a little diagram will help you envision the organization of a site (see Figure 10-16). At the top of the site is the home page — the first page that the reader sees. That page offers *hyperlinks* to other pages (documents) in the site. For example, the site in Figure 10-16 has a home page, a FAQs (frequently asked questions) page, a News page, a Sites page, and a Tips page.

If a site was geared more toward selling products than toward dispensing information, it may contain a different set of pages, as in Figure 10-17. Notice, however, that the organization of those pages remains the same as that shown in Figure 10-16 — the home page acts as the storefront and provides access to all other pages.

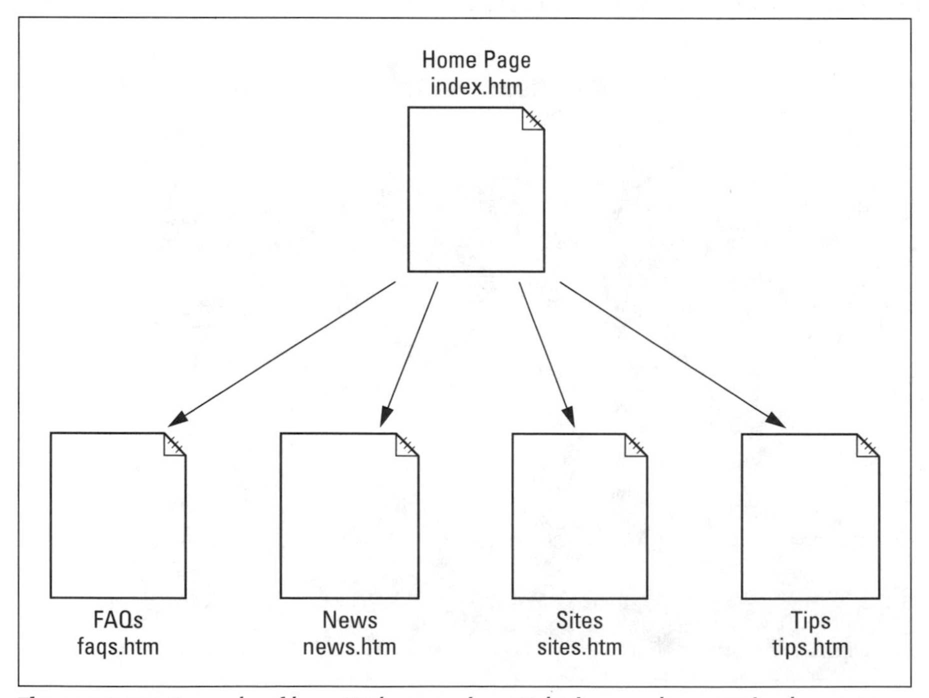

Figure 10-16: Example of how Web pages in a Web site may be organized.

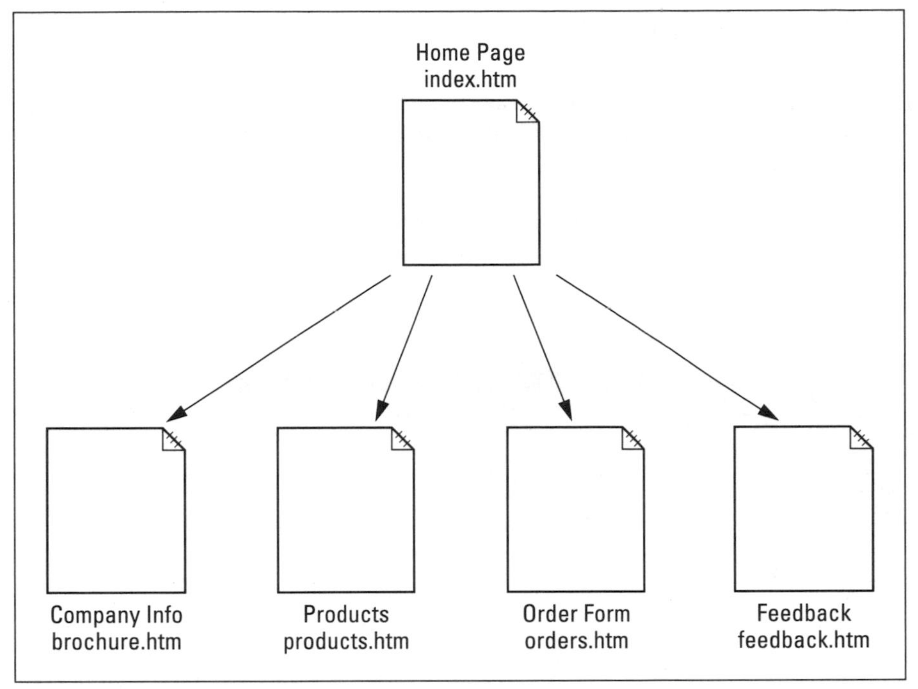

Figure 10-17: A second example of how Web pages in a Web site may be organized.

So What's in a Web Page?

If you grabbed any Web page off the World Wide Web and took a look "inside," you'd see that all Web pages contain basically two components:

✦ **Text.** The written information that the reader reads.

✦ **HTML tags.** Little codes that tell the Web browser how to format the text in the page.

HTML is an acronym for *Hypertext Markup Language,* which is the language that all Web browsers use to format Web pages on the screen. The HTML tags are, themselves, just text. What sets them off from regular text is a pair of angle brackets (<...>). In the next section, I demonstrate how these tags work. (There I'll assume that you are familiar with a simple text editor, such as Notepad or the old DOS EDIT program.)

An HTML demo

To demonstrate how HTML tags work, let's take a look at a sample Web page without HTML tags and then compare it to the same page with the HTML tags added. Figure 10-18 shows a simple text document that I created with Microsoft Notepad. Currently, the document contains text *only* — it does not have any HTML tags.

Notepad is a simple text editor that comes with Windows 95. You can access it by clicking the Start button, selecting Programs⇨Accessories, and then choosing Notepad.

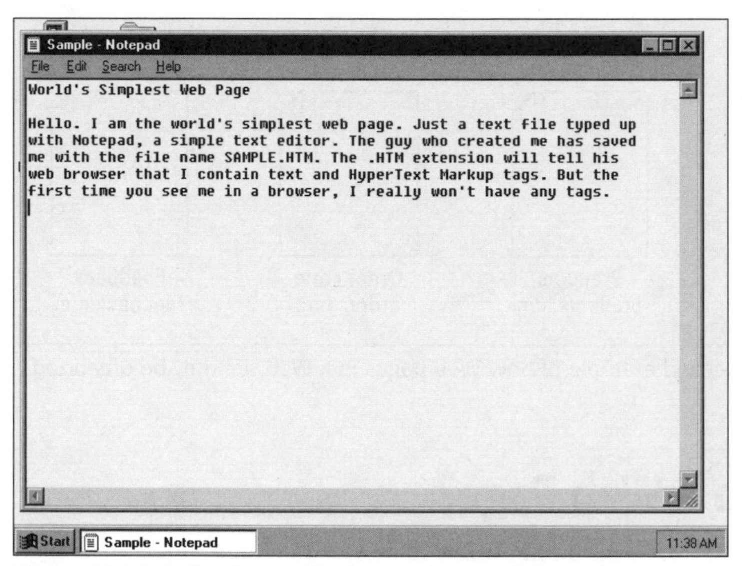

Figure 10-18: A simple text file document containing only text.

Now suppose that I save the document shown in Figure 10-18 to my hard disk using the filename Sample.htm and then I exit Notepad. From the Windows 95 desktop, I now launch my Web browser (Internet Explorer in this example). Rather than connecting to the Internet, I use the Web browser to open Sample.htm on my own hard disk. (To do that task, I just need to locate Sample.htm in My Computer and then double-click its filename. Alternatively, I could launch Internet Explorer, choose Cancel when it offers to connect me to the Internet, and then select File⇨Open⇨Open File to open the Sample.htm document.) The Web browser displays my text document as shown in Figure 10-19.

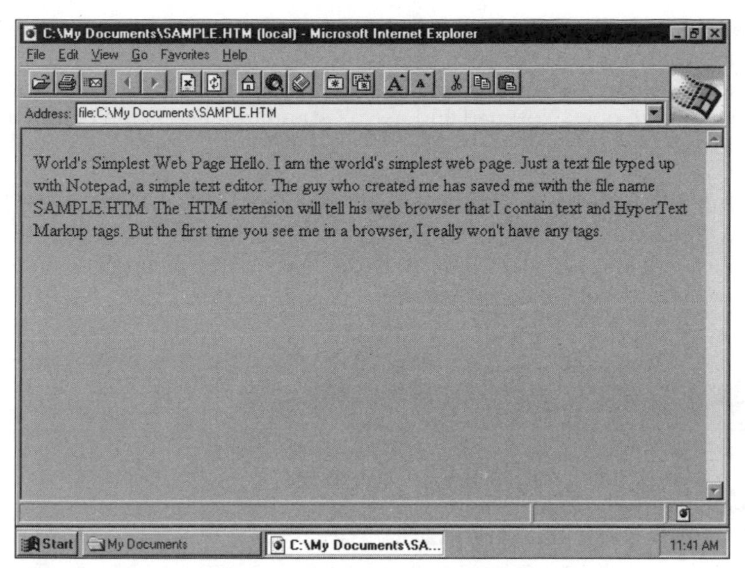

Figure 10-19: Sample.htm viewed from Internet Explorer.

Life Saver

Don't worry about all the details of using HTML tags just yet. In the next chapter, I show you exactly how to create, save, edit, and browse Web documents. For now, bear with me as I illustrate how HTML codes work in a document.

Notice that the Sample.htm document shown in Figure 10-19 does not have any formatting. Instead, Internet Explorer displays it as one long string of text. The reason why it appears in this format is because Sample.htm currently contains no HTML tags to *tell* Internet Explorer how to display the document.

What HTML tags look like

To spruce up the appearance of Sample.htm in Internet Explorer, we need to re-open it using Notepad (or some other editor) and insert some HTML tags. What does an HTML tag look like? Not much. Typically, it consists of a pair of angle brackets with one or more abbreviations in it. For example, the following HTML tag means "start a new paragraph":

```
<P>
```

Some HTML tags come in pairs. Symbol-wise, the first tag in the pair uses just the angle brackets. The ending tag, however, contains a forward slash (/) just after the first angle bracket. For example, the first HTML tag in the following code means "start the Heading 1 format." The second tag translates as "end the Heading 1 format."

```
<H1>   </H1>
```

Now you may be wondering, "How do I get those tags in there?" You cannot use the Web browser to put them in because a Web browser is strictly for *viewing* documents — not for editing them. Instead, you need to exit Internet Explorer to get back to the Windows desktop, then re-open Notepad and use its standard File⇨Open commands to re-open Sample.htm.

Once you have Sample.htm back on your Notepad screen, you can type in the HTML tags just as you'd type in text. For example, in Figure 10-20, I put an <H1> tag at the beginning of the heading line and an </H1> tag at the end of the heading line. I also placed a <P> tag at the start of each paragraph.

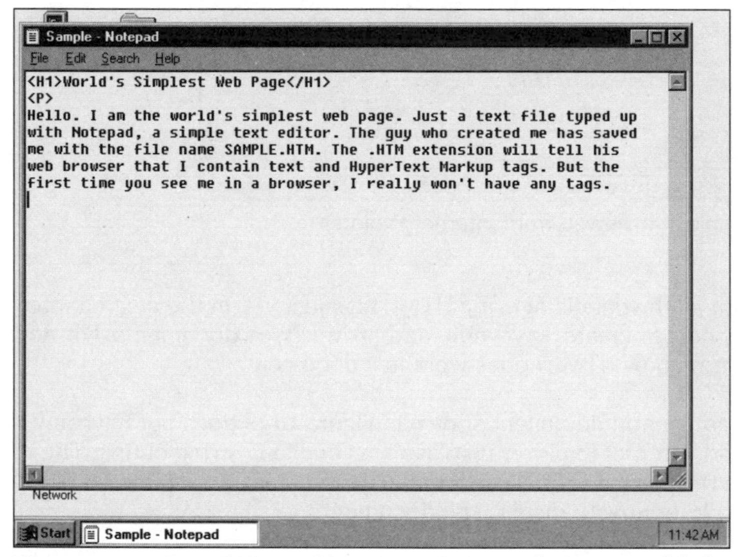

Figure 10-20: Sample.htm with <H1>, </H1>, and <P> tags added.

Once you've placed them in your document, you can save Sample.htm with these new tags added and then close Notepad. When you restart Internet Explorer (or any other Web browser) and re-open Sample.htm, lo and behold — the document looks *much* better (Figure 10-21).

Notice in Figure 10-21 that the HTML tags, <H1>, </H1>, and <P>, do not show up in the Web browser. That's because the Web browser interprets anything enclosed in angle brackets as formatting codes. Rather than display the code as text, the browser applies the format indicated by the code. The heading line in Figure 10-21 appears as large text because the <H1> code tells the browser to "switch to Heading 1 size format." The </H1> tells it when to stop displaying text in Heading 1 format. As such, the text that appears after the heading line is displayed in normal-sized text. The <P> code tells the browser where to start a new paragraph.

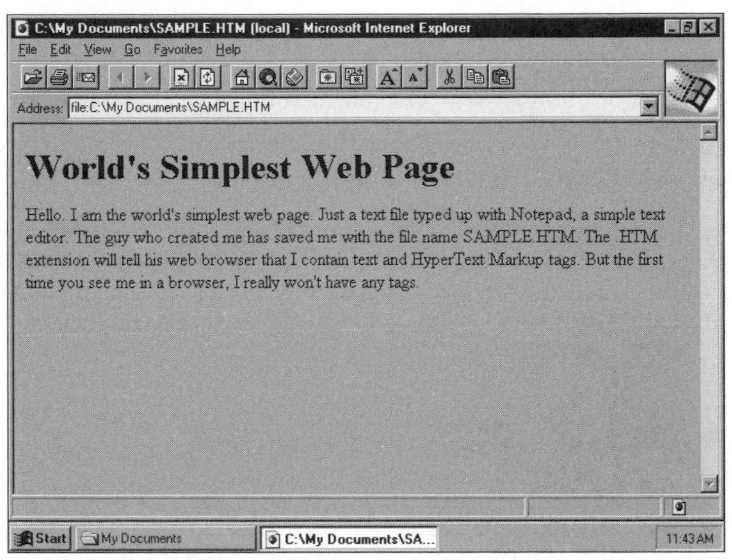

Figure 10-21: The document from Figure 10-20 as it appears in Internet Explorer.

That, in a nutshell, is what Web authoring is all about. Your Web document contains text for people to read, and HTML tags within the text tell the Web browser program how to format the text on the screen. As you learn in upcoming chapters, there are lots of HTML tags from which you can choose. This smorgasbord of tags enables you to be pretty specific about how you want your document to appear in a reader's Web browser.

As you also learn later, there are dozens of ways to *place* HTML tags into Web documents. These methods range from the rather archaic method I just demonstrated (manually typing the code through a text editor) to the modern, point-and-click, WYSISOWYG (pronounced *wizzy-sog*, an acronym for What You See Is Sort Of What You Get) method used throughout the rest of this book.

Sneak a Peek at Other People's Tags

Just about every page that you view on the World Wide Web consists of a text document with HTML tags in it. You can easily see this fact for yourself, if you like, because when you point your Web browser to a Web page, the Internet automatically downloads the entire Web page — HTML tags and all — to your computer. Of course, you do not see the HTML tags when you first view the Web page with your Web browser. But you *can* see the tags, if you want, by viewing the page's *source document*. To do so, try one of these methods:

✦ In Internet Explorer, right-click on a neutral part of the page (white space) and choose View Source from the shortcut menu.

✦ In Netscape Navigator, choose View⇨Document Source from the menu bar.

✦ In other Web browsers, choose View Source from the File or View menu or check that browser's help screens for information on viewing the *source*.

Figure 10-22 shows an example where I'm using Internet Explorer to view the home page for a site named Jungle Roses. In this example, I've already right-clicked on a neutral part of the document and chosen View Source. Instantly, the source document — the text and the HTML codes — appears in Notepad in a window that partially covers Internet Explorer.

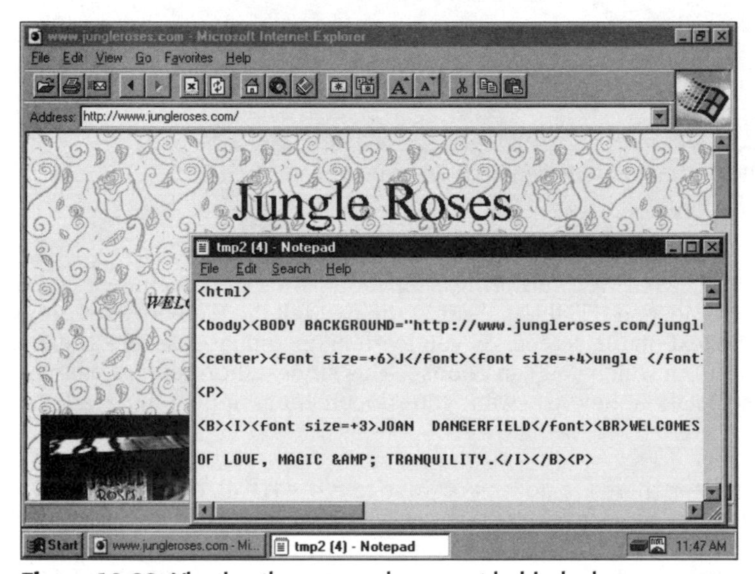

Figure 10-22: Viewing the source document behind a home page.

In Figure 10-22, I'm viewing one Web page in two different ways: as the Web browser's interpretation of the page and as the "pure source" document — text and HTML tags — via Notepad, a neutral text editor that doesn't interpret HTML tags.

Hot Stuff

I could choose File⇨Save from Notepad's menus in Figure 10-22 and save a copy of the Web page right onto my hard disk. Then I could use that page as sort of a template for designing my own page. This trick may come in handy when you start designing your own Web pages.

What about the pictures?

As you know, a Web site can contain more than just text and HTML tags. Most sites also contain lots of pictures and hypertext links. And some contain multimedia files such as sound, video, and even virtual worlds. But as you'll see, those non-text elements are not actually stored "in" the Web page document. The Web page document just contains tags that refer to the non-text files. For example, the tag

```
<IMG SRC = "MyPic.GIF">
```

tells the Web browser to "show an IMaGe (picture) here. The SouRCe (that is, the file that contains the image) is named "MyPic.GIF."

One look at the source document in Figure 10-22 may cause you to think "Yikes! That looks like some kind of secret code from another universe!" You're right, it does — but don't let that fact intimidate you, because you will rarely, if ever, have to type a bunch of weird-looking codes. As you learn in the next chapter, you can use Microsoft Word Internet Assistant (Word IA) to type a document using more familiar, point-and-click word-processing techniques. When you save your document, Word IA automatically creates the HTML tags for you.

Summary

In order to be a Web publisher/author, you first need to get a Web site — a place on the Internet that has its own URL. You then need to create some Web pages to put into that site. Let's review the major points covered in this chapter:

✦ The content (text) of your site is stored in Web pages on your Web site.

✦ The first page a reader comes to in your site is called the home page.

✦ Every Web page is basically a text document that contains regular text to be read by humans and HTML tags that tell the Web browser program how to display that text.

✦ Multiple Web pages are interlinked through hyperlinks — little, clickable hot spots on the screen.

✦ As you learn in Chapter 16, hyperlinks consist of simple HTML tags that you can put into your Web pages with just a few mouse clicks.

✦ ✦ ✦

Authoring Cool Web Pages with Word Internet Assistant

✦ ✦ ✦ ✦

In This Part

✦ ✦ ✦ ✦

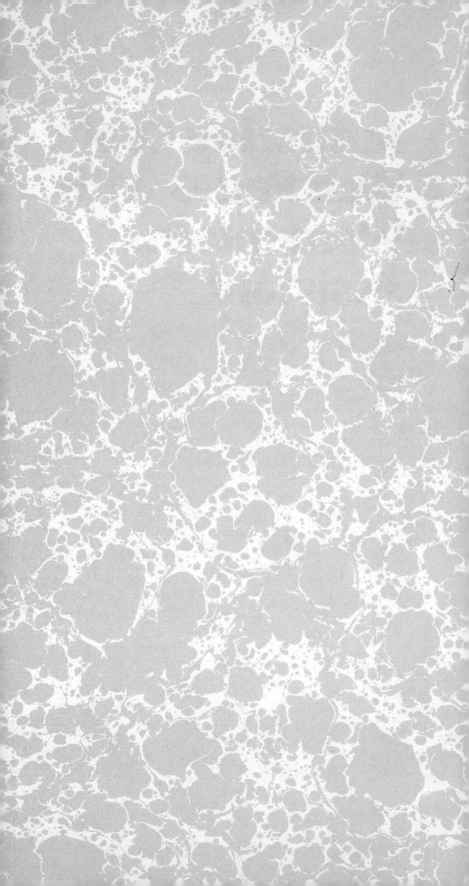

CHAPTER 11

Setting Up an Awesome Web Authoring Environment

✦ ✦ ✦ ✦

In This Chapter

Setting up Microsoft Word Internet Assistant (Word IA)

Installing Paint Shop Pro

Setting up quick shortcuts to your favorite authoring tools

Creating a folder for your Web pages

✦ ✦ ✦ ✦

With all the technical stuff about the Internet and Web sites now out of the way, we can move on to the creative, fun stuff — authoring Web pages. As a Web author, you'll need lots of good tools to make your work time efficient and your results fantastic. Hundreds of tools are available for Web authors, and I've tried plenty of them. I could spend the rest of this book just describing and comparing the various tools available.

This book is a how-to book though, not a product review book, so I'm not going to review countless tools. Rather, I'm just going to pick a few of these tools and demonstrate them throughout the chapters that follow. My criteria for selecting tools is totally subjective — I simply selected the tools that work best for me. I think these tools will work great for you, too.

Setting Up Word Internet Assistant

My favorite tool for authoring Web pages is Microsoft Word for Windows 95 (a.k.a. Word 7.0 with Internet Assistant, which I'll just refer to as Word IA throughout the rest of the book). This Microsoft Word product comes with the Microsoft Office for Windows 95 software suite. You can also purchase it separately at any computer store as a standalone product or as an upgrade to an earlier version of Word.

Currently, Microsoft is giving away the product for free, and you can easily download and install a copy from the Internet by following the instructions in the next section. I've also included a copy of Internet Assistant for Word 7.0 on the CD-ROM that comes with this book. If you do not have access to the Word Wide Web yet, you can install Internet Assistant from the CD-ROM.

Downloading the latest version of Word IA

Before you download Word IA, bear in mind that it is an add-on product for Microsoft Word. Word IA won't do you any good if you don't have Word installed. Also, two versions of Internet Assistant are available — one for Word 6.0 (of Windows 3.*x* fame) and the other for Word for Windows 95. You need to download whichever copy is appropriate for your current version of Word. Here are the steps to follow:

1. Start your Web browser (for example, Internet Explorer) and connect to the World Wide Web.
2. Point your browser to Microsoft's home page at `http://www.msn.com` (if you're not taken there automatically).
3. Choose Microsoft Products.
4. Click on Internet Assistant (you may need to scroll down a little to get to that option).
5. You should come to a page that lets you download Internet Assistant, as in Figure 11-1.
6. Click whichever option describes the version you want to download (such as for Word 6.0 or Word 95) and follow the instructions that appear on screen.

Web publishers sometimes rearrange their Web sites, so if you don't find Internet Assistant when you follow these steps, go to Microsoft's home page and search for *Internet Assistant* to get to the appropriate page.

After you have completed all the instructions that appear on screen, Word IA should be downloaded and already installed on your computer. To verify that the product was installed, do one of the following:

✦ From the Windows 95 desktop, click the Start button, click New Office Document, and click the General tab.

✦ If you are already in Microsoft Word, choose File➪New from Word's menu bar and click the General tab.

Either way, you should see a Word template icon for HTML or HTML.DOT, as shown in Figure 11-2 (near the mouse pointer). You use this template whenever you want to create a new Web page. For the moment, you can just click Cancel — we'll create a Web page in the next chapter. If you are currently in Microsoft Word, you can choose File➪Exit from Word's menu bar to get to the Windows 95 desktop.

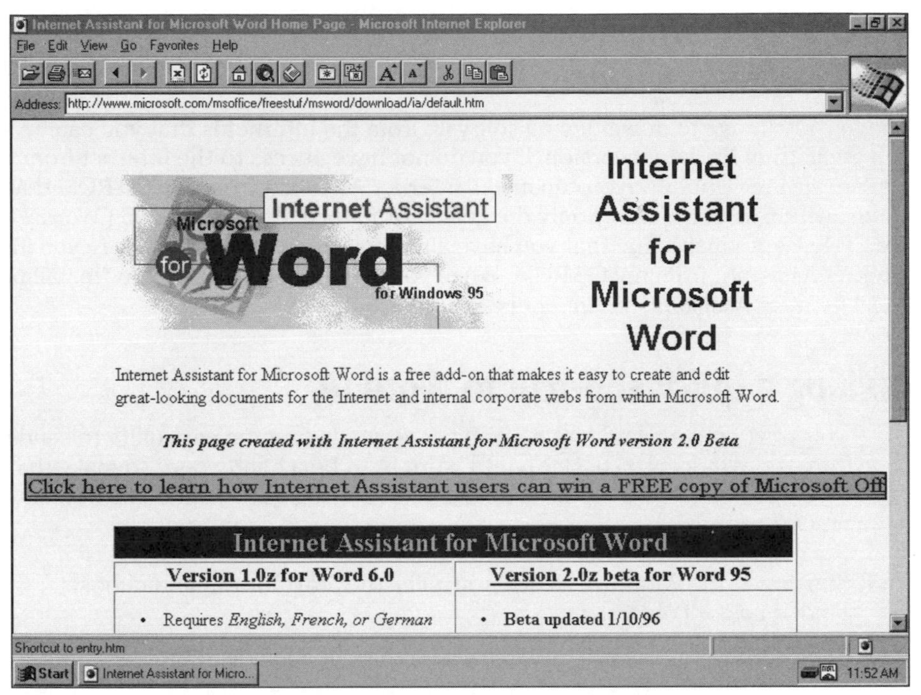

Figure 11-1: The Web page for downloading Word Internet Assistant.

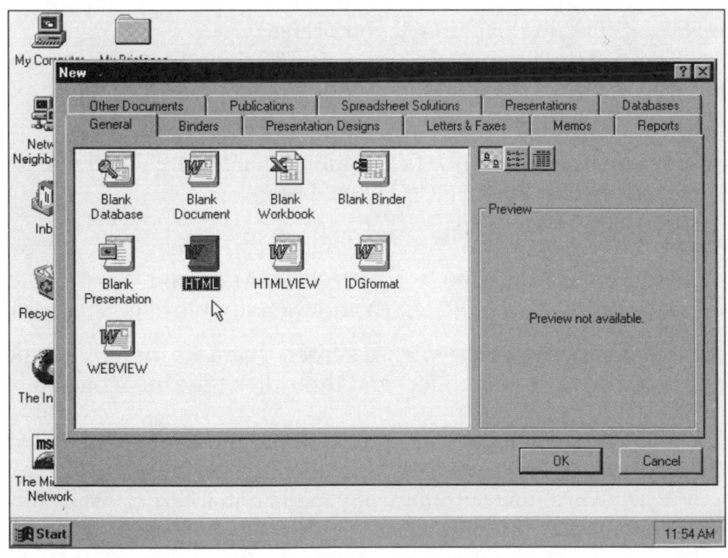

Figure 11-2: The HTML (or HTML.DOT) template icon appears after a successful installation of Internet Assistant.

Installing Internet Assistant from the *Web Publishing Uncut* CD-ROM

The big advantage to downloading software from the Internet is that you can be sure you are getting the latest version. If you do not have access to the Internet from where you are sitting right now, you can install Internet Assistant from the CD-ROM that comes with this book. I have only the version for Word for Windows 95 (Word 7.0) on the CD-ROM, so make sure that you have already installed Word 95 before you install Internet Assistant from my CD-ROM. When you are ready to go, refer to "Installing Word Internet Assistant" in Appendix A for instructions.

Making a quick shortcut to Word IA

Once you start creating and editing Web pages, you'll find the capability to send a Web page from the Windows 95 desktop into Word IA to be a handy one. To make that task as easy as possible, take a moment to add Microsoft Word to your Send To menu. The following list tells you how:

1. Starting at the Windows 95 desktop, click the Start button and choose Find➪Files or Folders.
2. Type **sendto** (one word) and make sure that the Include Subfolders option is selected (checked).

Hot Stuff

Using Find to get to the SendTo folder is entirely optional. On most PCs, you can simply type **C:\WINDOWS\FIND** to get to the SendTo folder, and you can open it through My Computer or Windows Explorer, if you prefer.

3. Click the Find Now button. Look for a folder named SendTo (most likely located in the C:\WINDOWS folder), as shown in Figure 11-3.
4. Double-click the SendTo icon to open that folder. Chances are you'll already see some shortcut icons in that folder, as in Figure 11-4.
5. Within the SendTo folder, choose File➪New➪Shortcut.
6. Use the Browse button to locate the startup icon for Microsoft Word (typically, C:\MSOFFICE\WINWORD\WINWORD.EXE) and then double-click that icon.
7. Choose Next, and when you see the Wizard screen that asks for a title, type **Word** (or **Microsoft Word**, if you prefer) and then click the Finish button.

Your SendTo folder should now contain a shortcut that points to Microsoft Word, as shown in Figure 11-5. When you send an HTML document (a file with the `.htm` or `.html` extension) to Word, Word now automatically loads it in Internet Assistant and displays your document, all ready for editing.

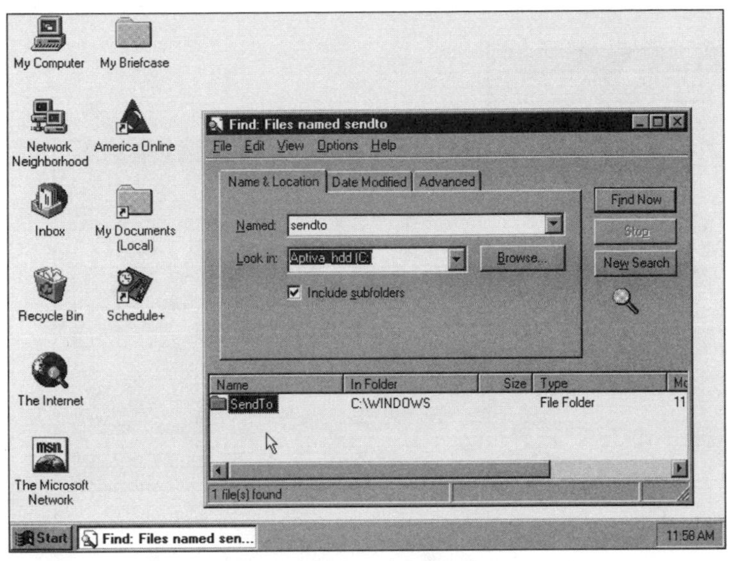

Figure 11-3: The SendTo folder in C:\WINDOWS.

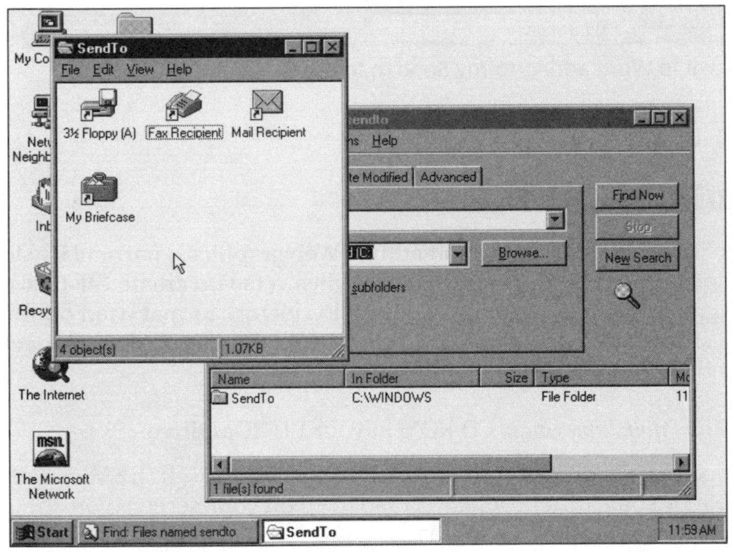

Figure 11-4: The SendTo folder already contains a few shortcuts but we'll be adding more.

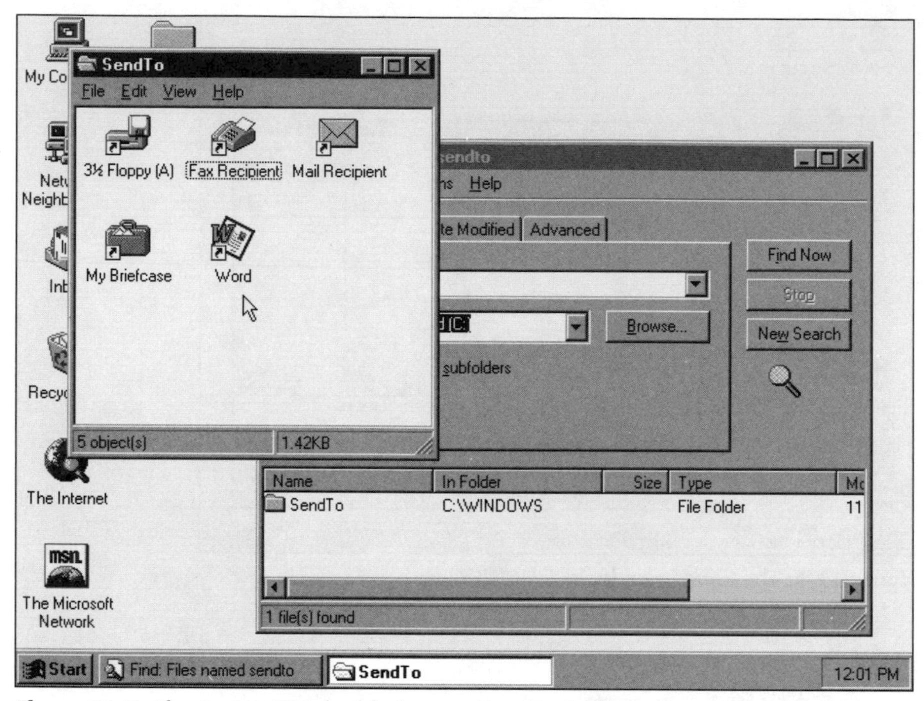

Figure 11-5: Shortcut to Word added to my SendTo folder.

Installing Paint Shop Pro

I like to use Paint Shop Pro for creating and editing Web graphics. I particularly like the latest 32-bit version because it supports long filenames, lets you create GIF files with transparent backgrounds, and also supports the JPEG picture format used on the Web. I included a shareware version of Paint Shop Pro on the CD-ROM in the back of this book. Follow these steps to install that program:

1. Insert the *Web Publishing Uncut* CD-ROM in your CD-ROM drive.
2. Close any open applications on your Windows 95 desktop. (If the Microsoft Office toolbar or some other toolbar is displayed on your screen, you should close it before installing a new program.)
3. From the Windows 95 desktop, click the Start button and select Run.
4. Type (or browse to) ***D*:\paintshp**, but substitute the drive letter for your CD-ROM drive in place of *D*.
5. Double-click the Setup (or Setup.exe) icon and follow the instructions on screen to install the 32-bit shareware version of Paint Shop Pro.

After you have installed Paint Shop Pro, you can run it as you would any other program. Typically, you just need to click the Start button, select Programs⇨Paint Shop Pro, and choose Paint Shop Pro-32 Bit. The system will confront you with a "nag screen" that encourages you to register the product. I hope you'll do so because it's a great program and the author deserves to be paid. By registering the product, you also get rid of the nag screen and make yourself eligible for some free future upgrades.

Creating a quick shortcut to Paint Shop Pro

You may want to take a moment to create a quick shortcut to Paint Shop Pro. You'll see the handiness of this shortcut when we get to Chapter 21. Use the same basic procedure you used to create the SendTo shortcut to Microsoft Word. The following list gives you the exact steps to follow:

1. Starting at the Windows 95 desktop, click the Start button and choose Find⇨Files or Folders.
2. Type **sendto** (one word) and make sure that the Include Subfolders option is selected (checked).
3. Click the Find Now button. Look for a folder named SendTo, most likely located in the C:\WINDOWS folder.
4. Double-click the SendTo icon to open that folder.
5. Within the SendTo folder, choose File⇨New⇨Shortcut.
6. Use the Browse button to locate the startup icon for Paint Shop Pro (typically, C:\PSP\PSP.EXE) and then double-click that icon.
7. Choose Next, and when you see the Wizard screen that asks for a title, type **Paint Shop Pro** and then click the Finish button.

Your SendTo folder should now contain a shortcut that points to Paint Shop Pro as in Figure 11-6. You can then close the SendTo folder and Find window before beginning the next section.

Figure 11-6: A shortcut to Paint Shop Pro added to my SendTo folder.

Making a shortcut to Netscape Navigator

If you have Netscape Navigator, you might want to create a SendTo shortcut to that product. That way, you can right-click any .htm or .html file and decide whether to view it in Internet Explorer or Navigator right on the spot. To add Navigator to your SendTo menu, locate the file NETSCAPE.EXE and add a shortcut to its icon to your SendTo menu group.

Keep in mind that Word IA tends to support Internet Explorer features more than it supports Navigator features. So, just to simplify matters, you might want to view your Web pages in Internet Explorer first.

Note that when you switch from Internet Explorer to Navigator, and vice versa, a message will appear asking if you want to make the current browser your default browser. There is no big commitment involved in this; you can just choose Yes when prompted. Once you choose a default browser, double-clicking a .htm or .html file will open that file in the default browser. If you want to open the file with the "other" browser, don't double-click. Just right-click the icon and choose SendTo and the browser you want to use.

Getting the latest version of Paint Shop Pro

If you want to keep abreast of current versions of Paint Shop Pro or check out some of Jasc's other great offerings, point your Web browser to `http://www.jasc.com`. I have found the quality of all its programs to be superb and the pricing to be very, very reasonable. This site is definitely worth a look.

Making a Shortcut to Internet Explorer

As you author your Web pages, you'll occasionally want to open them in your favorite Web browser to see how they will look once they are actually published on the Web. Adding your Web browser to your SendTo menu makes the task of viewing local Web pages very easy. Once again, you can use the same general techniques used to create the SendTo shortcuts for Word and Paint Shop Pro to make a shortcut for any Web browser you own. If you want to add Internet Explorer to your SendTo menu, follow these steps:

1. Starting at the Windows 95 desktop, click the Start button and choose Find⇨Files or Folders.
2. Type **sendto** (one word) and make sure that the Include Subfolders option is selected (checked).

3. Click the Find Now button. Look for a folder named SendTo, most likely located in the C:\WINDOWS folder.
4. Double-click the SendTo icon to open that folder.
5. Within the SendTo folder, choose File⇨New⇨Shortcut.
6. Use the Browse button to locate the startup icon for Internet Explorer (typically, C:\PROGRAM FILES\PLUS!\MICROSOFT INTERNET\IEXPLORE.EXE), and then double-click that icon.
7. Choose Next, and when you see the Wizard screen that asks for a title, type **Internet Explorer** and then click the Finish button.

Making a Shortcut to Notepad

You also may find it handy to open your Web pages with Microsoft's Notepad program from time to time. Notepad takes you right to the source, where you can view and tweak text and HTML tags. Typically, your computer automatically installs Notepad when you install Windows 95. As a result, all you need to do is create the shortcut by following the standard procedure:

1. Starting at the Windows 95 desktop, click the Start button and choose Find⇨Files or Folders.
2. Type **sendto** (one word), and make sure that the Include Subfolders option is selected (checked).
3. Click the Find Now button. Look for a folder named SendTo, most likely located in the C:\WINDOWS folder.
4. Double-click the SendTo icon to open that folder.
5. Within the SendTo folder, choose File⇨New⇨Shortcut.
6. Use the Browse button to locate the startup icon for Notepad (typically C:\WINDOWS\NOTEPAD.EXE), and then double-click that icon.
7. Choose Next, and when you see the Wizard screen that asks for a title, type **Notepad** and click the Finish button.

If you added all the shortcuts that I recommended, your SendTo folder should now look something like Figure 11-7. (To put your own icons into alphabetical order, just choose View⇨Arrange Icons⇨by Name from the SendTo folder's menu bar.)

Now you can close all your open windows to get back to the Windows 95 desktop. You'll see just how handy all those shortcuts can be as you read upcoming chapters.

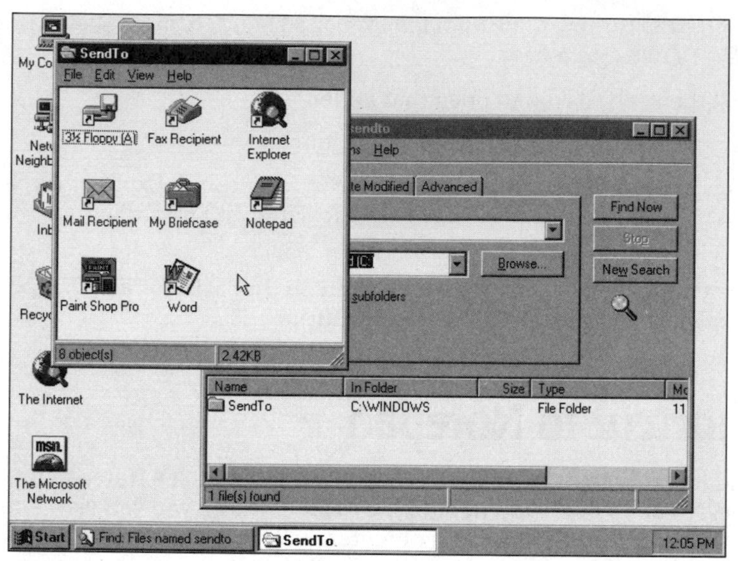

Figure 11-7: Shortcuts to good Web authoring tools in the SendTo menu.

Making a Folder for Your Web Pages

One last little thing before you start authoring your Web site documents: You want to create a folder, right off the bat, for storing all documents, graphics, and other files that you plan to put on your Web site. You should keep *all* files, and *only* the files, that you plan to later upload to your Web site in this folder. That way, when you are ready to do the upload, you can just copy all files from your site folder to your actual site.

I usually keep a subfolder named Parts within the site folder. In this subfolder, I keep stuff related to the Web site that I don't plan to upload to it. For example, if I have some clip art images in bitmap (.BMP) format for my site, I'll keep the .BMP files in the Parts subfolder. The converted GIF files, which will be uploaded, go in the parent folder. This is just one way to organize things so that you can easily find stuff when you need it. To use this type of organization, all you have to do to set up the folders is the following:

1. At the Windows 95 desktop, double-click your My Computer icon.
2. Double-click the drive where you want to store your local Web site documents (most likely drive C).
3. In the window that appears, choose File➪New➪Folder. A new folder named New Folder will appear.
4. Type your own folder name. For my example, I named the folder My Web Site.

Puzzled?

Throughout the book, I refer to the folder where you store your Web pages as your *My Web Site* folder. But you can, of course, give your folder any name you want.

5. Double-click the new folder to open it.
6. Within the new window that appears, select File➪New➪Folder once again. This time, type **Parts** as the name of this new folder.
7. Click somewhere just outside the new Parts folder to make sure that you saved the new name. Then close the My Web Site folder window.
8. To make things really easy, put a shortcut to the new folder on your desktop. That is, just right-drag the folder icon for My Web Site to the Windows 95 desktop. Release the right mouse button and choose Create Shortcut(s) Here. If you like, you can rename the folder.

Hot Stuff

Windows 95 automatically adds "Shortcut to . . ." to a new shortcut icon's name. I always delete those two words so that the system does not alphabetize the shortcuts under "S" on my desktop.

9. Now you can close all open windows.
10. Right-click some neutral area of the Windows 95 desktop and select Arrange Icons➪by Name.

Now you're cookin': Your Web authoring tools are ready to go, and (as you'll see) you can access any of these tools with just a couple of mouse clicks. You have a folder for your Web pages that has its own shortcut icon right on the desktop (see Figure 11-8). You even have a little subfolder for storing "incidentals." Life in the Web authoring lane is gonna be grand.

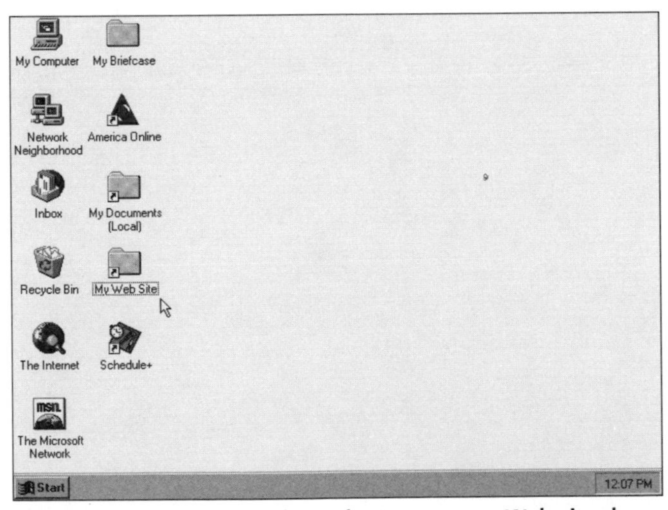

Figure 11-8: A handy desktop shortcut to your Web site documents.

Summary

Rather than getting right into authoring, we took a slight detour and spent a few moments setting up a great Web authoring environment on your PC. In this chapter, you learned the following:

- ✦ Microsoft Word Internet Assistant lets you author Web pages using the familiar word-processing techniques of Microsoft Word.
- ✦ Word Internet Assistant is free. But you must have Microsoft Word already to use it.
- ✦ Paint Shop Pro is a great tool for managing pictures that you use in your Web site. A copy of Paint Shop Pro (shareware version) is included on the CD-ROM that comes with this book.
- ✦ For quick access to a favorite Web authoring tool, add a shortcut to the Windows 95 SendTo menu (C:\WINDOWS\SENDTO).
- ✦ To make the tasks of managing your Web site and later copying your Web pages and related files easier, create a single folder for storing those items on your hard disk. Throughout this book, I refer to that folder as your My Web Site folder.

✦ ✦ ✦

Web Authoring with Internet Assistant

✦ ✦ ✦ ✦

In This Chapter

Creating your first Web page with Internet Assistant

Viewing your page with a Web browser

Word IA typing and editing basics

Applying styles to Web pages

Umpteen ways to view your Web page

Converting existing documents to Web pages

✦ ✦ ✦ ✦

It is (finally) time to start creating some Web pages. I first look at the process from a hands-on perspective. You can follow along to create and view your own first, simple Web page. Afterwards, I overview the main typing and editing tools and techniques that Word IA offers.

Creating a New Web Page

You can start creating a new Web page from the Windows 95 desktop or from within Microsoft Word:

1. Do one of the following:
   - If you have Microsoft Office and are at the Windows 95 desktop, click the Start button then choose New Office Document.
   - If you don't have Office, click the Start button and choose Programs⇨Microsoft Word.
   - If you're already in Microsoft Word, select File⇨New from Word's menu bar.
2. Click on the General tab and double-click on HTML (or HTML.DOT), as shown in Figure 12-1.

Puzzled? Whether or not the .DOT extension appears in the HTML icon's name depends on your current view options. You can set the extension viewing option through My Computer. To do this, double-click your My Computer icon, select View⇨Options, click the View tab, and select or clear the Hide MS-DOS file extensions check box as desired.

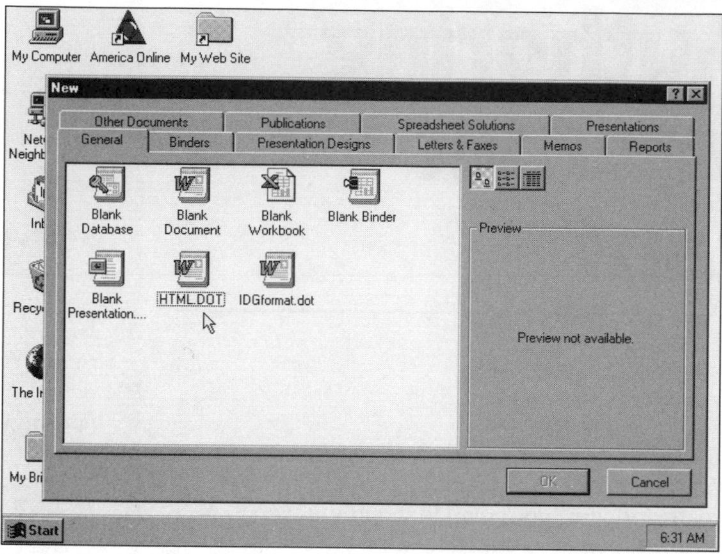

Figure 12-1: HTML (or HTML.DOT) is the template that you need to create a new Web page with Word IA.

After you do this task, you'll find yourself in Microsoft Word with a blank document displayed on your screen. Let's now take a look at how choosing HTML.DOT as your document template makes Word suddenly become Word IA.

What's special about Word IA

Word IA is, basically, Microsoft Word with Internet Assistant thrown in to enable you to create Web pages rather than printed documents. Some of the more common Web page features, such as hyperlinks and pictures, are readily available from the toolbars that appear on the screen (Figure 12-2). As always, you can point to any toolbar button to see its tooltip and display a brief description of that button in the status bar.

As you explore, you'll also discover lots of menu commands that deal specifically with Word IA. Perhaps the most important of these commands is Help⇨Internet Assistant for Word Help, which you can choose from the menu bar only while using the HTML.DOT document template.

If you are an experienced Word user, you may find that Word IA prevents you from doing lots of things that you used to do with Word. The reason is that Word IA supports only the relatively simple document formatting that the Web can use. Thus, any Word formatting features that the Web cannot support are hidden from you. You may find this irritating at first, but this setup is actually good because it saves you the frustration of finding out, the hard way, that "you can't do that on the Web."

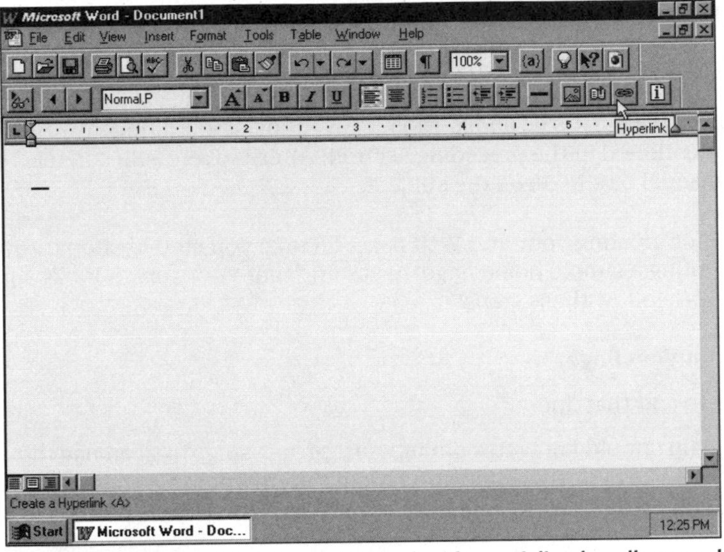

Figure 12-2: Word IA is Microsoft Word with specialized toolbars and menu commands.

Keep in mind that although many of your favorite formatting options may be gone, all of your general word-processing tools are still in place, including the following:

- ✦ Search and Replace
- ✦ Cut and Paste
- ✦ Go To
- ✦ Zoom
- ✦ Undo
- ✦ Repeat
- ✦ Center
- ✦ Spelling
- ✦ Thesaurus
- ✦ Hyphenation
- ✦ Auto-Correct

If you do not know how to use these Word features already, I recommend that you spend a little time learning them. These features are very useful tools, and they are easy to learn. Refer to your Microsoft Word manual or review the relevant "booklets" in Word's online help to learn more about them (from Word's menu bar, select Help⇨Microsoft Word Help Topics, click the Contents tab, and double-click the Typing, Selecting, and Editing entry).

Typing your first Web page

Typing up a Web page is pretty much the same as typing up any other document. I'm assuming that you already possess basic Word typing and editing skills, but if you don't, be sure to read the material under Typing, Selecting, and Editing in Word's online help, as I mentioned in the preceding section. Alternatively, you can read your Microsoft Word manual or a book on the subject.

To give you a feel for creating your first Web page, I'll take you step-by-step through the process of creating a simple home page. Assuming that your screen looks something like Figure 12-2, follow these steps:

1. Type **My First Web Page**.
2. Press Enter to end that line.

Life Saver

At the very least, you should know this about word processing: You can use the Backspace and Delete keys to erase text you typed. When typing a paragraph, press Enter only at the end of each paragraph, not at the end of each line.

3. Now type a few paragraphs. If you can't think of anything to type, just type these paragraphs:

```
Welcome to my first Web page. This being my first time,
I'm a little nervous about the whole thing. But I'm using
Microsoft Word Internet Assistant as my authoring tool.
And everyone assures me that doing so will make the job
easy. We'll see.

Well, I think that about wraps it up for my first Web
page. Thanks for stopping by, and you have a wonderful
day. OK?
```

4. Now let's apply a style to this document. Click anywhere in the My First Web Page title (or press Ctrl+Home to move the insertion point there).
5. Select Heading 1 from the Styles drop-down list in the toolbar (see Figure 12-3).

Immediately, the appearance of the first line changes, becoming larger and darker (see Figure 12-4) because you have applied the Heading 1 style to it. And that, in a nutshell, is how you create Web pages with Word IA. When you save the document, Word IA automatically inserts the appropriate HTML tags.

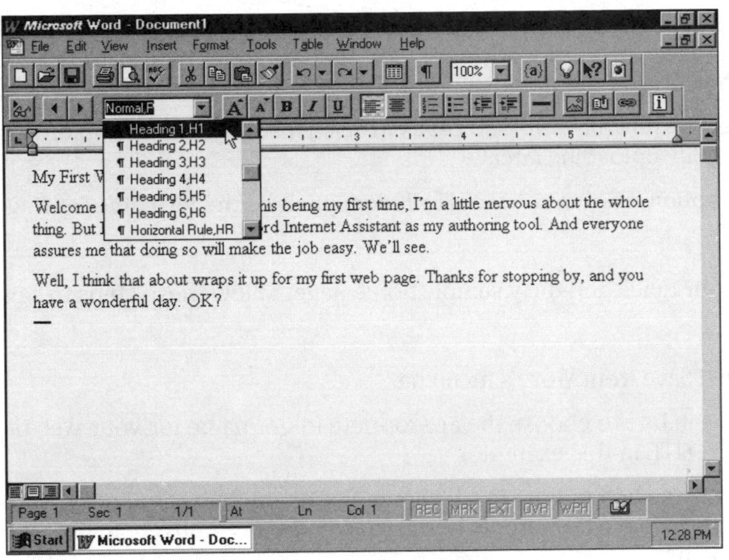

Figure 12-3: Word IA's Styles drop-down list.

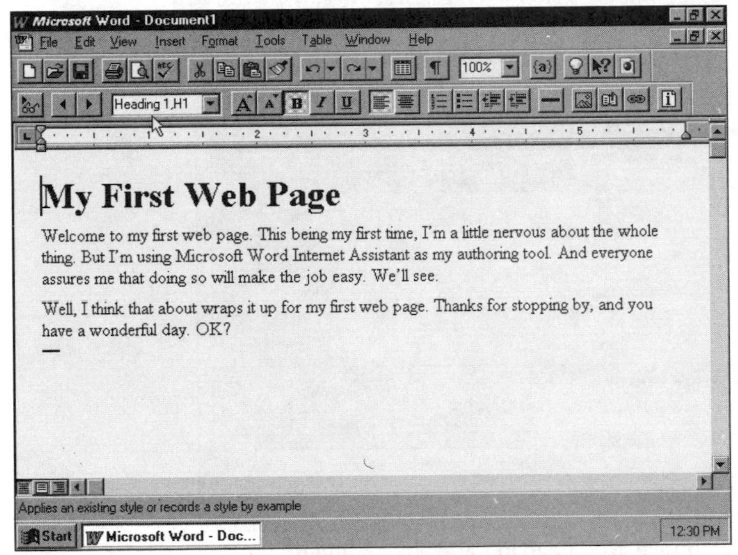

Figure 12-4: The Heading 1 style has been applied to the first line.

Naming and saving your Web page

You should keep a few things in mind when saving your Web page:

✦ Some services require you to name the home page (the page that browsers first encounter) `index.htm` or `index.html` or perhaps something else. If in doubt, check with your service provider.

✦ Don't forget to store all your Web pages in a single folder (for example, My Web Site) to simplify uploading later.

✦ If given an option, always choose HTML document as the format for saving your document.

Looking back at our quick-and-dirty sample home page, follow these steps to save your creation:

1. Choose File➪Save from Word's menu bar.
2. Use the Save in box to choose the appropriate folder name for your Web pages (C:\MY WEB SITE in this example).
3. Use the File name box to type in a filename (for example, `index.htm`). In Figure 12-5, I'm going to save the sample home page in the My Web Site folder with the name `index.htm`.

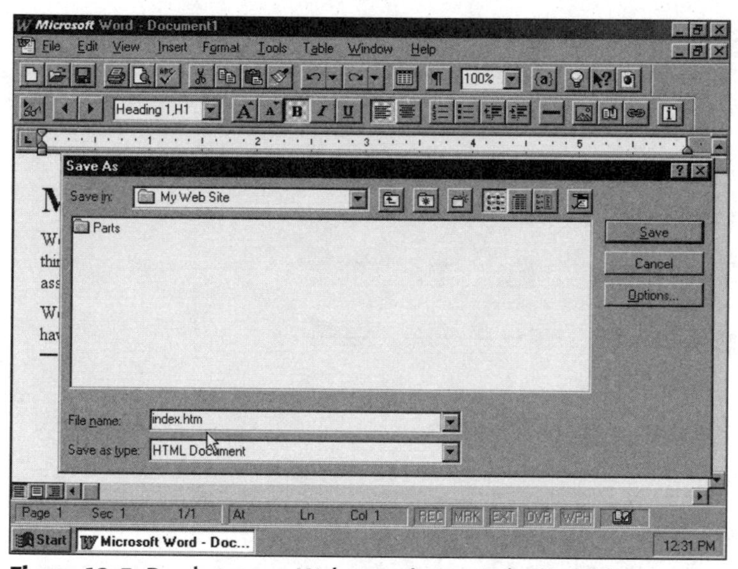

Figure 12-5: Ready to save Web page in My Web Site folder.

4. Click the Save button.

Word IA saves a copy of your document on disk. After you finish this task, you'll still be in Word IA with your document displayed on screen, so you can type in more text or make changes to the document if you want.

Saving your document every few minutes is a good idea. That way, if some mishap causes your PC to shut down, the most you stand to lose is a few minutes of work!

Exiting Word IA

To exit Word IA, just exit Word. That is, follow these steps:

1. Click the Close button in the upper-right corner of Word's window, or choose File➪Exit from Word's menu bar.
2. If you have made any changes since you last saved the document, Word prompts you to save those changes. Choose Yes (unless you're sure that you don't want to save recent changes).
3. If you are asked what format to save the document in, choose HTML document.

You have now created your first home page. Of course, only you can see it right now because you haven't published it yet. That is, you haven't moved it to a folder on a computer that's permanently connected to the Internet (unless you happen to be working directly on a Web server and have indeed put the document in a folder that's accessible through the Internet). That's okay for now because I doubt that you want to publish this particular page for all the world to see.

Index.html.htm

Before continuing, let me just say that if you *did* name your document `index.html` (or anything else with an `.html` extension), Microsoft Word probably added an extra `.htm` extension to the name you gave it. For example, suppose that I named my document `index.html`. When I open the folder named My Web Site (where I store all my Web pages), I see that the name of the file is actually `index.html.htm`, as shown in Figure 12-6.

You can easily fix this error: Just right-click the filename, `index.html.htm`, and choose Rename. Edit or retype the name to `index.html`. Click anywhere outside the new name to save it. Don't worry if you get a little message warning you about the effects of changing an extension — `.html` and `.htm` are treated the same. Chances are, you won't need to rename the document again in the future because Word only adds that extra `.htm` the first time you save the document.

To avoid the filename.html.htm problem, you can enclose the filename in double-quotation marks when typing it into the Save As dialog box. For example, if you type "**shmindex.html**" with the quotation marks in Word's Save As dialog box, the quotation marks will be removed and the file will have the name you intended, shmindex.html.

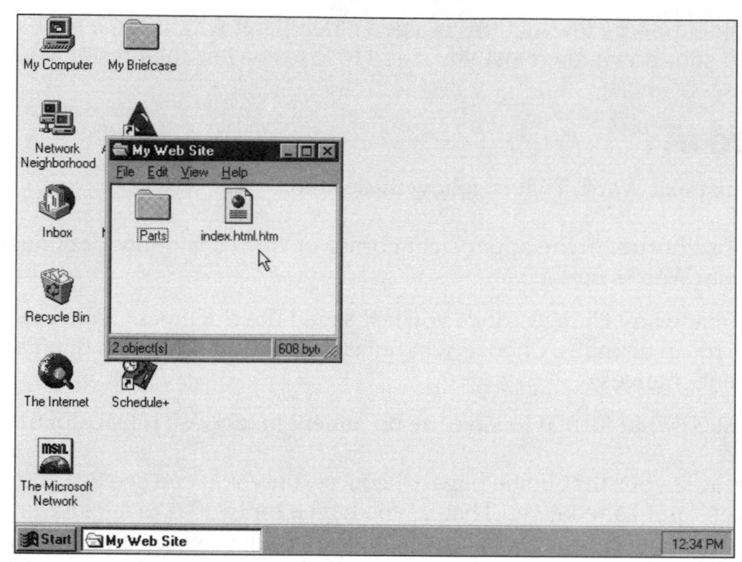

Figure 12-6: If you give a file a `.html` extension, Word adds `.htm` to that.

Keep in mind that you only need to use the four-letter extension, .html, if your Internet Service Provider requires it. If you create a Web page on a DOS-based PC, which only allows three-character extensions, go ahead and use the shorter three-character version (.htm). Then rename the file with a .html extension *after* you upload the file to the server that requires the four-letter extension. You can generally do this by using a simple Rename command in the FTP program that you use to upload pages to your server. But if you have any problems, I recommend that you ask your Internet Service Provider how to rename a file after it has been uploaded to the ISP's server.

Browsing your new Web page

If you want to see how your document looks when viewed through Internet Explorer or some other browser, just open the document with your browser. To do so, follow these steps:

1. Open the folder that contains the Web page (My Web Site in the example).
2. Double-click the Web page's icon. Or, right-click the Web page's icon, point to Send To, and choose Internet Explorer.

The document opens in your Web browser (see Figure 12-7) so that you can see it as the rest of the world will see it (after it's published). Of course, you can only *view* it. You can't navigate around and make changes because a Web browser only enables you to view Web pages — not create or change them.

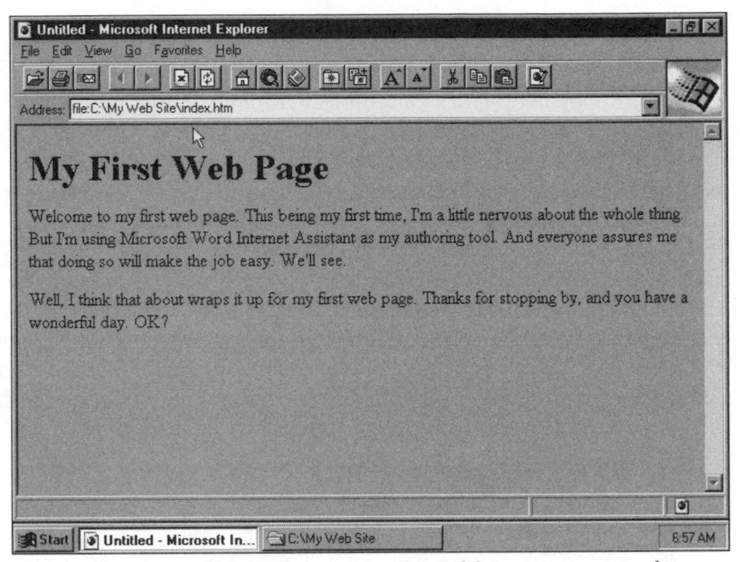

Figure 12-7: Your first Web page as viewed from Internet Explorer.

After you have finished viewing your first Web page, just close Internet Explorer to return to the Windows 95 desktop.

Hot Stuff

There's a quick shortcut you can take to get from Word IA to Internet Explorer. While you are in Word IA, just click the Preview in Browser button in the top toolbar. And here's a second tip: Some Web browsers, such as Netscape Navigator Gold 2.0, *do* allow you to switch to an edit mode and make changes to the page, right on the spot.

Word IA Basic Skills

The basic skills for creating your first Web page apply to all your Web pages. In a nutshell, you start or open a document using Microsoft Word and the HTML.DOT template. You type your text and then apply styles to that text to determine how it will look in the browser. Now let's take a closer look at these skills.

Opening a Web page for editing

Earlier in this chapter, I showed you how to create a new Web page by using the HTML.DOT document template in Microsoft Word. Of course, there are several instances when you want to re-open a document to make changes to it. You can re-open and edit your Web page at any time by using these standard Windows 95/ Word techniques:

Why does my document look different?

One of the most common questions people ask about Word IA goes something like this: "I closed and saved my document with a certain look. But then when I reopened the document, it looked different. What happened? Is this a bug?" Let me answer the last question first: No, it's not a bug.

What happened is that Word IA has "officially" converted your document to an HTML file. During this process, it removes any formatting features that will not carry over to the World Wide Web. The removal of tabs and indentations (that are not inside lists) is the most noticeable change.

It's important to remember that on the Internet, the reader's specific Web browser ultimately determines how your document will look on that person's screen. If you try to make your document look too perfect, you'll just end up frustrated because you cannot control the exact appearance of your document in every browser. Your best bet is to work with your document until you're reasonably satisfied with its appearance in Internet Explorer or your other favorite browser. But don't try to control the exact appearance of every detail.

✦ Click the Start button, select Documents, and if you see the name of the document you want to edit, just click on it.

✦ If you did as I suggested in Chapter 11, you can browse to the document by using the My Computer, Windows Explorer, or Find shortcuts you created. When you find the document, right-click the document's icon, select Send To, and choose Word from the shortcut menu.

✦ Alternatively, start Microsoft Word and click the File menu. If you see the name of the document that you want to open near the bottom of the File menu, just click its name. Otherwise, choose Open, browse to the document's folder, and then double-click its name or icon.

Typing and editing in Word IA

Word IA follows all the basic conventions of Windows word processing. For those of you who may be weak in those skills, here's a quick review of the basics:

✦ Whatever you type appears at the blinking *insertion point* (not at the mouse pointer).

✦ Pressing Backspace deletes the character to the left of the insertion point.

✦ Pressing Delete deletes the character to the right of the insertion point.

✦ You can move the insertion point to anywhere within existing text simply by clicking at the place where you want the insertion point to appear.

✦ You can also use the arrow keys, Home, End, and other cursor-positioning keys to move the insertion point. You can use the last two techniques to move the insertion point into existing text only; you cannot use them to move to a blank part of the page. If the insertion point is at the bottom of a page and you want to move further down, you need to insert more blank lines by pressing Enter. Likewise, if the insertion point is at the end of a line and you want to type further to the right, you must extend the line by pressing Spacebar or Tab.

Insert and Overwrite modes

When you type new text within existing text, the system typically inserts the new text. If you want to *replace* existing text, you can press Insert once to switch to Overwrite mode (an OVR indicator appears in the status bar). To switch back to Insert mode, press Insert again. In other words, the Insert key acts as a toggle, switching you between Insert and Overwrite modes.

Paragraph styles and character styles

When you open the Styles drop-down list in Word IA, you'll notice that some entries have a paragraph symbol preceding them. Other entries have an underlined letter a preceding them (see Figure 12-8). The ones marked with a paragraph symbol are called *paragraph styles* because Word automatically applies them to the entire current paragraph when you select them. The styles marked with a are called *character styles* because Word applies them only to the selected characters.

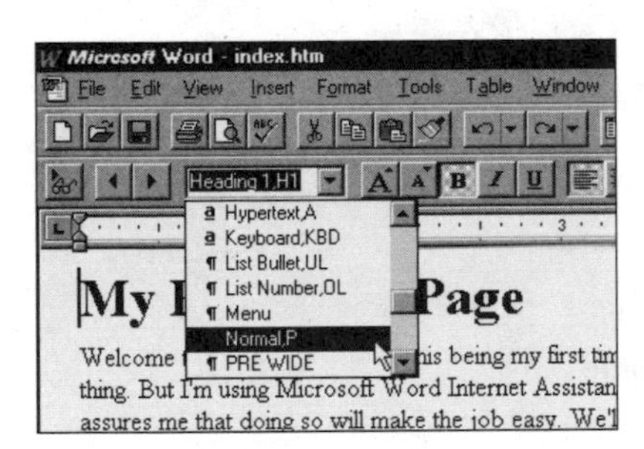

Figure 12-8: Paragraph styles and character styles in the Styles drop-down list.

Keep in mind that in word-processing parlance, a *paragraph* is any chunk of text that ends with a hard return (that is, any chunk of text that you end by pressing Enter). So, if you have a short heading followed by several block paragraphs, for example, the heading itself is a paragraph, as is each block of text that follows the heading. Earlier in this chapter, when you clicked on the short heading line and selected the Heading 1 style, you automatically applied that Heading 1 style to the entire heading.

Selecting text

Much of your work in Word IA involves selecting text that you want to work with. For example, if you want to cut, copy, move, or delete a chunk of text, or apply a character style to a chunk of text, you first need to select the text you want to work with. You can use the mouse, keyboard, or any combination of the two tools to select text.

Selecting with the mouse

There are several ways to select text using the mouse:

- ✦ Double-click a word to select that word.
- ✦ Triple-click a paragraph to select the entire paragraph.
- ✦ Select a body of text by dragging the mouse pointer through the text you want to select.
- ✦ Select lines of text by dragging the mouse pointer down the left margin through the lines you want to select.

Selecting with the keyboard

To select text using the keyboard, just hold Shift while moving the insertion point with the cursor-positioning keys. Table 12-1 summarizes the keyboard selection techniques.

Table 12-1
Selecting Text with the Keyboard

To Select	*Press*
Character right	Shift+right arrow
Character left	Shift+left arrow
Line	Shift+up arrow or Shift+down arrow
To beginning of line	Shift+Home
To end of line	Shift+End
To top of document	Shift+Ctrl+Home
To end of document	Shift+Ctrl+End
Entire document	Ctrl+A

Keep in mind that whenever you see an instruction to select text in this book, you can use whatever mouse or keyboard technique you find most convenient for you at the moment.

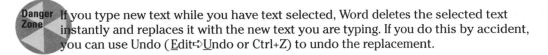

Danger Zone If you type new text while you have text selected, Word deletes the selected text instantly and replaces it with the new text you are typing. If you do this by accident, you can use Undo (Edit⇨Undo or Ctrl+Z) to undo the replacement.

Deselecting text

To deselect selected text, use the mouse to move the insertion point. Alternatively, you can move the insertion point by using any cursor-positioning key without holding Shift.

Applying styles

Once you get the hang of typing, editing, and selecting text, creating your Web page becomes largely a matter of applying styles to the text. This task is easy to do as well:

1. If you want to apply a paragraph style to an entire paragraph, place the insertion point anywhere in the paragraph then skip to Step 3.
2. To apply a character style, select the text to which you want to apply the style.
3. Choose a style from the Styles drop-down list or choose Format⇨Style from the menu bar, choose a style, and click the Apply button.

Hot Stuff While you are in the Styles list, you can type the first letter(s) of a style name to quickly jump to that part of the list. To select a style from the list, you can either click the option you want or press Enter while the highlighter is on the appropriate style name.

Changing/removing a style

If you apply a style to some text and then decide to remove that style or to apply a different style, just use the same basic process again. Follow these steps:

1. If you want to apply a paragraph style to an entire paragraph, just put the insertion point anywhere in the paragraph then skip to Step 3.
2. To apply a character style, select the text to which you want to apply the style.
3. Choose a different style, or to remove the style, choose the Normal, P style.

More Info For more general information about typing, editing, and using styles in Word, see your Microsoft Word Manual. Alternatively, you can choose Help⇨Microsoft Word Help Topics from Word's menu bar, click the Contents tab, and open the Typing, Selecting, and Editing and Formatting topics.

Ways to View Your Document with Word IA

While you are in Word IA, you can work with your document in any of several views: HTML Edit view (which you used to create your first Web page), HTML Source view, Full Screen view, Web Browse view, or Preview in Browser (for example, Internet Explorer's view). This book provides you with examples of how and when each view comes in handy as you progress through it. For now, I just want to give you some quick exposure to each view and tell you how to change views.

HTML Edit view

When you create and edit a Web page, you typically want to be in the HTML Edit view. This view provides you with the simple editing techniques described so far, where you select text and apply a style to that text.

HTML Source view

As mentioned earlier, Word IA automatically converts the styles you use to format your document to HTML tags. If you get curious and want to see what those tags look like, you can switch to the HTML Source view. Just select View⇨HTML Source from the menu bar. Figure 12-9 shows an example of this view. The weird codes in angle brackets (<>) are the HTML tags.

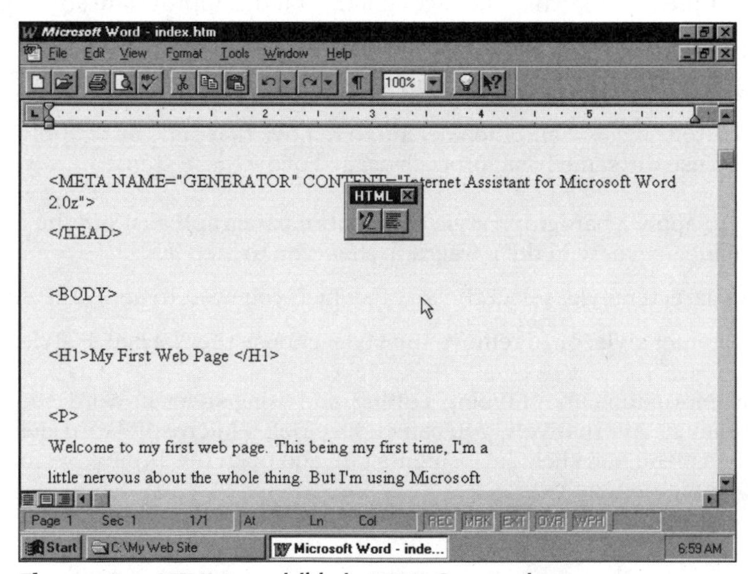

Figure 12-9: HTML tags visible in HTML Source view.

Notice the two small buttons in the floating toolbar near the middle of the screen. When you point to the button on the right, you'll see a tooltip titled Auto Format HTML. When you click that button, Word IA will color-code your document as follows:

✦ Black. Text that appears in Edit view, in the Web browser, and so forth.

✦ Red. HTML tags (visible only in the "source document" view).

✦ Blue. HTML attributes: Text that appears only within HTML tags in Source view.

You can edit the text, tags, and attributes in Source view, if you wish. But you probably won't want to mess with the HTML tags directly. Wait until you understand the HyperText Markup Language (HTML) in some depth. For now, you'll probably want to return to the previous Edit view to make any changes.

To edit some more, and also to stop viewing those HTML tags, just click the Return to Edit Mode button (the one with the pencil) in the floating toolbar.

Web Browse view

Word IA also offers a Web Browse view, where you can actually navigate through pages just as in a real Web browser. This view doesn't offer much in terms of editing, but it comes in handy for creating and testing hypertext links in your document. (We'll talk about hypertext links and the Web Browse view in some depth in Chapter 16.) For now, if you just want to take a peek at the Web Browse view, click the Switch to Web Browse View button in the toolbar (see Figure 12-10).

Figure 12-10: The Switch to Web Browse View button.

The lower toolbar in Word IA changes from one that offers editing to one that offers browsing tools. The little eyeglass button that you clicked to get here now shows a little pencil (see Figure 12-11).

Life Saver

If you suddenly lose the capability to navigate and edit within your document, chances are you're just in the Web Browse view. Click the Switch to Edit View button, or choose View⇨HTML Edit from the menus to fix the problem.

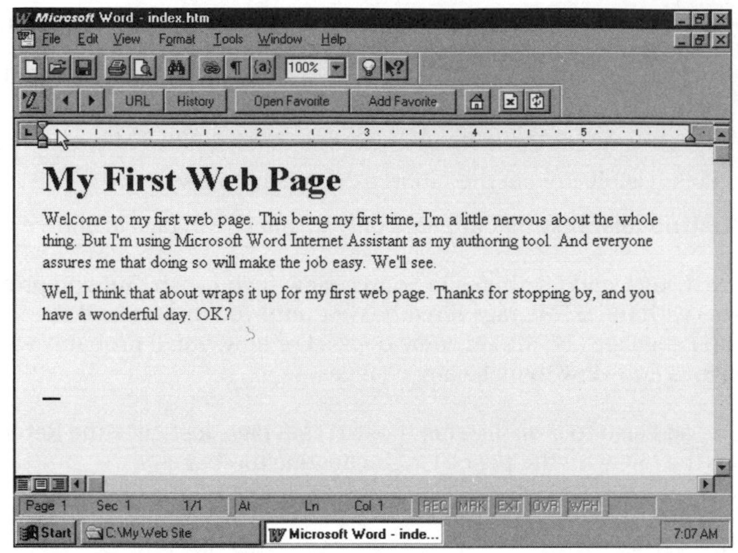

Figure 12-11: Word IA's Web Browse view, handy for creating and testing hypertext links.

When you want to get out of Web Browse view and back to normal editing, just click the Switch to Edit View button (with the little pencil) at the left end of the lower toolbar.

Full Screen view

Full Screen view removes the menu bar, status bar, and other doohickies from your screen so that you can get a larger view of your document. To get to this view, follow these steps:

1. Choose View⇨Full Screen.
2. If you want to see your toolbars, press Alt+V, choose Toolbars, select the toolbars to view (Standard and Formatting will probably be enough), and click OK.

When you want to return to Normal view, click the Full Screen button in the small floating toolbar (see Figure 12-12).

Web Browser Preview

To see exactly how your document looks to Web browsers, you can preview the document in an actual browser. Just click the Preview in Browser button on the toolbar. Your document opens up in your Web browser — most likely in Internet Explorer (see Figure 12-13).

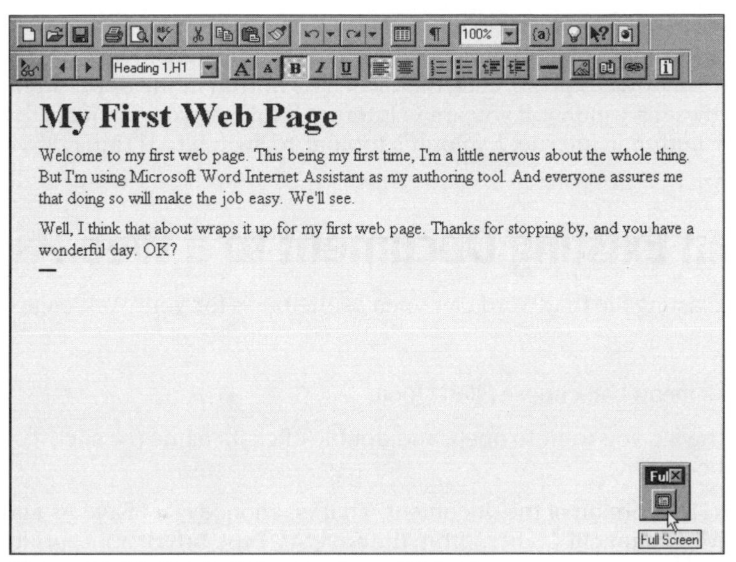

Figure 12-12: The Full Screen view with toolbars.

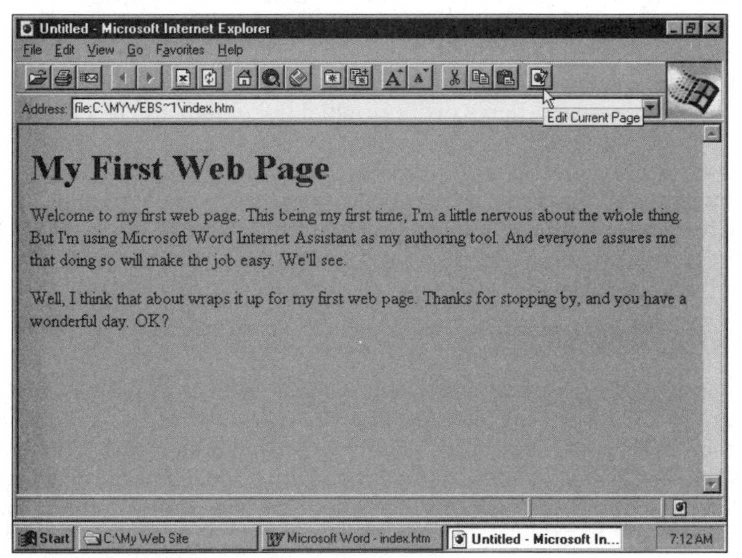

Figure 12-13: Document as shown in Web Browser Preview.

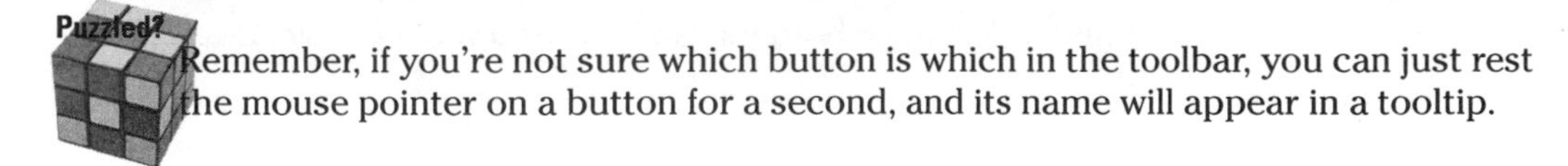

Remember, if you're not sure which button is which in the toolbar, you can just rest the mouse pointer on a button for a second, and its name will appear in a tooltip.

You cannot edit your Web page in the Preview view; this view only gives you a "reader's-eye view" of the document you authored. To return to the HTML Edit view, you must close the Preview window. To do so, click the Close (X) button in the upper-right corner of Web browser's window. If you are in Internet Explorer, you can just click the Edit Current Page button in Internet Explorer's toolbar to switch to HTML Edit view.

Converting an Existing Document to a Web Page

You can use any existing file that Word can open as the basis for your Web page. Here's how:

1. From Word's menu bar, choose File⇨Open.
2. Browse to the file you want to open, and double-click its name (or click its name, and then choose OK).
3. Create an HTML version of the document. That is, choose File⇨Save As and choose HTML Document (*.htm) from the Save As Type box. If appropriate, choose a new folder and filename for this version of the original document.
4. Apply styles to any headings, lists, or other text that need formatting.

Now you can treat the document on your screen as a Web page. For example, you can select styles from the Styles drop-down list as you did earlier in this chapter. This new document has a .htm extension, whereas your original document still has its original filename.

Hot Stuff

If the regular document you open has already been formatted with Word styles, you can map those styles to Web page styles. Look up mapping Word styles to HTML in the Help index for Word IA.

Lost in the translation

It's important (though not always easy) to remember that the World Wide Web only supports a handful of text formatting features. Many of the advanced — and some of the simplest — formatting features of Word have no equivalent in HTML. When Word IA encounters Word formatting features that it cannot translate, it flat-out removes them! Here is a list of some Word formatting elements that you cannot convert to HTML:

- Annotations
- Borders and shading (some table borders can be preserved, however)
- Captions
- Drawing layer elements

✦ Fields — only the result that the field produces is converted

✦ Footnotes and endnotes

✦ Frames (but top and bottom frame borders are converted to horizontal rules)

✦ Headers and footers

✦ Indented paragraphs (the paragraph stays, but the indent is lost)

✦ Index entries

✦ Page breaks and section breaks

✦ Revision marks

✦ Tabs in any paragraph style other than PRE and DL

✦ TOC entries

If you are a word-processing or desktop-publishing guru, you are likely to feel ripped off by HTML's lack of sophisticated formatting features. But don't worry, because there are plenty of things that you *can* do to control the format of your Web pages. You start learning about these formatting techniques in the next chapter.

Quick Access from the Desktop

Until now, I've talked about different ways to view your Web page using Internet Explorer as the basic starting point. If you set up your Web authoring environment as I suggested in Chapter 11, you also can get to and quickly open your document in a variety of views right from the Windows 95 desktop. To try out these methods, you should first exit Microsoft Word, if you haven't already done so (choose File➪Exit from Word's menu bar). Don't forget to save your work if Word prompts you to. The system takes you back to the Windows 95 desktop.

Now that you're there, here are some different ways to view/edit your Web page from the Windows 95 desktop:

1. Double-click the shortcut icon for the folder in which you store your Web pages.
2. Right-click the icon for the Web page you want to view, and select the Send To option on the shortcut menu, as in Figure 12-14.
3. Now you can choose any of the following ways to view/edit the document:
    - **Internet Explorer.** Displays the document as Web browsers will see it. You cannot (directly) edit the document in this view.
    - **Notepad.** Shows the "pure" Web page containing text and HTML tags. You can edit text and tags in this view.
    - **Word.** Takes you back to Word IA with the document ready for more editing.

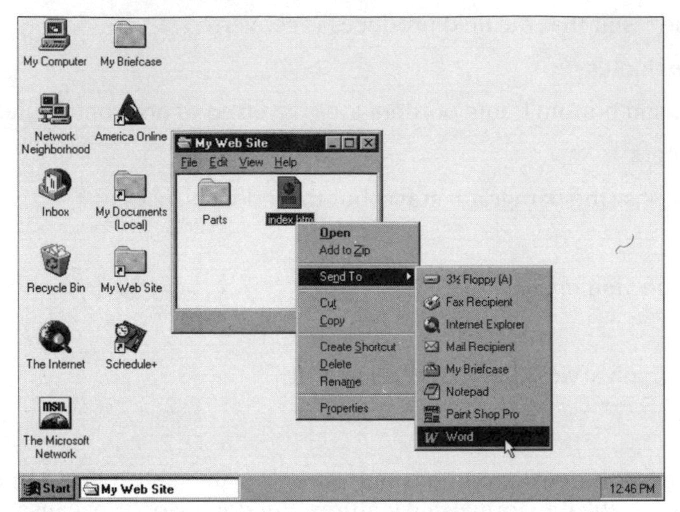

Figure 12-14: The SendTo menu makes it easy to send your Web page to Internet Explorer, Notepad, or Word.

You exit any of these views in the usual manner. For example, you can click the Close button in the upper-right corner of the window, or you can choose File⇨Exit from the menu bar.

Summary

Creating Web pages with Word IA is pretty much the same as creating regular Word documents. You just need to remember to start with the HTML.DOT document template. In this chapter, you learned the following:

✦ To create a Web page, start up Microsoft Word, choose File⇨New, and choose the HTML.DOT document template.

✦ Type, select, and edit as you normally would in Microsoft Word.

✦ To format a document, apply styles from the Styles drop-down list in Word IA's toolbar.

✦ When saving your Web page, be sure to give it a .htm (or .html) filename extension. Saving each Web page in your My Web Site folder is a good idea, too.

✦ To see your Web page from a Web browser, just double-click its document icon. Alternately, start your browser and open the page as a local document.

✦ Word IA offers several ways to view your Web page, including HTML Edit view (where you spend most of your typing and editing time), Web Browse view (which is handy for typing and creating hypertext links), Full Screen view, HTML Source view, and Preview in Web Browser.

✦ ✦ ✦

Formatting Your Web Page Text

In This Chapter

By now, you know that a Web page is a document containing text and HTML tags that tell the Web browser program how to display that text on the reader's screen. You also know that as an alternative to typing HTML tags manually, you can use Microsoft Word Internet Assistant (Word IA) to apply styles to any document. You can create, open, save, and browse your own Web pages — right? (You didn't skip too many chapters, did you?)

Now we can get into the nitty-gritty of formatting individual chunks of text within your Web pages.

Titling Your Web Page

You can give each Web page its own title. In Internet Explorer and most other Web browsers, the title appears in the title bar. I like to use my site name followed by the subject of the current page as my document titles. For example, the title for my coolnerds home page is *coolnerds - Home Page*. The title for my FAQs page is *coolnerds - FAQs*. These titles help readers see, at a glance, where in the whole World Wide Web they are at the moment.

You, of course, can title your own Web pages however you want. To title your Web page, follow these steps:

1. In Word IA, move the insertion point to the top of the document (press Ctrl+Home).
2. Click on Title in the Word IA toolbar, or choose HTML Document Info. You come to the dialog box shown in Figure 13-1.

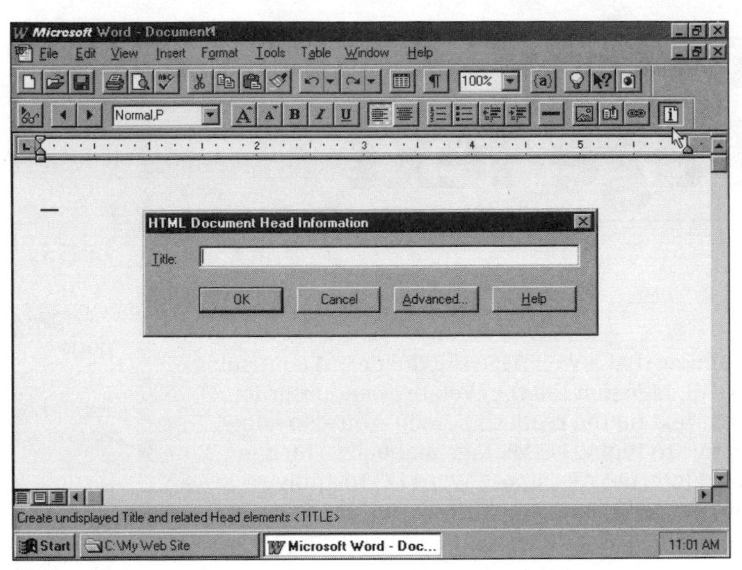

Figure 13-1: Word IA's dialog box for titling a Web page.

3. Type your own title and click OK.

The title does not actually appear in the document while you're viewing it with Word IA. In most Web browsers, however, the title does appear in the title bar (Figure 13-2). When viewing your Web page's HTML tags, you'll see the title enclosed between a pair of `<TITLE>...</TITLE>` tags near the top.

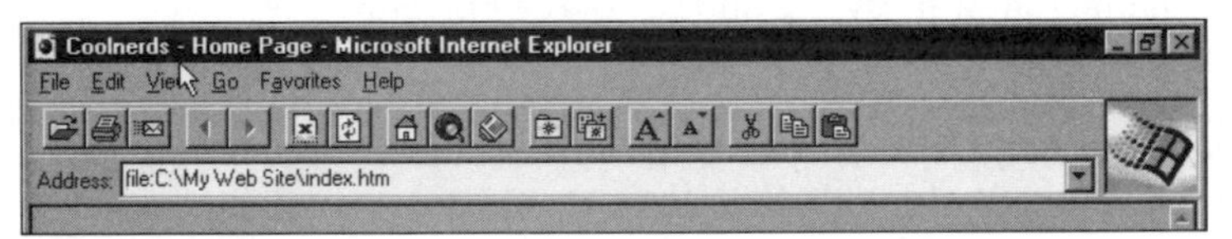

Figure 13-2: In Internet Explorer, the title appears in the application title bar.

Every document you create can have only one title. You cannot change titles halfway through a document.

Headings

Headings are generally used to show titles, topics, and subtopics within a body of text. Headings are used pretty universally in books, magazines, newspapers — all sorts of text. For example, the title at the beginning of this chapter is a large heading (a Heading 1).

After that, a slightly smaller heading appears that can be referred to as a Heading 2. Word IA offers six levels of headings: Heading 1, the largest level, down to Heading 6, the smallest.

All heading styles are paragraph styles, which means that if you click anywhere on a paragraph before selecting a style, the style is applied to the entire paragraph. (Remember, a "paragraph" consists of any text that ends with a hard return — a press of the Enter key — and can be a single short line.) To apply a heading to existing text, follow these steps:

1. Click the line of text that you want to display as a heading.
2. Choose a heading from the Styles drop-down list.

To give you an idea of how the various heading styles relate, Figure 13-3 shows an example where I've applied the Heading 1 style to the first line, the Heading 2 style to the second line, and so on within Word IA.

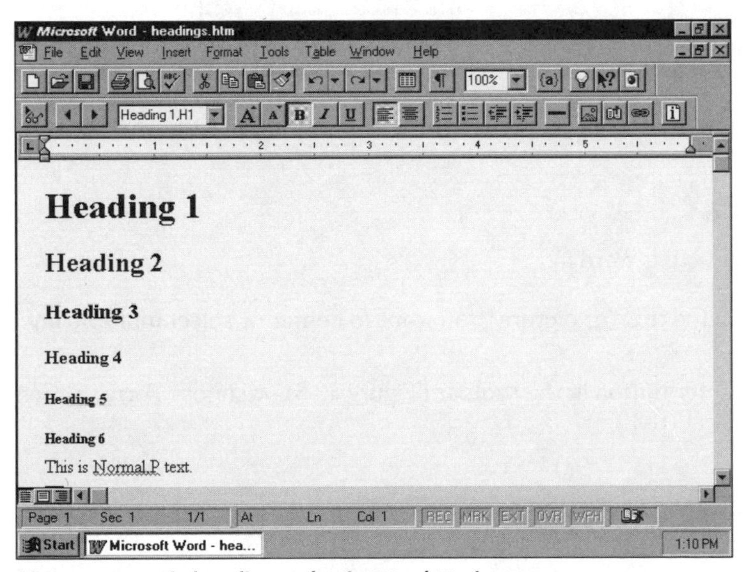

Figure 13-3: Six heading styles in Word IA view.

Puzzled?

Remember that the title discussed earlier appears in the Web browser's title bar. If you want a title or headline on your actual page, just type it as normal text on the page and then apply a heading style to it so it appears larger and darker than regular text.

Figure 13-4 shows this same text as displayed by Internet Explorer. Off to the right in Figure 13-4, I've opened a View Source window so that you can see the HTML tags that control the headings. For example, `<H1>` starts the Heading 1 style, `</H1>` ends that style, `<H2>` starts the Heading 2 style, `</H2>` ends that style, and so on.

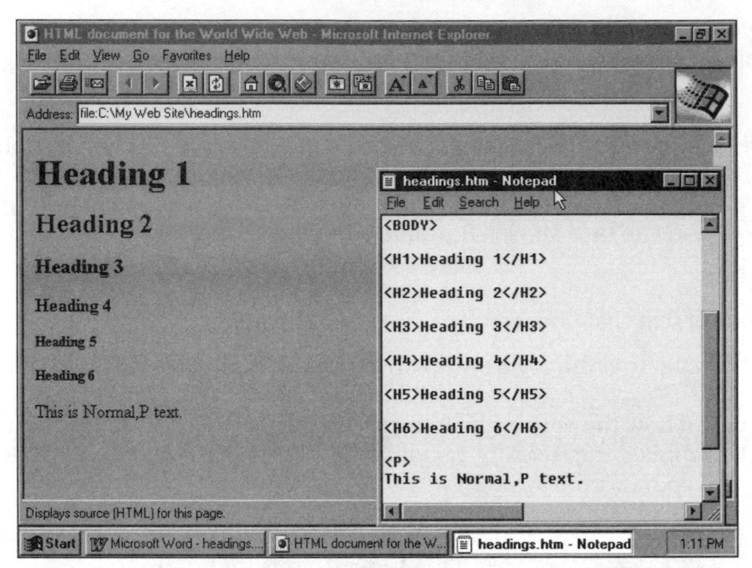

Figure 13-4: Heading styles as displayed by Internet Explorer and Notepad.

Centering Text

It's easy to center text in Word IA:

1. Just click on the text (or picture) you want to center or select multiple lines to center.
2. Click the Center button in the toolbar (Figure 13-5) or choose Format⇨Center Align or press Ctrl+E.

Figure 13-5: Just click the Center button to center text on your page.

If you change your mind, just re-click, or re-select, the centered text and click the Left Align button in the toolbar.

Normal Paragraph Style

By default, any new text that you type into a Web page is assigned the Normal,P style. The P stands for "paragraph," because this is the style applied to normal paragraphs. Here are a couple things that you should know about paragraphs:

✦ Don't bother to indent the first line in a paragraph. Most Web browsers ignore that indent.

✦ A paragraph, in word-processing parlance, consists of any chunk of text that ends with a hard return (which is inserted when you press Enter).

If you want to see exactly where the hard returns appear in your Word IA document, you can click the Show/Hide Paragraph button in the toolbar. Hard returns appear as paragraph symbols. For example, you can see a paragraph symbol at the end of the headline and at the end of the first regular paragraph in Figure 13-6. (Spaces have a little dot in the middle.) You can re-hide all those symbols by clicking the same toolbar button again.

Figure 13-6: Hard returns appear as paragraph symbols.

To apply the normal paragraph style to a paragraph, click on the paragraph and choose Normal,P from the Styles list. Alternatively, you can select multiple paragraphs and then choose Normal,P.

Paragraph breaks versus line breaks

Wherever you press Enter to end a line, the Web browser terminates the line and also displays a blank line. For example, in the following little poem, I pressed Enter at the end of each line:

The amphibian

keeled over

in the water

Kerplop

If you want to end a line but not insert a blank line, press Shift+Enter rather than Enter. In the following example, I pressed Shift+Enter at the end of each line:

The amphibian
keeled over
in the water
Kerplop

If you already inserted blank lines and need to get rid of them, just move the insertion point to the end of a top line and then press Delete to delete the paragraph break. Then press Shift+Enter to insert the line break.

When you have Show/Hide Paragraphs turned on, line breaks appear as little bent arrows rather than as paragraph marks. In your HTML source code, line breaks are represented by
 (break) tags rather than <P> tags.

Unformatting text

If you apply a style to a chunk of text and then later change your mind, you can always "undo" the style just by reapplying the Normal,P style. That is, click the paragraph or select the text you want to "unstyle." Then choose Normal,P from the Styles drop-down list.

HTML tag for paragraphs

The HTML tag for paragraph style is simply <P>. No ending tag exists for this style (that is, no </P>). Thus, when you view the HTML source for a document, you see a <P> atop just about every paragraph. A <P> by itself (followed by some other tag rather than text) displays a blank line in the document.

Boldface, Italic, and All That Jazz

You are probably familiar with basic text-formatting styles such as **boldface,** *italics,* and underscore. Word IA offers all three styles, plus a monospaced, "typewriter" style. Unlike paragraph styles, these are *character styles* — which means that the browser does *not* automatically apply them to the entire current paragraph. Instead, the browser applies these character styles only to the currently selected text. To use these styles, you need to follow these steps:

1. Select the text to which you want to apply the style.

More Info

If you are not sure what I mean by "select the text," go back to Chapter 12. Do not pass Go. Do not collect $200.

2. If you want to apply boldface, italics, or underlining, just click the appropriate toolbar button. Alternatively, you can press the appropriate shortcut key combination: Ctrl+B for Bold, Ctrl+I for Italic, and Ctrl+U for Underline.

3. If you instead want to apply the Strikethrough or Typewriter (monospaced) style, you need to choose the appropriate style from the Styles drop-down list.

To illustrate, in Figure 13-7, I applied the Bold, Italic, Underline, Strikethrough, and Typewriter styles to some text in the document. I magnified the view somewhat in this example, using the View menu options available in Word, to give you a closer look at the text.

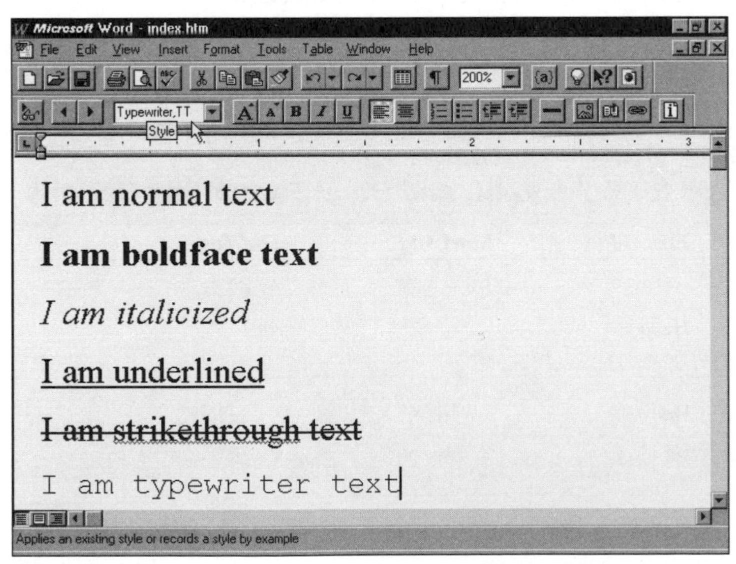

Figure 13-7: Examples of bold, italics, underlined, strikethrough, and typewriter styles.

Figure 13-8 shows the same document as it appears in Internet Explorer and also in Notepad (by right-clicking and choosing View Source). In Notepad, you can see some of the HTML tabs that Word IA placed in the document. Table 13-1 lists the HTML tags for these various text styles — just in case you're curious or ever want to go in and add or delete the tags manually.

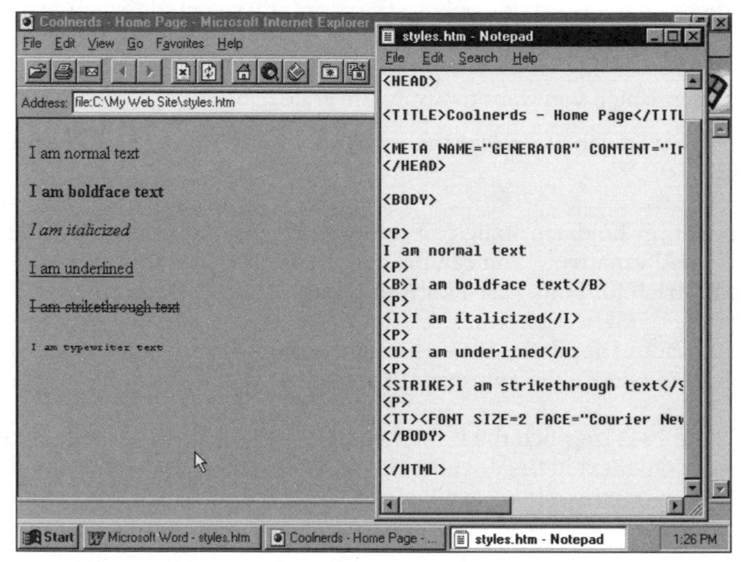

Figure 13-8: The document in Figure 13-7 shown in Internet Explorer and Notepad.

Table 13-1
HTML Tags for Bold, Italic, and Other Formatting Options

Style	*Example*	*Start Tag*	*End Tag*
Bold	**Hello**	<B>	</B>
Italic	*Hello*	<I>	</I>
Underline	Hello	<U>	</U>
Strikethrough	~~Hello~~	<STRIKE>	</STRIKE>
Typewriter	`Hello`	<TT>	</TT>

Logical Styles

HTML also offers some *logical styles*. These styles define the *role* played by a chunk of text rather than its specific appearance. For example, a logical style named CITE exists for citations, book titles, references, and so on. You cannot be completely sure how a particular Web browser will display the text you tag as CITE, however. For example, a Web browser for the legal profession may show a citation as underlined, like this example:

see Mickey vs. Minnie

A Web browser for the medical profession might display the CITE style in italics, such as

see *Evengood, J.G., Hormonal Ravings of Lab-Produced Mice.*

The following list summarizes the logical styles that are available and when you might use each:

✦ **Cite.** Use this style to identify citations, book titles, journal article titles, and other references to outside works. Most browsers display this style as italics.

✦ **Code.** Use this style to identify a chunk of programming language source code. Most browsers display this style in a monospaced font, such as Courier.

✦ **Emphasis.** Use this style to call attention to specific words. Most browsers display this style as italics.

✦ **Keyboard.** Use this style to identify text you want the reader to type exactly as shown. For example, you could use this style to show a URL. This style is typically displayed in a monospaced font.

✦ **Sample.** Use this style to display a literal sequence of characters, such as programming code. This style is typically displayed in a monospaced font with single quotation marks.

✦ **Strong.** Use this style to identify important warnings or other text you do not want the reader to overlook. This style usually appears in boldface on the reader's screen.

✦ **Variable.** Use this style to identify variables in formulas and equations. This style is typically displayed in italics.

To apply a logical style to existing text, follow these steps:

1. Select the text to which you want to apply the logical style.
2. Choose the appropriate style from the Style drop-down list.

Figure 13-9 shows examples of some logical styles as displayed by Internet Explorer, with Notepad giving a behind-the-scenes peek at the underlying HTML tags. Table 13-2 provides an example of the HTML tags used for each logical style.

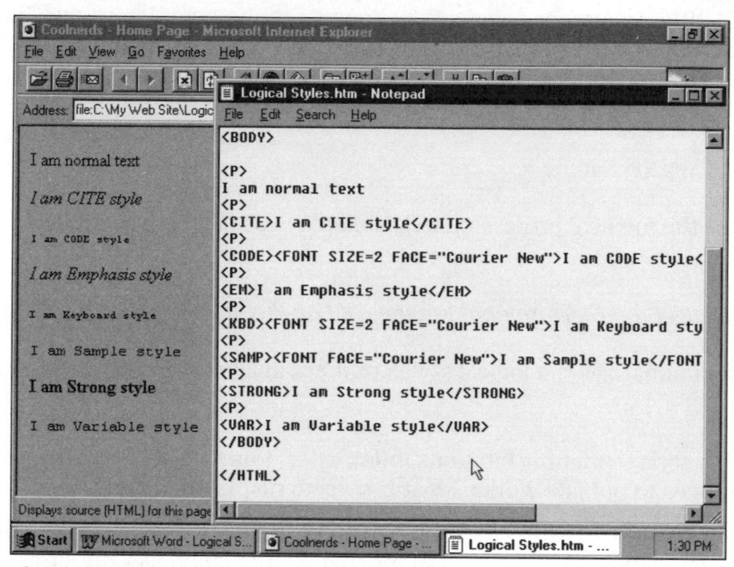

Figure 13-9: Examples of logical styles displayed in Internet Explorer and Notepad.

Table 13-2
Logical Styles and Their HTML Tags

Logical Style	*Example*	*Start Tag*	*End Tag*
Cite	*Smith and Jones*	`<CITE>`	`</CITE>`
Code	`X=10`	`<CODE>`	`</CODE>`
Emphasis	*Reply ASAP*	`<EM>`	`</EM>`
Keyboard	`Type Hello`	`<KBD>`	`</KBD>`
Sample	`'Print Sample'`	`<SAMP>`	`</SAMP>`
Strong	**Caution**	`<STRONG>`	`</STRONG>`
Variable	*$E=MC^2$*	`<VAR>`	`</VAR>`

Controlling Fonts

A *font* is a combination of a typeface, style, and size. The size of a font is generally measured in points, where one point = $^1/_{72}$ inch. Thus, printing text at 36 points creates letters that are about a half-inch tall when printed on paper. Figure 13-10 shows some examples of fonts.

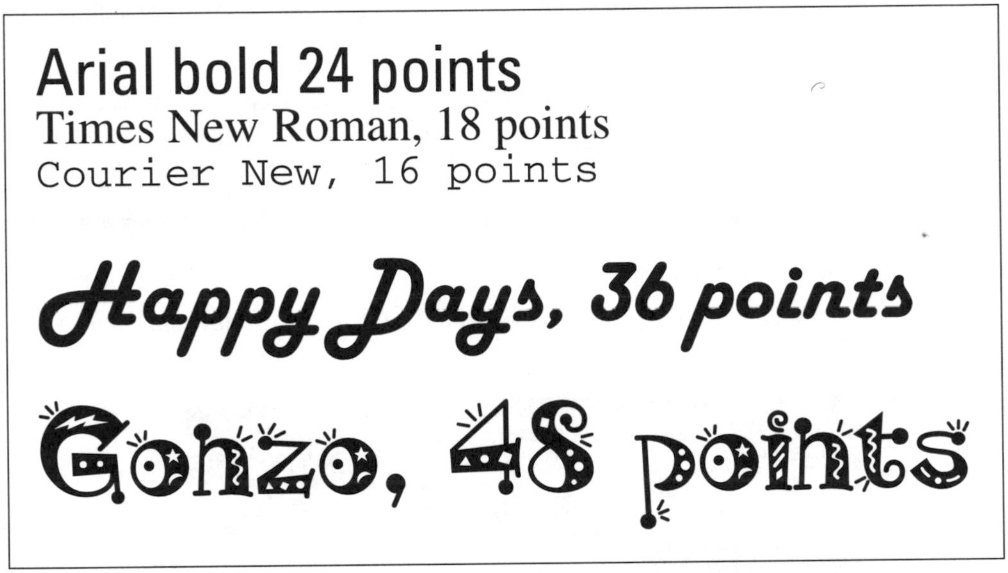

Arial bold 24 points
Times New Roman, 18 points
Courier New, 16 points
Happy Days, 36 points
Gonzo, 48 points

Figure 13-10: Some examples of fonts.

When you installed Windows 95 and Microsoft Word, these programs added a few new fonts to your font collection. You can also purchase fonts, individually, from most computer stores. The fancy Happy Days and Gonzo fonts in Figure 13-10 came from independent font vendors. Using fonts in *printed* documents is generally pretty easy. However, using fonts in Web pages is a very different story.

More Info To see what fonts your PC has available, click the Start button and choose Settings⇨Control Panel and then double-click the Fonts icon. Double-click any font to see what it looks like. You can use options from the File menu to install and print fonts. My *Windows 95 Uncut* book, published by IDG Books in 1995, covers fonts in detail.

The capability to control fonts in Web pages is very new, and not all Web browsers support it. Understanding that fonts are *never* downloaded to your reader's computer is also important. All you can do is *request* that the Web browser use a particular font to display some chunk of text. If that font is not available on your reader's PC, the Web browser will ignore your request and display your text in whatever font is available on your reader's PC.

Most PCs have at least a basic collection of sans serif (headline), serif (body text), and monospace (typewriter) fonts. For example, Arial and Helvetica are widely used sans-serif fonts. Times and Times New Roman are common serif fonts. Courier is a very common monspace font. If you request one of these fonts in your Web page, there is a very good chance that the reader will see these fonts.

On the other hand, if you request a fancy, decorative font such as Happy Days or Gonzo, there is a very good chance that the reader *won't* have that font. With that fact in mind, the bottom line on choosing fonts for Web pages is to stick with the absolute basics.

Life Saver A simple way around the fancy-font problem is to "capture" text in whatever font you want and save it as a graphic image. Then you can just treat the text as a graphic in your Web page. There's also Word Art, which lets you use fonts and shape text as well. You'll find more in Chapter 21.

To change the font of some text that you have already typed into your document

1. Select the text you want to change.
2. Choose Format⇨Font. You'll see the Font dialog box shown in Figure 13-11.

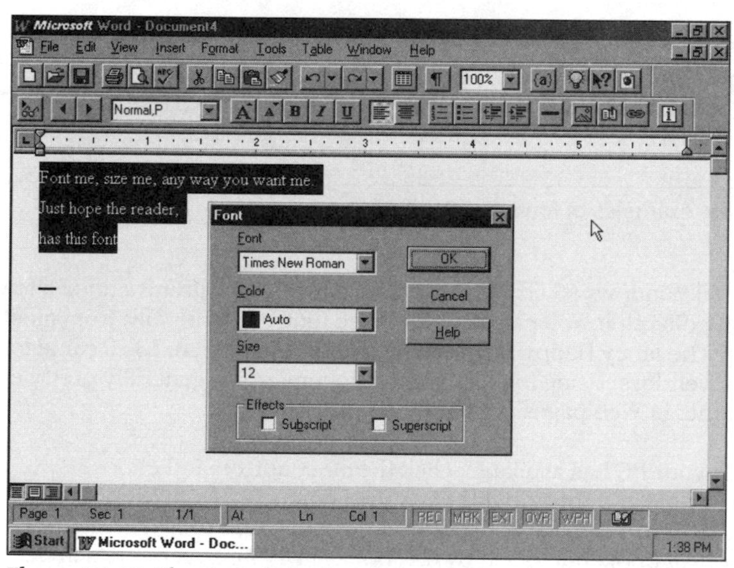

Figure 13-11: The Font dialog box in Word IA.

3. Choose a Font (typeface), Color, and Size, and then click OK.

Word IA applies the selected font, color, and size immediately. If you want to see how these elements look in your Web browser, just click the Preview in Browser button.

Relative sizing of fonts

Although the Font dialog box lets you pick a specific font size, the sizing is actually done on a relative basis. One reason for this fact is that points aren't exact measurements for displaying text on a screen. For example, text printed at 36 points will be physically larger on a 20-inch monitor than text of the same point size appearing on a tiny laptop monitor. Proportionally, the font will take up just as much space on the screen. But if you measured the text with a ruler on both screens, you'd find that the text on the big screen is larger than the text that appears on the small screen.

When you pick a font size, Word IA just assigns a single number, between 1 and 7, to the font size — 1 being the smallest size (about 9 points), and 7 being the largest (about 36 points.) You may find it easier to control the relative size of fonts rather than the exact point size. Here's how:

1. Select the text you want to resize.
2. Do one of the following:
   - To increase the size of the selected text, click the Increase Font Size button on the toolbar or press Ctrl+> or choose Format⇨Increase Font Size from the menus until you get to the size you want or until you reach the maximum size.
   - To decrease the size of the selected text, click the Decrease Font Size button on the toolbar or press Ctrl+< or choose Format⇨Decrease Font Size from the menus until you get to the size you want or until you reach the minimum size.

HTML tags for fonts

The HTML tags for fonts are `<FONT>` to start a new font and `</FONT>` to end that font. Within the `<FONT>` tag, the following attributes define the font that you want to use:

✦ **SIZE.** Defines the relative size of the font, where 1 is the smallest possible size, 3 is the "normal" body text size, and 7 the largest possible size.

✦ **COLOR.** Defines the color of the font, using hexadecimal *#rrggbb* format.

✦ **FACE.** Defines the typeface that you want to use.

For example, the tag shown in the following example specifies that the text should appear in the largest possible font size, in red, using the Arial typeface.

```
<FONT SIZE=7 COLOR=#FF0000 FACE="Arial">
```

More Info You can actually list several typefaces in the <FONT> tag, in order of preference. For example, this tag pair <FONT FACE="Arial","Lucida Sans">...</FONT> displays the text between the tags in Arial font if the reader's PC has Arial. If the reader's PC doesn't have Arial, it displays the text in Lucida Sans font. If the reader's PC has neither font, the text will be displayed in the default font for that browser (typically Times Roman). You can't enter a complex tag like this via Word IA's Edit mode. You'll need to manually type the tag through Notepad (Chapter 19) or some other text editor.

Superscripts and Subscripts

You can also size and position text as a superscript (small, raised) or subscript (small, lowered). To do so, follow these steps:

1. Select the character(s) you want to display as superscript or subscript.
2. From the menu bar, choose Format➪Font➪Subscript or Superscript, as appropriate.
3. Click OK.

The HTML tags for subscript are _{and}. The HTML tags for superscript are ^{and}.

Block Quotations

A block quotation is usually a chunk of text that's a direct quote from a different source and is too long to just enclose in quotation marks. Visually, a block quotation is just a chunk of text that's indented from the left margin (Figure 13-12).

To define a block quotation in your Web page

1. Click on the paragraph that you want to indent or select multiple paragraphs to indent.
2. Choose Blockquote from the Styles drop-down list.

Word IA inserts the appropriate HTML tags, <BLOCKQUOTE> and </BLOCKQUOTE>, at the start and end of the paragraph or the selected paragraphs.

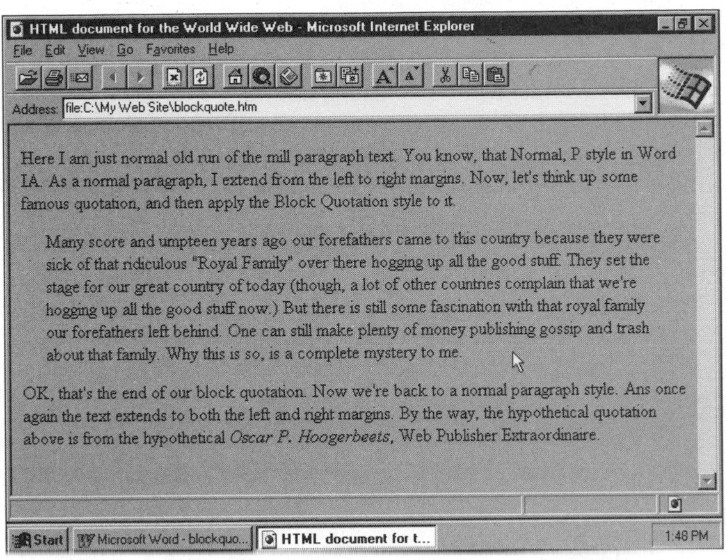

Figure 13-12: The indented paragraph is a block quotation.

Address Block

A somewhat standard procedure on the Web is to put the author's address at the bottom of the home page or at the bottom of all pages in the site. Doing so makes it easy for readers to send comments and questions to the author. Because adding address blocks is such a standard procedure, a pair of HTML tags exists that you can use to identify the address block. To identify an address block

1. Click the line or select the lines that you want to identify as your return address.
2. Choose Address from the Styles list.

In most browsers, the address line just appears in italics. Figure 13-13 shows an example where I applied the Address style to my own e-mail return address. In the open Notepad window, you can see the `<ADDRESS>` and `</ADDRESS>` tags surrounding that text.

Hot Stuff

If your ISP supports a "mailto" feature, you can set up a "hot" return address that will let readers send you an e-mail by simply clicking a hot spot. Check with your ISP, and see Chapter 18 for some general information on mailto and forms.

Horizontal Lines

You can insert a simple horizontal line — also called a horizontal rule — that extends across the width of the Web page to break up sections of your document. For example, in Figure 13-13, I placed a horizontal line above my return address.

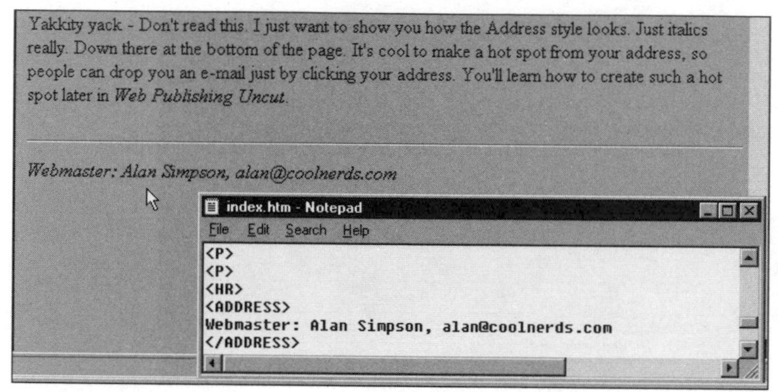

Figure 13-13: A horizontal line above my return address.

To insert a horizontal line in your own Web page, follow these steps:

1. Move the insertion point to a blank line where you want to place the horizontal line. If you need to add a blank line, move to the end of the line preceding the desired location and press Enter.
2. Click the Horizontal Rule button in the toolbar, or choose Insert⇨Horizontal Rule from the menu bar.

The horizontal line extends across the page. The HTML tag for the horizontal rule is `<HR>`.

Hot Stuff You can also use a graphic image as a horizontal line. See Chapter 15 for more details.

Please Stop Ignoring My Tabs and Spaces

If you have not discovered this practice already, you soon will. All Web browsers ignore any indents that you put into your Web page by using tabs or the Spacebar. For example, Figure 13-14 shows a document that uses lots of tabs and spaces to indent some self-explanatory text.

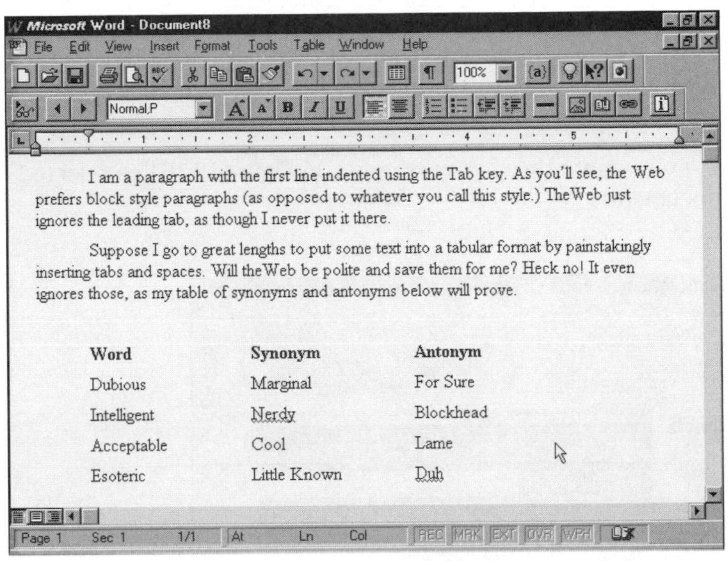

Figure 13-14: A document that uses tabs and spaces to format text.

Figure 13-15 shows how that same document looks in Internet Explorer (and probably any other Web browser). Clearly, Web browsers have no respect whatsoever for the Tab key or Spacebar.

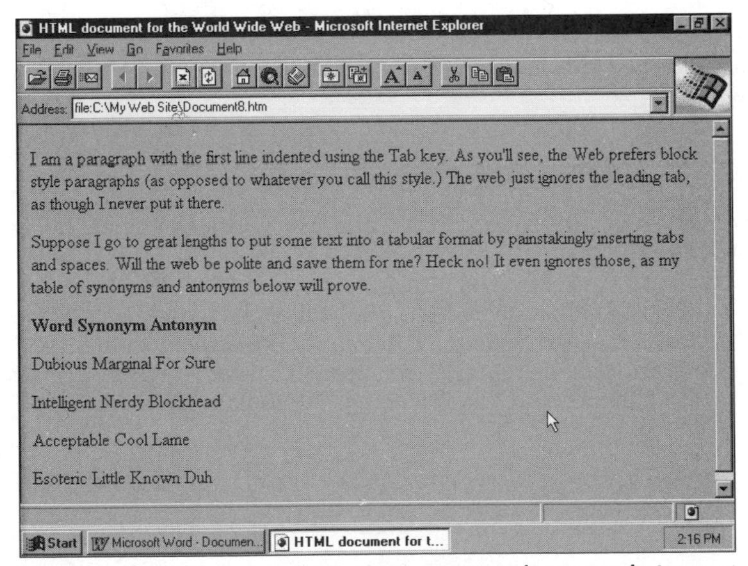

Figure 13-15: The document in Figure 13-14 as it appears in Internet Explorer.

One (albeit inelegant) solution to these indentation and formatting problems is to use the Preformatted, PRE style. This style tells the Web browser "Hey, don't mess with my spaces and tabs if you can help it." To apply the Preformatted style, follow these steps:

1. Select the text you want to style. For example, in Figure 13-16 I've selected all text in the document.

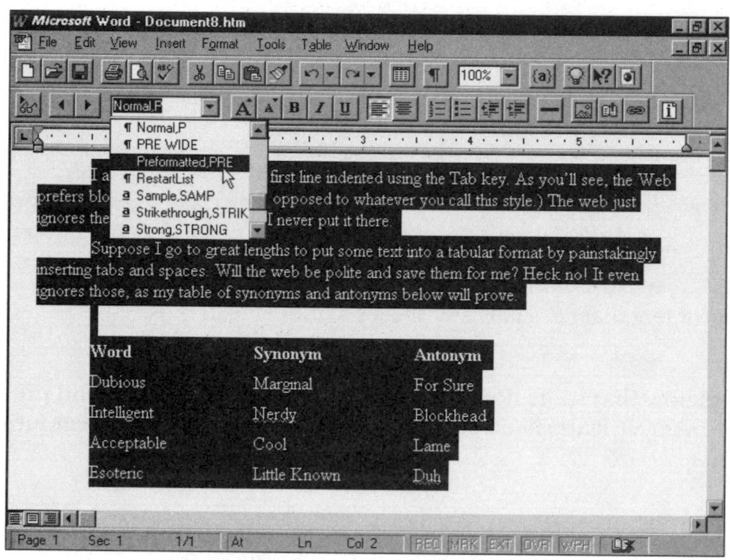

Figure 13-16: Some selected text about to be formatted with the PRE (Preformatted) style.

2. Choose Preformatted, PRE from the Styles drop-down list.
3. Word IA switches to a monospaced font. If necessary, insert or delete tabs and spaces to realign your text.

Word IA inserts a <PRE> tag at the top and a </PRE> tag at the bottom of the selection (which, of course, you cannot see in Word IA). When you view the document with a Web browser, the formatting of the text appears more like what you had originally intended — well, sort of. In this case, the text comes out looking something like Figure 13-17.

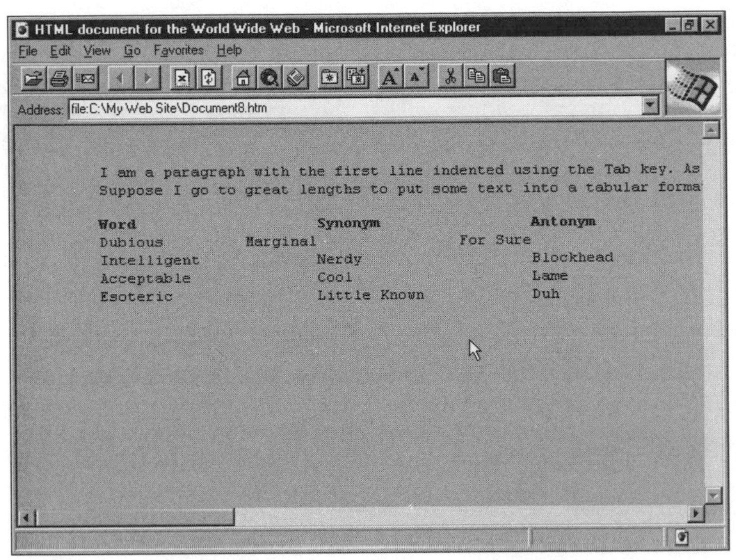

Figure 13-17: The document from Figure 13-14 after applying the Preformatted, PRE style.

Hmmmmm. The table isn't too bad. The Body paragraphs are a bit too wide for the browser screen though. I could go back to Word IA, tweak things around a bit, and fix this mess. But, as I mentioned earlier, this whole business of using the PRE style to conserve spaces and tabs is pretty inelegant (to put it mildly).

You may also notice a PRE WIDE style in the Styles list. This style is similar to <PRE> but includes the `WIDTH` attribute that, by default, sets the maximum width of each line to 132 characters. See also PRE in Appendix B for more information.

The better solutions to the formatting problem are lists (Chapter 14) and tables (Chapter 17). With lists, you can use the Increase Indent and Decrease Indent buttons on the toolbar to control the level of indentation of individual lines. With tables, you can put text neatly into rows and columns. Because of this fact, let's not spend any more time on the PRE style. There are better tools to work with.

Scrolling Marquee Text

Nothing catches a reader's attention like motion. If you have a special message that you want to call your reader's attention to, you can put that message into a scrolling marquee. The text will scroll onto the screen from the left or right edge of the screen. It is sort of like the scrolling marquee sign on New York's Radio City Music Hall. If you have browsed the Web using Internet Explorer, you have probably seen examples of text that scrolls across your screen.

As I write this chapter, Microsoft Internet Explorer 2.0 is the only browser that supports marquee text. Any reader viewing your page with another browser will still see the text — but that text remains motionless like the rest of the text on the page. So keep in mind that even though all readers will see the text, only those readers using Internet Explorer as their Web browser will see the text moving across the screen.

Creating marquee text is simple:

1. In the regular Edit mode of Word IA, move the insertion point where you want the text to appear — just as though you were typing in normal, non-moving text.
2. Choose Insert⇨Marquee. You'll come to the Marquee dialog box shown in Figure 13-18.

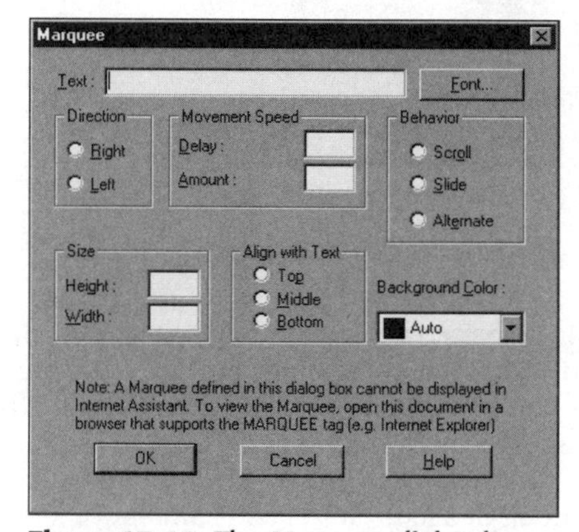

Figure 13-18: The Marquee dialog box.

3. Type the text of your message into the Text box.
4. Optionally, make other selections to define the appearance and behavior of the text as follows:
   - **Font.** Choose a font, keeping in mind that the font will be used only if the reader has that font on his/her PC, as discussed earlier in this chapter.
   - **Direction.** Choose whether you want the text to scroll to the Right or scroll to the Left. If you don't make a choice, the text will scroll in from the right. Optionally, choose Alternate under Behavior to make the text bounce back and forth.
   - **Movement Speed.** Delay — Enter the number of milliseconds to pause between each letter. The smaller the number, the faster the text moves. Amount — Enter the number of pixels you want the marquee text to move each time it is redrawn. The smaller the number, the smoother the marquee text moves.

- **Behavior.** Scroll — Text will scroll across and out of the marquee. Slide — Text will scroll to the opposite end of the marquee and stop there. Alternate — Text will scroll across the marquee, bounce off the opposite side, and scroll back the other direction.
- **Size.** Specify the Height and Width of the marquee in pixels.
- **Align with Text.** Specify how neighboring text, if any, will align to the scrolling marquee text. Choose Top, Middle, or Bottom.
- **Background Color.** Choose a background color for the marquee.

5. Choose OK.

In Word IA, your marquee text will be blue and unmoving. To see it scroll, you need to choose Preview in Browser, using Internet Explorer as your browser.

More Info The HTML tags for marquee text are `<MARQUEE>...</MARQUEE>`. Though Netscape Navigator 2.0 ignores those tags, you can create a similar effect in Navigator by using my custom banner( ) JavaScript function, which is discussed in Chapter 29.

Blinking Text

Netscape Navigator 2.0 supports blinking text. Internet Explorer does not, and there is no simple selection for blinking text in Word IA. But if you want to display blinking text to readers whose browsers support that feature, you just need to enclose the text in a pair of `<BLINK>...</BLINK>` tags. The following steps explain how to do that in Word IA.

More Info For more information on Netscape Navigator 2.0, see Chapters 33 and 34.

1. If you have already typed the text that you want to blink, select that text (just drag the mouse pointer through it). Then choose Edit⇨Cut or press Ctrl+X.
2. Choose Insert⇨HTML Markup from Word IA's menu bar.
3. In the dialog box that appears, type the tag **<BLINK>**.
4. If you selected and cut text in Step 1, press Ctrl+V now to insert that text.
5. Type **</BLINK>**, and make sure that you use a forward slash (/) not a backslash (\). You should see both tags and any text you pasted in between those tags as in Figure 13-19.

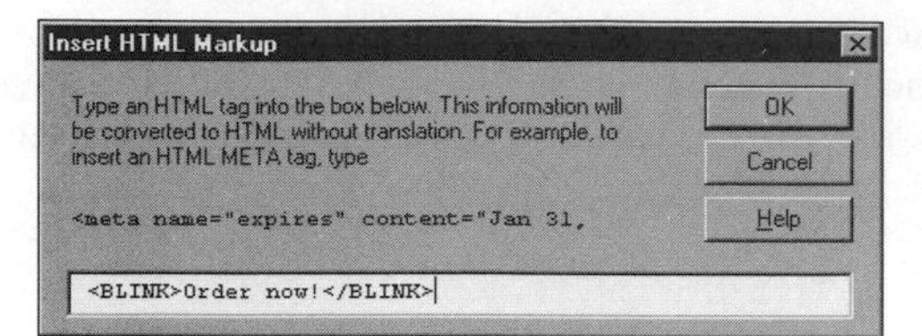

Figure 13-19: <BLINK>...</BLINK> tags around text that will blink.

6. Choose OK.

In Word IA, the <BLINK>...</BLINK> tags and any text in between will show on your screen in blue. To actually see the text blink, you'll need to open the page in a Web browser that supports blinking (such as Netscape Navigator 2.0).

Tags That Word IA Inserts without Asking You

When you view the HTML source for any Web page you create with Word IA, you are bound to see some HTML tags that you did not specifically request. Word IA puts these tags into your document automatically because most Web browsers expect to find them. These "uninvited" tags appear at the top and bottom of the document. The following list explains what they are and what they do:

- <HTML>...</HTML>: Marks the beginning and end of every Web page.
- <HEAD>...</HEAD>: Identifies the header section of the Web page, which contains information *about* the page — not text to be seen by the reader. The <TITLE> and <META> tags are placed within the <HEAD> tags.
- <TITLE>...</TITLE>: Specifies the title that appears in the title bar of the reader's browser.
- <META NAME="GENERATOR" CONTENT="...">: Contains information about the document that never appears on the reader's screen. Similar to File⇨Properties in Microsoft Word or File⇨Summary Information in WordPerfect, can contain information about the author, the date last edited, how the document was created, and so forth.
- <BODY>...</BODY>: Identifies the body of the page — the part the reader will view.

Figure 13-20 shows a sample document, in HTML Source view, so that you can see the codes that Word IA inserted automatically (I took out some blank lines to show all the tags). I only typed the sentence "My dog has fleas." Word IA inserted everything else on its own. In general, you want to leave those tags alone. Word IA knows where and when to insert them, and you shouldn't delete or modify them.

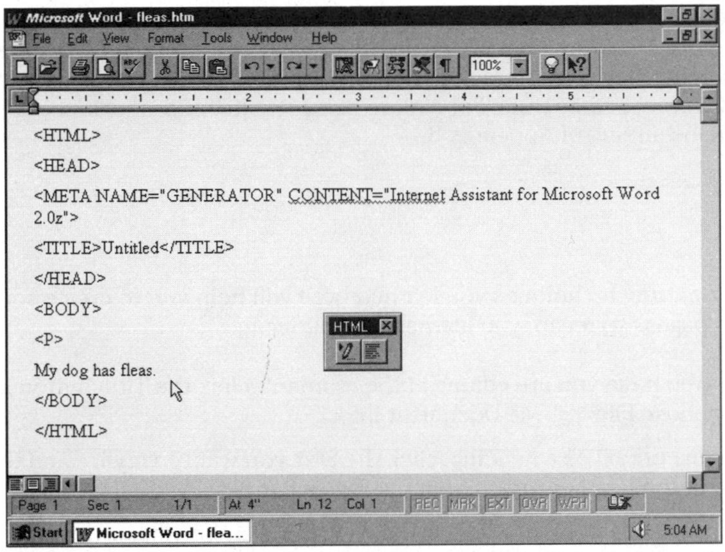

Figure 13-20: All of these tags (and some scrolled off the bottom of the screen) were inserted automatically by Word IA.

What About Those Strange "&" Things?

One last thing before closing this chapter: You may discover, when looking at the HTML source for your document, some weird-looking codes such as `&lquote` and `&ersand`. The reason is that the characters <, >, " (quotation mark), and & (ampersand) all have special meanings in HTML. If you want your Web browser to display one of these characters literally, rather than interpret the character as part of an HTML tag, you need to use the special & codes summarized in Table 13-3.

Table 13-3
Word IA Automatically Converts These Characters to These Codes

Character	*HTML Code*
& (ampersand)	`&`
" (quotation mark)	`"`
< (less than)	`<`
> (greater than)	`>`

Fortunately for you, Word IA converts those characters to the & codes automatically; you really don't have to do anything yourself. The only reason I even mention these codes is so that if you ever come across a strange-looking `&code:` , you'll know what it's all about and where it came from. For a more complete list of & codes, see "Character Data" near the beginning of Appendix B.

Summary

The basic text formatting techniques you learned here will help you to create some pretty fancy Web pages. To recap, you learned the following:

- ✦ To title the Web page you are editing at the moment, click the Title button in the toolbar or choose File⇨HTML Document Info.
- ✦ To define a line of text as a heading, click the text you want to stylize and then choose one of the heading styles from the Styles list.
- ✦ To "unstyle" text, click (or select) the stylized text and then apply the Normal,P style to it.
- ✦ To center text, click the line or select the text you want to center and then click the Center button in the toolbar or choose Format⇨Center Align. To "uncenter" text, click (or select) it and then click the Left button or choose Format⇨Left Align.
- ✦ To apply "weights" to text, such as boldface and italics, select the text you want to stylize. Then click the Bold, Italic, or Underline button in the toolbar.
- ✦ To change the typeface, relative size, or color of text, first select the text you want to change. Then choose Format⇨Font and make your selections. You can also resize text by selecting it and then clicking on the Increase Font Size and Decrease Font Size buttons in the toolbar.

✦ ✦ ✦

Lists, Lists, and More Lists

In This Chapter

Typing bulleted lists

Typing numbered lists

Editing lists

Indenting lists

Menu, directory, and definition lists

Lists are a great way to format text to give it a "quick read" look and feel. Lists also are great for presenting step-by-step instructions. I'm a big fan of lists, as you can tell simply by flipping through the pages in this book. Lists are even more important on the Web, because people generally do not like to read paragraph text on computer screens. In this chapter, we take a look at the many different ways that you can incorporate lists into your Web pages.

Bulleted Lists

People often use bulleted lists to break up text that does not fit into a paragraph, to present a summary, or to give that "quick read" look and feel to text. For example, every chapter in this book starts with a bulleted list titled "In This Chapter." Similarly, every chapter ends with a bulleted list that reviews the topics covered within that chapter. You'll find plenty of bulleted lists within the chapters as well.

Bulleted lists are also called *unordered lists* because the items in the list are not numbered. In fact, the HTML tag for starting a bulleted list is `<UL>`, which stands for *u*nordered *l*ist.

The easiest way to create a bulleted list is to simply type the entire list, pressing Enter after each item. Then select the list and apply the List Bullet,UL style. Here are the exact step-by-step instructions:

1. Type the first item in your list.
2. Press Enter.
3. Type the next item in your list.
4. Repeat Steps 2 and 3 until you have typed the entire list.
5. Select the list and then click on the Bulleted List button (Figure 14-1).

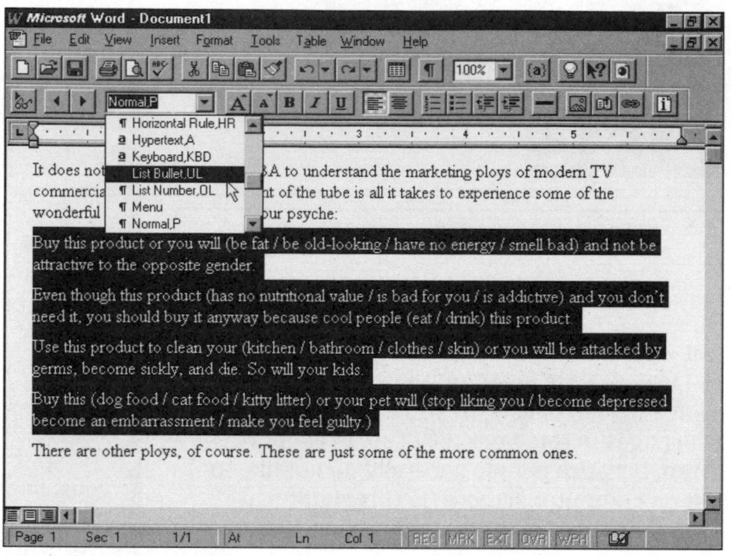

Figure 14-1: List of items selected before applying Bulleted List style.

Word IA automatically applies bullets to the list for you, as in Figure 14-2.

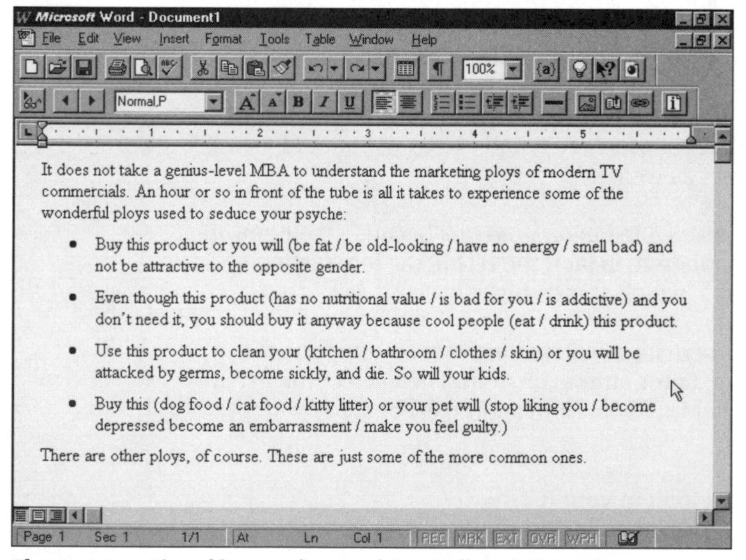

Figure 14-2: List of items after applying Bulleted List style.

The HTML tag to start a bulleted list in a Web page is <UL>. The code to end the list is </UL>. Each bulleted item within the list starts with an <LI> (list item) tag. If you ever happen to peek at the HTML tags behind the scenes, your bulleted list will look something like Figure 14-3.

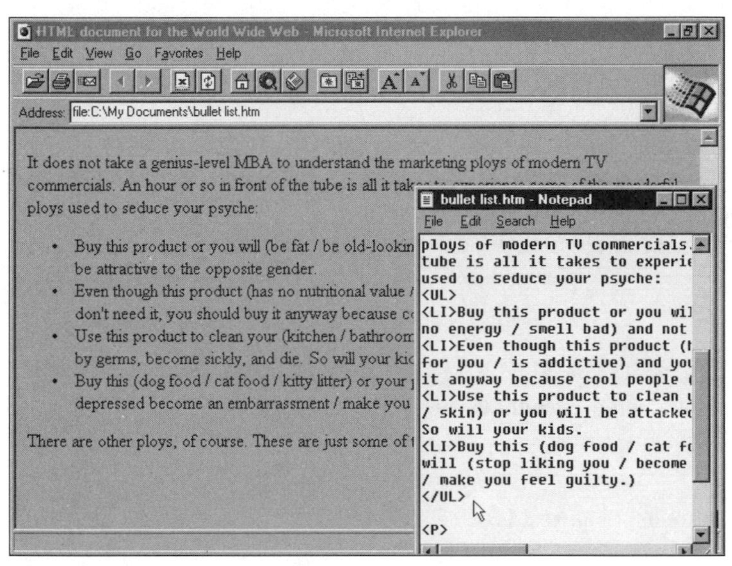

Figure 14-3: Word IA creates HTML <UL>, <LI>, and </UL> tags.

For tips on changing the list, see "Editing Lists" later in this chapter.

Hot Stuff

You can get fancy and use tiny graphic images in place of bullets (see Chapter 15). Some browsers, including Netscape Navigator, also support custom bullet characters named square, circle, and disc. Use Notepad or some other text editor to specify the bullet character as the type attribute in the <UL> tag, like this: `<ul type=square>` or `<ul type=disc>`.

Numbered Lists

A numbered list is perfect for times when you want to give your reader step-by-step instructions. To create a numbered list, do the following:

1. Type the first list item as a sentence. Don't put the number in front of the sentence.
2. Press Enter.
3. Type the next list item, again without numbering.
4. Repeat Steps 2 and 3 above until you've typed the entire list (Figure 14-4).

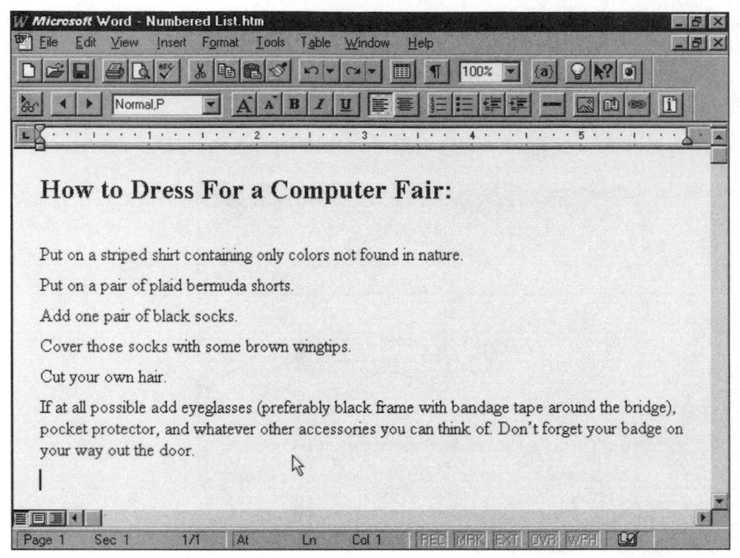

Figure 14-4: Type a numbered list without numbers, pressing Enter at the end of each item.

5. Select the entire list (Figure 14-5).

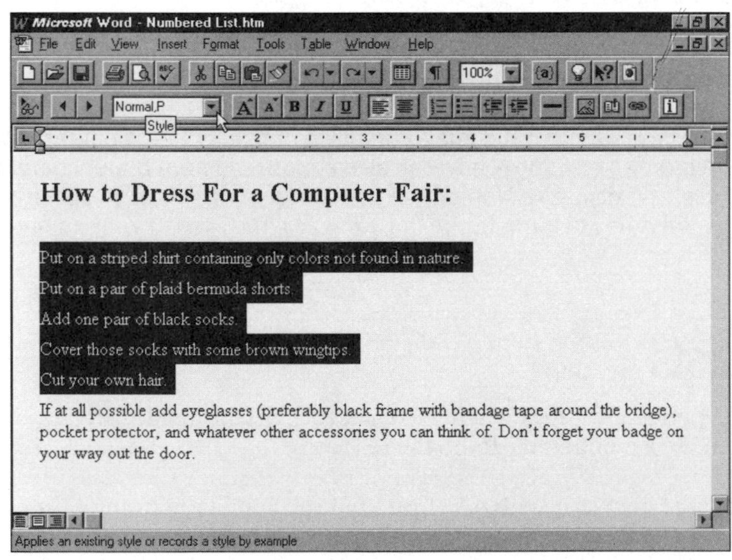

Figure 14-5: To convert to a numbered list, first select the list.

6. Click the Numbered List button or choose Format⇨Numbering from the menu bar.

More Info The HTML tags for numbered lists are <OL> to start the list and </OL> to end the list. The OL stands for *o*rdered *l*ist. As with all lists in HTML, a <LI> (list item) tag precedes the individual items of the list.

Word IA numbers and indents the list automatically, as you can see in Figure 14-6. If you start typing past the list and a list number appears at the start of your text, you can switch to Normal,P style to turn off list numbering. That is, click anywhere in the first paragraph following the list and then choose Normal,P from the Styles drop-down list.

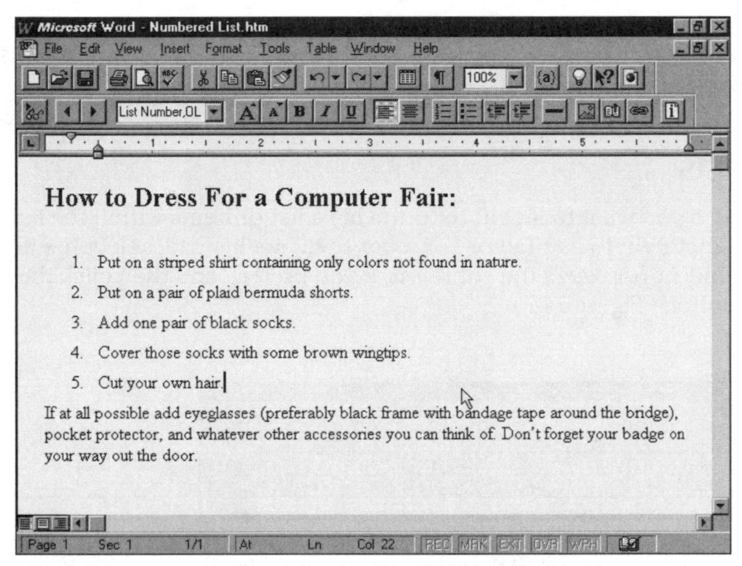

Figure 14-6: Word IA numbers and indents the list for you.

Editing Lists

If you type your list and then apply a list style to it, creating a list is pretty easy. Going back and changing a list can be a little tricky, however. Here are some tips that make the task of editing your lists a bit easier:

- ✦ Never use the Tab key or Backspace key to indent/outdent list items. Use the Increase Indent and Decrease Indent buttons on the toolbars instead.
- ✦ Never type in leading numbers or bullets yourself. Type your list item without those items, and then apply the appropriate style to the item, if necessary.
- ✦ To insert an item, move the cursor to the end of the line preceding the location where you want to make an insertion and then press Enter. Type your new item at the current cursor position.

✦ To delete a list item, select the entire item (triple-click it). Then press Delete.

✦ To move an item, select the item (triple-click it) and then choose Edit⇨Cut or press Ctrl+X. Next, move the insertion point to the end of the line preceding the point where you want to move the item and press Enter to insert a line. Select Edit⇨Paste (or press Ctrl+V). You may end up with an extra blank list item, but you can just press Delete to delete that item.

✦ If your list gets really messed up, select the list and apply the Normal,P style to it. Fix all indents and outdents so that all list items are evenly aligned to the left margin. Then reselect the list and reapply the Number or Bullet list style.

Hot Stuff

If your Web site will contain any lengthy lists or lists that need to be updated from time to time, be sure to try out the Coolsite program (Chapter 20) on the CD-ROM that came with this book. It may save you hours of time and headaches!

Indenting lists

As I've mentioned, if you want to indent (or outdent) a list or items within the list, you must avoid the temptation to use Tab or Spacebar to do so. Instead, select the item(s) that you want to indent (or select the entire list, if you prefer), and then click the Increase Indent button (Figure 14-7).

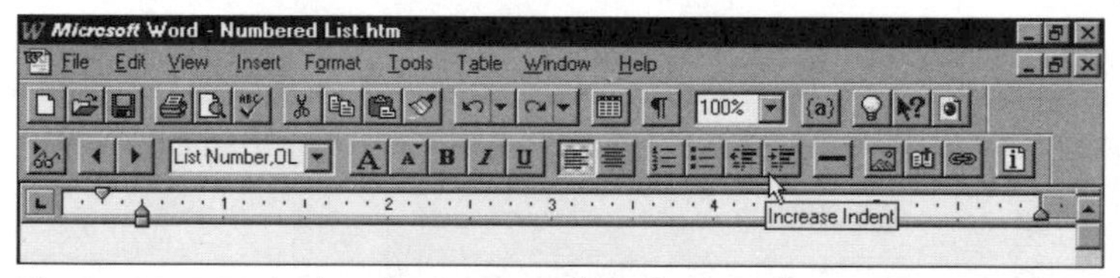

Figure 14-7: To indent list items, select them and use the Increase Indent and Decrease Indent buttons in the toolbar.

Every time you click the Increase Indent button, Word IA indents the selected list items further. If you go too far and want to outdent the items, just select the items you want to outdent and then click the Decrease Indent button as necessary to get to the level of indentation you want.

Combo numbered/bulleted list

If you want a list to contain more than one style, you should still type the list as normal lines of text. Then go back and apply design elements from the outside in. Figure 14-8 shows an example where I've typed a simple list using the normal paragraph style.

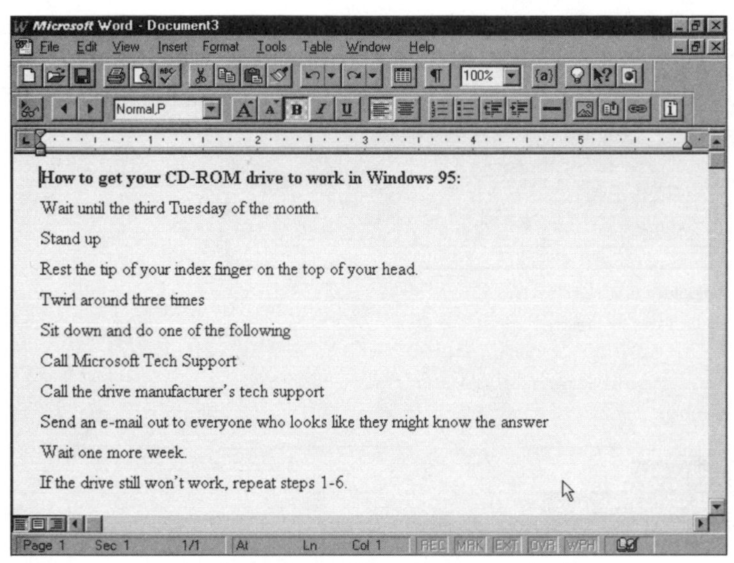

Figure 14-8: A simple list that will become a combo list.

Next, I select the entire list and click the Numbered List button. The result is shown in Figure 14-9. The list appears as a numbered list. Notice that items are numbered 1–10.

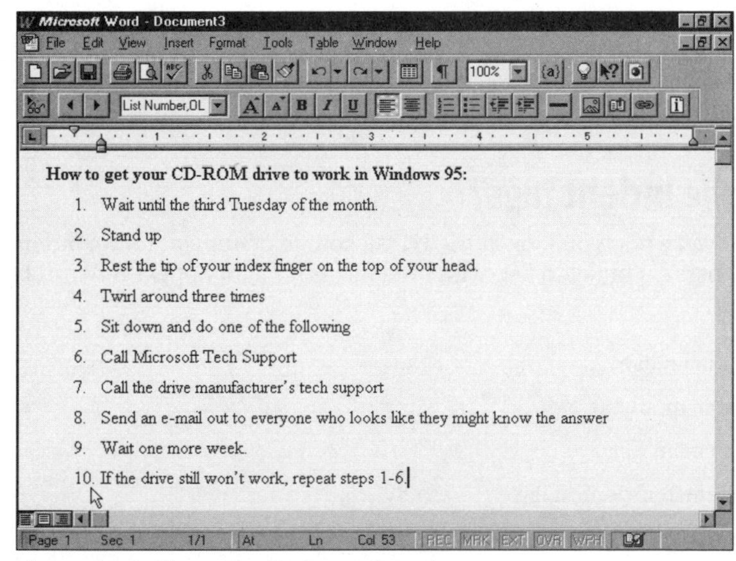

Figure 14-9: The entire list is numbered.

Now let's suppose that I really want Steps 6 through 8 to be options under Step 5, rather than steps of their own. No problem — I just select those three items (Figure 14-10).

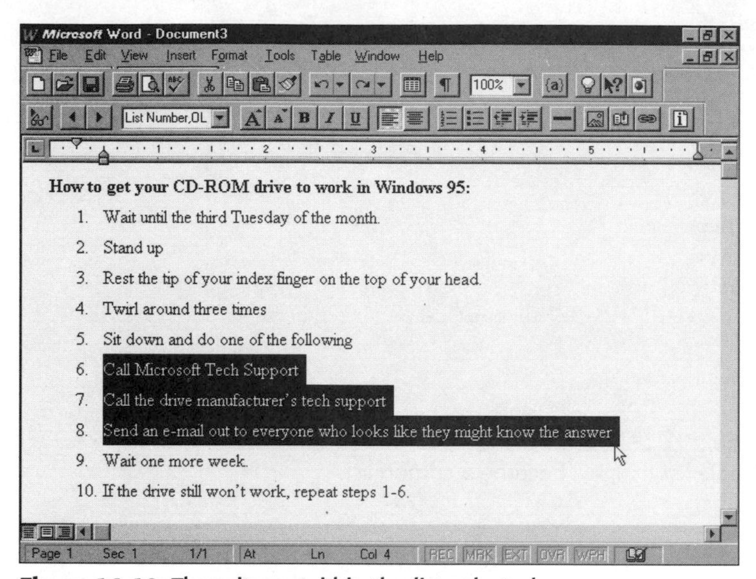

Figure 14-10: Three items within the list selected.

Next, I click the Bulleted List button to convert those three items to bulleted list items. I also can click the Indent button to indent them, if I want. The result is shown in Figure 14-11. Notice that Word IA automatically renumbers the list items to 1–7, which is the correct sequence for this modified list.

Where are the indent tags?

You may be surprised when you look at the HTML source document for an indented list. For example, here's a bulleted list, with indents, as it might appear in Word IA and your Web browser:

- First item in main list
- Second item in main list
- Third item in main list
    - First item in indented list
    - Second item in indented list
- Fourth item in main list

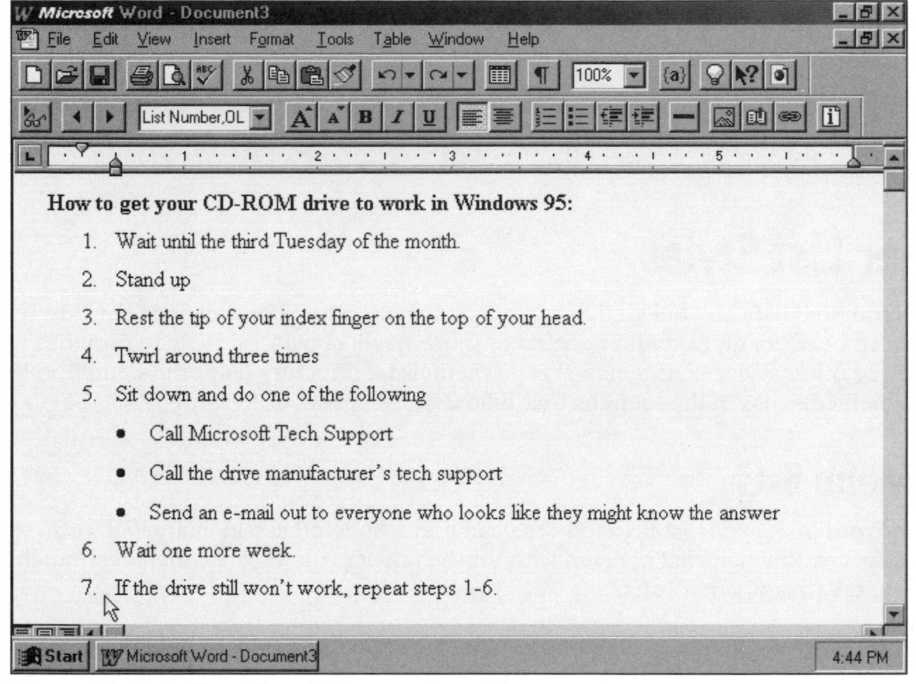

Figure 14-11: Bulleted list within a numbered list.

Here's how the same list looks when viewing the HTML source for the page:

```
<UL>
<LI>First item in main list
<LI>Second item in main list
<LI>Third item in main list
<UL>
<LI>First item in indented list
<LI>Second item in indented list
</UL>
<LI>Fourth item in main list
</UL>
```

As you can see, this list does not have any indent tags — or even any indents! What tells the Web browser to indent that one portion of the list is the new <UL>...</UL> tag pair that appears within the list. In HTML, whenever a new "start list" tag is encountered within an existing list, the items within the new list are automatically indented further than the previous list. As a result, the logic of the preceding list goes something like this:

```
<UL> (start of main list)
...
<UL> (start of indented list)
     ...
</UL> (end of indented list)
...
</UL> (end of main list)
```

Other List Styles

Numbered lists and bulleted lists are the most common types of lists. For that reason, Word IA offers quick toolbar access to those types of lists. HTML also provides for three other styles of lists, however — menu lists, directory lists, and definition lists, which I discuss in the sections that follow.

Menu lists

In Word IA, a menu list is exactly the same as a bulleted list. In many Web browsers, however, the menu list appears without the bullets. You create a menu list much like you create any other list:

1. Type each item in the list, pressing Enter after you type each item.
2. Select all the items in the list.
3. Choose Menu from the Styles drop-down list.

The list appears with bullets in Word IA. But in many browsers, including Internet Explorer, these bullets do not appear in front of the list items (Figure 14-12). I've also volunteered an alternative formatting technique for the example list, even though you didn't ask for one. Just giving you a little food for thought here — think of it as kind of an added bonus.

Directory lists

A directory list is formatted into columns across the screen — in some browsers, that is. Apparently, neither Internet Explorer nor Netscape Navigator support directory lists. But somebody's browser must because the `<DIR>` tags for directory lists are part of official HTML.

You use a directory list only if each item in the list is no more than 20 or so characters in length. In Word IA, you type the directory list as you would any other list: Just type each item and press Enter. After you finish typing the list, select it and choose the Directory, DIR style from the Styles drop-down menu.

Word IA inserts the appropriate HTML tags for you, although you may not notice any major changes to your list at first. To get the full effect, you need to close and re-open the Web page. That is, choose File⇨Close and save your current changes, and then click the File menu and open the document you just closed. You should see your items listed horizontally across the screen, in columns, such as in Figure 14-13.

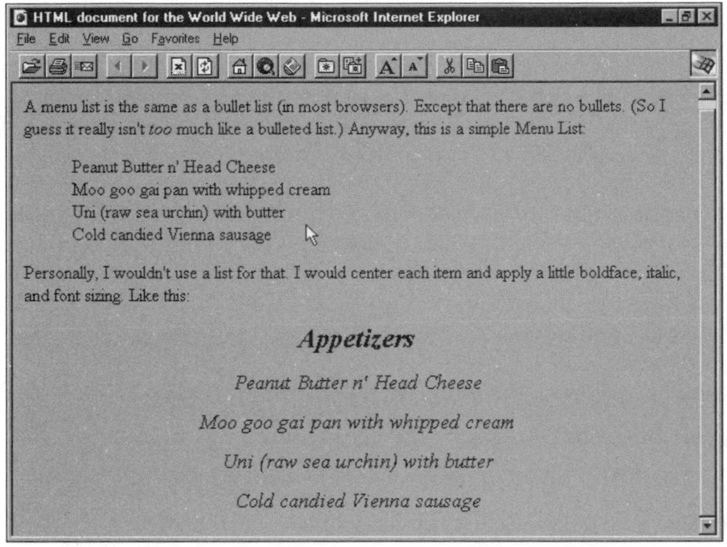

Figure 14-12: A menu list as displayed by Internet Explorer (no bullets).

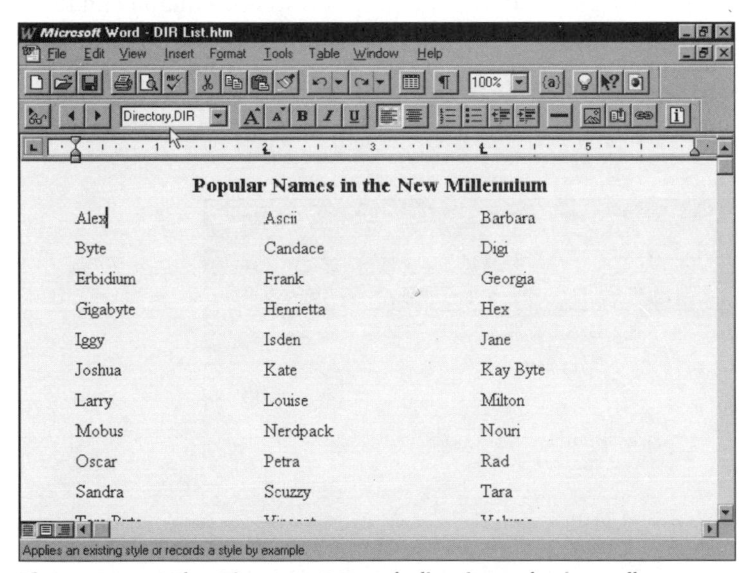

Figure 14-13: The Directory, DIR style lists items horizontally.

Unfortunately, the list appears as a single-column list in Internet Explorer and Navigator. (Go figure.) I'm not sure that you'd ever really want to use this type of list. You can, however, achieve a similar effect just by putting the list items in a three-column table (Chapter 17).

Definition lists

A definition list displays a list of terms with their definitions. For example, the glossary at the back of most books is a definition list. These lists are just a little trickier to create than the other type of lists because each row in the list actually contains two elements — the term to be defined and the definition of that term.

You also have two definition-list styles from which to choose: One is the Definition Compact, and the other is the Definition List. In Word IA, the Definition Compact style tightens up text slightly to reduce extra white space. Every Web browser I've seen, however, displays both styles in exactly the same format. Strange! Despite this fact, Word IA makes creating a definition list pretty easy:

1. Type the word that you want to define; then press Tab (pressing Tab is important).
2. Type the definition for the term and then press Enter.
3. Repeat Steps 1 and 2 to type your entire list of terms and their definitions.
4. To format the list as a definition list, first select the entire list.
5. Choose Definition List, DL (or Definition Compact) from the Styles drop-down list.

When Word IA applies the list style, it lists the terms down one column and the definitions down a second column, like the example in Figure 14-14. What's really weird, though, is that this list doesn't look anything like that in most Web browsers. In a browser, the list looks more like that shown in Figure 14-15, where each term is followed by its definition on the next line.

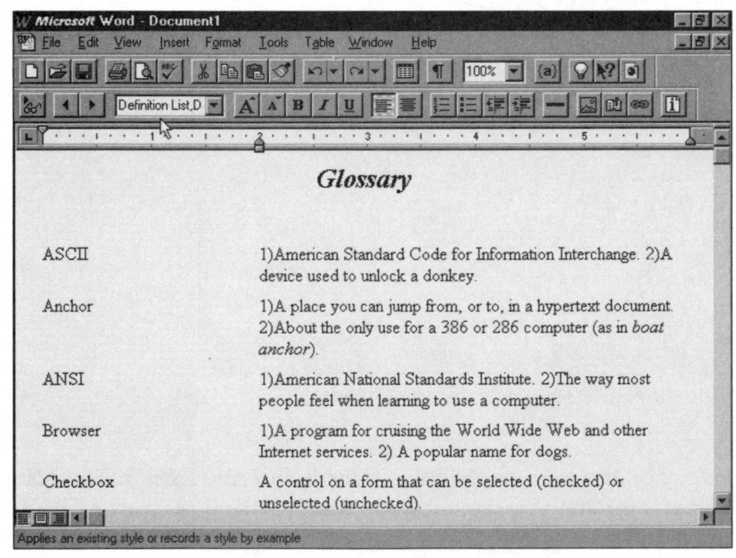

Figure 14-14: A definition list, as viewed in Word IA.

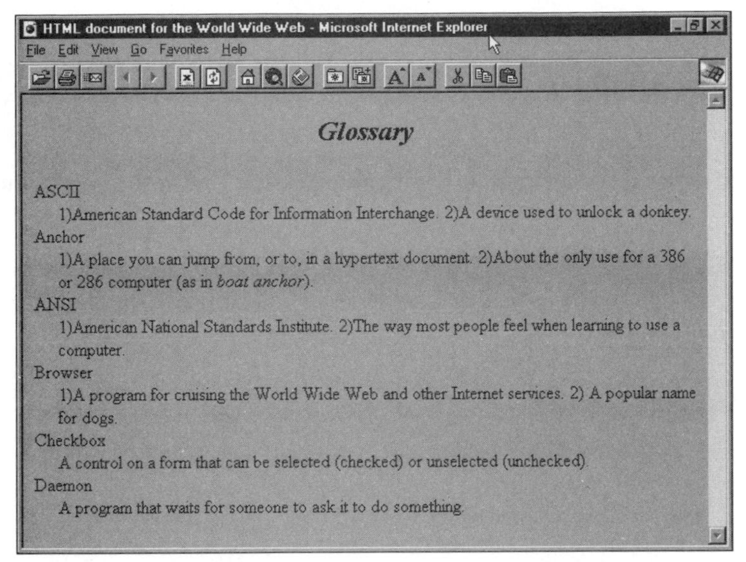

Figure 14-15: A definition list, as viewed in most other Web browsers.

For future reference, I should also point out that definition lists do not use the standard <LI> (list item) tag. Rather, a definition list uses the tags listed in Table 14-1.

Table 14-1
HTML Tags Used in Definition Lists

Element	*Tag*
Start definition list	<DL>
Term being defined	<DT>
Definition of the term	<DD>
End definition list	</DL>

Summary

Adding lists to your Web pages is pretty easy. In a nutshell, you just need to do the following:

- Type the list without typing numbers or bullets. Press Enter at the end of each list item.
- Select the list and apply one of the List styles to it.
- To indent items within the list, select the items you want to indent and click the Increase Indent button.
- If you make a major mess of your list, just apply the Normal,P style to it, then reapply one of the List styles.

✦ ✦ ✦

A Picture Is Worth Alotta Bytes

✦ ✦ ✦ ✦

In This Chapter

Where to get graphic images

Adding pictures to your pages

Sizing pictures

Aligning text to pictures

Adding background colors, textures, and watermarks

HTML tags for graphic images

✦ ✦ ✦ ✦

Pictures are both a blessing and a curse to Web authors. The blessing is that pictures make for a more interesting presentation than just text alone. (Imagine a newspaper or magazine with no pictures.) And, as everyone knows, a picture is worth a thousand words. Unfortunately, a picture also is worth many, many thousands of bytes, which means (1) it takes up lots of disk space and (2) it takes a long time to download to the reader's computer. You need to use pictures sparingly so that your readers don't die of old age while waiting for your images (pictures) to download.

More Info: If you have any troubles with graphic images, be sure to read Chapters 21 and 22. You'll find solutions to all kinds of common problems and learn some techniques to make your pictures look their best and move *quickly* across the Web.

Sources of Graphic Images

Many sources of graphic images are available to Web authors. In fact, just about anything you see can be used as a picture. In addition, you can create and display many things that you see only in your mind's eye at the moment. Figures15-1 through 15-3 show a handful of such examples, already plopped into Web pages and shown through Internet Explorer. Here's a quick written summary of sources:

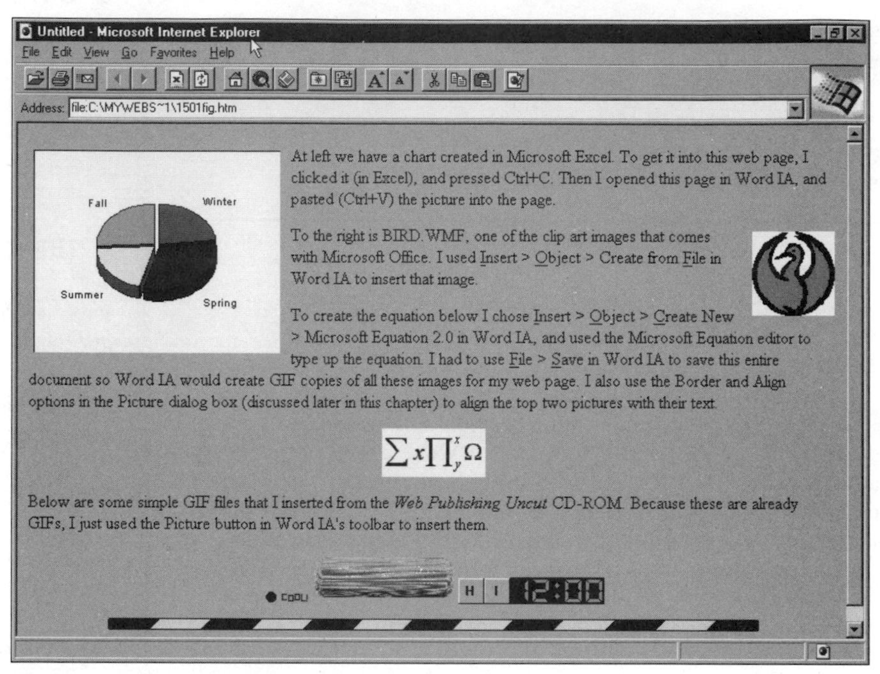

Figure 15-1: Sources of pictures (part 1).

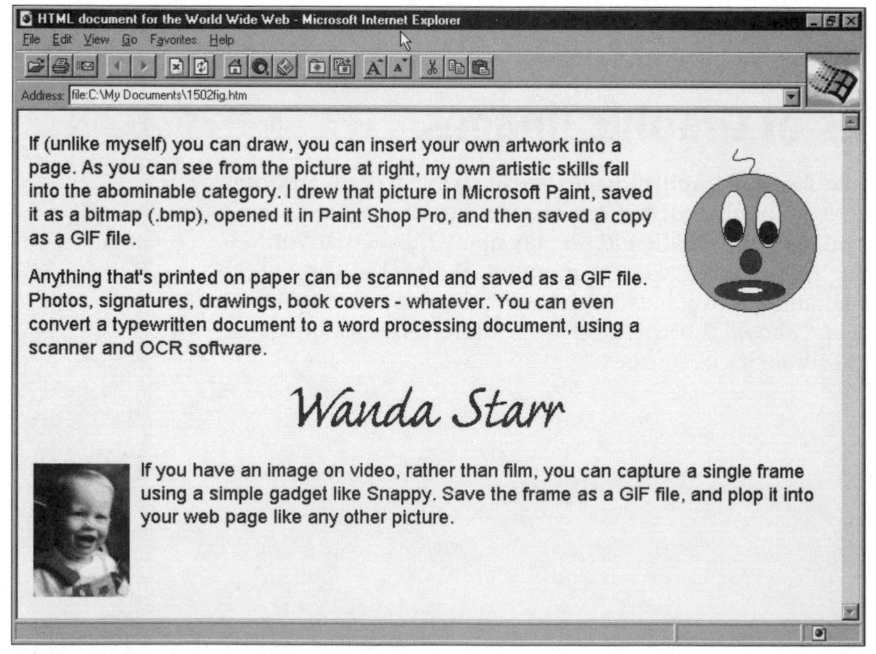

Figure 15-2: Sources of pictures (part 2).

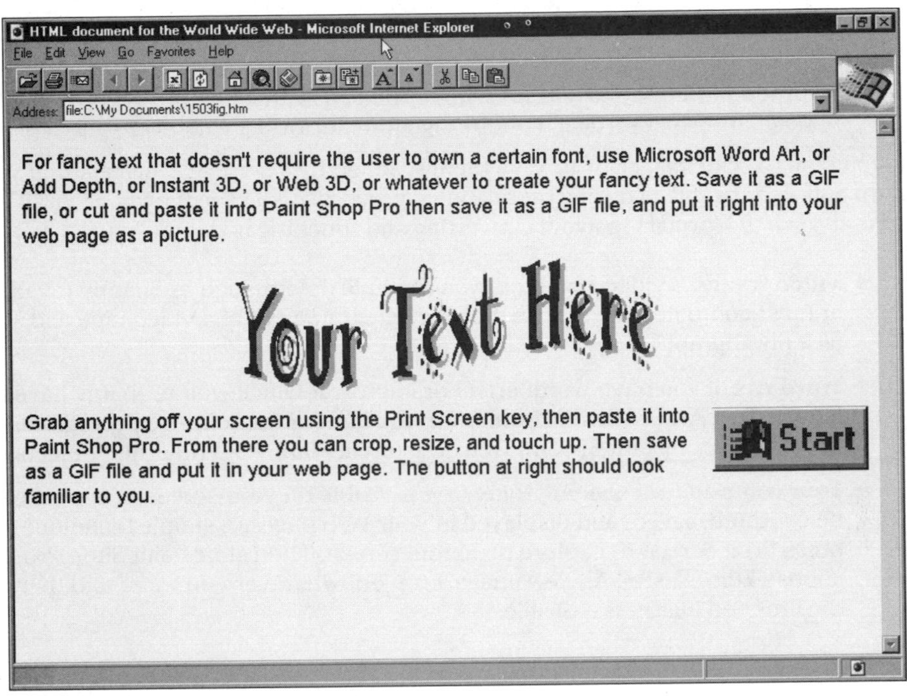

Figure 15-3: Sources of pictures (part 3).

✦ **Charts.** Any business charts or graphs that you create using Microsoft Excel or any other graphics program can be pasted into a Word IA document. Optionally, you can paste any chart into Paint Shop Pro, save it as a GIF file, and then insert it into your Web page by using the Picture button in Word IA.

✦ **Commercial clip art.** You can buy huge collections of ready-to-use clip art (and photographs) at most computer stores. Many formats can be read as-is right into Word IA, using the Insert➪Object➪Create from File commands. Word IA then creates a GIF file automatically when you save the page. Optionally, you can open any image in Paint Shop Pro, save it as a GIF file, and insert it into your Web page with the Picture button in Word IA.

✦ **Equations.** Both Microsoft Office and WordPerfect have equation editors built-in. You also can purchase sophisticated equation editors from many computer stores. To create an equation using Microsoft Equation, choose Insert➪Object➪Create New, as discussed in Chapter 21.

✦ **Free clip art.** Lots of places exist on the Web that let you download free clip art and background textures. For quick access to those sites, stop by the Web Authoring area in my coolnerds site at `http://www.coolnerds.com`, or scout around the *Web Publishing Uncut* CD-ROM (Appendix A).

Hot Stuff

You also can look up the words *clip art* in any search engine to find thousands of free buttons, bullets, lines, backgrounds, and other graphic images.

✦ **Freehand drawings.** If you can draw, you can use Paint Shop Pro or any other drawing program to create and save custom artwork for your site.

✦ **Scanned photographs and drawings.** You can scan and store anything that appears on paper — be it a photo, signature, drawing, whatever — as a picture.

Hot Stuff

If you plan to scan images or to have them scanned by a service, I suggest that you crop and size the image during the scanning process. Also save the image in GIF format (or JPEG format) to avoid converting and touching up later.

✦ **Video frame.** A video board or even a simple device such as Snappy (available at most computer stores) can grab a single frame out of a video tape and store it as a photograph.

✦ **Word Art.** If you have WordPerfect or Microsoft Office, you probably have some kind of Text Art or Word Art program. You also can purchase 3-D programs such as AddDepth, Instant 3D, and Web 3D to create fancy 3-D titles and objects.

✦ **Your computer screen.** Anything that is visible on your screen at any time can be captured, saved, and displayed in your Web pages. A simple technique is to press Print Screen to capture the entire screen. Then start Paint Shop Pro, choose Edit⇨Paste⇨As New Image, crop out whatever you want, and then save the cropped image as a GIF file.

When using other people's images, do keep in mind that many pictures are copyrighted. You cannot put such pictures into your Web site without express written permission from the holder of the copyright!

Inline images versus external images

There are two ways to offer graphic images to your Web browsing public:

✦ **Inline images.** Inline images appear automatically as soon as your reader opens your Web page. The images in Figures 15-1 to Figure 15-3 are all inline images, and this chapter is really about inline images.

✦ **External images.** External images are sort of optional for your reader. To view the image, the reader must click a hyperlink (underlined text, as in Figure 15-4), or a thumbnail (tiny picture or icon, as in Figure 15-5).

External images are a good way to offer large pictures that take a long time to download and are not really crucial to your general presentation. Give the reader a description of the picture and some idea of how long it will take to download. That way, you won't irritate the reader by making him or her wait through a 5- or 10-minute download to see something they may not really care to see.

More Info

External images are treated like other multimedia files (sound, video) and are discussed in Chapter 23.

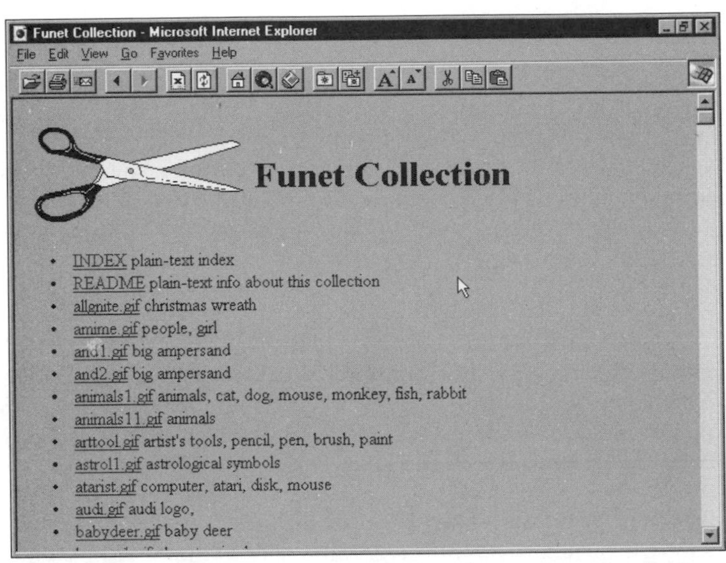

Figure 15-4: In this sample page, you can view a picture by clicking its hyperlink.

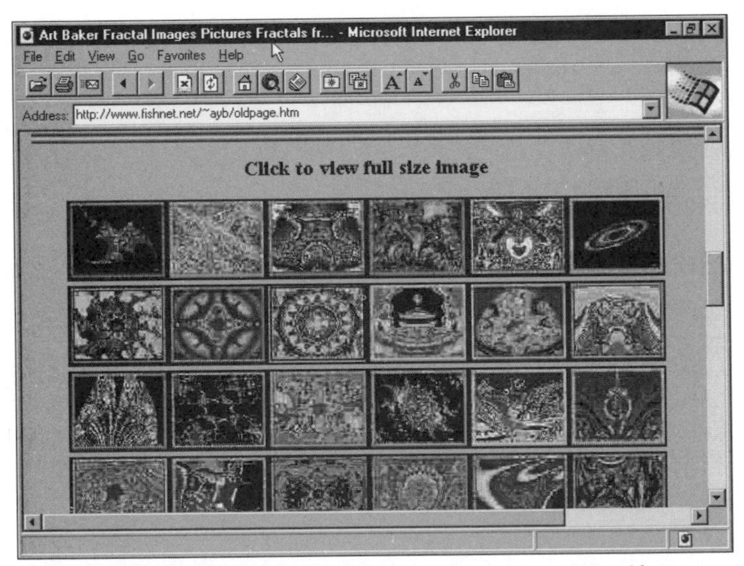

Figure 15-5: Small, inline thumbnails give you a preview of larger pictures to view.

GIFs and JPEGs

Inline images, which are the main focus of this chapter, have one major catch: They must be stored in GIF or JPEG format to work correctly. With Word IA, you can use the Insert⇨Object menu commands to insert other picture formats, including Windows bitmap (.bmp), Tagged Image File Format (.tif), Computer Graphics Metafile (.cgm), Paint (.pcx), Windows metafile (.wmf), and many others into your Web page. But when you save the Web page, Word IA converts the image to a GIF file and stores it in the same folder as the Web page. The Web page contains only a tag that refers to the image, as I'll discuss shortly.

If you want to have some control over the conversion from another format to GIF or JPEG, or if Word IA doesn't handle a conversion well, you can easily do the conversion yourself by using Paint Shop Pro. Converting pictures yourself gives you much greater control over the quality and size of the resulting picture. See Chapter 22 for more information on converting pictures to GIF and JPEG.

In case you're wondering *why* the Web likes only GIF and JPEG formats, the reason is that these formats were designed to compress graphic data as much as possible to speed transfer across phone lines. In fact, GIF is also called CompuServe GIF because CompuServe — one of the first online information services — developed the format to speed its own graphical online services.

One downside to GIF is that it only supports graphic images up to 256 colors. This limitation can make some pictures, particularly photographs, look grainy. JPEG, which is fairly new to the Web, can handle 240-bit graphics — which means it can handle pictures that contain millions of colors, such as photographs. I talk more about GIF and JEG in Chapter 22. For now, you just need to know that you will be limited to those two formats for inline graphics in your Web pages.

Relative versus absolute picture links

Your Web page document never actually contains any pictures. When you save your page, Word IA puts an `<IMG SRC...>` tag where the picture belongs. That `<IMG SOURCE>` tag tells the Web browser the location and filename of the picture to display. But the location on your PC may not be the same as the location on the Web server computer. Therefore, creating `<IMG SRC>` tags in your Web pages as *relative links* is important. That is, the tags should point to filenames but not to locations (folders or directories). For example, the following tag is a relative link to a picture stored in a file named mypic.gif:

```
<IMG SRC = "mypic.gif">
```

Because the filename is the only specific part of the tag, the reading Web browser assumes the image's location to be "the same directory that the Web page itself is on," without a specific drive or directory location.

The other type of link, where you do include a file's location in the tag, is called an *absolute link*. For example, the following tag is an absolute link because it specifies a folder named C:\MYWEBSITE as the location of the file named mypic.gif:

```
<IMG SRC = "c:\mywebsite\mypic.gif">
```

That link may work fine on your own PC, assuming that you have a folder named MyWebSite on drive C. But when you upload the page and graphic to your Web server, the server most likely will not contain a C:\MYWEBSITE folder. Hence the `<IMG SRC = "c:\mywebsite\mypic.gif">` points to a non-existent folder. Rather than showing the intended picture, the reader's Web browser will show only an "error picture," as in Figure 15-6, because it cannot find the requested folder.

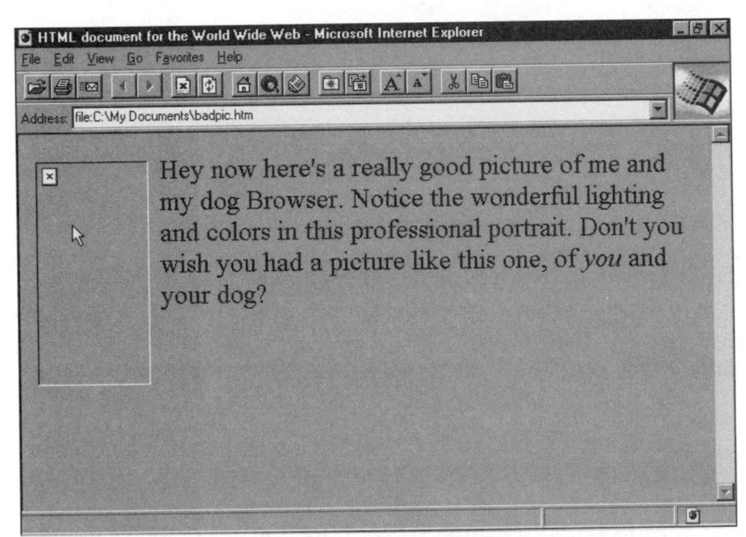

Figure 15-6: This Web page is trying to show a non-existent picture.

In general, Word IA is pretty good about using only relative links in your `<IMG SRC...>` tags. But being aware of the potential problems is good. Later in this chapter, I show you how to quickly fix this problem, should it occur.

Simplify picture management

To simplify the task of managing pictures in your site, I suggest that you gather up all the images you plan to use in a page and copy them to your My Web Site folder. In Figure 15-7, for example, I've copied some graphic images — which I've already converted to GIF format using Paint Shop Pro — into my own My Web Site folder.

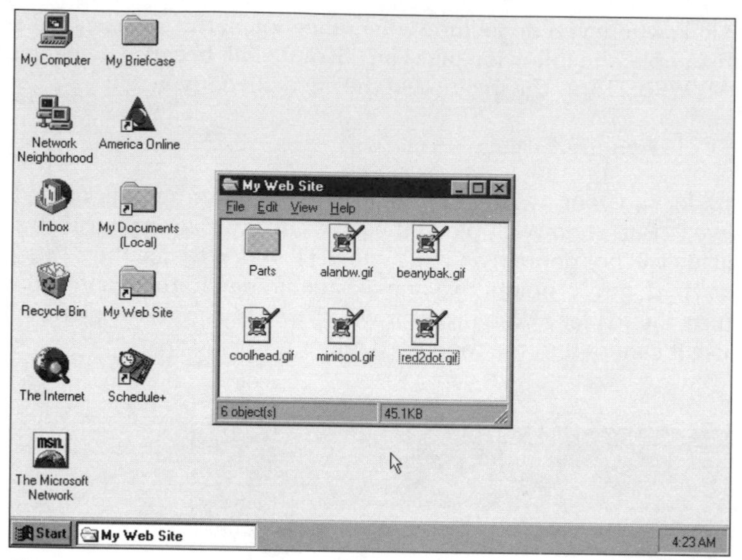

Figure 15-7: Some graphic images (GIF) files in my My Web Site folder.

When you use the Word IA Picture button to insert a picture into your page, be sure to choose the copy that resides in your My Web Site folder. That way, Word IA is sure to create a relative link to that picture. Also, when it comes time to upload your pages, the graphic images will be in the same folder as your pages, so you will be less likely to forget to upload all the images with your pages.

Inserting a GIF or JPEG Image

Whew! After all this yakking and prep work, you'd think putting a picture into a Web page was some big deal. Actually, this task is simple, as long as (1) the picture is already in GIF or JPEG format, (2) you know what picture you want to insert, and (3) you know where it's located on your hard disk.

1. Open (or create) your Web page with Word IA in the usual manner.
2. To ensure relative linking, save your Web page in your My Web Site folder (using File➪Save).
3. Move the insertion point to the approximate spot where you want the picture to appear, simply by clicking the spot.
4. Click the Picture button in the toolbar, or choose Insert➪Picture from the menu bar. You then see the dialog box shown in Figure 15-8.
5. Click the Browse button, and locate the picture you want to insert. In Figure 15-9, I'm about to insert the picture coolhead.gif from my My Web Site folder. When you find the picture, double-click it or click the OK button.

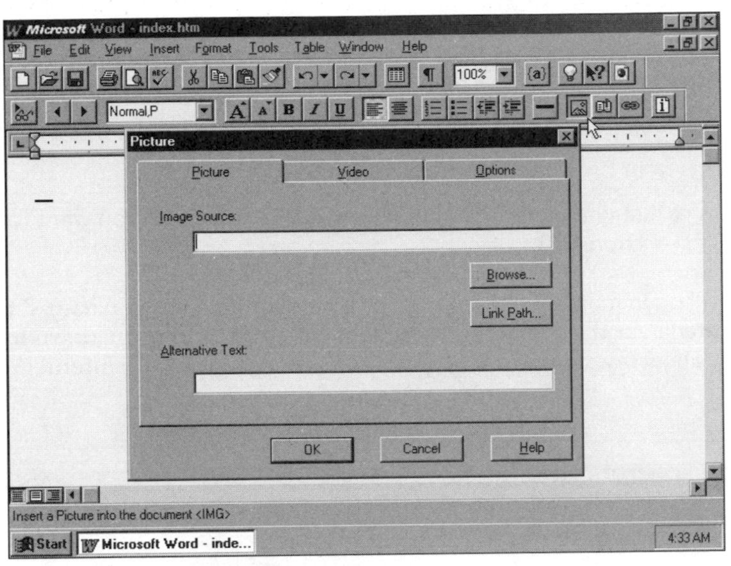

Figure 15-8: The Picture dialog box.

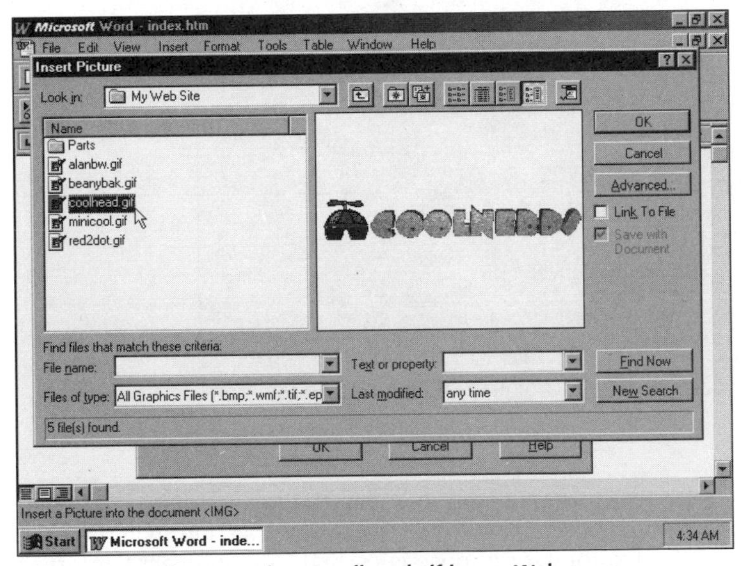

Figure 15-9: About to place coolhead.gif in my Web page.

6. Word IA takes you back to the Picture dialog box where you can choose the other options described in the sections that follow. Alternatively, just click OK to see how the picture looks right now. (You can easily go back and edit the picture later, if you want.)

The picture usually appears in your document right away, but don't worry if the picture doesn't show up immediately. The real "acid test" is whether or not it shows up in the Web browser. To see how the picture will look to your readers on the Web, take a peek at the document using your Web browser:

1. Click the Preview in Browser button on the toolbar.
2. Because you've just changed the document, Word IA will ask if you want to save those changes — choose Yes.

Your document will open in Internet Explorer (or whatever browser you use). If the picture is not located near the top of the document, you'll need to scroll down to it. Figure 15-10 shows how my sample document looks when viewed with Internet Explorer.

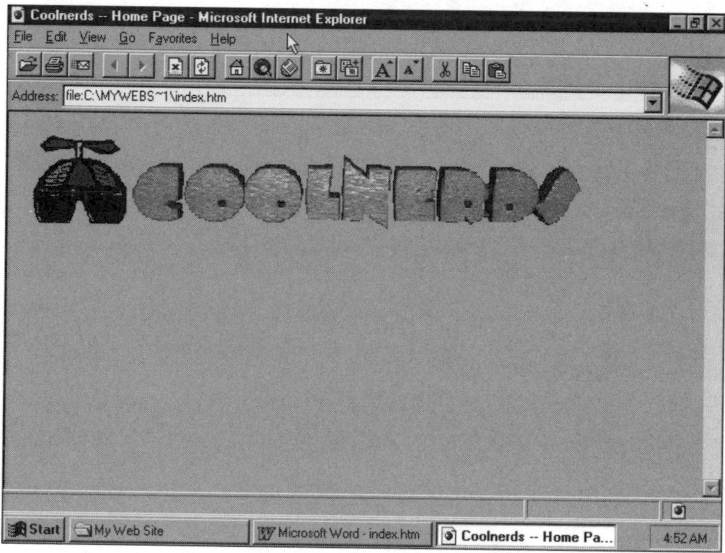

Figure 15-10: My document with coolhead.gif inserted, viewed from Internet Explorer.

After previewing your picture, don't forget that you need to close Internet Explorer and get back to Word IA to make changes. Just click the Close button in the upper-right corner of Internet Explorer, or choose File⇨Exit from Internet Explorer's menu bar.

More Info By the way, to create coolhead.gif, I used some commercial clip art from Art Parts, some 3-D tools, and the trusty Paint Shop Pro.

Inserting a Non-GIF or Non-JPEG Image

If the picture that you want to insert is not in GIF or JPEG format, you cannot use the Picture button to insert the picture. (Well, you *can,* but the picture won't show up in your Web browser!) You need to use the Insert⇨Object commands to insert .bmp, .cgm, .tif, .pcx, and all other non-GIF and non-JPEG formats. These steps tell you how:

1. Click at the approximate location where you want the picture to appear in your page to position the insertion point.
2. Choose Insert⇨Object⇨Create from File from Word IA's menu bar.
3. Click the Browse button, and work your way to the icon for the picture that you want to insert.
4. Choose OK to work your way back to your document after you've selected the picture you want. You should see a copy of the picture in your Web page now.
5. For convenience, have Word IA create a GIF version of this file right now. Choose File⇨Save from Word IA's menu bar.
6. When you see the Conversion of Pictures dialog box, choose Save Pictures.

Troubles opening graphic images

Word IA is pretty good about opening most graphic formats, but if you come across a picture that you cannot import, chances are that you just need to install the appropriate filter. You can easily fix this problem if you have your original Office 95 (or Word 95) floppy disks or CD-ROM lying around.

First, close all open applications so that you're at the Windows 95 desktop. Insert the original Office 95 (or Word 95) CD-ROM or floppy disk and run SETUP.EXE from that disk. When prompted, choose Add/Remove⇨Converters, Filters, and Data Access⇨Change Option⇨Graphic Filters⇨Change Option. Click on Select All if you just want to have access to all graphic types. Or, if you want to conserve disk space, check only the JPEG and GIF filters (if they are not already checked). Don't clear any existing check marks, though — otherwise, you'll remove that filter.

Choose OK and Continue until you see the message that Setup was completed successfully, and then choose OK. If you need further assistance, refer to your Microsoft Office for Windows 95 or Microsoft Word for Windows 95 manuals.

Word IA will make a GIF version of each non-GIF and non-JPEG image in the document and then store that GIF version in the same folder as the page. As soon as the conversion is finished, you can view the page with your Web browser.

The new files that Word IA creates when you save your document all have relatively simple names, such as Img00001.gif, Img00002.gif, and so on — both on the disk and in your Web page's HTML tags. Should you decide to rename one of these files, be sure to rename the reference to that picture in your page. Or, delete the picture from your page (in Word IA) and then re-insert it by using the Picture button.

Remember that when you upload pages to your Web server for publication, you must upload all the text (.htm and .html files) as well as *all* the pictures (.gif and .jpeg files) referred to by those pages.

Refining a Picture

After viewing your picture in a Web browser, you may decide to make some changes to it. You can control many elements, including size and position, from within Word IA. Most options are available right from the dialog box that appears when you first insert a picture. If you have already inserted a picture, you can easily get back to its dialog box in Word IA's HTML Edit view. Just click the picture to select it. Then click the Picture button in the toolbar. (You also can double-click the picture if it's a GIF or JPEG.)

Entering alternative text

Plenty of people on the World Wide Web still use text-based browsers such as Lynx. People with graphical browsers also have the option to turn off graphics so that they can browse from site to site more quickly. Whenever you put a picture into a Web page, you should include some alternative text that describes the picture for those people who won't see the picture automatically. Keep the text brief — just a short description of what the picture shows.

You can enter alternative text for a picture by using the dialog box that appears after you insert the picture into your page. Or, if you want to go back and add the alternative text later, follow these steps:

1. In Word IA (normal HTML Edit view), double-click the picture to get back to its dialog box.
2. Type your text into the Alternative Text option. For example, in Figure 15-11, I've typed **Coolnerds** into the Alternative Text field for the coolhead.gif image.
3. Click OK.

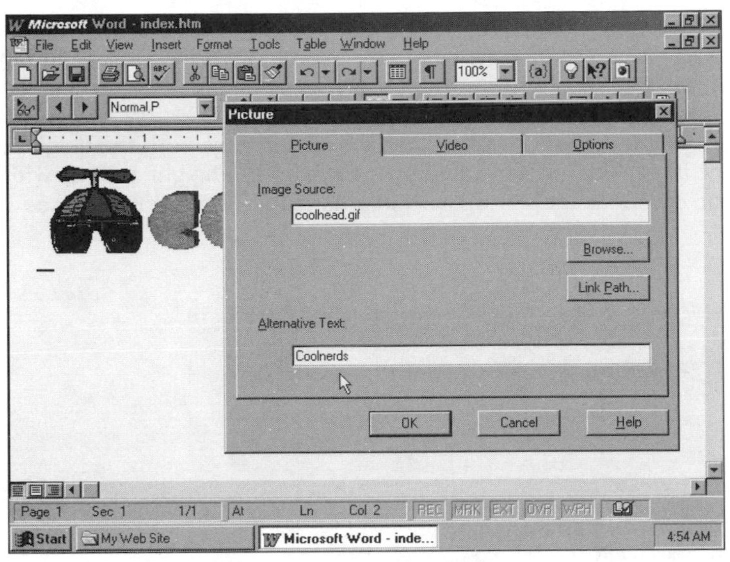

Figure 15-11: Alternative text for coolhead.gif image.

You won't see any change in your document, even if you switch to Internet Explorer. But a person browsing in a text-only mode will see your alternative text in place of the picture.

Sizing a picture

You also can determine the size of your picture in pixels. Most people use the 640 × 480 (pixels) or 800 × 600 (pixels) screen size. As a general rule of thumb, you don't want your picture to be more than 590 pixels wide. This ensures that the picture will fit on even the smallest screen width (640 pixels) and leaves an extra 50 pixels for the browser's window frame and scroll bar.

Setting a size for the picture can also speed downloading time. The reason is that the Web server can allot space for the picture before it downloads text and then wrap the text accordingly. After the text is downloaded (and visible on the reader's screen), the server then sends the picture to fill in the space you've allotted. (As you learn in Chapter 22, you can use Paint Shop Pro to determine the size of a picture in pixels.)

You also can set a different size for your picture. For example, let's say that the natural size of your picture is 100 × 100 pixels. But suppose that you want to display it at "icon size," which is 32 × 32 pixels. All you need to do is set the size of the picture to 32 × 32, and your picture will be squeezed into that size.

You are likely to encounter a few bizarre unpleasantries with this type of resizing, though; for instance, if you change the *aspect ratio* of the picture, then the picture will be distorted. For example, if the original picture is 105 × 126 pixels and you resize it to, say, 50 × 100 pixels, then the picture will be distorted to fit within that frame size. This distortion can produce an interesting effect in some pictures but is generally not what you want to see in photos or other pictures that need some degree of realism.

Preventing the distortion is easy: You just increase or decrease both the height and width by the same factor. For example, if you divide both the height and the width exactly in half, you get a smaller picture without changing the aspect ratio (see Figure 5-12).

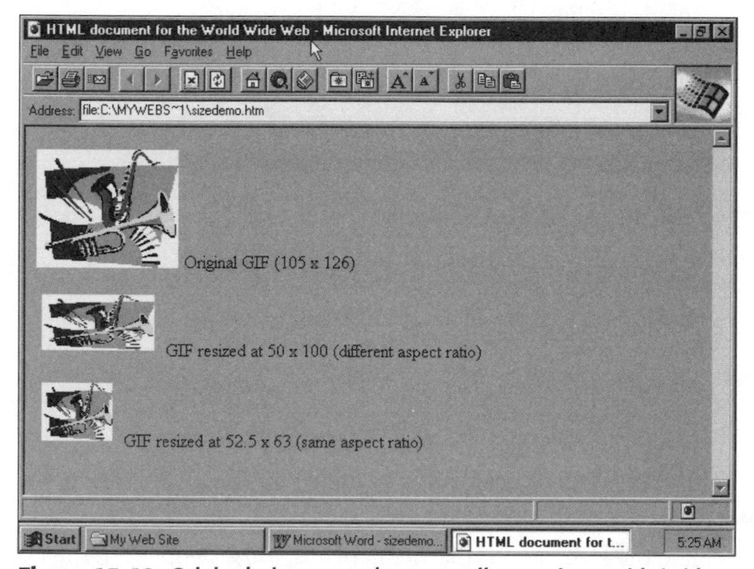

Figure 15-12: Original picture, and two smaller versions with/without same aspect ratio.

A second potential problem is that is if you change the size of a picture, it may become grainy or jagged-looking. It also may take on a checkerboard appearance. One trick that can help with that problem is to resample, rather than resize, the picture, as discussed in Chapter 22.

Hot Stuff

When you're scanning a photograph, try to size it accurately during the scanning process. That way, you won't have to resize it electronically after it has been stored on disk.

To set the size of a picture that's already in your Web page, follow these steps:

1. In Word IA, double-click the picture you want to size.
2. Click the Options tab.
3. Fill in the Height and Width options, as in the example shown in Figure 15-13.

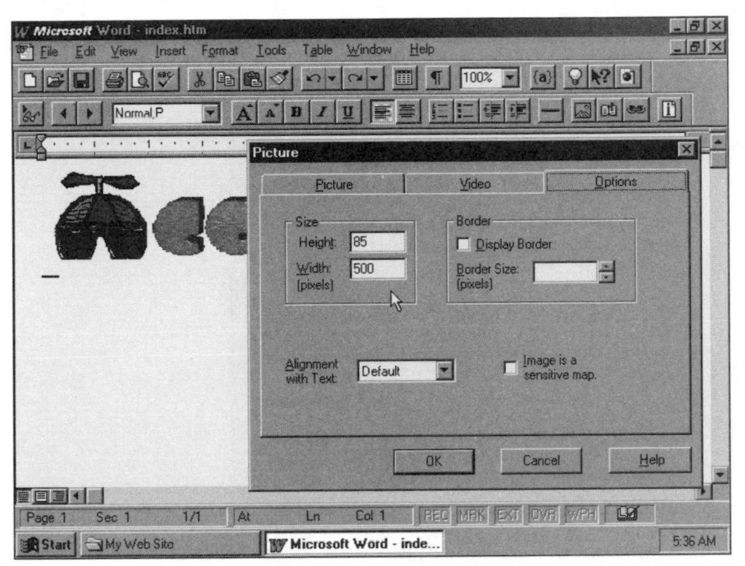

Figure 15-13: Use the Options tab to fill in the picture's height and width.

4. Click OK.

Again, don't expect any big changes to appear right away in Word IA. You'll first need to save the document and then preview it in your browser to see the picture as your readers will see it on their screens.

By the way, Paint Shop Pro shows you the size of a picture in *width × height × color depth* order. Word IA, however, asks for Height, then Width — the opposite order. Color depth has no bearing on the picture's dimensions in Word IA.

Centering a picture

To center a picture between the left and right margins, click on the picture once to select it (while in normal Edit view of Word IA). Then click the Center button in the toolbar or choose Format⇨Center Align from the menus.

Aligning text with the picture

You can align text next to a picture in any one of several ways. If you don't do anything to align text next to a picture, the result turns out like Figure 15-14, where one line of text aligns with the bottom of the picture. Subsequent lines start below the picture.

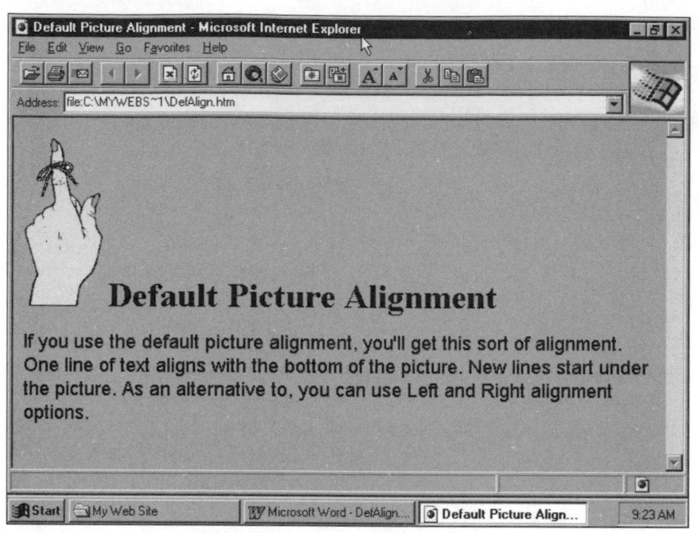

Figure 15-14: Default alignment of a paragraph next to a large picture.

You have two alignment options for wrapping text around a picture: Left and Right. Figure 15-15 shows examples of Left and Right alignment. Note that both figures are showing the document in Internet Explorer. The text does not wrap like that in Word IA.

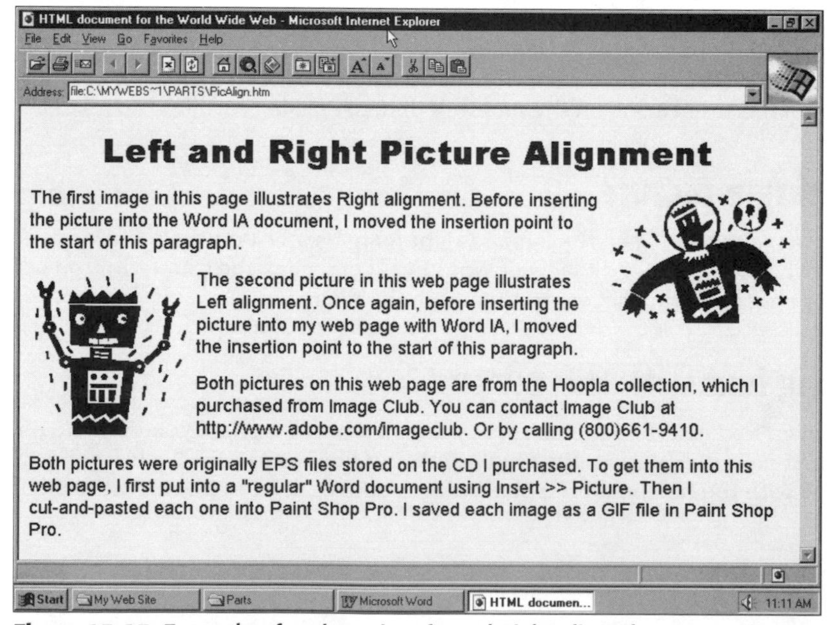

Figure 15-15: Example of a picture's Left- and Right-aligned text to a picture.

Seven other alignment options are available as well: Top, TextTop, Middle, AbsMiddle, Baseline, Bottom, and AbsBottom. None of these alignment options wrap text around a picture. Rather, they determine how a single line of text aligns next to a picture. You're more likely to use these alignment options with small images that act as bullets, thumbnails, or buttons. Figure 15-16 shows examples of these alignments. As you can see, the differences between some options are subtle, and as Table 15-1 explains, some alignment options are affected by other images within the same line.

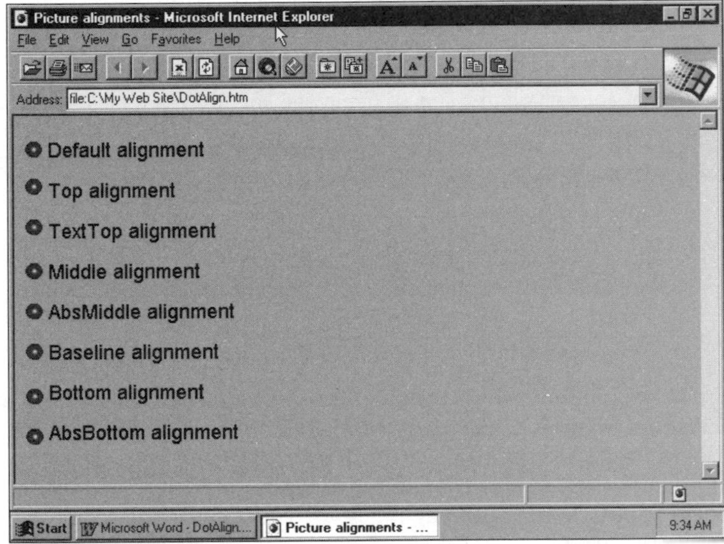

Figure 15-16: Examples of text alignment with a small picture.

Puzzled?

Not all Web browsers support all alignment options. If picture alignment is critical in your Web page design, be sure to check the alignment in a few browsers, if possible.

Table 15-1
Image Alignment Options

Option	*Description*
Default	Aligns inline graphics and text based on the default position determined by the reader's browser.
Left	Floats the image over to the first available space at the left-hand margin. Subsequent text wraps to the right of the picture.
Right	Floats the image over to the first available space at the right-hand margin. Subsequent text wraps to the left of the picture.

(continued)

Table 15-1 *(continued)*

Option	*Description*
Top	Aligns inline graphic with the top of the tallest item in the line. If the tallest item is another graphic, the top of the inline image will be aligned with the top of that graphic.
TextTop	Aligns inline graphic with the top of the tallest text in the line.
Middle	Aligns the middle of the inline graphic with the baseline of the text that appears on that line.
AbsMiddle	Aligns the middle of the inline graphic with the middle of the text that appears on that line, so the image and text are visually aligned at their middles.
Baseline	Aligns the bottom of the inline graphic with the baseline of the text.
Bottom	Same as Baseline above.
AbsBottom	Aligns the bottom of the inline graphic with the bottom of the text in the line so that the image and text are visually aligned at the bottom of each.

Be aware that Word IA *never* shows text alignment as it will appear in the browser. The reason for this fact is that Microsoft Word cannot wrap text around a picture unless you put a special Word frame around the picture. The World Wide Web does not support Word frames, however, so you cannot use that kind of frame when using Word IA. Here's how you go about choosing an alignment for your picture instead:

1. In Word IA (Edit view), select (click on) the picture that you want to realign and then click the Picture button in the toolbar to get to the picture's dialog box.
2. Click the Options tab.
3. Choose an option from the Alignment with Text dialog drop-down list.
4. Click OK.

To see the results of your selection, you must view the Web page with a Web browser. As usual, you can just click the Preview in Browser button in the toolbar to view your document in Internet Explorer.

Putting some space between text and a picture

You also can determine how much blank space surrounds your picture, from none up to six points. That space acts as a margin between the picture and any nearby text and images (Figure 15-17). To define a border for your picture, follow these steps:

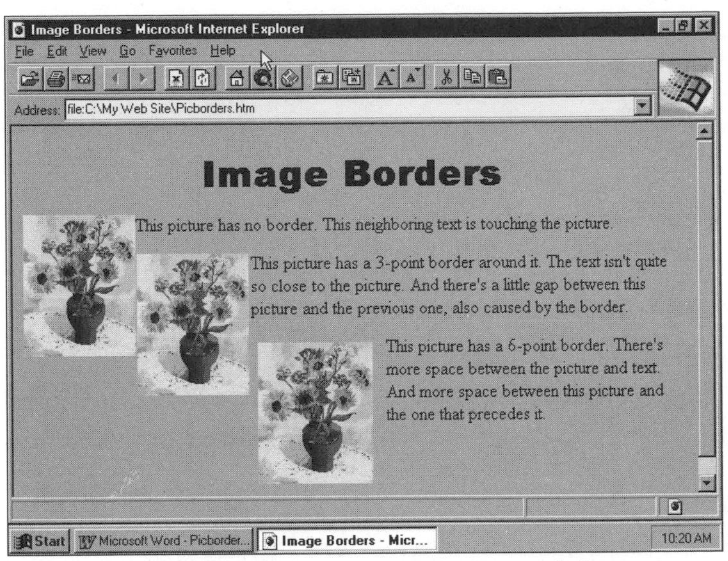

Figure 15-17: Examples of borders (margins) around pictures.

1. In Word IA (Edit view), double-click the picture you want to border with space to get to its dialog box.
2. Click the Options tab.
3. Select the Display Border option.
4. Enter the width of the border in pixels.
5. Choose OK.

As always, you need to view your document in Internet Explorer or some other Web browser to get an accurate view of the new space between your picture and its surrounding text.

Using Graphics as Horizontal Lines

You don't have to stick with the plain-vanilla lines that the <HR> tag in HTML provides. You can use any graphic image as though it were a graphic line. Lots of graphic lines are available on the Web. I've put a few sample graphic lines on the *Web Publishing Uncut* CD-ROM as well. Figure 15-18 shows a few examples.

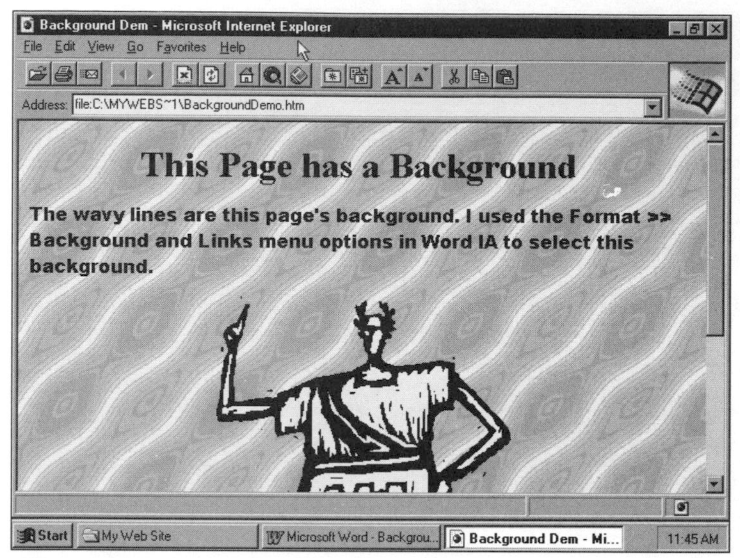

Figure 15-18: Some examples of images used in place of a regular horizontal rule.

Just insert the image as you would any other picture. If the image is much narrower than the browser width, try centering it for a better look.

HTML Tags for Pictures

Keep in mind that your Web page contains only text and HTML tags — but no pictures. When you insert a picture into a Web page, Word IA inserts an HTML tag that identifies the picture. The simplest HTML tag for a picture is `<IMG SRC>` (image source) followed by the name of the image to be displayed, such as this:

```
<IMG SRC="coolhead.gif">
```

Any optional attributes that you assign to a picture, such as alternate text and size, appear as attributes within the `<IMG SRC...>` tag. Thus, an IMG tag can be as complex as

```
<IMG SRC="mypict.gif" ALT="Beany Logo" HEIGHT="50" WIDTH="40"
      BORDER="2" ALIGN="RIGHT">
```

where the `ALT`, `HEIGHT`, `WIDTH`, `BORDER`, and `ALIGN` attributes relate to selections you made from the Picture dialog box. As always, if you want to edit the HTML tag directly, you can do so in the HTML Source view (choose View➪HTML Source from Word IA's menu bar). From there, you can use Edit➪Find to locate each `<IMG>` tag if you want to check them.

Background Colors, Textures, and Watermarks

You can add some uniqueness to your Web pages by controlling the background color and texture or by adding a watermark. Normally, the background on a Web page is gray. But you can change that background to some other color.

A texture can be a GIF or JPEG file, and it typically consists of a small image (100 × 100 pixels or less) tiled repeatedly on the page. When the reader scrolls through the text on your page, the texture scrolls along with the text. Figure 15-19 shows an example where I've used a freebie image from Radioactive Textures (`http://www.magicnet.net/rz/textures/`) as a background.

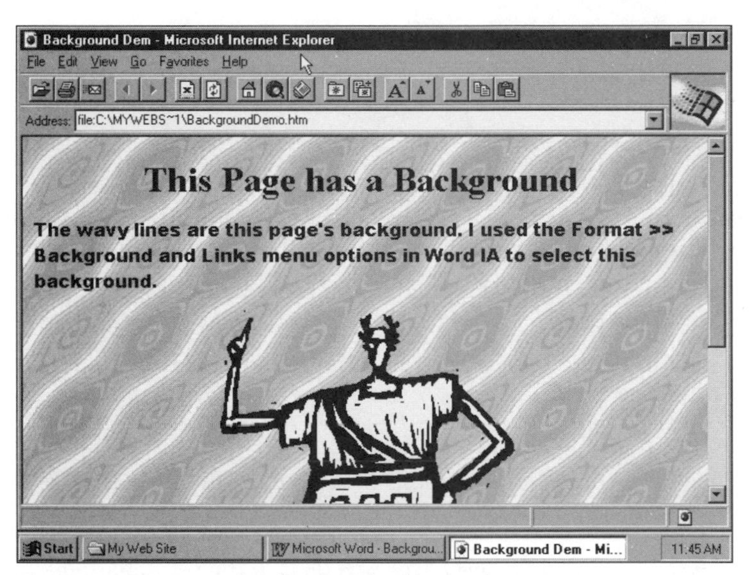

Figure 15-19: Example of a page background.

A watermark is similar to a texture, except that it remains stationary. That is, when the reader scrolls through text, the watermark in the background does not move. To add a color, texture, or watermark to your Web page, follow these steps:

1. With your Web page open in Word IA (Edit view), choose Format⇨Background and Links. You come to the Background and Links dialog box shown in Figure 15-20.

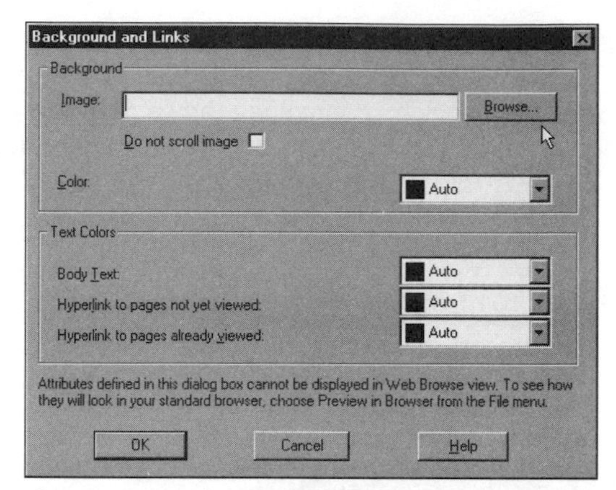

Figure 15-20: The Background and Links dialog box.

2. Now you have several choices:

   - If you want to specify an image to use as a texture or watermark, click the Browse button, navigate to your My Web Site folder, and choose the name of the GIF or JPEG file that you want to act as your background.
   - If you want to treat the background image as a watermark, select the Do Not Scroll checkbox.
   - If you want to define a color for your background, choose a color from the Color drop-down list.

Puzzled?

If you choose both a graphic image and a background color, that background color will be visible through any transparent portions of the background image. Chapter 22 explains how to select a transparent color for GIF images.

Puzzled?

You learn about *hypertext links* and *viewed hypertext links* in the next chapter.

3. Click OK when you're done.

You won't notice any change to the page's appearance in Word IA. To see how your Web page will look with its new background, preview the document in your Web browser (click the Preview in Browser button on the toolbar).

Danger Zone

As with most Web elements, background colors and textures are not supported by all Web browsers. Word IA does not show these features, either. To get an accurate view, you need to view your finished Web page from Internet Explorer or some other Web browser.

If you plan to use a graphic image as your background texture or watermark, remember to copy that file to your My Web Site folder — you'll need to upload that file along with your Web pages when you publish your pages later. The *Web Publishing Uncut* CD-ROM (Appendix A) contains some backgrounds you can try in your own Web pages. My Web site (`http://www.coolnerds.com`) points you to other sources of background images. Chapter 22 shows you some tricks for creating your own backgrounds.

HTML Tags for Backgrounds

When you choose a background color, texture, or watermark, Word IA inserts a `<BODY>` tag near the top of the document that describes the attributes you selected. Only the attributes you've selected appear within the tag. But let's say that you've defined a watermark, background color, and custom text colors. The resulting HTML tag may look something like

```
<BODY BGPROPERTIES="FIXED" BACKGROUND="mywtrmrk.jpg"
      BGCOLOR="#00ffff" TEXT="#000080" LINK="#ff0000"
      VLINK="#ff00ff">
```

where `BGPROPERTIES="FIXED"` means that the background image does not scroll with the page (that is, it's a watermark); `BACKGROUND="mywtrmrk.jpg"` specifies the name of the background image file; and `BGCOLOR`, `TEXT`, `LINK`, and `VLINK` define the colors of the background, body text, hypertext links, and viewed hypertext links, respectively. The colors are expressed as hexadecimal numbers, such as `"#00ffff"`. You need not concern yourself with doing this manually — you just choose a desired color from the Background and Links dialog box, and Word IA translates your selected color automatically.

As with any other picture, it's important that the `BACKGROUND=` attribute point to the name of a GIF or JPEG file located on the server drive. If you have any problems, make sure that you have uploaded the background image and also that the `BACKGROUND=` attribute refers to the correct location and filename.

Summary

Now you know how to get pictures into your Web page. As I mentioned ad infinitum, you learn a great deal more about working with graphic images in Chapters 21 and 22. For now, let's review the topics covered here:

- Pictures on the Web need to be in GIF or JPEG format. Word IA automatically converts most other graphic formats to GIF for you.
- The pictures themselves are not stored in your Web page. Rather, your Web page contains only an HTML tag `<IMG SRC...>` that defines where to place the picture and contains the filename of the picture.
- To insert a picture into your Web page, move the insertion point to the approximate spot where you want the picture to appear. Click the Picture button and choose the picture you want to view.
- To change a picture that's already in your Web page, double-click the picture to return to its dialog box.
- Provide some alternative text for each picture, so that people browsing in non-graphical modes can have some idea of what the picture would show.
- If you define the size of a picture in your Web page, your Web page will download it faster to your reader.
- To add a background color, texture, or watermark, choose Format⇨Background and Links from the Word IA menu bar.
- Remember that you must upload all pictures (GIF and JPEG files) along with your text documents (.htm files) when it comes time to publish your pages.

✦ ✦ ✦

C H A P T E R 16

Adding Hypertext Links

✦ ✦ ✦ ✦

In This Chapter

Creating links among your Web pages

Creating bookmarks: Links to specific spots within a page

Creating links to other Web sites

HTML tags for bookmarks and hyperlinks

Using Web Browse view to test your links

✦ ✦ ✦ ✦

Perhaps the most important feature of the World Wide Web is its *hypertext links,* often called *hyperlinks* or *hot spots* for short. These are the "hot" areas — underlined text or blue-bordered images — that take the reader to a new Web page when clicked. A hyperlink can take your reader to another page in your Web site or even to a specific place on a specific page in your site. And, of course, a hyperlink also can take your reader to any other page in the entire World Wide Web.

Relative Hyperlinks versus URLs

In the preceding chapter, I mentioned that a reference to an image may be a relative link (one that points to a file in the current Web site) or a link to a specific folder and file. The same idea applies to hyperlinks. Basically, two kinds of hyperlinks exist:

- ✦ **Relative link.** If you want to send your reader to a page within your own Web site or to a specific place in the current Web page, you need to set up a relative link.
- ✦ **URL.** If you want to send the reader to a page that is located elsewhere on the Web — not within your own Web site — use a URL (also called a *fixed file link*).

In this chapter, we cover both types of links.

Creating Hyperlinks among Your Own Pages

To create a link to another page in your own Web site, you first must create the page to which you will be linking. Then create or open the page that will contain the link (using Word IA). Next, in the Word IA Edit view, perform the following steps:

1. If you have not already done so, save the current page. Both the page to be jumped to and the page where you are placing the hyperlink must have filenames.
2. Select the text that you want to act as the hyperlink, or select (click once on) the picture that will act as the hot spot.
3. Click the Hyperlink button in the toolbar, or choose Insert⇨Hyperlink from the menus. You come to the Hyperlink dialog box shown in Figure 16-1.

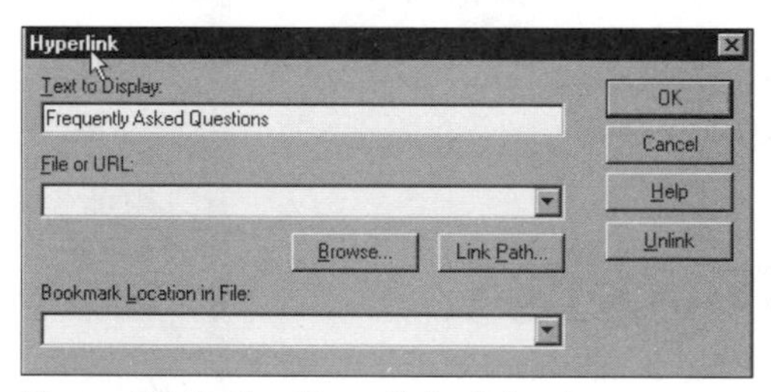

Figure 16-1: The Hyperlink dialog box.

4. Type the name of the file that you want to link to, or use the Browse button to select the name of the page to which you want to link. For example, in Figure 16-2, I want the hyperlink to take the reader to a document (page) named `faqs.htm` (which, presumably, I created and saved earlier).

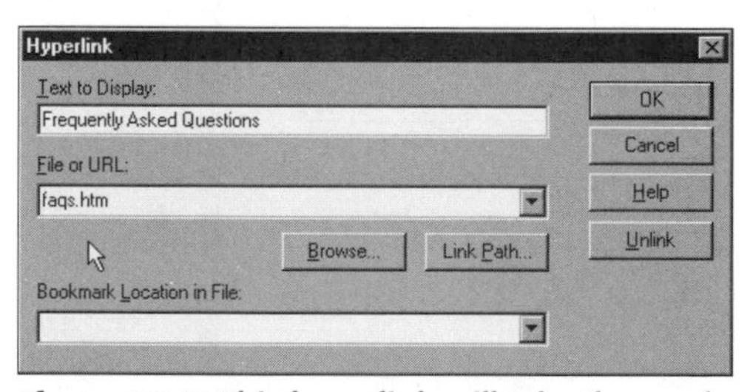

Figure 16-2: This hyperlink will take the reader to `faqs.htm` in my Web site.

5. Click OK.

Word IA underlines the selected text and makes it whatever text color you assigned to hypertext links (the default color is blue). If you selected a picture rather than text in Step 2, you may not notice anything different about the picture. But you'll be able to test its "hyperlink power" when you get to the Web Browse view in just a moment.

Clicking the hyperlink won't do anything while you are in Edit view. The reason is that Edit view is for, well, editing — not browsing. When you click a hyperlink in Edit view, the link just appears selected. Once you have selected a link in this manner, you can click the Hyperlink button in the toolbar to get back to the Hyperlink dialog box and make any changes to the link, if you like.

If you *double-click* a link in Edit view, Word IA loads the linked page. But you will probably prefer to use Web Browse view, discussed a little later in this chapter, to test your hyperlinks.

Creating a text hyperlink

Creating a hyperlink is very easy — just a few mouse clicks, really. But let's go through the process using a couple of sample documents to further illustrate what's involved. Suppose that I have already created two Web pages, one named `index.htm` and the other named `faqs.htm`, in my My Web Site folder (Figure 16-3). I want to create a hyperlink that takes the reader from `index.htm` to `faqs.htm`.

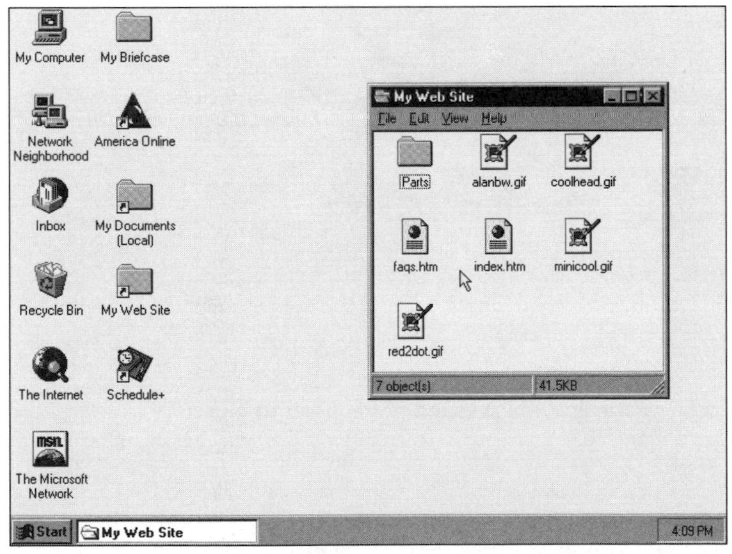

Figure 16-3: My Web Site folder contains two Web pages named `index.htm` and `faqs.htm`.

Now let's say that I want to make a link from `index.htm` to `faqs.htm`. I open `index.htm` in the usual editing mode of Word IA. I select the text that I want to act as the link, as shown in Figure 16-4. Next, I click the Hyperlink button and define `faqs.htm` as the file or URL to which I want to link. After I click OK, the selected text looks like a link, as shown in Figure 16-5.

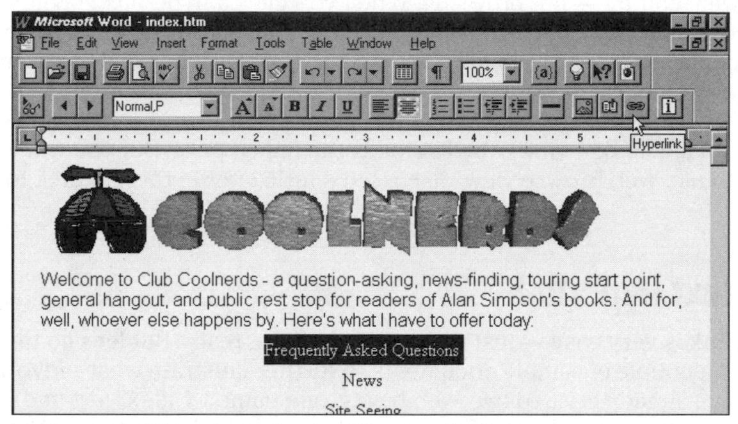

Figure 16-4: The selected text will act as the link.

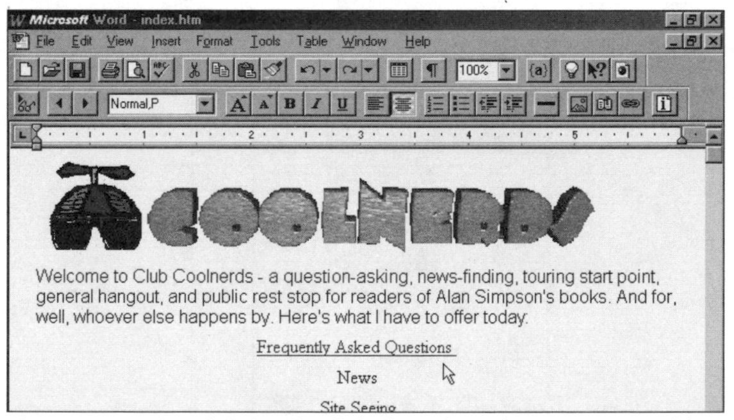

Figure 16-5: After defining the link, the selected text appears in blue and is underlined.

I'm done with that link. Now I can close and save `index.htm` or continue editing it and defining more links. Let's look at another example of creating a link.

Creating a picture hyperlink

Suppose that I now want to put a hyperlink from `faqs.htm` back to `index.htm`. In this example, let's say that I already have a small image named minicool.gif that I want to use as the hot spot. First, I need to open `faqs.htm` and get the insertion point to where I want to put the link. In this example, I'm going to put the link at the bottom of the page and center it. First, I use the Picture button to insert the button. Then I click the Center button to center the image. Next, I click the picture once to select it, as in Figure 16-6.

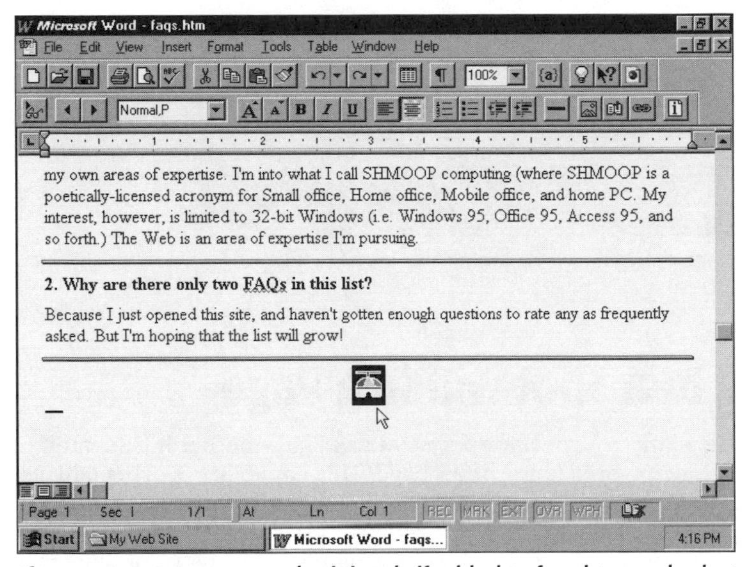

Figure 16-6: Image named minicool.gif added to faqs.htm and selected.

Once again, I click the Hyperlink button in the toolbar to get to the Hyperlink dialog box. I browse to (or type) `index.htm` as the name of the document to which I want to link and then click OK. The button now has a blue frame around it to indicate that it is a hot spot (Figure 16-7).

Now I can do more editing, define more hyperlinks, or close and save `faqs.htm` — whatever is convenient. In Web Browse view, which I discuss in a moment, you can hop back and forth between `index.htm` and `faqs.htm` to test both links.

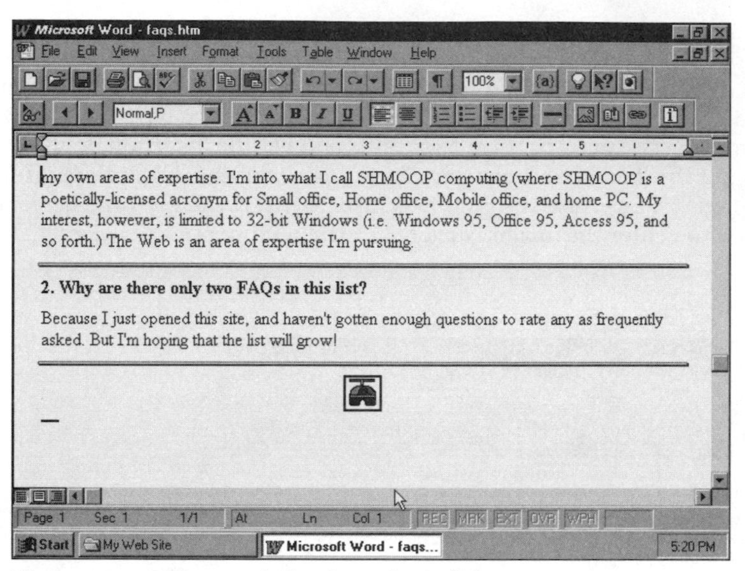

Figure 16-7: An image defined as a hyperlink.

Hyperlinking to a Spot within a Page

You also can create a link to a specific spot within a page, whether it is located on the page the reader is viewing or in some other page. This capability is especially useful for letting the reader go to a particular place in a list without scrolling through the list. For example, say that I've created a categorized list of Web sites for my reader to explore. These URLS are contained in a Web page named `urls.htm` (or whatever). When the reader first browses to that page, he or she is taken to an outline of sites organized by category and subcategory, as in Figure 16-8.

Clicking a link takes the reader directly to that part of the list. For example, if the reader clicks on Fun stuff in Figure 16-8, he/she is taken right to that category of sites, as shown in Figure 16-9. From there, the reader can click any site name to jump right to that site.

Looking behind the scenes at the `urls.htm` page, it's important to note that this is just one page. That is, rather than having the outline in one page and each site description located in a separate page, I've combined the outline and all the site descriptions into a single page. This setup makes the job easier from the authoring end. To do this, I use a sort of "internal link" within `urls.htm`. Creating this kind of link is a simple two-step process:

1. Create a bookmark (the place to which you'll be jumping).
2. Create a hyperlink to the bookmark (at the place from which you'll be jumping).

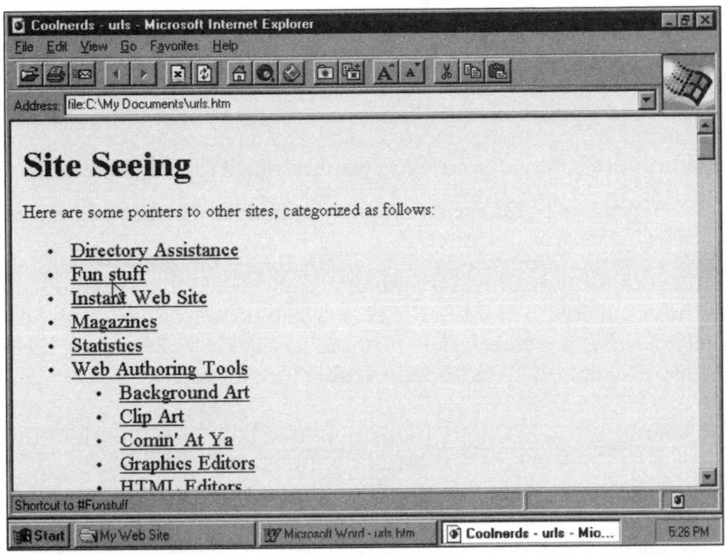

Figure 16-8: Categories and subcategories presented in an outline format act as hyperlinks to specific sites to explore.

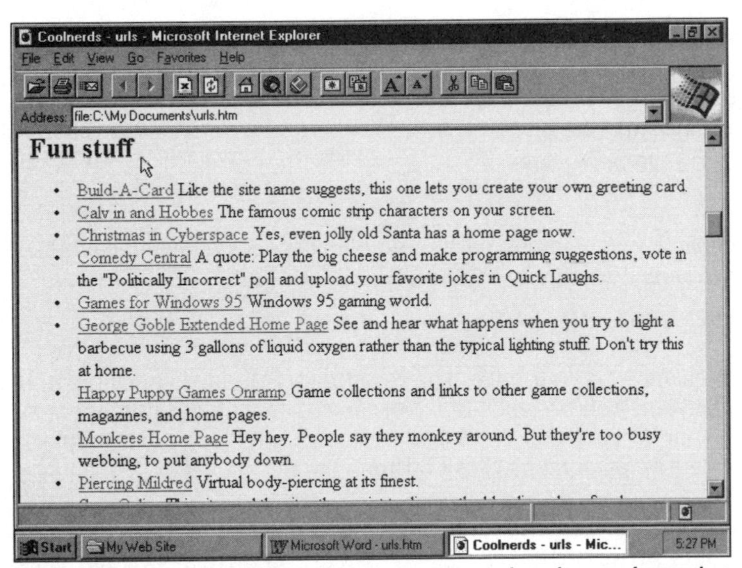

Figure 16-9: Clicking Fun stuff in Figure 16-8 takes the reader to that category of sites.

Puzzled?

You may hear the term *anchor* used in place of bookmark. Actually, anchor is the official HTML term for any spot in a page to which you can jump or from which you can jump.

Creating a bookmark

To create a bookmark, open (in Word IA's normal Edit view) the page that you want to contain the bookmark. Then follow these steps:

1. Move the insertion point to wherever you want to place the bookmark.
2. If you want the hyperlink to take the reader to a specific word or phrase within a paragraph, select that word or phrase.

More Info

If you do not select text before creating a bookmark, you create what is called an *invisible bookmark,* which is just a point in the text. If you do select text first, you create what is called a *visible bookmark.* The terminology is kind of strange, though, because neither type of bookmark is especially visible in your page!

3. Click the Bookmark button in the toolbar, or choose Edit⇨Bookmark from the menus. You come to the Bookmark dialog box shown in Figure 16-10.

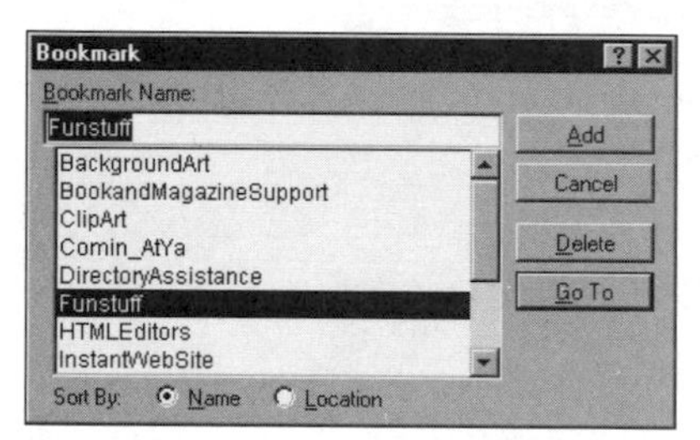

Figure 16-10: The Bookmark dialog box lets you create/change bookmarks.

4. Type a brief name for this bookmark — no blank spaces allowed. Each bookmark within a single document must have a unique name.
5. Click the Add button.

You won't see any changes in your page. The resulting HTML tag is invisible in both the Edit view and in your Web browser. But you can create a link to this bookmark from anywhere in your Web site, as discussed next. You can close the Bookmark dialog box at any time by clicking its Close button.

Hot Stuff

You can use Word's Go To feature to jump to any bookmark in your current page. Choose Edit⇨Goto (or press Ctrl+G), choose BookMark, choose a bookmark name, and then click the Go To button.

Creating a hyperlink to a bookmark

After you have defined a bookmark, you can create as many links to it as you want. The links can be located within the same page or on any other page within your Web site. Here's how to create the link:

1. If you haven't already done so, open (in Word IA) the page into which you want to place the hyperlink to a bookmark.
2. Select the text or the picture that will act as the hot spot for the hyperlink.
3. Click the Hyperlink button in the toolbar, or choose Insert⇨Hyperlink from the menus.
4. If the bookmark is in the same page that you are editing at the moment, open the drop-down list from the Bookmark Location in File field (Figure 16-11), choose the name of the bookmark to which you want to jump, and then click OK. You can now skip Steps 5 and 6.

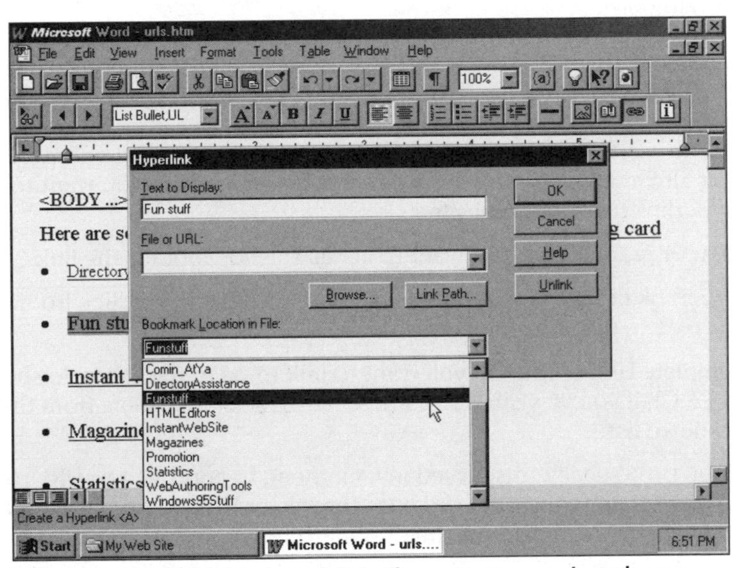

Figure 16-11: If the bookmark is in the current page, just choose the bookmark from the drop-down list.

5. If the bookmark is in some document other than the one you are currently editing, first use the Browse button to select the name of the document that contains the bookmark.
6. Next, in the Bookmark Location in File field, type the name of the bookmark to which you want to jump.
7. Click OK.

That's all there is to it. You can use the Web Browse view, which we'll discuss in a moment, to test the link.

Hot Stuff

Actually, I need to make a small confession. I used the Coolsite program (Chapter 20) to create the `urls.htm` page. Coolsite automatically created the outline, bookmarks, and hyperlinks for me. Thus, the process can be even easier than what I've just described.

Creating a Hyperlink to Another Web Site

Your Web site also can contain links to other sites that may be of interest to your reader. In general, other Web authors will be more than happy to have you send readers to their sites. But it never hurts to check in advance before you actually create a link to another site. You can just drop the Webmaster or author a note, asking if it is okay to reference his or her site in your site. Typically, if you just browse to the bottom of the home page at a site, you'll find a link that lets you send e-mail directly to the Webmaster or author.

Creating a link to another site is about the same as creating a link within your own site. The only difference is that you need to enter the complete URL of the site to which you are linking. Here are the exact steps:

1. If you haven't already done so, open (in Word IA) the page that you want to contain a hyperlink to an external site.
2. Select the text or graphic that you want to act as the hot spot for the link.
3. Click the Hyperlink button in the toolbar or choose Insert⇨Hyperlink from the menus. You come to the Hyperlink dialog box.
4. Type the complete URL of the site you want to link to, as in the example shown in Figure 16-12. Or, if you've visited the site recently, select its name from the File or URL drop-down list.

Hot Stuff

You can use the Web Browse view, discussed in a moment, to copy a site's URL to the Clipboard. Then, rather than typing that URL into the File or URL text box, click within that text box and press Ctrl+V to paste in the Clipboard text.

5. If you happen to know the exact name of a specific bookmark within the page to which you want to jump, you can enter that bookmark name in the Bookmark Location in File field.
6. Click OK.

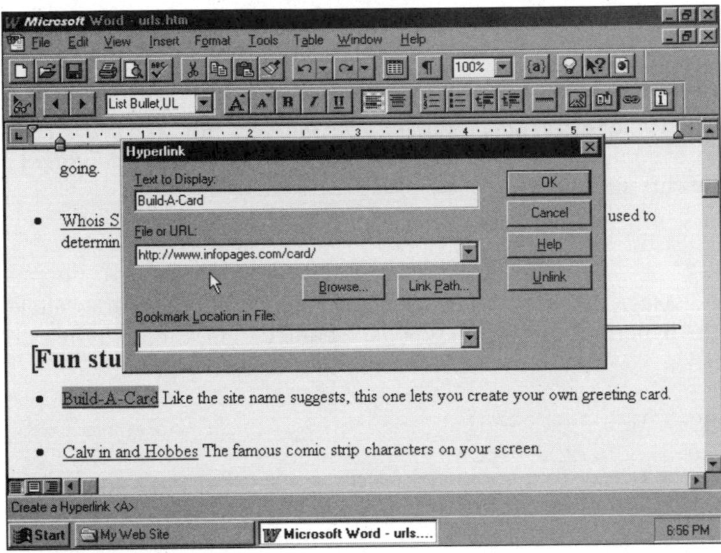

Figure 16-12: Typing the complete URL of the bookmark to which you want to jump.

You need to get online to test this type of link. If you like, you can exit Word IA, open your home page in Internet Explorer (or some other Web browser), and test your link from there. Or, as an alternative, you can use the Web Browse view in Word IA to browse the Web and edit your own Web pages at the same time.

HTML Tags for Hyperlinks and Bookmarks

HTML tags handle the actual links and bookmarks in your Web pages. As always, the tags are only visible in the HTML Source view or a similar view (such as Notepad's). Word IA creates the tags automatically, so you may never have to type the tags yourself, but I want to show you what the tags look like so that you know what you are looking at when you view an HTML page's source.

The basic tag for hyperlinks and bookmarks is `<A>`, which stands for *anchor*. Whether the tag acts as a hyperlink or bookmark depends on whether it contains the `NAME` or `HREF` (Hypertext Reference) attribute. The HTML tag for a bookmark is

```
<A NAME = "bookmarkname">
```

where *bookmarkname* is whatever name you gave the bookmark. For example, if you create a bookmark named FunStuff, the HTML tag for that bookmark would be the following:

```
<A NAME = "FunStuff">
```

The general syntax of a hyperlink is

```
<A HREF = "destinaton">
```

For example, the following tag displays the text *Fun Stuff* as a hot spot. When the reader clicks that hot spot, the browser takes him or her to a bookmark named FunStuff within the current page:

```
<A HREF="#FunStuff" >Fun Stuff</A>
```

The following tag displays the word *Home* as a hyperlink. When the reader clicks on the word Home, the hyperlink sends him to a page named `index.htm` in the current Web site:

```
<A HREF="index.htm" >Home</A>
```

If a hyperlink takes the reader to a bookmark within some other page, both the page name and bookmark name — separated by a # symbol — appear in the tag. For example, the following tag takes the reader to a bookmark named FunStuff within the page named `urls.htm` when the reader clicks it. The hot spot for the link is the text Fun Sites:

```
<A HREF="urls.htm#Fun Stuff" >Fun Sites</A>
```

A link to another Web site contains the complete URL of that site. For example, this tag highlights the words *Alan's Site* in the page. Clicking that text takes the reader to `http://www.coolnerds.com`:

```
<A HREF="http://www.coolnerds.com" >Alan's Site</A>
```

In these examples, the hyperlink consists of a little piece of text — such as *Alan's Site* in the preceding example. If your hot spot is a graphic image rather than a chunk of text, the `<IMG...>` tag for the picture replaces that little chunk of text just before the closing `</A>` tag. In the following example, a picture named minicool.gif is the hot spot. (The alternate text for that hot spot for non-graphical browsers is *Back*.) Clicking this hot spot takes the reader to a page named `index.htm` within the current Web site.

```
<A HREF="index.htm" ><IMG SRC="minicool.bmp" ALT="Back"></A>
```

I've been promising to discuss the Web Browse view, where you can actually try all your links without leaving Word IA. Let's talk about that now.

Testing Hyperlinks with Web Browse View

If you click on a hyperlink while in Word IA's normal Edit view, not much happens. The hyperlink appears highlighted, but you do not go anywhere. To test your links without leaving Word IA, switch from Edit view to Web Browse view. As you may recall, you simply click the Switch to Web Browse view button at the far left side of the toolbar (a pair of eyeglasses) to do so.

Once you are in Web Browse view, the formatting toolbar turns into a Web browsing toolbar. Because this view is about browsing rather than editing, it has buttons such as URL, History, Open Favorites, and so on (Figure 16-13).

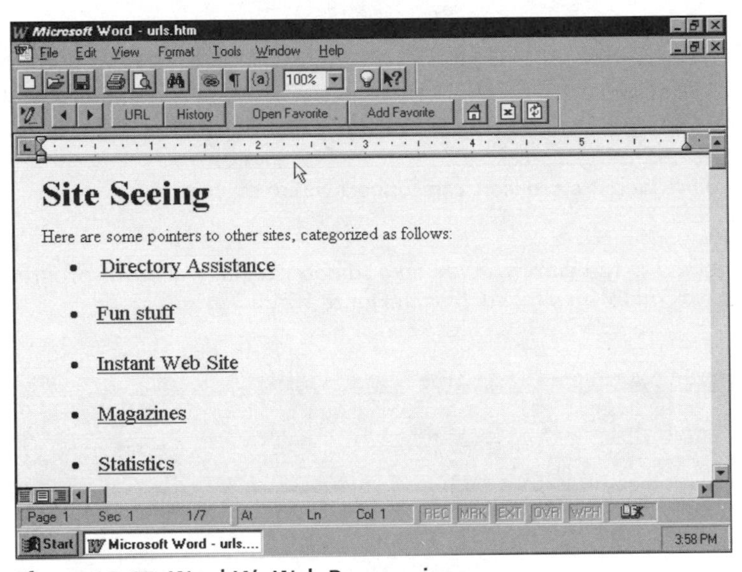

Figure 16-13: Word IA's Web Browse view.

The main beauty of Web Browse view is that it activates your hyperlinks and thus is a great way to test those links. You can even test links to other sites on the Web. When you click a hot spot for such a site, Word IA gives you the option to connect to the Internet right on the spot, as shown in Figure 16-14.

Figure 16-14: Word IA's Web Browse view can connect you to the Net.

Once you're connected to the Web, you see an odometer telling you your progress in connecting to the external Web site, such as in Figure 16-15.

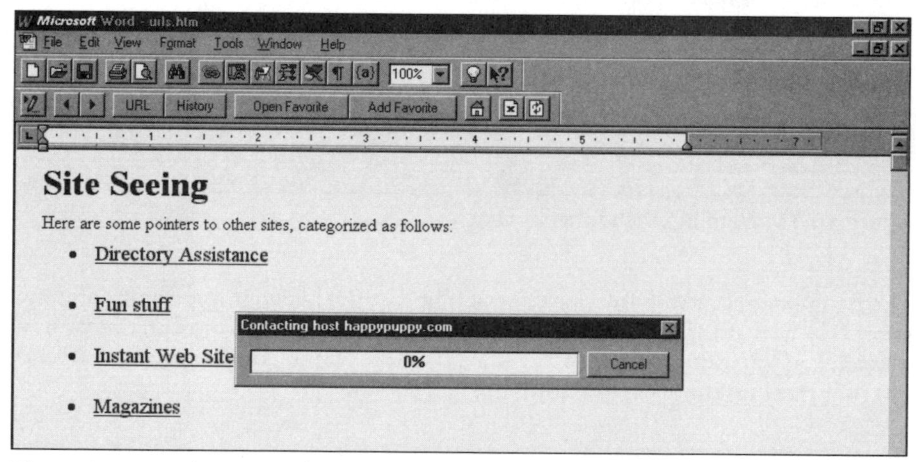

Figure 16-15: Going to another site in Word IA's Web Browse view.

Hot Stuff

You can test a hyperlink right from Edit mode. Just double-click, rather than click, the hot spot.

Web Browse view buttons

Most toolbar buttons in Word IA's Web Browse view work the same as equivalent buttons in a "real" Web browser:

- ✦ **Switch to Edit View.** Takes you out of Web Browse view and back to the normal Edit view for creating and editing Web pages.
- ✦ **Go Back.** Takes you back to your last anchor point.
- ✦ **Go Forward.** Takes you forward to the anchor point from which you just backed up.
- ✦ **URL.** Lets you type in the URL of a site you want to visit.
- ✦ **History.** Displays a list of recently visited sites. To return to a site, click the site name and then click the Go To button.
- ✦ **Open Favorite.** Shows a list of the sites you've added to your Favorite Places in Web Browse view.
- ✦ **Add Favorite.** Adds the site you are currently viewing to your list of favorites.
- ✦ **Home.** Takes you to Word IA's home page.
- ✦ **Stop.** Cancels a download that is taking too long.
- ✦ **Reload Document.** Loads the most recent copy of the document into the browser to ensure that you're viewing current text and graphics.

Handy Web Browse view features

In addition to the Browsing button, the Web Browse view offers two handy features: Copy URL and Reload. The following sections describe how to activate and use these features:

Copy URL

You can click the Copy Hyperlink button or choose Edit⇨Copy Hyperlink to copy the current page's URL to the Windows 95 Clipboard. Afterward, you can paste (Ctrl+V) that URL into any of your pages that you're editing. This method is a handy way to type a long URL and make sure that you get it right.

Reload

If you edit a page, save it, and then go to Web Browse view, you may not see your changes right away. Don't panic — you just need to reload the page from disk. Choose File⇨Reload from the menu bar.

Web Browse view gotchas

Even though Word IA's Web Browse view acts much like a real browser, keep in mind that it is not. You also should never assume that the Web Browse view of a page matches how the same page looks in a real Web browser, such as Internet Explorer or Netscape Navigator. For example, unlike a real browser, the Web Browse view never displays background images or textures. The format of text and graphics in the Web Browse view is much different from how the format looks in a real browser.

Life Saver

If you suddenly lose the capability to navigate and edit within your page, chances are you're in the Web Browse view. Click the Switch to Edit View button or choose View⇨HTML Edit from the menus.

Use the Web Browse view for what it was intended: as an aid to creating Web pages that gives you some ability to test links and copy URLs. If you want to see how a page *really* looks on the Web, use the Preview in Browser button or view it in an actual Web browser such as Netscape Navigator.

Web Browse view isn't as speedy as a real browser. In fact, it can be unbearably slow on some machines. You can use these three little tricks to help Word IA run at the fastest speed possible on your PC:

- ✦ Turn off automatic image loading (Choose View⇨Load Images). You won't see any images until you turn the feature back on, but you won't have to wait for them to appear, either.
- ✦ Close any programs that you are not using. The more resources you give to Word and Word IA, the faster the programs can work.
- ✦ Try using the Full Screen view (choose View⇨Full Screen as discussed in Chapter 12).

Changing/Deleting Hyperlinks and Bookmarks

There are lots of ways to change and delete hyperlinks and bookmarks. In your regular HTML Edit view, you have the following options:

- ✦ To change a hyperlink, click it once to select it and then click the Hyperlink button in the toolbar to get back to its dialog box.
- ✦ To delete a hyperlink, click it once to select it and then press Delete.
- ✦ To delete a bookmark, click the Bookmark button, click the name of the bookmark you want to delete and then click the Delete button.
- ✦ To move a bookmark, move the insertion point to the new location for the bookmark, type the bookmark name, and click the Add button. The new bookmark replaces the old one.

Of course, you also can go into HTML source and work on the HTML tags directly. We get into that type of editing in Chapter 19. As I have already mentioned, if you use Coolsite (Chapter 20) to create lists, it automatically creates outlines, bookmarks, and hyperlinks for you. That feature saves you a great deal of time otherwise spent messing around with tags.

Summary

Most Web sites consist of three main elements: text, pictures, and hyperlinks. At this point, you have the capability and knowledge to create all those things. For all intents and purposes, you are a real Web author now.

But there is also lots more that you can do on the Web, as you learn in the chapters coming up. Let's take a moment to review what you learned in this chapter:

- ✦ To turn an existing word, phrase, or image into a hyperlink, select the text or picture and click the Hyperlink button in the Word IA toolbar.
- ✦ To create a bookmark (a specific "landing place" within a page), click the spot or select the text where you want the reader to land. Click the Bookmark button, type a bookmark name, and then click the Add button.
- ✦ To test your hyperlinks without leaving Word IA, switch to Web Browse view.
- ✦ The Coolsite app that came with this book is useful for maintaining lists and automatically creates outlines, bookmarks, and hyperlinks for those lists.

✦ ✦ ✦

CHAPTER 17

Working Miracles with Tables

In This Chapter

Creating and editing a table

Sizing and positioning a table

Table borders and colors

Aligning pictures to tables

Alphabetizing table rows

Converting tables to text, and vice versa

Tables are one of the best new features to hit the Web. Unfortunately, new also means not widely supported yet. I can show you all kinds of cool things that you can do with tables in your Web site, but I cannot guarantee that all of your readers will be able to *see* your tables the same way that you've formatted them.

On the upside, I think just about everyone knows that tables are sorely needed in Web sites, so it shouldn't be long before all graphical browsers support the capability to create and see them. I'm hoping that, by the time you read this book, tables will be supported by virtually all graphical browsers. Of course, only time will tell. In the meantime, I show you how to make special copy of your table that even people with ancient Web browsers can appreciate.

What Is a Table?

A *table,* in the Web sense, is pretty much the same thing as a table in print publishing: text that is organized into columns and rows for easy reference. For example, Figure 17-1 shows a simple schedule-type table viewed from Internet Explorer.

You also can put pictures in tables. For example, in Figure 17-2, each button is actually within a table cell. The borders within the table are hidden here, so it doesn't really look much like a table. That's okay though, because in this case we want each button to look like it is sitting on the back surface.

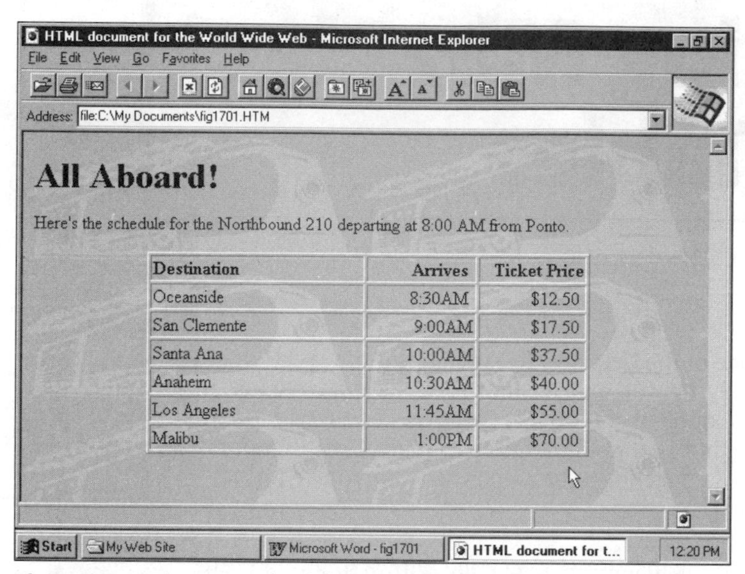

Destination	Arrives	Ticket Price
Oceanside	8:30AM	$12.50
San Clemente	9:00AM	$17.50
Santa Ana	10:00AM	$37.50
Anaheim	10:30AM	$40.00
Los Angeles	11:45AM	$55.00
Malibu	1:00PM	$70.00

Figure 17-1: The train schedule is a table created in Word IA.

Figure 17-2: Each button on this page is actually in a table cell.

You can get real fancy with tables, giving a page the appearance of having columns. Microsoft has some pretty good examples at its site (Figure 17-3). The text hyperlinks and short passages of text are set up in borderless table cells.

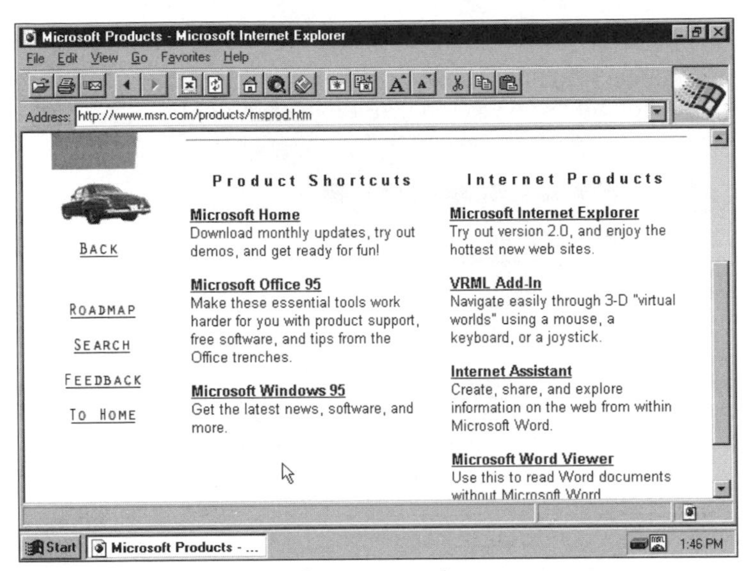

Figure 17-3: A table gives this page a columnar appearance.

Some simple terminology goes with tables: rows, columns, and cells. A *cell* is a single square within the table — the place where a row and column meet (Figure 17-4).

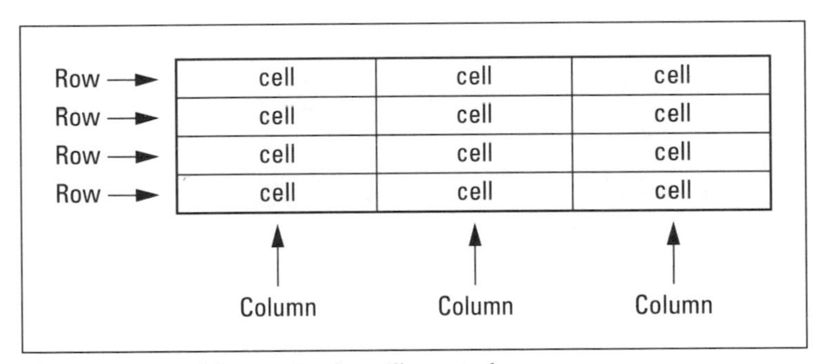

Figure 17-4: Table terminology illustrated.

Creating and Editing Tables

Creating a table is easy. You just follow these steps:

1. In Word IA's normal Edit view, move the insertion point to the approximate spot where you want the table to appear in your Web page.

2. Do one of the following:

   - Click the Table button in the toolbar and drag out a table with the number of rows and columns you want in your table (Figure 17-5).

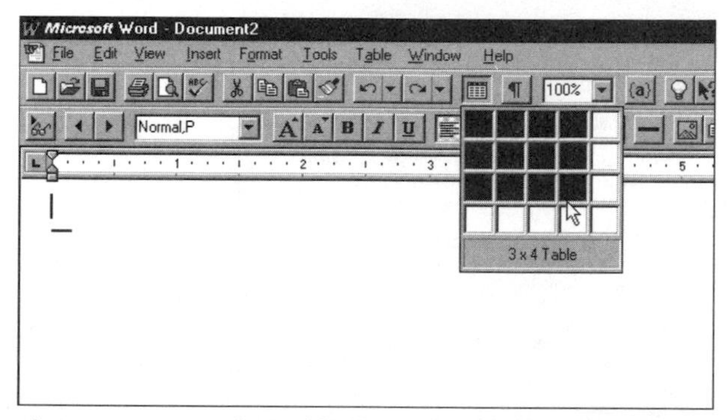

Figure 17-5: Use the Table button to drag out a table size.

   - Alternatively, choose Table➪Insert Table, specify the number of rows and columns you want, leave the Column Width setting at Auto, and click OK.

The table appears in your document with empty cells. Small dotted lines represent the table's gridlines (Figure 17-6).

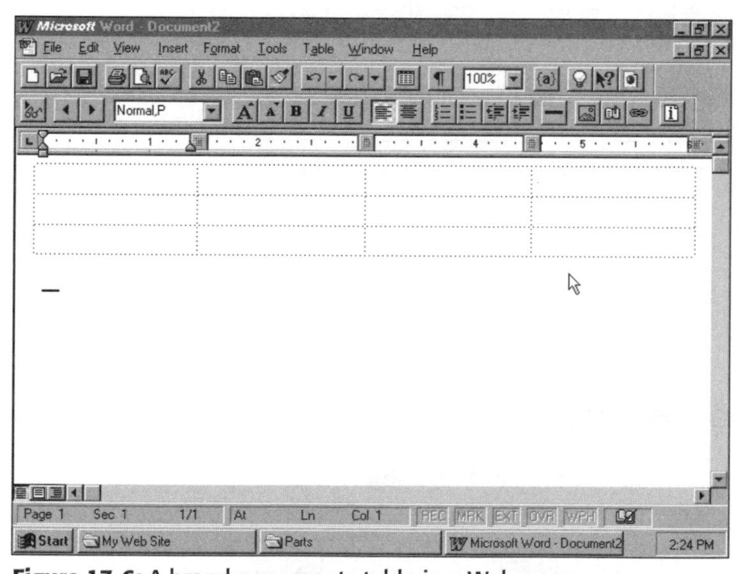

Figure 17-6: A brand new empty table in a Web page.

Navigating and filling a table

Moving around in a table is easy to do, as is placing text or a picture into the cell. Just do the following:

- ✦ To go to a cell, click the cell. You also can use the arrow keys or Tab and Shift+Tab to move from cell to cell.
- ✦ To enter text into a cell, move the insertion point to the cell you want and start typing.
- ✦ If you press Enter while typing in a cell, the entire row grows by a line. If you do this by accident, you can press Backspace to erase the hard return. Alternatively, you can turn on the Show/Hide Paragraphs button and delete the lone paragraph symbol.
- ✦ If you fill in the last cell and then press Tab, you automatically create a new, empty table row.
- ✦ To place a picture in a cell, click in the cell and then click the Picture button in the toolbar.

Be aware that if you view an empty table in a browser, the table appears as a tiny square. The reason is that the table is automatically sized to display its contents in the browser. If the table has no contents, it becomes practically invisible. To really see the table, you need to put some text and/or pictures into it before you view the page with a browser.

Selecting within a table

You can select and work with text inside table cells in the usual manner. You also can select specific cells, columns, rows, or the entire table to help speed editing and formatting tasks. Selected cells always appear in reverse-color. In Figure 17-7, for example, I've selected the entire second row. The following list describes how to select items within a table:

- ✦ To select text within a cell, drag the mouse pointer through the text you want to manipulate.
- ✦ To select an entire cell that already contains text, click just to the left of the text.
- ✦ To select a row, click just to the left of the row you want (click outside the table). You also can click the row you want to select and choose Table➪Select Row.
- ✦ To select a column, click at the very top of the column, right on the border line. Alternatively, click anywhere within the column and choose Table➪Select Column.

✦ To select multiple adjacent cells, drag the mouse pointer through the cells you want to select.

✦ To select the entire table, click anywhere inside the table and choose Table➪Select Table.

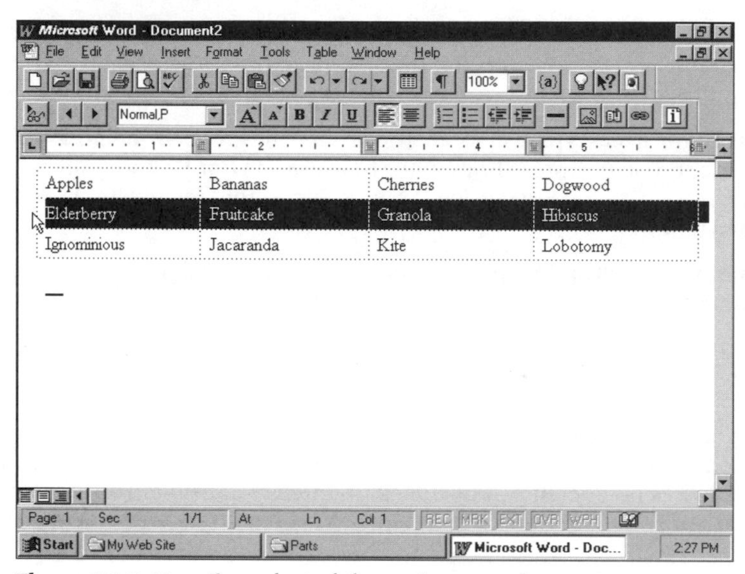

Figure 17-7: Here I've selected the entire second row.

Moving, inserting, and deleting rows and columns

Other easy, table-related tasks include moving things around in a table and changing the size of a table by inserting or deleting rows and columns. The following list explains how:

✦ To move a column, select the entire column (or columns) first. Then point to the middle of a cell within the selection, drag it to its new location, and release the mouse button. Optionally, choose Edit➪Cut to delete the selected column(s), click the new location for those columns, and choose Edit➪Paste Columns.

✦ To move a row, select the row (or rows) that you want to move. Choose Edit➪Cut. Click on the spot where you want to place the deleted row(s), and choose Edit➪Paste Rows.

Hot Stuff

If you want to rearrange table rows into alphabetical order, use the sorting techniques described later in this chapter.

✦ To insert a row within a table, click the location where you need a new row and choose Table➪Insert Rows. A new blank row appears above the row in which the insertion point is located.

✦ To add a new row to the bottom of a table, move to the end of the last cell in the table and press Tab.

✦ To delete a row, select the row(s) you want to delete and choose Table➪Delete Rows from the menus.

✦ To insert a new column within a table, select a column, then choose Table➪Insert Columns. The new column appears to the left of the selected column.

✦ To delete a column, select the column(s) you want to delete and choose Table➪Delete Columns.

Defining a header row

A header row in a table contains the titles that go across the tops of the columns. The contents of these cells are automatically centered and boldfaced for you. Several sample tables in this chapter contain heading rows, including Figure 17-14 (top row), Figure 17-16 (row containing *Milk, A, B1,* and so forth), and Figure 17-22 (row containing *When you know:* . . . and so forth).

To define a header row in your own table, follow these steps:

1. Select the row that contains the text that you want to act as titles atop the columns.
2. Choose Table➪Cell Type➪Table Header➪OK.

You won't see the effects of this command right away because Word IA needs to process the underlying HTML tags. You can see the effects, however, if you close the document (File➪Close➪Yes), and then re-open the same file (choose File➪and the appropriate name from the bottom of the File menu).

Captioning a table

You can give your table a caption that appears above or below the table. Unlike the header row, which contains a title for each column in the table, a caption is just a single cell that spans the entire width of the table. To caption a table, perform the following steps:

1. Click anywhere within the table that you want to caption.
2. Choose Table➪Caption.

3. Type the caption, and select its position from the dialog box that appears (Figure 17-8).

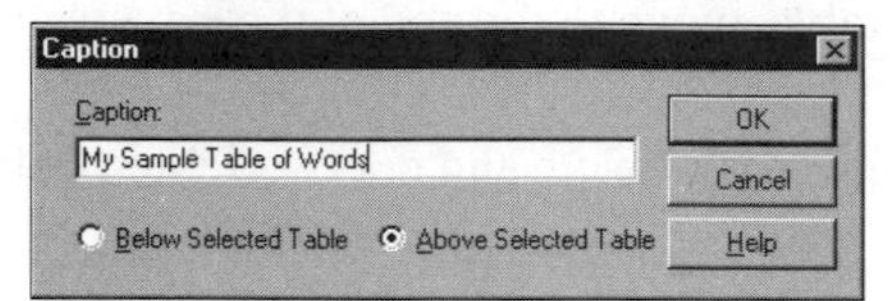

Figure 17-8: Dialog box for captioning a table.

4. Click OK.

The caption becomes part of the table, as in the example shown in Figure 17-9.

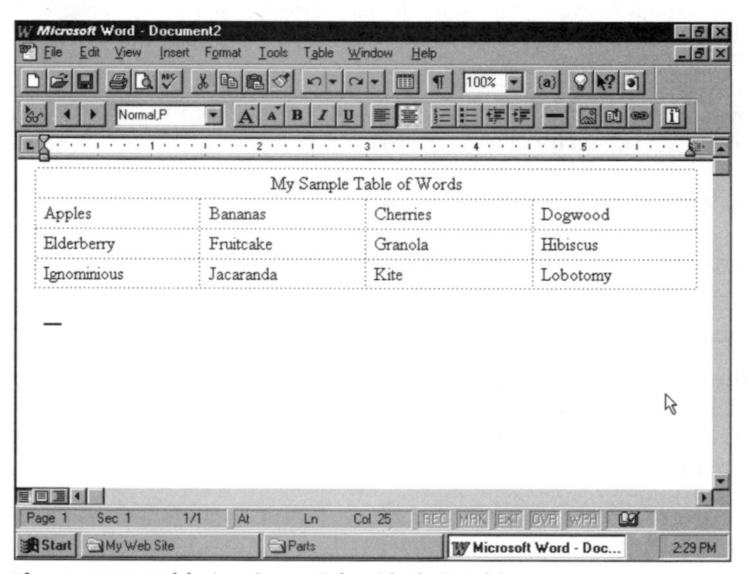

Figure 17-9: Table captions stick with their tables.

The caption is actually a new row added to the table. It appears as a single cell because its cells are automatically merged into a single cell. I talk more about merging cells a little later in this chapter.

Positioning a table on the page

If your table is narrower than the width of the browser window, you can determine how you want the table placed: either aligned with the left margin or centered (Figure 17-10).

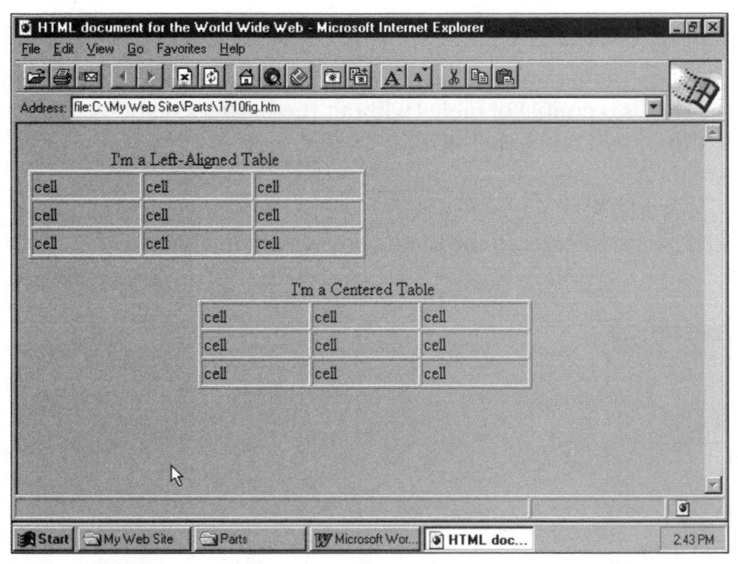

Figure 17-10: Example of a left-aligned and a centered table.

To change the alignment of the entire table:

1. Click anywhere within the table and then choose Table➪Align.
2. In the Entire Table section of the dialog box that appears, choose Left or Center.
3. Click OK.

What's with the blue asterisks?

As you format a table, you may notice a blue, underlined asterisk (*) appearing next to the table and within table cells. The asterisks signify that you are working in WYSIWYG (What You See Is What You Get) mode, which, in turn, means that the appearance of the table in Word IA exactly matches the appearance of the table in your Web browser. In fact, the blue asterisk actually means that the table formatting information has already been converted to, and is stored in, HTML tags. The asterisks never show up in a Web browser, so there is no need to delete them.

Showing/hiding borders

In Figure 17-1 (the train schedule), you saw a sample table with borders displayed. Figure 17-2 and 17-3 shows a couple of tables without the borders displayed. To turn borders on or off in your own table, do the following:

1. Click anywhere in the table.
2. Choose Table⇨Borders to get to the dialog box shown in Figure 17-11.

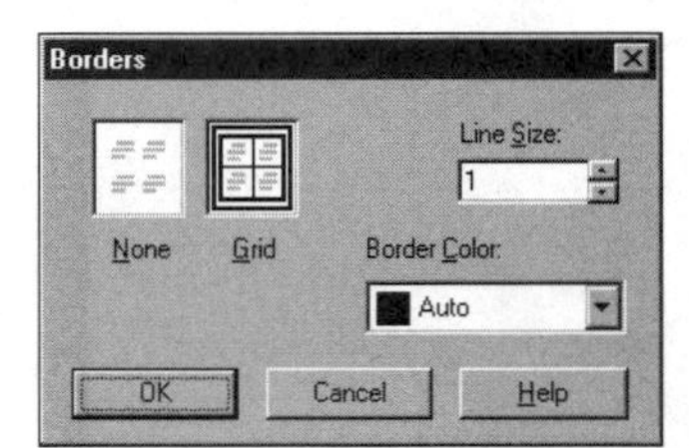

Figure 17-11: The Borders dialog box.

3. If you want your table to have visible borders, choose Grid and then choose a Line Size and Border Color. (In Figure 17-1, the size is 1pt and the color is Auto.)
4. Click OK.

In Edit view, the grid changes from dots to a solid line. To see the actual results, however, you need to look at the table from a browser (click the Preview in Browser button).

Showing/hiding gridlines

The difference between borders and gridlines may seem a little confusing. The Borders command on the Table menu refers to the borders that appear in the browser. You may also notice a Gridlines command on the Table menu. That option refers only to the gridlines that appear in Word IA while you are editing. Personally, I can't think of why you'd want to hide those gridlines. But if you do, click anywhere in the table and choose Table⇨Gridlines. If you change your mind, just choose Table⇨Gridlines again.

Aligning text within cells

You can decide how you want the contents of each cell to be aligned within the cell. In general, you'll probably want to left-align or center text. Numbers and dates look better when you right-align them, as Figure 17-12 illustrates. To align a cell's contents, follow these steps:

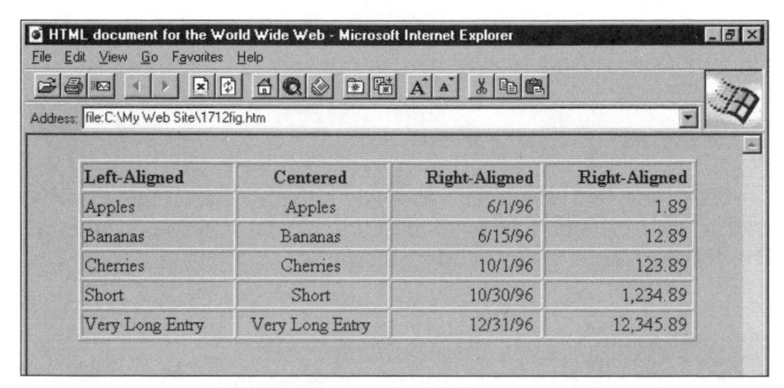

Left-Aligned	Centered	Right-Aligned	Right-Aligned
Apples	Apples	6/1/96	1.89
Bananas	Bananas	6/15/96	12.89
Cherries	Cherries	10/1/96	123.89
Short	Short	10/30/96	1,234.89
Very Long Entry	Very Long Entry	12/31/96	12,345.89

Figure 17-12: Left, Center, and Right alignment within a table.

1. Click the cell whose contents you want to align.

Hot Stuff

Personally, I've found this technique to work *some* of the time but not *all* the time. If it doesn't work, you'll just have to align some cells individually.

2. Choose Table➪Align to get to the Align dialog box shown in Figure 17-13.

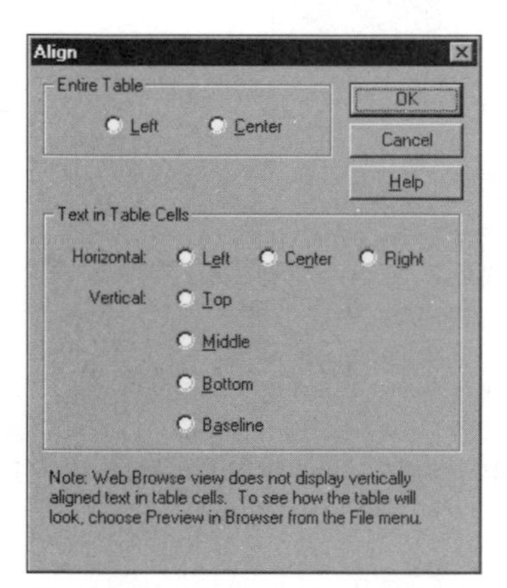

Figure 17-13: The Align dialog box.

3. Next to Horizontal in the Text in Table Cells section, choose an alignment option: Left, Center, or Right.
4. Click OK.

Hot Stuff

In right-aligned cells, you may find that the text lines up too close to the border. You can insert a little gap by typing a space after the text or number in each cell.

Aligning cell contents vertically

You can specify how text and pictures align vertically across a row. This alignment is most apparent when some columns have only one line of text whereas others have lots of text or pictures. Figure 17-14 shows some examples.

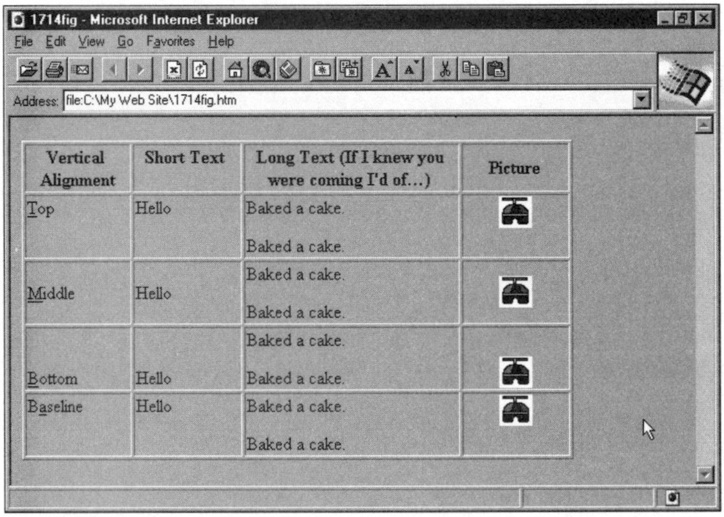

1714fig - Microsoft Internet Explorer

File Edit View Go Favorites Help

Address: file:C:\My Web Site\1714fig.htm

Vertical Alignment	Short Text	Long Text (If I knew you were coming I'd of...)	Picture
Top	Hello	Baked a cake. Baked a cake.	
Middle	Hello	Baked a cake. Baked a cake.	
Bottom	Hello	Baked a cake. Baked a cake.	
Baseline	Hello	Baked a cake. Baked a cake.	

Figure 17-14: Examples of vertical alignment within cells.

To vertically align cell contents, follow these steps:

1. Select the cell(s) you want to realign. You can select a column or the entire table if you like.
2. Choose Table⇨Align to get to the Align dialog box.
3. In the Text in Table Cells section, choose one of the Vertical alignment options: Top, Middle, Bottom, or Baseline.
4. Click OK.

The Baseline option affects the entire row and causes all row items to align along a single baseline. To get an accurate view of how the table will look when published, be sure to preview the page in your Web browser.

Coloring Your Table

You can color all cells within your table or give each cell a different color. Here's how:

1. If you want to color the entire table, click anywhere within the table. If you want to color specific cells, select those cells. You can select entire rows or columns if you want.
2. Choose Table➪Background Color to get to the Background colors dialog box shown in Figure 17-15.

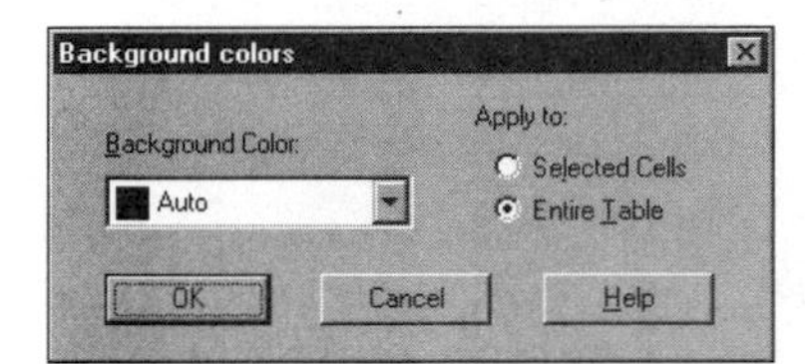

Figure 17-15: The Background colors dialog box.

3. If you want to color just the selected cells, choose Selected Cells.
4. Choose a color under Background Color. Note that the Auto option is actually no color (transparent) in most Web browsers.
5. Click OK.

Figure 17-16 shows an example of a table where I've colored the first column and the first row under the caption white. The remaining cells are set to Auto background color, which is transparent in most browsers. (I've also sized the columns in that example, using the techniques I'll describe in the next section.)

When you first get back to the table, it may look as though the wrong color was applied. That's only because the cells may still be selected. If you unselect these cells by clicking a single cell within the table, you see their true colors.

Be aware that if you color specific cells and then go back and color the entire table, the new color will *not* affect the cells you colored previously. The Entire Table option colors only cells that have never been colored before. To change the color of cells that you colored individually, you must re-select those cells, go back to the Background Colors dialog box, choose Selected Cells again, and then choose the new color for those cells.

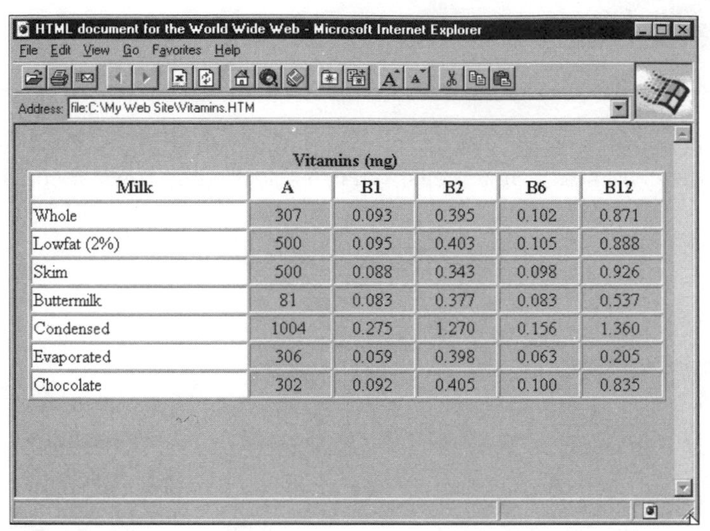

Milk	A	B1	B2	B6	B12
Whole	307	0.093	0.395	0.102	0.871
Lowfat (2%)	500	0.095	0.403	0.105	0.888
Skim	500	0.088	0.343	0.098	0.926
Buttermilk	81	0.083	0.377	0.083	0.537
Condensed	1004	0.275	1.270	0.156	1.360
Evaporated	306	0.059	0.398	0.063	0.205
Chocolate	302	0.092	0.405	0.100	0.835

Figure 17-16: One row and one column are white; the rest are Auto-colored.

Currently, Netscape Navigator 2.0 does not support table cell background colors. Supposedly, however, the next version of Navigator (currently code-named "Atlas") will support this feature.

Sizing Columns

A Web browser typically sizes a table to its contents automatically. For example, suppose that I create a table containing hyperlinks to various pages within some hypothetical Web site, as in Figure 17-17. Although I've turned on the borders and centered all the text within the cells, something still doesn't look quite right.

To create the hyperlinks within the table, I used the standard technique described in Chapter 16. That is, after typing text into a cell, I selected that text, clicked the Hyperlink button, and specified the destination page.

If I widen each column, and perhaps color the table and increase the font size of (or boldface) the text within the table, the table stands out much more, as in Figure 17-18.

There are a couple of ways to size table columns — one using *WYSIWYG* (What You See Is What You Get) sizing and another using *automatic* sizing. With WYSIWYG sizing, you manually set the width of each column. What you see on your Word IA screen is exactly what all your readers will see with their Web browsers. With automatic sizing, no direct correlation exists between what you see in Word IA and what your readers will see. Instead, the reader's Web browser will size the table columns on its own.

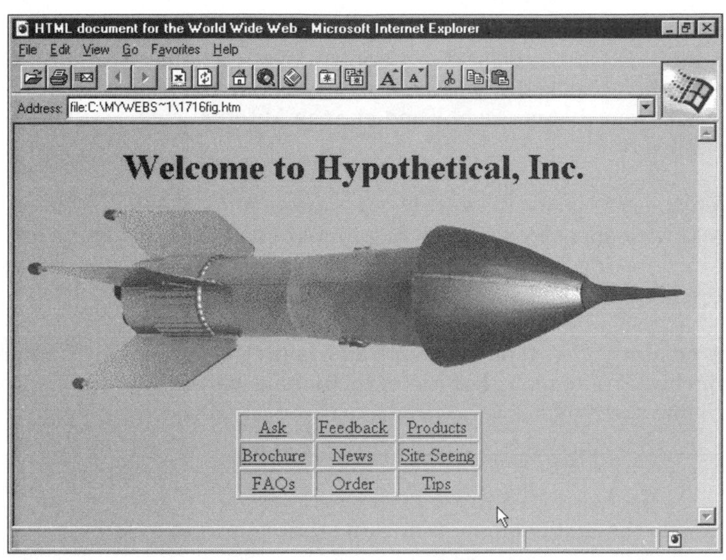

Figure 17-17: Hyperlinks to other pages organized into a table.

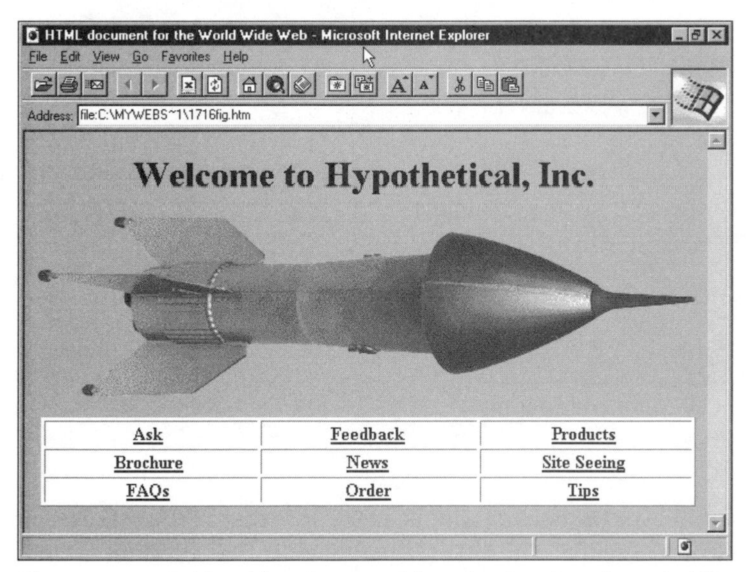

Figure 17-18: Table with columns widened, colored, and text boldfaced.

You can choose which sizing method you want from the Cell Width and Spacing dialog box (shown in Figure 17-19). If you want direct control over column widths, leave the WYSIWYG Column Widths checked. If you want to leave column sizing up to the reader's Web browser, clear that check box and choose Automatically Sized in the Cell Width area of the dialog box.

My personal preference is to go for the WYSIWYG approach. As a general rule of thumb, you can get a nice effect by sizing each column equally and sizing the entire table to about six inches wide. The table in Figure 17-18 is six inches wide, and, as you can see, it fills the screen pretty nicely on a 640 × 480 desktop area.

The arithmetic for creating other table elements also is pretty easy if you assume a total width of six inches for the table. For example, to make two equal-width columns, you make each column three inches wide. To make three equal-width columns, make each column two inches wide, and so on. Here's how you go about setting those column widths:

1. Click anywhere in the first column of the table that you want to size.
2. Choose Table⇨Cell Width and Spacing to get to the dialog box shown in Figure 17-19.

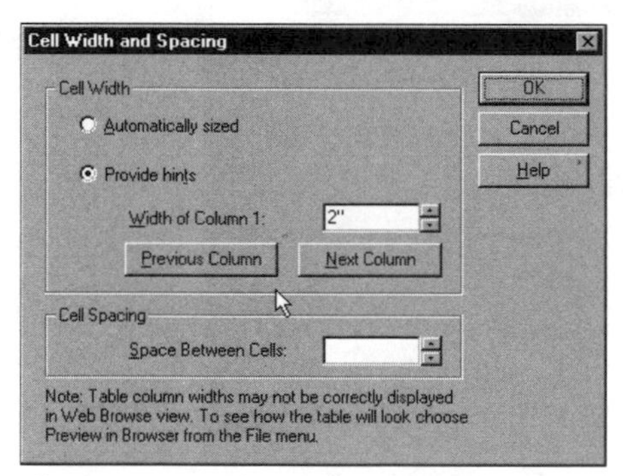

Figure 17-19: The Cell Width and Spacing dialog box.

3. For tight control over the column widths, make sure that WYSIWYG Column Widths is selected and then choose the Provide hints radio button.
4. Enter a measurement for the first column, in inches, next to Width of Column *x*.
5. Click the Next Column button to move on to the next column in the table.
6. Repeat Steps 4 and 5 until you have sized each column in the table.
7. Optionally, you can choose Space Between Cells to add a little blank space between each column.
8. Click OK.

Hot Stuff

You can specify cell widths as percentages of overall table width by inserting your own HTML markup tags (see Chapter 19). Also, to change the units of measure for specifying cell widths, you can choose Tools⇨Options⇨General⇨Measurement Units.

Your table is resized in your Edit window. For a truly accurate picture, however, you need to use Preview in Browser to view how your readers will see the table.

Aligning Pictures to Tables

You can "float" a picture to the left of a table. For example, to create the page shown in Figure 17-20, I first inserted the picture of the key by using the standard Picture button (no table). Within the Picture dialog box, I used the Options tab to set the Alignment with Text option to Left.

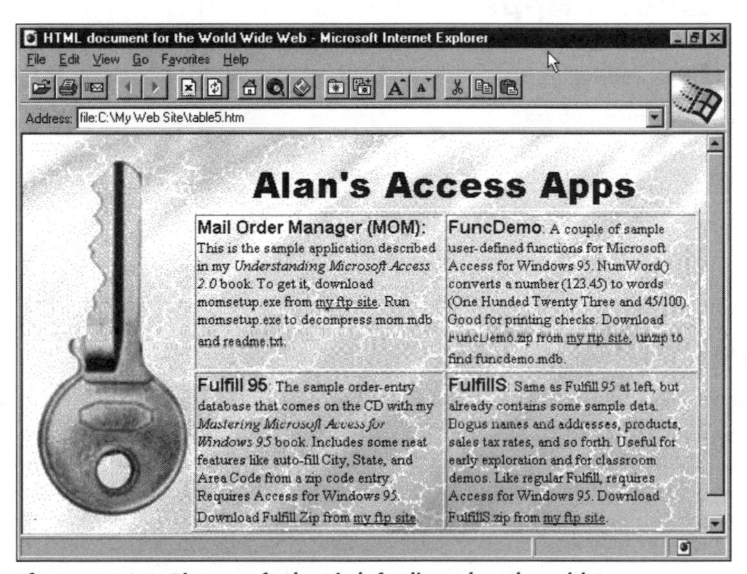

Figure 17-20: Picture of a key is left-aligned to the table.

Then I created the table just to the right of the picture. I sized each column to approximately two inches, making the total width of the table approximately four inches and leaving a couple of inches for the picture of the key. The text, *Alan's Access Apps,* is the table caption displayed in a large Arial Black font.

Hot Stuff

I could hide the borders in the table shown in Figure 17-20 to give the text a columnar look. It would look something like the sample Microsoft page I showed you back in Figure 17-3. If I did that, I'd probably make each column narrower, and put more space between the columns. Those changes would help put a bigger gap between the columns and compensate for the lack of a visible border between the columns.

I should warn you that in Edit view, the table always appears to be under the picture, as in Figure 17-21. As usual, to get the real picture, you need to take a quick peek using the Preview in Browser button.

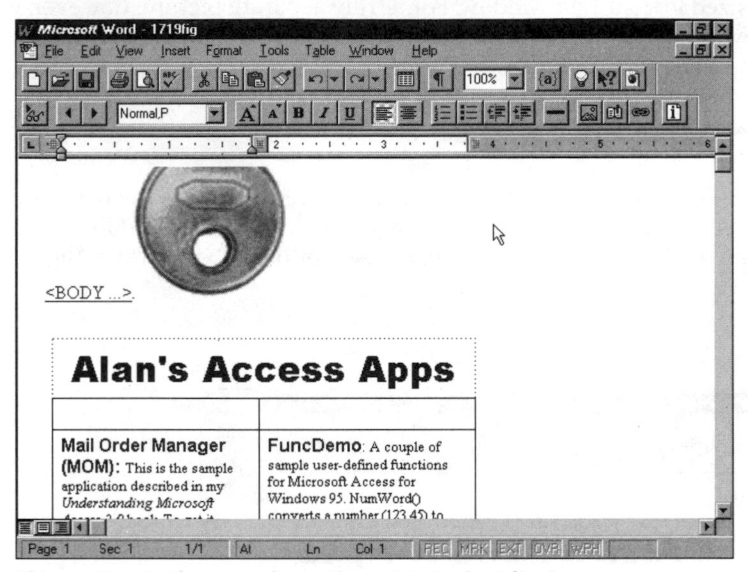

Figure 17-21: The page from Figure 17-20 in Edit view.

Merging and Splitting Cells

You can merge and split cells across columns. Merging cells removes the borders from inside the cells — handy for creating centered titles within a cell. To demonstrate what I mean, take a look at the table in Figure 17-22. Notice that the subtitles MASS AND WEIGHT and LIQUID VOLUME have blank cells next to them. In a Web browser, these blank cells look really weird, as in Figure 17-23.

To fix the problem, you can merge the cells that contain those subtitles into a single wide cell. Then, if you like, center the text within that cell. First, here are the general instructions for merging cells:

1. Select the cells you want to merge.
2. Choose Table⇨Merge Cells.

That's it. Say that I want to merge the cells that contain subtitles in my table. First, I select all cells across that row, as in Figure 17-24.

Converting Common Measurement Units		
When you know:	You can find:	If you multiply by:
MASS AND WEIGHT		
fluid ounces	grams	28
pounds	kilograms	0.45
short tons	metric tons	0.9
LIQUID VOLUME		
ounces	milliliters	30
pints	liters	0.47
quarts	liters	0.95
gallons	liters	3.8

Figure 17-22: MASS AND WEIGHT and LIQUID VOLUME have blank cells to the right.

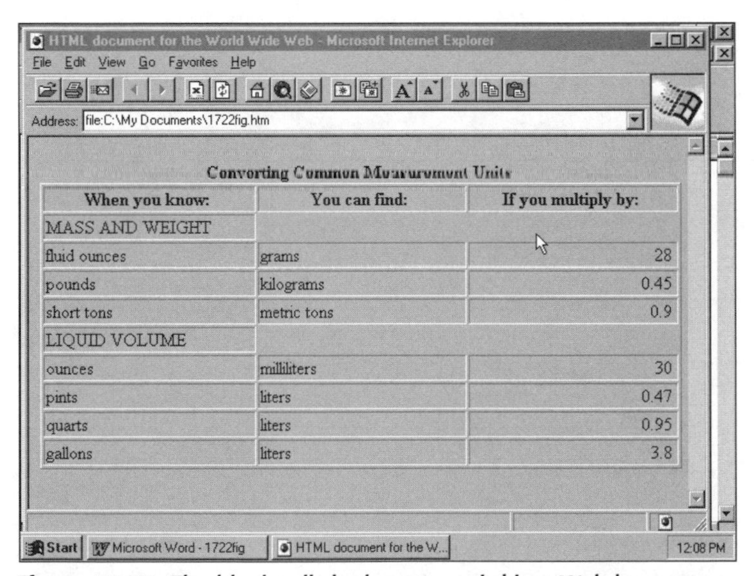

Converting Common Measurement Units		
When you know:	You can find:	If you multiply by:
MASS AND WEIGHT		
fluid ounces	grams	28
pounds	kilograms	0.45
short tons	metric tons	0.9
LIQUID VOLUME		
ounces	milliliters	30
pints	liters	0.47
quarts	liters	0.95
gallons	liters	3.8

Figure 17-23: The blank cells look pretty weird in a Web browser.

Then I choose Table⇨Merge Cells. The selected cells become one cell. I can then click the Center button to center the text within that wide cell.

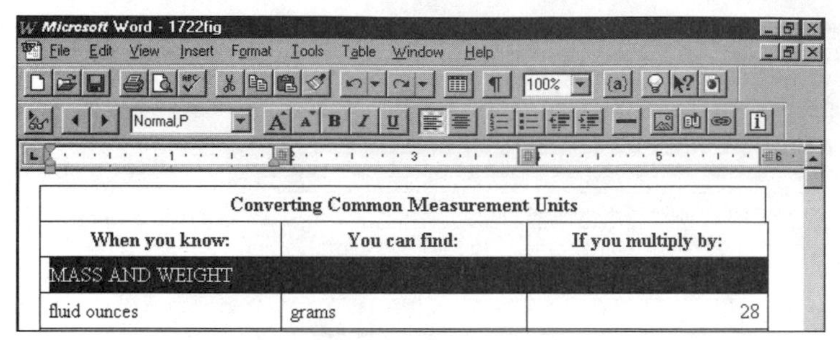

Converting Common Measurement Units		
When you know:	**You can find:**	**If you multiply by:**
MASS AND WEIGHT		
fluid ounces	grams	28

Figure 17-24: The cells that I want to join are selected.

Puzzled? If your merged cell becomes two rows wide, you simply need to delete the extra paragraph mark in the cell. Move to the end of the text in the cell and press Delete. Alternatively, you can turn on Show/Hide Paragraphs and remove the extra paragraph symbol in the cell.

I repeat the process for the row containing the LIQUID VOLUME subtitle, and my table ends up looking like Figure 17-25 (in Edit View). As you can see in Figure 17-26, this table looks better in the browser as well.

Converting Common Measurement Units		
When you know:	**You can find:**	**If you multiply by:**
MASS AND WEIGHT		
fluid ounces	grams	28
pounds	kilograms	0.45
short tons	metric tons	0.9
LIQUID VOLUME		
ounces	milliliters	30

Figure 17-25: MASS AND WEIGHT and LIQUID VOLUME centered in merged cells.

A potential problem with merged cells is that they make it practically impossible to go back into the table and resize columns. That is, you can do it — but the results are really wacky because some rows have more columns than others. If you need to resize columns after the fact, I suggest that you re-divide any merged cells back into the original number of columns. Then resize the columns. To split a cell into multiple columns, follow these steps:

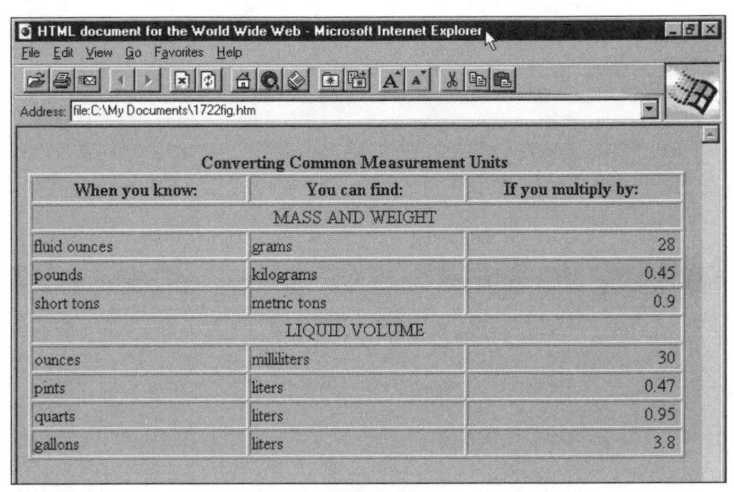

Converting Common Measurement Units

When you know:	You can find:	If you multiply by:
MASS AND WEIGHT		
fluid ounces	grams	28
pounds	kilograms	0.45
short tons	metric tons	0.9
LIQUID VOLUME		
ounces	milliliters	30
pints	liters	0.47
quarts	liters	0.95
gallons	liters	3.8

Figure 17-26: Figure 17-25's table in the Web browser.

1. Click the cell you want to split (or select multiple cells).
2. Choose Table⇨Split Cells.
3. Choose the number of columns that you want to split the cell(s) into.
4. Click OK.

Hot Stuff

Chapter 28 illustrates an interactive version of the sample conversion table shown here. If you have a JavaScript-capable browser such as Netscape Navigator 2.0, you also can try out the interactive version found on the *Web Publishing Uncut* CD-ROM or in my Web site at http://www.coolnerds.com. This version is located in the JavaScript area.

HTML Tags for Tables

The HTML tags for tables seem pretty hairy (er, I mean, "complex") when you view the HTML source. They are not quite so complex when you break them down, though. But what do you care? You use Internet Assistant, so you may never have to manually tweak table tags. But to help you recognize the tags in the future, Figure 17-27 shows a fairly simple table in Internet Explorer and the behind-the-scenes HTML tags that format the table. The following is a quick explanation of the tags.

<TABLE>: All tables start with a <TABLE> tag. If the table has a border, that attribute is defined in this tag. For example, <TABLE BORDER="1"> defines the start of a table with a 1-point border.

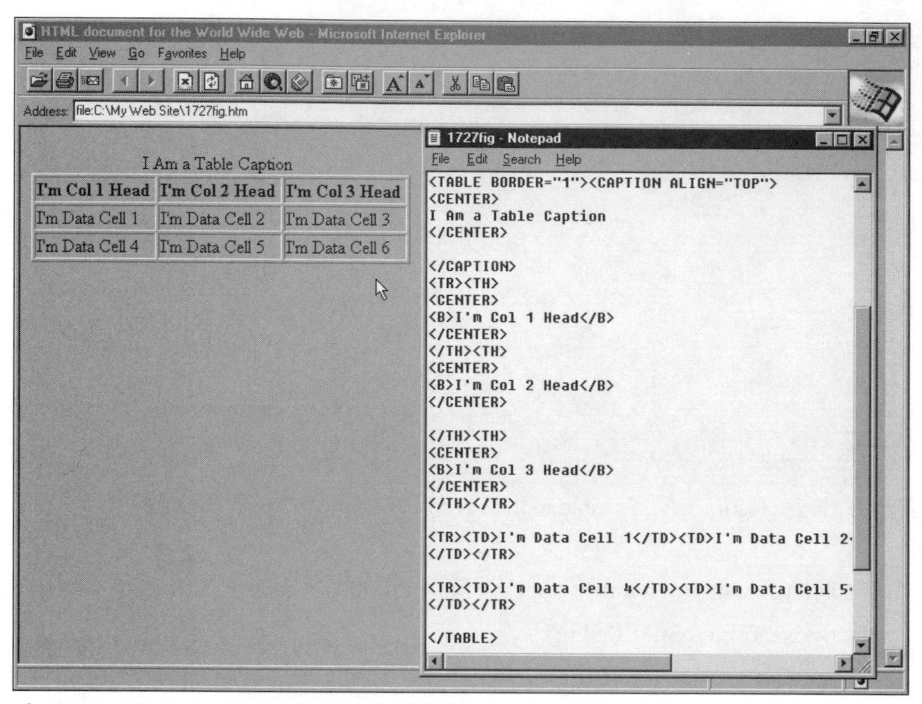

Figure 17-27: A simple table and the HTML tags that define it.

<CAPTION>...</CAPTION>**:** This tag identifies the table caption. The first tag usually contains an ALIGN attribute that identifies the position of the caption as "TOP" (above the table) or BOTTOM (below the table).

<TR>**:** This tag marks the beginning of each row in the table. Within the row, each cell is defined as either a table header (<TH>) or a table data (<TD>) cell.

<TH>...</TH>**:** These tags mark the beginning and end of a single cell defined as a table header. Typically, they contain the <B>...</B> (boldface) and <CENTER>...</CENTER> tags that boldface and center the contents of the cell.

<TD>...</TD>**:** These tags mark the start and end of each data cell. The contents of the cell, as well as any formatting tags for that cell, are contained within these tags.

</TR>**:** This tag marks the end of a table row.

</TABLE>**:** This tag marks the end of the table.

More Cool Table Tricks

The material covered so far in this chapter lets you create just about any table imaginable. But there are a few other tricks I feel compelled to mention before moving on to another topic.

Sorting (alphabetizing) table rows

You can sort (alphabetize) the rows in your table based on any column in the table. You also can select multiple columns for the sort, to get a sort-within-a-sort effect. For example, take a look at the small table in Figure 17-28. The names within the table do not appear in any particular order.

If I sorted the rows into alphabetical order by the first two columns, Last Name and First Name, the rows would be reshuffled into alphabetical order by Last Name. The First Name column would act as the tie-breaker should any rows have identical last names in them. Hence, sorting the table in Figure 17-28 by its first two columns produces the result shown in Figure 17-29. The rows are alphabetized, and within the identical Smith entries, the rows are alphabetized by first name: Annette, then Petra, then Zeke. Just like the real phone book.

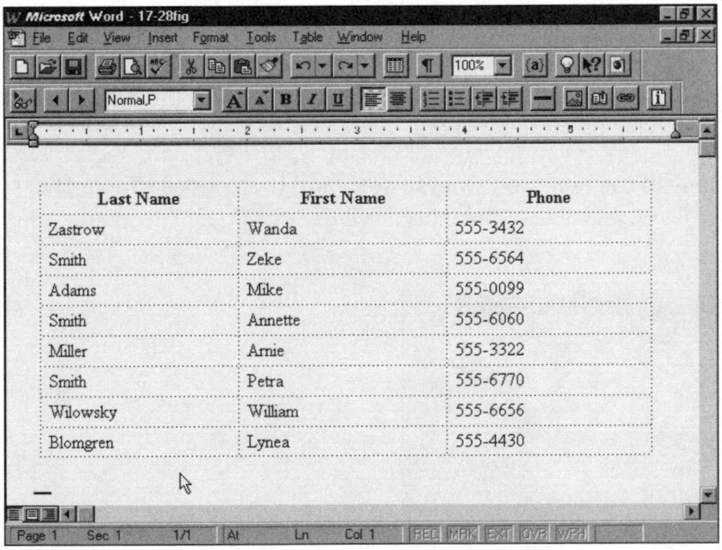

Last Name	First Name	Phone
Zastrow	Wanda	555-3432
Smith	Zeke	555-6564
Adams	Mike	555-0099
Smith	Annette	555-6060
Miller	Arnie	555-3322
Smith	Petra	555-6770
Wilowsky	William	555-6656
Blomgren	Lynea	555-4430

Figure 17-28: Table with rows in random order.

Last Name	First Name	Phone
Adams	Mike	555-0099
Blomgren	Lynea	555-4430
Miller	Arnie	555-3322
Smith	Annette	555-6060
Smith	Petra	555-6770
Smith	Zeke	555-6564
Wilowsky	William	555-6656
Zastrow	Wanda	555-3432

Figure 17-29: Table from Figure 17-28 after sorting on first two columns.

One small potential problem with sorting is that if your table has header rows and a caption, the header rows get sorted along with the rest of the rows. To avoid this problem, you can delete the caption row before you sort. Alternatively, let the rows fall where they may, then cut and paste the header rows back to the top of the table. Other than that, sorting is pretty easy to do:

1. Click anywhere in the table you want to sort, and then choose Table⇨Sort. You come to the dialog box shown in Figure 17-30.

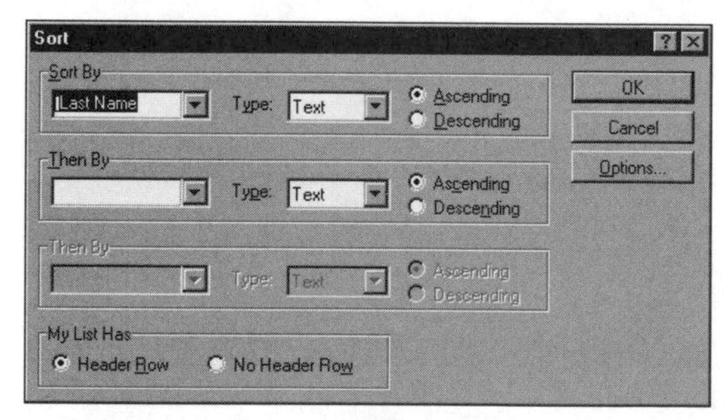

Figure 17-30: The Sort dialog box.

2. Choose the column to sort by, and then select either Ascending (A to Z) or Descending (Z to A).

3. If you want to define tie-breaker columns, choose column names and orders from the Then By boxes.
4. If your table has a header row, choose Header Row in the My List Has section.
5. Click OK.

Word IA sorts the rows right after you click OK. Then you're done!

Converting text to a table

You may have already typed some text and put it into rows and columns using tabs and spaces. You can easily convert that text to a table. But to get the right results, you need to understand *how* Word IA converts text to a table. Simply stated, each line will be converted to a table row. Within a line, each tab will mark the beginning of a new table column. The trick here is to make sure that only one tab character exists per column *before* you do the conversion. The verification process is easy to do, as this example will show.

First, take a look at Figure 17-31. There's some text organized into rows and columns. Each column may appear to be separated by a single tab. But looks can be deceiving.

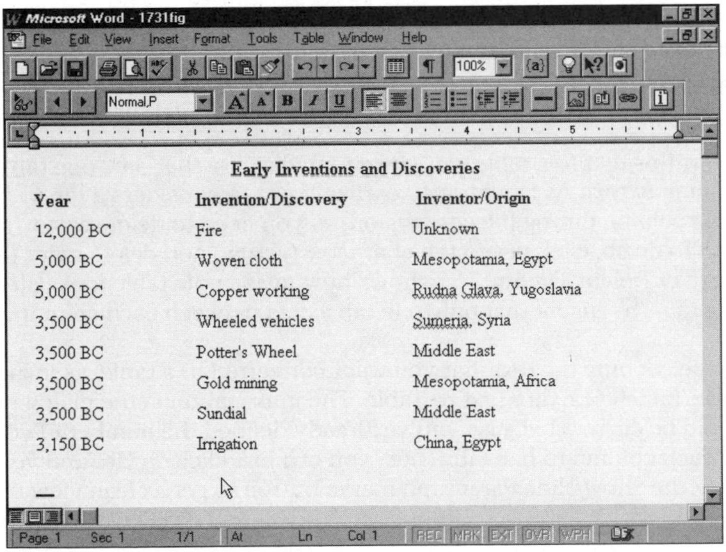
Microsoft Word - 1731fig
File Edit View Insert Format Tools Table Window Help
Early Inventions and Discoveries
Year Invention/Discovery Inventor/Origin
12,000 BC Fire Unknown
5,000 BC Woven cloth Mesopotamia, Egypt
5,000 BC Copper working Rudna Glava, Yugoslavia
3,500 BC Wheeled vehicles Sumeria, Syria
3,500 BC Potter's Wheel Middle East
3,500 BC Gold mining Mesopotamia, Africa
3,500 BC Sundial Middle East
3,150 BC Irrigation China, Egypt
Page 1 Sec 1 1/1 At Ln Col 1

Figure 17-31: Text typed into rows and columns using tabs.

To make sure, you need to turn on the Show/Hide Paragraphs feature (click the button in the toolbar). You now can see the actual tabs (represented as arrows) and the hard returns that end each row, as shown in Figure 17-32.

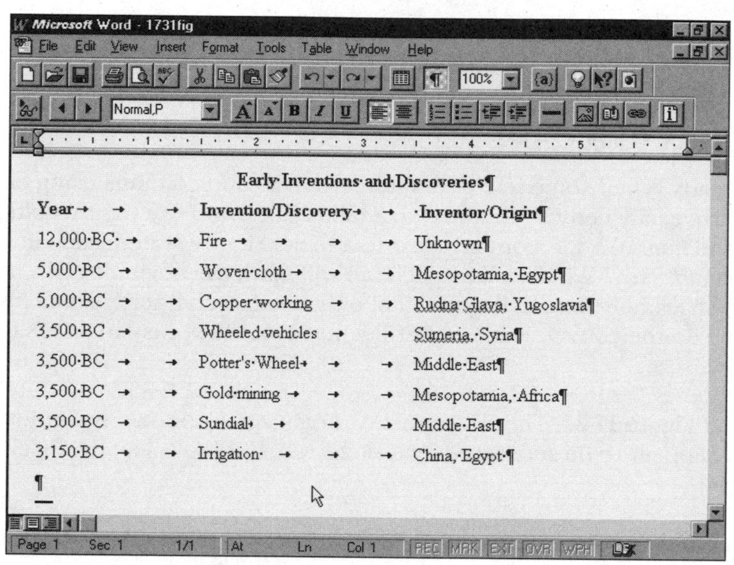

Figure 17-32: Tabs (right arrows) and hard returns (paragraph marks) are now visible.

To properly convert this text to a table, you need to make sure that only one tab exists between each column of text. As I mentioned earlier, Word IA considers a tab to be the start of a new table column during the conversion, so you need to delete any extra tabs between columns. To do so, click near a tab character (arrow) and delete extra tabs by using Backspace or Delete. Figure 17-33 shows how my sample table looks after removing all extra tabs, to ensure that only one tab exists between each column.

Next, you want to select only the text that you want converted to a table, as in Figure 17-34. Then choose Table➪Convert Text to Table. The information in the dialog box that appears should be correct because you've already defined the number of columns by limiting each column to one tab. Thus, you can just click on OK, and you are done. You can click the Show/Hide Paragraph marks button to get a clean view of the results, as in Figure 17-35.

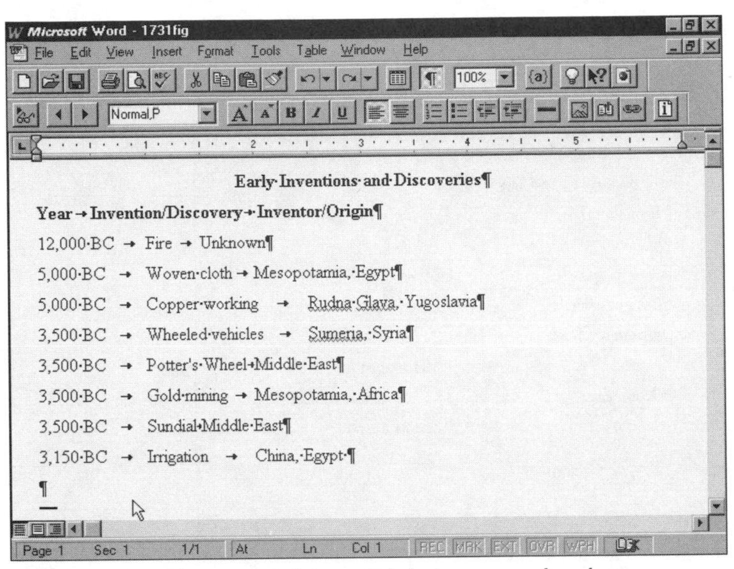

Figure 17-33: One, and only one, tab between each column.

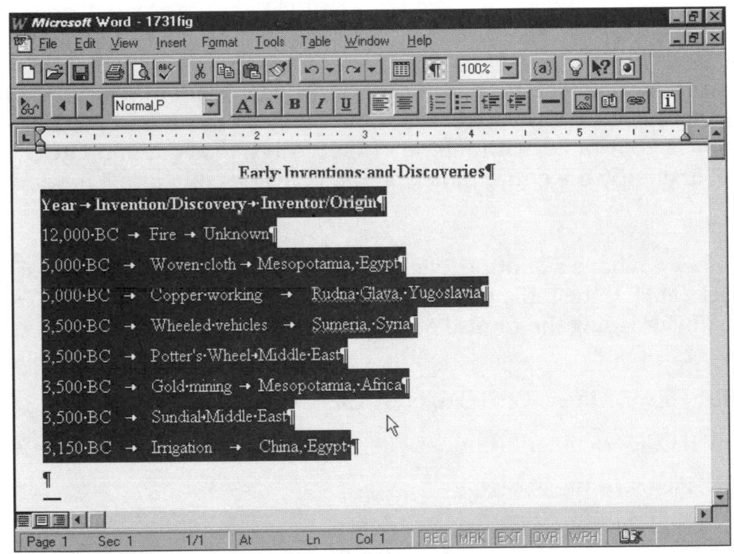

Figure 17-34: Text to be converted to a table is selected.

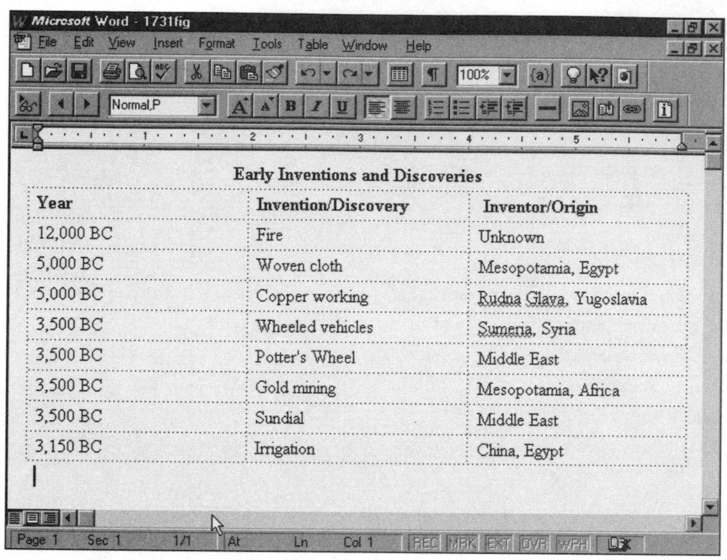

Early Inventions and Discoveries

Year	Invention/Discovery	Inventor/Origin
12,000 BC	Fire	Unknown
5,000 BC	Woven cloth	Mesopotamia, Egypt
5,000 BC	Copper working	Rudna Glava, Yugoslavia
3,500 BC	Wheeled vehicles	Sumeria, Syria
3,500 BC	Potter's Wheel	Middle East
3,500 BC	Gold mining	Mesopotamia, Africa
3,500 BC	Sundial	Middle East
3,150 BC	Irrigation	China, Egypt

Figure 17-35: Conversion to a table is complete.

Converting a table to text

As I mentioned earlier, not all Web browsers support tables. Readers who view your table without an appropriate browser will see something of a mess. You may want to make an extra copy of your table, without the <TABLE> tags, to accommodate these readers. To do so, first copy the entire table and then paste a copy into a new document as follows:

1. If the table *does not* have a caption, click anywhere in the table and choose Table⇨Select Table. If the table does have a caption, select all the rows *except* the caption (by dragging the mouse pointer down the left margin next to the rows you want to select).
2. Choose Edit⇨Copy or press Ctrl+C to copy the table to the Clipboard.
3. Create a new HTML document (choose File⇨New⇨HTML (or HTML.DOT)⇨OK).
4. Choose Edit⇨Paste, or press Ctrl+V.

Let's say that your copied table now looks like Figure 17-36.

To convert the table to text

1. Click anywhere inside the table.
2. Choose Table⇨Select Table.
3. Choose Table⇨Convert Table to Text.

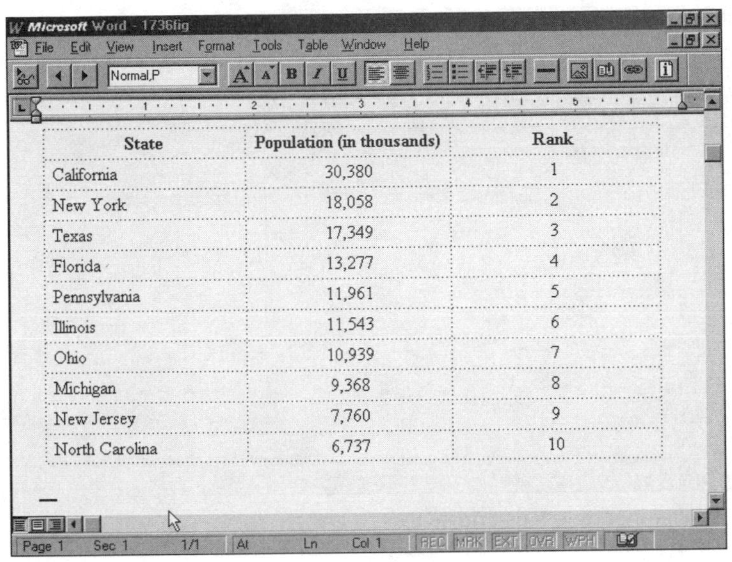

State	Population (in thousands)	Rank
California	30,380	1
New York	18,058	2
Texas	17,349	3
Florida	13,277	4
Pennsylvania	11,961	5
Illinois	11,543	6
Ohio	10,939	7
Michigan	9,368	8
New Jersey	7,760	9
North Carolina	6,737	10

Figure 17-36: Copied table before converting to text.

4. Choose Tabs and then OK.
5. The text of the table should still be selected, so now would be a good time to convert it using the monospace *PRE* format. Choose Preformatted,PRE from the Styles drop-down list.

Your table may look pretty ugly at first, as in Figure 17-37. But all you need to do is insert tabs and spaces to realign the text into columns, as in Figure 17-38.

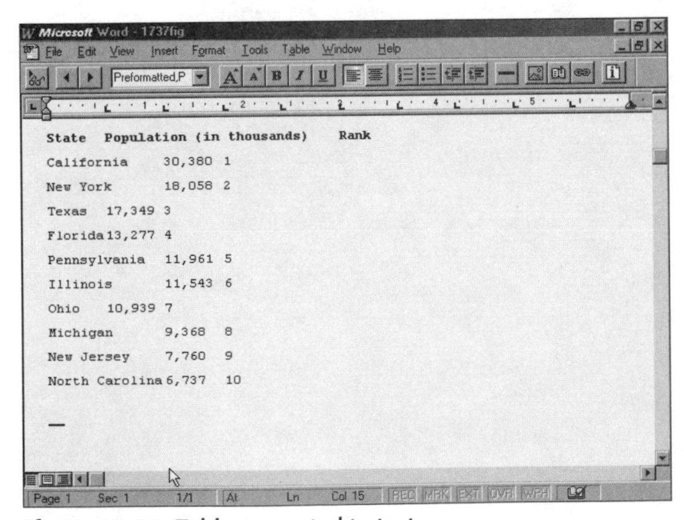

Figure 17-37: Table converted to text.

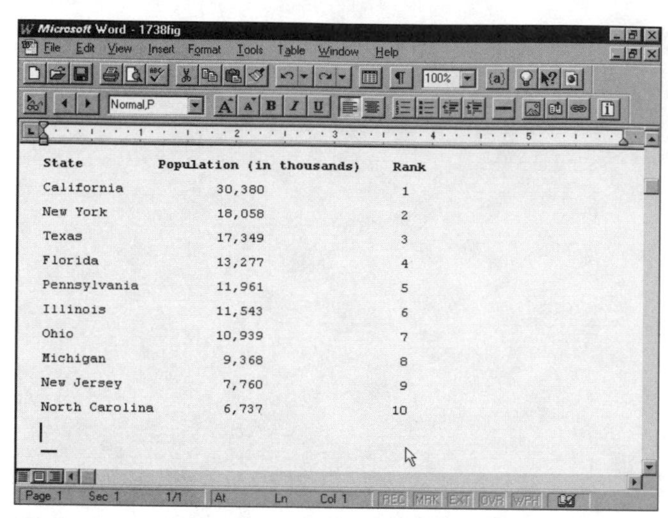

State	Population (in thousands)	Rank
California	30,380	1
New York	18,058	2
Texas	17,349	3
Florida	13,277	4
Pennsylvania	11,961	5
Illinois	11,543	6
Ohio	10,939	7
Michigan	9,368	8
New Jersey	7,760	9
North Carolina	6,737	10

Figure 17-38: Table after inserting tabs and spaces to realign columns.

In most Web browsers, the converted text looks identical to Figure 17-38 because you applied the PRE style (introduced back in Chapter 13) to the text. If you look at the HTML tags for the page, you should see a `<PRE>` tag above and a `</PRE>` tag below the converted table.

Now you can go back to the original table and put in a hyperlink that says something like *If the table is a mess, try the other view.* Have that hyperlink pull up the page that contains the converted table. In the page that contains the converted table, add a hyperlink that takes the reader back to the previous page or to wherever seems appropriate in your site.

Summary

Tables are mighty handy, and can be used in all kinds of creative ways within a Web site. The most important points to remember are as follows:

✦ To create a table, click the Insert Table button and drag out a mini-table with the number of rows and columns you want in your table.

✦ To fill a table, move the insertion point to wherever you want to type and type the cell's contents.

✦ All commands for working with the table, whether you want to work with the entire table or just selected cells within a table, are located in the Table pull-down menu.

✦ Use the Table⇨Borders commands to show/hide table borders in Web browsers.

✦ Use the Table⇨Cell Width and Spacing command to set an approximate size for each column in your table.

✦ If you want the table to fit in most Web browser windows, keep its width equal to or less than six inches.

✦ To accommodate Web browsers that do not support tables, consider making a text version of your table formatted with the Preformatted, PRE style.

✦ ✦ ✦

Interactive Webbing with Forms

✦ ✦ ✦ ✦

In This Chapter

Adding fill-in-the-blank forms to your site to get information from your readers if your ISP supports forms

Creating forms

Text boxes, radio buttons, check boxes, drop-down lists, and all that jazz

How your reader's responses will look when you get them

Testing your forms

✦ ✦ ✦ ✦

Web publishing becomes much more interesting when you enable your readers to give you feedback, make suggestions, publish tips, and ask questions. Forms can do all that and more. Web publishing can become profitable when you let people order products or join your mailing list. Regardless of the type of information you want to get from readers, you'll use a *form* to get that information. In this chapter, I show you how to create forms for your Web site using Word IA.

Web Forms

Unless you've been living on some other planet, you surely know what a form is. You've probably filled in hundreds of forms in your lifetime. If you can't think of a specific example, see if this rings a bell: income tax form (ugh). The electronic forms that appear on the Web usually are not as odious as Uncle Sam's 1040. Figure 18-1 shows a somewhat more appetizing form on the Web.

Puzzled? As far as I know, a real business named Click-A-Pizza does not exist on the Web. That form was made up for this book. But if you search Yahoo! or some other engine for pizza, you may find a pizza joint in your area that delivers.

Form fields

Field is the technical term for a "blank" that appears on one of those fill-in-the-blanks forms. Several varieties of fields exist that you can use on your Web forms. Each field type is designed to handle a specific type of response from the reader.

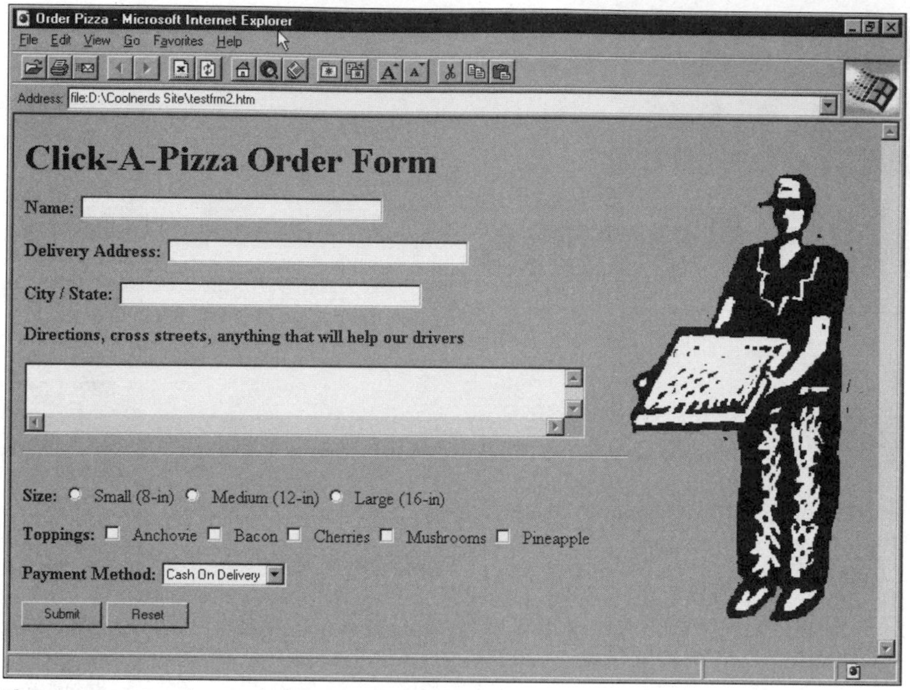

Order Pizza - Microsoft Internet Explorer

File Edit View Go Favorites Help

Address: file:D:\Coolnerds Site\testfrm2.htm

Click-A-Pizza Order Form

Name:

Delivery Address:

City / State:

Directions, cross streets, anything that will help our drivers

Size: Small (8-in) Medium (12-in) Large (16-in)

Toppings: Anchovie Bacon Cherries Mushrooms Pineapple

Payment Method: Cash On Delivery

Submit Reset

Figure 18-1: An electronic form on the Web.

Text fields

Text fields let the reader type in text. There are two types of text fields: Single Line fields and Multi-Line fields. In Figure 18-2, the Name, Delivery Address, and City/State fields are all Single Line text fields. The larger Directions . . . field is a Multi-Line field.

Name:

Delivery Address:

City / State:

Directions, cross streets, anything that will help our drivers

Figure 18-2: Examples of Single Line and Multi-Line text fields.

Check box

You use a check box to accept a yes/no answer or to enable a reader to make several selections from a list of options. Figure 18-3 shows some examples of check boxes. Unlike Figure 18-1, here I arranged the check boxes vertically rather than horizontally.

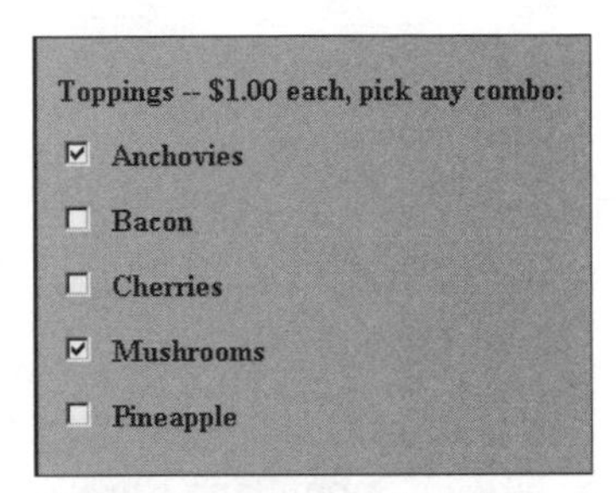

Figure 18-3: Examples of check box form fields.

Radio buttons (option buttons)

Radio buttons, also called *option buttons,* can accept a single choice from a list of mutually-exclusive options. These buttons are called radio buttons because they work like the buttons on older car radios — pushing in a button automatically "unpushes" whatever button happens to be pushed in. Thus, only one button can be selected at a time. Figure 18-4 shows examples of radio buttons, again arranged vertically.

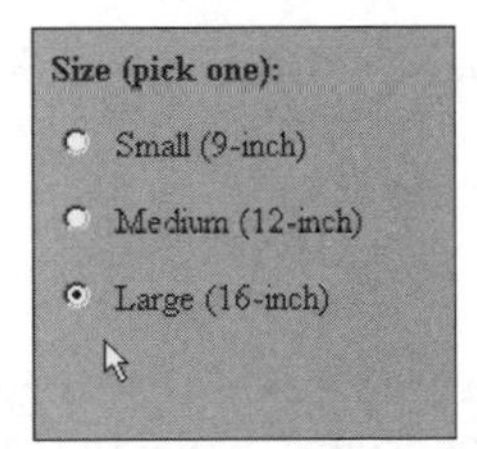

Figure 18-4: Examples of radio button form fields.

Drop-down list (select list)

A drop-down list is another way to present a list of mutually-exclusive options. This type of field takes up less room than a set of radio buttons because the options stay hidden until the reader clicks on the drop-down list button. You've no doubt seen many examples of these lists, such as the Styles list in the Word IA toolbar. Figure 18-5 shows an example of a drop-down list on a Web form, with the list already open.

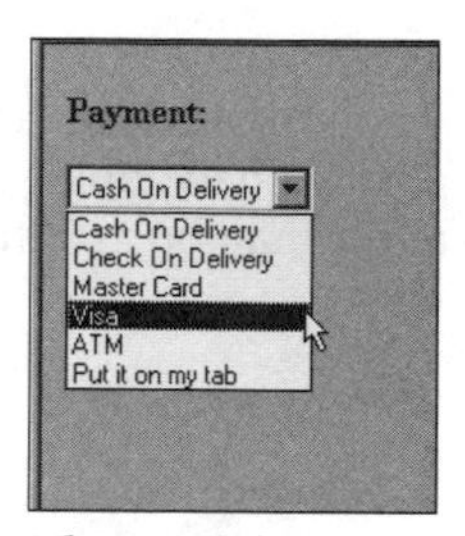

Figure 18-5: A drop-down (select) list on a form.

Command buttons

A Web form typically contains two command buttons labeled Submit and Reset. When the user clicks the Submit button, the completed form is sent to the recipient — usually yourself. Clicking the Reset button clears all the fields in the form. Figure 18-6 shows the Submit and Reset buttons at the bottom of a sample form.

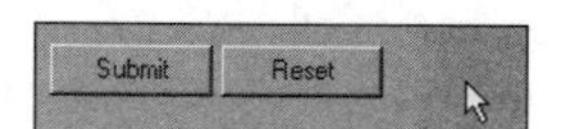

Figure 18-6: The Submit and Reset buttons on a Web form.

You can create custom buttons with custom labels by using JavaScript (see Part V).

Where the Form Data Goes

An important part of creating a form is figuring out where the data from the form goes after the reader hits the Submit button and how it's going to get there. Word IA won't ask you for this information until you create the Submit button. But when it *does* ask for that information, you'll be faced with the somewhat hair-raising dialog box shown in Figure 18-7.

Unfortunately, I can only offer a little assistance at filling out this dialog box because your Internet Service Provider determines how you fill in the lower options. Typically, you can find the information you need by searching for words like *forms* and *mailto* in your ISP's site.

Danger Zone

Before you even bother with forms, check with your ISP to make sure that you *can* do forms in your site. Many free personal-publishing sites do not offer support for forms.

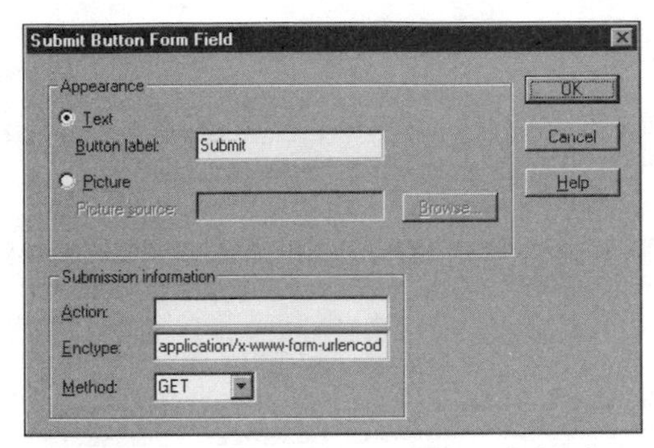

Figure 18-7: Word IA presents this dialog box when you create your form's Submit button.

I have noticed that many ISPs offer a feature called the POST method and the mailto?*emailaddress* action. This means that when you fill out the dialog box in Figure 18-7, you type

```
/cgi/bin/mailto?your_email_address
```

as the Action and choose POST as the method. For example, I've done just that with my own e-mail address in Figure 18-8. Be aware that the entry for the Action prompt is cut off. I've actually entered `/cgi-bin/mailto?alan@coolnerds.com` where `alan@coolnerds.com` is my own e-mail address — the place to which I want the reader's responses to be sent.

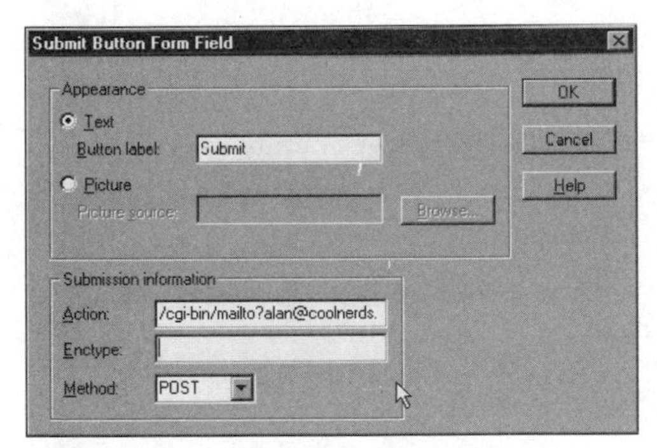

Figure 18-8: My form's Submit button.

If you want to know exactly how to fill in the blanks for the Submit button on your own form, I suggest that you contact your ISP. If you ask the ISP staff for what you specifically need, you'll probably get a specific answer. If possible, fax or e-mail a letter like the one in Figure 18-9 to the ISP staff. While you're waiting for a reply, you can work on everything *but* the Submit button in your form.

CGI, BIN, POST, GET — huh?

The `/cgi-bin` label is fairly common on the Internet. This is the name of a directory on the Web server where Common Gateway Interface (`cgi`) and Binary (`bin`) programs are stored. These are pre-written programs that you can use rather than create yourself. My ISP offers a *mailto* program that I can use to get forms sent to a particular e-mail address. I just need to specify the location (`cgi-bin`) and program name (`mailto`) and then follow that with a question mark (`?`) and the address I want the stuff mailed to (`alan@coolnerds.com` in this example).

The POST method is primarily for mailing data from forms. You use the GET method to send information to programs that send information back. For example, when you use Microsoft's All In One search page to search Excite, Yahoo!, or whatever, your search request is sent from Microsoft's page to the search engine with a GET method.

How the data is delivered

When the reader clicks that Submit button, the contents of the form (not the form itself) will be sent to you (or whatever e-mail address you specify). For example, let's say that I actually go into the pizza business and put the Click-A-Pizza form in my Web site. A reader pops in and fills out the form as in Figure 18-10.

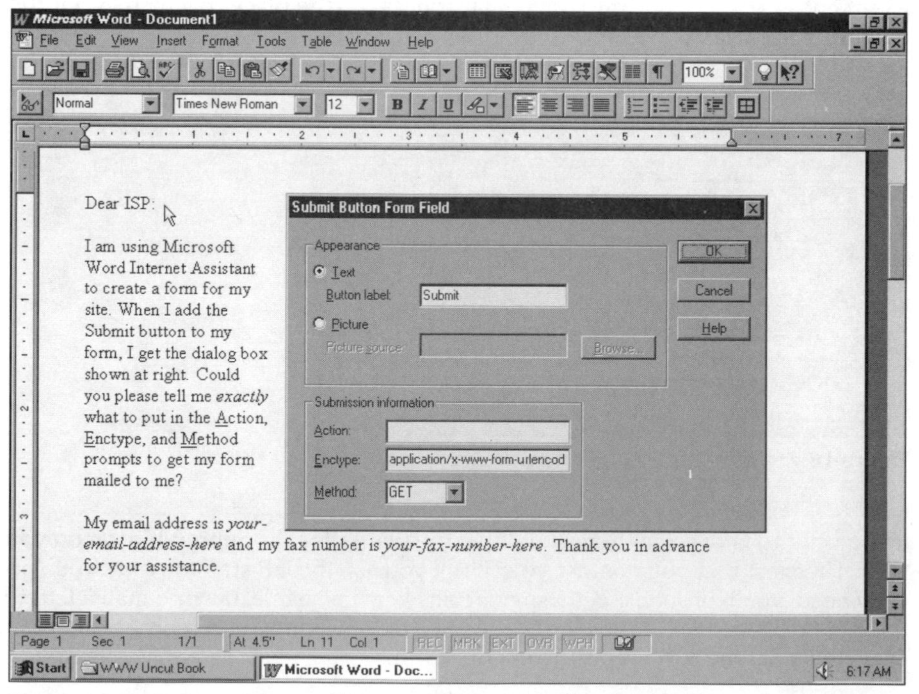

Figure 18-9: Get your ISP to tell you *exactly* how to fill in the blanks on the Submit dialog box.

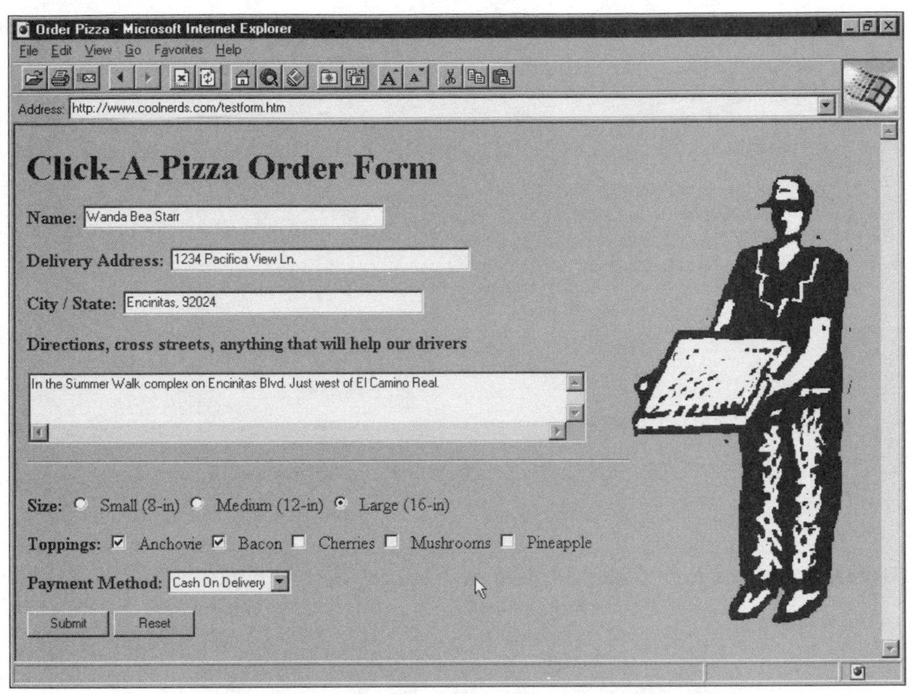

Figure 18-10: A reader has filled in the Click-A-Pizza form.

When the reader clicks the Submit button, the form data is then automatically sent to my e-mail address. When I check my e-mail, I see the message. When I open the message, it looks something like Figure 18-11.

The junk at the top is just the usual e-mail header stuff, which you can ignore (in this instance). The actual data from the form follows the header. My ISP sends the data with the field name (which I provided) followed by the reader's entry. For example, *Address* is the name of a field, and *1234 Pacifica View Ln.* is what the reader typed into the form.

Notice that the order of the data doesn't match the order of the fields on the form. That's because my ISP alphabetizes the entries, based on field name, for me. Thus the order is Address, Anchovies, Bacon, and so on. Personally, I don't like having the fields alphabetized by name. In fact, I use a special naming scheme to get around the problem. When naming fields (which you learn to do in a moment), I start each field name with a two-digit number. For example, I named the first field 01Name, the second field 02Address, the third field 03City, and so on. When "alphabetized," these field names come back to me in the format shown in Figure 18-12, which I prefer to the alternative format.

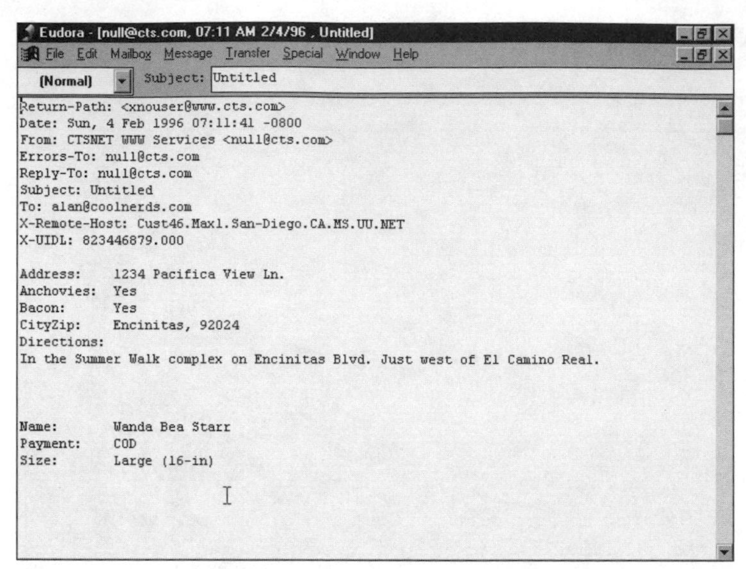

Figure 18-11: Data from Click-A-Pizza form in Figure 18-10.

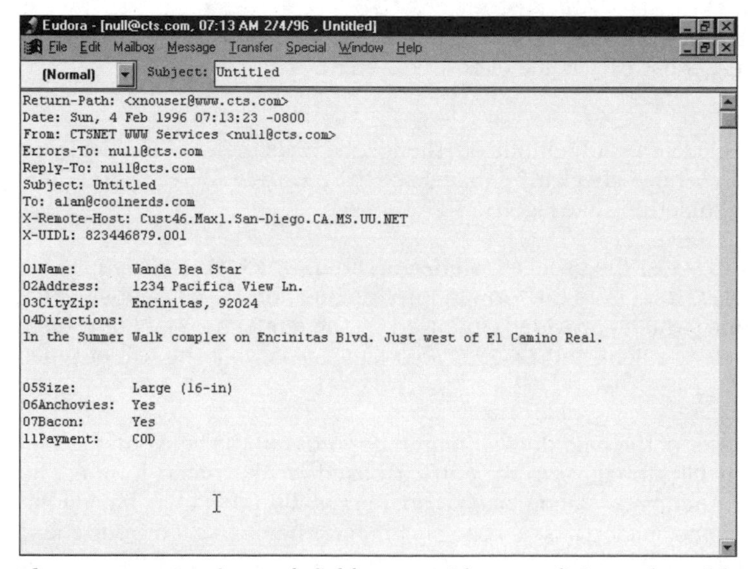

Figure 18-12: Starting each field name with a two-digit number tricks the ISP's alphabetizing scheme.

Whether or not you care to use a similar naming scheme in your own forms is entirely up to you.

You also may notice that some fields appear to be missing. The only ones missing are check boxes that the reader left blank. Looking back at Figure 18-10, you can see that the reader did not request Cherries, Mushrooms, or Pineapple. Those three fields are the very ones missing from the form.

If you're wondering about the big gap under *Directions,* that's caused by the fact that I allowed up to three lines of text for that field in my form. When the form data gets mailed to me, that field takes up three lines in the e-mail message as well — even if the reader didn't use all three lines.

Keep in mind that I'm showing you an *example.* Exactly how your form data looks when it's e-mailed to you largely depends on your Internet Service Provider.

Creating a Form

Creating a form with Word IA is pretty easy. You can add a form to an existing Web page or create a new Web page. If you're creating a new page for the form, be sure to use the HTML (or HTML.dot) template as usual. If you plan to put a headline, picture, or some text at the top of the form, you can put those items in first. Then follow these steps:

1. Move the insertion point to the place where you want to start the form in your document, and choose Insert⇨Form Field. You'll (probably) see the message shown in Figure 18-13.

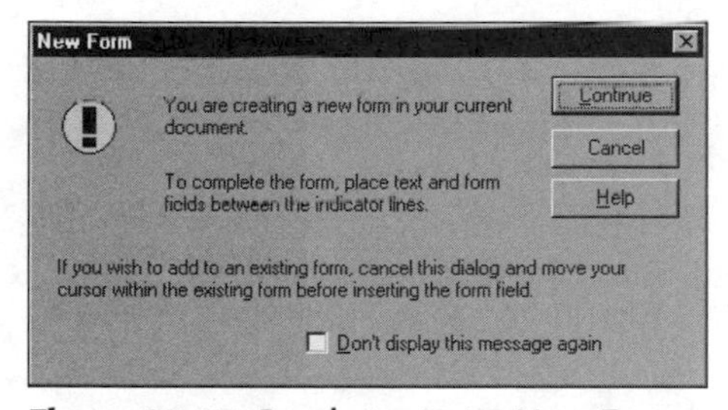

Figure 18-13: Ready to start a New Form.

2. Click the Continue button, and you notice several new items on your screen, as shown in Figure 18-14:

   - **Form Field dialog box.** The large Form Field dialog box lets you choose the type of field you want to add. You can click its Cancel button to move it out of the way, if you like. The smaller Forms toolbar lets you add fields.

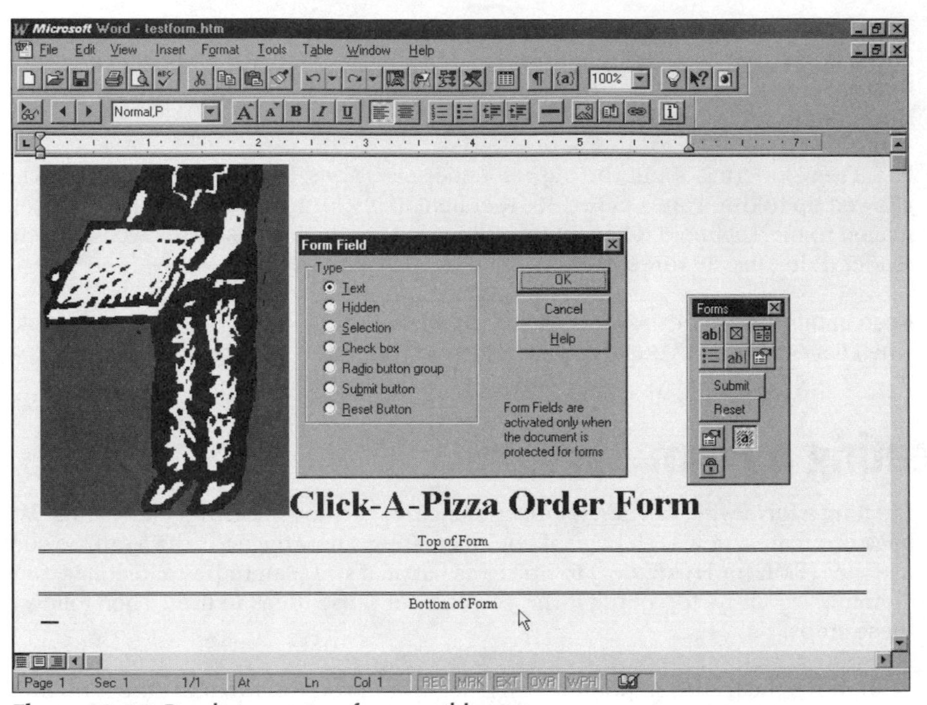

Figure 18-14: Ready to create a form on this page.

- **Forms toolbar.** The Forms toolbar, which is "floating" by default, also lets you add fields to your form. Like all toolbars, you can park it at any edge of the screen. To make it float again, drag it toward the center of the screen. Each button has a tooltip that you can view simply by pointing to the button for a couple of seconds.
- **Top and Bottom of Form.** A pair of lines show you the top and bottom of the form. All of your form fields must be between those lines. The space between the lines grows to accommodate as many fields as you care to add.

3. Now you can type text normally and add fields as you go along. I'll discuss each field type in the next section.
4. At the end of the form, add your Submit and Reset buttons. Then save the entire Web page with the usual File➪Save commands.

As you add fields to your Web page, they won't look like much in the Edit view. What appears in their place is a little shaded rectangle that acts as a placeholder for the field, like the examples shown in Figure 18-15. (If you can't even see the rectangles, click the Form Field Shading button in the Forms toolbar to turn on the shading.) To see how the field will look to your readers, preview the page with your Web browser.

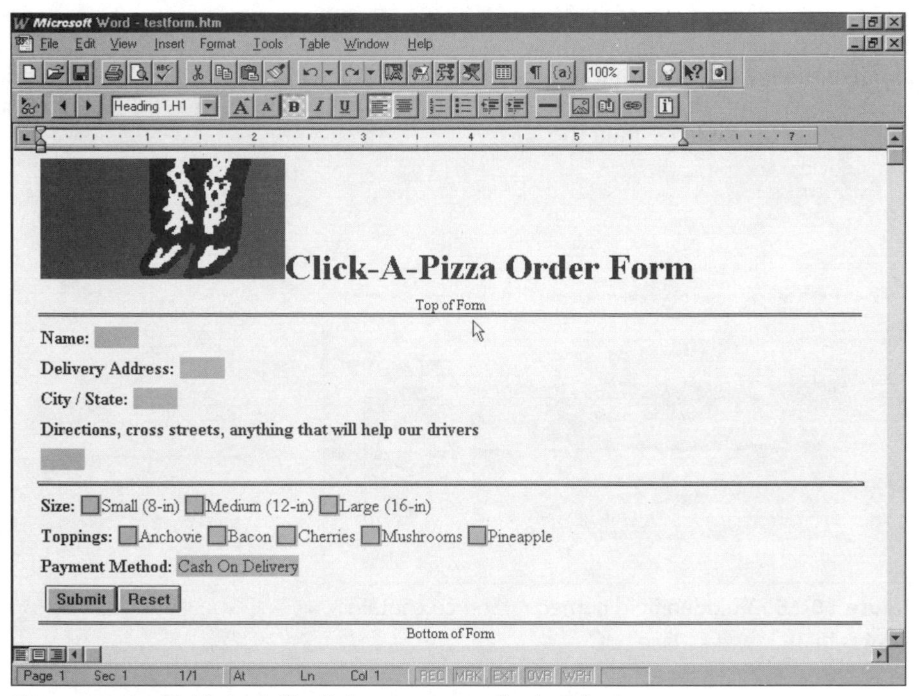

Figure 18-15: Fields look like little gray rectangles in Edit view.

Puzzled? If nothing seems to happen when you click on Preview in Browser, try minimizing the Word application window. Chances are that Internet Explorer is displaying your page behind it. After you're done previewing your form, close Internet Explorer and then click the Microsoft Word button in the taskbar to restore Word to its previous size.

Add a hidden field

Your form can contain hidden fields. These are fields that send information along with the rest of the fields on the form. But the reader never sees the field. You may want to use a hidden field to send information to yourself. For example, if your Web site has several forms in it, you may want to use a hidden field to send yourself the name of the form that the user filled in.

Life Saver If you lose the Forms toolbar (or any other toolbar for that matter), choose View⇨Toolbars and select the name of the toolbar you want to display (Forms, in this example) so that its check box contains a check. Then click OK. Optionally, right-click on a neutral area between buttons on any toolbar and choose the toolbar you want to view.

To create a hidden field, click the Hidden Form Field button in the Forms toolbar. You'll come to the dialog box shown in Figure 18-16. Type in a name for the field (you can use the leading two-digit number scheme, if you like) and a value for the hidden field. For example, if you filled out the dialog box as I did in Figure 18-16, your e-mail from the form would contain the line:

```
00Source:             Click-A-Pizza
```

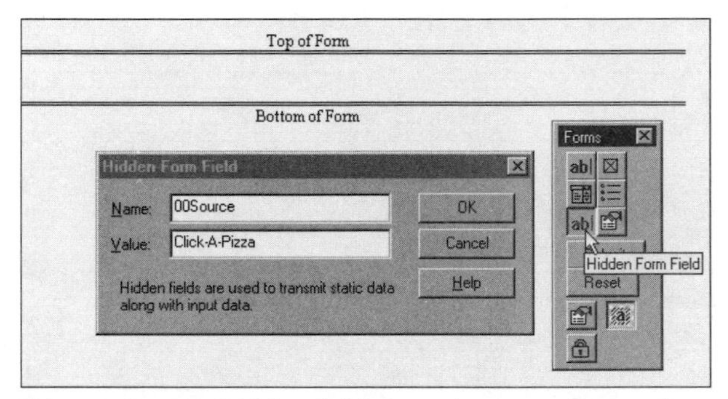

Figure 18-16: A hidden field named 00Source contains Click-A-Pizza when sent.

Add a text box field

To add a text box field to your form, click the Text Box Form Field button in the Forms toolbar (the first button). You'll come to the Text Form Field dialog box shown in Figure 18-17. Type in a Name for the field you're creating and then choose one of the following types: Single line, Multiple line, or Password. (If you choose Password, the reader will only see asterisks when typing in the field.)

If you choose Single line or Password, fill in the maximum number of characters that the reader can type and the visible size of the prompt. In Figure 18-17, I've set both widths to 75 characters.

If you choose Multiple Line, you can define the maximum number of characters and the number of lines that display on the screen. For example, in Figure 18-18 I'm defining a multiple line field named 04Directions that can contain a maximum of 1,024 characters (1K). The visible prompt on the reader's screen will be 75 characters across and three lines tall.

If you choose either Single Line or Multiple Line, you also can fill in some default text. Default text appears already typed into the field, but the readers can replace that text with whatever they want. Some authors use messages to the readers as the default text, such as "*Type your name right here.*"

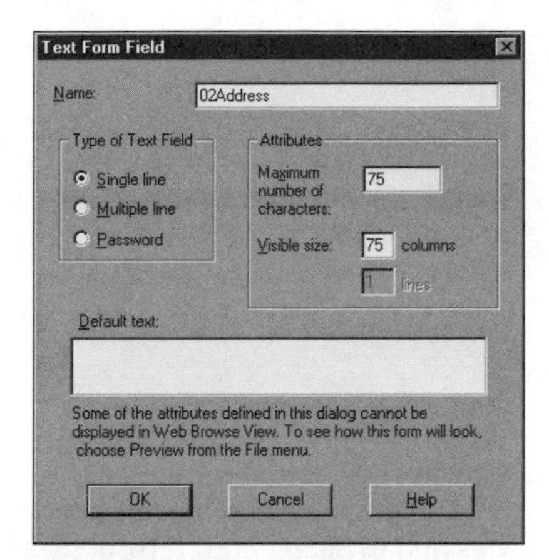

Figure 18-17: Creating a single-line text field named 02Address.

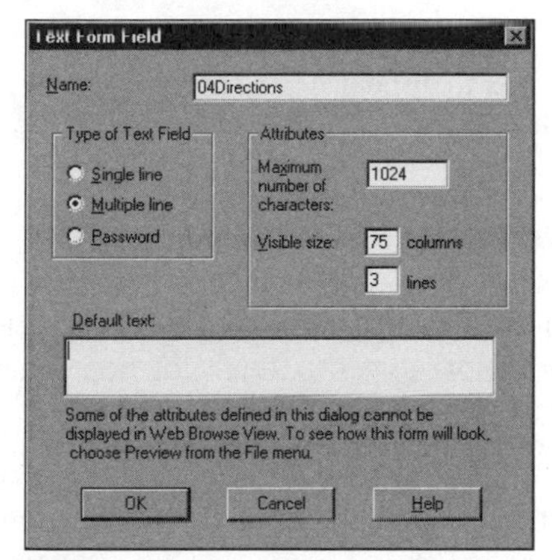

Figure 18-18: Creating a multiple line text field named 04Directions.

Add a check box

To add a check box field to your form, click on the Check Box Form Field button in the Forms toolbar. You'll come to the Check Box Form Field dialog box. Type in a name for the field and a value for the field if the user chooses the option. In Figure 18-19, for example, I've created a check box field named 06Anchovies. If the reader selects that box, the 06Anchovies field takes on the value *Yes,* which means it shows up in my e-mail as

```
06Anchovies:      Yes
```

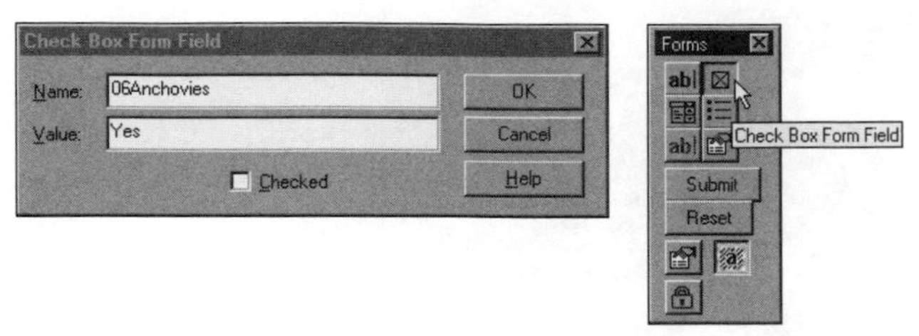

Figure 18-19: Creating a check box named 06Anchovies that will contain Yes if the reader checks the check box.

If the reader *doesn't* select a check box, nothing is returned on the form. Back in Figure 18-10, for example, the reader selected Anchovies and Bacon. If you look at the e-mail I received from that form, you see that 06Anchovies and 07Bacon both returned Yes. The Cherries, Mushrooms, and Pineapple field names do not even appear in the e-mail.

Danger Zone

Do not leave the Value option blank for any Check Box field. A simple value like Yes or True is all you need to fill in the Value option.

You also can decide how you want the check box to appear when the reader first sees it, whether that is as checked or not checked. In Figure 18-19, I've opted to display my check box empty (not checked) by default.

Add a drop-down list

If you want to add a drop-down list (a.k.a. Selection List) field to your form, click the Selection List Form Field button in the Forms toolbar to get to the dialog box shown in Figure 18-19. Give the field a name. Then type in an Option name and Value when selected and click the Add button for each item in the list. For example, the first item in my list in Figure 18-20 is Cash On Delivery. The Value for that selection is COD. As a result, when I get my e-mail from the form with that selection on it, the e-mail shows

```
11Payment:      COD
```

If you don't want the reader to be able to leave the field blank, you must define a default value for the field. First, click on the Advanced button, click on the item that you want to assign as the default selection, and choose Selected option is the default.

Add a radio button group

To create a radio button field, click the Radio Button Form Field button in the Forms toolbar. Assign a single name to the option. For example, I've named mine 05Size in Figure 18-21. Then type in a label for the first button and click Add. Type the label for the second button and click Add, and so on, until you've created a button for each option. In Figure 18-21, I've already added two options and am about to add a third. Click OK after defining the field.

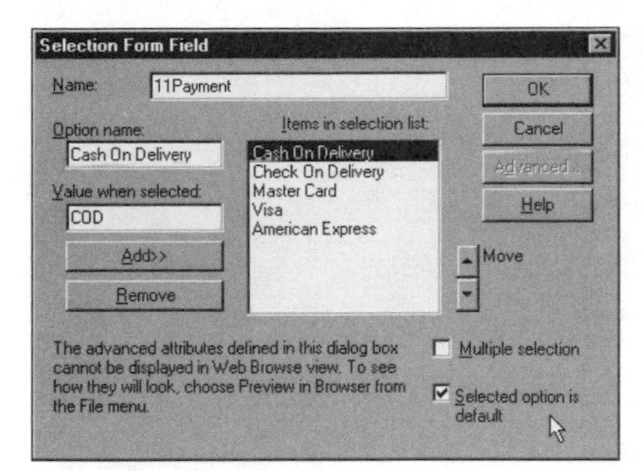

Figure 18-20: Creating a drop-down list named 11Payment that contains five items.

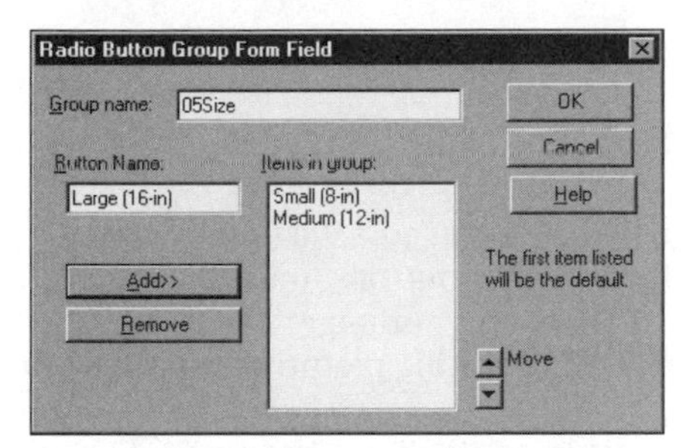

Figure 18-21: Creating a radio button group named 05Size. I'm preparing to add a third option to the list.

Add the Submit and Reset buttons

After you've entered all the fields that your form needs, you can add your Submit and Reset buttons. I already discussed the main options for defining your Submit button — Action, Enctype, and Method. Hopefully you'll be able to get the information you need from your ISP without too much fuss.

You also can change the appearance of the Submit button. For instance, when you create the Submit button, you'll see the dialog box shown in Figure 18-22. If you want the button to display text other than the word Submit (such as *Send It In!*), just type the text you want the button to display in the Button label prompt.

If you have a small bitmap image that you want to put on the button instead of text, choose the Picture option and use the Browse button to choose the name of the file that contains that picture.

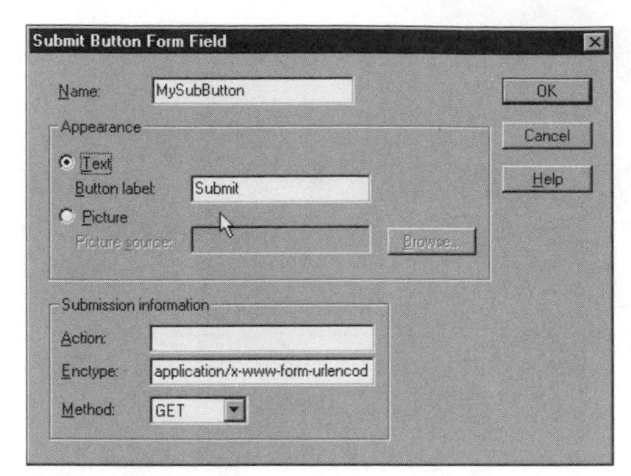

Figure 18-22: Dialog box for defining the Submit button.

Editing Form Fields

You can easily add, change, and delete form fields as you edit. Just don't forget that all fields for a single form, including the Submit and Reset buttons, must be placed between the Top of Form and Bottom of Form lines on your page. The techniques for editing fields are pretty much the same as those for editing pictures and other objects:

1. First, make sure that the Protect Form (little padlock) button on the Forms toolbar is "out" (not pressed in). That button, when pressed in, prevents you from editing all fields!
2. Select (click on) the field you want to change. Then do one of the following:
   - To delete the field, select it and then press the Delete key.
   - To move the field, select it and then drag it to its new location. Alternatively, you can choose Edit⇨Cut, click the destination for the move, and choose Edit⇨Paste.

Hot Stuff

If you have trouble typing text to the left of a field, select the field, choose Edit⇨Cut, type your text, and then choose Edit⇨Paste. Or, type the text into a blank line above the field. Then use the Delete key to "suck" up the field to the end of the current line.

   - To change the field's properties (that is, to get back to its dialog box), double-click the field. Or, in the case of the Submit and Reset button, select the button you want to change and then click the Submit or Reset button in the Forms toolbar again.

Danger Zone

The Protect Form button is really for "regular" Word forms. In an HTML document, it makes the fields act similar to the way they do on the Web. But it also prevents you from editing your fields, and that fact will drive you crazy if you do not notice that you have it pushed in!

Testing a Form

You can test the fields locally in your Web browser, but you can't really test the Submit button until you upload your page to your real site. You'll need to create a hyperlink link from your home page (or wherever) to your form as well, so that your readers (and you) can get to the form.

If at all possible, try viewing your form locally by using a few different Web browsers. A form that looks great in Internet Explorer may not look so hot in Mosaic or Netscape Navigator. Not that there's anything wrong with those other browsers — it's just that the "standards" on the Web are weak, and not all Web browsers display forms exactly the same. You may find that you need to tweak your form a bit here and there to make it look good in a variety of browsers.

When you do upload your form for public access, do yourself a huge favor: *Don't assume that the form will work!* If clicking the Submit button sends your form data reeling off into cyberspace lala land, you may never know it. And your readers will wonder why the heck you didn't respond to their requests.

Immediately after you upload the form, test it yourself by navigating to your site just as a reader would. Fill in the form, just as a reader would, and click the Submit button. Log off from the Web, wait a couple of minutes, and then check your e-mail. If you get the data you were expecting, then your form is safe and you can leave it in place.

If there are any problems with the form, you'll need to fix them right away and upload the corrected form to your site. You *don't* want to leave a non-functioning form in your site for too long! If you cannot fix the form right away, delete any hyperlinks to it so that readers won't stumble upon it while your form is in the virtual repair shop.

HTML Tags for Forms

Like everything else in your Web pages, form fields are controlled by HTML tags in your Web page. Figure 18-23 shows a sample form in Internet Explorer with the View Source window (Notepad) open, giving you a behind-the-scenes peek at some of the tags. Here I overview the main tags and attributes.

`<FORM>`**:** Each form starts with a `<FORM>` tag. The action and method that you define for the Submit button are actually stored as attributes of the FORM tag. For example, the full `<FORM>` tag for my pizza form is `<FORM ACTION="/cgi-bin/mailto?alan@coolnerds.com" METHOD="POST">`.

`<INPUT>`**:** Each field on the form is defined with an `<INPUT>` tag. Attributes within the INPUT tag define the name, type, and other properties of a form. If no type is defined, then the field is a text box. For example, `<INPUT NAME="Address" VALUE="" MAXLENGTH="75" SIZE=75>` is the tag for the text box named Address. The following list provides more examples:

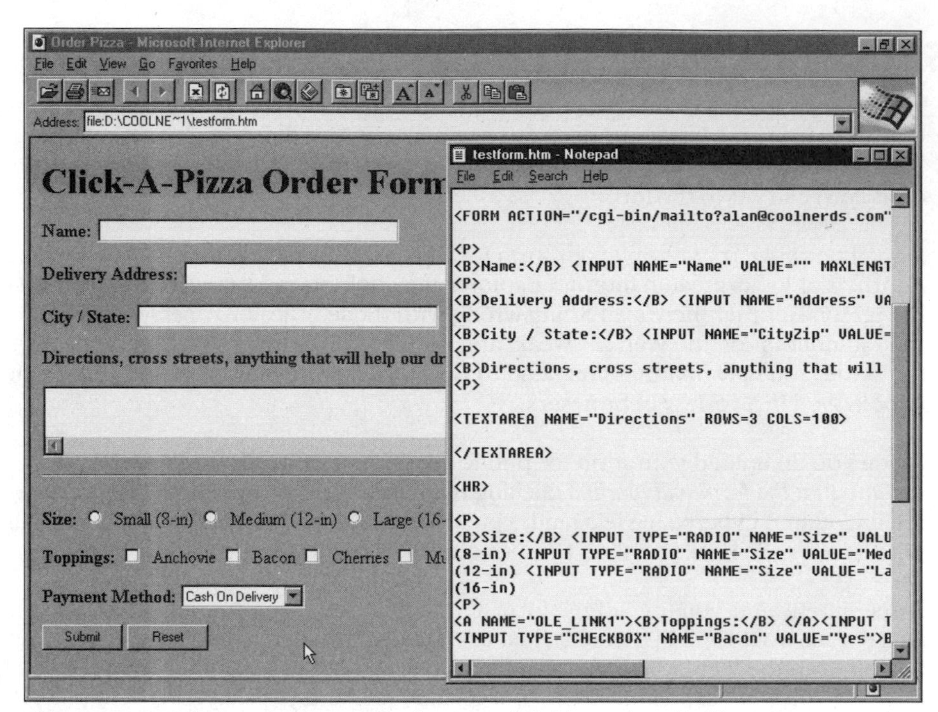

Figure 18-23: Like most things Web, forms and fields are handled by HTML tags.

- ✦ `<INPUT TYPE="CHECKBOX" NAME="Anchovies" VALUE="Yes">` is the tag for a check box.
- ✦ `<INPUT TYPE="RADIO" NAME="Size" VALUE="Small (8-in)">` is the tag for one button in a radio button group.
- ✦ `<INPUT TYPE=SUBMIT VALUE="Submit">` and `<INPUT TYPE=RESET VALUE="Reset">` are the tags for the Submit and Reset buttons.

`<TEXTAREA>`**:** The Multiple Line text box uses a slightly different coding, starting with `<TEXTAREA>` and some attributes and ending with `</TEXTREA>`, as in this example: `<TEXTAREA NAME="Directions" ROWS=3 COLS=100>...</TEXTAREA>`.

`<SELECT>`**:** Drop-down lists (Select Lists) do not use an `<INPUT>` tag. Instead, you enclose a select list with `<SELECT>` and `</SELECT>` tags and place `<OPTION>` tags in between. The codes look something like these examples: `<SELECT NAME="Payment">`, `<OPTION VALUE="COD">Cash On Delivery... </SELECT>`.

`</FORM>`**:** Marks the end of the form.

There's actually a lot more to forms than HTML tags. The JavaScript language (Part V) lets you create *hyper-interactive* forms that interact with the reader.

Lining Things Up

For the true perfectionist, the way that HTML lines up form fields can be a little irritating. For example, Figure 18-24 shows a sample form in the regular way that Internet Explorer displays forms — with the field "blank" pulled up pretty close to the text that precedes it.

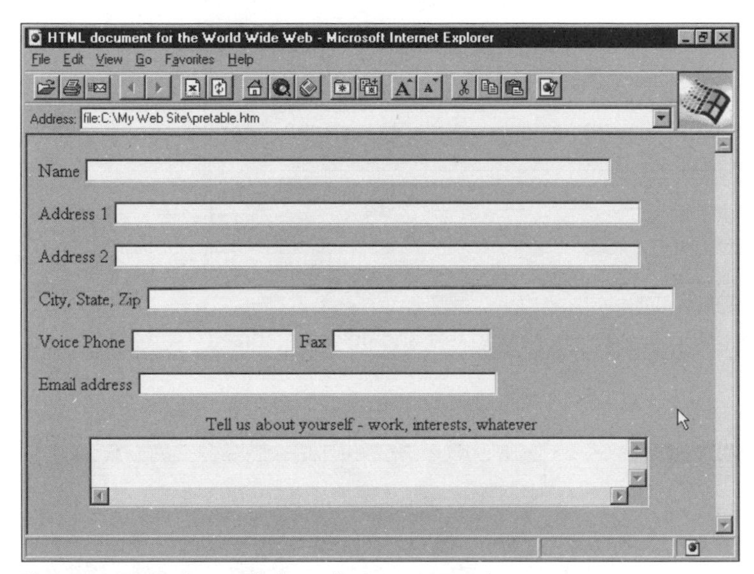

Figure 18-24: A sample form in Internet Explorer.

You can use a table, or several tables, to get a tidier appearance, as in the example shown in Figure 18-25. To use a table, I suggest that you first create a form, in Word IA, and put in a single, hidden field. That way, you'll be able to see the lines that mark the top of the form and the bottom of the form.

Once you can see the top and bottom of the form, you can put the insertion point between the lines and then press Enter a bunch of times to make some space. Then, within the lines, create a blank table. In the left column of that table, type the text that you want to appear next to the form field. Then use the Table➪Align➪(Vertical) Right to right-align the text within the cell. Then, in the cell to the right, use the standard Insert➪Form Field commands to insert a form field. Use the Table➪Cell Width and Spacing commands to set the column widths.

Although it is *possible* to merge and split cells in a table, sizing those cells can be difficult. As an alternative, if you need more cells in a row, consider creating a new, separate table. For example, Figure 18-26 shows the Word IA view of the form from Figure 18-25. As you can see, I put the Voice and Fax phone numbers in their own four-column table.

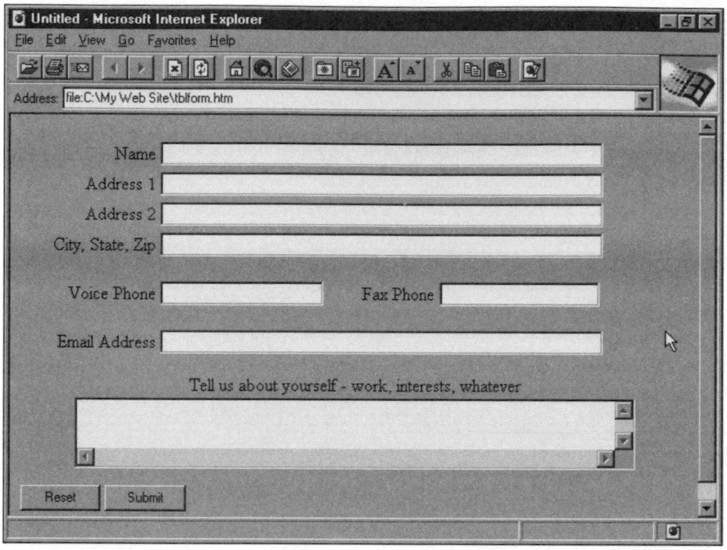

Figure 18-25: Form from Figure 18-24 with text and fields organized into a table.

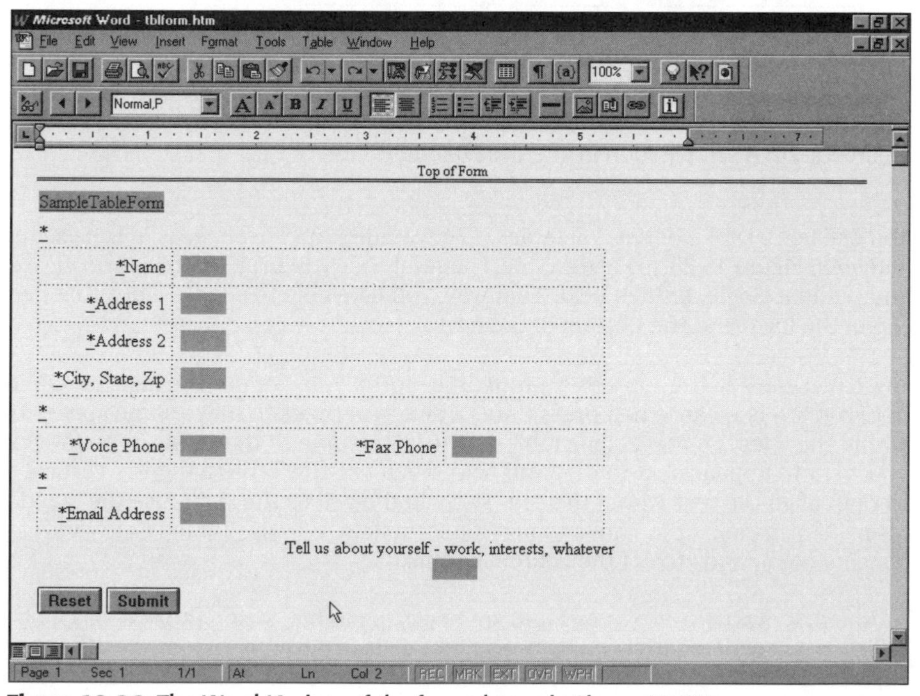

Figure 18-26: The Word IA view of the form shown in Figure 18-25.

I used tables to align prompts and fields in my sample *hyper-interactive* order form described in Chapter 32. But in that example, I turned on the table borders, so you can actually see the cells (Figure 18-27). That form is on the *Web Publishing Uncut* CD-ROM (Appendix A) if you want to take a look. It's also on my Web site, `www.coolnerds.com`, in the JavaScript area. Be aware that you must use a JavaScript-capable browser, such as Netscape Navigator 2.0, if you want the form to automatically calculate and display subtotals and totals.

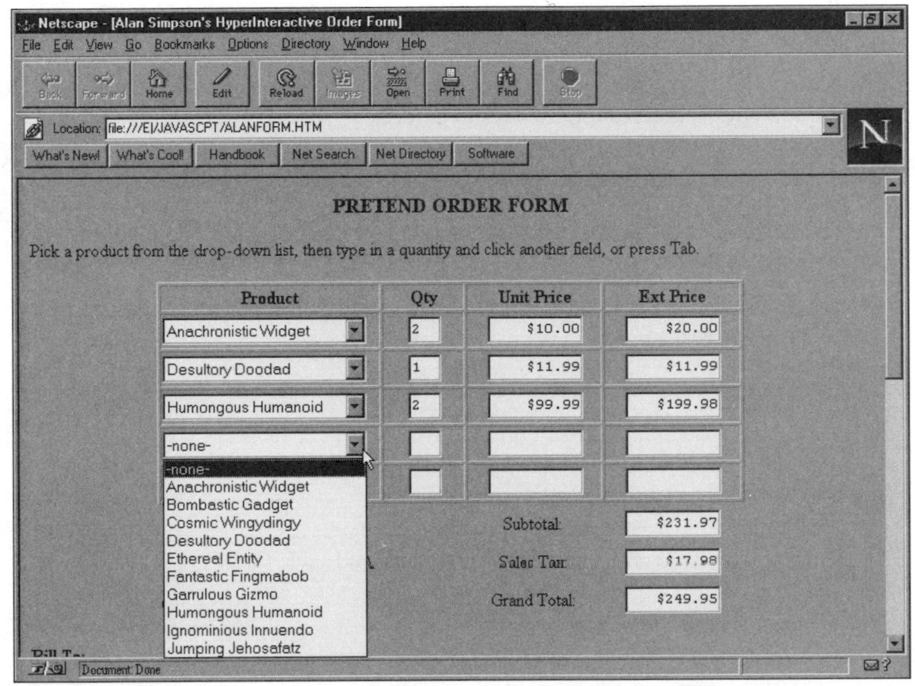

Figure 18-27: In this example, form fields are in a table with visible borders.

Summary

In this chapter, you learned how to create interactive forms for your Web site. This chapter covered the following topics:

- ✦ Before you create a form, you need to check with your ISP to make sure that it supports forms. You also need to get instructions on how to fill in the blanks on the Submit button's dialog box.
- ✦ To create a form, click at the spot where you want the form to begin and choose Insert⇨Form Field.
- ✦ To add fields to your form, choose buttons from the Forms toolbar and follow the instructions that appear on the screen.
- ✦ Be sure to keep all form fields, as well as the Submit and Reset buttons, between the Top of Form and Bottom of Form lines that appear in your page.
- ✦ To get an accurate view of the fields on your page, be sure to view the page with a Web browser.
- ✦ After you upload a form, test it immediately by filling it in and submitting it, just as a reader would.

✦ ✦ ✦

CHAPTER 19

Tweaking HTML Tags

✦ ✦ ✦ ✦

In This Chapter

Inserting custom tags directly into your page

Making a "hot" return address

Adding programmer comments

Color coding and editing HTML tags in HTML Source view

Using Notepad for quick, direct editing of a page

✦ ✦ ✦ ✦

The only thing that is constant about the World Wide Web is change. Browsers change, HTML specifications change, and new capabilities come onto the scene everyday. As you learn more about HTML and try to keep up with those changes, you may find that you need to add some new tags to your page — tags that Word IA does not yet support. Adding these tags is not a problem, though, because there are several ways to add new HTML tags to the Web pages you've created with Word IA.

Sometimes you may want to get into the HTML source of your Web page to make small, subtle changes that you cannot easily make from Word IA's Edit view. For example, you may want to get rid of a blank line by replacing a <P> (paragraph) tag with a
 (line break) tag. In this chapter, we look at the many ways you can work more directly with HTML tags.

Inserting New Tags in Word IA Edit View

A simple way to insert a new tag into a document is to stay in Word IA's normal HTML Edit view and use the HTML Markup command. The following are the exact steps for performing this task:

1. Move the insertion point to where you want to insert an HTML tag in your document.
2. Choose Insert➪HTML Markup to get to the dialog box shown in Figure 19-1.

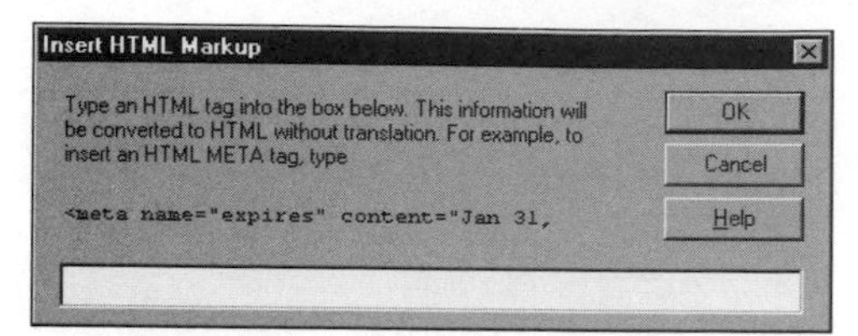

Figure 19-1: The Insert HTML Markup dialog box.

3. Type in the tag exactly as its syntax demands, including the opening and closing brackets (<>), and then click OK.

If you're not sure of the exact syntax required by a tag, look up the tag in Appendix B or one of the electronic references described near the beginning of Appendix B. In Word IA's Edit view, the tag will be colored blue. Let's look at a couple of quick examples.

Creating a hot return address

My ISP (and many others) let you treat the word *mailto* as an anchor that your reader can jump to in order to start his or her own e-mail and send a message. The syntax for this tag looks like this:

```
<a href = "mailto:emailaddress">hot text</a>
```

where *emailaddress* is the address to which the reader's message will be sent and *hot text* is the underlined hyperlink text in the document. Suppose that I want to add a hyperlink that reads *Send Feedback* in the address line of my home page. When the reader clicks that hyperlink, I want the reader's e-mail editor to pop up with my e-mail address already typed into the To portion, so that the reader can easily type and send me a note.

For starters, I open my page in Word IA and move the insertion point to where I want the *Send Feedback* hyperlink to appear. I choose Insert⇨HTML Markup and type the following, as shown in Figure 19-2:

```
<a href = "mailto:alan@coolnerds.com">Send Feedback</a>
```

Hot Stuff

To insert the copyright symbol in my Web page, I just selected Insert⇨Symbol from Word's menu bar and then chose that symbol from the table of symbols that appears.

After I click OK, the entire tag appears in blue in the Edit view. To see what it will look like in a Web browser, I just need to click the Preview in Browser button. After I do this, only the hyperlink text `Send Feedback` appears, blue and underlined like all hyperlinks. Figure 19-3 shows how this example turned out in Internet Explorer.

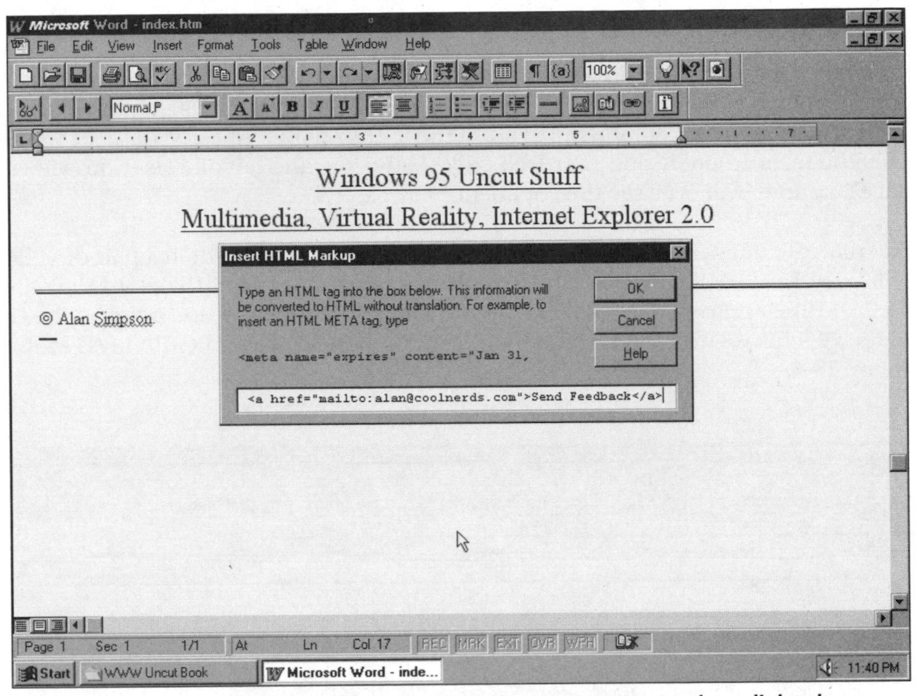

Figure 19-2: Inserting a "mailto" tag by using the Insert HTML Markup dialog box.

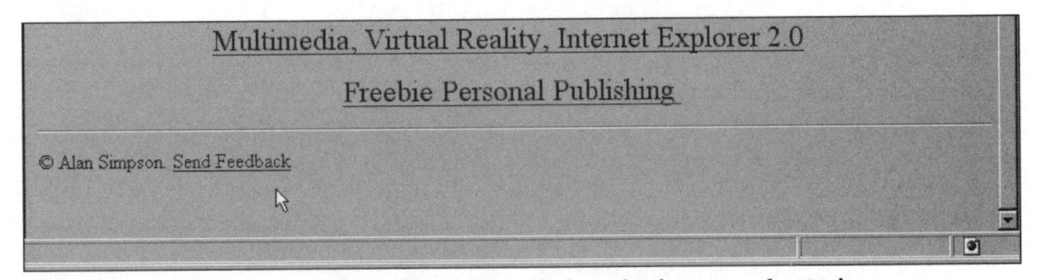

Figure 19-3: The new Send Feedback hyperlink at the bottom of a Web page.

Of course, if you decide to create such a hyperlink in your own Web page, you'll want to test it right after uploading the page. That is, navigate into your Web site just like a reader on the Web would and then use the Send Feedback link to type yourself a little e-mail message. Check your e-mail in a few minutes; if you receive your own message, you know that the link works. (If you don't receive the e-mail message, you should probably ask your ISP for information on how to set up a similar capability from its Web server.)

Adding comments

In programmer jargon, a note to one's self is called a *comment.* In a Web page, a comment is any text that appears only in the HTML Source view — never in the Web browser. You can use comments to store the author name, revision date, or whatever else you want to put inside your Web page. Only you, and anyone else who views the page's source, will ever see the comment.

To create a comment in HTML, you simply enclose the comment in a pair of `<COM-MENT>` and `</COMMENT>` tags. For example, suppose that I want to record the date of the last time I revised a particular page. I could move the insertion point to the top of the page, choose Insert➪HTML Markup, and type the comment (with tags) as in Figure 19-4.

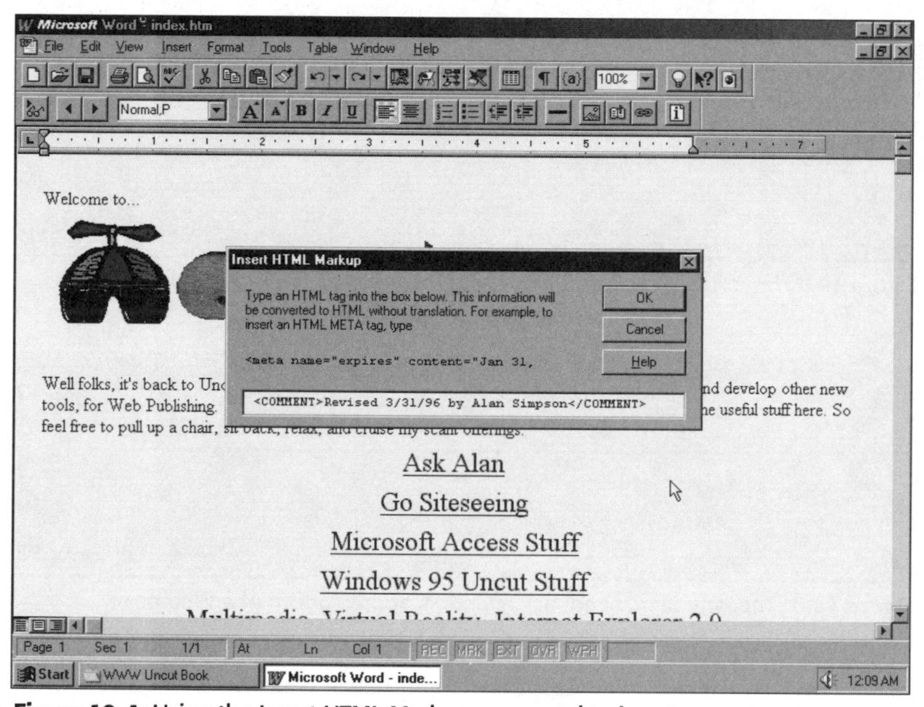

Figure 19-4: Using the Insert HTML Markup command to insert a comment.

After I click OK, the comment appears in blue in HTML Edit mode. That way, I can easily see it while editing my page (Figure 19-5). The comment will never appear in a Web browser.

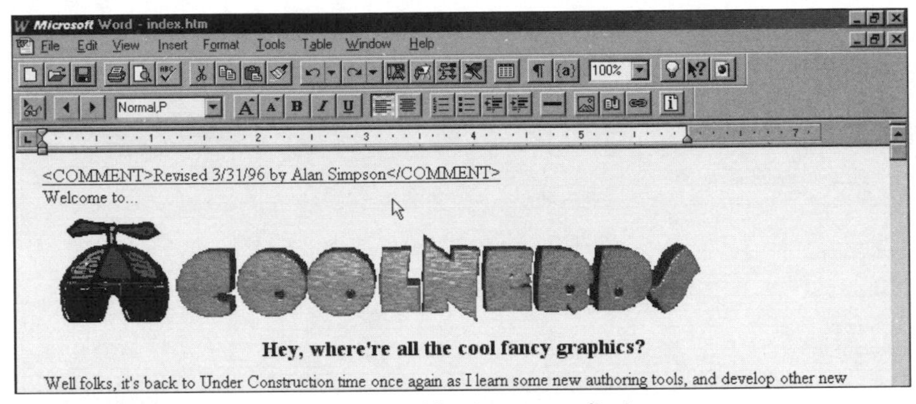

Figure 19-5: The comment appears in blue in HTML Edit view.

As an alternative to spelling out the word *comment* within the tag, you can start a comment with this symbol, <!, and end the comment with a single angle bracket, >. For example, I could have typed the comment in Figure 19-5 as:

```
<! Revised 3/31/96 by Alan Simpson >
```

Tweaking Tags in HTML Source View

To change (rather than insert) HTML tags in your Web page, you can use the HTML Source view. As you may recall, to get to the Source view, you choose View⇨HTML Source from Word IA's menus. Alternatively, you can right-click a neutral part of the page and choose HTML Source from the shortcut menu that appears.

When you get to the HTML Source view, you'll notice two little buttons in a floating toolbar. The button with the little pencil on it takes you back to the Edit view. The other button, Auto Format HTML, is very handy for working directly with tags. When you click that button, Word IA color-codes the Web page as follows:

- ✦ HTML tags appear in magenta.
- ✦ HTML attributes appear in boldface.
- ✦ Values assigned to attributes appear in blue.
- ✦ All other text remains black.

Obviously, I can't show you the exact colors here in a black-and-white book. But Figure 19-6 should give you some idea of how the page will look.

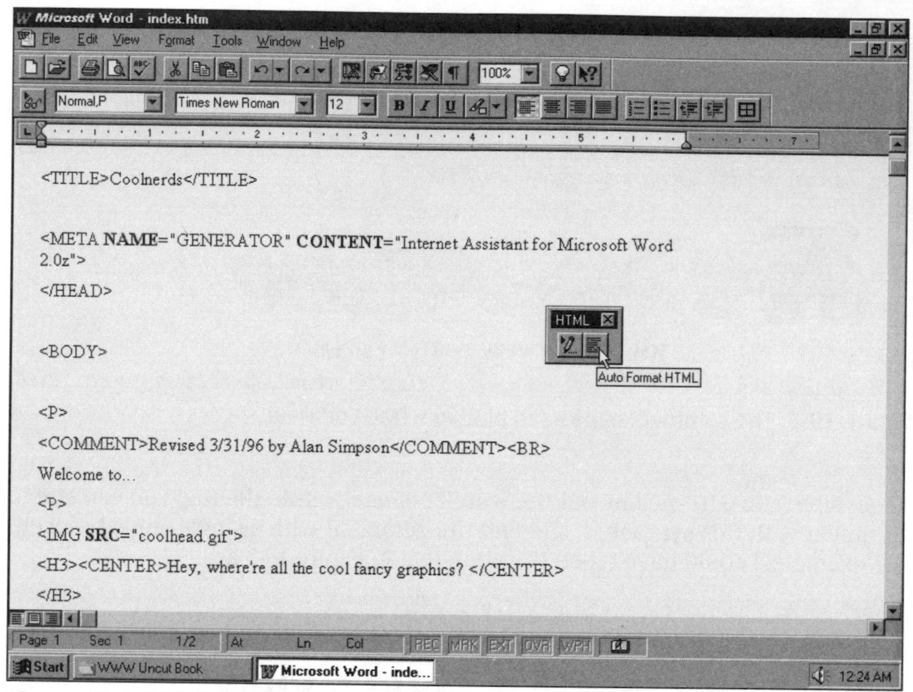

Figure 19-6: A Web page in HTML Source view.

The document is fully editable in HTML Source view. You can get right to the nitty-gritty attributes of every tag — a feat not really possible in the regular Edit view. You can add, change, and delete text and tags to your heart's content.

Keeping in mind that this view is really for working on tags, however, is important. The line breaks, tabs, spaces, and so on that appear in this view are virtually ignored by both the Edit view and Web browsers. As a result, anytime that you make changes to a page in this view, I recommend that you take the following steps to *really* see the results of your changes:

1. Switch back to the Edit view.
2. Close the document (File➪Close➪Yes).
3. Re-open the document (File➪*filename*).
4. Click the Preview in Browser button.

Once you complete this process, you now can see the page exactly as your readers will see it.

Tweaking Tags with Notepad

Once you have saved a Web page, it becomes an HTML document. As such, it is just a simple text file that you can edit with any simple text editor — Notepad, for instance. I often find myself popping into a Web page with Notepad just to make a small, simple change here and there. If you set up your Send To menu as I discuss in Chapter 11, you can easily hop right into Notepad from the Windows 95 desktop. Here's how you do it:

1. Use My Computer, Windows Explorer, or Find to locate the Web page you want to edit.
2. Right-click the filename for the page and choose Send To⇨Notepad.

In Notepad, you really get the pure, unadulterated view of what's in that Web page. Notepad does not provide you with color coding or any other frills. As far as tools go, you have your basic File, Edit, Search, and Help menus (see Figure 19-7). That's all Notepad provides you. After you've finished editing the page, just choose File⇨Exit and save your changes in the usual manner.

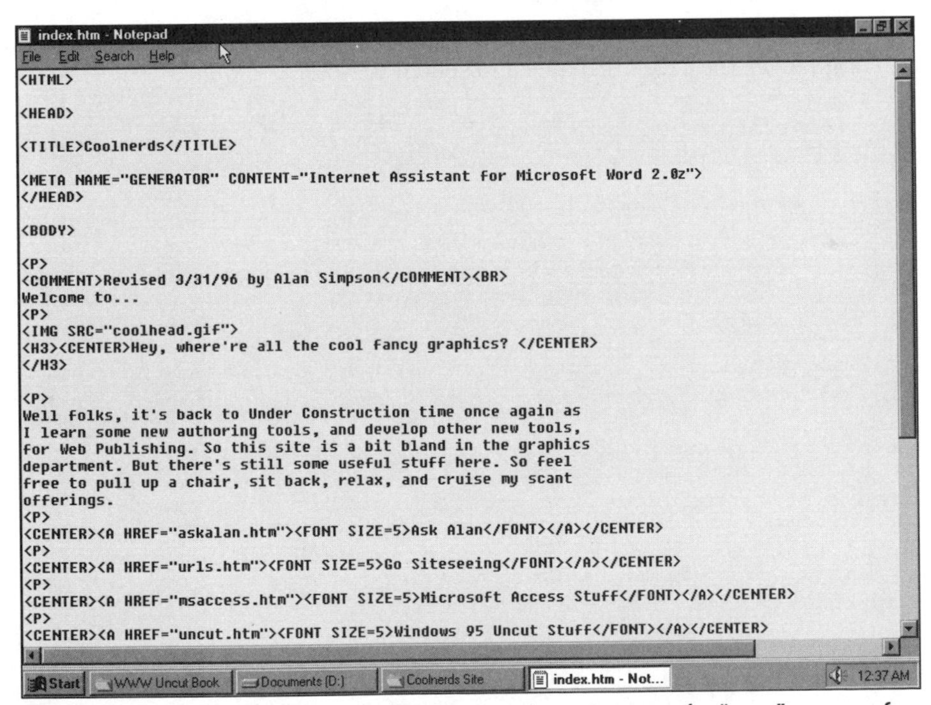

Figure 19-7: Windows' Notepad editor is a good way to get at the "pure" source of a Web page.

As you'll see in later chapters, I often use Notepad to insert features that Word IA currently does not support, such as frames and JavaScript code.

Summary

Although Word IA gives you a nice WYSIWYG environment for authoring Web pages, it's nice to be able to get to the real source of the page from time to time. That way you can add, tweak, and delete tags and text directly. The basic techniques you can use are summarized in the following list:

- In Word IA's normal Edit view, you can choose Insert⇨HTML Markup to type a tag directly into your document.
- To add, change, or delete tags, you can switch to the HTML Source view. Just choose View⇨HTML Source, or right-click the page and choose HTML Source.
- In the HTML Source view, you can click the Auto Format HTML button to color-code the page to more easily distinguish between text, tags, attributes, and the values assigned to attributes.
- If you're at the Windows 95 desktop and want to do a quick edit to a page, just right-click the page's filename and send it to Notepad.

✦ ✦ ✦

Even Cooler Web Pages

✦ ✦ ✦ ✦

In This Part

✦ ✦ ✦ ✦

Coolsite: Instant Web Site

In This Chapter

What Coolsite is all about

Installing and starting Coolsite

Defining your home page

Creating FAQs, news, sites, and tips lists

Generating Web pages from Coolsite

Testing your generated pages

Cool Coolsite tricks

Coolsite is a handy-dandy little shareware application that I created to make it easy to manage lists in Web pages. Basically, Coolsite lets you type up your lists just by filling in forms. You can click a button at any time, and Coolsite will create HTML versions of those lists. It automatically inserts all the list tags (<LI> and so forth) and lots of bookmarks and hyperlinks to make it easy for your readers to find information in your site.

Here's a quick example. Figure 20-1 shows a sample frequently asked question (FAQ) typed into Coolsite. Notice that it has a topic, a question, and an answer.

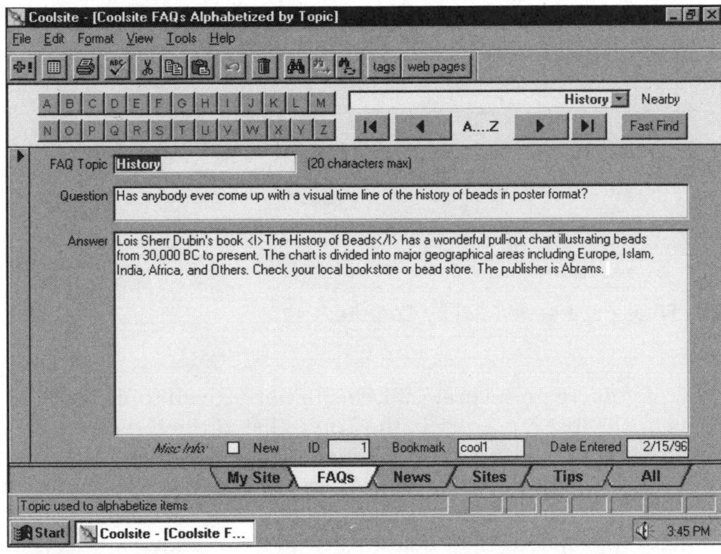

Figure 20-1: A frequently asked question typed into Coolsite.

For the sake of example, let's say that I've typed in several FAQs under the topics History, Magazines, and Product Catalogs. Now I'm ready to publish them in my Web site. I just need to click the HTML button in Coolsite's toolbar and follow a few simple instructions on the screen. Coolsite creates the appropriate HTML page for me.

To verify it, I could just open up that generated Web page by using my favorite browser. And voilà, there's my list of FAQs as shown in Figure 20-2. Notice the little list of topics at the top of the list — each of those topics is a hyperlink to an FAQ within the list. Thus, the reader can jump to FAQs about a particular topic without having to scroll up and down through the list and read all the questions.

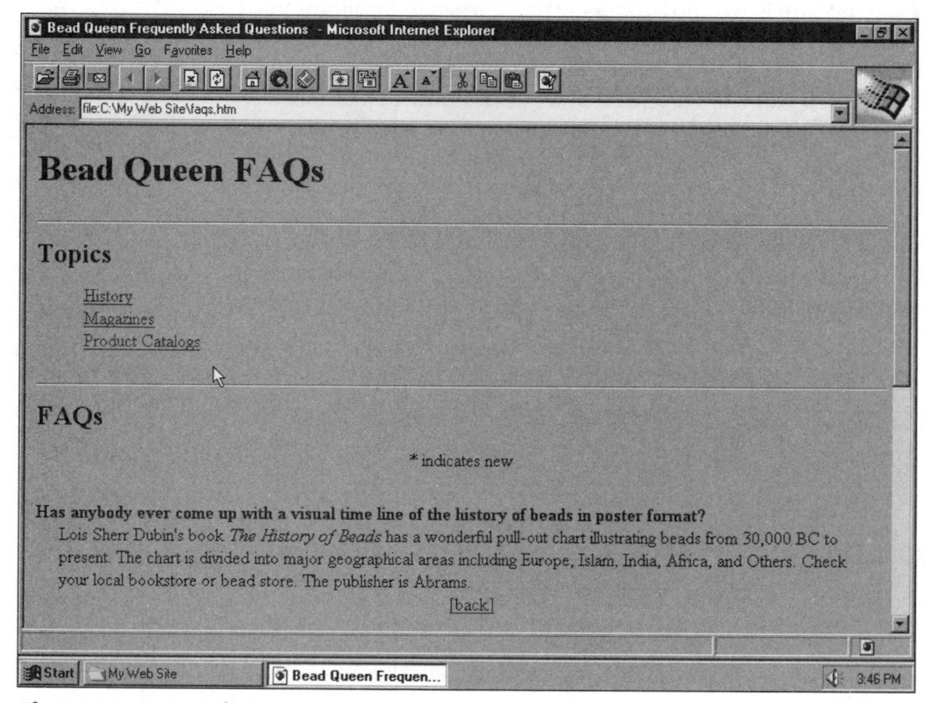

Figure 20-2: Sample FAQs page generated by Coolsite.

I should mention that if you create several list items under a given topic name, that topic name stills appears as just one entry in the Topics list at the top of the page. The items in the list are alphabetized by topic, which means that all items dealing with a particular topic are grouped together in the list. When your reader clicks on a topic, his or her Web browser sends the reader to the *first* item under that topic. Any other items dealing with that topic appear right below the first item. That enables your reader to scroll down through adjacent items to browse all items dealing with a certain topic.

That, in a nutshell, is what Coolsite is all about. You create individual items in FAQs, news, sites, and tips lists — just by filling in the blanks on the screen. Coolsite then turns all your entries into Web pages complete with hyperlinks, list tags, and other HTML bells and whistles.

I've tried to make Coolsite user-friendly enough for anyone to learn and use, and I've also included a copy of Coolsite on the CD-ROM that came with this book. You're welcome to use Coolsite as a tool for authoring your own Web site. But Coolsite *is* copyrighted, which means you cannot sell it or give it away as a value-added or promotional thing on a CD-ROM or in a book. Okay? So let's talk about installing and using Coolsite on your PC.

The topics list at the top of the generated Web page uses a `<DIR>` list format. Browsers that support this tag actually spread the list across three columns rather than down a single column. It's strange that Internet Explorer doesn't support `<DIR>`!

Installing Coolsite

To install Coolsite the quick-and-easy way, follow these steps:

1. Close any open programs and windows to get to the Windows 95 desktop.
2. Insert the *Web Publishing Uncut* CD-ROM in your CD-ROM drive.
3. Click the Start button, and point to Settings➪Control Panel.
4. Double-click Add/Remove Programs.
5. Click Install➪Next➪Browse and browse to (or type) ***D:*\COOLSITE\DISK1\SETUP** (where ***D:*** is the drive letter for your CD-ROM drive). Your command-line option should look something like *D:\COOLSITE\DISK1\SETUP.EXE.*
6. Click Finish.
7. Follow the instructions that appear on-screen.

You techies may discover that Coolsite is a Microsoft Access database application. If you have already installed Microsoft Access for Windows 95 on your PC, you can do the Compact installation.

When Setup gives you options for the type of installation you want, most of you will want to choose Typical. Just keep following the instructions on-screen until you see the `Coolsite Setup was completed successfully` message, and then click OK.

Starting Coolsite

You can start Coolsite at any time just as you would start any other program:

1. Click the Start button and point to Programs.
2. Point to Coolsite, and then click the Coolsite option.

You'll see a brief splash screen followed by the first screen of Coolsite. Note that if you are using an 800 × 600 (or greater) display, you'll also see a great deal of wasted space! To fix this, you can choose Restore and then resize the Coolsite window to the dimensions shown in Figure 20-3, which shows Coolsite displayed on a 600 × 480 screen.

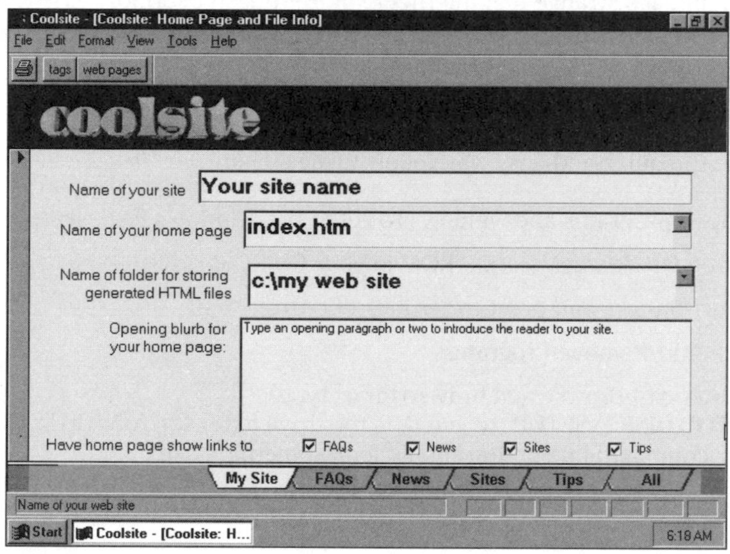

Figure 20-3: Coolsite's opening screen.

Make a desktop shortcut to Coolsite

You can create a desktop shortcut to Coolsite. Just right-click a neutral area of the Windows 95 desktop. Choose New⇨Shortcut from the pop-up menu that appears. Browse to C:\Coolsite, and choose All Files from the Files of type option near the bottom of the Browse dialog. Click the Coolsite (or Coolsite.mdb) icon, and choose Open. The command line should read C:\Coolsite\coolsite.mdb. Click Next, and then click Finish.

If you'd like to switch to the "link" icon, right-click the shortcut icon on the desktop, choose Properties, and click the Shortcut tab. Click Change icon, browse to C:\Coolsite, and click the Coolicon (or Coolicon.ico) icon. Choose Open⇨OK⇨OK. From now on, you can double-click the Coolsite icon on the desktop to start Coolsite.

Defining Your Site and Home Page

Notice the tabs along the bottom of Coolsite's window: My Site, FAQs, News, and so on. The My Site tab is where you define the following information about your site:

Name of your site

Type the name or title of your site into the Name of your site field. This info is simply a casual name for your site, like Coolnerds. *Do not* type a filename or URL in this field. The text you enter here will appear as the site's title at the top of the home page and at the top of every Web page that Coolsite generates.

Name of your home page

The Name of your home page field is where you type a filename. You use this entry to create hyperlinks from the various list pages back to your home page. Be sure to type the actual filename of your home page. If you plan to use the common index.htm or index.HTML as that name, you can just select the name from the drop-down list.

Name of folder . . .

At the Name of Folder prompt, type the drive and directory where you want Coolsite to store the pages it creates. You can use the suggested C:\My Web Site folder or any folder of your choosing.

Danger Zone

Coolsite overwrites like-named files within the folder. If you've already created a fancy home page or FAQs, News, Sites, or Tips pages, you may want to have Coolsite store its files in some other directory. That way, Coolsite won't overwrite your existing pages.

Opening blurb . . .

In the Opening blurb field, type a paragraph that describes your site. If you use Coolsite to generate your home page, this blurb appears just under the title of your home page.

Have home page show . . .

Finally, you need to decide which types of lists you want your home page to offer your readers. Place a check mark next to each type of list for which you want to create a hyperlink.

To give you an idea of what goes where when you actually create your Web pages, Figure 20-4 shows a hypothetical home page defined in the My Site tab in Coolsite. Figure 20-5 shows the Web page that Coolsite generates from that information.

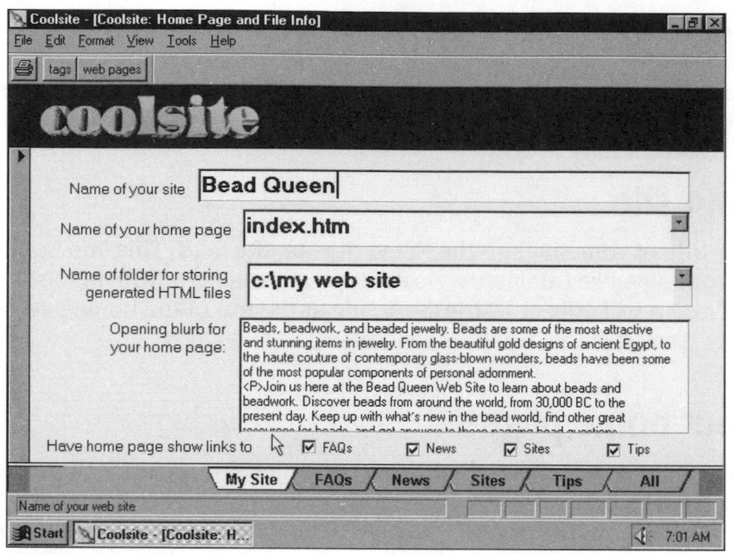

Figure 20-4: Some sample data typed into the My Site form.

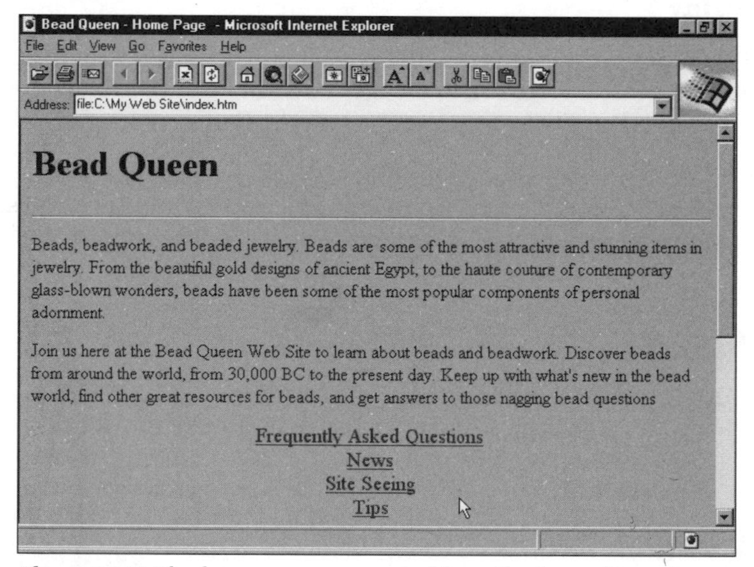

Figure 20-5: The home page generated from the form shown in Figure 20-4.

I realize that Coolsite doesn't create a particularly fancy home page, but that's okay because you're not stuck with that home page. You can use Word IA or another Web-page editing tool to create a home page that is as fancy as you like. Then you can create links from your custom home page to the various list pages that Coolsite helps you create. You can even cut and paste the links from the home page that Coolsite creates to add them to a fancy home page of your own creation.

Creating Your Lists

Managing lists rather than home pages is what Coolsite is really all about. You can create up to four of these commonly-used lists:

- **FAQs.** Use the FAQs tab to type your frequently-asked questions.
- **News.** If you want to have a News page, use the News tab to type those list items.
- **Sites.** It's always good to give your readers links to other sites that may interest them. Use the Sites tab to type these items.
- **Tips.** Everyone likes useful tips. If you plan to have a list of favorite tips in your site, use the Tips tab to type them.

Typing a list item is simple:

1. Click the tab that indicates which list you want to add the item to: FAQs, News, Sites, or Tips.
2. Click the Add Item button in the toolbar (the first button, which looks something like +!).
3. Fill in the blanks.

The forms you use to type in list items are very similar. Once you are in a form, you can use all the standard text-editing and navigation techniques that Windows offers. For example, you can move the insertion point to any field by clicking that field or by pressing Tab or Shift+Tab to move from field to field. I'll talk about the other navigation buttons that appear near the top of the form later in this chapter. But first, let me give you some pointers on how to type up the items in the various lists.

FAQs list items

As mentioned earlier, you use the FAQs tab to type the items for your frequently-asked-questions list. Figure 20-6 shows the FAQs tab with a sample item already typed in it.

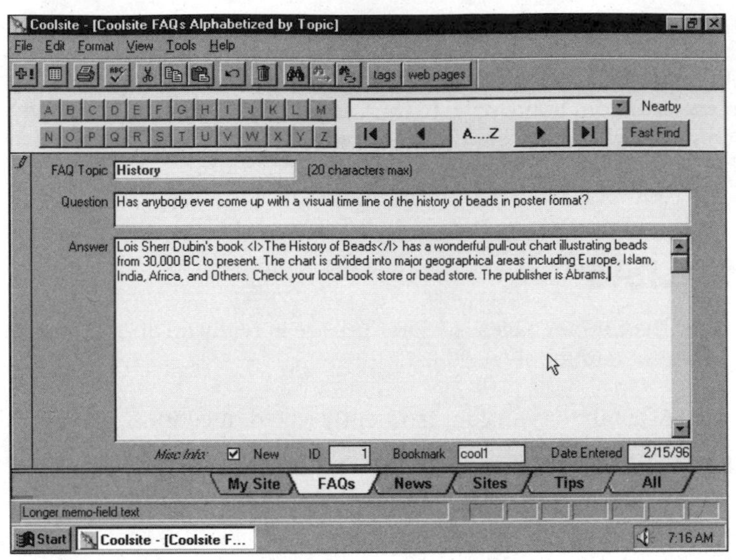

Figure 20-6: The FAQs tab with a sample FAQ already typed in.

Puzzled? In case you're wondering, the tags you see in Coolsite, such as `<P>`, `<I>`, and `</I>`, are just optional HTML tags that are inserted automatically. You also can manually type tags into your own text. More on this topic under "Inserting Custom Tags" later in this chapter.

When typing your own FAQ, put the following information into each field:

FAQ Topic

Type a short word or phrase (up to 20 characters), similar to the index entry at the back of a book, to describe the main topic of this FAQ. Your entry will become a hyperlink that the reader will click to get to the FAQ.

FAQ Question

Type the question portion of your FAQ. Be brief (up to 255 characters), and be specific. You want the reader to know exactly what question is being answered *before* he or she reads the answer.

FAQ Answer

Type the answer to the FAQ. There is no length-limit here — the answer can be as long as you want it to be. However, do keep in mind that every item you enter is a single item in a list — not an entire page. If you press Enter to start a new paragraph, Coolsite automatically inserts a `<P>` tag, which tells the Web browser to start a new paragraph.

FAQ Misc Info

Typically, you can ignore the Misc Info provided in Coolsite. This section contains additional information, but everything that appears there is filled in automatically by Coolsite. For example, the New field has a check mark when you type in a new item. (That check mark disappears after the item is published.) ID is a number that Coolsite assigns to each list item. Bookmark is the text that Coolsite uses as the bookmark when it generates your Web pages. The Date Entered field is automatically set to today's date.

News items

To type a news item, click the News tab and then click the Add Item button. Figure 20-7 shows the News tab with a sample story already typed in it. When typing your own stories, follow these guidelines:

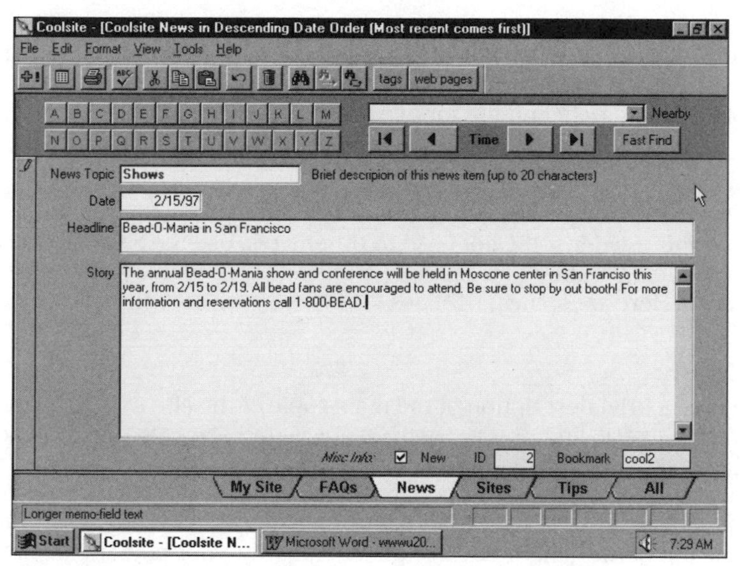

Figure 20-7: The News tab with a sample story already typed in.

News Topic

A short word or phrase (up to 20 characters) that reflects the main topic of the story. When you create your Web pages, Coolsite lists these topics at the top of the News page along with the date of each story to make it easy for your reader to focus on stories of interest to him or her.

News Date

The Date field is automatically filled in with today's date. You can replace it, however, with any date you wish. When Coolsite generates your Web pages, it lists stories in newest-to-oldest order. As a result, the date you type here affects where the story appears in the list of stories.

News Headline

This field displays a brief (up to 255 characters) headline for the story. The info displayed here is just like the headlines used in newspaper stories.

News Story

Type the story in the Story field. The story can be as long as you want it to be. As discussed later, this longer section can contain multiple paragraphs (each starting with a <P> tag and containing other HTML tags).

The Misc Info entries for News stories are similar to those for FAQs. They're filled in automatically, so you can ignore them if you like. There is no Date Entered field in Misc Info for news items. The story date of the story, which you entered near the top of the form, doubles as the Date Entered for news items.

Site-seeing

If you want to give your reader some hot links to other sites, use the Sites tab to type those references. Figure 20-8 shows an example of the Sites tab with a sample reference already filled in. Here are some guidelines for typing your own site references:

Site Topic/Category

In this field, you type a brief description of the main topic of the site to which you'll be sending the reader. As usual, limit this entry to 20 characters. You also can think of this entry as a category. For example, if you plan to provide your reader with links to several sites that cover petrified cheese, you may want to label each of those items with the topic *Petrified Cheese.* Whatever you enter here appears as a hyperlink in the topics listed at the top of the generated Sites page. This way, your reader can jump to a particular topic or category with a single mouse click.

Site Name

Type the casual name of the site here (not the URL). For example, *Coolnerds* is the name for my site. You could use *White House* as the site name if you're creating a link to the White House home page.

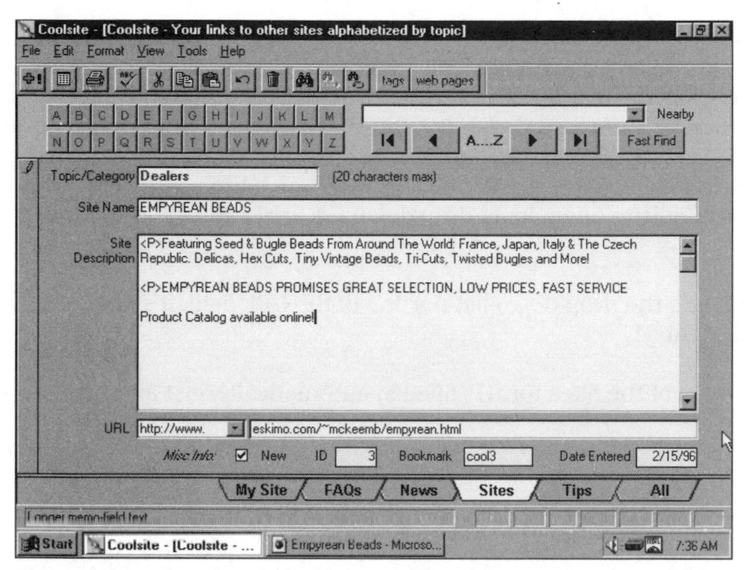

Figure 20-8: The Sites tab with a sample reference already typed in.

Site Description

Here you type a description of what the site is about, so that the reader can decide whether or not to visit it. You can, of course, type anything you like. For example, you may want to use it to provide your own personal review of a site or point out areas within the site that may be especially interesting to your readers. As with other lists, this entry can contain multiple paragraphs, preceded by `<P>` tags, as well as other HTML formatting tags.

URL

The URL field on the Sites page is the actual address of the site that your link takes the reader to. Two fields actually exist for this information. Most URLS start with the characters `http://www`, `http://`, or some other common lead-in. Rather than force you to manually type that prefix into every URL, Coolsite lets you pick the more common ones from a drop-down list.

Use the second half of the URL field to enter the rest of the URL. For example, if the URL you need to enter is `http://www.coolnerds.com`, you can just choose `http://www.` from the drop-down list and then type in `coolnerds.com`.

It's important to keep in mind that the URL you type is exactly what Coolsite will use in the hyperlink it creates. If you type the wrong URL or type the URL incorrectly, the link won't work. There is no margin for error on this one, so be careful.

Pasting a URL

If you happen to be cruising around in a Web browser or in Word IA's Web browse view, you can copy and paste any URL into Coolsite. Just copy it from wherever it appears on your screen and press Ctrl+C (or choose Edit⇨Copy from that program's menu bar). Then click the second (larger) field next to URL and press Ctrl+V. Alternatively, you can click the Paste button in Coolsite's toolbar. If the pasted URL has one of the lead-ins that Coolsite offers in its drop-down list, that URL will be split up automatically.

Danger Zone

Don't paste a URL into the drop-down list portion of the URL field. It's not built to handle that kind of entry!

The Misc Info section of the Sites form is filled in automatically, just as with the FAQs section.

Tip items

You probably get the picture by now, but let's take a quick look at the Tips tab anyway. To enter a tip, you just click the Tips tab and then click the Add Item button (if necessary) to get to a new blank form. Figure 20-9 shows the Tips tab with a sample tip already typed in.

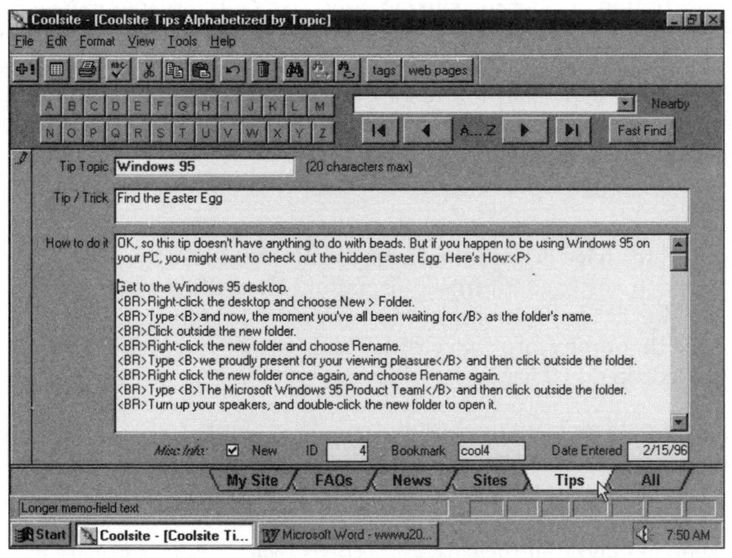

Figure 20-9: Coolsite's Tips tab with a sample entry already typed in.

Tip Topic

As with other types of lists, use the Tip Topic field to type a brief description (up to 20 characters) about the tip. Your entry here appears in the topics list at the top of the generated Tips page.

Tip/Trick

Here you type a sentence or so (up to 255 characters) that further describes what the tip is about. Give the reader enough information to determine whether or not the tip is something he or she wants to learn.

Tip "How to do it" field

The How to do it field is where you type the main body of your tip. Whether or not it is worded as a "how to" depends on the nature of the tip you're typing. If you want to give step-by-step instructions for the tip, you can manually insert the HTML tags for an ordered list (`<OL>`,`<LI>`, and `</OL>`) as I discuss later in this chapter.

The Misc Info section of the Tips tab is identical to that for FAQs and News. Coolsite automatically fills in the fields, so you can ignore them if you like.

Telling Coolsite to Create Your Pages

At any time, you can have Coolsite convert your list entries into actual Web pages that are ready for publishing. Here's how:

1. Click the *Web pages* button in Coolsite's toolbar. You'll come to the dialog box shown in Figure 20-10.
2. Fill in the blanks as follows:
   - In the Store All Pages On field, type the drive and folder where you want to store this batch of pages.

Puzzled?

By default, Coolsite stores all pages in whatever folder you specified in the My Site form. If you don't want to overwrite those pages with the ones you're about to create, however, you can specify a new folder for this run.

   - In the Create column, place a check mark next to each page you want Coolsite to create.
   - In the Topics column, include a check mark if you want Coolsite to list topics at the top of the generated page. (If the list is very short — say two or three items — you may not want to include topics.)
   - Under File Name, enter a filename for each of the pages. You can use the defaults, all of which have the standard `.htm` extension that Web pages use.

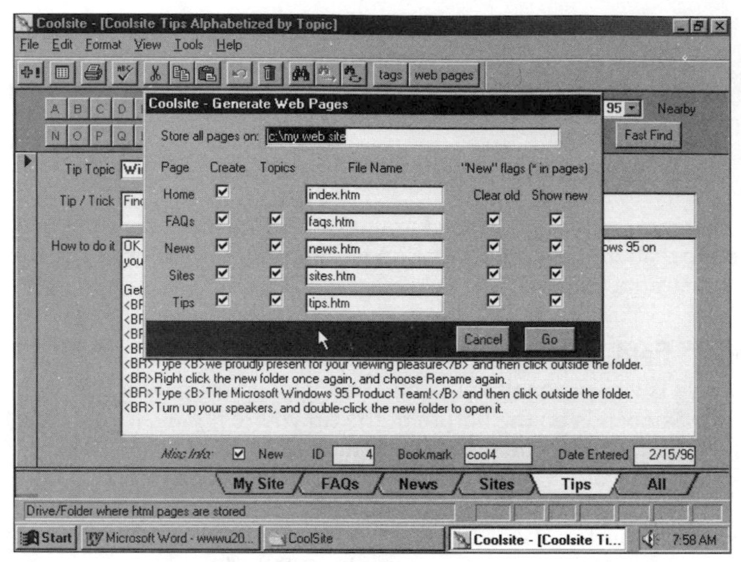

Figure 20-10: Coolsite's dialog box for generating Web pages.

- Whenever you generate pages with Coolsite, it marks new entries (those that have never been published) with an asterisk (*). If you want to keep the asterisks from the previous run, de-select the Clear Old check boxes for the appropriate pages. If you don't want Coolsite to flag new entries with asterisks, clear the Show New check boxes for the appropriate pages.

3. Click the Go button.

Coolsite will get to work and keep you informed of its progress. When it's finished creating your Web pages, you see a message like the one shown in Figure 20-11. Click OK to remove that dialog box.

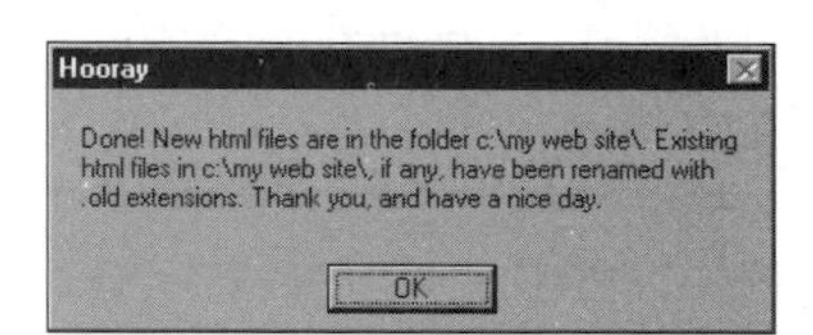

Figure 20-11: Coolsite has finished generating Web pages.

Testing Your Pages

To see how your pages will look on the Web, open one up with your Web browser. I'll take you through an example. First, I exit Coolsite (by choosing File➪Exit from its menu bar or clicking its Close button). Next, I open the folder in which I told Coolsite to store the pages — C:\My Web Site, in this example. (You can use My Computer, Windows Explorer, or Find to open the folder.) Once I've opened the correct folder, I see icons for the HTML documents that Coolsite created, such as in Figure 20-12.

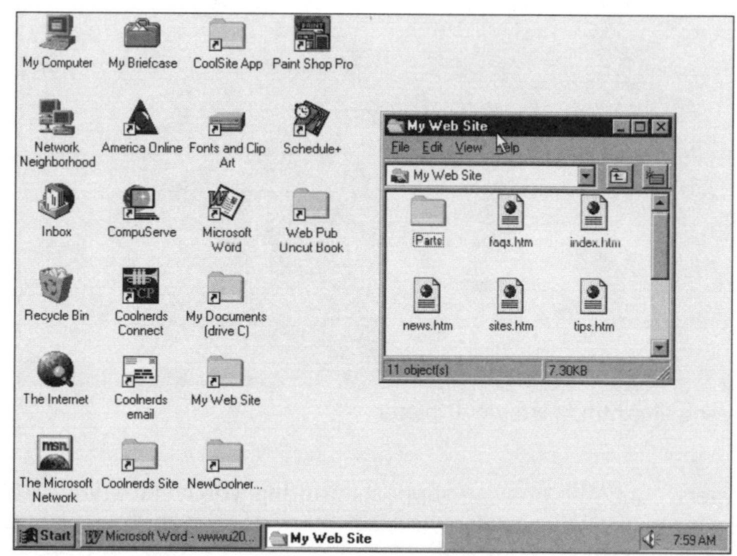

Figure 20-12: Documents that Coolsite created are in my C:\My Web Site folder.

To see how a page will look in a Web browser, double-click the page's icon. Or, if you've configured Windows to send .htm files elsewhere, you can right-click the icon and Send To your browser. Alternatively, you can start your Web browser and open the generated files from within the browser. It really doesn't matter which method you use because the pages are just your standard HTML documents.

In Figure 20-13, I double-clicked the sites.htm icon (after adding several sites to the list and re-generating the page). Here I've zoomed to a 1024 × 768 desktop area so that you can see the general structure of the page. The links at the top of the page are "hot" in the browser, so I can test them right now. I might also mention that the bottom of every generated page contains a hyperlink back to the home page.

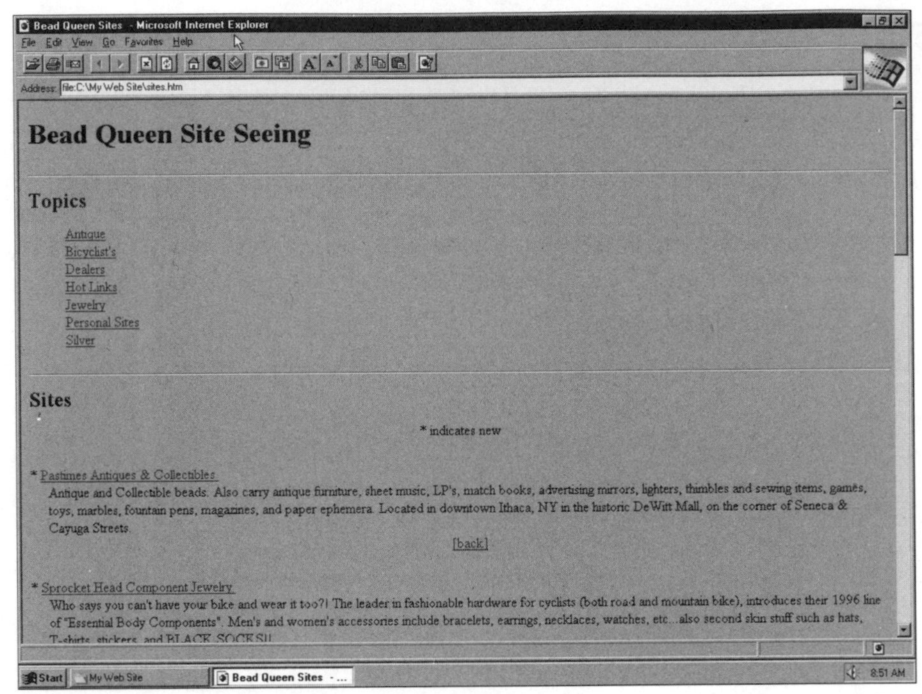

Figure 20-13: Viewing sites.htm in Internet Explorer.

Hot Stuff

If, like most browsers, your Web browser supports printing, you can use your Web browser to print your pages. You can also *view the source* if you want to peek at the tags that Coolsite put into the page for you.

Of course, the original copies of your lists are still in Coolsite. As a result, you can add new items, change existing items, and delete items at your convenience — then generate a new set of pages whenever you want.

Hot Stuff

If you regularly update your site, you're more likely to get return visitors.

Other Coolsite Goodies

Now that you know how to do the important stuff in Coolsite, I'll explain some of the little "extras" that help make the task of managing your lists a little easier.

Navigating and finding items

At the top of the FAQs, News, Sites, Tips, and All tabs, you'll find numerous navigation tools. These tools let you find stuff in your site quickly and (to some extent) follow the same model that your readers will follow. In other words, you can zero in on an item by first navigating to its topic and then going to the specific item.

For starters, click the tab that represents the list you want to search. For example, if you want to search your Sites list, click the Sites tab. If you want to search all lists, click the All tab. (This tab may come in handy if, say, you're looking for items about *Rockets* and don't care whether the items appear in FAQs, Tips, or so forth.) Next, click the one-letter "Rolodex" button that represents the first letter of the topic you're looking for.

Coolsite takes you to the first item within that topic. (If no topics start with the letter that you clicked, you won't be taken anywhere!) Once you're in the general vicinity of the item, you can click the Nearby drop-down button to peek forward and backward at nearby items (see Figure 20-14). If you see the item you want in the list, click the item, and Coolsite takes you right to it.

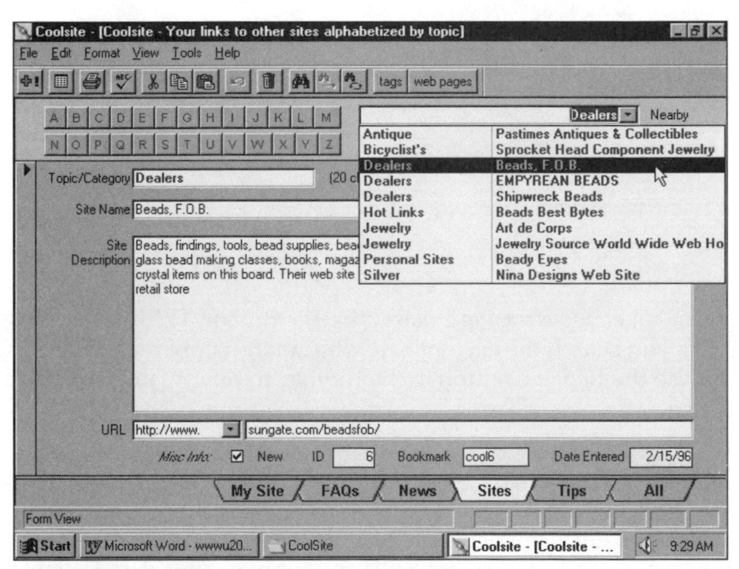

Figure 20-14: Use the Nearby drop-down list to peek ahead or behind at nearby items.

You also can use the First, Previous, Next, and Last buttons located under the Nearby list to scroll through items in your list. In all but the News lists, the items are listed in alphabetical order by topic. Clicking the scroll buttons takes you from topic to topic within the list. In the News list, however, items are in age order — as a result, scrolling ahead takes you to older items, whereas scrolling back takes you through newer items. Clicking the First... button takes you to the top of the list, which is the most recent news story.

You also can search for any word or phrase within the current list (or all lists, if you're in the All tab). Click the Fast Find button to get to the little dialog box shown in Figure 20-15. Type the word or phrase you're looking for, and then click the Find button. You'll come to the first occurrence of that word or phrase. If this is not the item you're looking for, click the Find Next button in the toolbar until you do find the item you're looking for.

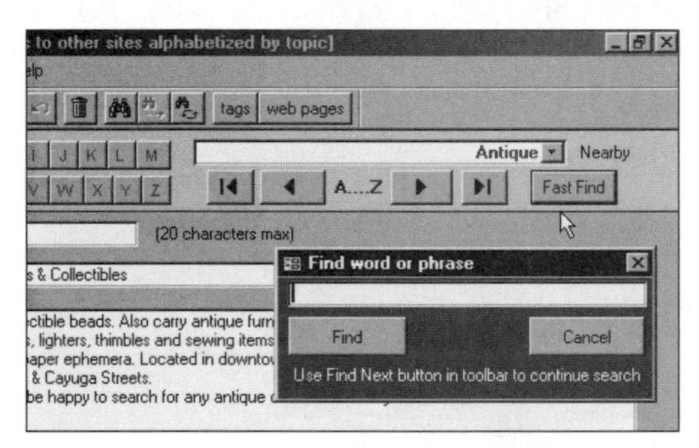

Figure 20-15: Use Find Fast to quickly locate a word or phrase.

For fussier searches, you can use the Find button in the toolbar. This button presents a dialog box that lets you search the current field only, match upper- and lowercase, and so on. You can use the Replace button in the toolbar to do a search-and-replace just as you would in a word processor.

List view versus Form view

You do not always have to deal with only one item at a time. To browse through the items in a list format, click the List View button in the toolbar. Your data is displayed in a list format such as the example shown in Figure 20-16.

In this view, you can use the scroll bars to move around the list. You can widen and narrow columns by dragging the bar that separates the column headings. You also can move columns by dragging the entire column head to the left or right. In addition, you can adjust the font, row height, grid, and colors to your liking.

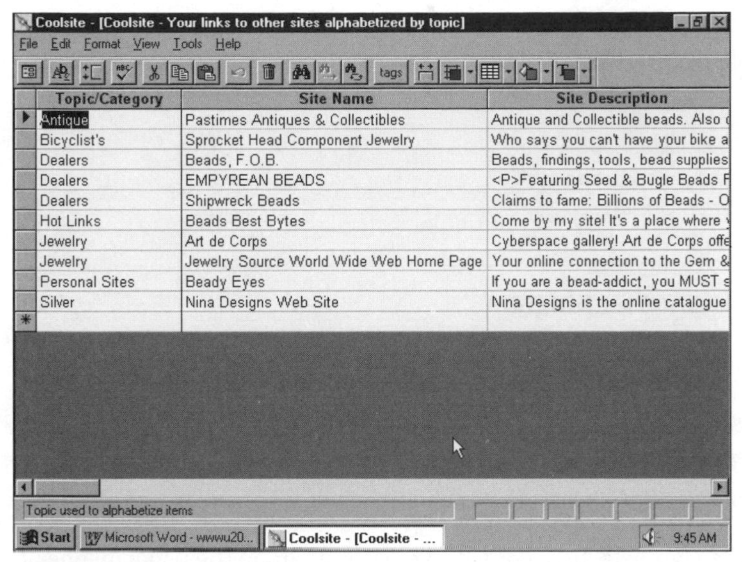

Figure 20-16: The List view of sites.

The changes to the font, colors, and so forth that you make in the List view affect only the List view. Those changes do not carry over into the Form view or the generated HTML documents.

To return to the Form view, click the Form View button in the toolbar.

Moving, copying, and deleting items

If you want to move an item from one list (say, News) to another list (say, FAQs), first get to the item that you want to move. Then click the All tab. There you can use the Belongs In List option to put the item in a different list. You may need to re-word some of the text to make it appropriate for the new list. For example, if you moved text from the News category to the FAQ category, you'll need to change the news headline into an FAQ question.

Duplicating an item

To copy all text in a list item, you can *clone* the item. Here's how:

1. Go to the item you want to clone.
2. Choose Edit⇨Clone from Coolsite's menu bar.
3. You'll see a message asking for verification. Click Yes to proceed.

When the copy is complete, the cloned record is visible in the All tab and you'll see the message shown in Figure 20-17. Click OK, and perform whatever changes are needed to make this new, cloned record different from the original.

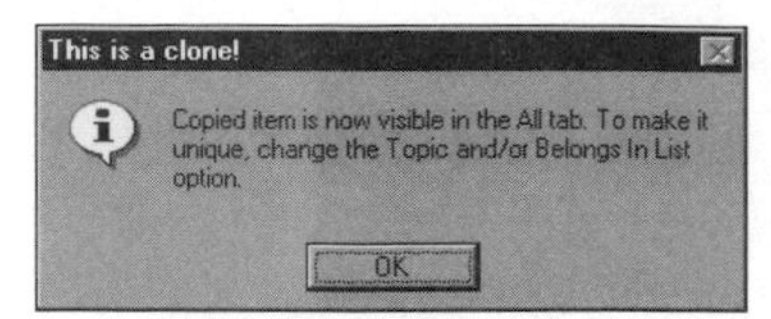

Figure 20-17: Message indicating that list item has been cloned.

Copying data to another program

You can cut and paste data from Coolsite to other Windows applications: Just select the text you want to copy. Alternatively, you can do one of the following:

- ✦ To select the entire item, click the large vertical bar near the left edge of the form or choose Edit➪Select Record.
- ✦ To select all items in the list, choose Edit➪Select All or press Ctrl+A.

After you've made your selection, copy it to the Clipboard in the usual manner. For example, either click the Copy button in the toolbar, press Ctrl+C, or choose Edit➪Copy from the menu. (Or, to delete the selected text, choose Cut rather than Copy.) At this point, the selected text is located on the Clipboard. To paste the text elsewhere, access the document with some other Windows program, position the insertion point, and choose Edit➪Paste from that program's menu bar. Alternatively, you can press Ctrl+V.

For more information on performing basic cut-and-paste actions between programs in Windows, please refer to your Windows documentation.

Exactly how the pasted text looks depends on the application into which you paste the text. If you're looking to get fairly clean text, try pasting into Notepad. If the format of the pasted text isn't good for your needs, try this instead: Generate the pages, open the page in Web browser, and then select and copy text from the browser screen. Alternatively, you can open the generated .htm document with Microsoft Word and then select and copy it from within Microsoft Word.

Deleting an item

To delete the item on your screen, click the Delete Record (little trash can) button in the toolbar. But pay attention to any warning you see. You cannot undo this type of deletion.

Your Coolsite list items are actually stored in a database where each item is considered to be a *record*. Hence, you'll occasionally see the word *record* used to describe a single item in a list.

Inserting custom tags

You can type HTML tags right into your list items. Here are a few pointers before I tell you how to do so:

✦ Coolsite automatically creates bookmarks and links to those bookmarks. As a result, don't bother putting an `<A NAME...>` tag in every item.

✦ Each item is already a member of a list (FAQs list, News list, and so on). Coolsite automatically inserts the `<LI>` and other list tags when you generate your Web pages, so there is no need to type them yourself.

Remember that each item is a member of a list and that the entire list is downloaded to your reader. Therefore, it's probably *not* a good idea to put pictures into your list. Instead, create any large, fancy pages by using Internet Assistant (or a similar program). Then just add hyperlinks to those pages in the list.

Basically, there are three ways to get tags into your pages: automatically, semi-automatically, and manually.

Automatic tags

While you are typing the larger portion of a list item, Coolsite automatically inserts two tags as you work:

✦ `<P>`: This tag marks a paragraph and is inserted when you press Enter.

✦ `<BR>`: This tag marks a line break and is inserted when you press Shift+Enter.

The difference between the two tags (in most Web browsers) is that `<P>` adds a blank line before starting the following paragraph. `<BR>` simply breaks the line and starts anew on the next line.

You can manually insert and delete `<P>` and `<BR>` tags to your heart's content. The important thing to remember is that Coolsite (and most other programs) will ignore those tags. They *appear,* but they don't do anything to the format of the document.

On the other hand, Web browsers pay attention *only* to the tags and not to the line breaks visible in Coolsite. Keeping this straight will probably be tough until you're accustomed to HTML. Basically, however, you just need to remember to put a `<P>` tag somewhere between the end of one paragraph and the start of another. If you don't want the reader to see a blank line between the paragraphs, insert `<BR>` instead of `<P>`.

Semi-automatic tags

The Format menu in Coolsite offers quick access to some of the more common HTML tags, such as `<B>` for bold and `<I>` for italics. Here's how to insert those tags:

1. If you want to format existing text, select that text.
2. Choose Format from Coolsite's menu bar (Figure 20-18), and choose an option from that menu.

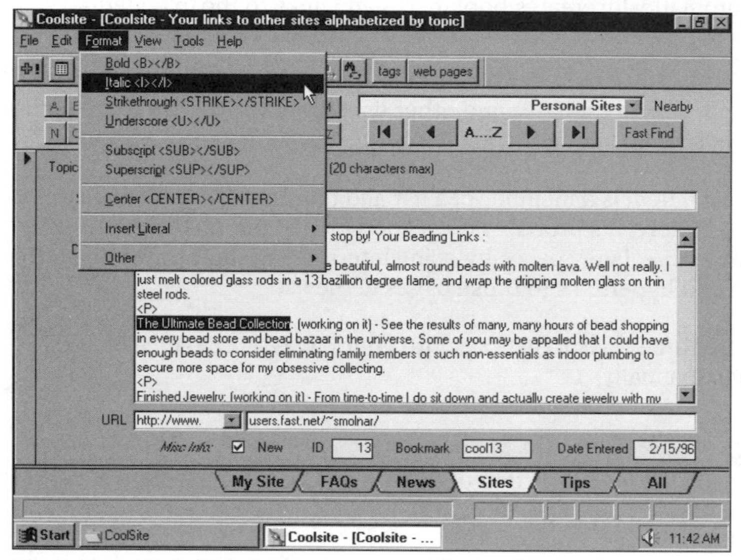

Figure 20-18: Coolsite's Format menu offers quick access to commonly-used HTML tags.

If you selected text in Step 1, the start tag appears at the beginning of the selection and the end tag appears at the end of the selection. If you didn't select text first, the tags appear right beside each other, like this:

```
<I></I>
```

In this example, any new text you type between the tags will be italicized when displayed in a Web browser.

Manual tags

You can manually insert any valid HTML tag into the short (255-character) and longer portions of your list items. Just type the tag as you would type text. That is, position the insertion point and start typing.

Remember that every item in Coolsite is, by itself, an item within a list. Keeping that in mind, you don't want to get *too* carried away with your HTML tags. Nonetheless, you occasionally may want to manually insert a small list within a list item. For example, you could insert `<OL>`, `<LI>`, and `</OL>` tags to create a small numbered list within one of your list items, as shown in Figure 20-19.

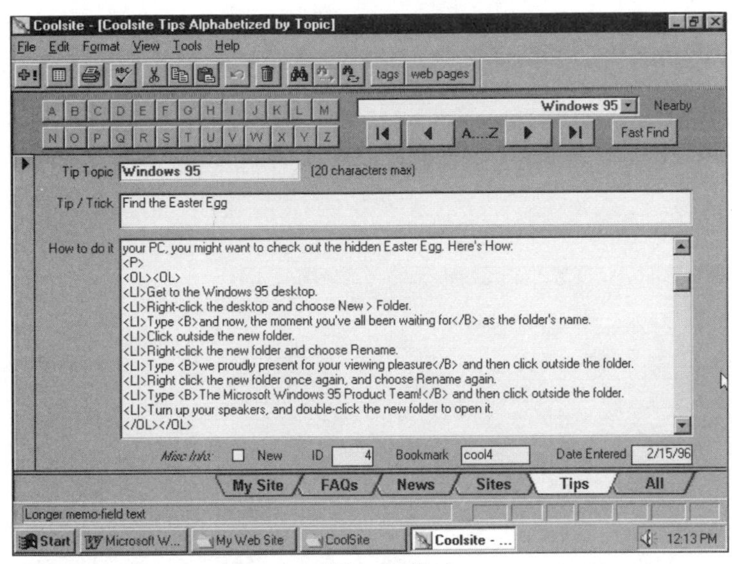

Figure 20-19: HTML tags typed into a list item.

As with HTML tags, Coolsite never tries to interpret these manually-inserted tags. But when you generate your HTML pages and view them with a Web browser, the browser interprets the tags. For example, Figure 20-20 shows the tip from Figure 20-19 as viewed in Microsoft's Internet Explorer.

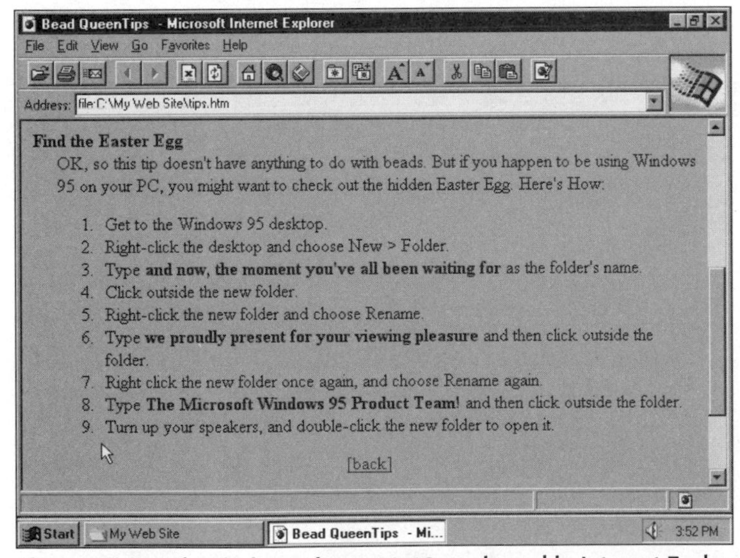

Figure 20-20: The tip from Figure 20-19 as viewed in Internet Explorer.

In Figure 20-19 and Figure 20-21, I doubled the <OL> and <UL> tags to increase the level of indentation in the final document. If you do this, make sure that you include a closing code (</OL> or </UL>) for each starting code.

Figure 20-21 shows a similar trick used to create a bulleted (unordered) list in another list item, using <UL>, <LI>, and </UL> tags. Figure 20-22 shows the Web browser view of that list.

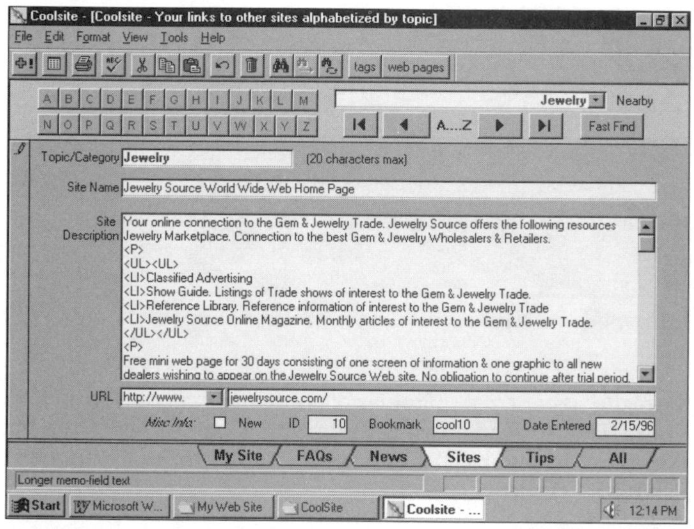

Figure 20-21: Using <UL>...</UL> tags to create a bulleted list within a list item.

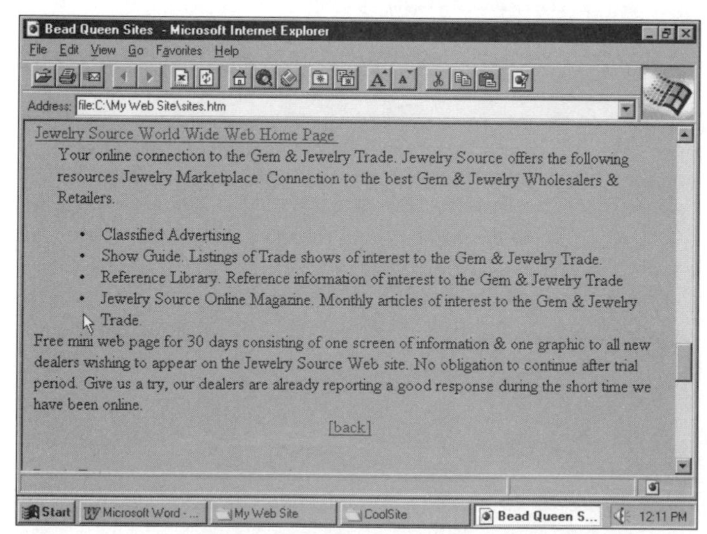

Figure 20-22: The list item from Figure 20-21 as viewed by Internet Explorer.

You can even add hyperlinks to your list items using the standard `<A HREF...></A>` tags. For example, Figure 20-23 shows a hyperlink to `http://www.coolnerds.com` added to a list item in the Bead Queen tips.

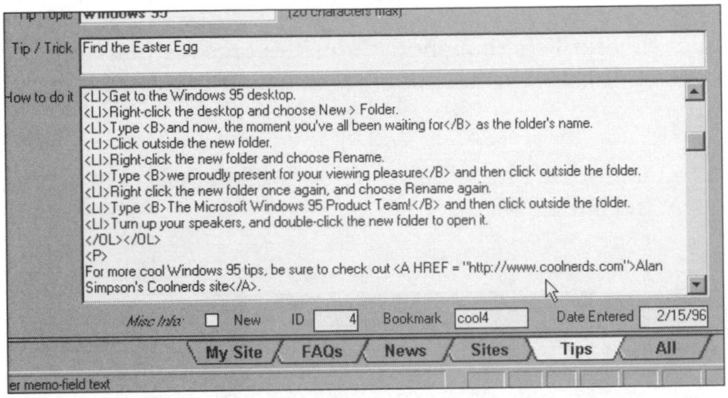

Figure 20-23: A hyperlink manually typed into a list item.

The main trick to manually typing tags is knowing *what* to type. If you forget the exact HTML tags needed to get a certain effect, you can just pop up Coolsite's HTML Tags Quick Reference (Figure 20-24). Click the Tags button in the toolbar or choose View➪Tag Reference.

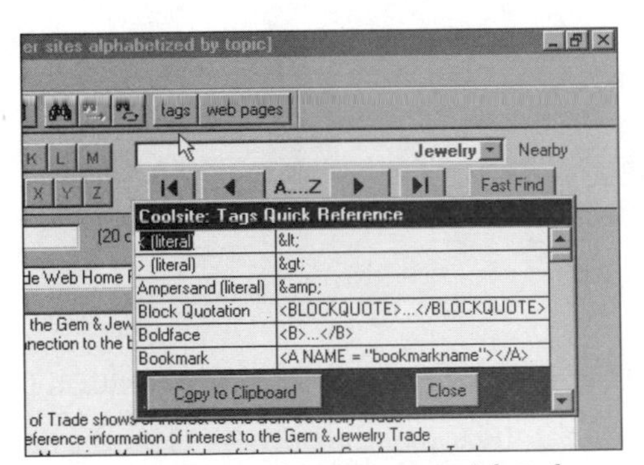

Figure 20-24: Coolsite's Tags Quick Reference window lets you look up a tag in a jiffy.

You can copy a tag from the Quick Reference into the Windows Clipboard. Just click anywhere in the row of the tag you want to copy (you don't need to select text first) and click the Copy to Clipboard button. Now close the Tags reference dialog box. Click wherever you want to paste the tag in your list item, and then paste it (by clicking the Paste button in Coolsite's toolbar, pressing Ctrl+V, or choosing Edit➪Paste).

Printing your lists

In most cases, the best way to view and print your list will be through your Web browser after you've generated the pages. This method enables you to see the information as your readers will see it.

If you'd like printed copies of your lists that show Coolsite's tags (or just your own tags), however, you can use Coolsite's Print capability to whip out a hard copy. To do this task, follow these steps:

1. Click the Print button in Coolsite's toolbar, or choose File⇨Print. You'll come to the dialog box shown in Figure 20-25.

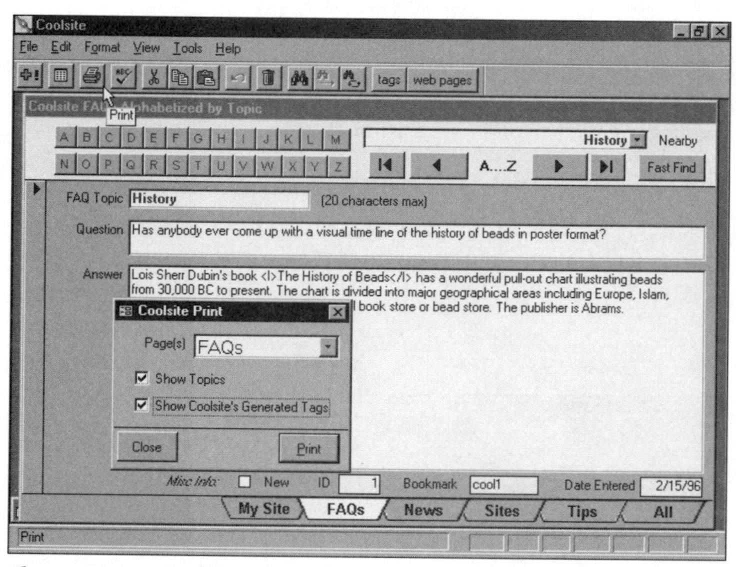

Figure 20-25: Coolsite's own Print dialog box.

2. Choose the page (or all pages) that you want to print from the drop-down list.
3. If you *don't* want to print the topic list at the top of the page(s), clear the Show Topics check box.
4. If you don't want to see the HTML tags that Coolsite generates, close that check box.
5. Click OK.

Remember that the printed copy is really for reviewing the contents of your lists. The exact formatting of the printed lists may not match how the lists look in a Web browser.

Today's Coolsite

I have to confess that, even as I write this chapter, I'm working the last few bugs out of Coolsite. But I don't anticipate any problems in creating a bug-free clean version to ship with this book. The version you receive will be dubbed version 1.0. I may even add some new features before the shipping date, such as an online help file.

In the meantime, however, if you have any questions or are wondering about new versions, just stop by my Web site (`http://www.coolnerds.com`) and lurk around the Web Publishing area to find current information on Coolsite. If you come up with any good ideas for future versions of Coolsite, please let me know. I'm *always* wide open to suggestions.

Uninstalling Coolsite

If you ever need to uninstall Coolsite, follow these steps:

1. Click the Start button, point to Settings, and choose Control Panel.
2. Double-click Add/Remove Programs.
3. Click Coolsite and then click Add/Remove.
4. Choose Remove All⇨Yes. You'll probably need to restart your computer when you're done.

Summary

Let's do the mandatory summary of what we've covered in this chapter:

- ✦ Coolsite is a Windows 95 program that lets you type, edit, and manage text that will be organized into FAQs, News, Site References, and Tips in your Web site.
- ✦ You can install Coolsite from the *Web Publishing Uncut* CD-ROM that came with this book.
- ✦ The My Site tab in Coolsite lets you define your site name, opening blurb, a folder for storing your generated Web pages, and hyperlinks to other pages in your site.
- ✦ The FAQs, News, Sites, and Tips tabs enable you to define items for those kinds of lists.
- ✦ The All tab gives you access to all items in all your lists and is useful for finding words or phrases within list items, regardless of the list in which the item happens to be located.
- ✦ When you want Coolsite to generate Web pages from your lists, click the *Web pages* button in Coolsite's toolbar.
- ✦ Coolsite automatically creates HTML tags for formatting your lists and also creates hyperlinks that let the reader jump to any topic within a list.
- ✦ You also can insert your own HTML tags right into your Coolsite text either by simply typing the tag or by choosing some of the semi-automatic tags from Coolsite's Format menu.

✦ ✦ ✦

Charts, Word Art, and More

✦ ✦ ✦ ✦

In This Chapter

Inserting non-GIF and non-JPEG images into your Web page

Adding word art, equations, and org charts to your page

Pasting a business chart or other image into your Web page

Taking snapshots of your screen

✦ ✦ ✦ ✦

Chapter 15 looked at techniques for inserting images into your Web pages. As you may recall, it's especially easy to insert a GIF or JPEG image: Just click the Picture button in Word IA, specify a picture file, and select other options in the Picture dialog box. In this chapter and the next, I want to look at techniques for placing non-GIF and non-JPEG pictures in your Web pages. You can do this task in several ways:

✦ Use the Insert⇨Object commands from Word IA's menu bars to create or open the picture. Then let Word IA automatically create a GIF file from that object.

✦ Paste an object directly into your Web page, and let Word IA automatically create a GIF file from the object.

✦ Paste a "snapshot" of anything on your screen into Paint Shop Pro, save it as a GIF or JPEG file, and then insert it into your page with the usual Picture button.

In short, virtually anything you see on your screen can be placed in a Web page as a graphic image. In this chapter, I'd like to look at the various techniques for inserting pictures into your Web pages in more depth. Let's start with setting up a clip art library of images you may want to use in your pages.

Setting Up Your Clip Art Gallery

As you build up a collection of clip art images, photos, and other pictures, it becomes increasingly difficult to find the exact picture you need. Browsing around and peeking at the various pictures to find one that could appropriately fill empty space on a page is no longer so easy, either. A good solution to this problem is to invest a little time into organizing all your existing pictures into a *clip art gallery.* Several programs are available that enable you to create such galleries.

Installing missing office components

If you can't find some of the Office components discussed in this chapter — ClipArt Gallery, WordArt, Equation, or Org Chart — you simply may need to install them. To do so, you first need to grab your original Office CD-ROM or floppy disks. Then click the Start button and choose Settings⇨Control Panel⇨Add/Remove Programs. Click on the Microsoft Office option (or Microsoft Office Professional or Microsoft Word — whatever you have) and then click the Add/Remove button. Insert a disk as instructed on the screen.

When you reach the Setup window, click the Add/Remove button. Click on Office Tools, and then click the Change Option button. In the list of tools that appears, select the components that you want to add. (Don't clear any existing check marks unless you want to remove the corresponding components.) Click OK, then choose Continue, and follow any instructions that appear on the screen.

In this chapter, I use the Microsoft ClipArt Gallery as the example. I chose this particular program mainly because it comes with Microsoft Office for Windows 95. In fact, many of the individual components that come in Office also contain the ClipArt Gallery. So even if you only have one or two of those programs (such as Word and Excel), chances are the ClipArt Gallery is already installed on your PC.

To bring the ClipArt Gallery up-to-date with the clip art available on your PC, follow these steps:

1. In Word IA, choose Insert⇨Object from the menu bar.
2. Choose Microsoft ClipArt Gallery⇨OK.
3. If you've never used Microsoft ClipArt Gallery, you may see a dialog box asking if you want to update the gallery with some existing clip art. Choose Yes to start updating right now.
4. You'll come to the ClipArt Gallery (Figure 21-1) which may or may not already contain some pictures.
5. Choose Organize⇨Add Pictures.
6. In the dialog box that appears, browse to a folder that contains pictures and select the filenames of pictures that you want to add. For example, in Figure 21-2, I browsed to a folder named F:\ArtParts\Dingbats on my PC. Then I selected all pictures in the folder by clicking the first filename and Shift+clicking the last filename.

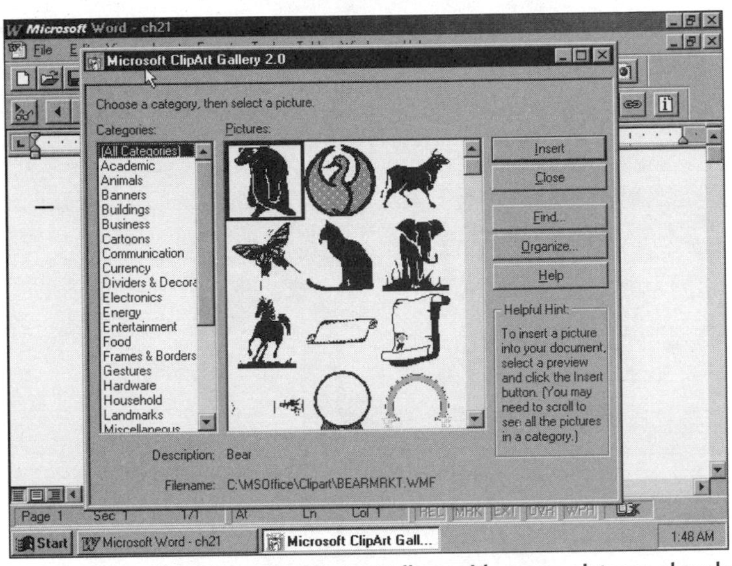

Figure 21-1: The Microsoft ClipArt Gallery with some pictures already in place.

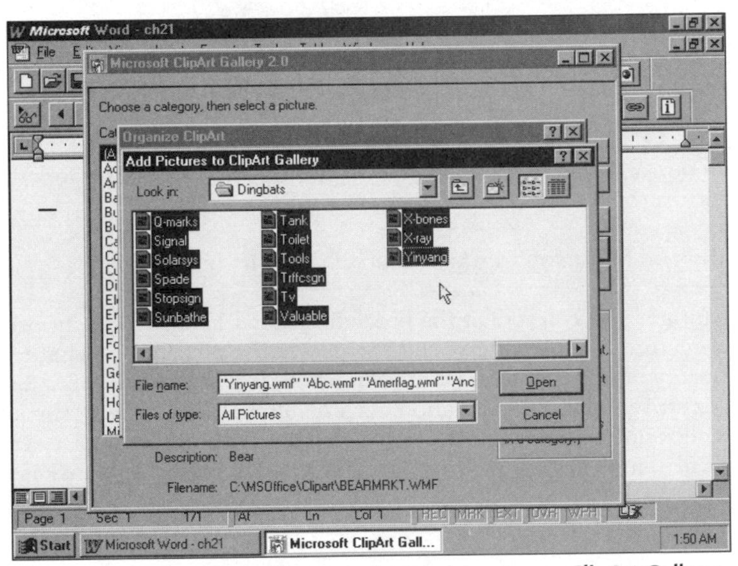

Figure 21-2: About to add some pictures to my own ClipArt Gallery.

7. Choose Open.

8. You'll see a dialog box like the example in Figure 21-3, giving you the chance to enter a description and category for each selected picture. To speed things along, you can just select one or more categories for all incoming pictures, choose the *Add all pictures to the selected categories* check box, and click OK.

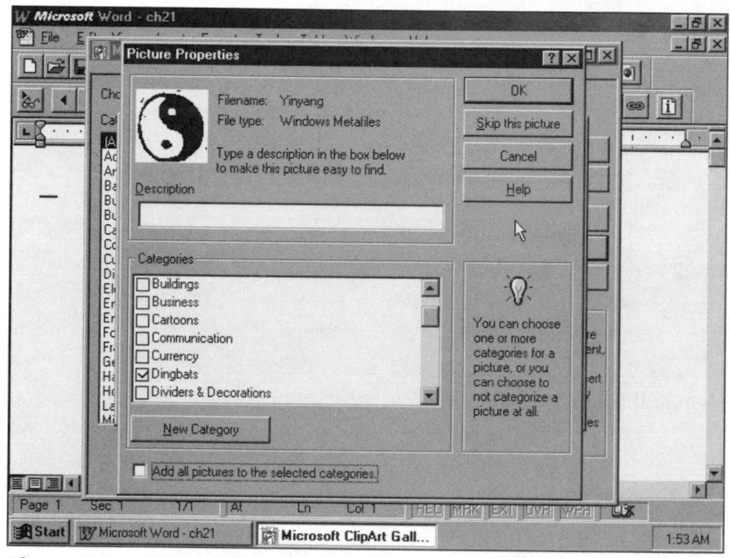

Figure 21-3: Options for a picture that I've added to the ClipArt Gallery.

9. Now you can repeat Steps 5 through 8 to add pictures from other folders to your ClipArt Gallery.

More Info

For more information on Microsoft ClipArt Gallery, peruse its online help.

At any time in the future, you can repeat the preceding Steps 1 through 4, choose Organize, add new pictures to the gallery, and reorganize the pictures — whatever is convenient. The beauty of it is that when you've finished, you'll have thumbnails of all your clip art images stored in a single location. As a result, you can browse through your pictures and click one to enter it into your Web page, without having to worry about the picture's filename, location, or format. You'll see how easy this task is in the next section.

Inserting Non-GIF Clip Art

If you have a picture to show in your Web site but that picture isn't stored in GIF or JPEG format, the easiest way to get it into your Web page is to use Insert⇨Object in Word IA's normal Edit mode. The following list provides the exact steps.

Hot Stuff

Before putting *any* pictures or objects in your Web page, be sure to save the page to your My Web Site folder. That way, all GIF files that Word IA generates end up in your My Web Site folder.

1. With your Web page in normal Word IA Edit view, click at the point where you want to insert the picture to position the insertion point.
2. Choose Insert⇨Object. Then follow these steps according to your situation:
   - If you've already added the picture to your ClipArt Gallery, choose Microsoft ClipArt Gallery, click on the picture you want, click on the Insert button, and skip the next step.
   - Otherwise, click the Create from File tab, use the Browse button to locate the filename of the picture you want to insert, click on the filename, and click OK (twice) to insert the picture into your document.

You now can size the picture to fit on your page. Click the picture so it has sizing handles. Drag any corner to size the picture to your liking. Keep in mind that Word IA never shows exactly how the text will wrap next to a picture, so don't waste time trying to align text to the picture now.

When you save the Web page, Word IA displays a dialog box titled Conversion of Pictures. Choose Save pictures to automatically create a GIF version of the picture, put it in the same folder as your Web page, and insert the `<IMG SRC = ...>` tag required to display the picture in your Web page. At that point, you can click the Preview in Browser button to see how the picture will really look when published. Figure 21-4 shows an example.

Figure 21-4: The YinYang.wmf clip art image in a Web page, as viewed by Internet Explorer.

There are a few disadvantages to using Insert⇨Object to add non-GIF and non-JPEG images to your Web pages. But there are also easy fixes. One disadvantage is that Word IA gives the GIF copy of each picture a generic, non-descriptive filename (the GIF images may be named img00001.gif, img00002.gif, img00003.gif, and so on). The simple fix to this disadvantage is to rename the file. Then you can go back to your Web page in Word IA, delete the image, and re-insert it by using the Picture button and the new filename. Alternatively, you can use Paint Shop Pro to convert the image to a GIF file and then copy it to your My Web Site folder *before* you put the picture into your Web page. Here you use the Picture button, rather than Insert⇨Object, to insert the GIF image.

A second disadvantage is that Insert⇨Object never attempts to give the picture a transparent background. The background color always shows up, as the example in Figure 21-4 illustrates. If you want to make the image appear to float within your Web page, you need to define the picture's background color as Transparent. As you learn in the next chapter, you can do that with Paint Shop Pro as well.

Finally, Insert⇨Object always uses the default settings for alignment with text, alternate text, and so forth. But those defaults are easy to change. Just click the picture in Word IA to select it. Next, click the Picture button to get to the picture's options. Choose your options and then click OK. In Figure 21-5, I gave the YinYang symbol a transparent background and right-aligned it with neighboring text.

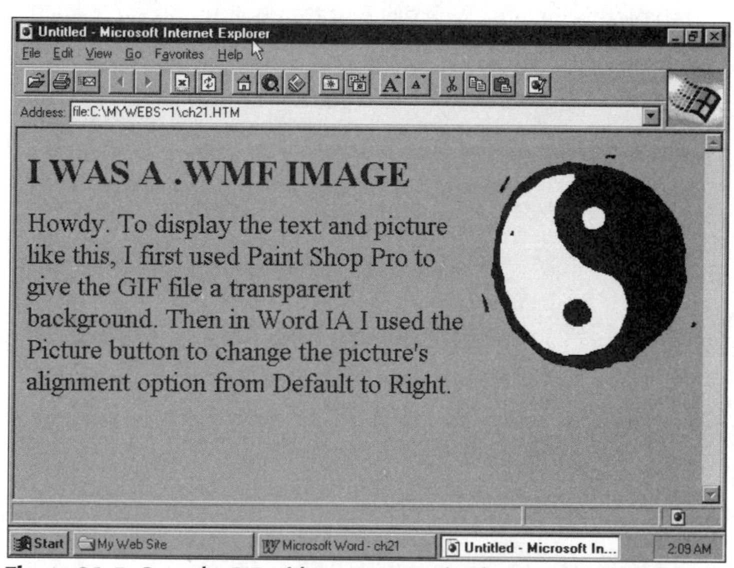

Figure 21-5: Sample GIF with transparent background and text alignment set to Right.

More Info Chapter 15 discusses aligning pictures with text, centering pictures, and performing other options for GIFs.

Creating New Pictures On-The-Fly

You can use Insert⇨Object to create new objects as you add them to your Web page. Again, when you save your page, Word IA automatically copies the objects to GIF files and puts the appropriate tag into your Web page. The three most common objects you're likely to create are word art, equations, and org charts.

Creating word art

Microsoft WordArt 2.0 is a fun and easy way to add some pizzazz to titles and other small chunks of text. To use it, follow these steps:

1. In normal Word IA Edit mode, click on the approximate spot where you want to position the word art.
2. Choose Insert⇨Object⇨Create New⇨MS WordArt 2.0⇨OK.
3. Type your own text to replace "Your Text Here."
4. Use buttons in the WordArt toolbar to assign a shape, font, and other characteristics to the text. For example, in Figure 21-6, I've typed the text *Web Publishing Uncut,* given it the Wave 1 shape, and applied a font and shadow.

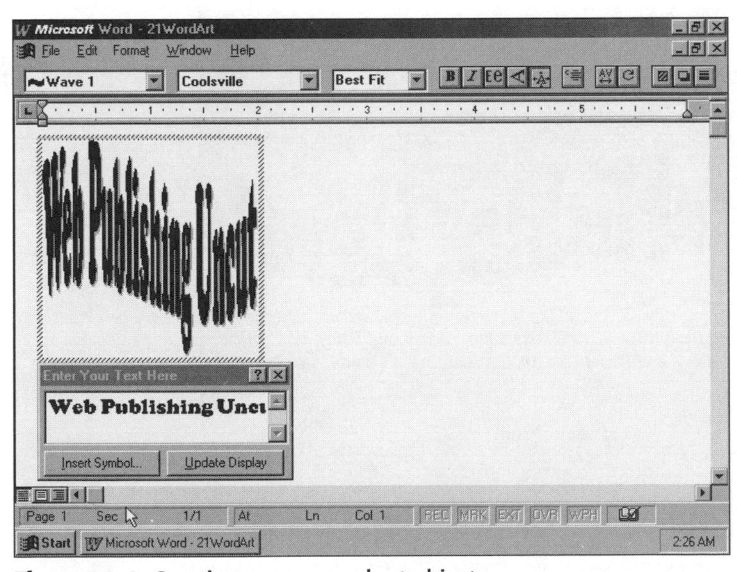

Figure 21-6: Creating a new word art object.

5. Click anywhere outside the word art picture to return to regular Word IA.

Once you're back in Word IA, you can size the word art picture in the usual manner. That is, click it once to select it so that it displays sizing handles. Then drag the sizing handle in whatever direction you want. If you have trouble getting the exact size you want, you may want to try the Stretch to Frame command. Double-click the word art picture to get back to the WordArt toolbar. Then choose Format⇨Stretch to Frame, or click the equivalent button in the WordArt toolbar. Click outside the word art picture to get rid of the WordArt toolbar and then try to resize the image.

Hot Stuff

Word art is sent to the reader as a graphic image, not text. As such, your reader sees the word art displayed in whatever font you used. The reader need not have that font on his or her own PC.

If you want to change the font, shape, color, or other attribute of your word art image after you've placed it in the Web page, double-click the image. You'll be taken back to the WordArt toolbar where you are free to make whatever changes you want.

When you save the current Web page, Word IA creates a GIF copy of the word art picture, following the standard *img0000x.gif* file-naming convention. When you view the page with your Web browser, you'll see the word art with a white background and perhaps not sized quite as you'd like it. If you want to give the word art a transparent background or want to have more control over its size, you can use Paint Shop Pro to modify the GIF file that Word IA created for you. For example, in Figure 21-7, I've given my sample word art a transparent background and a width of about 600 pixels.

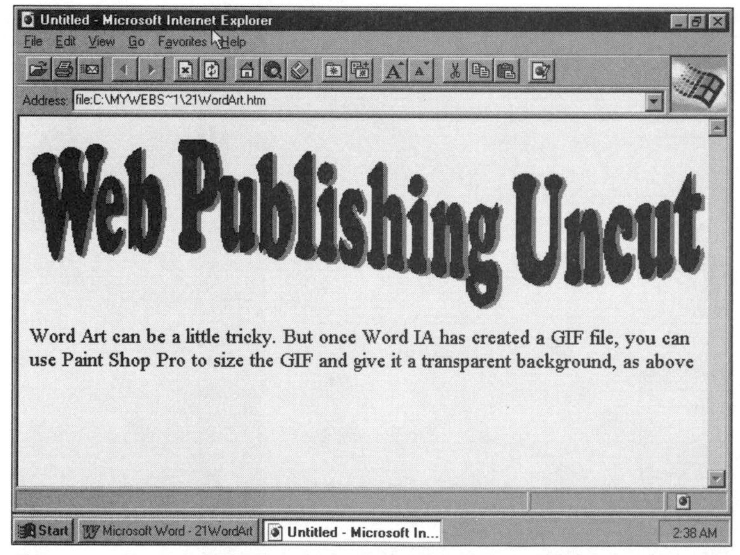

Figure 21-7: Web browser view of word art after giving it a transparent background and sizing it with Paint Shop Pro.

Creating equations

If you need to show equations in your Web page and you have Microsoft Office, you can use Microsoft Equation 2.0 to type the equation. Here's how:

1. With your Web page showing in the normal Word IA Edit mode, move the insertion point to the approximate spot where you want to place the equation.
2. Choose Insert⇨Object⇨Create New⇨Microsoft Equation 2.0, and then click on OK. The little equation editor pops up on your screen as in Figure 21-8.

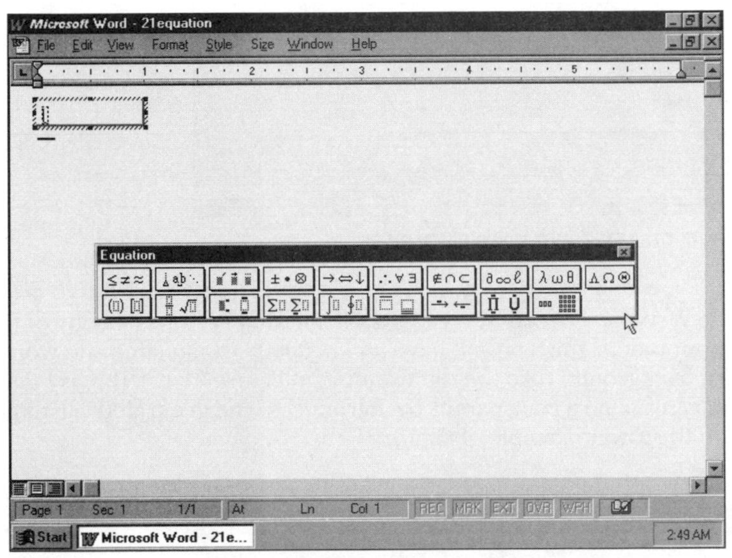

Figure 21-8: Microsoft Equation 2.0 editor on the screen.

3. Select the special symbols that you need in your equation. Type numbers and text (variable names) as regular characters.

More Info

For more information on using Microsoft Equation 2.0, refer to its online help while typing your equation.

4. After typing your equation, click anywhere outside the equation to return to normal Word IA editing.

You then can click the equation to display its sizing handles and drag any sizing handle to resize the equation. If you need to get back to the equation editor options, double-click the equation. In Figure 21-9, I've typed an equation and sized it to fit my Web page.

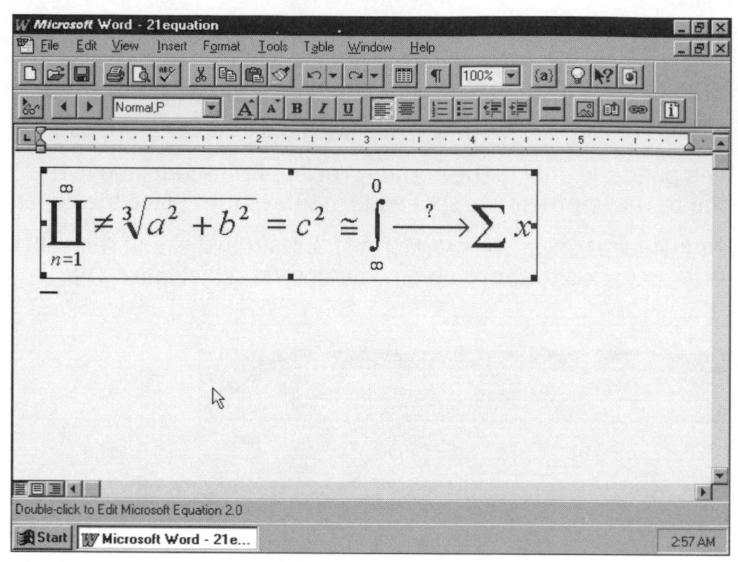

Figure 21-9: An equation typed into my Web page.

When you save the Web page, Word IA creates a GIF file that contains a copy of the equation. Like other objects, this one will have an img0000*x*.gif filename and won't have a transparent background (like the top example in Figure 21-10). But as I discuss in Chapter 22, you can assign a transparent background to the generated GIF to get the effect shown in the lower example of Figure 21-10.

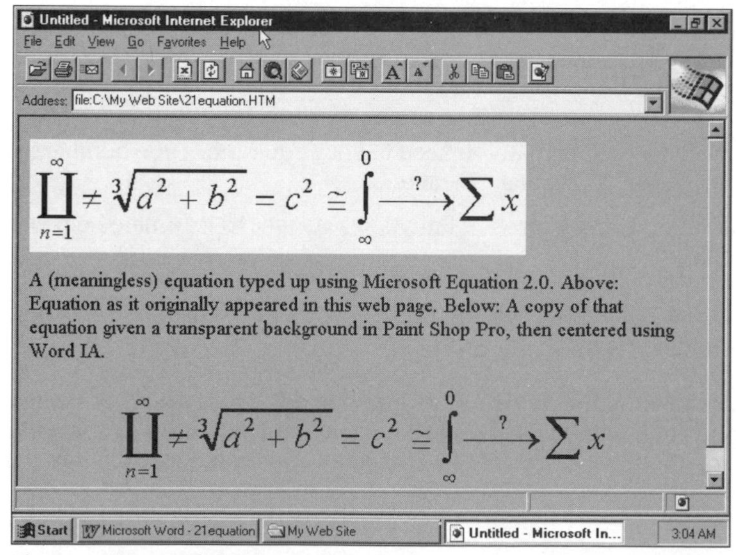

Figure 21-10: Web browser view of an equation in a Web page, with and without a transparent background.

Creating an org chart

You can easily create organizational charts (org charts) in Microsoft Office by using MS Organization Chart 2.0. Here are the steps to follow if you want to create an org chart and put it into a Web page:

1. With the Web page open in Word IA's normal editing mode, move the insertion point to the approximate location where you want the org chart to appear.
2. Choose Insert⇨Object⇨Create New⇨MS Organization Chart 2.0, and click on OK. A simple org chart and tools for editing it appear on the screen in Figure 21-11.

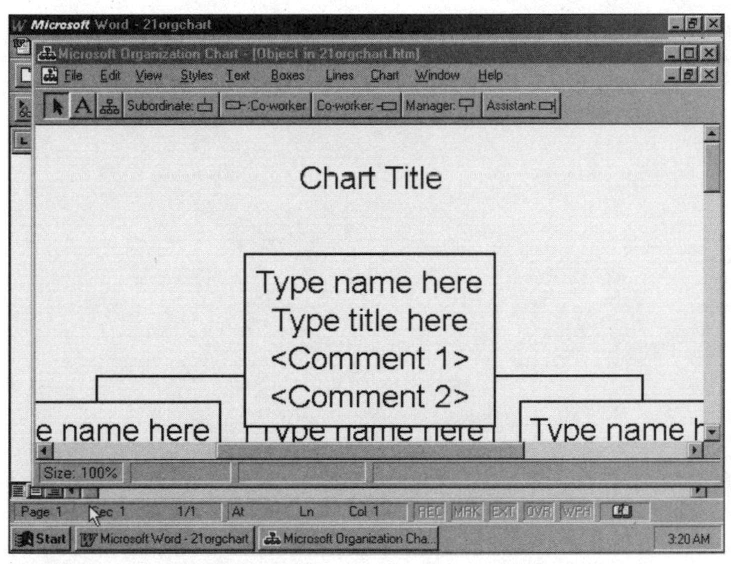

Figure 21-11: Ready to add an org chart to my Web page.

3. Type text where indicated. If you want to remove text, just leave it as-is. For example, to get rid of `<Comment 1>` and `<Comment 2>` in the top box, leave those items unchanged.
4. Use the menu commands and toolbar buttons in Organization Chart to add new levels, move things around, color cells, and so forth.

More Info

For more information on using MS Organization Chart, review its online help while you're creating an org chart.

5. Once you're happy with your org chart, choose File⇨Close and Return…⇨Yes to return to your page.

As with the other object types, you now can size the org chart by clicking it and dragging its sizing handles. If you need to make changes to the chart, just double-click it to get back to org-chart editing commands.

As with other objects, when you save the Web page, Word IA will create a GIF image of the org chart and store it in the same folder as the Web page itself. If you want, you can open the org chart with Paint Shop Pro and give it a transparent background color, as discussed in the next chapter. Figure 21-12 shows an org chart as it originally looked after entering it into a Web page and a copy of that same org chart with a transparent background and centered on the page.

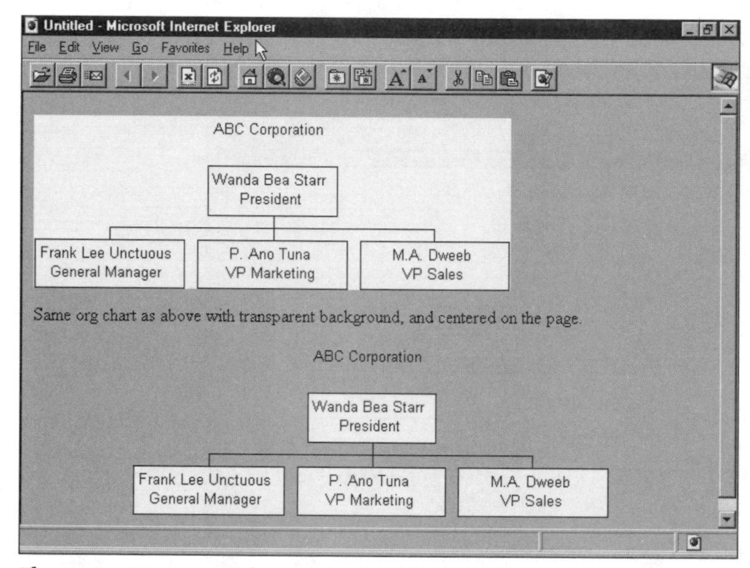

Figure 21-12: A sample org chart, with and without a transparent background.

Other objects

Word art, equations, and organization charts are examples of objects you can create and insert into your Web pages by using Word IA. When you choose Insert➪Object on your own PC, you'll see the full range of "OLE-aware" applications that you've installed on your PC. For example, Figure 21-13 shows the Object dialog box from one of my PCs.

Notice that the Object dialog box contains two tabs: Create New and Create from File. As a general rule, you only want to use Create New to embed objects that you really cannot create in any other way. For instance, Microsoft WordArt, Equations, and Organization Charts all have to be created in this manner.

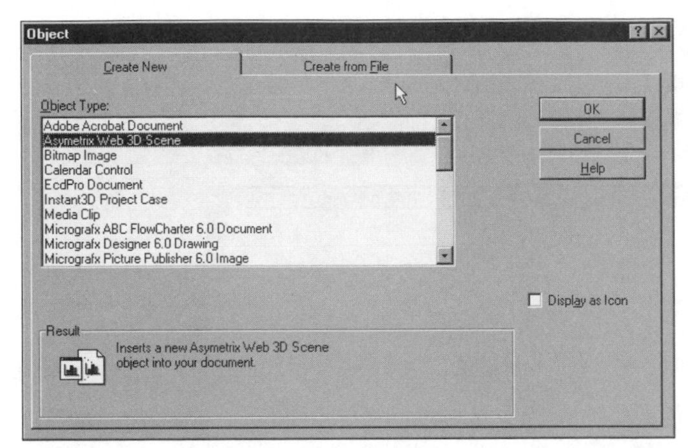

Figure 21-13: The Insert Object dialog box on one of my PCs.

For most other types of objects, you are probably better off creating the entire object and then saving it to disk, as per that program's instructions. When you want to embed that object in your Web page, choose Insert⇨Object⇨Create from File and just browse to the object's filename.

More Info

For more information on objects, read up on OLE (Object Linking and Embedding) in your Windows 95 documentation and in the manuals of any programs you plan to use to create such objects.

Unfortunately, there is no guarantee that Word IA will be able to convert *every* object to a GIF file. But even that is not a big deal, because if Insert⇨Object doesn't work, one of the next two methods discussed in this chapter will.

Paste an Object into Your Web Page

In many situations, you can just copy and paste a picture (or other object) right into your Web page. After you save the page, Word IA automatically creates a GIF file of that object and stores the GIF file in the same folder as the page itself. The classic copy-and-paste example is popping an Excel chart into your Web page.

Figure 21-14 shows a sample Microsoft Excel worksheet, where I typed some text and numbers in the first two columns. Next, I selected those two columns and used the Chart Wizard to create the simple pie chart shown in the worksheet. I also clicked on the pie chart (so it displays sizing handles). At this point, I choose Edit⇨Copy from Excel's menu bar to copy the chart to the Windows Clipboard.

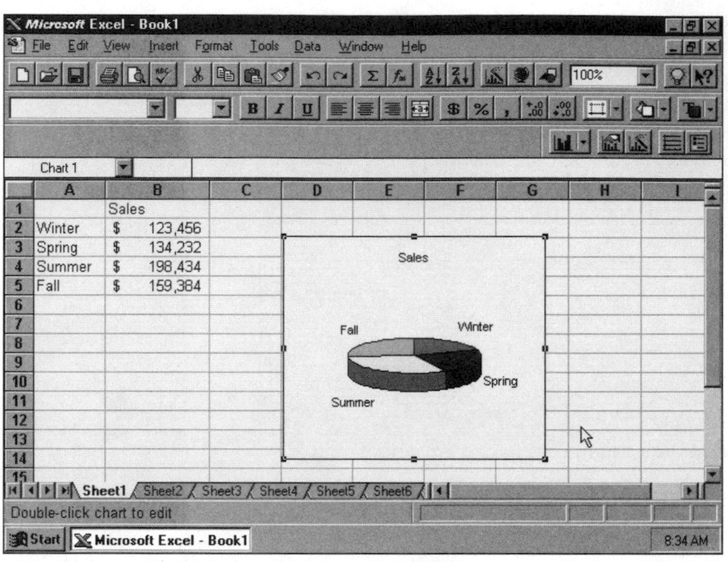

Figure 21-14: A chart in an Excel worksheet, selected and ready to copy.

When you get to this point with an object you want to add, you open up (or create) your Web page in Word IA's normal Edit mode. Move the insertion point to the approximate spot where you want the chart to appear, and choose Edit⇨Paste from the Word IA menu bar. When you save the Web page, Word IA asks if you want to save the pictures as well. Choose Save pictures, which prompts Word IA to create a GIF file of the chart and put it in the same folder as the Web page.

When you view the page with a Web browser, the chart will have a white background. Any neighboring text will align at the bottom of the chart. If you want to give the chart a clear background, you can open the chart's GIF file in Paint Shop Pro and assign a transparent background color. In Word IA, you can use the Picture button to align the text to your liking. For example, Figure 21-15 shows my sample pie chart embedded in a Web page, with a clear background and the picture right-aligned to the text.

Puzzled?

Actually, I cropped the image a little and enlarged the chart title a bit while I had it open in Paint Shop Pro.

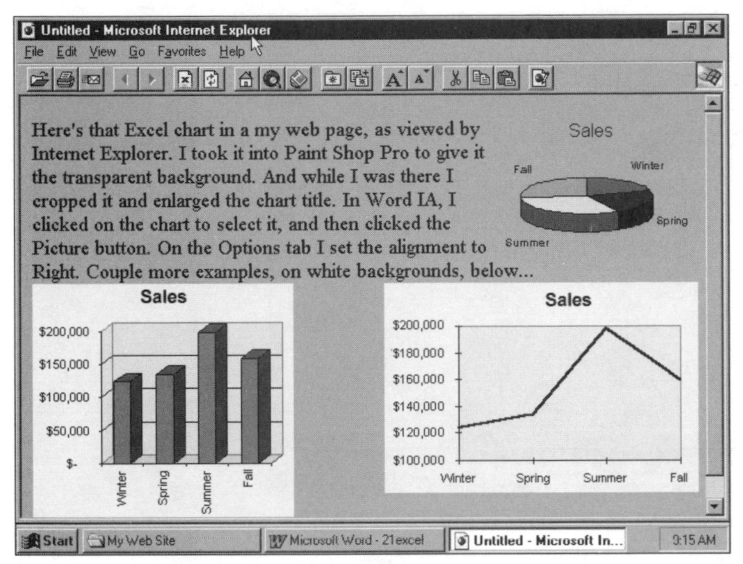

Figure 21-15: The Excel chart in a Web page, as viewed by Internet Explorer.

Take a Snapshot of the Screen

Unfortunately, Insert⇨Object and Copy⇨Paste won't work for every image that you may want to display in a Web page. When all else fails, you can always take a "snapshot" of the image on the screen. Clean it up in Paint Shop Pro, and save it in GIF format. Then use the Picture button in Word IA to place the picture in your Web page. Let's look at an example.

Suppose that I want to create a table using the Microsoft Word Normal.dot template and Table Wizard. In my Web document, I want to treat it as a graphic rather than as a table so that I can wrap some text around it and not worry about what fonts the reader has. First, I create a normal document in Word by choosing File⇨New and the Blank Document template. Then I use the standard tools in Word to create a table like the one shown in Figure 21-16.

Now I want to place a Print Preview version of this table in my Web document. To do this, I first choose File⇨Print Preview to get into that view. Once there, I can use the Zoom control to set the table to the approximate size I want it to be in my Web page, as shown in Figure 21-17.

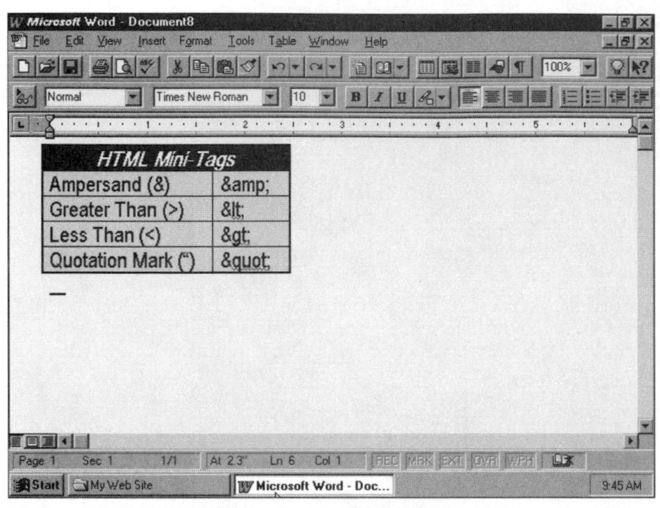

Figure 21-16: A table created in Word's Normal.dot template.

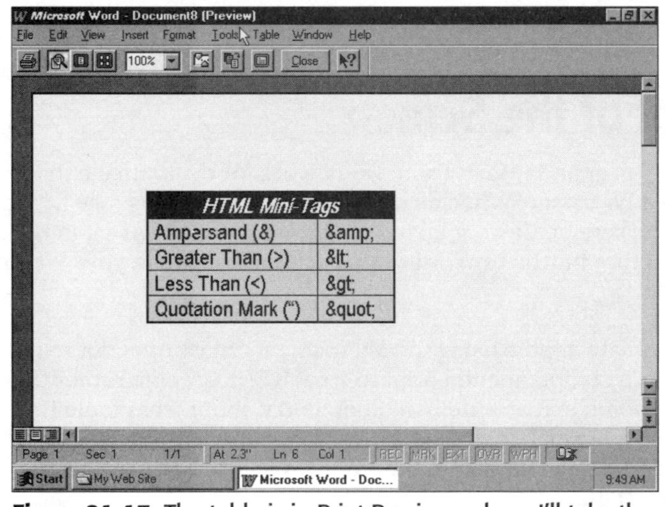

Figure 21-17: The table is in Print Preview, where I'll take the snapshot.

To take the snapshot, I simply press the Print Screen (Prt Scr) button. (On some computers, you may have to press Shift + Print Screen.) Nothing seems to happen, but behind the scenes, Windows has placed an exact snapshot of the screen onto the Windows Clipboard. At this point, I can Close Print Preview and exit Word, perhaps saving a copy of the current document as a backup in case I ever need a copy of the table in the future.

Next, I fire up Paint Shop Pro and choose Edit⇨Paste⇨As New Image. A dump of the entire screen appears as a picture in Paint Shop Pro. I then can use the Selection tool to drag a frame around the part I want to put into my Web page, as in Figure 21-18.

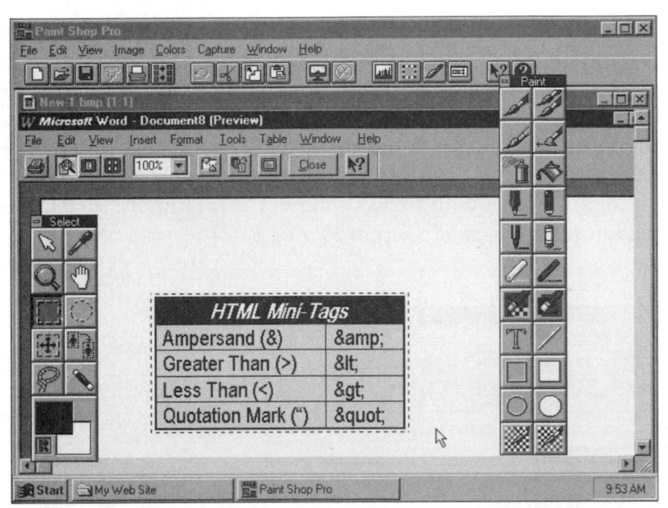

Figure 21-18: Ready to crop the table from the snapshot in Paint Shop Pro.

Once the selection is made, I choose Image➪Crop, and my table appears looking like a graphic image in Paint Shop Pro, as you can see in Figure 21-19. At this point, I could use File➪Save As in Paint Shop Pro to save the image as a GIF file and perhaps even assign a transparent background color. If I did that, I then want to save that GIF file in my My Web Site folder because, being that I saved the image as a GIF file, I will need to upload it to the server at some point to publish it.

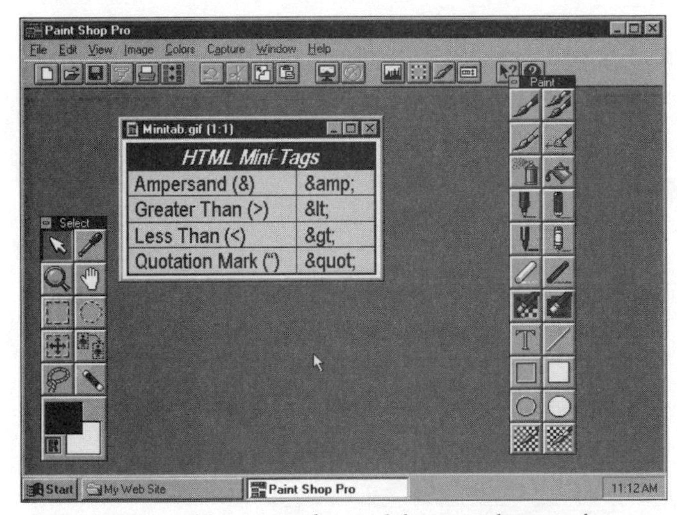

Figure 21-19: Table cropped out of the snapshot, ready to save as a GIF.

After I've saved the GIF file, I can fire up Word IA (that is, Word with the HTML.DOT template) and open or create my Web page normally. Once I've completed that task, I just use the Picture button in the Word IA toolbar to read in the GIF file. While I'm at it, I can set the picture alignment to Left or Right so that I can wrap text around the picture. In this case, I also opted to put a five-point border around the image (see Chapter 15 if you forgot how to do that). Initially, the text and picture may look something like Figure 21-20, but in the Web Browse view, the alignment kicks in and I get exactly the look I was hoping for, as shown in Figure 21-21.

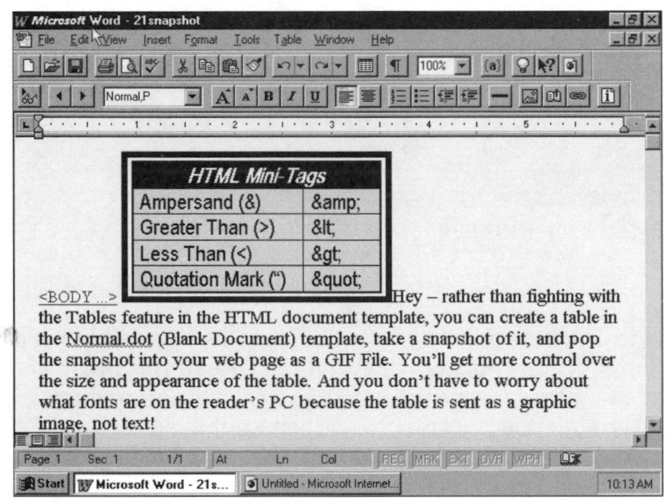

Figure 21-20: Word IA's view of the pasted-in table.

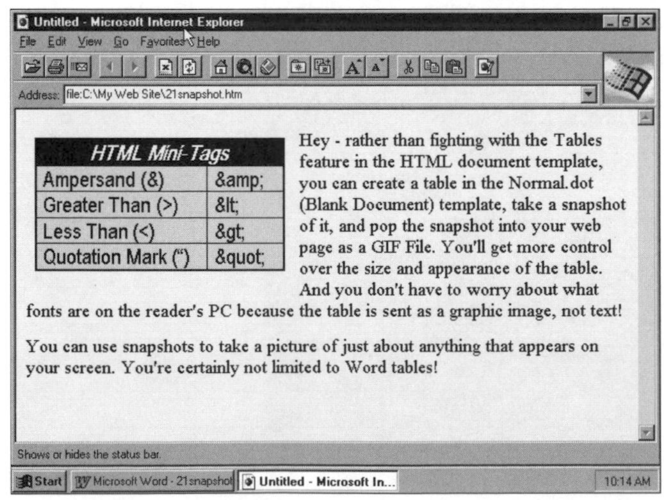

Figure 21-21: Internet Explorer's view of the Web page shown in Figure 21-20.

The snapshot approach works with *any* image that you can display on your screen. As always, you should try to size the image before you take the snapshot so that you don't have to resize it later in Paint Shop Pro or Word IA. Also, if the image quality on your screen isn't so hot, be sure to check your monitor's current color depth and desktop area settings. To do so, save any work in progress and close all programs to get to the Windows 95 desktop. Right-click the desktop, and choose Properties. Click the Settings tab, and choose a Color palette (depth) and Desktop area. You may even want to experiment with settings on some of the other tabs. When you're done, click OK and follow the instructions on the screen.

Summary

In this chapter, we've looked at lots of ways to get non-GIF and non-JPEG graphic images into your Web pages. As you'll see in the next chapter, yet another approach is to open the image in Paint Shop Pro and save it as a GIF or JPEG from there. But before we get to that method, let's review what you learned here:

✦ You can use the Insert⇨Object commands in Word IA to insert a non-GIF or non-JPEG image into a Web page.

✦ You also can paste many types of graphic images directly into a Web page.

✦ When you save your Web page, Word IA attempts to make a GIF image from the embedded object and then stores that object in the same folder as the Web page.

✦ You can use Paint Shop Pro (Chapter 22) to change any GIF file that Word IA creates. For example, you may want to give the picture a transparent background.

✦ Virtually anything you see on your screen can be captured as a snapshot, simply by pressing the Print Screen key.

✦ You can paste a snapshot into Paint Shop Pro, crop it, and save it as a GIF or JPEG file to put into your Web page.

✦ The bottom line is, if you can *see* an image on your screen, you can *display* it in your Web page.

✦ ✦ ✦

Improving Your Image(s)

✦ ✦ ✦ ✦

In This Chapter

Opening and converting graphic images with Paint Shop Pro

Resizing and cropping images

Getting graphics to the reader in a jiffy

Creating interlaced "fade-in" GIFs

Creating transparent-background GIFs

✦ ✦ ✦ ✦

Let's get one thing straight before I start this chapter. Even though this chapter has to do with art in your Web site, I don't want to imply that I am an artist. Any pictures I show you in this chapter (other than photographs) are most likely from some clip art collection. Granted, I may change many of the pictures. But I don't claim that I'm making them better by changing them! I tell you this for two reasons: First, I don't want anyone to think that I'm trying to pass myself off as a graphic artist. And second, I want you to know that if you can't draw worth beans either, you are not entirely helpless. There are lots of things you can do with Paint Shop Pro to improve your images, even if you are artistically challenged (or, as in my case, artistically defeated, vanquished, and left for dead).

Throughout this chapter (and the book), I use Paint Shop Pro, which is included on the *HTML Publishing Bible* CD-ROM. If you haven't done so already, you may want to install Paint Shop Pro on your own PC. See Chapter 11 if you need help with installing Paint Shop Pro and creating SendTo shortcuts to the program.

Overview of Paint Shop Pro

Paint Shop Pro is a great graphics program that's very capable, yet simple to learn and use. I'm not going to try to teach you everything there is to know about the program here, but I do want to give you the quick lowdown on "how you work it" so that you can start being productive with it right away.

More Info You also can get more help with Paint Shop Pro by pressing the Help key (F1). When you register your copy, you'll also get a complete printed manual.

The first thing you need to be aware of is that Paint Shop Pro can open graphics files in any format listed in Table 22-1. After you get an image into Paint Shop Pro, you then can choose File⇨Save As to save the picture as a GIF or JPEG file for use in your Web pages.

Table 22-1
File Formats That You Can Open with Paint Shop Pro

Format	*Typical Extension*
Windows bitmap	.bmp
CorelDRAW!	.cdr
Computer Graphics Metafile	.cgm
Windows Clipboard	.clp
Dr. Halo	.cut
Device independent bitmap	.dib
Micrografx Draw	.drw
Autodesk	.dxf
Encapsulated PostScript (image only)	.eps
Ventura/GEM	.gem
CompuServe GIF	.gif
Hewlett-Packard Graphics Language	.hgl
Electronic Arts	.iff
GEM Paint	.img
Huffman compressed	.jif
Joint Photo Expert Group	.jpg
Deluxe Paint	.lbm
MacPaint	.mac
Microsoft Paint	.msp
UNIX portable bitmap	.pbm
Kodak Photo CD	.pcd
Zsoft Paintbrush	.pcx
UNIX Portable Graymap	.pgm
Lotus/Pixtor/PC Paint	.pic
Portable Network Graphics	.png
UNIX Portable Pixelmap	.ppm
Photoshop	.psd
Sun Microsystems Type 1	.ras
Unencoded pixel data	.raw

Format	*Typical Extension*
Run-Length Encoded	.rle
Truevision	.tga
Windows Metafile	.wmf
Tagged Image File Format	.tif
WordPerfect Graphics File	.wpg

There are two main ways to get a file into Paint Shop Pro:

- ✦ If you're already in Paint Shop Pro, choose File⇨Open, as in most programs, and browse to the name of the file that you want to open.
- ✦ Or, if you've added Paint Shop Pro to your Send To menu (Chapter 11), you can right-click the icon for any graphic file and choose Send To⇨Paint Shop Pro.

You also can copy and paste images into Paint Shop Pro. You can use the *snapshot* technique as I did at the end of Chapter 21. Or, in many cases, you can select an object (such as a WordArt object) and choose Edit⇨Copy. Then open (or click within) Paint Shop Pro and choose Edit⇨Paste from its menu bar.

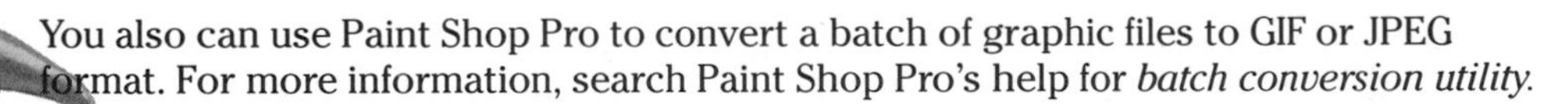

You also can use Paint Shop Pro to convert a batch of graphic files to GIF or JPEG format. For more information, search Paint Shop Pro's help for *batch conversion utility.*

Once you have an image in Paint Shop Pro, you'll probably do most of your work with tools in the Paint toolbox and Select toolbox (Figure 22-1). You can turn these toolboxes on and off by using simple commands on Paint Shop Pro's View menu. When you point to a tool in either toolbox, the status bar near the bottom of the screen tells you the name of the tool and also provides brief instructions on how to use the tool.

Using the Paint tools

The Paint tools let you draw, color, erase, change colors, and so on. Critical to understanding how to use these tools are the concepts of *foreground color* and *background color.* At any given moment, you essentially are working with these two colors. The current foreground and background colors are always displayed in little boxes near the bottom of the Select toolbox (Figure 22-2). (I suppose that they appear at the bottom of the Select toolbox rather than the bottom of the Paint toolbox because the Select toolbox has more room.)

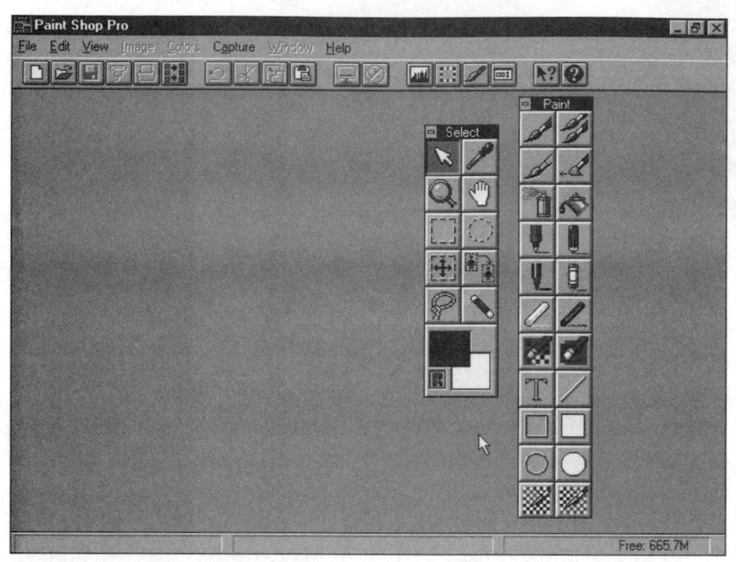

Figure 22-1: The Paint toolbox and Select toolbox in Paint Shop Pro.

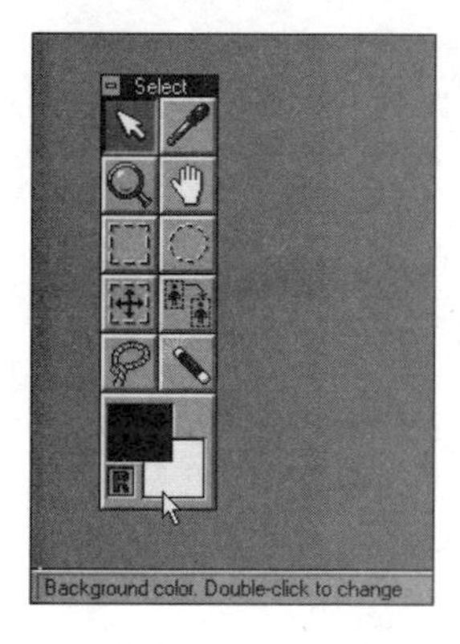

Figure 22-2: The foreground color and background color.

You have several ways to tell Paint Shop Pro which colors you want to use as the foreground and background:

✦ To simply reverse the two colors, click the R button.

✦ To pick a new foreground or background color from a palette, double-click the color you want to change. If the palette that appears is too complex, double-click the color that best resembles the color you want and then choose an actual color from the simpler dialog box that appears.

✦ You also can use the Eyedropper tool to set the colors. Click on the Eyedropper tool in the Paint toolbox. Then in your picture, click on whatever color you want to use as the foreground and right-click on whatever color you want to use as the background.

Paint Shop Pro often refer to the terms *foreground color* and *background color.* These terms *always* refer to the colors currently chosen in the little boxes at the bottom of the Paint toolbox. (That fact is why understanding the concepts of foreground and background color is so important to using Paint Shop Pro successfully.)

Hot Stuff

If you mess up while using a Paint tool, choose Edit⇨Undo to undo the mess. Undo undoes all operations that you performed with the current tool or everything up to the last time you saved the picture, whichever is most recent.

Using the Select tools

The Select tools enable you to isolate a part of a picture in order to crop, copy, delete, re-color, or perform other tasks on it. The Select tools do not really care about the currently selected foreground and background colors, so don't let the fact that this toolbox houses those colors confuse you. To use a Select tool, you typically click the tool you want and then click (or perhaps drag, depending on the tool you are using) within the picture to make your selection.

You also can find a very handy Magnifier tool in the Select toolbox. Even though it doesn't let you select, per se, it does let you zoom in on any portion of the picture to get a closer look at what you're doing and perform detail work. To use the Magnifier, just click the tool and then click the area you want to magnify as many times as necessary to get the magnification you want. To "unmagnify," choose View⇨Normal Viewing (1:1) from the menus.

Sizing a Picture (Width × Height)

GIF and JPEG images are *bitmap images,* which means they basically consist of collections of dots. All bitmap images have one thing in common — they are difficult to resize. When you change the size of a bitmap image, you encounter some distortion, especially jaggies (jagged edges) and sometimes moiré patterns (checkerboard patterns). As a rule, you always should try to size an image while you are creating it. For example, while you are scanning an image, use the scanning software's program to define the size of the scanned image before you actually save the image. If you are creating a bar chart, word art, or some other object, try to define the size of the image while you are in the program creating the image. (You can even just eyeball the size when you're working on the screen.)

Of course, you cannot always control the original size of a picture. For example, when you purchase clip art, each image is whatever size it is. As a result, there will be times when you need to resize an image to place it in your Web page. Here I show you a couple of techniques for resizing an image in Paint Shop Pro — with the goal of keeping distortions to a minimum.

Thinking in pixels

First and foremost, you need to start thinking of sizes in terms of pixels. A pixel is basically one little dot on the screen. There is no telling what screen resolution your reader will be using while viewing your page. To play it safe, though, you can assume that your readers will use a standard area of 640 × 480 (pixels). Some of that space is taken up by the reader's browser. Hence, for you, as publisher, it's probably best to think of a *page* as being approximately 600 pixels wide by approximately 400 pixels tall.

By *page* in this context, I mean the amount of stuff the reader can see on the screen at one time, without scrolling. Your actual Web page, of course, can be much larger than 600 × 400 pixels. The reader simply needs to scroll to areas that are out of view.

To help you get a feel for sizes, Figure 22-3 shows a sample Web page with a checkerboard background, viewed at the "standard" resolution of 640 × 480. On that page, I've placed four rectangles. The gray rectangle is 600 × 300 pixels. The black one is 300 × 100, the white one is 100 × 165, and the little see-through one is icon-size — 32 × 32.

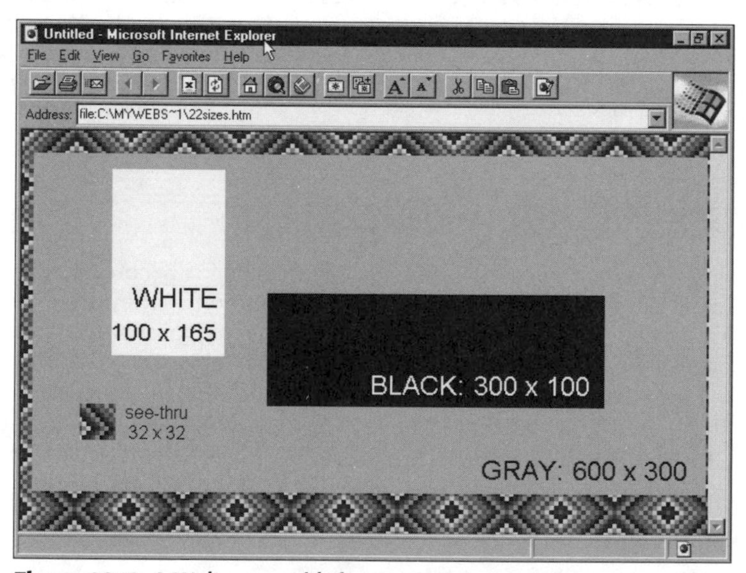

Figure 22-3: A Web page with four rectangles on it.

Resize and resample

A couple of last-minute recommendations before I go on to the how-to: Remember that the larger the picture, the longer it takes to download to your reader. Try to be frugal. Also, in the steps that follow, I recommend that you work with copies of the original file when resizing. Although it's not absolutely necessary to do so, it's a good idea to keep the original intact just in case you need it again in the future. Here's how I recommend that you resize a picture in Paint Shop Pro:

1. With your picture on the screen in Paint Shop Pro, choose the Arrow tool (the first button in the Select toolbox).
2. Click once anywhere on the picture, and choose Edit➪Copy. Next, choose Edit➪Paste➪As New Image. A duplicate of your picture appears.
3. Save this new copy as a GIF (or JPEG) file. That is, choose File➪Save As, choose the GIF or JPEG format, enter a filename, and choose OK.
4. Now choose Image➪Resize to get to the dialog box shown in Figure 22-4.

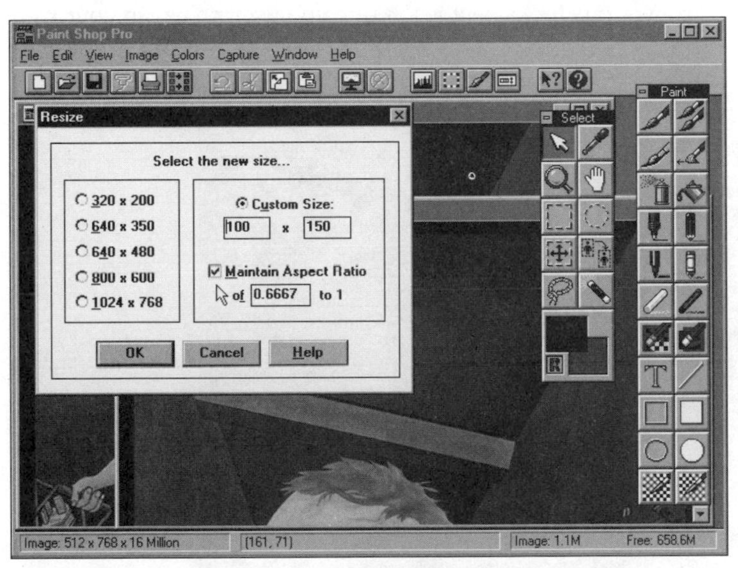

Figure 22-4: About to resize an image in Paint Shop Pro.

5. To minimize distortion, choose Custom Size and enter a width or height measurement only. Next, select (check) the Maintain Aspect Ratio check box and then click OK.
6. For good measure, I'll have you try the Resample technique of resizing the original image, just to see if the results are better. Click on the original image again, and choose Edit➪Copy.

7. Choose Edit⇨Paste⇨As New Image to make a duplicate of the original image on your screen.
8. Click on the new copy, and save it as a GIF or JPEG file again (File⇨Save As). Use a new name for this second copy.
9. You can resample only high-resolution images, so you need to increase the color depth to 16.7 million colors in this copy. If possible, choose Colors⇨Increase Color Depth and increase the depth to 16.7 million colors. (If you can't do this task, it simply means that the picture is already at 16.7 million colors. No problem.)
10. Choose Image⇨Resample. To keep the same settings as the first copy you made, click on OK.
11. Now choose filenames from the Window menu until you can see the original and both copies on the screen.

In Figure 22-5, you can see the large original picture and two smaller copies of it. I doubt that you'll be able to discern much difference in the quality of the resized and resampled images in this book, but take a close look at your own images to see which one looks best. Whichever one looks best is the one you want to use in your Web page.

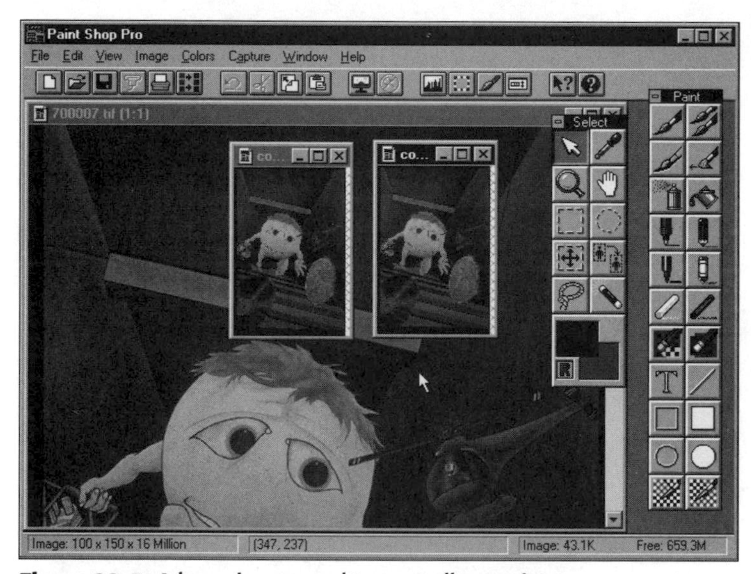

Figure 22-5: A large image and two smaller copies.

In case you're wondering, the basic difference between resizing and resampling is that resampling attempts to smooth out the jaggies by filling in missing pixels through a process of *interpolation* — sort of "inferring" what would be the appropriate color based on nearby colors. In most cases, resampling produces better results. But there's no harm in trying out both methods to see which works best for the picture you're using at the moment.

For more information on resizing and resampling, search Paint Shop Pro's help for *Resizing an Image.*

Cropping an image

Cropping an image, as you probably already know, is just a matter of getting rid of any unnecessary background stuff. For example, looking back at my alien picture in Figure 22-5, suppose that I want to make a smaller, more square picture that includes only the alien. In that case, I click on the original picture again and go through the Edit⇨Copy, Edit⇨Paste⇨As New Image ritual again to make a clone of the original picture.

Next, I click on the Rectangular Select tool in the Select toolbox and then drag a frame around the part of the image that I want to keep. Then I choose Image⇨Crop so that my new image contains only the stuff that appears inside the selection marquee, as shown in Figure 22-6. Don't forget to save the new image as a GIF or JPEG file for use in your Web page.

Figure 22-6: Use the Rectangular Selection tool and Image⇨Crop commands to crop any portion of a picture.

A little touch-up

You may have noticed a slight problem with my cropped alien picture: The helicopter blade is still showing. That image is out of context now that the rest of the helicopter has been cropped out, as you can see in the left-hand copy of the image in Figure 22-7. In the picture on the right, you can see that I've made the helicopter blade disappear. To do so, I used the Clone Brush tool in the Paint toolbox.

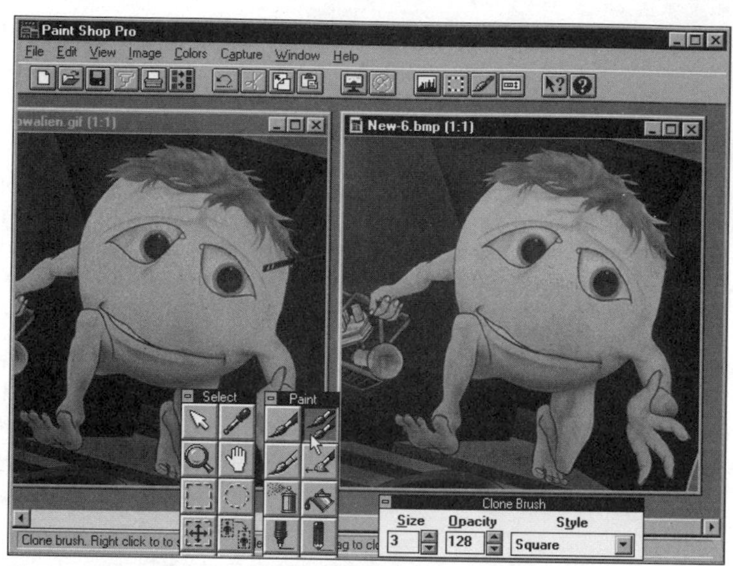

Figure 22-7: Helicopter blade removed through color cloning.

You have lots of ways to touch up pictures in Paint Shop Pro — the Clone Brush is just one of them. Unfortunately, I don't have the 100 pages needed to get into all of those methods. Instead, you may want to experiment with various tools on your own to get a feel for what's possible. You also can use the online help and the printed manual that comes with the registered version of Paint Shop Pro to help learn the various touch-up tools available. Meanwhile, I need to focus on topics that are of specific importance to Web publishing — and this next topic definitely falls into that category!

Controlling Image Quality and Download Time

Of special interest to Web authors are the Color Count commands on the Colors menu. These commands are important because of a basic formula for colors that goes like this: The greater the color depth, the better the quality of the picture. But there is a cost associated with using more color: The higher the color depth, the larger the file (in bytes), and hence the longer it takes to send across the Internet to your reader's PC.

Figure 22-8 shows an example of how large a photograph would be, byte-wise, at various color depths. You also can get some idea of the degradation of picture quality as you go from 16.7 million colors down to 2 (though, in truth, this is a color photo displayed on a screen, not in a black-and-white book, so this figure only gives you a rough idea).

16-million color JPEG	17KB
256-color GIF	8KB
Gray scale GIF	8KB
16-color GIF	4KB
2-color GIF	1KB

Figure 22-8: How large, byte-wise, a photograph is at various color depths.

It's impossible to say exactly how long any one image would take to send to a reader. The actual time depends on the speed of the reader's modem, how busy the server is, and even the amount of general traffic on the Internet. But considering that the highest-quality photo is 17KB in size and the lowest quality is 1KB in size, we can say that the high-quality photo is going to take 17 times longer to download than the low-quality one.

Puzzled?

GIF files can contain a maximum of 256 colors. JPEG (which stands for Joint Photographic Experts Group) files always contain 16.7 million colors. Originally, only GIF files were used on the Web. JPEG was added later to allow for high-quality photographs at 16.7 million colors.

Picking a color depth

Your goal, as a Web author, is to try to find a happy balance between picture quality and download time. There is a simple way to do this in Paint Shop Pro:

1. Choose Colors⇨Count Colors Used to see how many colors are actually used in your picture, just to get an idea of how many colors you really need.
2. Choose Colors⇨Decrease Color depth to try the next lowest color depth.
3. If you lose too much quality in Step 2, choose Edit⇨Undo to go back up to the higher. Otherwise, repeat Step 2 and try a lower color depth.

Remember, the farther down you go in color depth, the faster your image will get to your reader. Table 22-2 shows some general guidelines for acceptable color depths and types of pictures. But again, try out various color depths and trust your own eye to make your decision.

Table 22-2
Some General Guidelines on Picture Type and Color Depth

Picture Type	*At Least*	*Perhaps Required*
Color photograph	256 colors	16.7 million colors
Black-and-white photograph	Gray scale	16.7 million colors
Filled-line art (comic book pictures, logos, and so on)	16 colors	256 colors
Black-and-white line drawings	2 colors	2 colors

If you decide to save a picture at 16.7 million colors, you'll need to use the JPEG (.jpg) format to do so. If you try to save that picture as a GIF file, Paintshop Pro will make you reduce its color depth to 256 colors first.

Measuring height and width

You also can speed up graphic downloads by specifying the exact size, in terms of height and width, of the picture in your Web page. If the Web server knows how large the picture is going to be, it sends all the text first, leaving just enough room for the pictures. If the server doesn't know the size of the picture, it must send some picture info and then some text to format the page properly. That process, from the reader's perspective, makes the page seem as though it is taking longer to download.

To determine the exact width and height of a picture, open the picture in Paint Shop Pro. Click on the picture's title bar, and you'll see the dimensions of the picture in the status bar, in the format *width × height × color depth.* For example, the little beanie picture in Figure 22-9 measures 100 pixels wide by 90 pixels tall, with a color depth of 256.

To speed up your graphics, you need to find every instance of this graphic image in your Web pages and type in the dimensions. Use Word IA for this step. That is, do the following:

1. Open the Web page in Word IA's normal Edit mode.
2. Select (click on) the picture whose dimensions you now know.
3. Click on the Picture button in Word IA's toolbar and then click on the Options tab.

Danger Zone

Paint Shop Pro shows *width × height.* Word IA asks for this information in the opposite order — height first then width. Make sure that you type in the numbers correctly, or your picture may look quite strange in a Web browser.

4. Type the height and width as in the example shown in Figure 22-10.

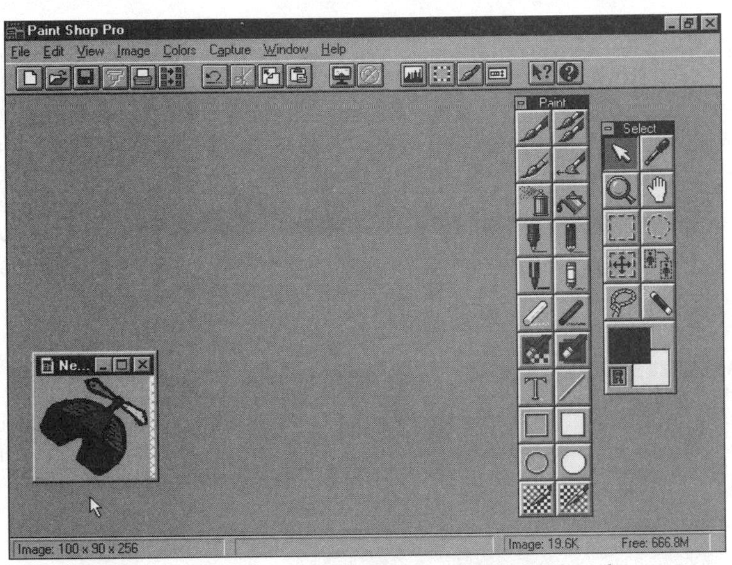

Figure 22-9: As you can see in the status bar, this Paint Shop Pro image measures 100 × 90 × 256.

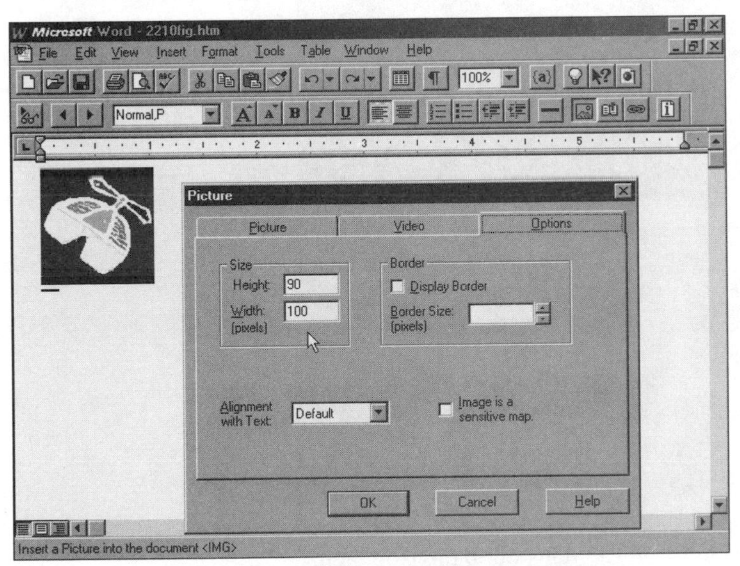

Figure 22-10: Defining the height and width of a picture.

5. Click OK.

You won't notice any change on your screen. Behind the scenes, however, Word IA adds height and width attributes to the `<IMG SRC = >` tag that displays the image.

Going in and checking the color depth of every image and then typing the height and width of every image in your Web site can be a tedious process. But if you do those tasks consistently, your page will definitely download faster. As a result, your readers are less likely to become impatient and click the Stop button. Your readers also are more likely to halt the image-downloading process if they think they can get to your pages without the long, drawn-out wait.

Creating Fade-In Images

One of the unique features of the GIF picture format is its capability to *fade* a picture into view on the reader's screen. You've probably seen examples of images that slowly come into focus on your screen. Figure 22-11 shows such an example.

Figure 22-11: An interlaced GIF starts out blurry and then comes into focus.

The official term for a fade-in image is *interlaced.* Although these images don't get to the reader any quicker than non-interlaced graphics, they *appear* to come in faster because the reader gets a sneak preview of the image. You can actually scroll ahead to other areas of the page if the image doesn't look that interesting.

Creating an interlaced GIF is simply a matter of saving the file in the Interlaced format. Here's how to do so in Paint Shop Pro:

1. In Paint Shop Pro, open the image that you want to fade into the reader's screen.
2. Choose File⇨Save As from Paint Shop Pro's menu bar.
3. Choose a location (most likely, your My Web Site folder) and a filename for the picture.
4. Under List Files of Type, choose *GIF - CompuServe.*
5. Under File Sub-Format, choose *Version 89a - Interlaced,* as in Figure 22-12.

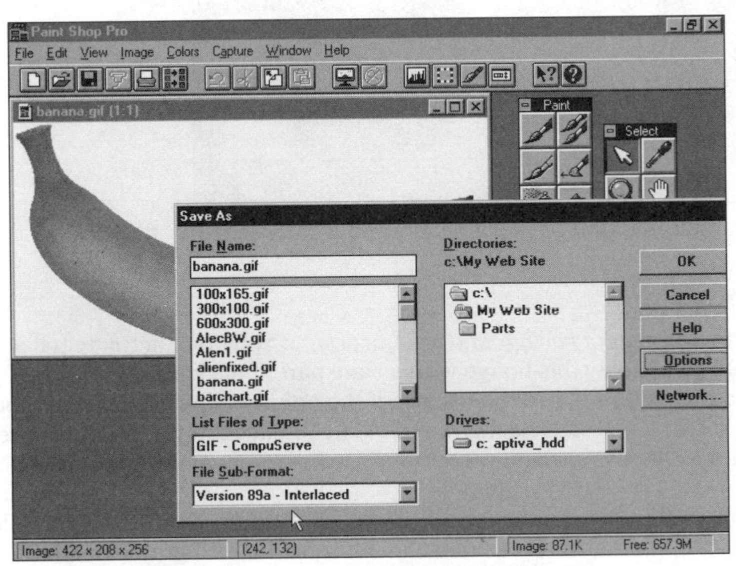

Figure 22-12: Saving an interlaced GIF in Paint Shop Pro.

6. Click OK to save the interlaced image.

That's all there is to it. If you haven't already done so, you can insert the GIF into a Web page by using the standard Picture button in Word IA. Anyone who views that page on the Web sees the image fade into view on his or her screen.

Creating Transparent Background GIFs

A transparent background GIF is one that appears to float on the page. Figure 22-13 shows an example of an image with and without a transparent background.

Figure 22-13: Example of a GIF image with and without a transparent background.

Actually, the term *transparent background* is a misnomer. You don't actually tell a graphics program to "display this image with a transparent background." Rather, you pick one color in the picture to be transparent. If the color you pick happens to be the same as the color of the picture's background, *then* you effectively get a transparent background. Let me show you what I mean.

Figure 22-14 shows a Web page with a checkerboard-like background and three GIF images. The GIF image contains three colors — black, white, and gray. The first (topmost) image is displayed with no colors set to transparent. The second image is displayed with white defined as the transparent color. The third image has gray defined as its transparent color.

As you can see, with white set as the transparent color, the image appears to float because the background happens to be white. Setting gray as the transparent color, however, gives the image an entirely different look. The gray body of the bird is transparent — not the background of the picture.

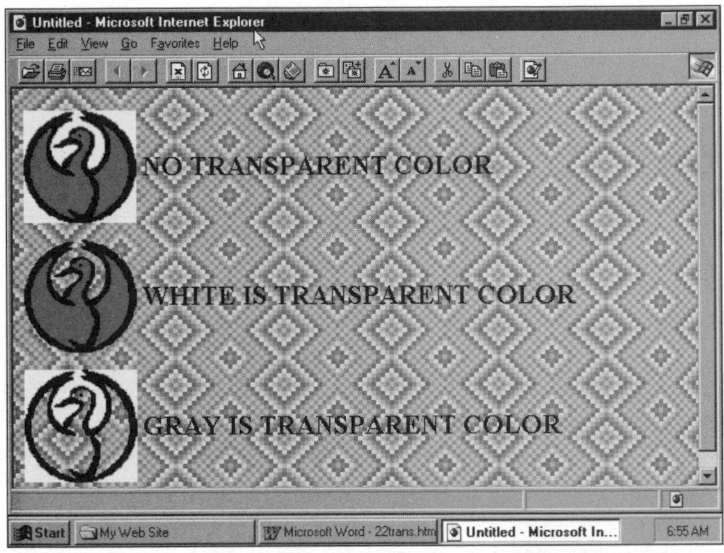

Figure 22-14: GIF image with white and then gray defined as the transparent color.

Defining transparency with Paint Shop Pro

Keeping in mind what you just learned about transparency, let's now look at how you go about picking which color will be transparent in your GIF file, using Paint Shop Pro as your graphics program:

1. If you haven't already done so, open the image in Paint Shop Pro with the standard File⇨Open commands.
2. Use the Colors menu to choose your color depth *before* you choose a transparent color.
3. Click the Eyedropper tool in the Select toolbox.
4. Right-click whatever color in your picture you want to set to transparent. The background color at the bottom of the Select toolbox turns to whatever color you right-clicked.
5. Click the Arrow tool to deactivate the Eyedropper tool.
6. Choose File⇨Save As.
7. Under List Files of Type, choose *GIF - CompuServe;* and under File Sub-Format, choose *Version 89a-Interlaced* (or *Version 89a-Noninterlaced* if you don't want to have the image fade in on the reader's screen).

8. Click the Options button in the Save As dialog box. You come to the dialog box shown in Figure 22-15.

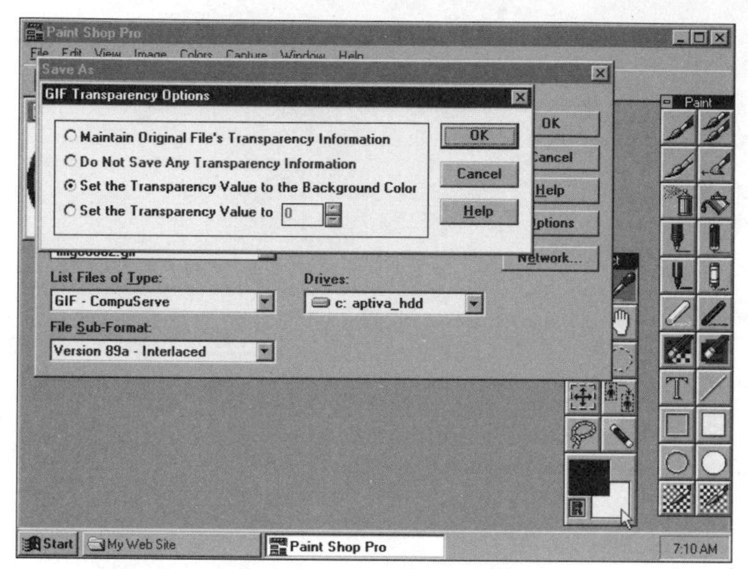

Figure 22-15: GIF Transparency Options dialog box.

9. Choose the third option, *Set the Transparency Value to the Background Color.* Remember that the term *Background Color* here refers to the background color defined in the Select toolbox — located near the mouse pointer in Figure 22-15.
10. Click OK.
11. If you haven't already done so, choose the folder (under Directories), specify the File Name for this image, and then click OK.

You can now insert the picture into any Web page by using the standard Picture button in Word IA. The transparency you selected will be apparent only in your Web browser — not in Word IA.

Assigning a transparent background for black-and-white pics

A picture that is truly black-and-white (no grays) can present a bit of a problem in the transparency department. For example, take a look at the org chart in Figure 22-16. If I make white the transparent color, then the background and the boxes in the chart will be transparent. Only the black lines and text will remain visible.

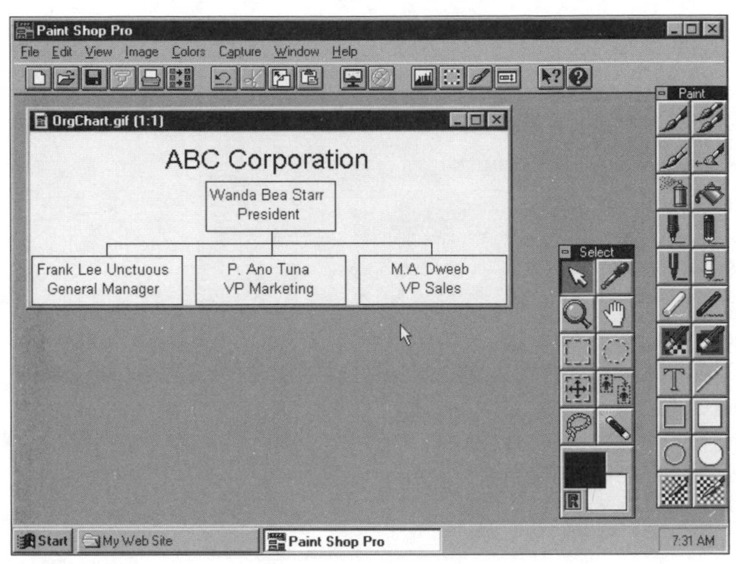

Figure 22-16: A true black-and-white picture.

If I want the picture to actually show the boxes as white, I need to come up with a third color to play the role of transparent color. I could pick any color: red, yellow, and so on. Because this is not a color book, however, I'll use gray as the transparent color. I first need to color gray anything that I want to make transparent in this picture. Here is how I'd go about making that happen.

The first thing I do is choose Colors⇨Decrease Color Depth (or Increase Color Depth) to set this picture's color depth to 16 colors. (I really need only three colors, but 16 colors is as close as I can set the color depth.) I save the file as a GIF file (if it wasn't already a GIF) to make sure that I can define a background color.

Next, I double-click the Foreground Color box at the bottom of the Select toolbox. I need to come up with a unique third color, so I double-click some empty box in the little palette that appears and then click on the gray color (or whatever color I planned to use as the transparent color), as shown in Figure 22-17. Clicking OK twice takes me back to my picture. The foreground color, as defined in the Select toolbox, is now gray.

Now I can choose the Flood Fill tool from the Paint toolbox and then click every area in my picture that needs to be gray. When you do this task, you may need to use the Magnifier to zoom in on the little spaces within letters so that you can fill those, too. For example, in Figure 22-18, I've zoomed in very close on the ABC Corporation title, re-selected my Flood Fill tool, and started coloring in the white space within letters.

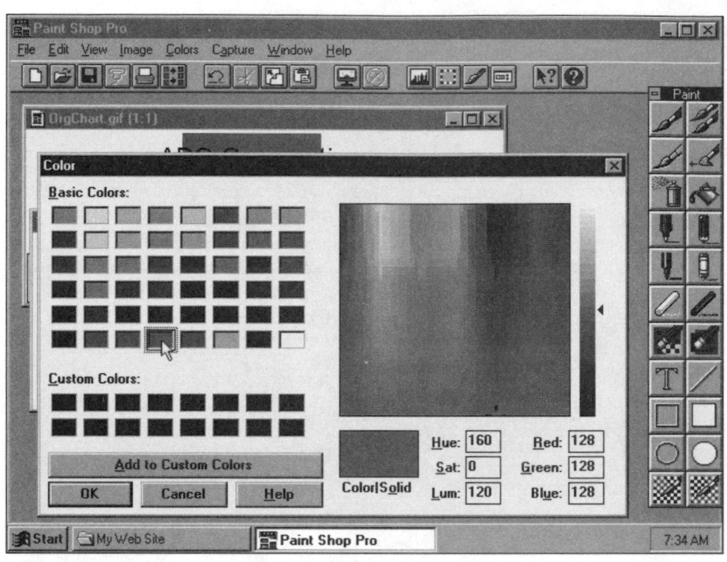

Figure 22-17: Choosing a color to add to the palette.

Figure 22-18: Zoomed in tight to flood-fill white space within letters.

Next, I return to Normal view (View➪Normal Viewing (1:1)) and take a good look to make sure that everything that needs to be transparent, and *only* those things that need to be transparent, are colored gray. Then I set gray as the background color (by clicking the Eyedropper tool and right-clicking the gray area in my picture), so that the background color defined at the bottom of the Select toolbox is the same color I want to define as transparent in my picture. In Figure 22-19, I've done all that and am ready to proceed.

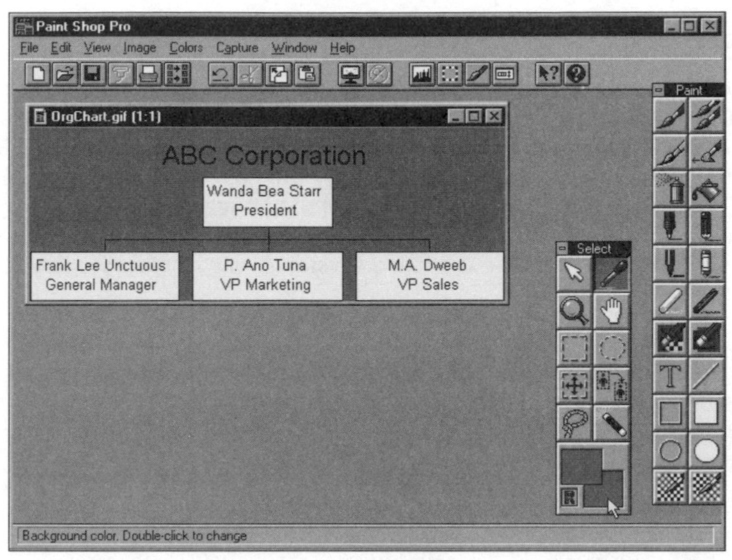

Figure 22-19: All transparent areas are gray, and gray is the selected background color (near the mouse pointer).

As my final step, I choose File➪Save As➪Options➪*Set the Transparency Value to the Background Color*➪OK➪OK. Now I can exit Paint Shop Pro (File➪Exit). Next, I go back into Word IA and put the GIF file into a Web page with the usual Picture button. When I view the page in a Web browser, what once was gray is now transparent, as Figure 22-20 shows.

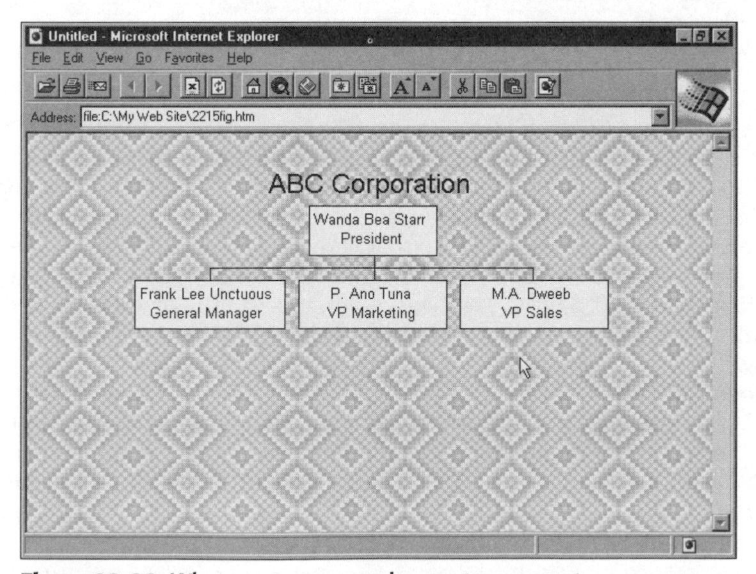

Figure 22-20: What once was gray is now transparent.

Creating Custom Backgrounds

You can use a small logo or picture as a background image. But if that image has too much contrast, the text on top of that background will be hard to read. Here are a couple of tricks that you can try to convert a favorite image into a background. First, open the image in Paint Shop Pro. Click on the image, and choose Edit➪Copy and Edit➪Paste➪As New Image. Click on the new copy of the image, and select Colors➪Adjust➪Brightness/Contrast. Crank up the Brightness to high, and perhaps the Contrast to low, so that the new image is a faded version of the original (Figure 22-21).

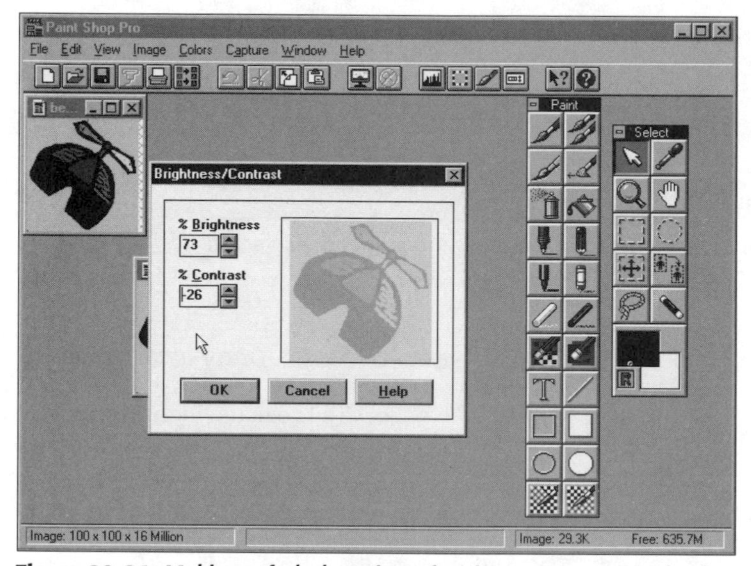

Figure 22-21: Making a faded version of an image to use as a background.

Save the faded version as a GIF or JPEG with a new filename (in your My Web Site folder). Here's a second cool effect you can try: Click on the new copy of the image, and choose Edit➪Copy and Edit➪Paste➪As New Image again. Click on the new copy, and choose Colors➪Gray Scale. Next, choose Image➪Special Filters➪Emboss. The new image has an embossed effect, similar to that shown in Figure 22-22 (near the mouse pointer). You may want to turn up the brightness on that copy, too, by using the Colors➪Adjust command. Save the embossed version as a GIF or JPEG file with yet another name.

You now can close Paint Shop Pro and use Word IA to open any Web page. Once you're in Word IA, choose Format➪Background and Links and use the Browse button to browse to and select one of your new background images. Then click the Preview in Browser button to see how it looks in a Web browser. In Figure 22-23, I'm trying on the embossed version for size.

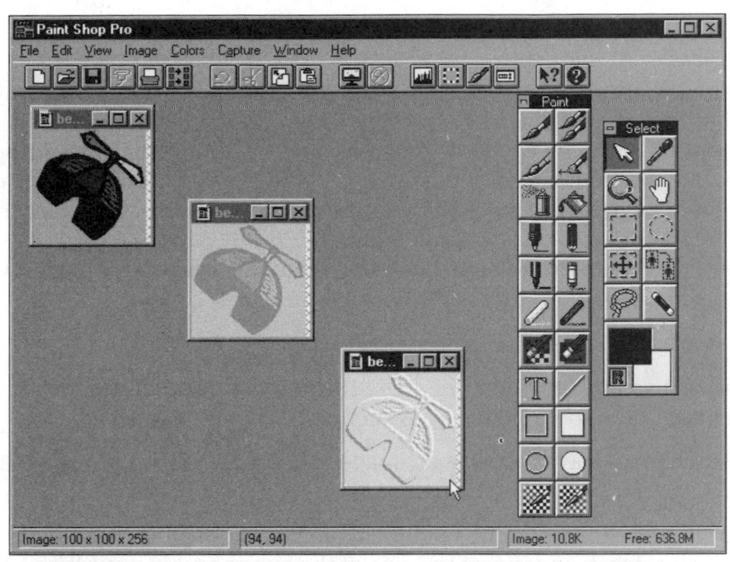

Figure 22-22: Faded and embossed versions of beanie image.

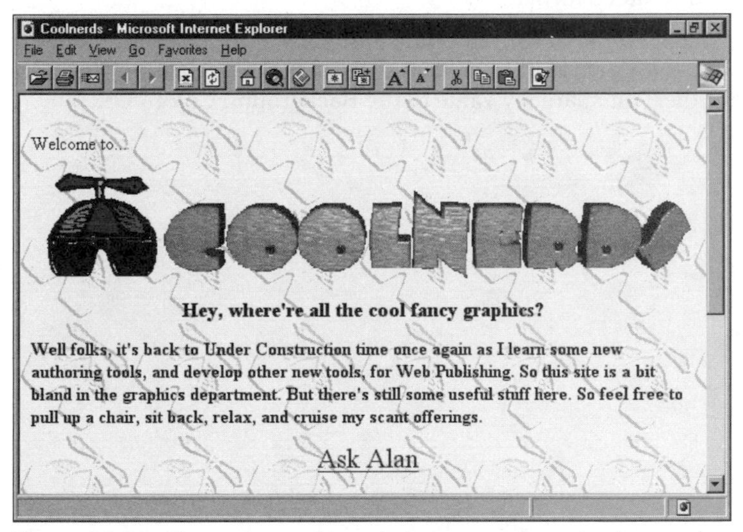

Figure 22-23: The embossed beanie image used as a background.

Summary

Whew! Enough already about graphic images! It seems like I've been yakking away on that topic for days. My original disclaimer still applies — I don't claim to be an artist, and I have no intention of telling you how to make your site look good from a graphic-arts perspective. But as a Web author and publisher, you do need to know some of the basics. Here's a list of some of the more important points covered in this chapter:

✦ You can use Paint Shop Pro to open images in many formats and also to save those images in GIF or JPEG format.

✦ You also can paste images into Paint Shop Pro.

✦ Most tools you use in Paint Shop Pro are in the Paint and Select toolboxes, which you can show/hide from the View menu.

✦ There are three main ways to resize an image in Paint Shop Pro: resize, resample, and crop.

✦ To get your graphic images to the reader as quickly as possible, use the smallest acceptable color depth and define the size of the image within your Web page.

✦ To create a fade-in GIF image, simply save the image in Compuserve - GIF, Version 89a - Interlaced format.

✦ To create a transparent-background GIF, set the background color on the Select toolbox to the color you want to make transparent. Then choose File⇨Save As⇨Options⇨Set the Transparency Value to the Background Color⇨OK.

✦ ✦ ✦

Maniacal Multimedia

✦ ✦ ✦ ✦

In This Chapter

Multimedia helper apps and Netscape plug-ins

Adding background sound and inline video

Adding sound bytes and movie clips to your site

Treating large graphics as multimedia files

Letting people download files from your Web site

✦ ✦ ✦ ✦

Multimedia, as you probably know, is sort of a catch-all term for non-textual forms of communication — sound and video being the most common examples. A multimedia PC basically is a PC equipped with a sound card, speakers, and a VGA or better monitor. Multimedia programs abound, encompassing everything from games to interactive reference guides. On a standalone PC, you typically buy a multimedia program on CD-ROM. You take it home, perhaps go through a little installation procedure, load the program, and voilà — your multimedia program comes to life.

Multimedia on the Web is a little different. In Web browsing, the server sends pictures and raw text containing some HTML tags to your PC. The browser on your PC is responsible for interpreting the text, tags, and pictures into something meaningful. The same holds true for multimedia. The server sends the "raw" video file or sound file, and your Web browser, or some other program on your PC, plays that file.

The "or some other program on your PC" is typically what's called a *helper app, viewer, player,* or *plug-in.* Before you start publishing multimedia, you should be familiar with how the reader will experience it on the Web. Therefore, I encourage you to obtain some players or plug-ins and visit some multimedia sites. I explain how to do that at the start of this chapter.

Helper Apps and Plug-Ins

Many different formats of multimedia are on the Web — and lots of players for them. Fortunately, the players are almost always free and are easy to install. It's just a matter of knowing where to look for them. The best way to get the latest-and-greatest version of a help app or plug-in is simply to download it from the World Wide Web to your own PC.

Windows helper apps

One of the best places on the Web to find multimedia helper apps for Windows is *The Ultimate Collection of Windows Socketware (TUCOWS)*. To get there, point your Web browser to `http://www.tucows.com`. When you reach the site, choose the location nearest you, as instructed on the screen. Then work your way through Software➪Non Winsock Applications to get to the screen that offers audio applications, image viewers, movie viewers, and so on (Figure 23-1).

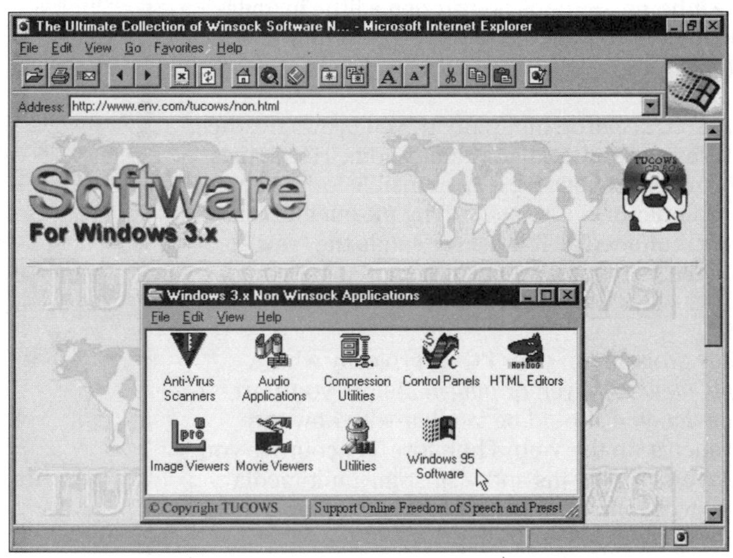

Figure 23-1: TUCOWS has tons of great helper apps and viewers.

Netscape Navigator 2.0 Plug-Ins site

Netscape Navigator version 2.0 (and later) supports *plug-ins* that treat external multimedia like inline objects. If you have Navigator 2.0, you'll definitely want to take a look at what's available and consider taking advantage of these new capabilities in your own Web pages. For more info and the latest news, point your Web browser to `http://home.netscape.com/comprod/products/navigator/version_2.0/plugins/index.html` (Figure 23-2). Or pop over to coolnerds (`http://www.coolnerds.com`) and take the one-click jump route.

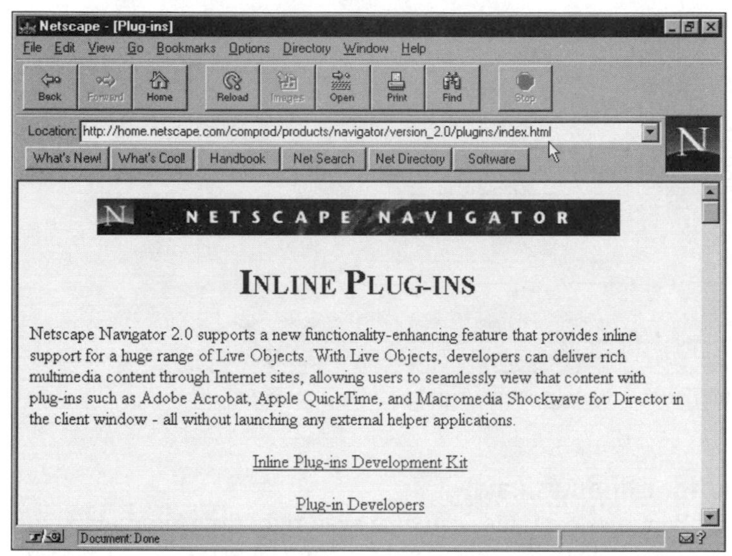

Figure 23-2: The Inline Plug-Ins site for Netscape Navigator 2.0.

Sound file players

Sound files come in many formats, including .au, .voc, .aif, .mid, .cmf, .snd, .iff, .wav, and more. The Windows Sound Recorder, which came with Windows 95, can play a .wav file and also kicks in automatically when Internet Explorer finds one. For other sound formats, you'll need to download some helper apps. TUCOWS has lots of great sound players and editors (Figure 23-3).

For Netscape plug-ins, browse over to the Netscape Plug-Ins site and check out Crescendo by LiveUpdate, RealAudio by Progressive Networks, ToolVox by Voxware, and whatever else is new when you get there.

Video file formats and players

Video files also come in several different formats. Both the TUCOWS site and the Netscape 2.0 Plug-Ins site offer great players. Here's a little information about some of the more widely-used video formats for Windows.

Figure 23-3: TUCOWS has lots of great sound editors and players.

Microsoft Video for Windows (.avi)

Microsoft Video for Windows (.avi) files can be played right from Internet Explorer. The Authorware Professional for Windows (AVI Pro) and NET TOOB viewers on TUCOWS also are good viewers for .avi files.

Motion Picture Experts Group (.mpeg or .mpg)

MPEG is quickly gaining acceptance as *the* format for video on PCs. From TUCOWS, check out VMPEG Lite, NET TOOB, MPEG Movie Player 32-bit, and Stream Works. At Netscape's Plug-Ins site, take a look at PreVu by InterVu. Also check out the MPEG Archive at `http://www.cs.tu-berlin.de/~phade/mpeg.html` (Figure 23-4).

Apple QuickTime (.qtw)

You can view Apple QuickTime videos on many different platforms, including Windows 95. To download the latest freebie QuickTime viewer, point your browser to `http://quicktime.apple.com`. Or check out `http://www.astro.nwu.edu/lentz/mac/qt`. For Netscape plug-ins, cruise over to the Netscape Plug-Ins site. To try out some QuickTime moves (after you download the viewer), search Yahoo! for *quicktime*.

Shockwave

Shockwave lets people who create multimedia titles with Macromedia Director compress their works to a reasonable size for downloading over the Internet. To see a Shockwave presentation, you need the Shockwave viewer. For more information and a free viewer, point your Web browser to `http://www.macromedia.com`.

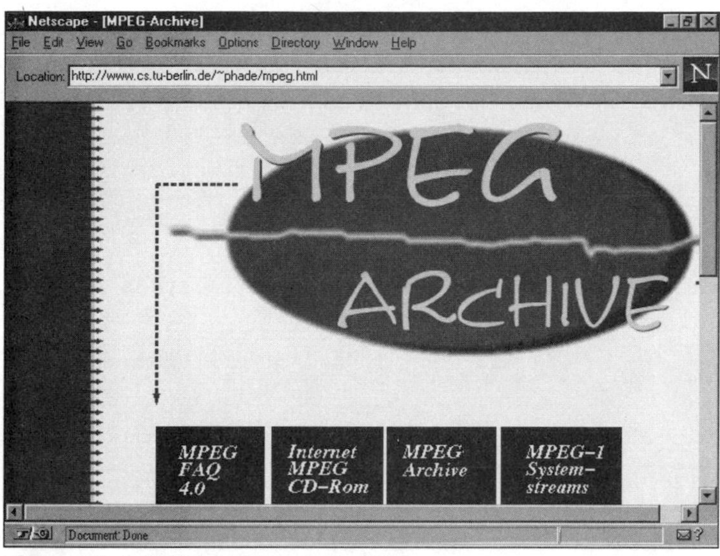

Figure 23-4: MPEG archive on the Web.

Finding Multimedia Files

Several sites on the Web now dish up sound and video. You can use these sites to test your helper apps and plug-ins. In some (though certainly not all) cases, you can even download multimedia files for use in your own Web pages. Check out some of the sites in Table 23-1 to get started.

Hot Stuff

As an alternative to typing all these lengthy URLs, you can just hop over to coolnerds (`http://www.coolnerds.com`) and click your way to the sites. You can also search Yahoo or any other search engine for *sound, video,* or *multimedia.*

Table 23-1
Sites That Use Sound and Video

Site Name	*URL*
Auricular	`http://www.nanothinc.com:80/Auricular`
Jesse's Movies	`http://www.uslink.net~edgerton/index.html`
Morphing Shmorphing	`http://www.wr.com.au/sc/morph.html`
Movies!	`http://tausq.resnet.cornell.edu/mmedia.htm`
Open Virtual Reality	`http://www.nist.gov/itl/div878/ovrt/OVRTmovies.html`

(continued)

Table 23-1 *(continued)*

Site Name	***URL***
QT Gallery	`http://129.186.85.60/gallery.html`
The Daily WAV	`http://www.idir.net/~shockwav/dailywav.html`
The Sound Page	`http://www.ucsalf.ac.uk/pa/soundp/sphome.htm`
The Synergy Workshop	`http://www.eirenet.net/cork/synergy/freeclip.html`
TV Bytes	`http://themes.parkhere.com/themes`

Creating Multimedia Files

Creating multimedia files is a bit more complex than viewing them, and an in-depth explanation of how you go about this task is beyond the scope of this book. I can give you some pointers to get you started. To create audio files, you need a sound card capable of recording (most are) and the appropriate software. You can create .wav files by using the Windows 95 Sound Recorder applet. To create other formats or to convert from one format to another, use Cool Edit, WHAM, or any other shareware app available for Windows from the aforementioned TUCOWS.

Creating video is considerably more complicated and perhaps best left to the pros. Typically, you need a video camera (unless you're swiping pre-recorded material) and a video capture card for your PC. Then you also need appropriate software, such as Adobe Premiere, to do your editing and compression. All these items are fairly expensive and require a substantial investment of time to learn.

If you are interested in creating "flying logos" rather than live video, take a look at Crystal Flying Fonts Pro from CrystalGraphics, available at most computer stores. It is very easy to learn and a blast to use. For more information, contact CrystalGraphics, Inc., 3110 Patrick Henry Drive, Santa Clara, CA 95054, 408-496-6175, `http://www.awa.com/nct/forms/crystal.com`. Or stop by the (unofficial) Flying Fonts Support Page at `http://www.interdine.com/interdine/Flying-Fonts/ffsp.html`. I've also included some examples of Flying Fonts videos on the *Web Publishing Uncut* CD-ROM.

If the Reader Doesn't Have the Right Viewer

You may be thinking "What happens if I put a sound/video file in my site and my reader doesn't have the appropriate viewer?" They won't be able to see/hear the file. But beyond that, nothing too catastrophic happens. If your reader is using Internet Explorer 2.0, he/she sees a message like the one shown in Figure 23-5. If the reader is using Netscape Navigator 2.0. the message looks like Figure 23-6. Other browsers offer similar simple messages.

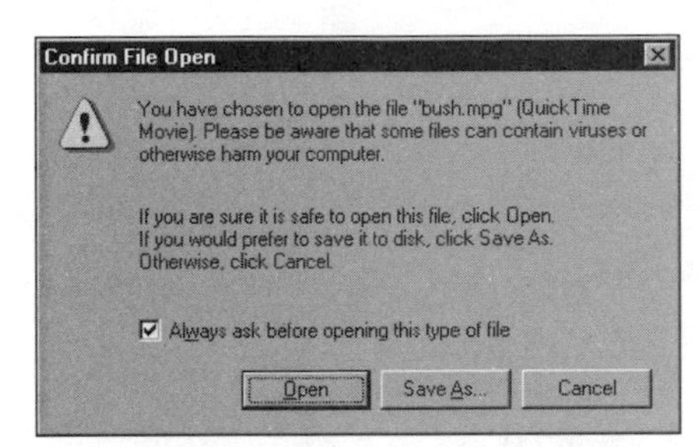

Figure 23-5: Internet Explorer's "no can do" message.

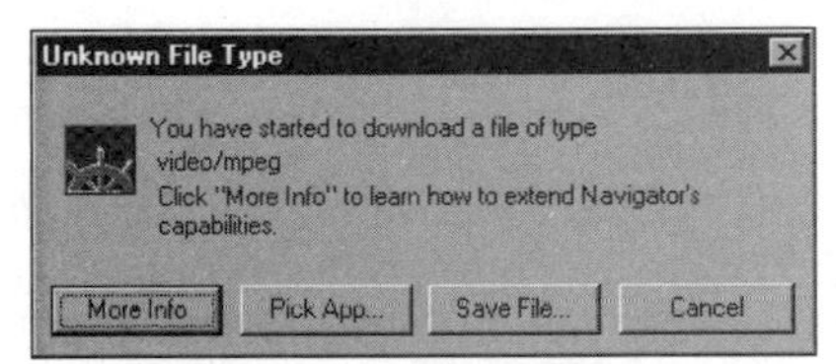

Figure 23-6: Netscape Navigator's "no helper app" message.

One thing you can do, to be courteous to your readers, is tell them what helper app or plug-in they need and provide a hot link to a site that will let them download that app. For example, the courteous publisher in Figure 23-7 makes it quite clear that visitors need Netscape Navigator 2.0 and Shockwave to take full advantage of the site and also provides quick access to both products.

It's simple enough to find appropriate download sites yourself. Just search Yahoo! or any other search engine for the name of the helper app or plug-in for which you are looking. Check out each site, and when you find the one that offers the download, put that URL into your hyperlink.

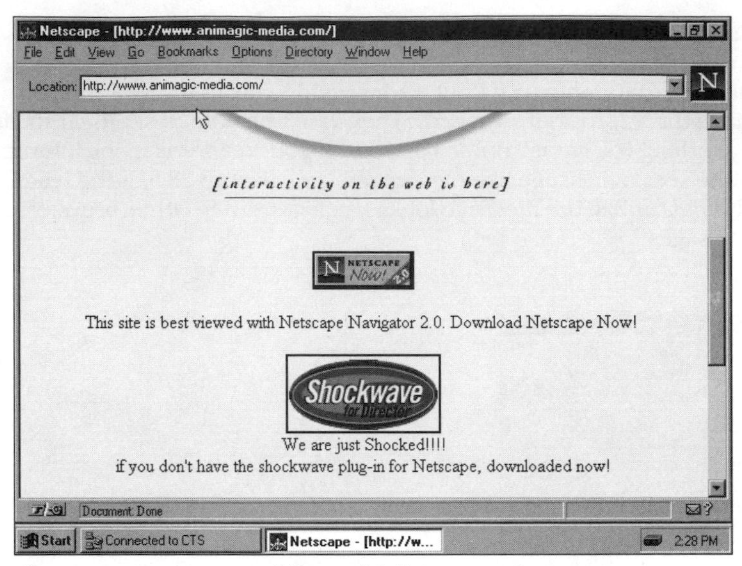

Figure 23-7: A page providing quick links to Navigator 2.0 and Shockwave.

Adding Multimedia to Your Site

There are two ways to add multimedia capabilities to your Web site: As *inline multimedia,* which plays automatically when the reader opens the page, or as *external media,* which the reader must download and play outside the Web browser. I'll talk about the external type first.

Including external media in your Web pages actually is a very simple task. Just create a hyperlink to the sound or video file in the format

```
<A HREF = "filename">
```

where *filename* is the name of the file with the extension. Figure 23-8 shows a hypothetical example — a Web page viewed via Internet Explorer containing links to a variety of videos and sound files. Figure 23-9 shows the HTML source for that document.

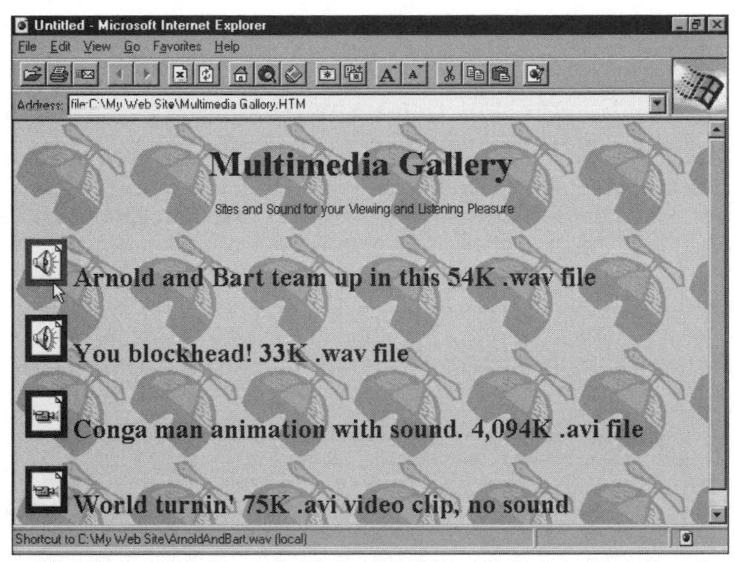

Figure 23-8: Web browser of a page offering links to external media.

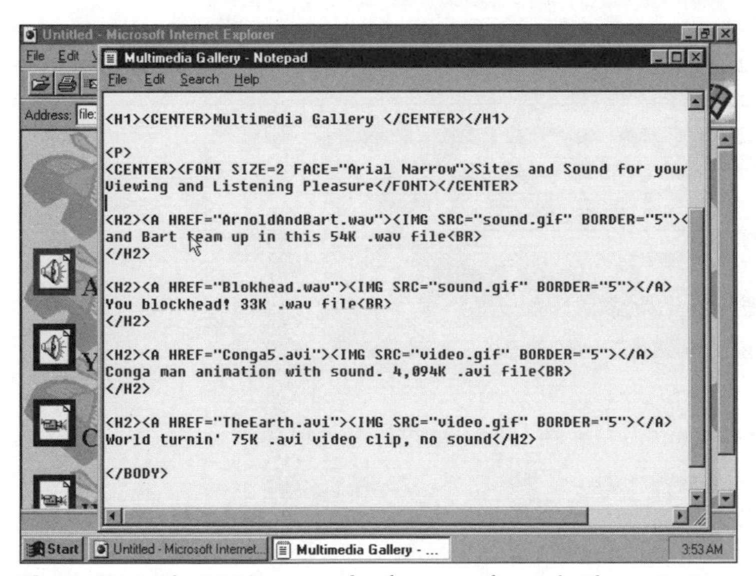

Figure 23-9: The HTML source for the page shown in Figure 23-8.

The following are the step-by-step instructions for including external media in your Web pages:

1. Move or copy the multimedia file to your My Web Site folder (so you don't forget to upload it with the rest of your pages later).

Hot Stuff

Want to use the little sound and video icons from Figure 23-8 in your own pages? No problem. You can find them under "Buttons" in the Images (Web Art) folder on the *Web Publishing Uncut* CD-ROM, as well as at my `http://www.coolnerds.com` site.

2. If you want to use a thumbnail (small GIF file) as the hyperlink, insert that picture into your Web page by using the standard Picture button in Word IA. If you want to use text as the hyperlink, just type that text. (You can do both, of course.)
3. Select the text or GIF that will act as the hyperlink.
4. Click the Hyperlink button in Word IA's toolbar, and type the name of the multimedia file or use the Browse button to choose the name of the multimedia file (Figure 23-10).

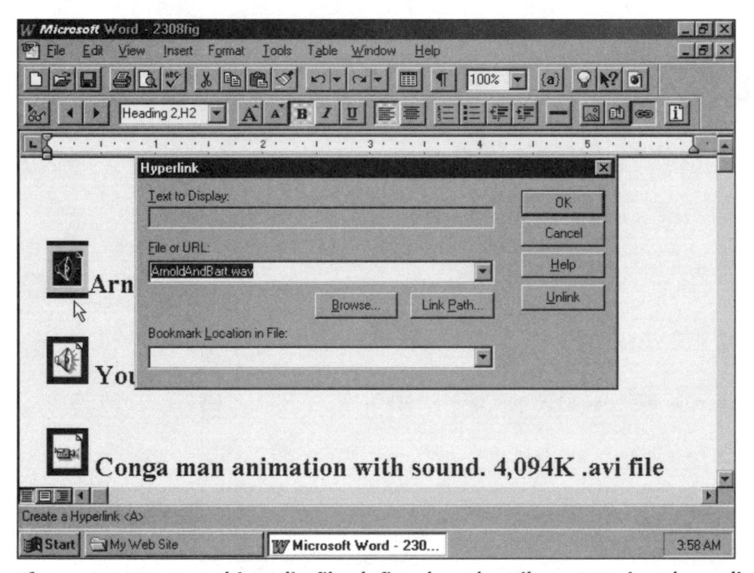

Figure 23-10: A multimedia file defined as the File or URL in a hyperlink.

5. Click OK.

That's it — you're done. You can test the link locally by viewing your Web page in your favorite browser and then clicking the link (assuming, of course, that you've installed the appropriate viewer or plug-in).

Inline Multimedia

Inline multimedia is multimedia that plays automatically as soon as the reader opens the page. Well, maybe I better rephrase that. Inline multimedia is downloaded automatically with the page, and after waiting for however long it takes for the multimedia file to get there, the reader automatically sees the video moving or hears the sound file playing without having to specifically request it. Hmmmm. Maybe that's a little too wordy. How about this: Inline multimedia is multimedia the reader gets whether he or she wants it or not. Like an inline GIF image, inline multimedia is just part of the page. Two basic types of inline multimedia exist: background sounds and video.

Automatic background music

A *background sound* is a sound file that plays automatically as soon as the reader opens the page. Internet Explorer supports background sound files in either .wav or .au formats. By the time you read this, there will no doubt be plug-ins for Netscape Navigator 2.0 that support a variety of inline sound formats.

When choosing a sound file as your page's theme song, remember that your reader has to wait for that file when he or she opens your page. Therefore, keep the file small. If you find a small *loop* (a musical piece that can be played repeatedly to sound like an ongoing tune), that's great. You can download the sound file once and then have it play repeatedly on the reader's PC. Defining a background sound is simple:

1. Be sure to copy the .wav or .au sound file to your My Web Site folder so that you don't forget to upload it later.
2. Using Word IA, open (or create) the Web page that will play the sound.
3. Choose Format⇨Background Sound from Word IA's menu bar to get to the dialog box shown in Figure 23-11.

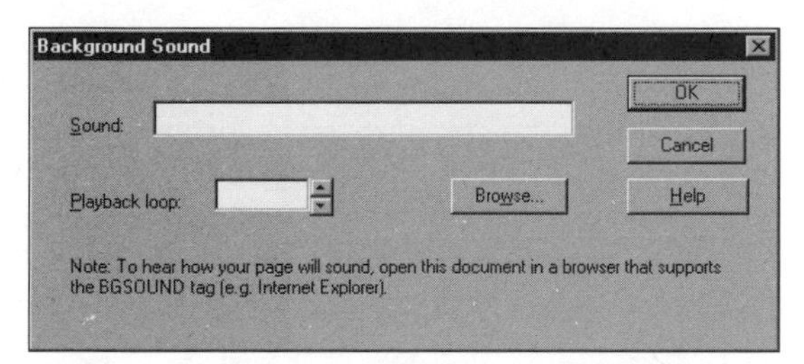

Figure 23-11: Word IA's Background Sound dialog box.

4. Enter the name of the sound file or use the Browse button to browse to it.

5. If you want the sound to play repeatedly, specify the number of repetitions in the Playback Loop spin box. If you want the sound to keep playing the entire time while the reader is viewing the page, click the down arrow once to choose INFINITE.

6. Click OK.

In Word IA, you only see the `<BGSOUND...>` tag in your document, To actually hear the sound, you need to preview the page in Internet Explorer or any other browser that supports background sounds. The sound is simply ignored by any browser that doesn't support the `<BGSOUND>` tag.

Inline video

An *inline video* is much like an inline picture. It downloads automatically as soon as the reader opens the page and then plays inside a frame on the page. You need to give some serious thought to using this feature for a couple of reasons. First, it takes a *really* long time to download even a short, tiny video clip. It takes so long, in fact, that I doubt you'd even want to include an inline video on your home page. Readers will get impatient and move along to some other site. You can, of course, put the inline video on some other page and provide a link to that page. But you should warn the reader that the page takes some time to download because of the video clip.

Second, if you're thinking of putting some of your own favorite camcorder clips on the Web, you better pick ones with *very* compelling content. And remember to keep them short. A reader who waits an hour to see a few minutes of "Baby's First Meal" or "Kitty Does the Jerk" is likely to end up irritated. On the other hand, a video of someone lighting a barbecue with three gallons of liquid oxygen (`http://ghg.ecn.purdue.edu`) or removing a malodorous beached whale with half a ton of dynamite (`http://www.xmission.com/~grue/whale/`) — those videos might be worth the wait. (Neither of those is treated as an inline video, however. Both are optional and give ample warning about the impending wait.)

A better use for an inline video may be a small "moving image" consisting of a few frames played repeatedly on the user's screen. I cannot really show you an example on a printed page, but if you can imagine the globe spinning or the letters in *One-Click Travel* dancing around in their frame in Figure 23-12, then you may be able to get the idea. Each of those videos contains only a few frames played repeatedly to give the appearance of constant motion.

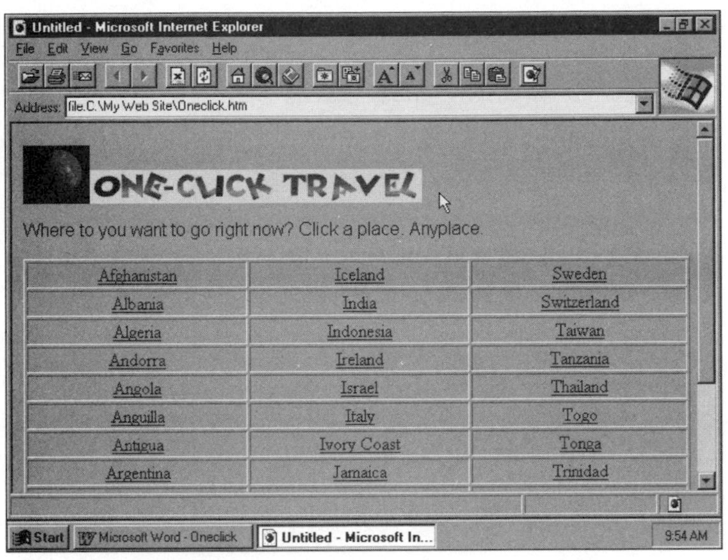

Figure 23-12: Small inline videos can add some pizzazz to a page without taking an eternity to download.

Hot Stuff

By the time you read this, many Web browsers will support animated GIFs — small moving images that will be much easier to create than videos. For more information, stop by my Web site at `http://www.coolnerds.com` or search the Web for *animated GIF.*

Microsoft Internet Explorer 2.0 supports inline videos as long as the video is in .avi format. Numerous plug-ins that enable Netscape Navigator 2.0 to display inline videos are available for download. These plug-ins support .avi, .mpeg, and other formats. Once you have your video file on disk, follow these simple steps to display it as an inline video in your Web page:

1. Be sure to copy the video file to your My Web Site folder so that you won't forget to upload it with the rest of your pages.
2. Use Word IA to open (or create) the Web page that will display the inline video.
3. Move the insertion point to the approximate spot where you want the video to appear on the page.
4. Click the Picture button in Word IA's toolbar, or choose Insert⇨Picture.
5. Click the Video tab to get to the dialog box shown in Figure 23-13.

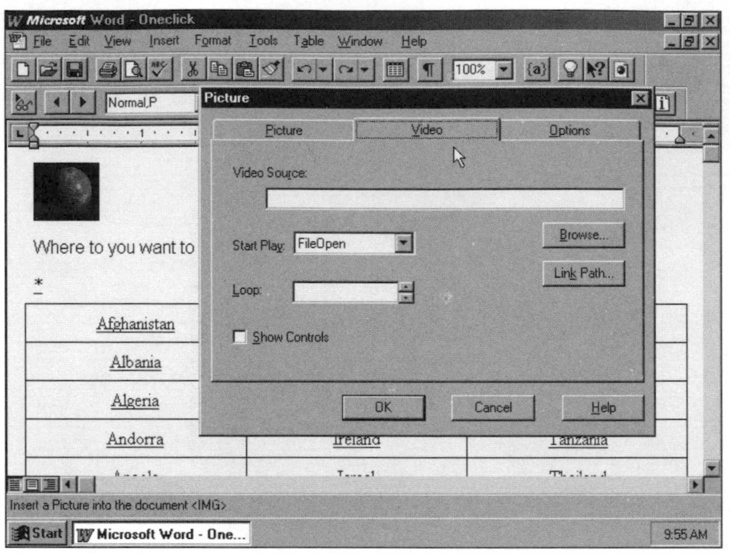

Figure 23-13: Dialog box for inserting an inline video.

6. Type the filename of the video, or use the Browse button to select it.
7. Next to Start Play, specify when you want the video to start playing: FileOpen (as soon as the reader opens the page) or MouseOver (when the user points to the video frame on the page).
8. If you want the video to play repeatedly, specify how many times it should repeat in the Loop spin box. Or click the down arrow once to choose INFINITE.
9. If you want to give the reader the power to start, stop, and rewind the video, choose Show Controls. (Figure 23-14 shows how a video frame with controls appears in Internet Explorer.)
10. If you like, you can click the Options tab and specify the Size, Border, and Alignment with Text options just as you would with a static GIF picture.
11. Click OK.

In Word IA, you may see only an *Image Not Loaded* message, indicating where the video is located. In the HTML Source view, you see the HTML tag `<IMG DYNSRC=...>` where the video will be played. To actually see the video in action, however, you must view the page in a Web browser that supports inline videos.

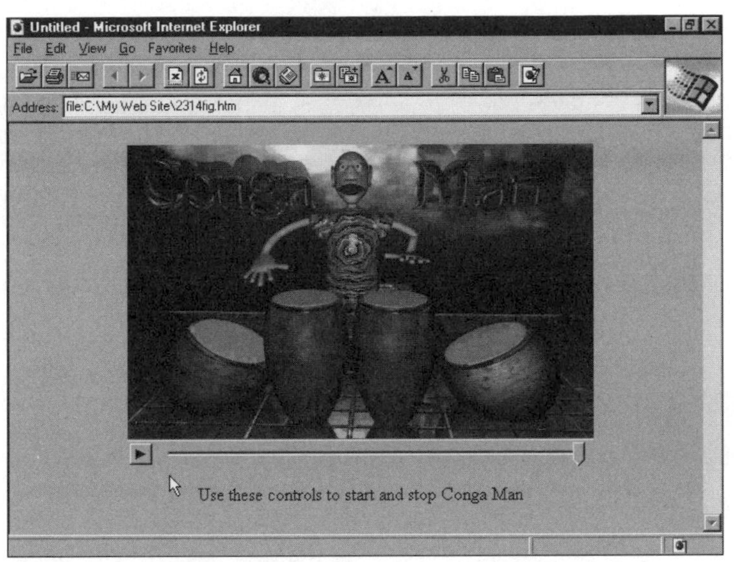

Figure 23-14: Internet Explorer's view of a video with Show Controls activated.

Treating Large Graphics as Multimedia Files

I've mentioned in earlier chapters that if you have any large graphics files, you may want to treat them as external, rather than inline, images. Perhaps put the thumbnails in a *gallery* where the reader can get a quick glimpse of the thumbnails. Tell the reader how large the file is for each thumbnail so that he or she can estimate download time, as in the example shown in Figure 23-15.

Creating picture thumbnails

To create the thumbnails of pictures, open the larger picture in Paint Shop Pro. Then you can do either of the following: Use the Rectangular Selection tool to select a small, representative portion of the picture, then use Choose Edit⇨Copy, Edit⇨Paste⇨As New Image to make a smaller image. Save this small image as a GIF file.

Optionally, you can make a mini-version of the entire picture. Click the picture (in Paint Shop Pro), and choose Edit⇨Copy, Edit⇨Paste⇨As New Image to make a copy. Use the Image⇨Resize or Image⇨Resample commands (Chapter 22) to shrink the copy. Save the smaller copy as a GIF file.

(continued)

(continued)

Or, do both. Copy some representative portion of the larger image to a smaller new image. Then shrink the smaller image down to icon size.

Once you have the small GIF file for use as a thumbnail, you can plop it into your Web page by using the Picture button in Word IA (Chapter 15). To use the thumbnail as a hyperlink, click it, click the Hyperlink button in Word IA's toolbar, and then specify the name of the larger image as the File or URL.

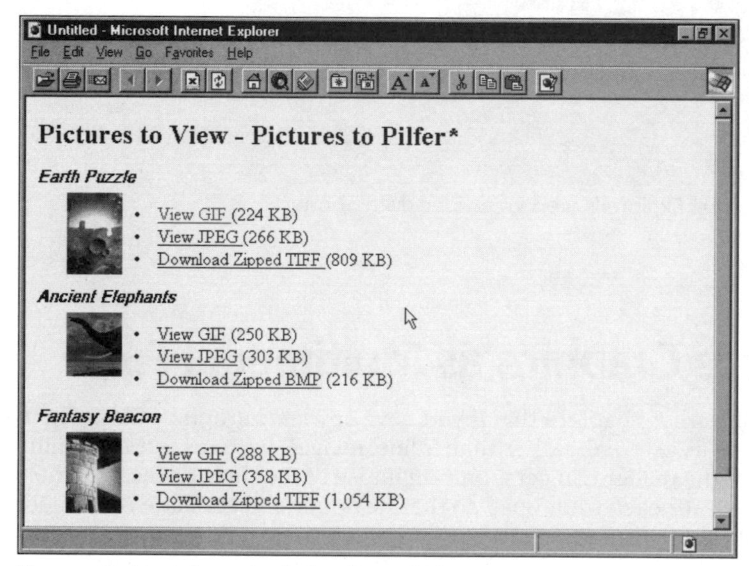

Figure 23-15: A hypothetical gallery of pictures.

To create a gallery like the example shown, I suggest that you do the following for each image in the gallery: Open, in Paint Shop Pro, the large image, and save a copy of it to your My Web Site folder in either GIF or JPEG format (or both, to give the reader a choice). Then make a little thumbnail of the photo by cropping or shrinking a copy of the original, and save the little thumbnail as a GIF file, also in your My Web Site folder.

After you've done that for all photos, open (or create) a Web page in the usual manner with Word IA. Pull in the thumbnail for any one photo and type any text to go along with that photo. To make the hyperlink, select the photo or a chunk of text and click the Hyperlink button. Make the destination (File or URL) for the hyperlink the name of the larger picture, as shown in Figure 23-16.

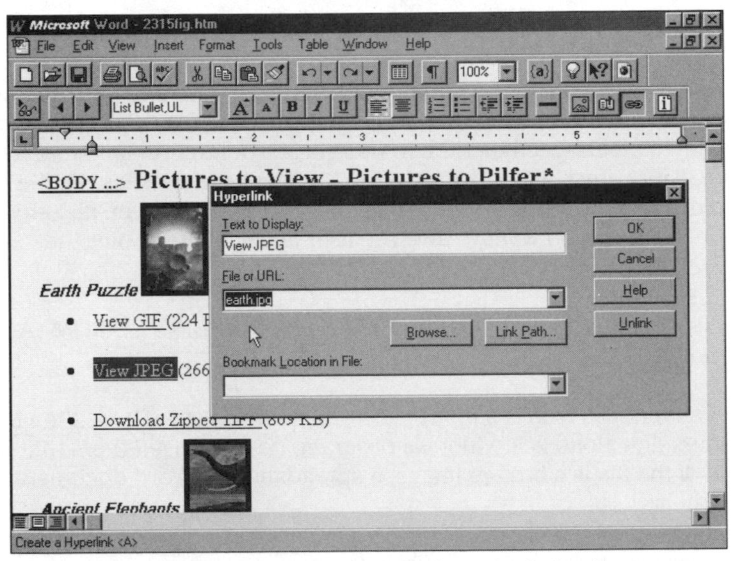

Figure 23-16: Creating one entry for the hypothetical gallery page.

After you're done, don't forget to upload the gallery pages, little thumbnails, and larger images to your Web server. By the way, I should mention what happens when the reader clicks on a hyperlink to a larger picture. The picture replaces the current page in the Web browser (Figure 23-17). If the picture is larger than the screen area, the reader can just scroll around by using the scroll bars. After viewing the picture, clicking the Back button takes the reader back to the previous page.

Figure 23-17: Viewing the full-sized JPEG image of *Ancient Elephants*.

Letting People Download Files

You can let people download programs and documents from your site in the same way you let them download multimedia files and large graphics — by putting the file on your Web site and then creating a hyperlink to that file. I wouldn't recommend letting the reader download just *any* file in this manner. When the browser sees the file coming, it tries to display it in some viewer. To get around that problem, just zip (compress) the file to which you want to give the user access. Then point the hyperlink to the Zip file.

Hot Stuff You can use WinZip, which is included on the *HTML Publishing Bible* CD-ROM (Appendix A) to zip and unzip files.

Remember, however, that the Web is a multi-platform environment. Thus, if the file you're letting readers download is a Windows program, be sure to *tell* them that it is a Windows program. If the file is a bitmap image, a spreadsheet, a Word document, or so on, be sure to tell them.

When the reader clicks your link, he/she is likely to see a message saying that no viewer exists for the file. One of the readers' options will be to Save (or Save As). Give your readers instructions telling them that this happens, and instruct them to choose the Save (or Save As) option.

You can see back in Figure 23-15 that I've allowed readers of that (hypothetical) page to download zipped copies of the original TIF or BMP versions of the pictures. The files that the reader will download are Zip files, which I created on my PC and uploaded to my site with the rest of the files. The hyperlinks to those files are the usual kind you create with the Hyperlink button in Word IA. The File or URL for the hyperlink is just the name of the Zip file. Figure 23-18 shows part of the source document for that page. You can see that all hyperlinks, for the pictures as well as the Zip files, are just your standard `<A HREF = ...>` tags. (The `<IMG SRC=...>` tags are thumbnails.)

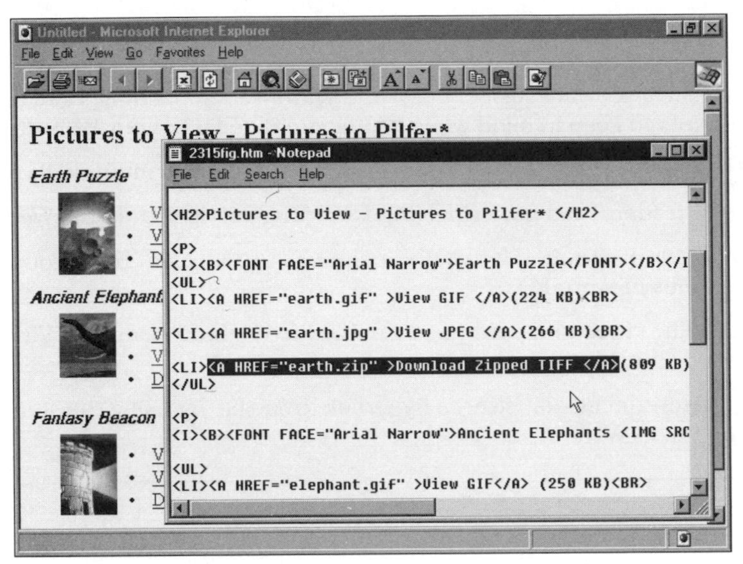

Figure 23-18: Part of the source for the gallery pages shown in Figure 23-16.

Summary

Multimedia is the fastest growing segment of World Wide Web publishing. Here are some important points to keep in mind when adding multimedia to your Web site:

- ✦ Most Web browsers require helper apps or plug-ins to display multimedia files.
- ✦ You (and your readers) can get helper apps and plug-ins right from the Web.
- ✦ To insert a background sound into a Web page, use the Format⇨Background Sound commands in Word IA.
- ✦ To insert an inline video into your page, use the Picture button and the Video tab in the dialog box that appears.
- ✦ To insert any external media, insert a hyperlink to the file by using the standard Hyperlink button in Word IA.

✦ ✦ ✦

Creating Clickable Image Maps

✦ ✦ ✦ ✦

In This Chapter

Examples of clickable image maps

Creating the GIF file for an image map

Using Map This! to define the hot spots

Testing and troubleshooting clickable image maps

Providing alternatives for non-graphical browsers

✦ ✦ ✦ ✦

You've no doubt seen clickable image maps on your Web browsing tour. An image map is basically a picture — a GIF file — with clickable hot spots on it. Each hot spot is a hyperlink to some bookmark, page, or Web site. Here are some examples: In Figure 24-1, you see an opening page for The Spot (`http://www.thespot.com`). Each star within the picture is a hot spot that you can click to go somewhere.

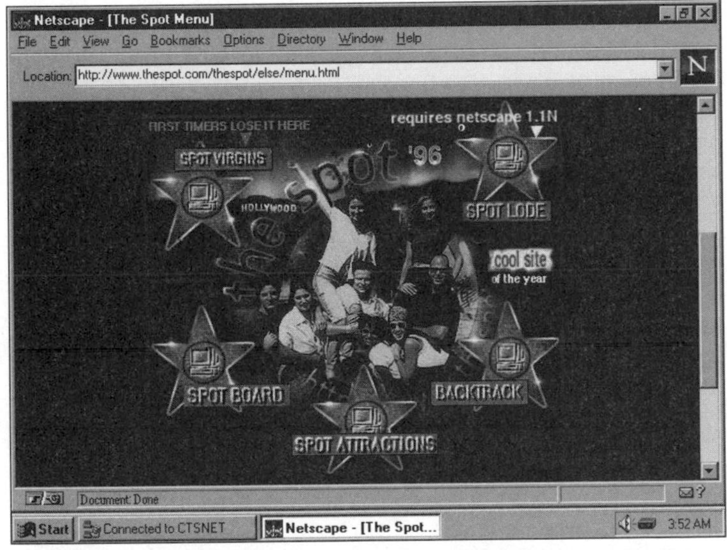

Figure 24-1: Stars in The Spot's page are clickable hot spots.

Microsoft's home page (`http://www.msn.com`), shown in Figure 24-2, opens with an image map. The little graphics down the left and right sides of the picture are all hot spots.

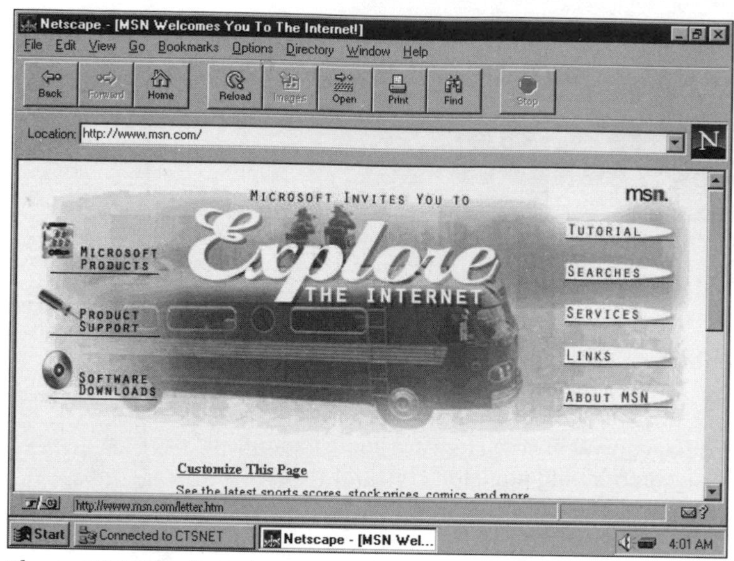

Figure 24-2: The bus picture contains several hot spots.

Image maps are often used as button bars or navigation bars within a Web site. For example, Figure 24-3 shows the navigation bar that appears on many of Netscape's pages (`http://home.netscape.com`).

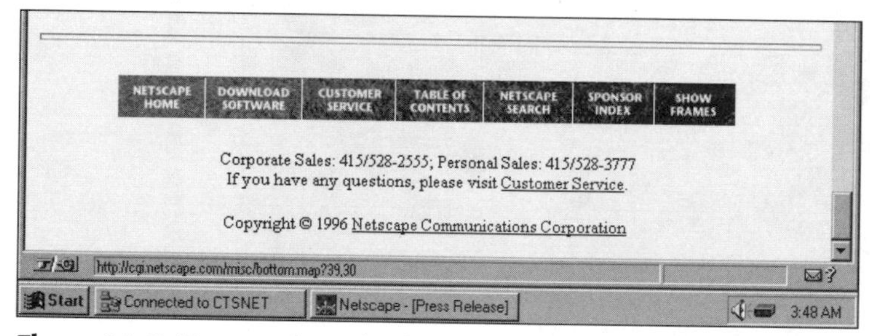

Figure 24-3: Netscape's navigation bars are clickable image maps.

Historically, creating clickable image maps has been a royal pain in the neck. Different servers required different approaches. Fortunately, those days are now over, thanks to *client-side image mapping* (CSIM). With CSIM, the reader's Web browser takes care of all image mapping — you just need to insert the GIF image and the map into your Web page. The map actually consists of a series of HTML tags that define what happens when the reader clicks on different regions of the map.

Some great (and free) tools are available that make image mapping easy. One such tool, called *Map This!,* is included on the *HTML Publishing Bible* CD-ROM. You also can find it online at `http://galadriel.ecaetc.ohio-state.edu/tc/mt/`. In this chapter, you learn how to create client-side image maps, using Map This! as your tool. For information on installing and starting Map This!, please refer to Appendix A.

Step 1: Create the GIF Image

The GIF image for a clickable map is *just* a GIF image. You can create it with any drawing program, such as Paint Shop Pro. Of course, the image needs to give the reader some clue as to where to click to get a result. For this chapter, I created a navigation bar image map that looks like a series of buttons. Figure 24-4 shows that GIF image in Paint Shop Pro, which I've named navbar.gif (for *navigation bar*).

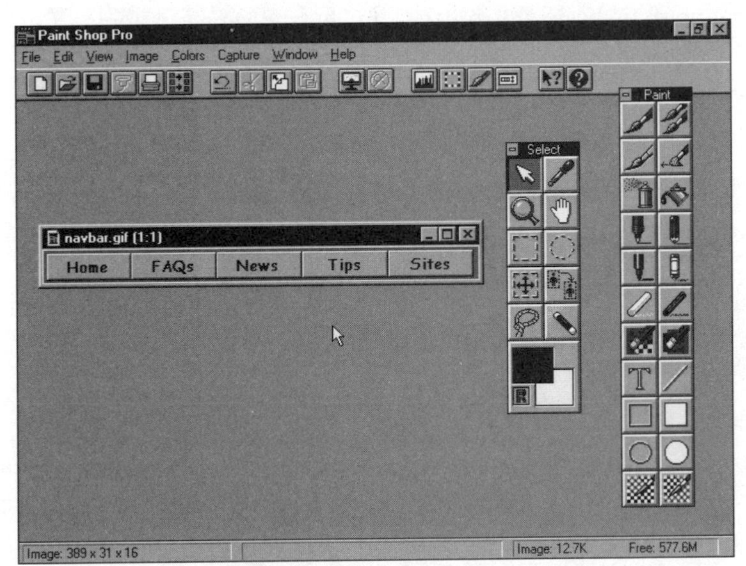

Figure 24-4: The GIF image I'll use as the example in this chapter.

Once you have your GIF image, save it to your My Web Site folder. When it is time to publish your site, you need to upload that image with the rest of your pages. You can exit Paint Shop Pro before you move onto the next step.

More Info

In case you're curious, I actually created the navigation bar in Microsoft Access. (Like most application development tools, Access has features that enable you to easily draw buttons and such.) Then I took a snapshot of the bar and pasted it into Paint Shop Pro. In Paint Shop Pro, I cropped the snapshot down to size and then saved it as a GIF file named navbar.gif.

Step 2: Define the Map

A clickable image map always consists of two parts — the GIF image, which you created in Step 1, and the map, which defines the hot spots and the action to take when the reader clicks a particular hot spot. I'll have you use Map This! to create that map. Here's how to get started:

1. From the Windows 95 desktop, start Map This!
2. Let's first set up some basic preferences for client-side image mapping. Choose File⇨Preferences to get to the General Preferences dialog box. Choose CSIM under Default Map Type. Then clear the Require Default URL check box as in Figure 24-5. Click OK.

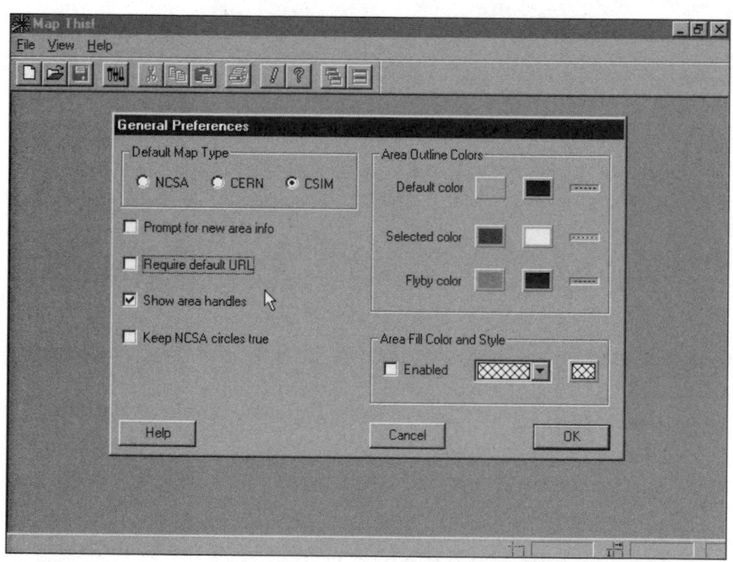

Figure 24-5: Set up Map This! preferences for client-side image mapping.

3. Now you need to add the GIF file. Choose File⇨New⇨Let's Go Find One.
4. Browse to the folder that contains your GIF file and choose its name. For example, in Figure 24-6, I've opened my navbar.gif image. (You may need to size the GIF's document window to see the entire image.)

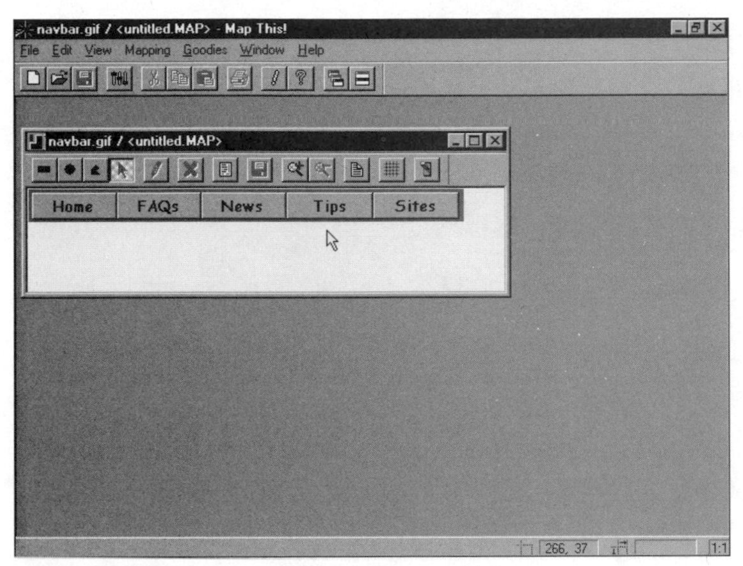

Figure 24-6: My navbar.gif image in Map This!

You can press F1 or click a Help button (if one is available) to learn more while you're in Map This! You may want to stop by the Map This! home page to see what's new. Point your Web browser to `http://galadriel.ecaetc.ohio-state.edu/tc/mt/`.

Now you need to map out each hot spot in the image and describe where the reader will be taken when he or she clicks that hot spot. You may want to "zoom in" on your image a little, using the magnifying glass button, to do this part of the procedure.

1. First, open the Area List window by choosing View⇨Area List.
2. Click one of the first three buttons just above your GIF image to indicate the shape you want to map out: Rectangle, Circle/Oval, or Polygon.
3. Now drag a frame around one hot spot. For example, in Figure 24-7, I've dragged a frame around the Home button in my GIF. Notice that the Area List window now contains a reference to that area, titled *1:rect.*

Neatness definitely counts when defining your hot spots. Don't let them overlap. If you need to resize a hot spot after you've released the mouse button, drag any sizing handle within the hot spot. To delete a hot spot, click its reference in the Area List and then click the Delete button there.

4. In the Area List, click the reference to the spot you just defined (*1:rect,* in this example), and then click the Edit button in the Area List.

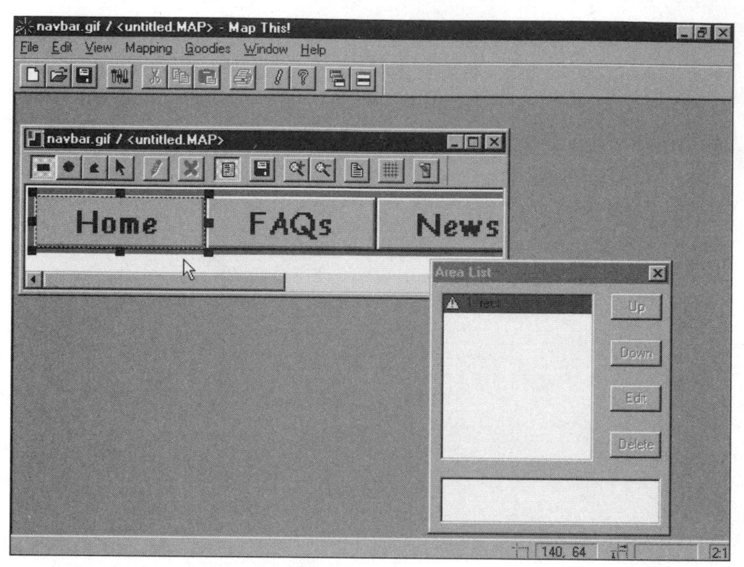

Figure 24-7: Defining my first hot spot in Map This!

5. Type the URL (or just the filename for a page within your own site) to indicate where you want this hot spot to take the reader. Optionally, you can enter a comment for your own future reference. Here my home page is named index.htm, so I want the Home hot spot to take my reader to index.htm, as in Figure 24-8.

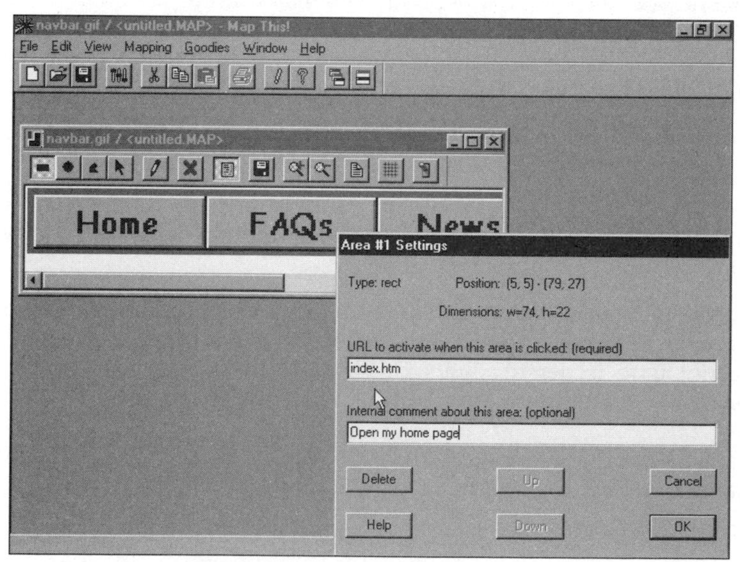

Figure 24-8: My Home button takes the reader to my home page, index.htm.

6. Click OK from the Area Settings dialog box. The Area List now includes the optional internal comment you entered, as you can see in Figure 24-9.

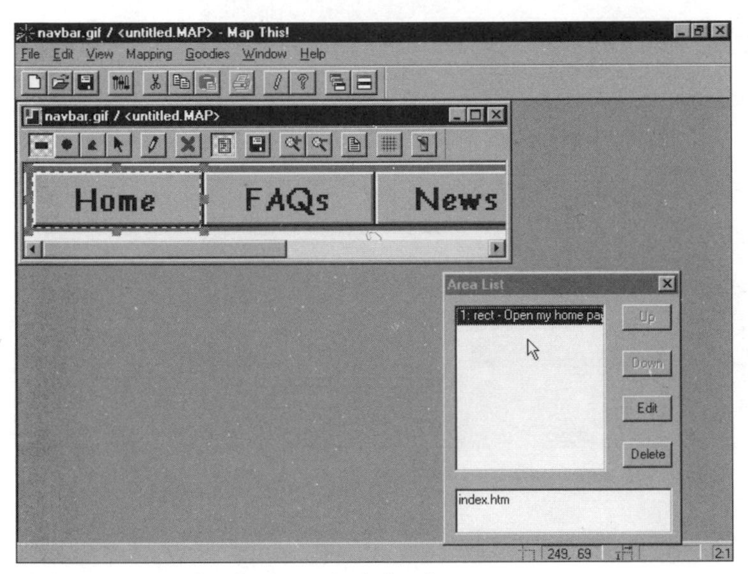

Figure 24-9: My first hot spot is defined.

7. Now you need to repeat Steps 3–6 to define every hot spot within your image.

Figure 24-10 shows how Map This! looks after I've defined the hot spot for each button in my GIF image. Table 24-1 shows which URL I've assigned to each button.

Table 24-1
Where Each Hot Spot Takes My Reader

Hot Spot	*URL*
Home	`index.htm`
FAQs	`faqs.htm`
News	`news.htm`
Tips	`tips.htm`
Sites	`sites.htm`

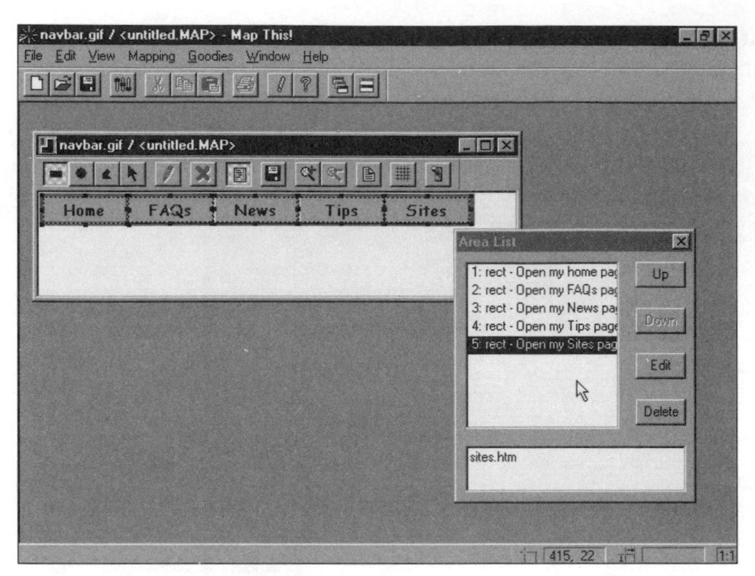

Figure 24-10: All my hot spots defined.

Step 3: Save the Map

Now that you've defined the map, you need to save it. Here's how:

1. Choose File➪Save and then click the Map Info button to define the map.
2. Enter a descriptive title that will be easy to remember. For example, I would name mine *navbar map* because this map goes with the nabar.gif image.
3. Fill in the rest of the blanks to your liking, but be sure to select CSIM under Map file format, as in Figure 24-11.

Puzzled? The dialog box in Figure 24-11 says that a default URL is required. That's not true with client-side image maps. You can leave that option blank. If the reader clicks some neutral part of the image map, the click will be ignored. It's not necessary to send the reader to some default URL.

4. Choose OK after filling in the Map Info dialog to get back to the Save As dialog box.
5. Now you need to choose a location and filename for the map. You'll want to keep a few things in mind here:
   - You won't actually upload the map file to your Web site. Rather, you'll be inserting its HTML tags into your Web pages. Thus, you may want to store the file in your My Web Site\Parts folder.
   - When creating a client-side image map, you must use the .htm extension in the filename.

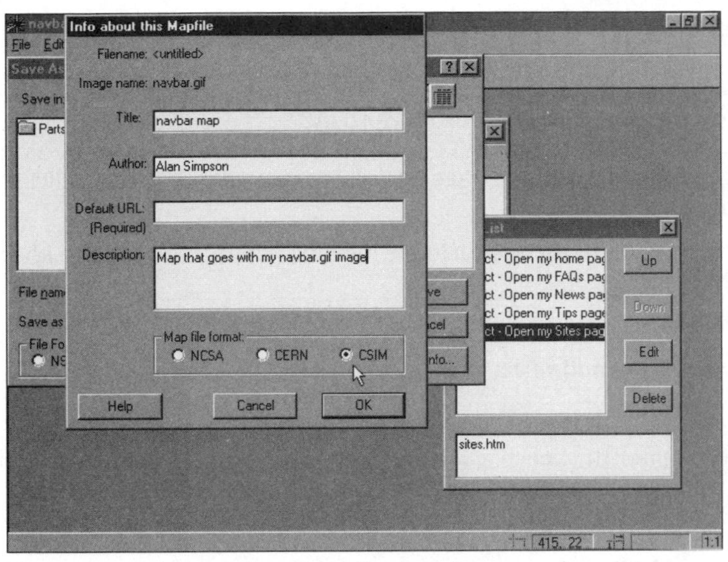

Figure 24-11: Information about the map for my navbar.gif image.

   • As always, use a filename you can remember later.

6. In Figure 24-12, I'm about to name my map file as navbar.htm, and I will put it in my My Web Site\Parts folder. Click on Save to complete the job.

7. You now can exit Map This! (choose File⇨Exit or click its Close button).

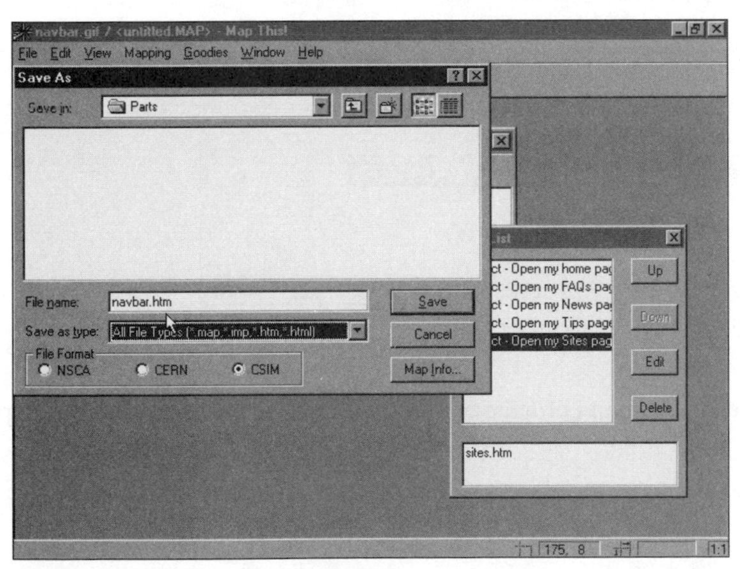

Figure 24-12: Saving my image map as navbar.htm in my My Web Site\Parts folder.

Step 4: Put the GIF into the Web Page

You have your GIF image and your map. Now it's time to put them into a Web page. I first show you how to insert the GIF by using Word IA:

1. In Word IA, open (or create) the page into which you want to put the clickable image map.
2. Move the insert point to the approximate location where you want the image to appear in the page.
3. Click the Picture button, and then browse to and select the name of the GIF file.
4. Click the Options tab and select the Image is a sensitive map option.
5. Click OK.
6. If you want to center the image, click the Center button in the Word IA toolbar. Figure 24-13 shows an example where I've inserted the navbar.gif picture into a simple Web page named index.htm.

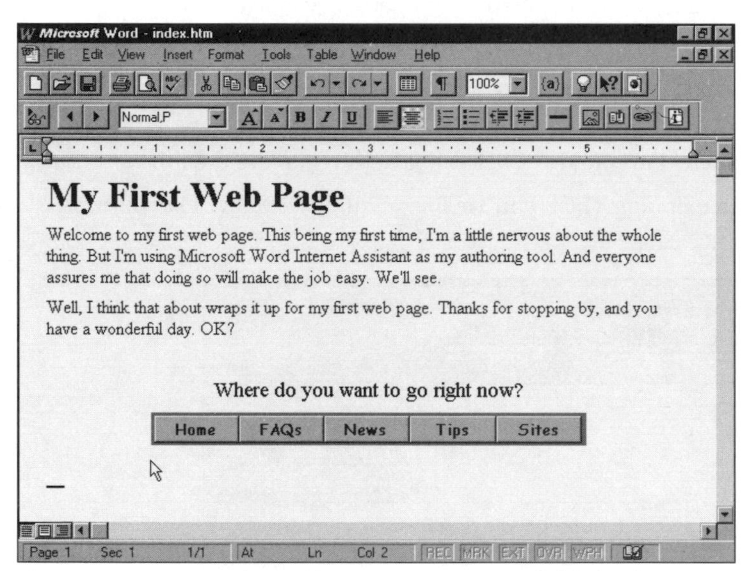

Figure 24-13: My navbar.gif image in a page named index.htm.

Now you need to get the map (htm file) created by Map This! into the same Web page.

Step 5: Put the Map into the Web Page

Earlier I said that an image map really consists of two components — the GIF file and the map. The map in client-side image mapping is made up of a set of HTML tags. You just inserted the GIF file, so now you need to insert the map. Map This! has already created the map for you. You need to find it and yank it into your page.

1. Move the insertion point to just above the GIF picture you inserted in the preceding steps (or to the left side of that picture).
2. Choose Insert⇨File.
3. Under Files of Type near the bottom of the Insert File dialog box, choose All Files (*.*).
4. Browse to wherever you told Map This! to save the map, and click on the map name. In my example, I need to get to My Web Site\Parts\navbar.htm, as in Figure 24-14.

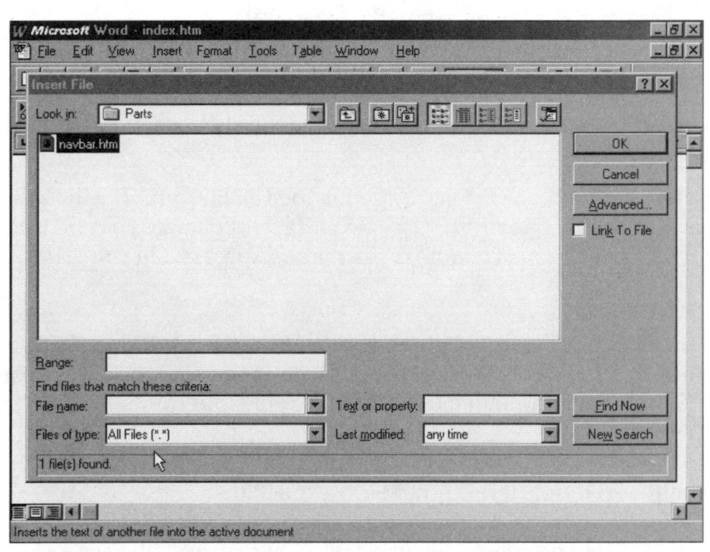

Figure 24-14: About to insert the My Web Site\Parts\navbar.htm file into the current Web page.

5. Click OK.
6. The tags that appear look pretty funky (Figure 24-15), but don't worry about that just now. You're not quite done yet.

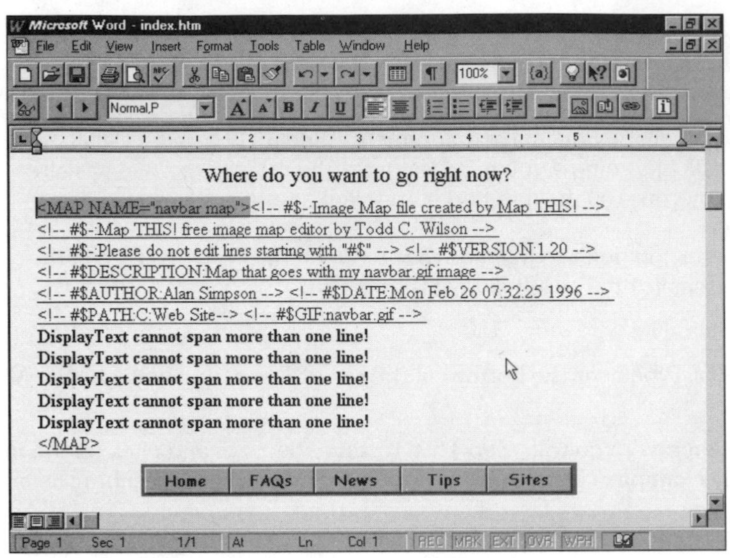

Figure 24-15: The <MAP NAME>...</MAP> tags that Map This! created are in my index.htm Web page now.

7. Now you have a little tag-tweaking to do. From the Word IA menu bar, choose View⇨HTML Source⇨Yes.
8. You need to get to the <IMG SRC= ...> tag for the GIF file, which will look something like <IMG SRC="navbar.gif" ISMAP>, and change that ISMAP to USEMAP="#mapname" where *mapname* is the name expressed in the <MAP NAME =...> tag.

Figure 24-16 shows an example. I've highlighted the <MAP NAME => tag so that you can see it easily. If you look at the IMG SRC tag at the bottom of the screen, you can see that I've made the USEMAP attribute equal to the name defined in the MAP NAME tag (*navbar map,* in this example).

And that should about wrap it up. Here's how to do a quick test:

1. Return to normal Edit mode (click the little pencil button and choose Yes).
2. Click the Preview in Browser button in the Word IA toolbar.
3. In your Web browser, point to any hot spot. The status bar should show a Shortcut to... message, as in Figure 24-17.

If you've created the page that the hot spot links to, you should be able to click the hot spot and arrive at that page. Click the Back button in your browser's toolbar to return to the previous page.

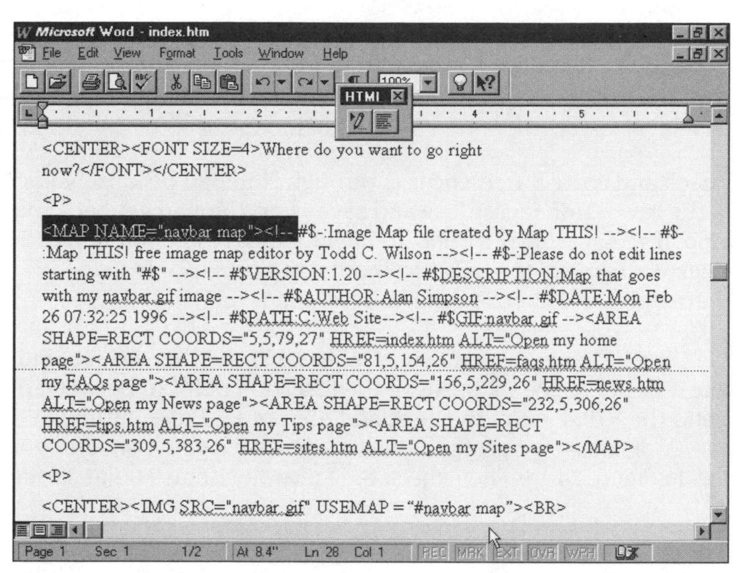

Figure 24-16: Changed ISMAP to USEMAP="#*mapname*" in the IMG SRC tag.

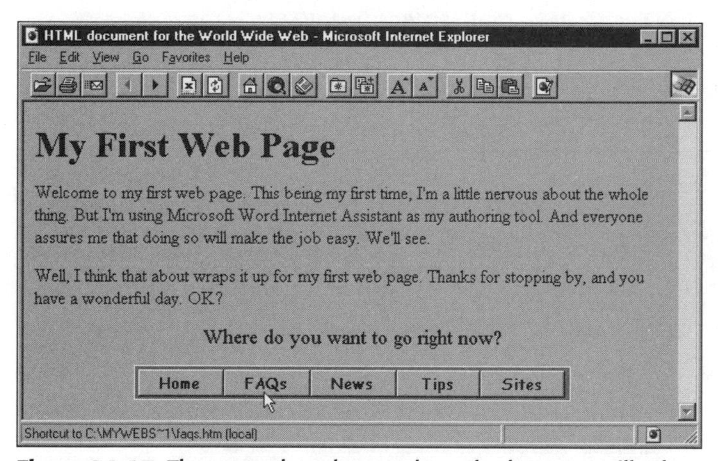

Figure 24-17: The status bar shows where the hot spot will take me.

Troubleshooting Image Maps

If you have any trouble with your image map either before or after you upload the page(s) to your Web site, I recommend that you do the following: First, make sure that your Web browser supports client-side image mapping. Internet Explorer 2.0 and Netscape Navigator 2.0 both do. If you are not using a browser that supports client-side image mapping, the image map won't do anything when you click a hot spot.

A second potential problem centers around using relative versus absolute URLs. All references to pages, and the reference to your GIF file, should be *relative* in the sense that they do not specify a location. Otherwise, as discussed earlier, the folder names at your actual Web site may not match the folder names on your PC.

The best way to check and correct references is through Notepad because you can work directly with the raw HTML tags. Close and save everything to get back the Windows 95 desktop. If you set up your Send To menu as suggested in Chapter 11, you can simply right-click the name of the page that contains the clickable map (index.htm, in my example) and choose Send To⇨Notepad.

When you open the page in Notepad, you may want to separate the tags into individual lines to make it easier to see them. Move the insertion point to between the > that ends one tag and the < that starts the next, and then press Enter. Although the tags are a little scary looking at first glance, you can see what's going on after you tidy up the lines a bit, as in Figure 24-18. Then check the following items and make any necessary changes:

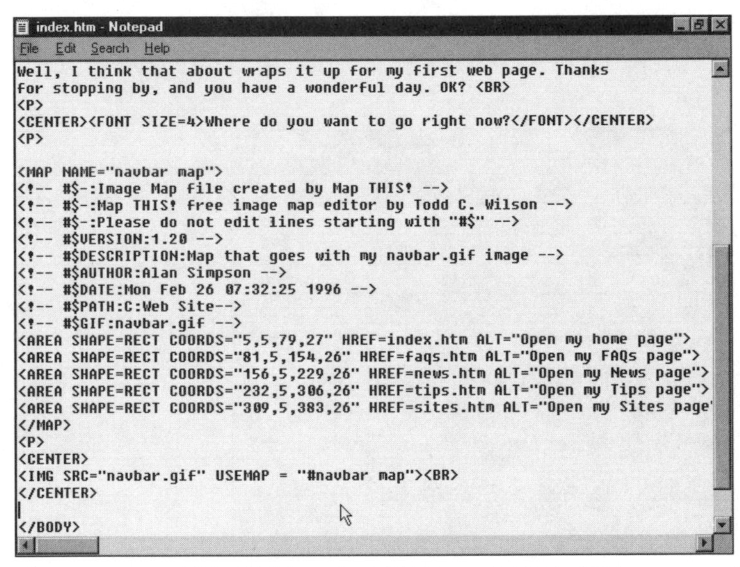

```
Well, I think that about wraps it up for my first web page. Thanks
for stopping by, and you have a wonderful day. OK? <BR>
<P>
<CENTER><FONT SIZE=4>Where do you want to go right now?</FONT></CENTER>
<P>

<MAP NAME="navbar map">
<!-- #$-:Image Map file created by Map THIS! -->
<!-- #$-:Map THIS! free image map editor by Todd C. Wilson -->
<!-- #$-:Please do not edit lines starting with "#$" -->
<!-- #$VERSION:1.20 -->
<!-- #$DESCRIPTION:Map that goes with my navbar.gif image -->
<!-- #$AUTHOR:Alan Simpson -->
<!-- #$DATE:Mon Feb 26 07:32:25 1996 -->
<!-- #$PATH:C:Web Site-->
<!-- #$GIF:navbar.gif -->
<AREA SHAPE=RECT COORDS="5,5,79,27" HREF=index.htm ALT="Open my home page">
<AREA SHAPE=RECT COORDS="81,5,154,26" HREF=faqs.htm ALT="Open my FAQs page">
<AREA SHAPE=RECT COORDS="156,5,229,26" HREF=news.htm ALT="Open my News page">
<AREA SHAPE=RECT COORDS="232,5,306,26" HREF=tips.htm ALT="Open my Tips page">
<AREA SHAPE=RECT COORDS="309,5,383,26" HREF=sites.htm ALT="Open my Sites page'
</MAP>
<P>
<CENTER>
<IMG SRC="navbar.gif" USEMAP = "#navbar map"><BR>
</CENTER>

</BODY>
```

Figure 24-18: `<MAP NAME...>`, `</MAP>`, and `<IMG SRC = ... USEMAP>` tags in my index.htm document.

- ✦ Note the exact map name in the `<MAP NAME>` tag and make sure that the `USEMAP =` attribute in the `IMG SRC` tag is spelled exactly the same as that name. In `USEMAP`, however, that name must be preceded by a # character.
- ✦ You can ignore all tags that start with `<!`, as these comments don't affect how the image map behaves.

✦ Each `<AREA SHAPE...>` tag should point to a local document with no folder name (such as faqs.htm, not C:\My Web Site\FAQs.htm>).

Danger Zone

Don't forget that your Web server may be a Unix machine, and Unix is case-sensitive to filenames. Your actual filenames and any references to those files within your HTML tags should use only lowercase letters!

✦ In the `IMG SRC =` tag, make sure that the name of the GIF file does not contain a location. For example, it should be *navbar.gif,* not *\My Web Site\NavBar.GIF.*

When you close the page, make sure that you choose Yes if Notepad asks about saving the changes. Test it again in any Web browser that supports client-side image mapping.

Copying an Image Map

If you want to put the same image map into several Web pages, you can copy and paste the map image source tags from one page to the next. For example, in Figure 24-19, I've selected everything I need to place an exact duplicate of my navbar image map into another page. I just need to choose Edit⇨Copy to copy that stuff to the Windows Clipboard.

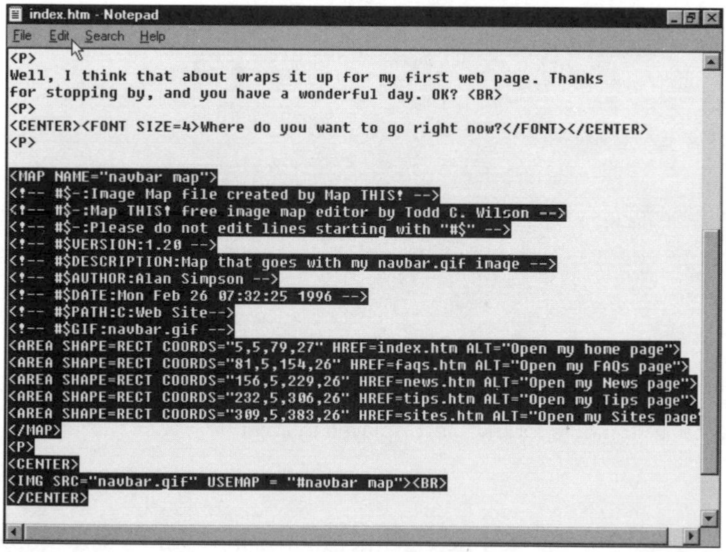

index.htm - Notepad

File Edit Search Help

```
<P>
Well, I think that about wraps it up for my first web page. Thanks
for stopping by, and you have a wonderful day. OK? <BR>
<P>
<CENTER><FONT SIZE=4>Where do you want to go right now?</FONT></CENTER>
<P>

<MAP NAME="navbar map">
<!-- #$-:Image Map file created by Map THIS! -->
<!-- #$-:Map THIS! free image map editor by Todd C. Wilson -->
<!-- #$-:Please do not edit lines starting with "#$" -->
<!-- #$VERSION:1.20 -->
<!-- #$DESCRIPTION:Map that goes with my navbar.gif image -->
<!-- #$AUTHOR:Alan Simpson -->
<!-- #$DATE:Mon Feb 26 07:32:25 1996 -->
<!-- #$PATH:C:Web Site-->
<!-- #$GIF:navbar.gif -->
<AREA SHAPE=RECT COORDS="5,5,79,27" HREF=index.htm ALT="Open my home page">
<AREA SHAPE=RECT COORDS="81,5,154,26" HREF=faqs.htm ALT="Open my FAQs page">
<AREA SHAPE=RECT COORDS="156,5,229,26" HREF=news.htm ALT="Open my News page">
<AREA SHAPE=RECT COORDS="232,5,306,26" HREF=tips.htm ALT="Open my Tips page">
<AREA SHAPE=RECT COORDS="309,5,383,26" HREF=sites.htm ALT="Open my Sites page
</MAP>
<P>
<CENTER>
<IMG SRC="navbar.gif" USEMAP = "#navbar map"><BR>
</CENTER>
```

Figure 24-19: Stuff I need to copy to duplicate image map in other Web pages.

Then I can open any other Web page, using Notepad, move the insertion point to the approximate location of where I want the image map to appear, and then choose Edit⇨Paste to paste in the tags.

More Refined Image Maps

Some of you may be thinking "Hey Alan, that's all really cool. But isn't it a little tacky to use the same navigation bar in every page? After all, why should the FAQs page have a button to go to the FAQs page, when the reader is already *in* the FAQs page?" The answers to those questions are "Yes" (it is tacky) and "Because the author of the pages was too lazy to create five separate navigation bars." Given the fact that I *am* the author, I suppose it behooves me to be a little more considerate of my Web site readers. Here's what I would do if I were in a suitably magnanimous mood:

First, I create five separate navigation bar GIFs. In each GIF, I could eliminate the button for the current page. But, because I'm feeling extra magnanimous, instead I show the button for the current page as being "pushed in." Now my navigation bar not only gives the reader quick access to other pages, but it also presents a quick reminder of where the reader is at the moment. Figure 24-20 shows my five new navigation bar GIFs in Paint Shop Pro. Notice that each is named in accordance with the page it belongs in (such as homebar.gif, faqsbar.gif, and so on).

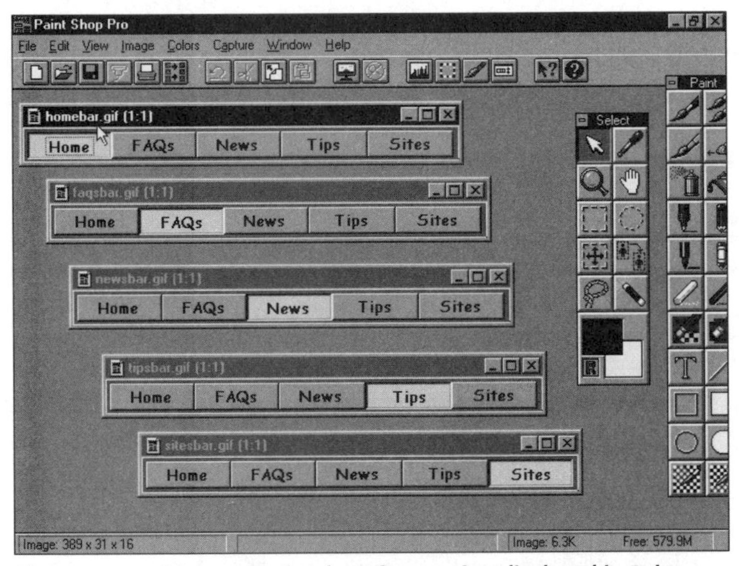

Figure 24-20: Five navigation bars for my site, displayed in Paint Shop Pro.

I reserve the right to be a little bit lazy here. Rather than using Map This! to map out each of these bars, I'm just going to copy the Map This! tags from navbar.gif into each Web page. Then I modify the tags to display the appropriate bar for that page. I also disable the hot spot for the current page so that if the reader does click on the button for the current page, nothing happens.

First, I open index.htm in Notepad and change the tags so that the image source is homebar.gif rather than navbar.gif. Then I "comment out" the AREA that makes the Home button hot, as shown in the following example (changes are shown in boldface). To comment out a line, I just put an exclamation point right after the opening < marker for the appropriate AREA SHAPE tag. Once converted to a comment, the Web browser ignores everything between <*!* and > in that line.

```
<MAP NAME="navbar map">
<!-- #$-:Image Map file created by Map THIS! -->
<!-- #$-:Map THIS! free image map editor by Todd C. Wilson -->
<!-- #$-:Please do not edit lines starting with "#$" -->
<!-- #$VERSION:1.20 -->
<!-- #$DESCRIPTION:Map that goes with my navbar.gif image -->
<!-- #$AUTHOR:Alan Simpson -->
<!-- #$DATE:Mon Feb 26 07:32:25 1996 -->
<!-- #$PATH:C:Web Site-->
<!-- #$GIF:navbar.gif -->
<! -- AREA SHAPE=RECT COORDS="5,5,79,27" HREF=index.htm ALT="Home
      page"->
<AREA SHAPE=RECT COORDS="81,5,154,26" HREF=faqs.htm ALT="FAQs
      page">
<AREA SHAPE=RECT COORDS="156,5,229,26" HREF=news.htm ALT="News
      page">
<AREA SHAPE=RECT COORDS="232,5,306,26" HREF=tips.htm ALT="Tips
      page">
<AREA SHAPE=RECT COORDS="309,5,383,26" HREF=sites.htm ALT="Sites
      page">
</MAP>
<P>
<CENTER>
<IMG SRC="homebar.gif" USEMAP = "#navbar map"><BR>
</CENTER>
```

I then copy those same tags into my faqs.htm page. There, I reactivate the `<AREA SHAPE` tag for going to the home page and comment out the `<AREA SHAPE` tag that would take the reader to the FAQs page. I also change the image source for the map to faqsbar.gif, as follows:

```
<MAP NAME="navbar map">
<!-- #$-:Image Map file created by Map THIS! -->
<!-- #$-:Map THIS! free image map editor by Todd C. Wilson -->
<!-- #$-:Please do not edit lines starting with "#$" -->
<!-- #$VERSION:1.20 -->
<!-- #$DESCRIPTION:Map that goes with my navbar.gif image -->
<!-- #$AUTHOR:Alan Simpson -->
<!-- #$DATE:Mon Feb 26 07:32:25 1996 -->
<!-- #$PATH:C:Web Site-->
<!-- #$GIF:navbar.gif -->
<AREA SHAPE=RECT COORDS="5,5,79,27" HREF=index.htm ALT="Home
      page">
```

```
<!--AREA SHAPE=RECT COORDS="81,5,154,26" HREF=faqs.htm ALT="FAQs
       page"->
<AREA SHAPE=RECT COORDS="156,5,229,26" HREF=news.htm ALT="News
       page">
<AREA SHAPE=RECT COORDS="232,5,306,26" HREF=tips.htm ALT="Tips
       page">
<AREA SHAPE=RECT COORDS="309,5,383,26" HREF=sites.htm ALT="Sites
       page">
</MAP>
<P>
<CENTER>
<IMG SRC="faqsbar.gif" USEMAP = "#navbar map"><BR>
</CENTER>
```

In my news.htm page, I do a similar task, commenting out the News hot spot and using newsbar.gif as the image map graphic.

```
<MAP NAME="navbar map">
<!-- #$-:Image Map file created by Map THIS! -->
<!-- #$-:Map THIS! free image map editor by Todd C. Wilson -->
<!-- #$-:Please do not edit lines starting with "#$" -->
<!-- #$VERSION:1.20 -->
<!-- #$DESCRIPTION:Map that goes with my navbar.gif image -->
<!-- #$AUTHOR:Alan Simpson -->
<!-- #$DATE:Mon Feb 26 07:32:25 1996 -->
<!-- #$PATH:C:Web Site-->
<!-- #$GIF:navbar.gif -->
<AREA SHAPE=RECT COORDS="5,5,79,27" HREF=index.htm ALT="Home
       page">
<AREA SHAPE=RECT COORDS="81,5,154,26" HREF=faqs.htm ALT="FAQs
       page">
<! -- AREA SHAPE=RECT COORDS="156,5,229,26" HREF=news.htm
       ALT="News page"->
<AREA SHAPE=RECT COORDS="232,5,306,26" HREF=tips.htm ALT="Tips
       page">
<AREA SHAPE=RECT COORDS="309,5,383,26" HREF=sites.htm ALT="Sites
       page">
</MAP>
<P>
<CENTER>
<IMG SRC="newsbar.gif" USEMAP = "#navbar map"><BR>
</CENTER>
```

I then continue with this process until each page has a custom navigation bar. For example, Figure 24-21 shows the custom navigation bar at the bottom of my FAQs page, as viewed in Internet Explorer.

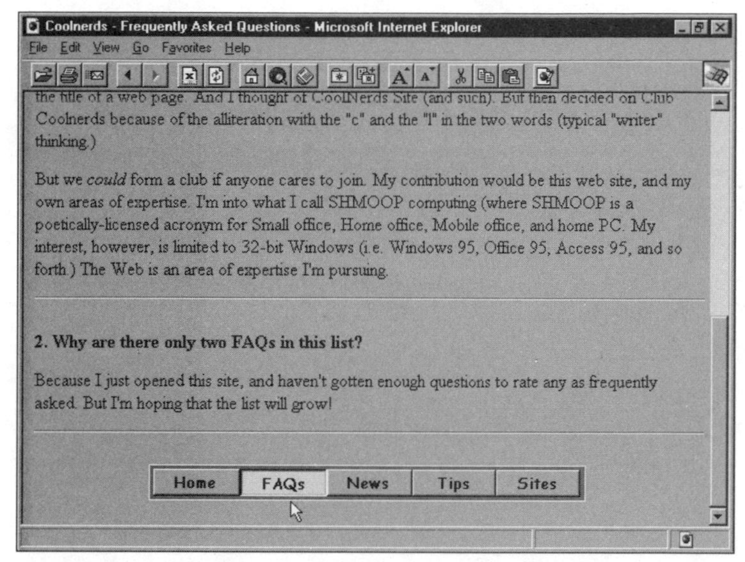

Figure 24-21: My FAQs page with its very own navigation map showing.

Navigation for Non-CSIM Browsers

A couple of problems are left to contend with in the clickable image map business:

✦ Readers who are browsing with graphics turned off or with non-graphical browsers won't even see the navigation bar.

✦ Readers whose browsers don't support client-side image mapping will see the navigation bar. But the navigation bar won't take them anywhere.

A simple solution to both problems is to create a text-only navigation bar and put it near the graphical one. This is pretty easy to do. I'll use my FAQs page as an example. First I open that page in Word IA, scroll down to the bottom, and put the insertion point just under the graphical image map. Then I type (literally) this line:

```
[Home][News][Tips][Sites]
```

Now I can select the word between any pair of square brackets and use the Word IA Hyperlink button to make that word a hot link to some other page. For example, in Figure 24-22, I've made the word *Home* a hyperlink to my index.htm page.

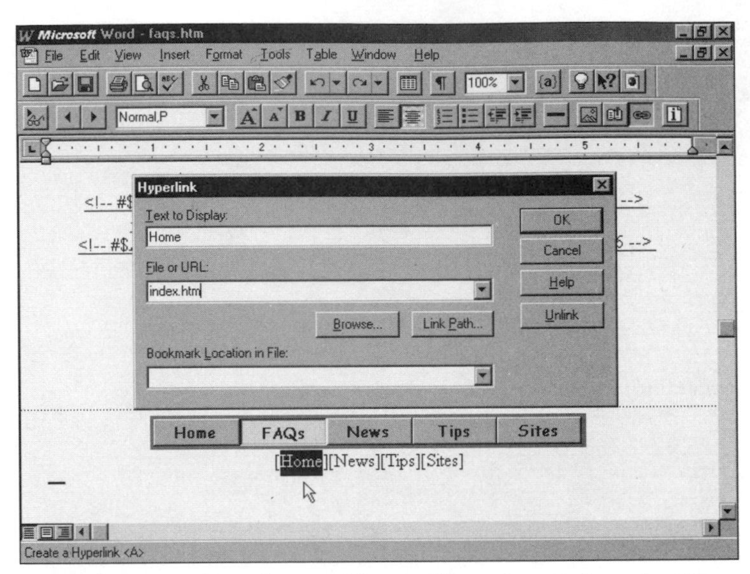

Figure 24-22: Making the word "Home" in my text-only navigation bar a hyperlink.

Figure 24-23 shows how the page looks when it contains both the graphical navigation bar and the text-only navigation bar. All bases are covered now — readers who have no graphics or client-side image mapping support can use the text-only navigation bar to get around.

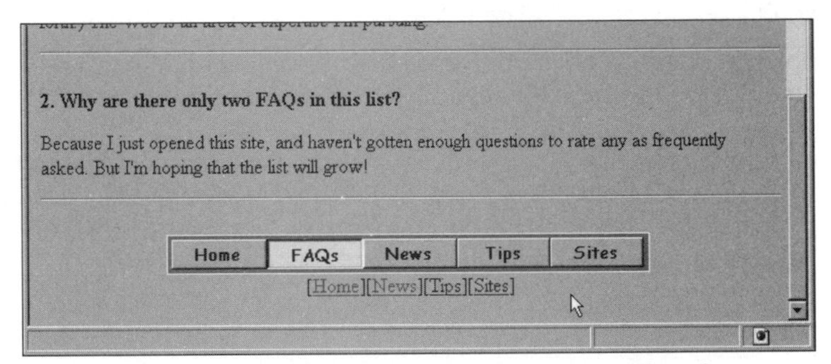

Figure 24-23: Both graphical and text-only navigation bars in my FAQs page.

Summary

Image maps are kind of fun and easy to create, as long as you have a good tool such as Map This! to work with. Let's review the basics:

- A clickable image map consists of a graphic image and a map (HTML tags) that defines hot spots within that image.
- You can create the graphic image by using any graphics program that can save GIF files.
- You can use Map This! to identify the hot spots and where the reader will be sent after clicking that hot spot.
- To create a client-side image map in Map This!, make sure that you choose CSIM as the map type and give the map filename a .htm extension when you save the map.
- To insert the image map into your Web page, first insert the graphic image with the regular Picture button in Word IA and then choose ISMAP in the Options tab.
- Use Insert⇨File in Word IA to insert the map (.htm file) that Map This! created for you.
- In the <IMG SRC =...> tag for the clickable image, change the ISMAP attribute to USEMAP " #mapname" where *mapname* is the name of the map defined in the <MAP NAME...> tag.

✦ ✦ ✦

Creating Netscape Frames

In This Chapter

What are frames?

HTML tags for frames

Incorporating frames into your own site

Supporting frame-incapable browsers

Nesting frames

Historically, a big problem with the Web has been the one-screen-at-a-time approach to things. Like old DOS programs, each page you open essentially takes over the screen. You cannot split the Web browser screen into separate little windows, each with some useful piece of information. With the release of Navigator 2.0, however, you *can* simultaneously display multiple Web pages in little window-like objects called *frames.*

Netscape — the folks who brought you frames — has, of course, implemented frames in its own home page. If you go to Netscape's site (`http://home.netscape.com`) by using Netscape 2.0, you come right to the home page divided into five frames (Figure 25-1).

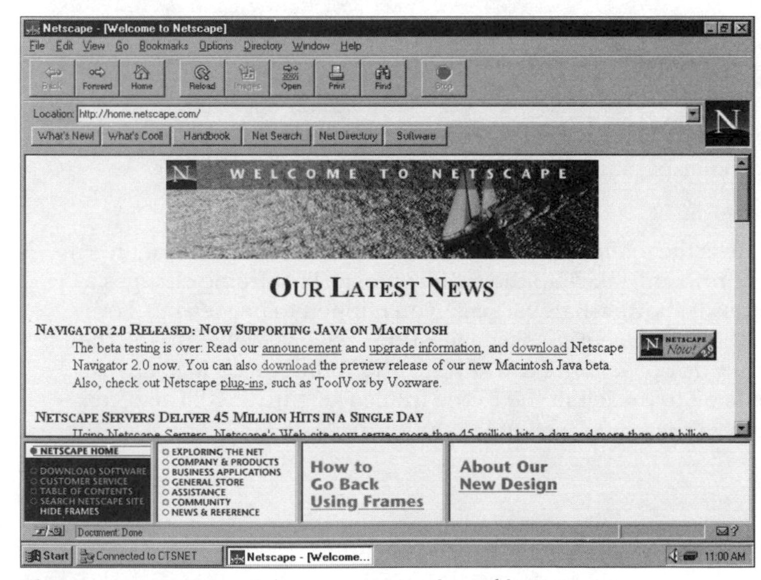

Figure 25-1: Netscape's home page as viewed in Netscape Navigator 2.0.

Webs Are Us (`http://www.websrus.com`), a company that provides a wide range of Internet solutions, uses frames simply, yet very effectively, in its new home page (Figure 25-2). The frame in the upper-left corner shows the company name and logo. That frame never changes, so you always know which site you are in. The frame below that one is a Table of Contents that you can scroll through (using the little scroll bar for that frame) to choose a new destination. The Table of Contents also remains on the screen throughout your visit.

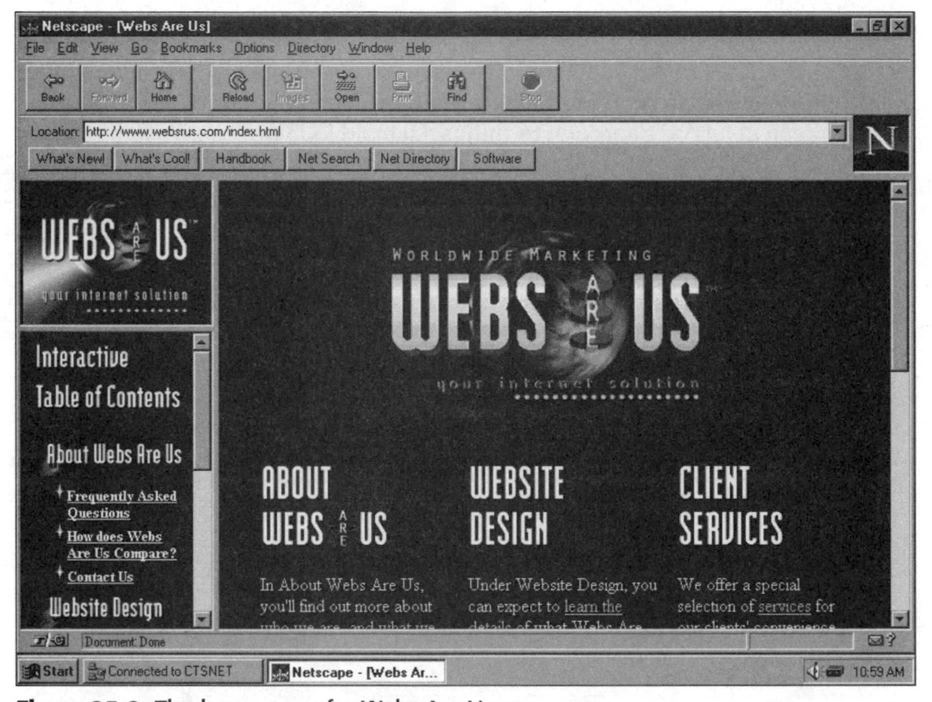

Figure 25-2: The home page for Webs Are Us.

The largest frame is the *main frame* (no pun intended) — a frame that, in traditional Web browsers, takes up the entire screen. That frame changes a great deal because it shows whatever page you happen to be viewing. For example, if I go to the Frequently Asked Questions page in Webs Are Us, the main frame shows that page. But I can still see the Webs Are Us logo and Table of Contents off to the left in their little frames (Figure 25-3). I also can still use the Table of Contents to jump to another page.

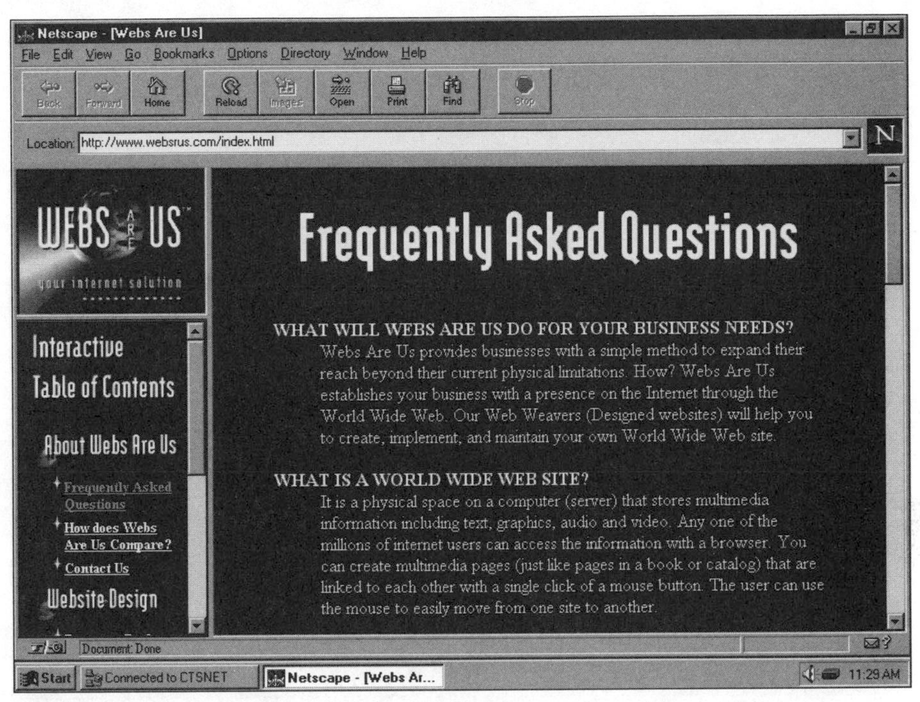

Figure 25-3: The FAQs page of Webs Are Us.

Puzzled? To scroll backward and forward through pages within a frame, right-click the frame and make a selection from the pop-up menu. Or, on a Mac, hold down the mouse button to make the pop-up menu appear. To print a page, click its frame and then choose File➪Print Frame from Netscape's menu bar.

A not-so-obvious advantage to the design used by Webs Are Us is that the reader can jump around quickly. Webs Are Us doesn't need to put its logo on every page because the logo is always displayed in the top left frame. By using this format, its pages can contain just text (or minimal graphics), which downloads more quickly to the reader.

Of course, there is no rule that says you have to use frames for navigation or logos. You may just want to have some fun with them. For example, Figure 25-4 shows a sample page designed somewhat along the vein of a newspaper's format. The top row shows the masthead, *Nerd News Gazette*. Each of the three columns beneath the masthead shows a separate Web page.

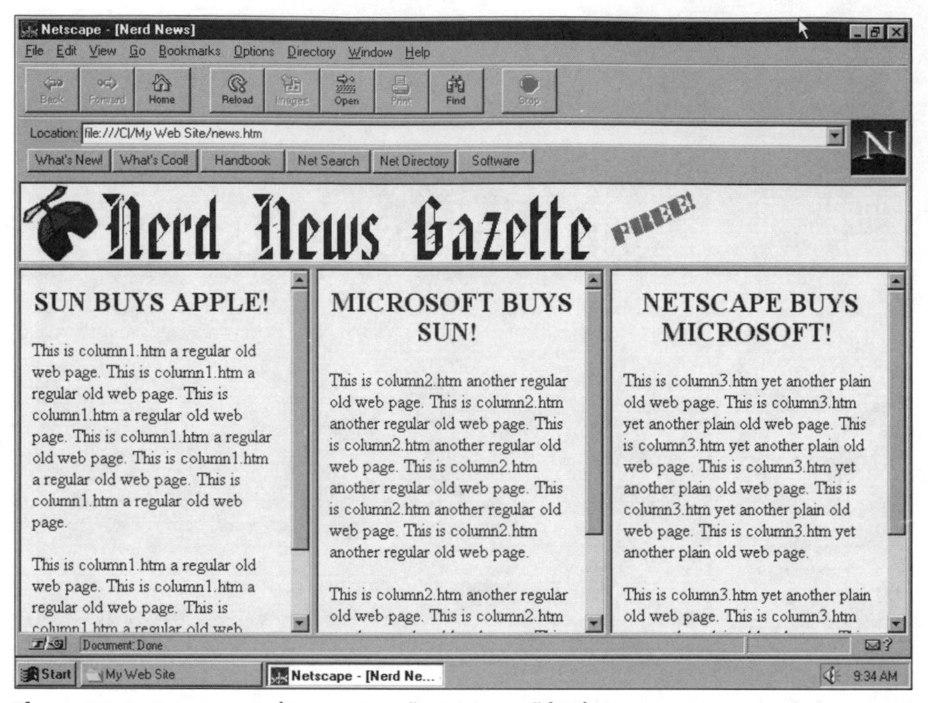

Figure 25-4: Frames used to create a "newspaper" look.

Frame Gotchas

Before I show you how to create frames, here is a couple of gotchas to keep in mind:

✦ Not all Web browsers support frames. When designing your site, make sure that frame-impaired browsers can still get around.

✦ I don't know of any nifty shareware programs that let you simply draw frames on the screen. You'll need to *hard code* the frames by manually typing the appropriate HTML tags.

I put some examples of pages containing already-defined frames on the *Web Publishing Uncut* CD-ROM, in a folder named *Frames.* If you find a page there that already has the frames laid out the way you want them, you're welcome to use it.

Tags for Frames

Because you must work directly with tags to create frames, I'll start off by describing how to define the tags. As always, I've also included these tags in the HTML Quick Reference (Appendix B), so you can look there for more information or quick reminders.

The <FRAMESET>...</FRAMESET> tags

The general layout of frames on the reader's screen is defined by one or more pairs of <FRAMESET>...</FRAMESET> tags. It's important to understand that the <FRAMESET>...</FRAMESET> tags replace the <BODY>...</BODY> tags that normally appear in a Web page. This means that a framed page has no body, per se. It has frames instead.

Danger Zone

All tags that normally appear between the <BODY> and </BODY> tags in a page must be placed between the <FRAMESET>...</FRAMESET> tags. If any tags that normally appear within the <BODY>...</BODY> tags are placed *outside* the <FRAMESET>...</FRAMESET> tags, the frames will be ignored. That fact can drive you outright crazy when you're trying to figure out why your frames aren't working! The <BODY> tags themselves are optional, but you can include them if you want to define body attributes such as background color and text color. The <BODY> tags also must be placed within the <FRAMESET>...</FRAMESET> tags.

The <FRAMESET> tag has two attributes: ROWS and COLS. Each attribute is followed by a *value list* that defines the number of frames and the size of each frame within the frameset. The number for these values can be expressed in one of three ways:

- ✦ **Pixels.** If you specify a row or column size as a number (such as 100), the browser interprets that as a specific size in pixels.
- ✦ **Percent.** If you specify a row or column size as a percent (such as 50%), the browser calculates the size as a percentage of however many pixels are on the reader's screen.
- ✦ If you specify a row or column size as an asterisk, the browser interprets that as "the rest of the space available on the screen." Multiple * can be used to proportion the available space. For example, "*,*" would create two equal-sized rows or columns. "2*,*" also would create two rows or columns, but the first would be twice as big as the second. Another way to say it is that "2*,*" gives the first row/column two thirds of the screen and the second row/column one third of the screen.

Note that the first measurement, pixels, is absolute (fixed). The other two are relative measurements. The reason for this type of setup is that you cannot determine how many pixels will be on your reader's screen. Some people may be browsing at 640 × 480, whereas others are browsing at 800 × 600, and still others are browsing at 1024 × 768 or higher. As a result, at least one measurement in your value list needs to be relative. The following are some examples.

The tags in this example tell the browser to divide the screen (or current frame) into two columns: The first column is 100 pixels wide, and the second column equals "the rest of the pixels on the reader's screen."

```
<FRAMESET COLS = "100,*">
...
</FRAMESET>
```

The next set of tags tells the browser to divide the screen (or current frame) into three rows. The first two rows are set to 25 percent of the available space; the last row consists of the remaining 50 percent:

```
<FRAMESET ROWS = "25%,25%,50%">
...
</FRAMESET>
```

In order to subdivide a column into rows, or a row into columns, you must *nest* the <FRAMESET> tags. But before I show you how to do that, I need to show you the next tag used in creating frames.

The <FRAME> tag

The frame tag defines a single frame — or *cell,* if you prefer to think of it that way — within a frameset. The <FRAME> tag has size optional attributes: NAME, SRC, MARGINWIDTH, MARGINHEIGHT, SCROLLING, and NORESIZE. There is no closing </FRAME> tag.

The NAME attribute

The NAME attribute lets you give each frame a unique name to make it easier to refer to a specific frame later. The name must begin with an alphanumeric character. For example, you can name your frames LOGO (for the frame that contains a logo), TOC (for a frame that contains a Table of Contents), and MAIN (for the main frame that displays an entire Web page).

The SRC attribute

The SRC (source) attribute defines what initially appears within the frame. The source can be the name of a page (.htm or .html file) within your own Web site, a URL, or the name of the GIF or JPEG image. A frame with no SRC specified is displayed as blank space.

The MARGINWIDTH attribute

The MARGINWIDTH attribute defines the width of the left and right margins within the frame in pixels. If omitted, the reader's Web browser assigns margins automatically.

The MARGINHEIGHT attribute

The MARGINHEIGHT attribute defines the height of the top and bottom margins within the frame in pixels. If omitted, the reader's Web browser assigns margins automatically.

The SCROLLING attribute

The SCROLLING attribute determines whether or not the frame has its own scroll bar. The options are YES — scroll bars are always visible, NO — scroll bars are never visible, and AUTO — scroll bars are visible only when needed. If you omit this attribute, the AUTO option is assumed.

The NORESIZE attribute

Typically, a reader can resize the frames on his or her screen simply by dragging the frame's border. If you do not want the reader to be able to resize a frame, add the NORESIZE attribute to the <FRAME> tag. Be aware that *any* frame adjacent to a non-resizable edge will also be non-resizable after you define the NORESIZE attribute. Thus, specifying a single frame as NORESIZE may actually prevent the reader from resizing several frames. If the NORESIZE attribute is omitted, the frame is resizable.

The <NOFRAMES>...</NOFRAMES> tags

The <NOFRAMES>...</NOFRAMES> tags identify a section of the page that will be displayed to the people viewing your page with a "frame-challenged" browser. Frame-capable browsers ignore everything inside the <NOFRAMES>...</NOFRAMES> tags.

Targeting Frames

Defining a set of frames adds a whole new dimension to how you display pages in your presentation. Simply telling the browser to "display this page" or "display that graphic" with tags is no longer sufficient. You now need to specify the item that you want to display *and* the frame in which it should be displayed. To accomplish this, you need to include a frame name in any tag that displays information, including <A> (anchor) tags, <AREA> tags, <FORM> tags, and <BASE> tags. Let's take a look at each in more detail.

Targeting from <A> tags

The anchor tag normally defines the filename or URL of the content to be displayed on the screen. For example,

```
<A HREF="news.htm">News </A>
```

typically shows the reader the page stored as news.htm within the current Web site, and that page fills the entire screen. In a framed site, you can display news.htm in a specific frame on the screen. To do so, add a TARGET="frame name"> attribute to the <A> tag.

For example, suppose that one of your frames is named *main,* and you want the news.htm page to appear in that frame. You need to change the preceding anchor tag to

```
<A HREF="news.htm" TARGET="main">News </A>
```

You can even display another site within a single frame. For example, the following <A> tag takes the reader to the home page of the site named http://www.coolnerds.com and displays the home page of that site in the frame named main:

```
<A HREF="http://www.coolnerds.com" TARGET="main">Visit Coolnerds
  </A>
```

Targeting from <AREA> tags

As discussed in the preceding chapter, client-side image mapping enables you to define hot spots using <AREA> tags. As part of that tag, you define what appears when the reader clicks the hot spot. For example, when someone clicks the hot spot that follows, it displays a page named faqs.htm to the reader.

```
<AREA SHAPE=RECT COORDS="81,5,154,26" HREF=faqs.htm>
```

In a frame-aware site, you need to add a TARGET= attribute to the <AREA> tag to define the frame in which the content will appear. For example, if you want to display faqs.htm in the frame named MAIN, you need to alter that <AREA...> tag as follows:

```
<AREA SHAPE=RECT COORDS="81,5,154,26" HREF=faqs.htm
      TARGET="main">
```

Targeting from a <FORM> tag

When a reader submits a form, typically the results of that submission take up a full screen as a page. The reader needs to click the Back button to get out of the page. In a framed site, you can tell the browser to display the results of the form submission in a specific frame, again by using the TARGET= attribute. For example, in this tag

```
<FORM METHOD=POST ACTION="/cgi-bin/
      mailto?alan@coolnerds.com:Ask_Alan" TARGET="main">
```

the results of a form submission are displayed in a frame named main.

Targeting from a <BASE> tag

You can use the <BASE> tag to define a default window for the preceding tags. Once you define a BASE target, any <A>, <AREA>, or <FORM> tag that doesn't include a TARGET= attribute will display its results in the frame you specify in the <BASE> tag. For example, you use the following tag to make the MAIN frame the default window for displaying new content:

```
<BASE TARGET="main">
```

Magic target names

There are four special target names that you can use in lieu of a specific target name. Note that each of these names begins with an underscore.

Danger Zone

The magic target names are the *only* ones that begin with an underscore character. When naming your own frames, you must start with normal alphanumeric characters.

TARGET = "_blank"

The _blank target name causes the new content to be displayed in a new, empty window. The window has no name and replaces the framed windows. When the reader clicks the Back button to back out of that page, the framed window is redisplayed.

TARGET = "_self"

The _self target name displays new content in the same window in which the link is located. This setup usually is the default if you don't specify a target name or a base target. If you do specify a base target, the _self magic word overrides it.

TARGET = "_parent"

In nested frames (which I'll discuss in a moment), the _parent target causes the new content to appear in the immediate `FRAMESET` parent of the document. This is the same as _self if the current frame has no parent.

TARGET = "_top"

This target causes the new content to be displayed on a full screen and can be used to break out of deeply nested frames.

That should clear everything right up, no? (Yeah, right.) Don't worry if this seems a little overwhelming. I didn't get it at first either. Let's take a step-by-step approach to the frame-making process and look at some examples.

Step 1: Rename Your Existing Home Page

Chances are, your Internet Service Provider requires you to name your home page index.htm, index.html, or something like that. If you plan to use frames in your site, you'll want the first file downloaded to the reader to be the one that defines the frames. So, if you already have a home page named index.htm or index.html, you should probably rename your home page (locally and on the server) to something else. In my example, I named the home page home.htm.

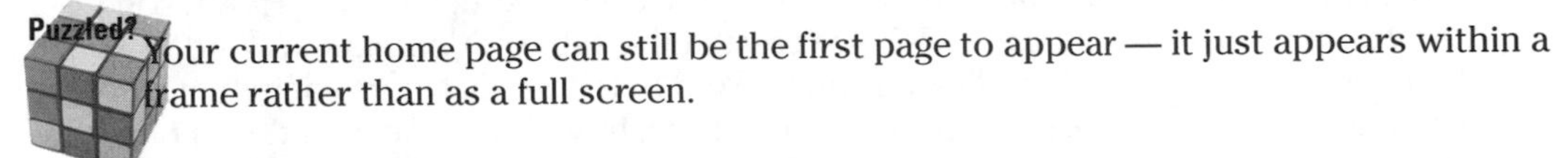

Your current home page can still be the first page to appear — it just appears within a frame rather than as a full screen.

Step 2: Create Some Frame Content

A frame can display any page or graphic image on the Web. It's not *necessary* to create new content for your frames. It generally makes sense to do so, however, so that you can take advantage of the smaller frames. For this example, I'm setting up a hypothetical site called Good Morning that presents three frames to the reader — a fixed frame that displays a logo, a scrollable frame that displays a Table of Contents of sorts, and a large main window. Figure 25-5 shows my goal.

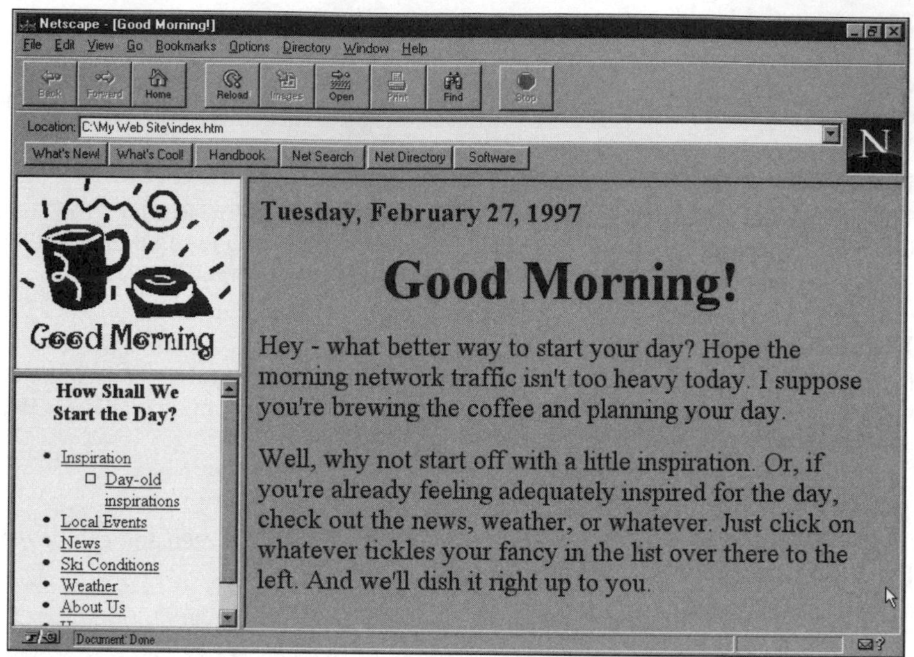

Figure 25-5: A hypothetical site that you learn how to build in this chapter.

First, I create a little logo by borrowing a piece of clip art and adding the words "Good Morning" to it. I need to be aware of the size of this image because I want it to fit perfectly within a frame on my page. I estimate that I'll need to make the first column in my site about 210 pixels wide so that the column itself is about 200 pixels wide and I still have 10 pixels left for the frame border. I want to make sure that my logo fits nicely in its frame, so I'll make it a little narrower than that 200 pixel measurement. Figure 25-6 shows the logo, which I've saved as mornlogo.gif. As you can see in Paint Shop Pro's status bar, this image is 190 pixels wide and 166 pixels tall.

Next, I need the Table of Contents. This element can consist of a regular HTML page created with Word IA. In Figure 25-7, I've created the Table of Contents in Word IA as a bulleted list. I used the Hyperlink button in Word IA to specify where each item in the list takes the reader. One small problem still exists, however — Word IA doesn't let me indicate a specific frame in which to display a page.

To get around that problem, I can insert a `<BASE TARGET>` tag into this document, using Insert⇨HTML Markup in Word IA. In Figure 25-7, I moved the cursor near the top of the document and have inserted the tag `<BASE NAME = "main">`. (Now I just need to remember to create a frame named main when I create the frames.) After typing the `<BASE NAME="main">` tag and clicking OK, I can save and close the morntoc.htm document.

Figure 25-6: My mornlogo.gif graphic image.

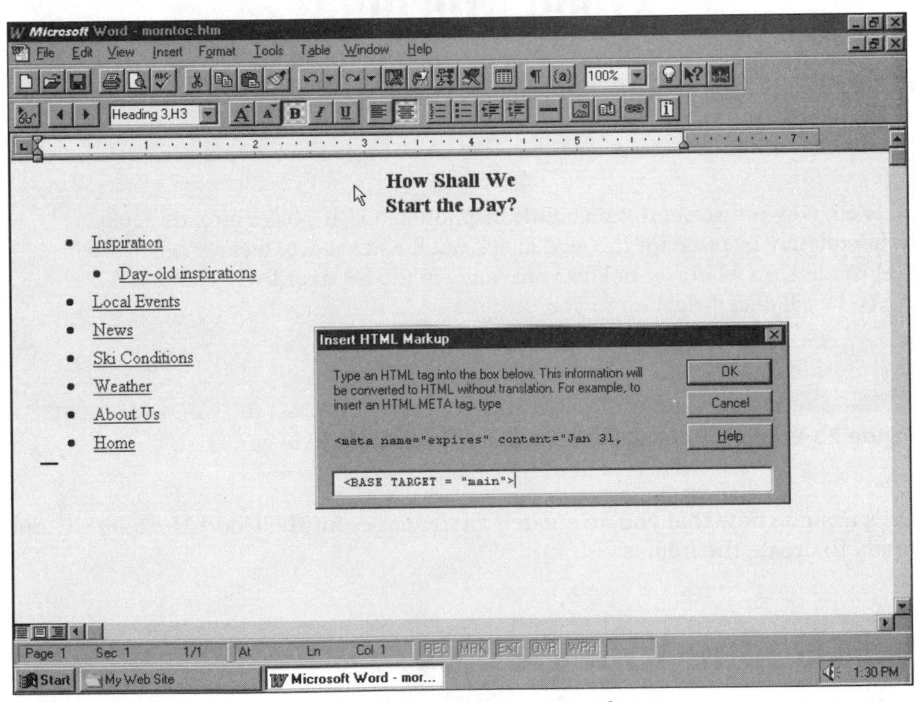

Figure 25-7: My Table of Contents, morntoc.htm, in Word IA.

Hot Stuff

You can use the HTML Source view in Word IA or open the completed document in Notepad to verify that the `<BASE TARGET="main">` tag is defined before the `<A HREF...>` tags.

The rest of the pages will appear in the larger window. Some links in the Table of Contents, such as weather and ski conditions, will take the reader to other sites on the Web. Some links, such as About Us and Home, will take the reader to local documents. I can create those documents in the usual manner with Word IA. For example, Figure 25-8 shows the home.htm page for my Good Morning site. That is the same page shown in Figure 25-5 and also is the first page that visitors will see.

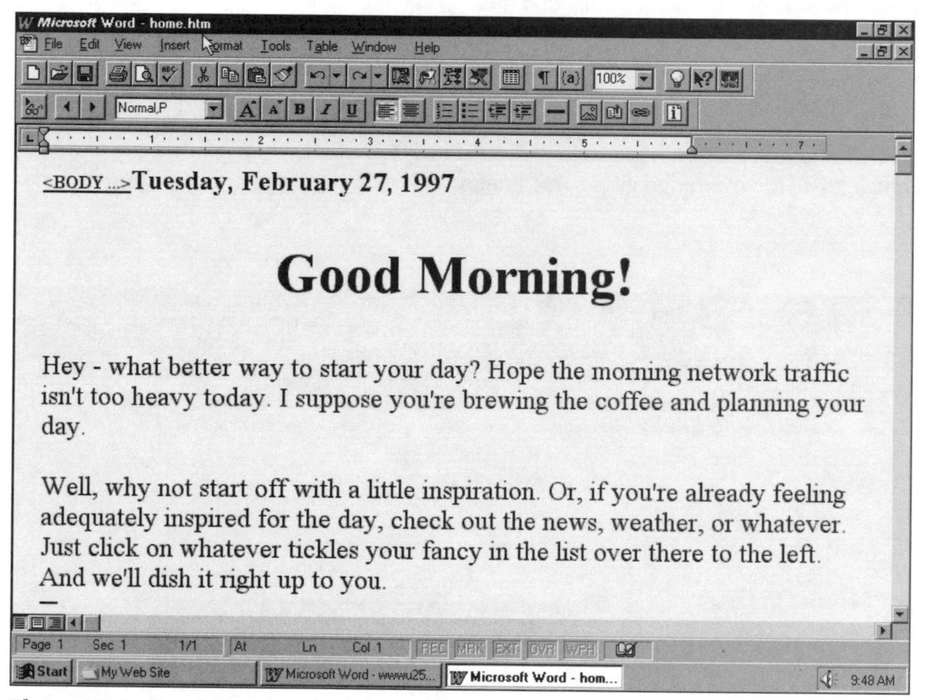

Figure 25-8: Good Morning site's home.htm page in Word IA.

Let's assume now that you've created all the pages for the Good Morning site and are ready to create the frames.

Step 3: Define Your Frames

As I mentioned earlier, if you want your frames to appear automatically when the reader first gets to your site, you need to define the frames in whatever page automatically opens first. For this example, assume that my ISP requires me to name that page *index.htm*. Using Notepad, I create a new document and manually type in the "usual" codes for a Web page, including <HEAD>...</HEAD> and the title. As mentioned earlier, the <FRAMESET>...</FRAMESET> tags replace the <BODY>...</BODY> tags in a page that defines frames, so I could type in those tags next.

For this example, I first want to divide the page into two columns. The left column will be 210 pixels wide. The second column will be however many pixels are left over. As a result, my index.htm page looks like Figure 25-9 for starters. (The <!...> tags are comments to explain, in English, the purpose of the tags that follow them. The Web browser ignores those comments.)

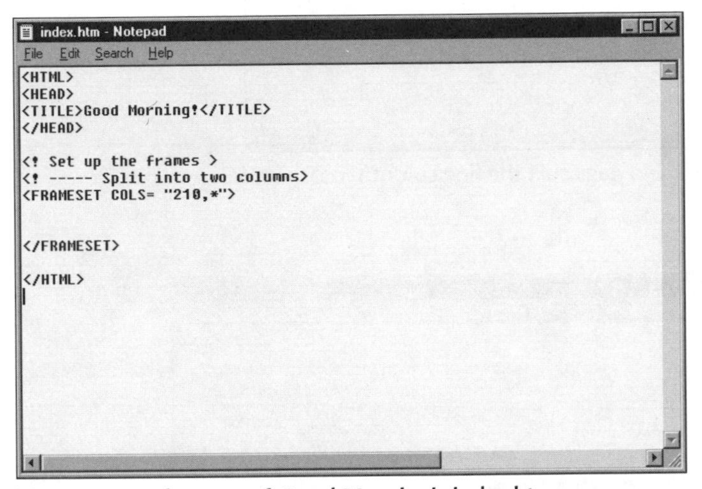

Figure 25-9: The start of Good Morning's index.htm page.

Now here's where it gets a little tricky. I want to divide the first column into two rows. To do that, I have to put in another <FRAMESET>...</FRAMESET> pair of codes to define two rows. I want those two rows to appear in the first column, so it's essential that this next <FRAMESET> tag appear immediately after the <FRAMESET> tag that defined the columns. I'll make the first row 180 pixels tall so that it can comfortably contain the mainlogo.gif image I created earlier. As always, I can add comments <!...> as notes to myself, as in Figure 25-10.

You may have noticed that I indented the nested pair of <FRAMESET>...</FRAMESET> tags. Technically, it's not necessary to do so, but it helps me see which </FRAMESET> tag goes with which <FRAMESET> tag.

The next step is to insert <FRAME> tags to name each frame, define what's to appear in each frame, and so on. I'll name the first (top) cell in the two new rows *logo,* and I'll name the second row *toc.* I'll set up the frames to display mornlogo.gif in the top cell and morntoc.htm in the bottom cell. I don't want any margins in either frame — I prefer a tight fit in this example. There is no need for the reader to scroll around in the cell that contains the logo, either. Instead, I'll define those two cells as shown in Figure 25-11.

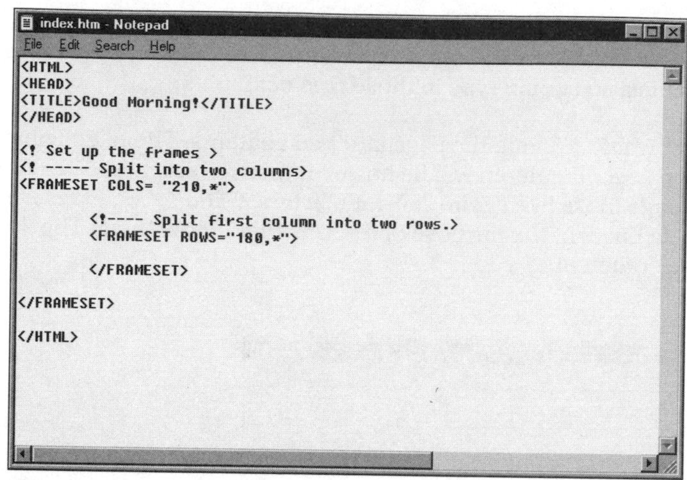

```
<HTML>
<HEAD>
<TITLE>Good Morning!</TITLE>
</HEAD>

<! Set up the frames >
<! ----- Split into two columns>
<FRAMESET COLS= "210,*">

        <!---- Split first column into two rows.>
        <FRAMESET ROWS="180,*">

        </FRAMESET>

</FRAMESET>

</HTML>
```

Figure 25-10: <FRAMESET> tags split the first column into two rows.

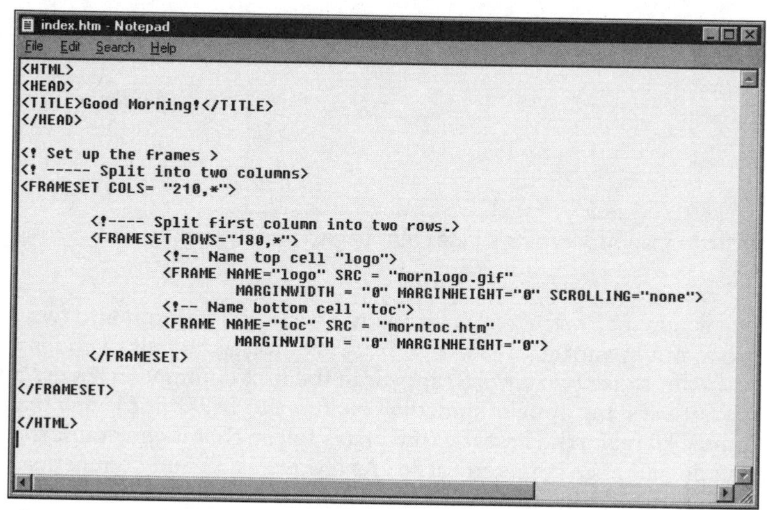

```
<HTML>
<HEAD>
<TITLE>Good Morning!</TITLE>
</HEAD>

<! Set up the frames >
<! ----- Split into two columns>
<FRAMESET COLS= "210,*">

        <!---- Split first column into two rows.>
        <FRAMESET ROWS="180,*">
                <!-- Name top cell "logo">
                <FRAME NAME="logo" SRC = "mornlogo.gif"
                        MARGINWIDTH = "0" MARGINHEIGHT="0" SCROLLING="none">
                <!-- Name bottom cell "toc">
                <FRAME NAME="toc" SRC = "morntoc.htm"
                        MARGINWIDTH = "0" MARGINHEIGHT="0">
        </FRAMESET>

</FRAMESET>

</HTML>
```

Figure 25-11: Top and bottom frames in the first column defined by <FRAME> tags.

I still haven't done anything with the second column. I'll name that frame main and display the home.htm page in it. This second column isn't divided into rows, so I need to get past the <FRAMESET>...</FRAMESET> tags for the rows but still stay within the <FRAMESET>...</FRAMESET> tags for the columns, in order to name that frame. Therefore, I put the <FRAME> tag between the two existing </FRAMESET> tags, as shown in Figure 25-12.

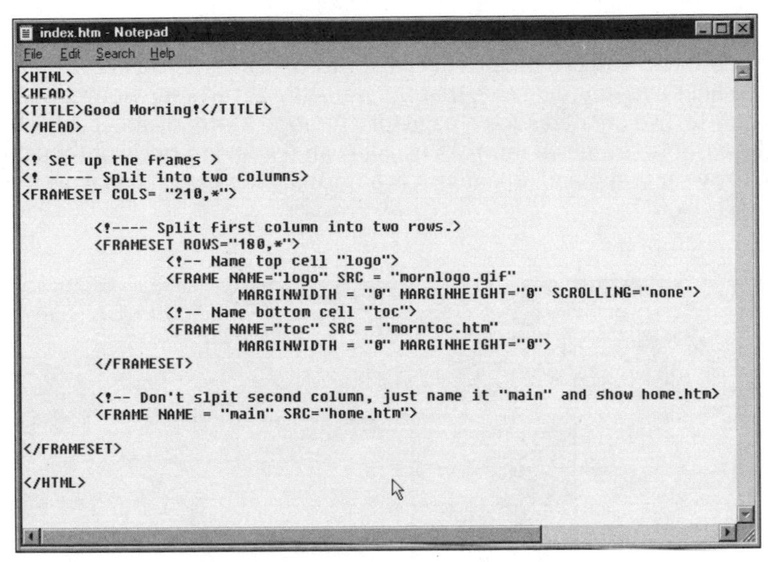

```
<HTML>
<HEAD>
<TITLE>Good Morning!</TITLE>
</HEAD>

<! Set up the frames >
<! ----- Split into two columns>
<FRAMESET COLS= "210,*">

        <!---- Split first column into two rows.>
        <FRAMESET ROWS="180,*">
                <!-- Name top cell "logo">
                <FRAME NAME="logo" SRC = "mornlogo.gif"
                        MARGINWIDTH = "0" MARGINHEIGHT="0" SCROLLING="none">
                <!-- Name bottom cell "toc">
                <FRAME NAME="toc" SRC = "morntoc.htm"
                        MARGINWIDTH = "0" MARGINHEIGHT="0">
        </FRAMESET>

        <!-- Don't slpit second column, just name it "main" and show home.htm>
        <FRAME NAME = "main" SRC="home.htm">

</FRAMESET>

</HTML>
```

Figure 25-12: Second column defined by a <FRAME> tag.

At this point, I'm basically done. I can save and close index.htm and then open it with Netscape Navigator 2.0 or any other frame-capable browser. If I do this, I will see exactly what I showed you in Figure 25-5.

Step 4: Consider Frame-Incapable Browsers

I do have one small problem remaining: Anybody who views this page with a frame-incapable browser is going to see nothing. Why? Because a regular browser will be expecting <BODY>...</BODY> tags. Those tags are not allowed in pages that have <FRAMESET>...</FRAMESET> tags, however. This problem alone deserves a pretty good-sized "Hmmmmm." But there's more.

Even if a reader *could* see the home page (home.htm) in Full-Screen view, he or she still wouldn't have any means of navigating around the site. The reason is that the hyperlinks for getting around in Good Morning are contained in a separate frame. Now I have a major "Hmmmmm" on my hands.

The solution lies in using the <NOFRAMES>...</NOFRAMES> tags, which mean something like this:

"If the reader is not using a frame-capable browser, show all the stuff between <NOFRAMES> and </NOFRAMES>. If the reader is using a frame-capable browser, *ignore* all the stuff between <NOFRAMES> and </NOFRAMES>."

What I need to do first is come up with a home page for people who do not have frame-capable browsers. You can create this page with Word IA, if you like. Don't forget to include links and anything else that the frame-lame browser won't be able to show. In Figure 25-13, I've created such a page for my Good Morning site. I named this page nfhome.htm (for no-frames-home). As usual, I can test it and tweak it by using the Preview in Browser command. Because it is a normal Web page, I can save it as such and then exit Word IA.

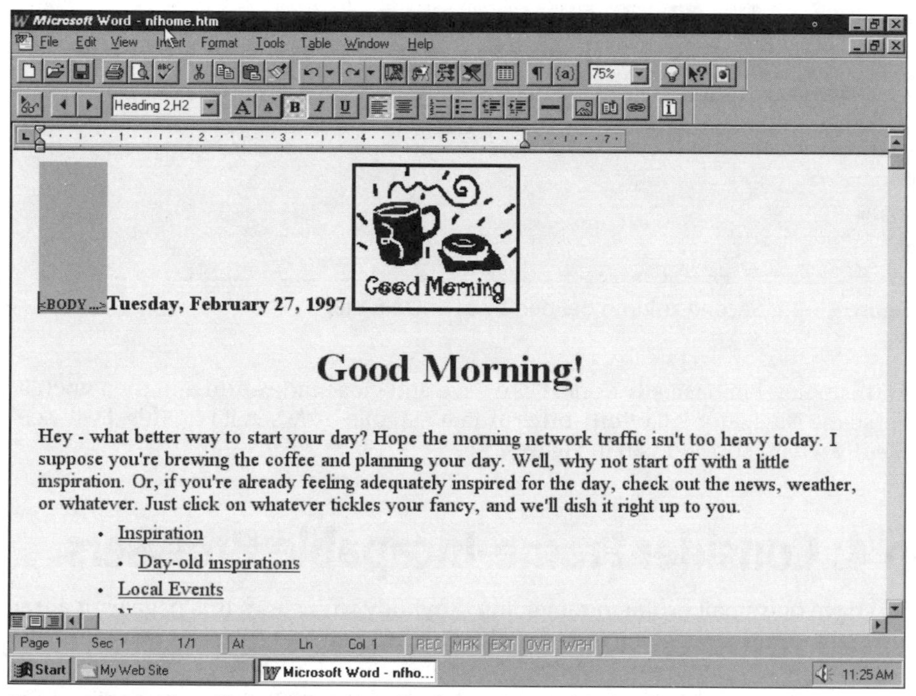

Figure 25-13: The nfhome.htm page for frame-incapable browsers.

Next, I need to open Good Morning's index.htm page and insert a pair of `<NOFRAMES>...</NOFRAMES>` tags somewhere under the first `<FRAMESET>` tag, as in Figure 25-14.

Now I need to open nfhome.htm in Notepad (not Word IA) because I really need to get to the nitty-gritty tag level. To do this, I can right-click nfhome.htm and Send To➪Notepad. Alternatively, I can start Notepad and use its File➪Open commands to open nfhome.htm. Once I've opened nfhome.htm, I need to select everything between, but excluding, the `<BODY>` and `</BODY>` tags, as shown in Figure 25-15.

```
index.htm - Notepad
File  Edit  Search  Help
<HTML>
<HEAD>
<TITLE>Good Morning!</TITLE>
</HEAD>

<! Set up the frames >
<! ----- Split into two columns>
<FRAMESET COLS= "210,*">

        <!---- Split first column into two rows.>
        <FRAMESET ROWS="180,*">

                <!-- Before we go any further, decide what to show frame-incapable browsers>
                <NOFRAMES>

                </NOFRAMES>

                <!-- Name top cell "logo">
                <FRAME NAME="logo" SRC = "mornlogo.gif"
                        MARGINWIDTH = "0" MARGINHEIGHT="0" SCROLLING="none">
                <!-- Name bottom cell "toc">
                <FRAME NAME="toc" SRC = "morntoc.htm"
                        MARGINWIDTH = "0" MARGINHEIGHT="0">
        </FRAMESET>

        <!-- Don't slpit second column, just name it "main" and show home.htm>
        <FRAME NAME = "main" SRC="home.htm">

</FRAMESET>
```

Figure 25-14: `<NOFRAMES>...</NOFRAMES>` tags in Good Morning's index.htm.

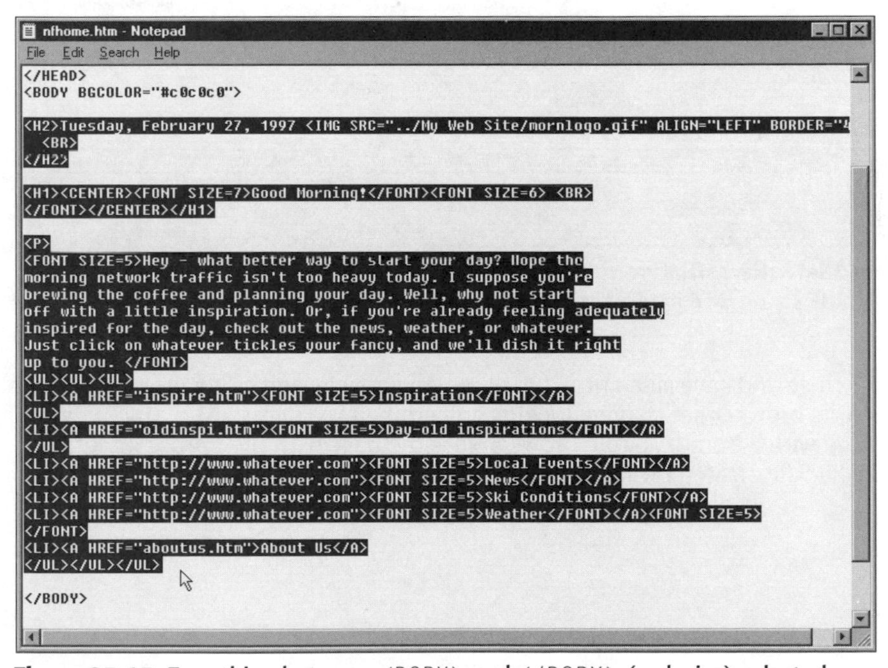

```
nfhome.htm - Notepad
File  Edit  Search  Help
</HEAD>
<BODY BGCOLOR="#c0c0c0">

<H2>Tuesday, February 27, 1997 <IMG SRC="../My Web Site/mornlogo.gif" ALIGN="LEFT" BORDER="
  <BR>
</H2>

<H1><CENTER><FONT SIZE=7>Good Morning!</FONT><FONT SIZE=6> <BR>
</FONT></CENTER></H1>

<P>
<FONT SIZE=5>Hey - what better way to start your day? Hope the
morning network traffic isn't too heavy today. I suppose you're
brewing the coffee and planning your day. Well, why not start
off with a little inspiration. Or, if you're already feeling adequately
inspired for the day, check out the news, weather, or whatever.
Just click on whatever tickles your fancy, and we'll dish it right
up to you. </FONT>
<UL><UL><UL>
<LI><A HREF="inspire.htm"><FONT SIZE=5>Inspiration</FONT></A>
<UL>
<LI><A HREF="oldinspi.htm"><FONT SIZE=5>Day-old inspirations</FONT></A>
</UL>
<LI><A HREF="http://www.whatever.com"><FONT SIZE=5>Local Events</FONT></A>
<LI><A HREF="http://www.whatever.com"><FONT SIZE=5>News</FONT></A>
<LI><A HREF="http://www.whatever.com"><FONT SIZE=5>Ski Conditions</FONT></A>
<LI><A HREF="http://www.whatever.com"><FONT SIZE=5>Weather</FONT></A><FONT SIZE=5>
</FONT>
<LI><A HREF="aboutus.htm">About Us</A>
</UL></UL></UL>

</BODY>
```

Figure 25-15: Everything between `<BODY>` and `</BODY>` (exclusive) selected.

Once selected, I choose Edit➪Copy to copy the selected text to the Windows Clipboard. Next, I need to re-open index.htm in Notepad, put the insertion point right between the <NOFRAMES> and </NOFRAMES> tags, and Edit➪Paste the text in between those tags. In Figure 25-16, I did just that. I then indented those pasted-in lines so that you can better see how the new lines fall between the <NOFRAMES> and </NOFRAMES> tags.

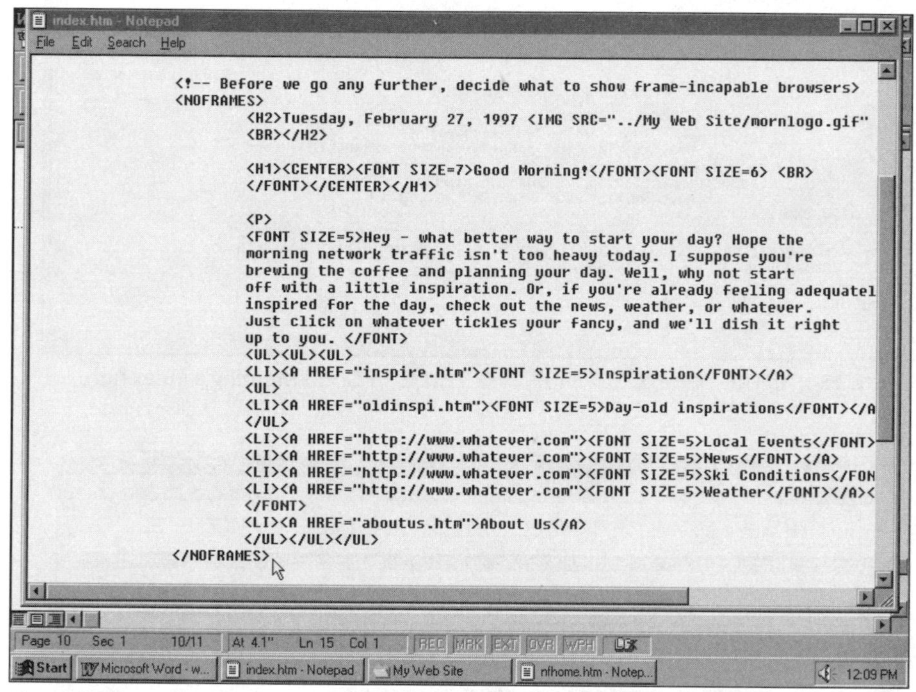

Figure 25-16: Raw HTML from nfhome.htm pasted between index.htm's <NOFRAMES>...</NOFRAMES> tags.

After I close and save index.htm, I'm done. Anyone viewing index.htm with a frame-incapable browser sees a page looking something like Figure 25-17. Anyone viewing the page with a frame-capable browser sees the page with the frames intact, as Figure 25-5 illustrated earlier in this chapter.

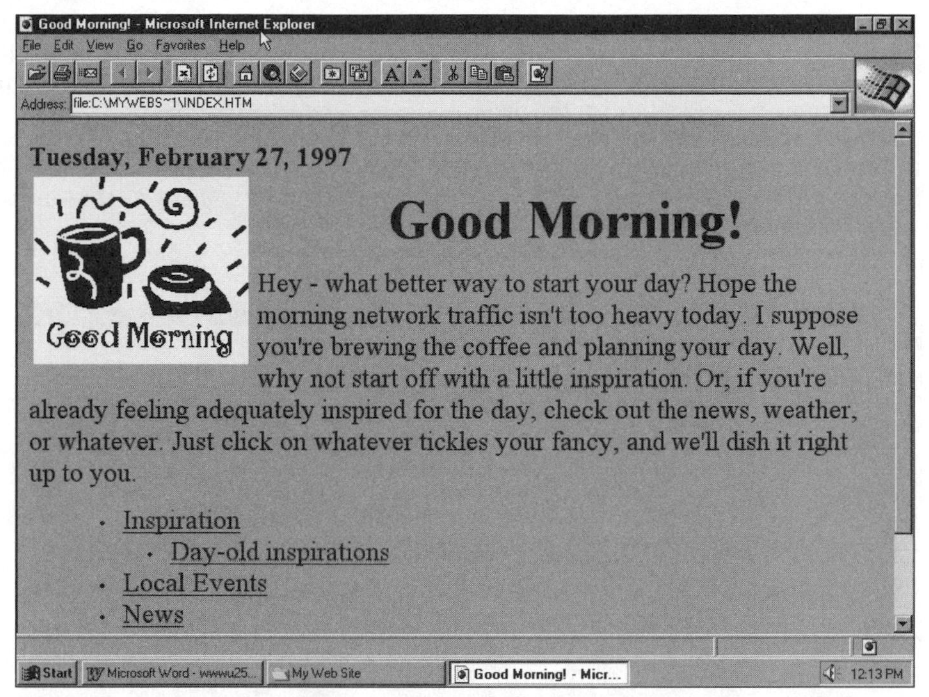

Figure 25-17. A frame-incapable browser's view of the new index.htm for Good Morning! page.

More on Nesting Frames

The way in which you organize your <FRAMESET> and <FRAME> tags defines how the frames will look. This process takes a little getting used to because the procedure is about as non-WYSIWYG as it can be. For example, take a look at this slightly modified version of the tags for my Good Morning site:

```
<! Set up the frames >
<! ----- Split into two columns>
<FRAMESET COLS= "*,210">
     <FRAME NAME = "main" SRC="home.htm">
     <FRAMESET ROWS="180,*">
          <!-- Name top cell "logo">
        <FRAME NAME="logo" SRC = "mornlogo.gif" MARGINWIDTH = "0"
              MARGINHEIGHT="0" SCROLLING="none">
          <!-- Name bottom cell "toc">
          <FRAME NAME="toc" SRC = "morntoc.htm" MARGINWIDTH = "0"
              MARGINHEIGHT="0">
     </FRAMESET>
</FRAMESET>
```

Your first reaction may be "Yeah, so it looks pretty much the same as the tags back in Figure 25-12. It's equally unintelligible." But because the tags are rearranged slightly here, I end up with a much different result, as Figure 25-18 illustrates. By defining the "main" frame before setting up the two rows, I've essentially told the browser to display the main frame and then split the second column into two rows. The moral of the story is that you must pay close attention to how you arrange your FRAME tags. Not that Figure 25-18 is "bad," per se — it just doesn't match what I was thinking of when I originally envisioned the page.

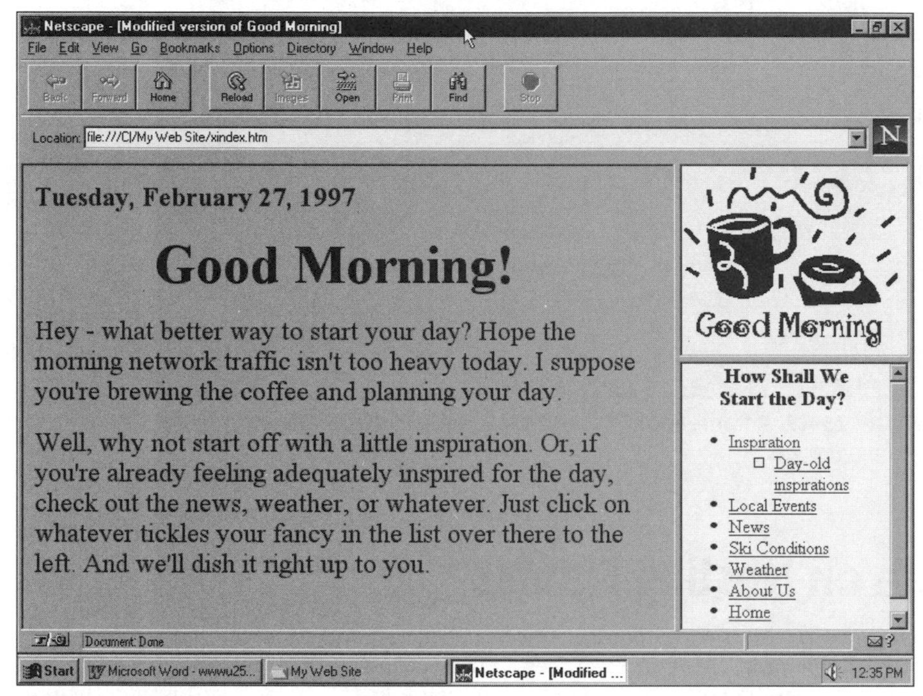

Figure 25-18: Results of rearranging <FRAMESET> and <FRAME> tags a little.

Here's a brain teaser for you: What happens if I put a link to some other framed site, such as Webs Are Us, in my Good Morning site, and then I specify my main window as the target, like this:

```
<A HREF="http://www.websrus.com" TARGET="main">Webs R Us</A>
```

Actually, when Good Morning shows the Webs Are Us page, it still displays in its framed format within my main frame, as shown in Figure 25-19.

In and of itself, this setup isn't so bad. But suppose that the Webs Are Us site contains a link to yet another framed site, such as Netscape's. You'll need to squeeeze Netscape's site into the main frame within the Webs Are Us display, and so on, until you are dealing with microscopically small frames!

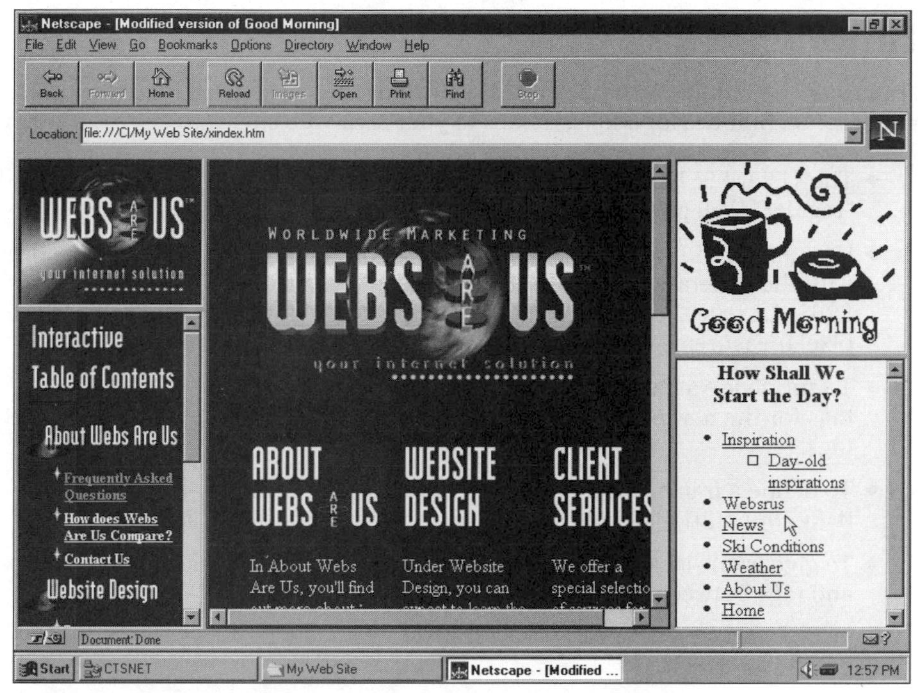

Figure 25-19: Displaying a framed site from within my framed site.

To prevent this kind of infinite nesting, you can use the _blank magic word, rather than a specific frame name, in your hyperlink. For example, the following tag displays the Webs Are Us page in a new window without showing Good Morning's frames at all. When the reader closes the Webs Are Us site, he or she returns to my Good Morning site with all its frames intact.

```
<A HREF="http://www.websrus.com" TARGET="_blank">Webs R Us</A>
```

Examples to Explore on Your Own

As I was writing this chapter, frames were a brand new feature of the Web and only a handful of sites had implemented them. By the time you read this chapter, however, I suspect you'll see many examples of framed sites. Remember, there are no secrets on the Web. If you come to a nicely framed page and are curious as to how the author set up the frames, choose View⇨Document Source from Netscape's menu bar to view the underlying tags.

For a quick tour of sites that use frames in their presentations, check out Netscape's list of sites. Point your browser to `http://home.netscape.com/comprod/products/navigator/version_2.0/frames/frame_users.html`.

Summary

Frames are definitely one of the hottest new things to hit the Web. Here's a quick review of techniques for adding frames to your own Web site:

✦ The <FRAMESET>...</FRAMESET> *replace* the <BODY>...</BODY> tags used in "regular" Web pages.

✦ Use <FRAMESET> to specify how may rows or columns to display on the page, with the general syntax <FRAMESET COLS ="values"> or <FRAMESET ROWS="values">, where *values* can be percents (for example, "50%,50%") or pixel measurements with a "rest of the screen" (*) value (such as "200,*").

✦ To subdivide a frame into rows or columns, nest the <FRAMESET>...</FRAMESET> tags for the new rows/columns within the existing <FRAMESET>...</FRAMESET> tags.

✦ To define a frame, use the <FRAME> tag with the optional NAME, SRC, MARGINHEIGHT, MARGINWIDTH, SCROLLING, and NORESIZE attributes.

✦ To give frame-incapable browsers access to your site, include appropriate text and tags between <NOFRAMES> and </NOFRAMES> tags.

✦ ✦ ✦

Hyper-Interactivity with JavaScript

✦ ✦ ✦ ✦

In This Part

✦ ✦ ✦ ✦

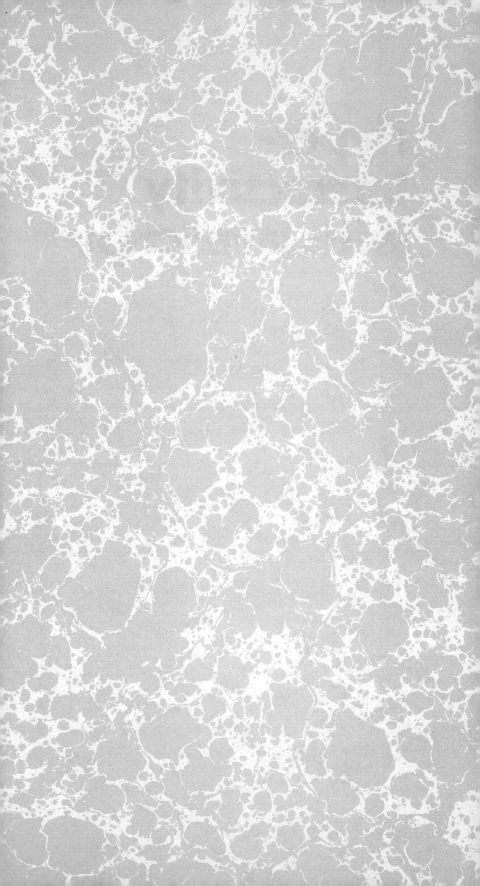

Creating JavaScript Programs

✦ ✦ ✦ ✦

In This Chapter

What is JavaScript?

Creating your first JavaScript script

Testing your script

Debugging your script

Making fancier scripts

✦ ✦ ✦ ✦

Programming is a technique of writing instructions that a machine (a computer) can carry out to perform some task. The reason you write programs on the Web is to make your Web pages "do something" on the reader's PC while the reader is viewing the page. The goal, in most cases, is to make your page interactive — and hence more dynamic — by presenting the reader with some options and then having the page "do something" in response to the choices they make.

The big catch to writing instructions for a computer to carry out is that you cannot write those instructions in plain English. Computers are much, much, much too stupid to understand a spoken language. Instead, you have to write your instructions in a *programming language* that the computer can interpret. In this book, the programming language you learn to use is called *JavaScript*.

More Info You'll often hear the term *code* used to refer to instructions written in a programming language. The reason for this, as you'll see, is that the language is like a "secret code" that only computers and programmers can understand.

As I was writing this chapter, JavaScript was very new. In fact, the only Web browser that even supports it is Netscape Navigator 2.0. I suspect that by the time you read this, many other Web browsers will support JavaScript. But before you drive yourself crazy trying to figure out why none of your JavaScript programs work, let me say this: *First and foremost, you need a Web browser that supports JavaScript.* If you don't already have one, you can download a copy of Netscape Navigator 2.0 from Netscape's site at `http://home.netscape.com`.

Creating Your First JavaScript Script

Before I start explaining what JavaScript is all about, I want to give you a feel for creating, "playing" (a.k.a. running, executing), and debugging JavaScript scripts. As a programmer, these tasks are what you'll do all of the time: Write some *code* (JavaScript instructions), try it out, and if you discover any mistakes, fix them (*debug* the code).

Be forewarned that if this is your first foray into computer programming, the code you're writing isn't going to be very meaningful to you. In fact, it will make about as much sense as this:

```
rt&* /{ Ew&%9 kluless@^% == && || bormetodeth %%<!ugh
```

Don't worry about that. First, you need to get a feel for the mechanics of typing, playing, and running JavaScript scripts, so that you *can* learn more about the language in a hands-on manner. Keep in mind that the basic mechanics of creating, playing, and debugging scripts here applies to all the JavaScript programs you'll ever write. So, even though the code you write may not mean anything to you, you're still giving your brain a headstart (no pun intended) on figuring out what this programming business is all about. Rest assured, you're not wasting your time.

Step 1: Open the page in Notepad

The first step to writing a JavaScript page is to open — using Notepad — the page that will contain the script. If you set up a Send To shortcut to Notepad, as suggested in Chapter 11, you just need to get to the page's icon in My Computer, Windows Explorer, or Find. Then right-click that icon and choose Send To⇨Notepad. The page that opens looks something like Figure 26-1.

As an alternative, you can start Notepad from the Windows 95 Start button (Start⇨Programs⇨Accessories⇨Notepad) to get to a blank Notepad document. Then choose File⇨Open within Notepad, choose All Files (*.*) under Files of type, and then locate and open your Web page.

Danger Zone

Do not use Word IA to write JavaScript code — it doesn't handle JavaScript well. After you become good at writing JavaScript, keep in mind that you'll want to use Word IA or some other WYSIWYG tool to create as much of the page as you can without JavaScript. Then, as a last step, you can use Notepad or some other text editor to add the JavaScript code.

You also can create a new Web page from scratch by using Notepad. Start up Notepad to get to a new, blank document. Next, type the basic "mandatory" tags, as shown in Figure 26-2. Then choose File⇨Save in Notepad and save the new document to your My Web Site folder with a .htm extension.

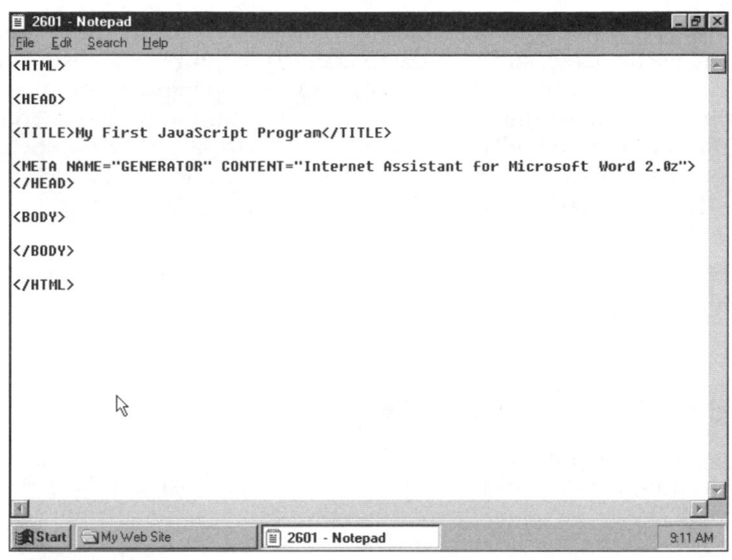

Figure 26-1: A page created in Word IA, opened in Notepad.

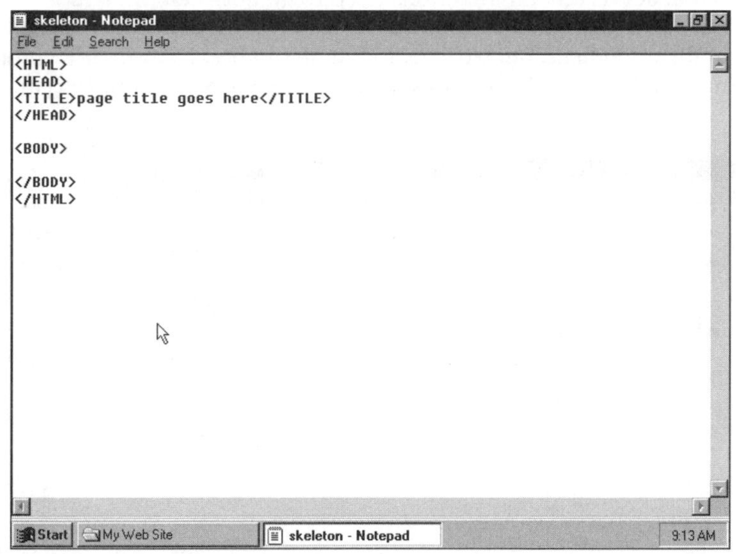

Figure 26-2: A new Web page, created from scratch, in Notepad.

Hot Stuff

If you create a skeleton HTML page like the one in Figure 26-2, you may want to save that page with a unique filename, such as skeleton.txt. In the future, whenever you want to create a new Web page in Notepad, you can start by opening skeleton.txt. To do this, change the text between the `<TITLE>...</TITLE>` tags to whatever you want the title of the new page to be. Then use File➪Save As to save the new document with whatever filename you want to give the actual Web page. For the real Web page, remember to use the .htm extension (or .html if your server requires that).

In the example I present here, I start with a "blank" HTML page like the one shown in Figure 26-2. First, I'll change the title to My First JavaScript Program and save it as JavaTest.htm.

Step 2: Type in the <SCRIPT> tags

Each JavaScript program must be enclosed within a pair of `<SCRIPT>...</SCRIPT>` tags. It's a good idea to specify JavaScript as the language being used in the script, simply by typing `LANGUAGE = "JavaScript"` into the first tag as an attribute.

In general, you want to make sure that the script is placed within the body of the document. Otherwise, it won't be executed. An exception to this rule exists — JavaScript scripts that act as custom functions need to go between the `<HEAD>...</HEAD>` tags, so that the functions are defined before they are called from scripts within the body of the document. But we'll get to that in Chapter 27. Let's not complicate things right now. In Figure 26-3, you can see where I've added the appropriate tags.

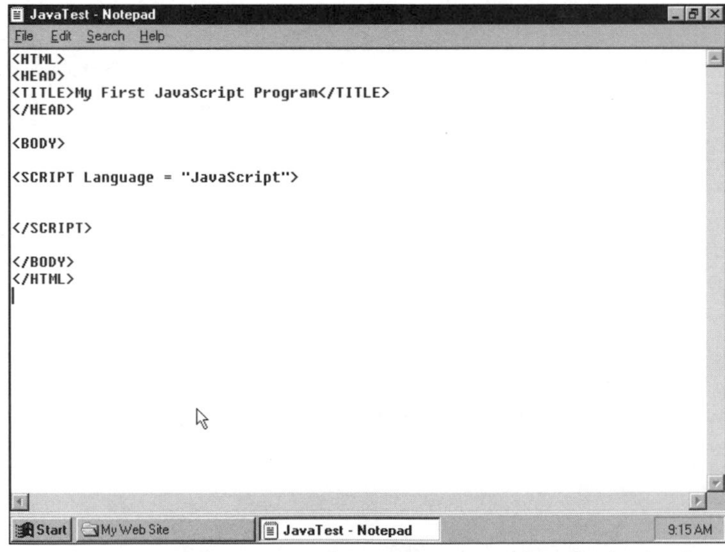

Figure 26-3: Tags for a JavaScript program typed into the body of a Web page.

Step 3: Hide code from non-JavaScript browsers

You need to be considerate of readers who are browsing the Web with non-JavaScript browsers. When those browsers encounter the <SCRIPT> tag, they ignore it — which means they treat the code within the tags as normal text. As a result, you are spilling a copy of the actual source code onto the reader's screen. This is not good. To prevent that problem, you need to put the code of the script between a pair of special comment tags that start with <!-- and end with //-->.

To do that, just type <!-- beneath the <SCRIPT> tag and //--> above the </SCRIPT> tag, leaving some room between to type in your script. You can type any text you want to the right of the <!-- tag, and to the right of the // in the last tag, as my example shows in Figure 26-4.

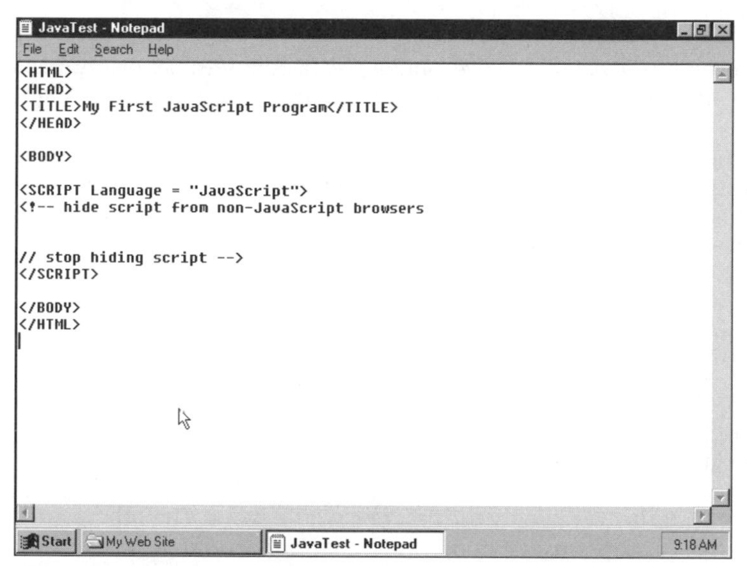

Figure 26-4: Comment tags (<!--. . . //-->) added to hide code from non-JavaScript browsers.

Puzzled? You can insert blank lines into a Notepad document just as you would a word-processing document. Move the insertion point to the start of a line and press Enter to move everything that appears below that point down. Then press the up arrow to move the insertion point back up to the blank line. Optionally, you can move the insertion point to the end of the line above the location where you want to insert a blank line and then press Enter.

Step 4: Type in the script

Once you have your <SCRIPT>...</SCRIPT> tags and comment tags in place, you are ready to type your script. Three very important points to remember are the following:

✦ Only valid JavaScript code can go between the <SCRIPT>...</SCRIPT> tags. Normal text and HTML tags won't work within the script tags.

✦ Any normal text and tags need to be typed outside of the <SCRIPT>...</SCRIPT> tags. JavaScript code should never be typed outside the <SCRIPT>...</SCRIPT> tags.

✦ JavaScript is case-sensitive. When typing JavaScript code, you must use the "official" upper- and lowercase conventions of the language. This is *very important,* and very irritating as well.

Puzzled? You'll hear the terms *script, program, code,* and *applet* used interchangeably. Basically, they all mean the same thing — "stuff written in a computer programming language."

The last requirement is typical of Unix-oriented stuff but completely foreign to Windows users. It's sure to drive you crazy until you get the hang of it. To show you how fussy JavaScript is, take a look at the sample JavaScript statements that follow. They all "say" the same thing:

```
time = today.gettime()
time=today.GetTime()
time=TODAY.GETTIME()
time=Today.getTime()
time=today.getTime
Document.Write (Time)
document.Write time
```

Of all those statements, however, only the first one would work. The others are incorrect because of improper use of upper/lowercase and would not be understood when you ran the script. So, suffice it to say that JavaScript is very, very, *very* fussy about proper use of upper/lowercase letters.

Just to put some icing on the cake, JavaScript, like all programming languages, is very, very, very fussy about *syntax*. By syntax, I mean the exact order and position of every word, curly brace ({}), dot (.), blank space, and so forth. There simply is no margin for error (or sloppiness) when it comes to syntax. And it takes quite a bit of time and experience to get accustomed to the syntax requirements of a programming language.

Life Saver Programming languages, in general, are not known for cutting people any slack. This is probably why most people hate programming. But keep in mind that no great tragedies will occur from your programming errors. All that happens is that your program doesn't run the way you wanted it to. But you can't break anything or hurt anything by writing sloppy code.

Enough yakking. Let's actually write our first JavaScript program, which will be the classic Hello World! program that just about everyone starts with. This program simply displays the message *Hello World!* on the screen. The command to print something in JavaScript is document.write(). In the jargon of object-oriented languages, however, it would be more correct for me to say "To display text on the screen, use the .write() method of the document object." Any way you say it, it means you need to type

```
document.write('Hello World!')
```

into your document. Note the upper/lowercase letters, parentheses, quotation marks ('), and the fact that the only space in the whole script line is the one between the words Hello and World. Figure 26-5 shows the line in place within the sample script. (The blank lines and indentations are entirely optional.)

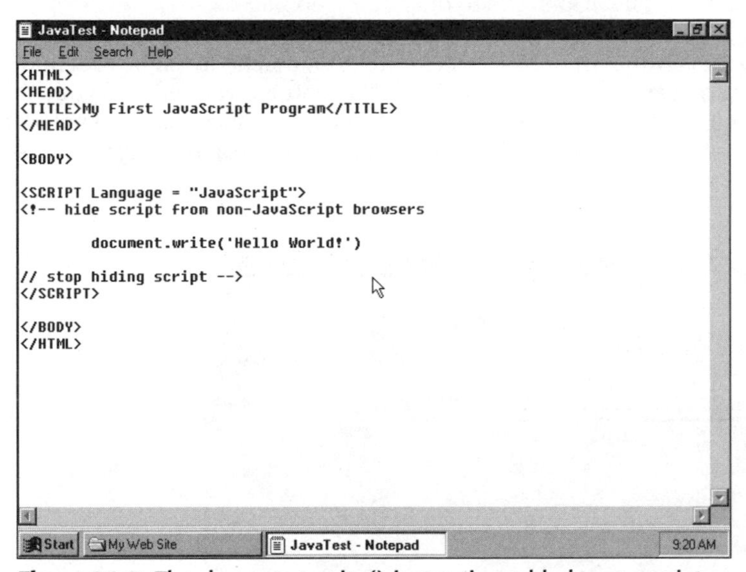

Figure 26-5: The document.write() instruction added to our script.

For our purposes, the script is now finished. You can close and save the script. To do so, click the Close button in the upper-right corner of Notepad's menu, or choose File➪Exit from Notepad's menu bar. Choose Yes when asked about saving your work. Make sure that you (1) put the file in a folder with your other Web pages and (2) give the filename the .htm extension so that your Web browser recognizes it as a Web page. For this example, say that I saved the file on my My Web Site page with the filename JavaTest.htm.

Step 5: Test and debug the script

To run your JavaScript program, you simply need to open the page that contains that script with a JavaScript-capable browser. You can use any one of the three normal techniques to do so:

✦ If Netscape Navigator 2.0 is your default browser, double-click the page's filename (JavaTest.htm in my example).

✦ Or, if you've added Navigator 2.0 to your Send To menu, right-click the page's filename (JavaTest.htm, in my example) and choose Send To➪Navigator.

More Info

If you need a reminder on how to add programs to your Send To menu, see Chapter 11.

✦ Or, start Netscape Navigator 2.0 on your system. (If it tries to log on to the Net, just cancel the logon process or click the Stop button to keep it from displaying a page.) Then use File➪Open File to open the Web page.

Because this script is within the <BODY> tags of the document, it will be executed automatically as soon as the page is loaded into Navigator. If you did everything right (and the fairy godmother of all programming languages is feeling magnanimous), the script runs without a hitch and proudly displays its message on the page, as illustrated by Figure 26-6.

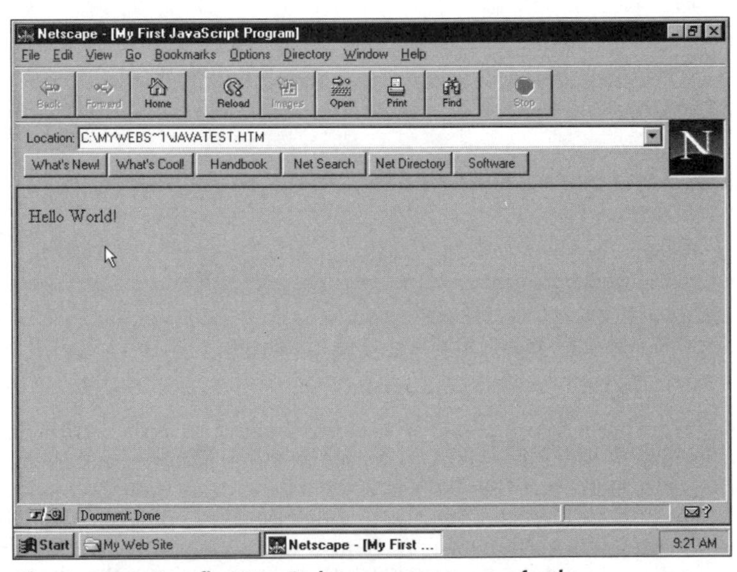

Figure 26-6: Our first JavaScript program ran perfectly.

I realize that this is a stupid script. After all, if I wanted my Web page to show Hello World! to the reader, I could have typed Hello World! between the `<BODY>...</BODY>` tags and eliminated the script altogether. But I never said that Hello World was a *useful* script — I just said it was an example script. I'll get to some useful scripts soon.

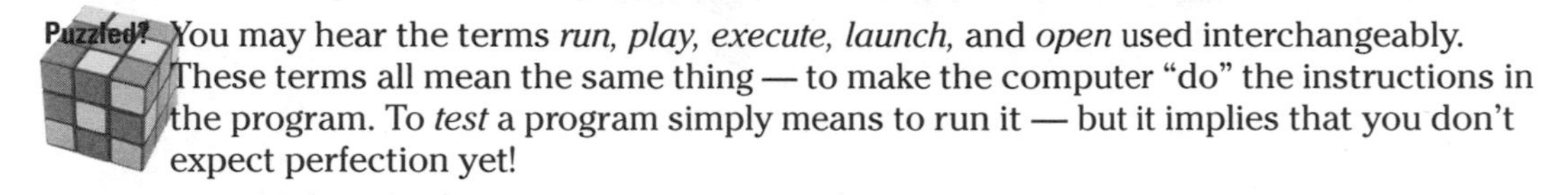

Puzzled? You may hear the terms *run, play, execute, launch,* and *open* used interchangeably. These terms all mean the same thing — to make the computer "do" the instructions in the program. To *test* a program simply means to run it — but it implies that you don't expect perfection yet!

Debugging Scripts

It's rare for a script to run perfectly on the first try. As I've mentioned, programming languages are very fussy about syntax, capitalization, and other stuff that we humans hardly even pay attention to. And it's *very* easy to make mistakes while you are typing a script.

When your Web browser comes across a mistake (an instruction it cannot understand), it displays an *error message* on the screen and stops running the script at that point. Figure 26-7 shows a sample error message. Many, many error messages exist other than the one shown. And I hate to tell you this, (but it's true), you'll probably get to experience just about all of them as you struggle your way through the low end of the JavaScript learning curve.

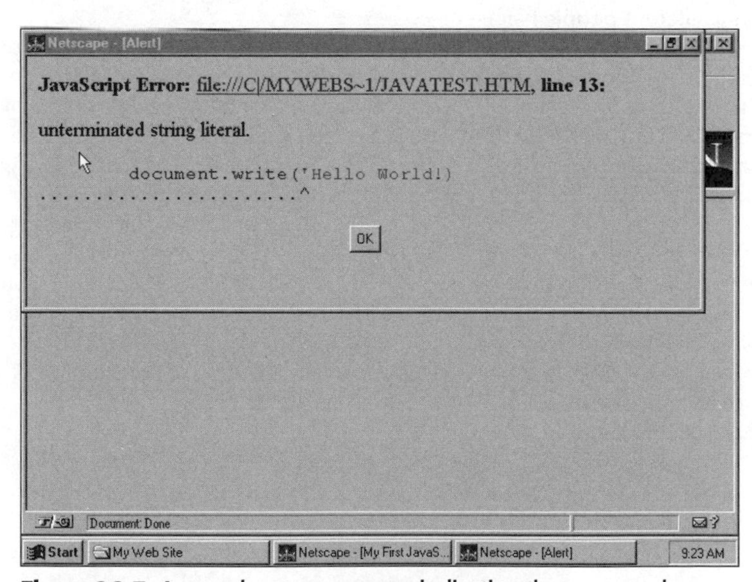

Figure 26-7: A sample error message indicating that you made a mistake while typing your script.

Most people sort of lapse into a "simian stare" when they see an error message. They're not quite sure if it is supposed to be there, if it is actually presenting useful information, or if the computer just went momentarily insane and arbitrarily put something weird and meaningless on the screen. Some people just sit there and wait for something else to happen. These are not good ways to respond to an error message.

The error message is there for some very good reasons:

✦ To inform you that there is an instruction in your script that the computer doesn't understand

✦ To give you some clue as to where it stopped understanding the script

✦ To give you some hints about what might be wrong with the script

Therefore, you want to be sure to read the message — not just ignore it.

After you read the error message, click the OK button in the error message window. If more errors exist in the script, you may see more error messages. Keep reading and clicking OK until no more error messages appear.

Beginner's responses to error messages

As a teacher and as a person who suffered through the early stages of learning to program myself, I've noticed that different people have different responses to error messages when first learning to program. Some people fall into the "simian stare," where they just stare at the screen and do nothing, acting as if they sit there long enough, the computer will fix the program and then finish running it. Sorry, it doesn't work that way. Once the last error has been found, the last error message just stays on the screen until you click that OK button.

Some people panic, thinking that they've somehow broken the computer. Trust me on this, you cannot break a computer by mistyping a JavaScript program. About the only way you can break a computer is by tossing it out of the window of a fairly tall building.

Some people take error messages personally – as though the computer is giving them a slap on the wrist for being naughty or stupid. If you fall into that category, try to change your attitude right away. Even experienced, professional programmers have to deal with dozens – if not *hundreds* – of error messages every day. The computer can't interpret even slightly-mistyped instructions because *it* is stupid. Dumb as a post, in fact. You're not the stupid one in the mix. If you take error messages personally, learning to program is going to be a long, difficult road.

I realize that the error messages aren't always that informative. You won't, for example, see an error message that says "Excuse me, but it looks like you may have forgotten to put a closing quotation mark right here" (and then show you where). Unfortunately, it just says something like `Unterminated string literal`. Nonetheless, the message does show you (approximately) where the browser had problems, and sometimes the message even appears in semi-plain English rather than pure nerdbrain argot.

Either way, you need to fix the script and try again. That means you need to close the Web browser window, re-open the Web page in Notepad, figure out what's wrong, and then fix it. Then you need to save the modified page, close Notepad, and re-open the page. You may need to repeat this little dance several times to get all the bugs out and have the JavaScript program run flawlessly.

Later in this chapter, I cover some of the more common error messages and their causes. Generally, though, when it comes to debugging (fixing broken scripts), we all have to fend for ourselves. Like programming, debugging is one of those skills that gets better with time and experience. For now, let's turn our attention back to the JavaTest.htm page and add some new tricks to it.

Adding a Loop to JavaTest.htm

What'ya say we add some "real" programming code to JavaTest.htm, such as a loop that repeats the document.write command ten times? To do so, you need to open — again using Notepad — the JavaTest.htm page. Then add this command above the document.write statement:

```
for (i = 1; i <= 10, i++) {
```

Below that statement, type a closing curly brace to mark the end of the loop. You may want to indent the document.write() statement, as I've done in Figure 26-8, just to make it easier to see which statement is contained within the loop.

Let's talk about exactly what that command means before testing it. The For statement, in JavaScript, uses the syntax

```
For (startvalue; condition; incrementvalue) {
     statements
{
```

The *startvalue* is an expression that identifies a variable for the loop to use and gives it some initial value. In this example, where the *startvalue* is i=1, you've told JavaScript that you're going to use a variable named i to act as a counter and that you're going to start off the loop by giving the i a value of 1.

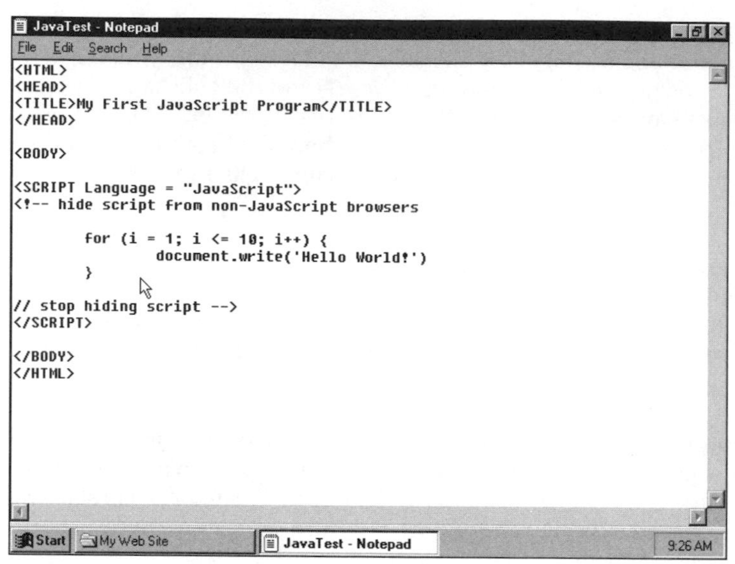

Figure 26-8: A "For" loop added to JavaTest.htm.

The *condition* portion tells JavaScript to "repeat this loop as long as this condition is true." In this example, i <= 10, you've told JavaScript to keep doing the loop as long as the variable i contains a number that is less than or equal to 10.

The *incrementvalue* tells JavaScript what to do to i for every pass through the loop. In the example, you used i++ as the incrementing value, which is an abbreviated way of saying "increase i by 1 with each pass through the loop." You could have stated that as i=i+1. But the shortcut method, ++, requires a little less typing. Notice that these three items are enclosed in parentheses and separated by semicolons.

The { *statements* } code after the loop tells the loop *which* statements to execute with each pass through the loop. The *statements* can be any number of valid JavaScript statements. All statements within — and only the statements within — those curly braces are executed with each pass through the loop. Any statements that come after the closing curly brace will not be executed until the loop has run its entire course.

To test your new, fancier script, close and save it as you normally would. Then re-open it in Netscape Navigator. If you typed everything just right, the script will print Hello World! on the screen ten times, as Figure 26-9 shows.

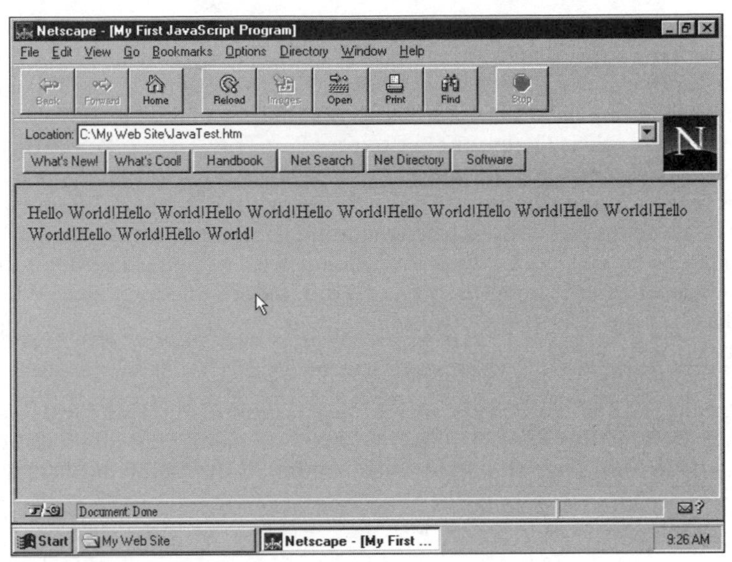

Figure 26-9: Results of the script in Figure 26-8.

Adding more goodies to JavaTest.htm

Let's assume that you have the newest version of JavaTest.htm finished (it ran okay — or it didn't run okay, but you fixed it). Now let's spice it up just a tad by adding some regular text and tags and by making a fancier document.write() statement. Close the Navigator window, and re-open JavaTest.htm in Notepad.

Now insert a blank line between the <BODY> and <SCRIPT> tags, and type <H1><CENTER>My First JavaScript Script</CENTER></H1><P> as it appears in boldface below:

```
<BODY>
 <H1><CENTER>My First JavaScript Script</CENTER></H1><P>
<SCRIPT LANGUAGE = "JavaScript">
```

Notice that you've typed in regular text and HTML tags, not JavaScript code. Because the new line is not JavaScript code, it needs to be placed outside the <SCRIPT>... </SCRIPT> tags.

Next, let's fancy-up the document.write() statement. Change it from its current state, which looks like this

```
document.write('Hello World!')
```

to this

```
document.write(i,'. Hello World!<BR>')
```

Notice that in front, I've added *i* just after the inside parenthesis, followed by a comma, a single quotation mark, and a blank space. Let me tell you what effect that has. By adding these characters, I've now told JavaScript to write the contents of the variable i into the document. (The i is not in quotation marks so it is treated as a variable rather than a literal, as I'll discuss in Chapter 27.) The , ”. *Hello World
’)* instructs JavaScript to “after typing the value of i, type a period, a space, *Hello World!* and *
*“. If you're wondering what the `<BR>` tag is about, that is the HTML tag for a line break. What is it doing here, you ask? Keep in mind that document.write() actually *writes to the document,* not to the screen. Thus, with each pass through the loop, this version will write `Hello World!<BR>` to the underlying document. When the browser re-displays the underlying document, it will view the `<BR>` tags as tags and show line breaks instead of the tags.

Just for good measure, let's add another chunk of regular text and HTML tags, this time below the script. Type this line between the `</SCRIPT>` and `</BODY>` tags near the bottom of the page. Your page should look like Figure 26-10 when you're finished.

```
<P><CENTER><BLINK>That's all folks! </CENTER></BLINK>
```

```
<HTML>
<HEAD>
<TITLE>My First JavaScript Program</TITLE>
</HEAD>

<BODY>

<H1><CENTER>My First JavaScript Script</CENTER></H1><P>

<SCRIPT Language = "JavaScript">
<!-- hide script from non-JavaScript browsers

        for (i = 1; i <= 10; i++) {
                document.write(i,'. Hello World!<BR>')
        }

// stop hiding script -->
</SCRIPT>

<P><CENTER><BLINK>That's all folks!</CENTER></BLINK>

</BODY>
</HTML>
```

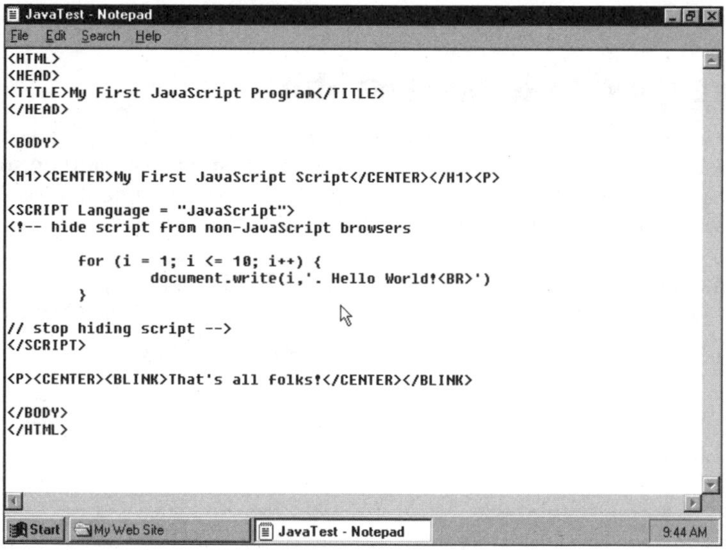

Figure 26-10: Some more changes made to JavaTest.htm.

To test the new version of JavaTest.htm, close and save it. Then re-open it with Netscape Navigator. This time, the page looks something like Figure 26-11, with *That's all folks!* blinking at the bottom of the screen.

Puzzled? If you don't see the blinking text at the bottom of the page, it may just be scrolled out of view. You can choose Options➪Show Toolbar to hide the toolbar buttons and make more room for the page. To redisplay the buttons, choose Options➪Show Toolbar again.

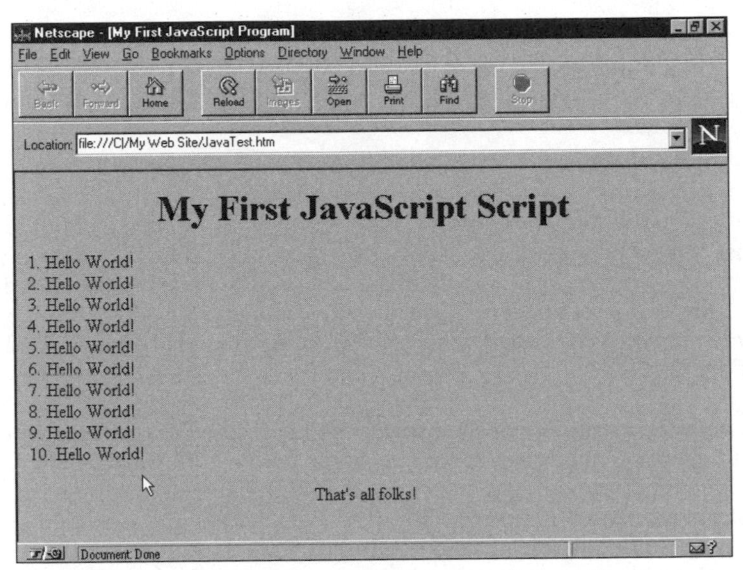

Figure 26-11: The page from Figure 26-10 as displayed by Netscape Navigator 2.0.

Help yourself

For those of you who are new to programming, let me say that I understand how foreign and ridiculous this whole business of writing, running, and debugging scripts can be. For most people, it takes time and practice for everything to sink in. It may help to just fool around with JavaText.htm. Open it in Notepad, make a change or two, save it, and re-open the page in Navigator to see the effects of your changes.

For example, you can try changing the For loop in JavaTest.htm so that it starts at 2, goes to 20, and increments by 2 with each pass through the loop, such as this:

```
for (i = 2; i <= 20, i = i + 2) {
```

Run that version and take a really good look at the result in Netscape Navigator. Then re-open JavaTest.htm in Notepad and try changing the loop so that it counts from 1 to 100. This time, though, take the `<BR>` out of the document.write() statement, like this:

```
for (i = 1; i <= 100; i++) {
     document.write(i,'. Hello World!')
```

and run that version. Here's another variation you can try after you've tried that the preceding one:

```
for (i = 1 i <= 100i = i++) {
     document.write(i,' - Turn me loose - ')
```

After that, you might try the more adventurous:

```
for (i = 1 i <= 100i = i++) {
     document.write(i,' - Turn me loose, <BLINK><B> caboose </
       B></BLINK>- ')
```

Perhaps try filling in your own name or words within the single-quotation marks in document.write(). Or try some other tags like italic `<I>...</I>` in place of bold `<B>...</B>`. Just have some fun. It may seem a little frivolous, but it's actually a very beneficial task. On the one hand, you get the hang of a programmer's life cycle, which is write/change code, test it, debug if necessary, write/change code, test it, debug if necessary ... *ad nauseum.* Programmers are good at programming because this is *all* they do most of the day.

Another benefit of this exercise is that the experience of changing a script and seeing the results of that change immediately helps the whole concept of programming sink in a little better. Most people never get it because they don't give their brains enough time to get it. I should warn you of one possible problem, though. Once you do get it, programming can be very addictive because it's fun. You've no doubt seen the characteristics of the addicted computo-nerd: Order out for pizza often (so you don't waste time preparing food). Drink lots of caffeine (so you don't waste time sleeping). Ignore people a lot (so you don't waste time talking). But heck, it's not the kind of addiction that will kill you or anything.

Common JavaScript Errors

I promised earlier that I would review some of the more common error messages (ugh) that are likely to pay you a visit while you're writing JavaScript code. Of course, I didn't conduct a scientific study to determine what the most common error messages are within various regions and cultures around the globe. What defines a common error message, for our purposes, is one that visits me quite often during my own JavaScripting shenanigans.

... is not defined

The *Something-or-other is not defined* error message is quite common and is usually caused by misspelling an object name or by using the wrong upper/lowercase letters. For example, the following JavaScript statement

```
Document.write(i,". Hello World!<BR>")
```

causes the error message *Document is not defined* to appear. Why? Because the *document* object name starts with a lowercase "d." The cure here is to change the statement to the following:

```
document.write(i,". Hello World!<BR>")
```

To see the exact syntax, spelling, purpose, and examples of a JavaScript statement, look it up in the alphabetical JavaScript reference presented in Appendix C, or any of the electronic references described there.

. . . is not a function

The *Something-or-other is not a function* error message means you either misspelled a method or property or used the wrong upper/lowercase. For example, the command that follows would cause the error message *Write is not a function* to appear:

```
document.Write(i,". Hello World!<BR>")
```

Fussy, fussy, fussy. I just hate this one. The cure is to change the statement so that it uses the proper upper/lowercase letters, like this:

```
document.write(i,". Hello World!<BR>")
```

Missing) . . .

The *Missing)* . . . (closing paragraph character) message means that JavaScript was expecting to find a closing parenthesis somewhere after an opening parenthesis. But didn't find one. For example, this For loop is missing a closing parenthesis:

```
for (i=1 ; i <= 10 ; i++ {
```

The fix is to re-open the script in Notepad, figure out where the missing parenthesis should go, and type it in, as follows:

```
for (i=1 ; i <= 10 ; i++) {
```

One VERY pesty problem

One of JavaScript's more difficult to trace problems occurs when a page contains one or more graphic images and JavaScript code. If every `<IMG...>` tag specifies a HEIGHT and WIDTH tag for the picture it displays, you'll generally have no problems. However, if any `<IMG...>` tags are used without those attributes, the script might behave incorrectly or not work at all! The only real solution here is to measure every picture in the page (you can do this with Paint Shop Pro, as we discussed in Chapter 22). And then make sure that every `<IMG...>` tag specifies the picture's correct size.

Missing (. . .

This error message basically alerts you of the same problem as the preceding one, but an open parenthesis character (rather than a closing parenthesis character) is missing somewhere.

Missing ; after for-loop initializer

This error message means that you forgot to put a semicolon in the *conditions* portion of a For loop statement. Maybe you accidentally typed commas instead, like this:

```
for (i=1 , i <= 10 , i++) {
```

The cure is to type the semicolons where they belong and remove any characters that don't belong, like this:

```
for (i=1 ; i <= 10 ; i++) {
```

Missing } in compound statement

The English translation of this error message is that you started off some hunk of statements with a curly brace ({) but forgot to type the closing curly brace (}). For example, the For loop that follows has no closing curly brace:

```
for (i=1 ; i <= 10 ; i++) {
     document.write(i,'. Hello World!<BR>')

//--> Stop hiding code
```

The cure is to figure out where the curly brace should be and then type it in, as follows:

```
for (i=1 ; i <= 10 ; i++) {
     document.write(i,'. Hello World!<BR>')
}
//--> Stop hiding code
```

Why so fussy? Because you're writing instructions for a *machine* to carry out, and machines have no brains. They cannot figure out what's wrong or make corrections — you *really* have to spell it out for them.

Syntax error

This message means that the computer could no longer understand the instructions but is not exactly sure why. The computer is guessing that some error exists in the syntax of the command — such as with the exact placement of spaces, parentheses, dots, curly braces, and so on. The cure is to go back into Notepad, find the syntax error, and correct it. The Syntax and Example headings in Appendix C can help you locate and correct syntax errors in your JavaScript statements.

Unterminated string literal

Every time I see this error message, I feel like telling the machine I'd be glad to terminate a few string literals right about now. This message means that you started to define some literal text like "Hello World" or "Yowsa." But you didn't put the closing quotation mark at the end of the literal. For example, the closing quotation mark at the end of `<BR>` that follows is missing:

```
document.write(i,'. Hello World!<BR>)
```

The fix is to figure out where the missing character goes and type it in, as follows:

```
document.write(i,'. Hello World!<BR>')
```

Note that you can use either ' and " to delimit literals. However, you must use the same character at both ends. For example, these are both okay:

```
document.write(i,'. Hello World!<BR>')

document.write(i,". Hello World!<BR>")
```

but this is not okay:

```
document.write(i,'. Hello World!<BR>")
```

You can alternate the ' and " characters to show one inside the other. For example, the following is a string literal enclosed in single quotation marks. But notice that a pair of double quotation marks also appear within the literal.

```
document.write('Jane said "Hello" to Manny')
```

The effect here is that the double quotation marks are treated just like any other normal character. A ' was used to mark the beginning of the literal, so any text up to the next ' is treated literally. The preceding JavaScript statement, when executed, displays this on the Web browser screen:

```
Jane said "Hello" to Manny
```

Out of Memory or machine hangs

"Machine hangs" isn't actually an error message; here I'm talking about when everything just stops working. This problem may occur if, say, JavaScript doesn't find an error but a loop that never achieves its termination condition (a.k.a. an *infinite loop*) has taken over and the rest of the computer sits there. Sometimes, the only way to get "unhung" is to press Ctrl+Alt+Del, hold down all three keys for a few seconds, and then release the keys. When Windows 95 provides you with some options as a result, you need to pick End Task. The task to end is Netscape Navigator.

Next, you need to get back into your script and find out why the loop tried to run forever. You may, for example, discover something like this:

```
for (i=1 ;1 <= 10 ; i++) {
```

Why would that loop try to run forever? Because the termination condition, 1 <= 10, is always true because one is always less than ten. What you probably intended to do was say "while *i* is less than or equal to 10," like this:

```
for (i=1 ;i <= 10 ; i++)
```

In this version, the variable i eventually will be greater than ten, because the i++ part adds one to i with each pass through the loop. When i = 11, the condition i <= 10 evaluates false, which stops the loop.

A mere sampling

There you have it — a tiny sampling of the many (many, many) mysterious error messages that may appear when you incorrectly type something in a JavaScript program. Remember that the error message (as irritating as it may be) *is* actually trying to help. Reading the message and paying attention to where the little caret character (^) in the message is pointing can help you isolate the problem to a single line in your script.

Summary

Let's review the basic mechanics of creating JavaScript scripts before getting into the more abstract overview of the JavaScript programming language:

- ✦ JavaScript is a programming language that can be interpreted by any JavaScript-capable Web browser.
- ✦ The term *code* refers to the actual instructions written on the JavaScript programming language.
- ✦ Typically, you'll use a simple text editor, like Notepad, to add JavaScript code to your Web pages.
- ✦ Any JavaScript code that you add to a Web page must be enclosed in a pair of `<SCRIPT Language="JavaScript">...</SCRIPT>` tags, to differentiate it from regular HTML tags and text.
- ✦ To hide JavaScript code from non-JavaScript browsers, enclose the code in a pair of `<!--` and `//-->` comment tags.
- ✦ To run (that is, play, test, execute) a JavaScript script, first close and save the page as a .htm (or .html) file. Then open the page with any JavaScript-capable Web browser.
- ✦ If your script contains any errors, you see an error message telling you roughly where the computer stopped understanding the instructions and providing a suggestion as to what the problem may be.
- ✦ The only way to get rid of an error message is to close the browser, re-open the page with a text editor, find and correct the problem, save the page, and re-open it in a JavaScript-capable browser.

✦ ✦ ✦

CHAPTER 27

JavaScript: The Big Picture

✦ ✦ ✦ ✦

In This Chapter

JavaScript programmer comments

JavaScript data (numbers and strings)

Expressions, variables, operators, and literals

JavaScript objects, properties, and methods

Event handlers, statements, and functions

JavaScript versus Java and Hot Java

✦ ✦ ✦ ✦

Now that you know the mechanics of creating, playing, and debugging JavaScript scripts, we need to take a step back and take a look at JavaScript from the big picture vantage point. As I've mentioned, JavaScript is a programming *language.* Like a spoken language, it consists of verbs, nouns, sentences, questions, and so on. But people in the computer industry do not use terms like *verb* and *noun* when describing programming languages. Instead, they refer to the various parts of the language using terms like *statements, objects, variables, operators, literals,* and so on.

I should warn you that if JavaScript is your first programming language, this whole business of variables, operators, and so forth can be a bit daunting. Your brain cells are likely to get tired trying to relate this stuff to things that exist in the real world — there really isn't anything in the real world that you can relate this stuff to! When it comes to foreign languages, programming languages are about as foreign as you can get.

If it is any consolation to you, remember that *all* programmers have suffered through the brain-drain of trying to learn their first programming language. Nobody is born knowing how to do this stuff. Your brain *can* learn the programming process. It may not be easy — you may flail around through these chapters and dozens of other peoples' programs for weeks or months before you become fluent in JavaScript. But the reward is that once you have mastered a programming language, you have much more control over your Web pages and your computer in general.

Enough with the pep talk. Let's pick apart JavaScript so that you can get a feel for some of the terminology and concepts that programmers use when discussing their programming endeavors.

JavaScript Programmer Comments

Comments are plain-English notes to yourself that you can put into your JavaScript scripts. You've already seen one type of comment — the <!-- and //--> pair of symbols used to hide an entire script from non-JavaScript browsers. These tags go just below the <SCRIPT...> and just above the </SCRIPT> tag, as you saw back in Figure 26-4 of the preceding chapter.

Within the body of your script, you can add two types of comments:

//	Starts a single-line comment that can begin anywhere on the line
/*...*/	Encloses a multiple line comment

Figure 27-1 shows examples of both types of comments added to your JavaTest.htm script.

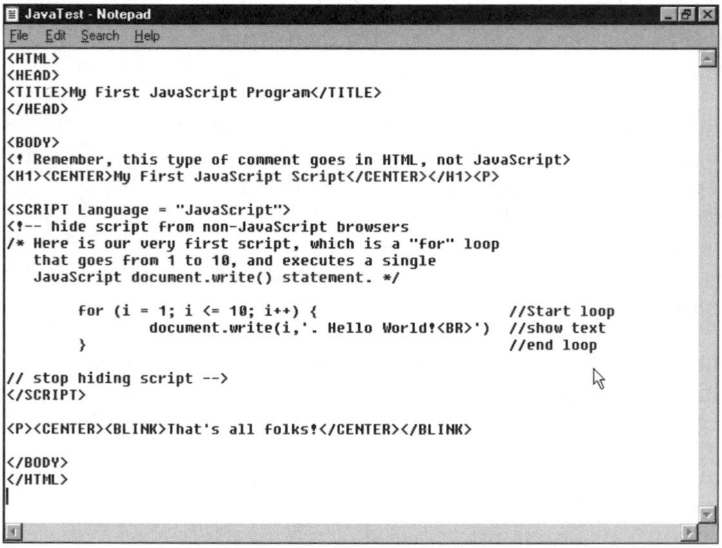

```
JavaTest - Notepad
File Edit Search Help
<HTML>
<HEAD>
<TITLE>My First JavaScript Program</TITLE>
</HEAD>

<BODY>
<! Remember, this type of comment goes in HTML, not JavaScript>
<H1><CENTER>My First JavaScript Script</CENTER></H1><P>

<SCRIPT Language = "JavaScript">
<!-- hide script from non-JavaScript browsers
/* Here is our very first script, which is a "for" loop
   that goes from 1 to 10, and executes a single
   JavaScript document.write() statement. */

       for (i = 1; i <= 10; i++) {                    //Start loop
              document.write(i,'. Hello World!<BR>')  //show text
       }                                              //end loop

// stop hiding script -->
</SCRIPT>

<P><CENTER><BLINK>That's all folks!</CENTER></BLINK>

</BODY>
</HTML>
```

Figure 27-1: This little script is just full of comments.

JavaScript Data: Numbers and Strings

Data is the general term used to describe information. For example, suppose that you present a fill-in-the-blank form on a Web page for your reader to fill out. Whatever the reader types into the form is the *data*. In general, all data is divided into two categories: *numbers* and *strings*.

A *number* is, well, a number. It is something you can do basic arithmetic with — add, subtract, multiply, and divide. For example, 123.45 is a number, as is 22. A *string* is a string of characters, so named because to a computer, all text is just meaningless strings of characters. For example, "Hello" is a string, as is "Jane Doe." So is "fldjsmkk fjlksdf" and "P.O. Box 630." Some of those strings may have meaning for you, but a computer views them all as meaningless strings of text that it stores in memory and puts up on the screen when told to do so.

JavaScript Expressions

Much of what you do when you write a program consists of telling the computer how to manipulate the data. To do that, you write *expressions.* Programming involves writing lots of expressions, which are little instructions that tell the computer what to do with data. Most expressions contain some combination of *operators, variables,* and *literals.* Let's take a look at what those items mean.

Operators

Operators are symbols that operate on data. You are probably already familiar with operators from basic arithmetic. For example, in the expression 1+1 = 2, the + sign is the operator. JavaScript uses all the operators that you'll find in any language. Here are some of the more commonly used operators:

+	addition (or string concatenation, discussed in a moment)
-	subtraction
*	multiplication
/	division
=	equals (assign a value to a variable)
>	is greater than
<	is less than
>=	is greater than or equal to
<=	is less than or equal to
==	is equal to (compare two values)
!=	is not equal to

JavaScript uses more operators than these, but this list should be enough to get you started. The full set of JavaScript operators and the rules of precedence are documented at the start of Appendix C.

Literals

A *literal* is a chunk of data that the program interprets literally. For example, the number 10 is a literal, as is the string "Hello There." Numeric literals are written as-is. String literals are enclosed in single quotation marks (') or double quotation marks ("). In the JavaScript statements that follow, 0 and -123.45 are numeric literals (numbers) and "Josey" and "Rod" are string literals:

```
x = 10
y = -123.45
a = "Josey"
b = 'Rod'
```

Variables

A variable, as opposed to a literal, is a *placeholder.* Basically, a variable is a name with no quotation marks around it that you use to "hold" some item of data. For example, say that you present a fill-in-the-blank form for your reader to fill out. When the reader enters his or her name, your JavaScript program can grab that name and store it on a variable, perhaps named personsName. Later, it can manipulate that chunk of data.

Here's another quick example: Suppose that your form is a fill-in-the-blank form that contains a blank for filling in the quantity of an item ordered and the unit price. You can store the reader's entries in a pair of variables named, say, qty and unitprice. To determine the total sale on that item, you can create a new variable named something like subtotal. Then you can store the quantity times the unit price in that variable, like this:

```
subtotal = qty * unitprice
```

Variable names in JavaScript must begin with a letter (a-z or A-Z) and cannot contain blank spaces. Also, you cannot use *reserved words* (listed in Appendix C) as variable names.

That line you just wrote, subtotal=qty*unitprice, is an *expression.* It contains three variable names (subtotal, qty, and unitprice) and two operators (= and *). As mentioned, all expressions basically consist of some combination of variables, perhaps literals, and operators. Some more examples follow, along with what they mean in English:

```
x = 10
```

means "stick the number 10 in the variable named x."

```
myname = "Alan Simpson"
```

means “stick the string ‘Alan Simpson’ in a variable named myname.”

```
qty = 2
unitprice = 5.50
subtotal = qty * unitprice
```

contains three expressions. The first puts the value 2 in a variable named qty. The second puts the value 5.50 in the variable named unitprice. The third expression puts 11.00 in the variable named subtotal (because 2 times 5.50 equals 11.00). Here’s another series of expressions:

```
firstname = "Jane"
lastname = "Doe"
fullname = firstname + " " + lastname
```

The first expression puts the string Jane in a variable named firstname. The second expression puts the string Doe into a variable named lastname. The last expression puts Jane Doe into a variable named fullname. Notice that when you add (+) strings, you do not get a sum. Instead, the strings are *concatenated* (a fancy term for “stuck together”).

What’s with the little " " that appears in the middle? If I made that expression look like this:

```
fullname = firstname + lastname
```

then the fullname variable would contain JaneDoe. You and I know that this result is wrong because a space should appear between the first and last name. The real problem lies in the fact that the computer doesn’t know a name from a pastrami sandwich. To the computer, Jane Doe is just another string. So, if you want a space to appear between the first and last name, you need to include that in the expression. Therefore, the meaning of the expression

```
fullname = firstname + " " + lastname
```

in English is “put the contents of the firstname variable, followed by a blank space (" "), followed by the contents of the lastname variable, into the variable called fullname.”

Although it is not necessary to do so, you can use the *var* statement to indicate that you are creating a new variable for the first time within a script. Precede the variable name with the word *var* and a space, as in these examples:

```
var qty = 2
var unitprice = 5.50
var subtotal = qty * unitprice
var firstname = "Jane"
var lastname = "Doe"
var fullname = firstname + " " + lastname
```

Note that the *var* word is used only where you are creating a variable — not to refer to an existing variable. For example, I used *var subtotal = qty * unitprice* rather than *var subtotal = var qty * var unitprice* because in that example, the variables named qty and unitprice have already been created.

You see many more examples of expressions in the sample scripts presented in the upcoming chapters. Most likely, you'll type numerous expressions while developing your own scripts. For now, I want to step away from this whole business of expressions and look at another major component of JavaScript — its *objects.*

JavaScript Objects

The term *object* is the official term for "thing." The real world consists of many objects (things). For example, if you look around your office, you see many objects: a keyboard, a mouse, perhaps a pencil sharpener, some pens, maybe a lamp. All of these things are objects. Some objects in the real world consist of many objects. For example, a car is an object. The car is made up of yet more objects — a motor, a steering wheel, tires, a radio, and a bunch of other objects.

While you're browsing the World Wide Web, your computer screen contains lots of objects. For example, in Figure 27-2, the screen contains the Netscape window. That window contains still more objects — some toolbars, a Location (address) box, and a document (Web page). The document itself contains some objects, such as text, HTML tags (which aren't visible at the moment), and a form. The form contains even more objects — text boxes (Name, Address, City, State, Zip), radio buttons (Male, Female), and more.

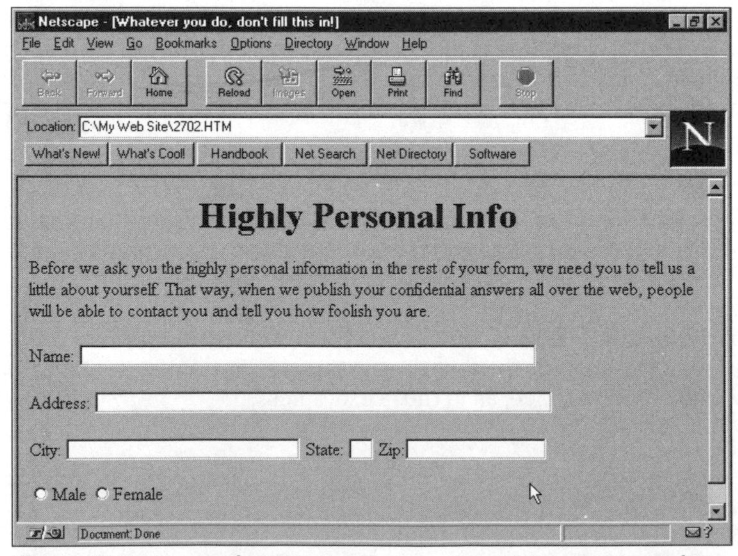

Figure 27-2: At any given moment, your computer screen contains many "things" (objects).

Object properties and methods

Each of the "things" on the screen in Figure 27-2 has certain characteristics which, in computer parlance, are called *properties*. For example, the document (Web page) has properties such as a background color and foreground (text) color. The Location box object has a property as well — the current URL shown in its text box (C:\My Web Site\2703.HTM in Figure 27-2). The history list that becomes visible if you click the drop-down list button in the Location box is another property of the Location box object.

Many objects on your screen have *behaviors,* or things they can do, in addition to characteristics. In computer parlance, the things an object can do are called its *methods.* For example, I can *go to* any URL in the history list by clicking that item. Thus, you could say that "go to" is a method of the history list. I also can *close* the current Web page (document), so you could say "close" is a method of the document object.

As strange as this concept of objects with properties and methods may sound, it is really not far removed from the real world. Objects in the real world have properties and methods, too (although I suspect you've never thought of the real world in those terms before). Let's use the car as a real world object. It has some properties, such as color, year, make, model, and a whole bunch of other characteristics. The car also has methods — things it can do — such as go, turn, stop, and so on.

Referring to objects, properties, and methods

Remember that when writing a program, you are essentially writing instructions that tell the computer to do something. Often, you want those instructions to do something to the objects on the screen. For example, you may want the program to tell the computer to go to some item in the history list. Or, you may want the computer to change the background color property of the document. In order to write such instructions, you need some way to refer to the various objects on the screen.

As I mentioned earlier, computers cannot understand English. Thus, you cannot write an instruction that says "Hey, take the reader to the second item in the history list" or "Let's surprise this reader by changing the background color to black and the foreground color to white." You need to use a more exact language to describe the things you want the computer to mess around with. In JavaScript, you use the *JavaScript Object Model* to refer to specific objects on the screen and the properties and methods of those objects.

The JavaScript Object Model

Lots of objects are available in JavaScript. Lots of properties and methods are available, too. At first glance then, the whole object model thing may seem a bit overwhelming. Ultimately, however, it all boils down to understanding that to refer to an object's property, you always use the following general syntax:

```
objectname.property
```

For example, to refer to the current document's background color, you use the syntax

```
document.bgcolor
```

You use the same general syntax to refer to an object's methods. However, methods usually end with a pair of closing parentheses. For example, to close the current document, you call upon its close method by using this syntax:

```
document.close()
```

In the sections that follow, I lead you on a whirlwind tour of some of the main objects available in JavaScript and show you some of the properties and methods of those objects. I need to ask two things of you first, however:

✦ Don't be concerned about the actual JavaScript code behind the scenes just yet. I get to that in the next chapter. Here I just want to show you some sample objects, properties, and methods.

✦ Don't consider this whirlwind tour to be exhaustive. There are even more objects and properties than those I present here. I do, however, demonstrate some of the objects that you are most likely to use.

I know this stuff may seem pretty abstract, but don't be intimidated by it. You are not stupid. Really understanding this stuff requires getting some hands-on practice with it. Thus, the process of learning JavaScript presents a problem similar to the chicken-and-egg quandry: You need some background information to understand what you're doing when you go "hands on," but you also need some hands-on experience to fully understand the background information.

If you just relax and go easy on yourself as you read these sections, you'll have an easier go of it. Don't expect to grasp it all in one chapter and say, "Ah yes, that's perfectly clear to me. I am now thoroughly fluent in the JavaScript programming language." That kind of "ah-hah" experience does come eventually, but you have to be willing to put in a little time to achieve that reward.

Okay — enough pep talk. On to the JavaScript objects.

The JavaScript document object

In JavaScript, the *document object* refers to "whatever Web page the reader is looking at right now" — which, incidentally, is also the document that contains the JavaScript code. Figure 27-3 shows a sample Web page in Netscape Navigator 2.0. That page shows you some of its own properties.

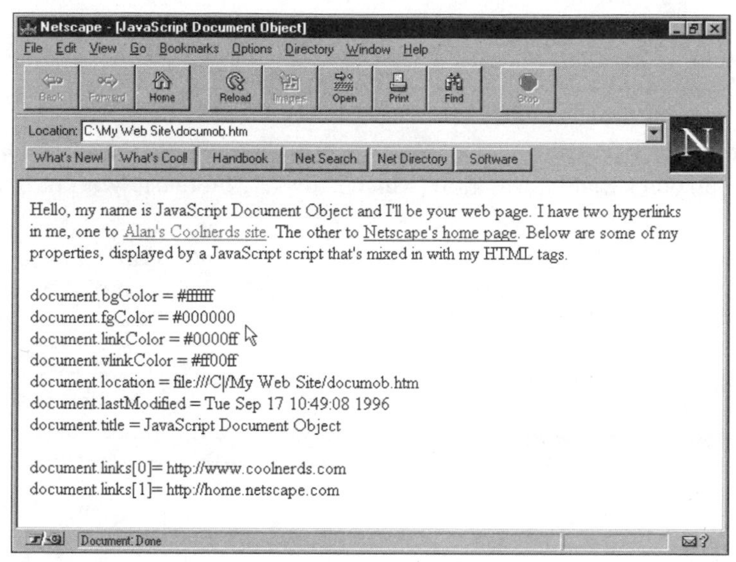

Figure 27-3: A sample Web page in Netscape Navigator 2.0.

Let's take a look at some of the page's properties, which are displayed on the screen:

✦ **Colors.** bgColor (background color), fgColor (foreground (text) color), linkColor, and vlink (visited link) color are all shown as color triplets. The JavaScript that shows this information has plucked the information out of the `<BODY "colors">` tag in the HTML source document (Figure 27-4).

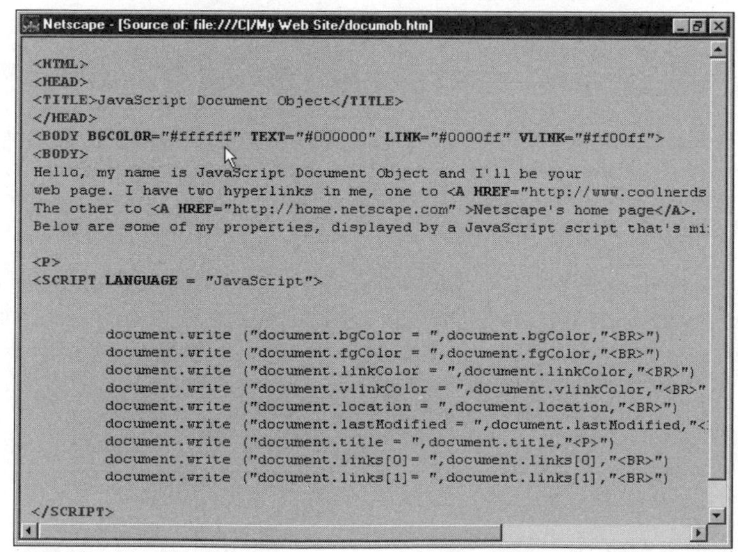

Figure 27-4: The HTML source for the Web page shown in Figure 27-3.

✦ **Location.** JavaScript knows where this document is located on the Internet and expresses it in "Web server" speak (though you can see that this location was built from the contents of the Location box, where the drive and folder are expressed in "Windows 95" speak).

✦ **Last Modified.** All files store information about when they were last modified. JavaScript can pluck that information (which is usually hidden) right out of the Web page.

✦ **Title.** JavaScript has plucked the document title, *JavaScript Document Object,* right out of the title bar at the top of the screen (well, actually, out of the `<TITLE>...</TITLE>` tags within the document).

Incidentally, in Figure 27-4, you can see the entire JavaScript that is showing the properties on the screen. It's nestled between a pair of `<SCRIPT...>...</SCRIPT>` tags. Don't worry about that fact for now — you learn how to write scripts in the next chapter.

The links array

The Web page back in Figure 27-3 contains a couple of links — one to my Web site, coolnerds, and another to Netscape's site. You can see some of the `< HREF...>` tags that define those links in the page's HTML Source View shown in Figure 27-4.

The links are objects, too. They are objects within the document object — but objects nonetheless (just like a motor is an object inside a car object). When your Web browser reads a page, it makes a little list of all link objects that appear in the page. You never see the list, but it is there. When the browser finishes making its list, it even records how many items were added to the list.

Netscape and Notepad only

Throughout these next few chapters, I show everything with Netscape Navigator 2.0 for one very important reason. As I write this chapter, Navigator 2.0 is the only Web browser that supports JavaScript. If you try to view a page that contains JavaScript by using Internet Explorer or some other browser, the script will either be ignored or (worse yet) be displayed on the screen in its "raw" form, like text. For now, you *must* use Navigator 2.0 to view your (and my) scripts.

I also use Notepad, rather than Word IA, to write many scripts in upcoming chapters. The reason is that Word IA doesn't support JavaScript. In fact, if you write a script in Word IA, chances are Word IA will ruin the script when it tries to generate the HTML document. You can still use Word IA to create all non-JavaScript portions of the page, but once you start putting JavaScripts into the document, you can no longer use Word IA as your Web page editor. Bummer, I know.

The fancy programming term for a list is *array.* More specifically, a list is an array of *subscripted variables,* where the subscript is a number that represents the item's position in the list. To complicate things further, JavaScript numbers items in arrays starting at zero rather than one. Despite all the fancy terminology and weird numbering, a list array is not such a difficult thing to grasp. Here's how a list array works:

While the browser is reading the page, if it encounters a link, it stores information about that link as link[0] (pronounced *link sub zero*). When the browser comes to another link, it stores that link as link[1] (pronounced *link sub one*). This process continues until it has finished reading the entire page.

You can get at the array of links via JavaScript by using the standard object.property syntax. However, when you refer to an object located within another object, you need to work your way from the larger (more general) object to the specific object. The general object, in this case is the *document* object. The specific objects are *links,* so the naming syntax looks like this:

```
document.links[x].property
```

where *x* is the subscript — the object's position in the list.

Take a look at Figure 27-5, where a JavaScript is showing information about the links in the current document. Notice how each of the weird document.links.whatever identifier returns (shows) some tidbit of information about the (invisible) links list and individual items within the list

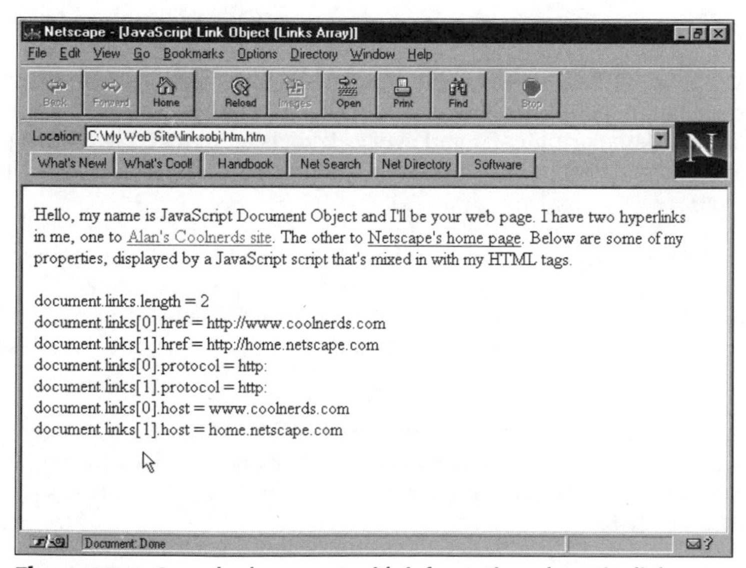

Figure 27-5: Sample document with information about its links displayed by a JavaScript script.

✦ **document.links.length.** Returns how many link items are in this particular document.

✦ **document.links[0].href.** Returns the hyperlink reference (URL) of the first link (link[0]) in the list (`http://www.coolnerds.com`).

✦ **document.links[1].href.** Returns the hyperlink reference (URL) of the second link (link[1]) in the list (`http://home.netscape.com`).

✦ **document.links[0].protocol.** Returns the protocol (everything up to the // in the URL) of the first link in the list.

✦ **document.links[1].href.** Returns the protocol (everything up to the // in the URL) of the second link in the list.

✦ **document.links[0].host.** Returns the host name (the URL minus the protocol) for the first link in the list.

✦ **document.links[1].host.** Returns the host name (the URL minus the protocol) for the second link in the list.

You may be thinking, "Big deal. So JavaScript can get at things on the screen if I just tell it the weird name of the thing. What good does that do *me?*" JavaScript can change that information, use that information to make decisions, and use that information as parts of commands that it executes by itself. But before I get into all that, please bear with me as I introduce you to just a few more JavaScript objects.

The string object

As I mentioned earlier, a *string* is a chunk of text (such as "Hello") as opposed to a number (such as 123.45). The string may be something you define in your JavaScript program, or it may be something your reader typed while filling in a form on your site. The string may even be the result of a links array. It doesn't matter *where* the string comes from because to JavaScript, each and every string is an object. Each string has its own properties (such as a length), as well as a set of methods (things JavaScript can do to the string).

The page in Figure 27-6 illustrates a property (length) and some methods applied to a string object. The string object in this example is stored in a variable named personname, using the expression personname = "Jane Doe." The length property defines the length of that string. The various methods (toUpperCase, toLowerCase, and so forth) act upon that string.

I don't want you to be concerned with any nitty-gritty details of JavaScript just yet. But to prove to you that there is a JavaScript behind the scenes and also for future reference when you know how to read and write JavaScript, Figure 27-7 shows the HTML source for Figure 27-6.

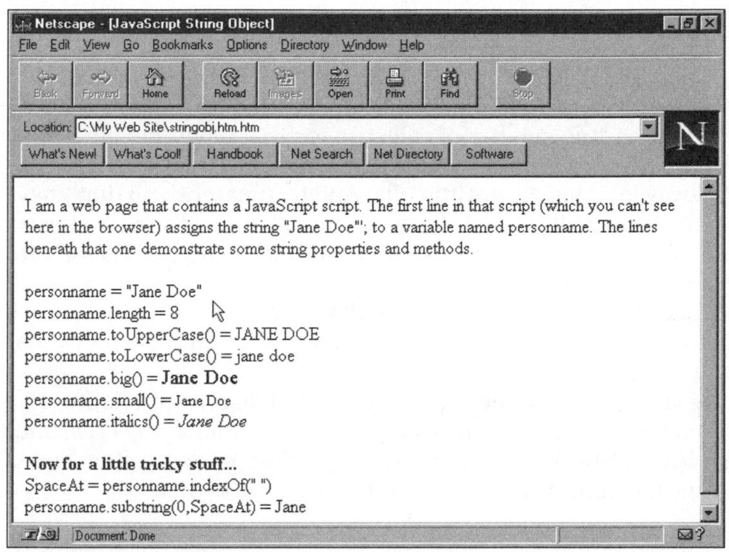

Figure 27-6: A string object property (.length) and some string properties.

```
Netscape - [Source of: file:///C|/My Web Site/stringobj.htm.htm]

<HTML>
<HEAD>
<TITLE>JavaScript String Object</TITLE>
</HEAD>
<BODY BGCOLOR="#ffffff" TEXT="#000000" LINK="#0000ff" VLINK="#ff00ff">
<BODY>
I am a web page that contains a JavaScript script. The first line in that s
The lines beneath that one demonstrate some string properties and methods.
<P>
personname = "Jane Doe"<BR>
<SCRIPT LANGUAGE = "JavaScript">


        personname = "Jane Doe"
        document.write ("personname.length = ",personname.length,"<BR>")
        document.write ("personname.toUpperCase() = ",personname.toUpperCas
        document.write ("personname.toLowerCase() = ",personname.toLowerCas
        document.write ("personname.big() = ",personname.big(),"<BR>")
        document.write ("personname.small() = ",personname.small(),"<BR>")
        document.write ("personname.italics() = ",personname.italics(),"<P>
        document.write ("<B>Now for a little tricky stuff...</B><BR>")
        SpaceAt=personname.indexOf(" ")
        document.write ('SpaceAt = personname.indexOf(" ")<BR>')
        document.write ('personname.substring(0,SpaceAt) = ',personname.sub
```

Figure 27-7: The HTML source behind the page shown in Figure 27-6.

Puzzled? You may find the tricky example in Figure 27-7 especially puzzling. But please don't waste any brain cells pondering that right now. I explain the string object and string manipulation in more detail when we get to Chapter 29.

The date object

JavaScript's date object is an invisible place where it stores dates and times. JavaScript really doesn't have a date "data type" per se. What the date object does is convert a date and time as "the number of milliseconds that have transpired since January 1, 1970." This is funky, no doubt, but treating dates as numbers gives JavaScript some leeway in doing date arithmetic. And fortunately, you don't have to be too concerned about the milliseconds because the date object's properties and methods automatically convert "normal" dates to and from milliseconds for you.

Danger Zone

Currently, JavaScript cannot store or manipulate dates prior to 1/1/70. Future releases of JavaScript may fix that problem. But for now, you're limited to fairly recent dates.

You can create date values and put them in variables, as I discuss in Chapters 28 and 29. You also can grab the datemodified property from a document object. In addition, you can grab the current date and time right out of the computer's system clock. This last method is the most common and is defined by using the syntax

```
variable = new date()
```

where *variable* is any legitimate JavaScript variable name.

Figure 27-8 illustrates some exercises with date properties and methods using JavaScript. Future chapters provide some more detailed (and practical) examples.

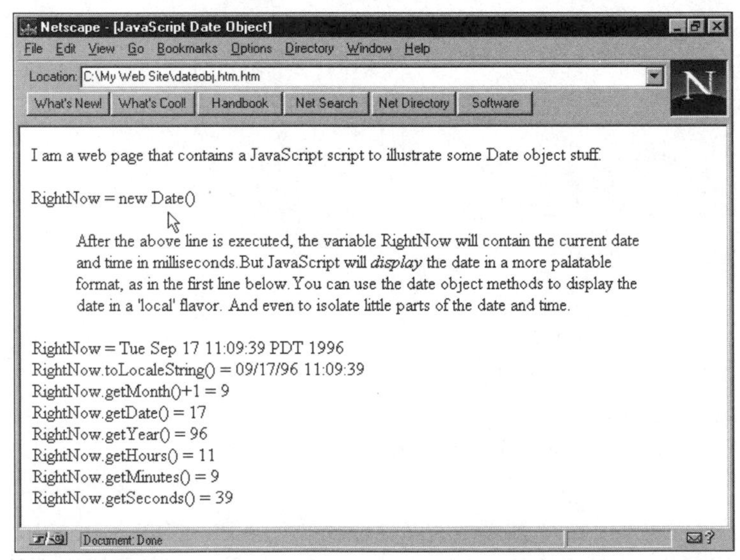

Figure 27-8: Some examples of manipulating JavaScript's date object.

Other objects

Yoo hoo. Are you still awake? There are still lots more objects, properties, and methods in JavaScript. Rather than go into detail right now, I'll just summarize what they are and what they refer to. The important thing here is to get a feel for the object.property and object.method() technique for referring to objects. The following is a list of the other JavaScript objects that I discuss in upcoming chapters and in Appendix C:

✦ **anchor object (anchors array).** This object contains a list of all bookmarks (anchor points) in the current document, as defined by `<A NAME=...>` tags within the document.

✦ **button object.** This is a push-button on a form. You can use this object to create custom buttons. The button object has an event handler, which lets you define an action that JavaScript should take when the reader clicks the button.

✦ **check box object.** This object is a check box on a form. Its Value property lets a JavaScript program see if the box is currently clear or selected. An onClick event handler lets a script respond to a reader's selection immediately.

✦ **elements array.** This array is a list of all controls (text boxes, radio buttons, check boxes) that appear in a single form.

✦ **form object (forms array).** This object is a list of all forms in the current Web page. It also provides a means of dealing with individual chunks of data on the form. This object is used in conjunction with the elements array to create *smart forms* that interact with the reader.

✦ **frame object (frames array).** This object contains a list of all frames (Chapter 25) currently displayed on the screen and also provides a means for jumping from frame to frame, opening new frames, and so on.

✦ **hidden object.** This object is a hidden object on a form that sends you (the publisher) data, but that isn't visible to the reader.

✦ **history object.** This object contains a list of all items in the History list. Back, Forward, and Go methods let a script move through URLs automatically.

✦ **location object.** This object contains information about the current Web page's URL. Properties such as hostname, pathname, hash, and search let you isolate small portions of the current document's URL.

✦ **Math object.** This object is sort of a built-in calculator that can do square roots, trigonometric operations, and other, more complex math.

✦ **navigator object.** This object contains information about the version of Navigator in use.

✦ **password object.** This object contains information about a Password field on a form. Its Value property, combined with an onBlur event handler, lets a script test a reader's password immediately upon entry.

✦ **radio object.** This object contains information about radio buttons on a form. It includes properties, methods, and event handlers to test and manage radio buttons from a JavaScript program.

✦ **reset object.** This object is the Reset button on a form.

✦ **select object (*options* array).** This object is a selection list (drop-down list) or scrolling list (list box) on a form. The *options* array stores the possible selections for each list. Other properties and methods enable scripts to respond immediately to a reader's selection.

✦ **submit object.** This object is the Submit button on a form.

✦ **text object.** This object is a single, text-box field on a form. Properties, methods, and event handlers enable a JavaScript program to respond to and evaluate a reader's entry immediately.

✦ **textarea object.** This object is a larger (multi-line) text box on a form. As with other form controls, properties, methods, and event handlers enable a script to respond to a reader's entry immediately.

✦ **window object.** This object is the top-level object for each document, location, and history object. Numerous properties and methods let a JavaScript program display custom messages to your reader, manipulate frames, and much more.

JavaScript Statements

Normally, your JavaScript code is executed left to right, top to bottom, in exactly the same way you would read a list of instructions:

```
<SCRIPT Language = "JavaScript">
     I get executed first
            Then I get executed
            I get executed third
            I am executed last
</SCRIPT>
```

JavaScript statements let you build *loops* into your script so that some commands can be executed several times. There also are *decision-making* statements that let you build logic into the script — for example, *if (such-and-such) then {do these commands}*. The code within the curly braces is executed only if *such-and-such* is true. Table 27-1 provides a quick summary of JavaScript's statements.

Table 27-1
Quick Summary of JavaScript Statements

Statement	*Description*
Decision-making	
if(condition) {code}	Executes *code* only if *condition* proves true.
if(condition) {code1} ***else*** {code2}	Executes *code1* if *condition* proves true. If *condition* proves false, executes *code2.*
(condition) ***?*** value1 **:** value2	Though technically an operator, the ? operator provides an "immediate if" function. If *condition* proves true, returns *value1.* Otherwise, returns *value2.*
Loops	
for (start,while,increment***)*** {code}	Sets up a loop with a built-in counter starting at *start* value and automatically increments by *increment* value with each pass through the loop. The *code* in curly braces are executed as long as the condition in *while* proves true.
while (*condition*) {*code*}	Repeats *code* in curly braces for as long as *condition* proves true.
break	Terminates a loop immediately and passes execution to the first statement after the loop.
continue	Sends execution back to the top of the loop immediately to start the next iteration of the loop.
Object Manipulation	
for (*properties* **in** *object*) {*code*}	Sets up a loop that executes *code* once for each of the *properties* within the specified *object.*
objectName = **new** *objectType* (*parameters*)	Creates a new object with the *objectName* you specify, of the type specified in *objectType,* with the properties specified in *parameters.*
this	Refers to the current object, or the calling object in a method.

(continued)

Table 27-1 *(continued)*

Statement	*Description*
with (*object*) {*code*}	Specifes that *object* is the object to be used when executing *code* in the curly braces.
Miscellaneous	
function *name*(*arguments*) {*code*}	Creates a custom function with the *name* you specify. The function accepts values listed as *arguments.* The *code* within curly braces is the JavaScript statements executed when the function is executed.
return *value*	Terminates a custom function and returns *value* to the code that called the function.
var *name*	Creates a new variable with the *name* you specify.

Remember that JavaScript statements are documented more fully in Appendix C.

JavaScript Event Handlers

JavaScript *event handlers* are those parts of the language that tell JavaScript *when* to carry out some action. The event handlers go into regular HTML tags. For example, the tag that follows displays a button captioned Recalc on the reader's screen:

```
<INPUT TYPE="button" VALUE="Recalc" onClick="recalc(this.form)">
```

When the reader opens the page that contains this tag, he or she sees a button named Recalc on the screen. The button just sits there initially. When the reader clicks on the button, however, the onClick event handler jumps into action and calls upon a JavaScript function named *recalc()* to do something with the page the reader is viewing.

You see many practical examples of these event handlers in forthcoming chapters. For now, just make a mental note that an event handler is a thing that tells a page *when* to play a script. Table 27-2 summarizes the JavaScript event handlers.

Table 27-2
Summary of JavaScript Event Handlers

Event Handler	*Occurs When*
onClick	The reader clicks on a button, hyperlink, or some other clickable object on the page.
onChange	The reader changes the contents of a text box or some other item on a form.
onFocus	The reader has moved the insertion point into a text box or other form item.
onBlur	The reader has moved the insertion point out of a text box or other form item.
onMouseOver	The reader is pointing to a link or other "pointable" object on the screen.
onSelect	The reader selects an item from a list on a form.
onSubmit	The reader clicks the Submit button on a form.
onLoad	The reader first opens a Web page.
onUnload	The reader exits the current Web page.
HREF=javascript:	The reader clicks on a hot spot in a clickable image map.

Built-In Functions

JavaScript offers three built-in functions, summarized in Table 27-3.

Table 27-3
JavaScript's Built-In Functions

Function	*Purpose*
eval(*string*)	Executes *string* as though it were a JavaScript expression, statement, or sequence of statements.
parseFloat(*string*)	Converts *string* to a floating point number. Example: parseFloat("123.45xyv") returns 123.45.
parseInt(*string*)	Converts *string* to an integer. Example: parseInt("123.45xyv") returns 123.

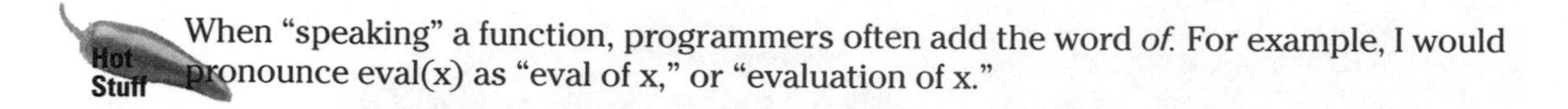

When "speaking" a function, programmers often add the word *of*. For example, I would pronounce eval(x) as "eval of x," or "evaluation of x."

JavaScript Tips, Tricks, and Gotchas

Here are some quick JavaScript tricks and techniques. If you are new to programming or new to object-oriented languages, some of these items will seem strange and outright meaningless. Don't worry — you're not stupid. You just haven't seen them used in context yet. You'll see them in context when you study the sample scripts presented in upcoming chapters, as well as other peoples' scripts on the Web.

Using quotes in statements

As in regular HTML, quotation marks in JavaScript have "meaning." Sometimes, however, you want the quotation marks to be taken literally, not as meaningful characters. JavaScript makes it pretty easy to do this. You just have to alternate between single quotation marks (') and double quotation marks ("). For instance, if you want a string to include double quotation marks, enclose the entire string in single quotation marks, such as this:

```
var reply = 'Mac said "Hello Joe", how's your day going?'
document.write (reply)
```

When the document.write( ) statement is executed, it displays this on the screen:

```
Mac said "Hello Joe", how's your day going?
```

Semicolons (;)

You may notice that many JavaScript programmers put a semicolon at the end of each line in their scripts. Technically, however, the semicolons are only required if you want to put several statements on a single line. For example, the following line

```
a = 20; b = 45; c = 213
```

is the same as this:

```
a = 20;
b = 45;
c = 213
```

which is the same as this:

```
a = 20
b = 45
c = 213
```

Problems with printing

A problem currently exists with printing in JavaScript: You can't do it. That is, when you (or your reader) print the page on the screen, the printed output contains only the standard HTML text. Any text that has been placed on the page by JavaScript's document.write( ) or document.writeln( ) method will not be printed.

This rates as a pretty substantial problem. But Netscape has promised to rectify the problem in future versions of Navigator.

Custom dialog boxes

JavaScript can display custom dialog boxes on your reader's screen. You have three types of dialog boxes to choose from:

- **alert().** Displays an alert (!) box with your message, an OK button, and an audible beep.
- **confirm().** Displays your message, OK and Cancel buttons, and an audible beep.
- **prompt().** Displays your message, a prompt for user input, and OK and Cancel buttons.

Here's a simple script that presents an example of each type of dialog box when opened with Netscape 2.0. Each dialog box, however, appears on the screen and waits for the user to click a button. Thus, if you actually type in and run this dialog box, you see the alert message first. After you click its OK button, you see the confirm box. When you click a button there, you then see the prompt box.

```
<HTML><HEAD></HEAD><BODY>
<SCRIPT Language = "JavaScript">
     //show an alert message box.
     alert("Your message here")

     //show a confirm message box.
     confirm("Your message here")

     //show a prompt message box.
     prompt("Your message here","Someone types here")
</SCRIPT></BODY>
```

Figure 27-9 shows how each of those messages looks on the screen. Remember, however, that if you actually run the little script, the boxes appear one at a time.

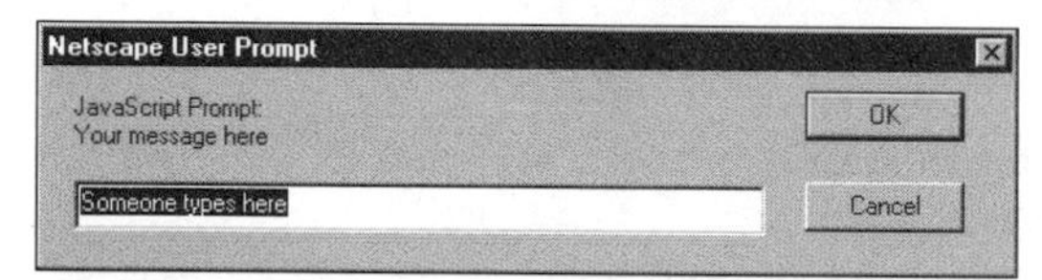

Figure 27-9: Examples of JavaScript custom dialog boxes.

Converting data types

Technically, JavaScript has only two data types: numbers and strings. You can use the parseInt and parseFloat functions mentioned earlier in Table 27-3 to convert strings to numbers. To convert a number to a string, just assign an empty string ("") plus the number to a variable. Here is an example with comments:

```
var xnum = 123.45     //variable xnum contains the number 123.45
var xstring = ""+123.45     //variable xstring contains the
      string "123.45"
var xint = parseInt(xstring)     //variable xint contains the
      number 123.
```

Dates, numbers, and strings

Though no Date data type exists per se in JavaScript, there is a date object. The date object includes numerous functions to convert dates to strings and numbers, and vice versa. Because a date is an object, you use the *new* keyword to create a new variable that contains a date. For example, the following statement puts the current system date in a variable named now:

```
var now = new Date()
```

Now assume that this statement is executed when the system clock is at 12/18/96 12:30 p.m. The variable named now contains a date object which, when displayed on the screen using a document.write(now) statement, looks something like this:

```
Wed Dec 18 12:30:00 PST 1996
```

Although the result looks like a string, it is not. It is, instead, a date object. There are, however, numerous "to," "get," and "parse" methods that you can use on the date object to convert the date and time object to numbers and strings. Figure 27-8 earlier in this chapter showed some examples of those methods.

I know this all seems pretty funky. It gets even funkier though when you start converting string and numbers to dates. For example, to convert a string to a date object, you need to create a new date object, then use the *parse* method to put a specific date (expressed as a string) into that object. Here is a sample series of statements:

```
myDate = new Date()                    //create a date object named
      myDate
myDate.setTime(Date.parse("Dec 15, 1996"))      //Set the myDate
      object to 12/15/96.
Document.write (myDate)                    //displays  Sun Dec 15
      00:00:00 PST 1996
```

Notice that myDate is neither a string nor a number. It is a date object. Thus, to manipulate myDate, you need to use the to and get methods of the date object. (Yikes!)

To convert numbers into a date, use the UTC (Universal Coordinated Time) method of the date object to convert numbers to a date value. The following statements illustrate the basic technique:

```
//Create a new date object named gmtDate
gmtDate = new Date(Date.UTC(96, 11, 15, 2, 30, 0))
//Show gmtDate on the screen
document.write(gmtDate)      //displays Sun Dec 15 10:30:00 PST
      1996
```

In the last example, you may be wondering where the Dec for December came from. To make things extra confusing, JavaScript numbers dates from 0 (for January) to 11 (for December). Hence, the 96,11,15 numbers translate to 12/15/96. (Don't blame me, I didn't create JavaScript. I'm just telling you the facts.)

Date arithmetic

Some of you may wonder how on Earth one can do date arithmetic with all of these quirks. This point is where JavaScript goes from the funky to the sublime. As I mentioned earlier, the date is *internally* stored by JavaScript as a number representing the number of milliseconds transpired since 1/1/70. Typically, you do not see those numbers. You can, however, use the getTime() method of the date object to get that number. The following example illustrates this method assuming that the PC's clock has the current date set to 12/15/96:

```
// create a new date object named orderDate, with today's date.
orderDate = new Date()
milliDate = orderDate.getTime()     //convert orderDate to
      milliseconds since 1/1/70.
//show orderDate and millDate.
document.write ("orderDate = ",orderDate,"<BR>")
document.write ("milliDate = ",milliDate,"<BR>")
```

The output of these statements looks like this (again, assuming that the script is executed on 12/16/96, at noon):

```
orderDate = Mon Dec 16 12:00:00 PST 1996

milliDate = 850766403230
```

where 850766403230 is the number of milliseconds that have elapsed since 1/1/70. Using this information, how do you calculate the date 30 days from the orderDate? milliDate+30 won't do the trick because 30 at this scale is 30 milliseconds — $^{30}/_{1000}$ of a second. Instead, you need to figure out how many milliseconds are in one day. To do that, you can create the following expression:

```
oneMilliday = (24 * 60 * 60 * 1000)
```

In milliseconds, a day is 24 hours $\times$ 60 minutes $\times$ 60 seconds $\times$ 1,000 milliseconds (or 86,400,000 milliseconds, to be exact). Thus, the date 30 days from orderDate is the order date plus 30 times oneMilliday. You follow the preceding expressions with these expressions:

```
oneMilliday = (24 * 60 * 60 * 1000)          //calculate one day
      as milliseconds
dueDate = new Date()                   //create a new date object
      named dueDate
dueDate.setTime(milliDate + (30 * oneMilliday) //Set the time of
      dueDate to orderDate + 30 days
document.write ("dueDate = ",dueDate)     //display the dueDate
```

Hot Stuff

Personally, I find this whole method of managing dates to be much too taxing on my wimpy brain cells. Hence, I've created my own set of custom date functions to make this task a little easier. These custom date functions are included on the *Web Publishing Uncut* CD-ROM for your taking and are discussed in Chapter 29.

The last line displays

```
dueDate =  Wed Jan 15 12:00:00 PST 1997
```

If you were to check a calendar, you'd see that January 15, 1997 is indeed exactly 30 days after December 16. That, in a very complicated nutshell, is how dates work in JavaScript. It's solid proof that truth is indeed stranger than fiction.

Mixing data types

Despite the rather complicated approach to managing some data types, mixing them together in variables or document.write() statements is pretty easy. When assigning the values to a variable, use the + operator to combine them. Be sure to enclose any literals in quotation marks. For example, when you execute this little script

```
<SCRIPT Language = "JavaScript">
        var x = 9
        var name = "Ashley"
        var msg = name + " is " + x + " years old."      //Stick
      x, name, and some literals together in msg.
        document.write (msg)                  //display msg.
</SCRIPT>
```

it displays the following:

```
Ashley is 9 years old.
```

To mix data types in a document.write() statement, you can use either commas or the plus sign to delimit (separate) the literals from the variables. You do not need to explicitly convert data types. Here is an example:

```
<SCRIPT Language = "JavaScript">

var kidName = "Alec"         //kidName is a string
var age = 4                //age is a number

bdate = new Date()
bdate.setTime(Date.parse("Mar 31, 1992"))      //bdate is a date
mo = bdate.getMonth()+1                 //mo, day, and yr are
      numbers
day = bdate.getDate()
yr = bdate.getYear()
bdateStr = mo+"/"+day+"/"+yr            //mix numbers with literal
      strings (/)

//display literals and variables, and a break (<BR>) tag.
document.write (kidName,"'s birthday is ",bdateStr,". This year
      he'll turn ",age,".<BR>")

</SCRIPT>
```

The output of that script, when executed, is

```
Alec's birthday is 3/31/92. This year he'll turn 4.
```

Creating Custom Functions

When you start exploring other peoples' scripts, the first thing you'll discover is that virtually all programmers organize their code into *functions.* These functions appear between the <HEAD>...</HEAD> tags and then are called upon by scripts within the <BODY>...</BODY> section of the Web page.

There are many advantages to organizing JavaScript code into functions. First, once you create a function, you can easily cut and paste it into whatever page you're working on at the moment, so you don't have to "reinvent the wheel" every time you need a script to do some job. Secondly, you can test and debug the function once. After you are confident that it works, you just call it as needed. You don't have to retype and re-debug the script every time you use it. Finally, the whole approach enables you to build up your own collection of user-defined functions (UDFs, or *custom functions*) relevant to your own work almost as though you get to create your own programming language, with capabilities and syntax *you* design into it yourself.

What is a function, anyway?

Now that I've given you the pitch on functions, I better explain what they are. A function is a little *routine,* written in JavaScript, that has a name (which you give it) and a purpose (which you write into it). For example, you can create a function called calctax( ) that calculates the sales tax for any number in any form.

Note the parentheses at the end of the name in calctax( ). All functions end in parentheses. You can pass values to the function simply by putting the value (or a variable that represents the value) inside the parentheses. For example, you can design your calctax( ) function so that it can accept a single number. Then say that you have a variable named TotalSale in the body of your Web page. To create a new variable named SalesTax, you can use the following relatively simple command:

```
SalesTax = calctax(TotalSale)
```

It helps to think of the parentheses as standing for the word *of.* For example, the preceding statement reads as *SalesTax equals calctax of TotalSale.*

All functions *return* some value. Thus, when you enter a statement such as

```
SalesTax = calctax(TotalSale)
```

you assume that the calctax( ) function will calculate the sales tax and *return* that number. That returned number is what gets stored in the SalesTax variable in the preceding example.

Swiping JavaScript code

Like I always say, there are no secrets on the World Wide Web. If someone's Web page has a neat little JavaScript in it, you can easily look at the *source code* for that script. You can look at the source code for the entire page, in fact. The exact steps for doing this task in Netscape Navigator are a little different from the steps you take in Internet Explorer, but they are not too tough.

If the page you are viewing is in a Netscape frame, be sure to click on the appropriate frame first. Then choose View⇨Document Source from Navigator's menus. That shows you the entire source document. To make a copy, press Ctrl+A (for Select All) or drag the mouse pointer through whatever part you want to copy. Then press Ctrl+C to copy the selected text to the Windows Clipboard.

Next, click the Start button and choose Programs⇨Accessories⇨Notepad. When Notepad opens, click inside its blank document window and press Ctrl+V, or choose Edit⇨Paste from Notepad's menu bar. To save the copy, choose File⇨Save As from Notepad's menu bar, and choose a folder on your own PC. When you name the file, be sure to give it the .htm extension.

How to create a custom function

So how does one go about creating a custom JavaScript function? Beats me. (Just kidding.) You basically do the same things you'd do to create a regular JavaScript script but with two added rules:

- ✦ You define all functions between the <HEAD> and </HEAD> tags in the page.
- ✦ The function must start with *function {* statement and end with a } character.

The reason for putting all functions between the <HEAD> and </HEAD> tags is that you want the reader's Web browser to be aware of all functions available in the page before it actually starts displaying the page on the screen. That way, you can write JavaScript statements that call up your custom functions from anywhere within your Web page and know for sure that the reader's Web browser has already "seen" all functions defined in that page.

The exact syntax for defining a function in JavaScript is

```
function name(parameters) {
   statements
         }
```

where *name* is the name you want to give the function, *parameters* are names assigned to any data that gets passed to the function, and *statements* are normal JavaScript statements that define what the function does.

Let's look at an example. Suppose that I want to create a calctax() function that calculates the sales tax on whatever number is passed to it. In my state, the sales tax is 7.75 percent (or 0.0775 in decimal format). My calctax() function might look something like this:

```
   function calctax(anynumber) {
return (0.0775 * anynumber)
      }
```

In the body of my Web page, I can enter the following JavaScript statement to calculate the sales tax on the value currently stored in a variable named TotalSale:

```
TotalSale = 100.00
SalesTax = calctax(TotalSale)
```

When JavaScript executes the SalesTax = calctax(TotalSale) statement, it substitutes in the value for TotalSale (100.00 in this example). For a split second, the function looks something like SalesTax=calctax(100). Then it passes the 100.00 to the calctax() function, which multiplies 100 by 0.0775, resulting in 7.75. The calctax() function then returns that value (7.75), so for a split second, the statement looks something like SalesTax = 7.75. That statement is the one that JavaScript actually executes. By the time the execution cycle reaches the next line in the script, the variable SalesTax contains the number 7.75.

Don't forget that the function must be defined in the head of the page. Once defined, it can be called from anywhere (below the definition) in the page. For example, Figure 27-10 shows how the calctax() function and SalesTax= statements may look in a real Web page:

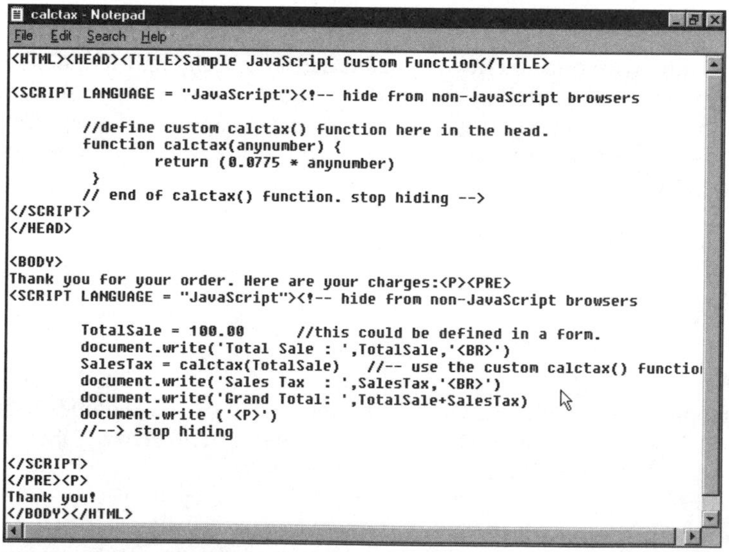

```
calctax - Notepad
File Edit Search Help
<HTML><HEAD><TITLE>Sample JavaScript Custom Function</TITLE>

<SCRIPT LANGUAGE = "JavaScript"><!-- hide from non-JavaScript browsers

        //define custom calctax() function here in the head.
        function calctax(anynumber) {
                return (0.0775 * anynumber)
         }
        // end of calctax() function. stop hiding -->
</SCRIPT>
</HEAD>

<BODY>
Thank you for your order. Here are your charges:<P><PRE>
<SCRIPT LANGUAGE = "JavaScript"><!-- hide from non-JavaScript browsers

        TotalSale = 100.00      //this could be defined in a form.
        document.write('Total Sale : ',TotalSale,'<BR>')
        SalesTax = calctax(TotalSale)    //-- use the custom calctax() functio
        document.write('Sales Tax  : ',SalesTax,'<BR>')
        document.write('Grand Total: ',TotalSale+SalesTax)
        document.write ('<P>')
        //--> stop hiding

</SCRIPT>
</PRE><P>
Thank you!
</BODY></HTML>
```

Figure 27-10: The calctax() function defined in the head, called up from the body of the page.

Want to see some more examples of functions? Trust me, you will. Most of the sample Web pages presented in the following chapters contain plenty of JavaScript functions for your perusal.

Custom function to reload a page

JavaScript statements in a Web page are generated from the top down. There is no way for JavaScript to change just a part of a page that's on the reader's screen already. That is, JavaScript cannot change a formatted page without reloading the entire page. You may come across a situation, however, in which you really need to update the page that the reader is viewing. For future reference, here's how to do it. First, create a function — perhaps named reloadme() — in the head of the page, like this:

```
<HTML><HEAD>
<SCRIPT Language = "JavaScript">

     //define the reloadme() custom function.
     function reloadme() {
          location = '#'
     }
</SCRIPT>
</HEAD>
```

When you need to reload the page, execute the reloadme( ) function. In the following example, I've created a button that, when clicked, reloads the current page:

```
<BODY><FORM>
<!Example of how a button would call reloadme().
<INPUT type="button" value= "Update Form" onClick="reloadme()">
</FORM></BODY></HTML>
```

In the preceding examples, *location* is a JavaScript object and *onClick* is a JavaScript event handler. Within the <BODY> tags, everything except the onClick event handler is HTML, not JavaScript.

Well, dear reader, I want you to know that I realize your head is probably spinning right now and that you're wondering if any of this will ever make sense to you. Once you see some examples of JavaScript in action, though, it will all start to make sense. I have lots of examples coming at you starting in the next chapter. There is, however, one more general JavaScript issue that I'd like to discuss before closing this chapter. This question may already be on your mind . . .

Is JavaScript the Same as Java?

I'm sure that many of you have heard of Java and Hot Java. Let me clarify that JavaScript is *not* the same as Java or Hot Java. Let's take a break from JavaScript for a moment and talk about Java so that you can see the differences.

Java is a complete programming language designed to create applications — standalone programs, such as your browser, word-processor, spreadsheet, and graphics programs. Currently, most standalone programs are written in a language called C or C++. Java is a language that is very similar to C++, except that it has cross-platform capability. Let me explain.

When you write a program in C/C++, you need to target that program for a specific platform (operating system). For example, you need to create a Windows version of the program, a separate Macintosh version of the program, and perhaps a Unix version and other versions. If you write the program in Java, however, you do not need to create those separate versions. The same program can run on all platforms. This advantage is a big one in today's online world, where different computer platforms are hooked together via the Internet.

Programming languages such as C, C++, and Java fall into a category called *low-level languages.* By *low-level,* I don't mean disadvantaged and I certainly don't mean easy. Low-level, in this context, means "more like the way computers work than the way people think." To the contrary, a high-level language is one that uses a form closer to English — closer to the way *people* think.

A low-level language such as C or Java can take years to learn and master. I'm sure that you'll hear all kinds of hype and hoopla to the contrary — that these languages are fun and easy. But trust me on this — when you really sit down to learn these programming languages, words such as fun and easy will not pop into your mind. That is, except in the context of "If this is fun and easy, then I must be completely brain dead."

Let me put it another way: When you first learned to use a computer, you probably started with a program such as your Web browser or perhaps a word-processing system such as Microsoft Word. Whatever program you used, I'm sure that you had to invest some time and brain cells to develop mastery. That time was invested in learning to *use* the program. When you get into low-level languages such as C, you're no longer trying to learn to *use* a program such as Word. You're trying to learn to *create,* from scratch, a program such as Word, which is a much larger undertaking. It is not unlike the difference that exists between learning to *use* a VCR versus learning to *create* a VCR from scrap metal.

If you look at this process in the context of being a Web author/publisher, you can safely say that any low-level language — be it assembly language, C, C++, or Java — provides *major* overkill for what 99.9 percent of users need to do. Big software companies like Netscape know this fact. As a result, they often create alternative *scripting* languages, like JavaScript, for the 99.9 percent of people who need a little more flexibility in designing their Web pages — but don't want to make a lifelong career of learning a more complex, low-level language. JavaScript *exists* because so many of us fall into the 99.9 percent category.

Hot Stuff

Even if you do plan to learn Java, you'd do well to learn JavaScript first. The *low-end* of the learning curve will be much easier. In addition, everything you learn during that phase carries over to learning the lower-level languages.

So, where does that other product, Hot Java, fit into this scheme? It doesn't. Hot Java is not a programming language. It is a Web browser, just like Microsoft Internet Explorer and Netscape Navigator. Hot Java was the *first* browser to support programs written in Java, but it is not the only one. Netscape Navigator 2.0 also provides Java support. I'm pretty sure that Microsoft Internet Explorer and many other browsers will soon follow suit.

Differences between JavaScript and Java

As I've said, one big difference between Java and JavaScript is simply that JavaScript is much easier to learn and use. JavaScript is more than adequate for most Web publishers' needs. To give you a feel for the difference, I'll show you the steps involved in creating a simple "Hello World" program in Java and then show you the steps for creating the same program in JavaScript.

"Hello World" in JavaScript

You've already done a simple "Hello World" program in JavaScript (Chapter 26), but let's review the basics. In JavaScript, all you need is some kind of simple text editor, like Notepad, so that you can open a Web page and type in a script, as in this example:

```
<HTML>
<HEAD>
<TITLE>My first Java script</TITLE>
</HEAD>
<BODY>
<SCRIPT LANGUAGE="JavaScript">
     document.write("Hello World")
</SCRIPT>
</BODY>
</HTML>
```

You can now save the HTML file because you are done. To play the script, open the Web page (HTML file) with Netscape Navigator 2.0. To make the script available to the world (that is, to everyone on the Web who has a JavaScript-capable browser), copy the HTML file to your Web server — just as you would any other normal Web page.

"Hello World" in Java

The process for creating a simple "Hello World" program in Java is pretty cumbersome. First, you need to get a copy of the Java Developerment Kit (JDK) from Sun Microsystems and install it on your PC. Then you need to tweak the AUTOEXEC.BAT file on your PC so that the Java directory appears in the DOS PATH statement.

With JDK installed, you can write your Hello World applet. First, you fire up your favorite text editor (in this case, Notepad) and type this little program:

```
import java.awt.Graphics;
public class Howdy extends java.applet.Applet {
public void paint (Graphics g) {
g.drawString("Hello World", 5, 25);
}
}
```

After typing, you save that program with some filename — perhaps *howdy.java* in this case. Then you need to compile that program. To do that, you need to go out to the old DOS command prompt and enter a command like this:

```
javac howdy.java
```

The javac program from JDK kicks in, creates a compiled copy of the program, and stores that copy in a file named *howdy.class.* Now you need to jump through some hoops to make your Web page run the program. First, you need to open (or create) the Web page. Then add the following commands shown in boldface:

```
<HTML>
<HEAD>
<TITLE>My first Java applet</TITLE>
</HEAD>
<BODY>
<APPLET CODE="howdy.class" WIDTH=150 HEIGHT = 25>
</APPLET>
</BODY>
</HTML>
```

To see the results, you save the HTML file and then open it with some browser that supports Java — such as Hot Java or Netscape Navigator 2.0. The browser locates and executes the howdy.class script.

I'm sure you'll agree that the Java approach is more complicated than that taken by JavaScript. Granted, both Java and JavaScript are programming languages. I'm not saying that either one is particularly fun, easy, or user-friendly — all programming is tedious, rough on the brain cells, and frustrating until you get the hang of it. But I think you'll agree that the JavaScript approach to doing things involves a great deal less hassle than the Java approach.

Quick summary comparison

For those of you who are familiar with modern programming languages, Table 27-4 provides a quick summary comparison of JavaScript and Java. If you're not a programmer, don't worry about it. You still can become a hotshot JavaScript programmer without understanding anything presented in the table.

Table 27-4
Quick Summary Comparison of JavaScript and Java

JavaScript	*Java*
Interpreted by client (reader's Web browser)	Compiled on server before execution on client
Code is integrated into HTML document	Applets are stored as separate files that are called upon from HTML pages
Secure: Cannot write to client's disk	Secure: Cannot write to client's disk
Object-based, but no classes or inheritance	Object-oriented applets consist of object classes with inheritance
Dynamic binding: Object references checked at runtime	Static binding: Object references must exist at compilation

Summary

A brainful of JavaScript important trivia still awaits you. In the next chapter, you start using this lofty knowledge to create some practical scripts. First, however, let's review what you learned in this chapter:

- JavaScript is a programming language that lets you write instructions for your Web page to carry out on the reader's PC.
- Like all programming languages, JavaScript consists of many elements, including variables, operators, expressions, statements, and functions.
- JavaScript is an object-oriented language, which means that it includes a syntax for referring to *things* that are visible on the screen or available on the reader's PC.
- All objects have properties (characteristics) and methods (things they can do). To refer to an object's property, you use the general syntax *object.property*. To refer to a method, you use the general syntax *object.method( )*.
- Event handlers in JavaScript let you call up your scripts in response to some event that occurs on the reader's PC while viewing your page. That is, event handlers determine *when* a script is executed.
- Most JavaScripts that you explore will contain a list of JavaScript custom functions, which are defined in the page's <HEAD> . . . </HEAD> area. Those functions then are called from within the <BODY> . . . </BODY> tags.
- JavaScript is not the same as Java. But if you're thinking of learning Java, you'd do well to learn JavaScript first.

✦ ✦ ✦

Fun with JavaScript

In This Chapter

Custom navigation buttons

An interactive conversion table

An on-screen JavaScript calculator

An on-screen digital clock

It's time to leave the general discussion, put on our propeller beanies, and start writing some real code. In this chapter, I want to show you some real JavaScript scripts and then pick them apart line-by-line so that you can see the logic behind them. This gives you a chance to "reverse engineer" some real JavaScript programs to see what makes them tick. This exercise also gives you some tools, techniques, and food for thought in creating your own scripts.

Custom Navigation Buttons

Let's start out with a simple yet useful script that places some navigation buttons on a Web page. Figure 28-1 shows the bottom of a sample Web page where I've added five custom navigation buttons. The buttons are as follows:

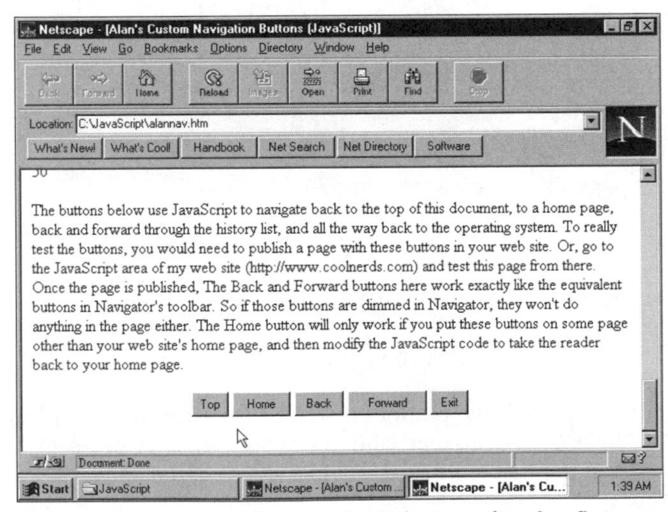

Figure 28-1: Bottom of a sample Web page showing five custom navigation buttons.

✦ **Top.** Returns the reader to the top of the page.

✦ **Home.** Returns the reader to this site's home page.

✦ **Back.** Sends reader back one page in the history list (same as the Back button in the Navigator toolbar).

✦ **Forward.** Sends reader forward one page in the history list (same as the Forward button in the Navigator toolbar).

✦ **Exit.** Presents an "Are you sure?" confirmation box and, if the reader clicks OK, closes the Web browser.

When the reader clicks the Top button, he or she is taken to the top of the page, which, in this example, looks like Figure 28-2. (The purpose of the numbered lines is to give the page some length so that you can test the Top button.)

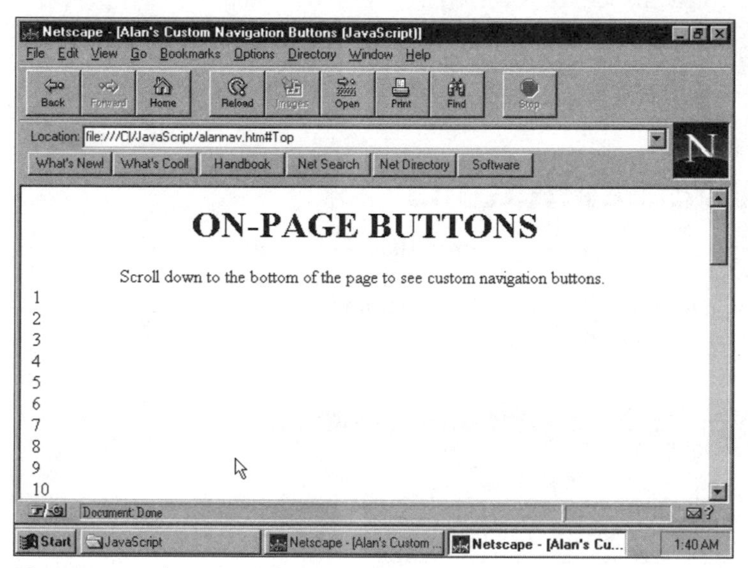

Figure 28-2: The top of the page that contains the sample navigation buttons.

Clicking the Exit button presents the reader with a message like

```
Are you sure you want to exit Navigator?
```

followed by OK and Cancel buttons. If the reader clicks OK, the Navigator window shuts down. If the reader clicks Cancel instead, the `Are you sure...` message disappears and Navigator and the current page remain on the screen.

The Home, Back, and Forward buttons act like their equivalents in the Navigator toolbar. It may seem silly to reproduce those buttons here, but when we start talking about JavaScript and frames (Chapter 30), you'll see how similar buttons can make it easier for your reader to navigate within a single frame.

Also, I should point out that if you type in this page and try it out, the Home, Back, and Forward buttons may not work locally. However, once published on your site, those buttons will work. If you like, you can open this page in my site to test the buttons. Point your browser to `http://www.coolnerds.com`, go to my JavaScript section, and locate the Custom Navigation Buttons example.

The confirm box

Let's look at the code behind the scenes for my custom navigation buttons. Figure 28-3 shows the top half of the source for the document in Notepad. As you can see, the page contains one custom JavaScript function named makesure(), which looks like this:

```
<SCRIPT Language = "JavaScript"><!-- hide from non-JS browsers.
     function makesure() {
          msg="Are you sure you want to exit Navigator?"
          response = confirm(msg)
          if (response == true) {
               self.close()
          }
     }
// end of makesure() function, stop hiding -->
</SCRIPT>
```

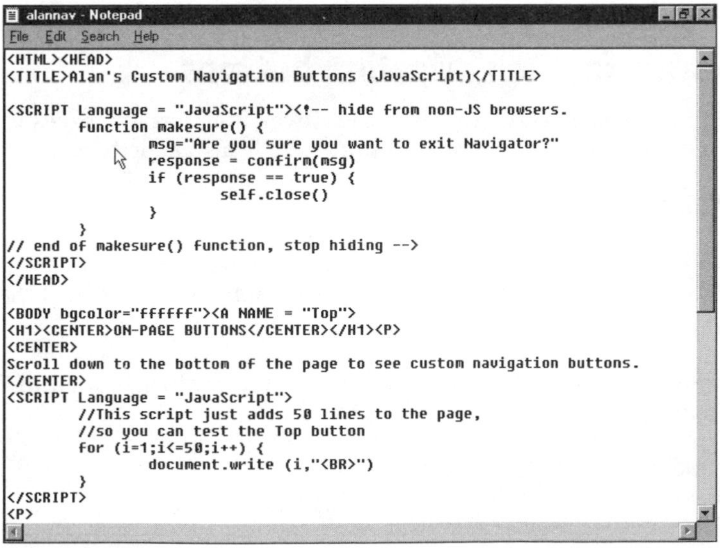

```
alannav - Notepad
File  Edit  Search  Help
<HTML><HEAD>
<TITLE>Alan's Custom Navigation Buttons (JavaScript)</TITLE>

<SCRIPT Language = "JavaScript"><!-- hide from non-JS browsers.
        function makesure() {
                msg="Are you sure you want to exit Navigator?"
                response = confirm(msg)
                if (response == true) {
                        self.close()
                }
        }
// end of makesure() function, stop hiding -->
</SCRIPT>
</HEAD>

<BODY bgcolor="ffffff"><A NAME = "Top">
<H1><CENTER>ON-PAGE BUTTONS</CENTER></H1><P>
<CENTER>
Scroll down to the bottom of the page to see custom navigation buttons.
</CENTER>
<SCRIPT Language = "JavaScript">
        //This script just adds 50 lines to the page,
        //so you can test the Top button
        for (i=1;i<=50;i++) {
                document.write (i,"<BR>")
        }
</SCRIPT>
<P>
```

Figure 28-3: Top half of the source for custom navigation buttons page.

Because makesure( ) is a custom JavaScript function, it is defined in the head of the document. This function is not *executed* right away — it is just *defined* so that other JavaScript code in the body of the document can call it up. The first thing makesure() does is create a variable name msg (for message) and put a plain-English message into that variable:

```
msg="Are you sure you want to exit Navigator?"
```

The next line displays that message in a confirm( ) dialog box. If the reader clicks the OK button, the variable named *response* contains the value **true**. If the reader clicks the Cancel button, the variable named *response* contains **false.**

```
response = confirm(msg)
```

The if( ) statement that follows says "If the *response* variable contains **true,** then close this window (using a JavaScript *self.close()* method).

```
if (response == true) {
      self.close()
}
```

If the reader clicks on Cancel, *response* contains **false,** so the self.close( ) statement will be ignored and basically nothing else happens on the screen (except that the *Are you sure . . .* message disappears). This is exactly what you want to happen in this case.

Hot Stuff

Here are a couple of little shortcuts for testing to see if a variable contains true or false. To test for true, you can just use the variable name, if you prefer. For example, instead of putting *if(response == true)* in my script, I could have put *if (response).* To test for false, you can use the long method (*if (response == false)*) or the not(!) operator with just the variable name (*if (!response)*).

Other prep stuff for the navigation buttons

There is more to the custom navigation buttons, however, than just the makesure( ) custom function. For starters, notice that in Figure 28-3 I've also added the tag

```
<A NAME = "Top">
```

next to the opening <BODY> tag. That tag is a regular HTML bookmark — not JavaScript code. As you'll see shortly, however, I'll use that bookmark as the target for my custom Top button.

I also need to type in this little routine, which has absolutely nothing to do with the navigation buttons:

```
<SCRIPT Language = "JavaScript">
     //This script just adds 50 lines to the page,
     //so you can test the Top button
     for (i=1;i<=50;i++) {
```

```
            document.write (i,"<BR>")
        }
</SCRIPT>
```

The purpose of this script is just to type 50 lines into the Web page so that I have a way to test the Top navigation button. This loop is the reason for the lines extending down the page in Figure 28-2. I felt it was easier to type up this little script than to type 50 or so lines into the document.

The navigation buttons

The navigation buttons themselves are handled with minimal JavaScript. These buttons consist of some button objects defined with <INPUT> tags, whose actions are defined with the onClick( ) method of JavaScript. Figure 28-4 shows the source for the bottom half of the page containing the custom buttons.

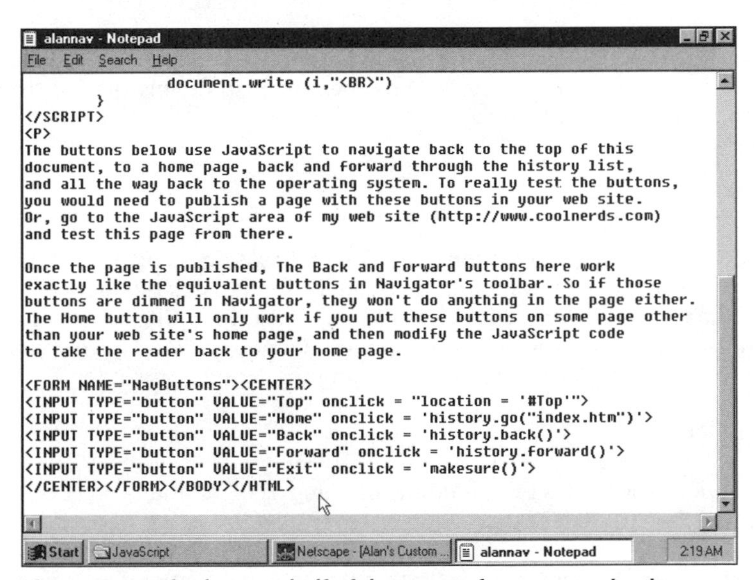

```
            document.write (i,"<BR>")
        }
</SCRIPT>
<P>
The buttons below use JavaScript to navigate back to the top of this
document, to a home page, back and forward through the history list,
and all the way back to the operating system. To really test the buttons,
you would need to publish a page with these buttons in your web site.
Or, go to the JavaScript area of my web site (http://www.coolnerds.com)
and test this page from there.

Once the page is published, The Back and Forward buttons here work
exactly like the equivalent buttons in Navigator's toolbar. So if those
buttons are dimmed in Navigator, they won't do anything in the page either.
The Home button will only work if you put these buttons on some page other
than your web site's home page, and then modify the JavaScript code
to take the reader back to your home page.

<FORM NAME="NavButtons"><CENTER>
<INPUT TYPE="button" VALUE="Top" onclick = "location = '#Top'">
<INPUT TYPE="button" VALUE="Home" onclick = 'history.go("index.htm")'>
<INPUT TYPE="button" VALUE="Back" onclick = 'history.back()'>
<INPUT TYPE="button" VALUE="Forward" onclick = 'history.forward()'>
<INPUT TYPE="button" VALUE="Exit" onclick = 'makesure()'>
</CENTER></FORM></BODY></HTML>
```

Figure 28-4: The bottom half of the source for same navigation buttons page.

Take a look at the code behind the navigation buttons, line by line. First, these HTML tags define a form and center the buttons defined in the following examples:

```
<FORM NAME="NavButtons"><CENTER>
```

The <FORM> tag is necessary because the <INPUT> tags do nothing if they're not enclosed within <FORM> tags. The first button, titled *Top,* is defined by this tag:

```
<INPUT TYPE="button" VALUE="Top" onClick = "location = '#Top'">
```

Notice that the onClick event handler for this tag is "location='#Top'". Here I'm using the JavaScript location object to send the reader to a bookmark named Top, which was defined near the <BODY> tag by using the <A NAME = "Top"> tag.

The Home button is defined by this tag:

```
<INPUT TYPE="button" VALUE="Home" onClick =
      'history.go("index.htm")'>
```

In this tag, the onClick event handler for this tag uses the *go()* method of the history object to send the reader to a page named index.htm. In your own Web site, you want to replace index.htm with the name of your site's home page.

The next tag defines the Back button, which uses the *back()* method of the JavaScript history object to send the reader back one page in the history list:

```
<INPUT TYPE="button" VALUE="Back" onClick = 'history.back()'>
```

The following tag defines the Forward button, which uses the *forward()* method of the JavaScript history object to send the reader to the next page in the history list (the page the reader just backed out of, if any):

```
<INPUT TYPE="button" VALUE="Forward" onClick =
      'history.forward()'>
```

The tag that follows defines the last button, Exit. Because exiting Navigator is a pretty big step to take, you want to make sure that the reader did not click this button by accident. Rather than just assigning self.close( ) to this button's onClick( ) event handler, you can use the makesure( ) custom function defined earlier. This gives the reader a chance to change his/her mind before closing the Navigator window.

```
<INPUT TYPE="button" VALUE="Exit" onClick = 'makesure()'>
```

The </CENTER> and </FORM> tags terminate the opening <FORM> and <CENTER> tags defined at the top of these <INPUT> tags.

That, in a nutshell, is how the custom navigation buttons work. Remember, though, that some of the buttons won't work until you publish them in an actual Web site.

More Info This section of the navigation buttons sample page uses the *function* statement and the button, history, and location objects referenced in Appendix C. The <FORM> and <INPUT> tags are HTML tags, not JavaScript, and therefore are referenced in Appendix B and Chapter 18.

A Conversion Table

Let's look at another Web page that uses JavaScript to provide a little interactivity. In this example, you present the reader with a simple page for converting miles to kilometers, or kilometers to miles. The reader can type any number of miles into the miles form field, click anywhere outside the field, and the form field to the right will show that value converted to kilometers. For example, in Figure 28-5, the reader has entered 10 as the miles entry and the kilometers field to the right shows that 10 miles equals 16 kilometers. Likewise, the reader can type in known kilometers in the lower form field and the miles form field to its right will show that value converted to miles.

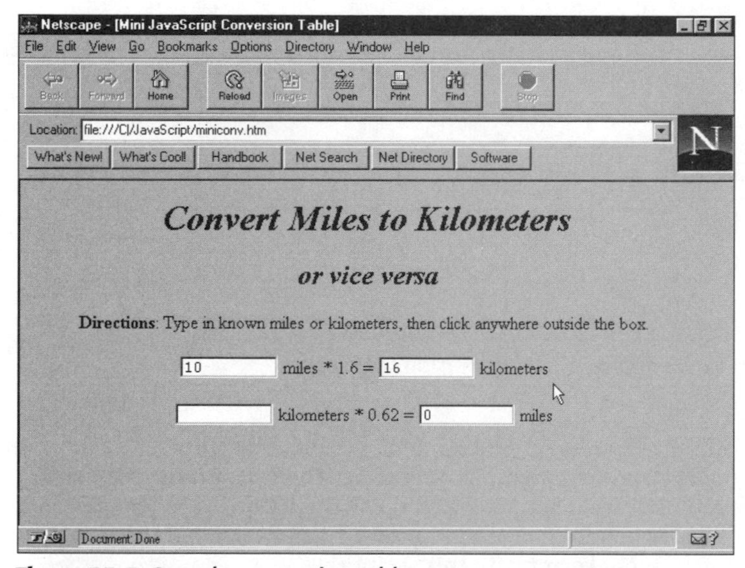

Figure 28-5: Sample conversion table page.

To see how this page does its thing, you need to look at its source. Figure 28-6 shows (roughly) the top half of the source for this page. Of particular importance is the custom calc( ) function, which does the calculations. Let's take a look at that custom function in detail.

Like any custom JavaScript function, calc( ) is defined between `<SCRIPT>` tags within the head of the document. It starts off with this comment and function statement:

```
//define the calc() custom function.
function calc(val,factor,putin) {
```

In this example, the calc( ) function expects to receive three values, including one named val, which is the value to be converted. For example, if the reader wants to convert ten miles to kilometers, val receives a value of 10.

The second parameter, factor, is the conversion factor. For example, when the reader wants to convert miles to kilometers, the factor value is 1.6. The last parameter, putin, is the name of the form field where calc displays the calculated result.

```
miniconv - Notepad
File  Edit  Search  Help
<HTML><HEAD>
<TITLE>Mini JavaScript Conversion Table</TITLE>
<SCRIPT LANGUAGE="JavaScript">  <!-- hide script
        //define the calc() custom function.
        function calc(val,factor,putin) {
        if (val == "") {
                val = "0"
        }
        evalstr = "document.ConverTable."+putin+ ".value = "
        evalstr = evalstr + val + "*" + factor
        eval(evalstr)
}
// end of calc() function. Unhide script -->
</SCRIPT>
</HEAD>

<BODY>
<! Show headings and directions>
<H1><CENTER><I>Convert Miles to Kilometers</I></CENTER></H1>
<H2><CENTER><I>or vice versa</I></CENTER></H2><P><P>
<CENTER>
<B>Directions</B>: Type in known miles or kilometers, then click anywhere out
</CENTER>

<! Set up the form fields>
<FORM NAME = "ConverTable">
<CENTER>
```

Figure 28-6: Part of the source of the conversion table page.

This script has one small potential problem that you need to trap before it becomes a problem. If the reader tries to convert a blank value, the script returns an error message. To prevent that from happening, you use the following if() statement to tell JavaScript that "if val is blank, change that to zero." JavaScript can handle the zero, so you've trapped the potential error with this script:

```
if (val == "") {
     val = "0"
}
```

Next, calc() builds an executable JavaScript command from the parameters it has received. Suppose that the name of the form field into which you want to place the result is ckilos, as passed to the putin argument. When JavaScript executes the first statement

```
evalstr = "document.ConverTable."+putin+ ".value = "
```

it causes the variable named evalstr to contain

```
document.ConverTable.ckilos.value =
```

The next statement expands evalstr to include the val parameter and the factor parameter:

```
evalstr = evalstr + val + "*" + factor
```

Let's say that 10 was passed as the val parameter and 1.6 as the factor parameter. After that statement executes, the variable named evalstr contains:

```
document.ConverTable.ckilos.value = 10 * 1.6
```

The last statement in the calc( ) function uses JavaScript's built-in eval( ) function to evaluate the string stored in the evalstr variable. By *evaluate,* I mean "to execute the string as though it were a JavaScript statement":

```
        eval(evalstr)
}
```

When the eval( ) function executes *document.ConverTable.ckilos.value = 10 * 1.6,* it puts the result of 10 times 1.6 into a form field named ConverTable.ckilos. Of course, it wouldn't work right now because you haven't created a form field named ConverTable.ckilos. That part is done in the body of the page. If I scroll down to the lower half of the conversion table page (Figure 28-7), you can see the <BODY> tags with <FORM> and <INPUT> tags.

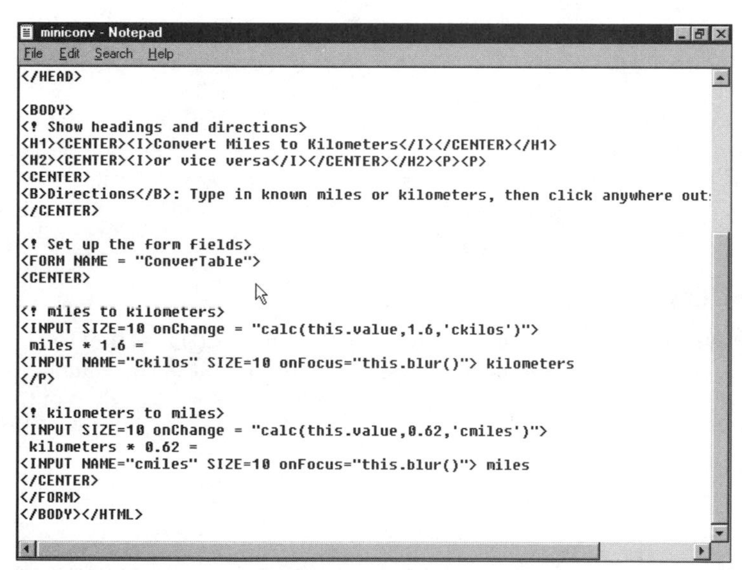


```
</HEAD>

<BODY>
<! Show headings and directions>
<H1><CENTER><I>Convert Miles to Kilometers</I></CENTER></H1>
<H2><CENTER><I>or vice versa</I></CENTER></H2><P><P>
<CENTER>
<B>Directions</B>: Type in known miles or kilometers, then click anywhere out:
</CENTER>

<! Set up the form fields>
<FORM NAME = "ConverTable">
<CENTER>

<! miles to kilometers>
<INPUT SIZE=10 onChange = "calc(this.value,1.6,'ckilos')">
 miles * 1.6 =
<INPUT NAME="ckilos" SIZE=10 onFocus="this.blur()"> kilometers
</P>

<! kilometers to miles>
<INPUT SIZE=10 onChange = "calc(this.value,0.62,'cmiles')">
 kilometers * 0.62 =
<INPUT NAME="cmiles" SIZE=10 onFocus="this.blur()"> miles
</CENTER>
</FORM>
</BODY></HTML>
```

Figure 28-7: The body of the conversion table Web page.

The <FORM NAME = "ConverTable"> tag defines a form which, in this page, is named ConverTable. Let's skip down to the first <INPUT> tag in this form:

```
<INPUT SIZE=10 onChange = "calc(this.value,1.6,'ckilos')">
```

Notice that the onChange event handler for the first form field is "calc(this.value, 1.6,'ckilos')". After the reader changes the value in this field, the calc( ) function is called with the current contents of the field (this.value) as the first parameter (val), 1.6 as the second parameter (factor), and ckilos as the third parameter (putin). Thus, if the reader enters 10 as the value to convert, calc( ) is going to put the product of 10 * 1.6 in a field named ckilos in the form named ConverTable.

Where is the ckilos form field? Right under the first `<INPUT>` tag in the source, as you can see in the following example. Notice how I used the NAME attribute to give the form field its name:

```
<INPUT NAME="ckilos" SIZE=10 onFocus="this.blur()"> kilometers
```

The form name ConverTable was already defined in the NAME attribute of this form. As a result, the "full object" name for this form field is actually document.ConverTable.ckilos, which is exactly where the calc( ) function places its results when called from first `<INPUT>` tag.

You use the same idea, with different parameters, to convert kilometers to miles in these two `<INPUT>` tags:

```
<! kilometers to miles>
<INPUT SIZE=10 onChange = "calc(this.value,0.62,'cmiles')">
<INPUT NAME="cmiles" SIZE=10 onFocus="this.blur()"> miles
```

Here the conversion factor is 0.62 and the putin field is cmiles. You can see that name in the `NAME` attribute of the second tag. When the reader changes the value in the "kilometers: field, the calc( ) function is called with the new value in that field (this.value), a conversion factor of 0.62, and *cmiles* as the name of the field to put the result into.

Read-only fields

Notice that only the first `<INPUT>` tag in each pair calls the calc( ) function to perform a calculation. The second form field is just for showing the result of the calculation. Thus, you really don't want your reader to type anything in the second field of that pair. To prevent the reader from typing into those form fields, I've added this little JavaScript statement to each of those two input tags:

```
onFocus="this.blur()"
```

where onFocus is an event handler that triggers as soon as the reader moves the insertion point into a form field. The blur( ) method moves the *focus* out of the form field. (It doesn't physically remove the insertion point, but it makes it impossible to change the contents of the form field.) What *onFocus="this.blur()"* says, in English, is "if the reader moves the focus into this form field, 'blur' the focus so he or she can't make changes." It sounds kinda weird, but it works.

More Info The main JavaScript elements used in this sample script are *function* and *if()* statements and eval( ) function, all referenced in Appendix C.

A bigger conversion table

The calc( ) custom function can be used to convert any value, provided that you know the conversion factor. Figure 28-8 shows a much larger conversion table example, artificially stretched to show as much of the page as possible. You can find the entire page on the *HTML Publishing Bible* CD-ROM and in my coolnerds Web site, under the filename alanconv.htm.

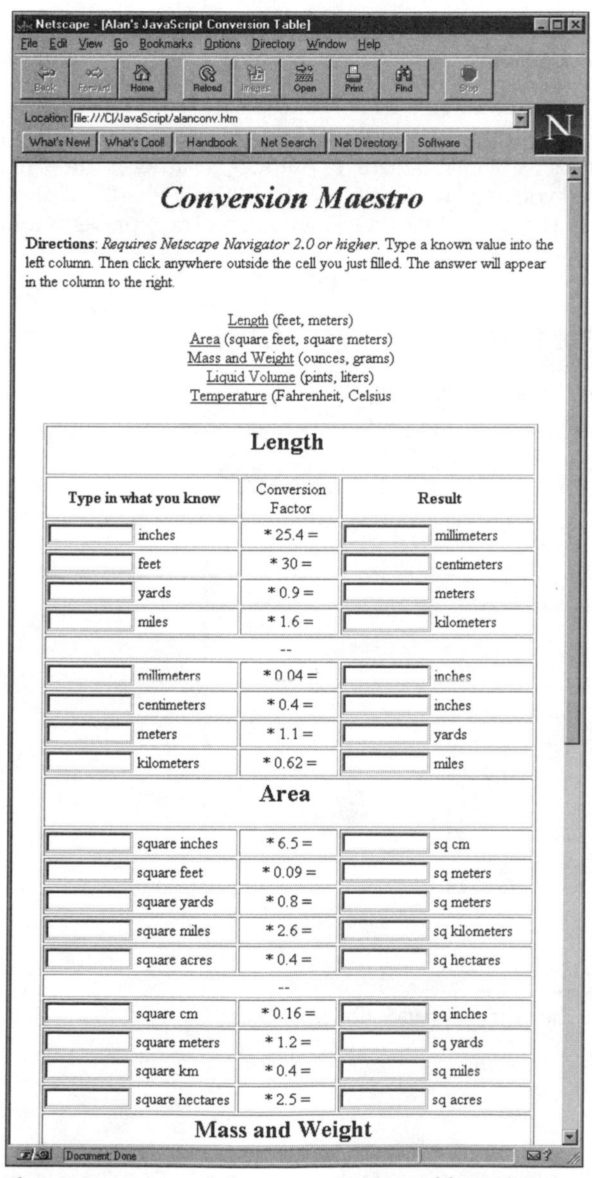

Figure 28-8: A much larger conversion table Web page.

If you view the source of alanconv.htm, you see a bunch of table tags (<TD> and <TR>) and you'll think I must have spent many hours creating that page. Actually, however, I didn't. I created most of the page — including the text, bookmarks and links, the table, and form fields — with Word IA. That task was pretty easy. Then I opened the HTML document that Word IA created and pasted in the calc( ) function and the various NAME = attributes, onChange, and onFocus event handlers. The creation process wasn't nearly as complicated as the source code makes it look.

An On-Screen Calculator

Just about every JavaScript programmer gets the urge to create a little on-screen calculator somewhere along the learning curve. When I went looking around the Web for JavaScript ideas, I found dozens of calculators. (That fact is rather ironic when you consider that in Windows 95, all you need to do is click Start⇨Programs⇨Accessories⇨Calculator.) My contribution to the world of JavaScript calculators is presented in Figure 28-9.

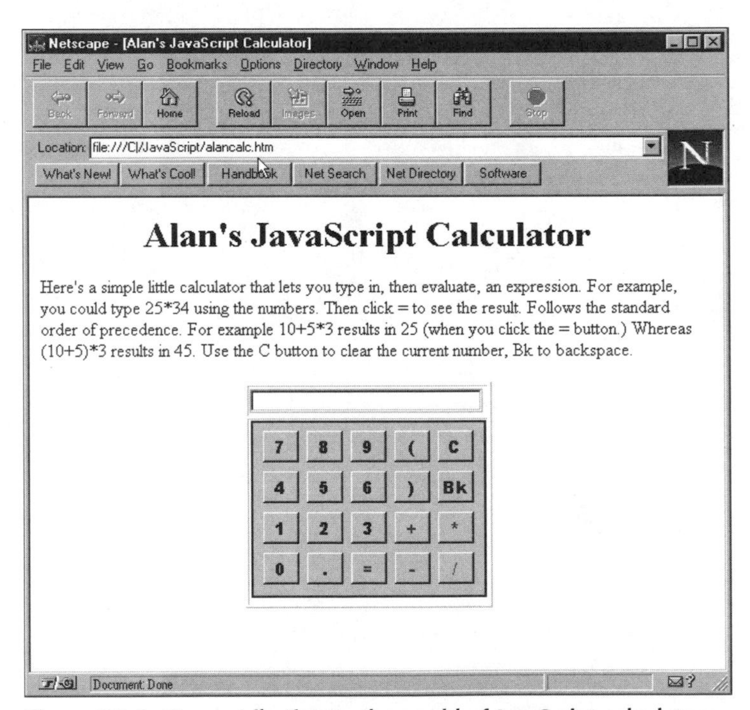

Figure 28-9: My contribution to the world of JavaScript calculators.

In the sections that follow, I explain exactly how I created this little calculator and then explain the underlying JavaScript code that makes it work.

Calculator's GIF image and map

First, I created a little GIF file named calcbttn.gif, shown in Figure 28-10, in Paint Shop Pro. (Actually, I created the buttons in Microsoft Access and then cut and pasted them into Paint Shop Pro to save as a GIF file.)

Figure 28-10: Calcbttn.gif in Paint Shop Pro.

Then I used Map This! (Chapter 24) to create a client-side image map for calcbttn.gif. Next, I created most of the actual Web page in Word IA. First, I typed in the text and then added a little table with two rows and one column. In the top cell, I used Insert➪Form field to insert a text box within. Then I used the Picture button to insert calcbttn.gif into the bottom cell. I had to tweak the sizes, alignments, and centering of things a bit, but eventually my page ended up looking like Figure 28-11 when viewed in Word IA.

Calculator JavaScript functions

With the preliminary work out of the way, it was time to start editing the page by using Notepad. First, I created some custom JavaScript functions to do the work of the calculator. Figure 28-12 shows that collection of functions near the top of the source of the Web page. Let me describe what each one does.

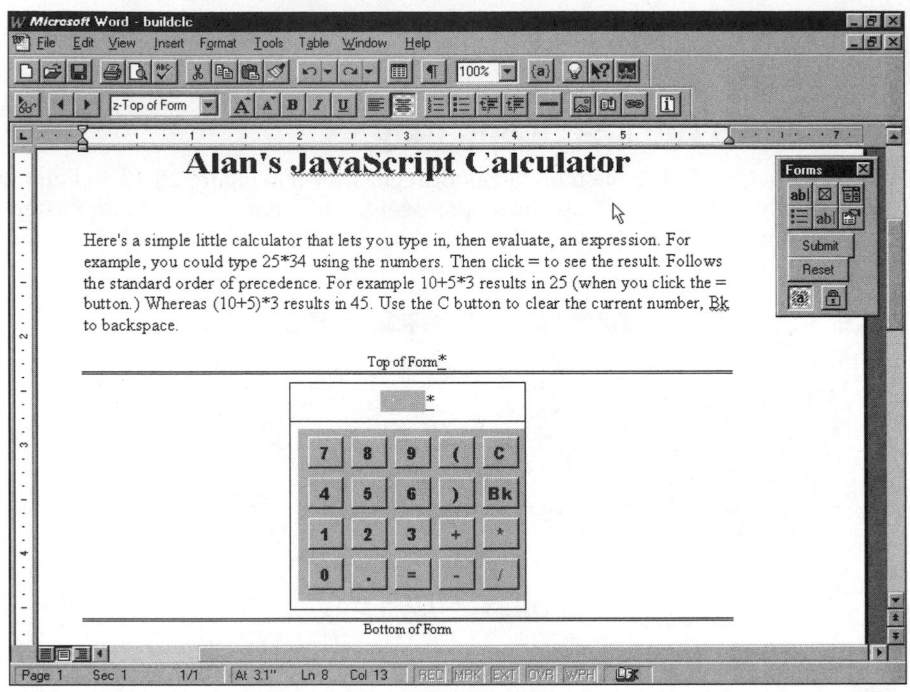

Figure 28-11: My JavaScript calculator Web page in Word IA.

```
alancalc - Notepad
File  Edit  Search  Help
<HTML>
<HEAD>
<META NAME="GENERATOR" CONTENT="Internet Assistant for Microsoft Word 2.0z">
<TITLE>Alan's JavaScript Calculator</TITLE>
<SCRIPT Language = "JavaScript">

function pad(anystr) {
        document.calc.shownum.value += anystr
}

function calcit() {
        document.calc.shownum.value = eval(document.calc.shownum.value)
}

function clearit() {
        document.calc.shownum.value = ""
}

function backspace() {
        curvalue = document.calc.shownum.value
        curlength = curvalue.length
        curvalue = curvalue.substring(0,curlength-1)
        document.calc.shownum.value = curvalue
}
</SCRIPT>
</HEAD>

<BODY BGCOLOR="blanchedalmond">
```

Figure 28-12: Custom JavaScript functions added to alancalc.htm.

Objects versus variables

A big difference exists between assigning a value to a variable and assigning a value to an object. Assigning a value to a variable is simple: Just script it as *variablename = value*, such as x=10. But a variable is a simple thing — just a temporary placeholder in memory to stick some string or number you want to use later in the script.

An object is an actual item on the screen. And, unlike a variable, an object can have several properties and methods, including, but not limited to, a value. As discussed earlier in this book, an object also may be a component of some larger object. For example, a text field is an object that belongs to a larger object — a form. A form is an object that belongs to yet a larger object — the document.

To refer to an object, you need to start from the largest object and point your way down to the specific object. For example, document.calc.shownum means "in the current document, within the object named *calc*, the specific object named *shownum*." But keep in mind that that one object can have many properties. To specifically refer to the *contents* of that object, you need to tack on the .value property. Hence, *document.calc.shownum.value* is how, in JavaScript, you say "the contents of a field named shownum, in the form named calc, in the current document."

The little pad() function that follows accepts a string named anystr:

```
function pad(anystr) {
     document.calc.shownum.value += anystr
}
```

In a moment, you see where anystr gets its value. The *document.calc.shownum.value += anystr* statement in the pad() function takes whatever is currently in the form field named calc.shownum and sticks whatever is in anystr onto the end of that field's current value. I used the shortcut += operator to do this. That operator means "*variable* equals itself plus *variable.*"

The second custom function shown in the following example, named calcit(), takes whatever is in the calc.shownum form field and replaces it with the evaluation of that value, using the JavaScript's built-in eval() function:

```
function calcit() {
     document.calc.shownum.value =
       eval(document.calc.shownum.value)
}
```

For example, if calc.shownum.value contains the string "5 * 10", the eval function executes it to come up with the product 50 and replaces the original string with the new value 50.

The third custom function named clearit() sticks an empty string (" ") into the cacl.shownum form field. Thus, it clears the contents of that field.

```
function clearit() {
     document.calc.shownum.value = ""
}
```

Finally, the custom backspace script that follows uses the length property and substring() method of JavaScripts string object to peel off the last character from the contents of the calc.shownum form field. From the reader's perspective, this process looks the same as that which takes place when you press the Backspace key in most programs:

```
function backspace() {
     curvalue = document.calc.shownum.value
     curlength = curvalue.length
     curvalue = curvalue.substring(0,curlength-1)
     document.calc.shownum.value = curvalue
}
</SCRIPT>
```

Pulling the calculator together

The next step was to assign appropriate names to the form and input field in the body of the page. You can see that I've named the following form *calc* (in the <FORM> tag) and named the field *shownum* (in the <INPUT> tag), both of which match the names I made up for my custom functions.

```
<FORM NAME = "calc"><P>
<CENTER><TABLE BORDER="1"><TR><TD WIDTH=213>
<CENTER>
<INPUT NAME="shownum" VALUE="" MAXLENGTH="25" SIZE=25>
</CENTER>
</TD></TR>
```

The <TABLE>, <TR>, and <TD> tags all are HTML tags for the table that contains the calculator. Word IA created those tags for me automatically.

Next, I imported the image map I created with Map This! and set each hot spot to call the appropriate custom function. You cannot use event handlers, such as onClick, in <AREA. . .> tags. You can, however, have a hot spot call a JavaScript function by setting the HREF attribute to *javascript:* followed by the name of the JavaScript function. For example, the following example shows the <AREA> tag for the 1 button in my calcbttn.gif image. Notice that it passes the character '1' to my custom pad() function.

```
<AREA SHAPE=RECT COORDS="10,80,40,106" HREF=javascript:pad('1')>
```

The next example illustrates the `AREA` tag for the = button in my calculator. This button, when clicked, calls up the calcit( ) function.

```
<AREA SHAPE=RECT COORDS="89,116,119,141" HREF=javascript:calcit()>
```

The following listing shows the whole collection of them after setting all `HREF=` attributes to the appropriate functions and parameters. It looks like a great deal of work, but Map This! did most of the labor.

```
<MAP NAME="calcmap">
<!-- #$-:Image Map file created by Map THIS! -->
<!-- #$-:Map THIS! free image map editor by Todd C. Wilson -->
<!-- #$-:Please do not edit lines starting with "#$" -->
<!-- #$VERSION:1.20 -->
<!-- #$AUTHOR:Alan Simpson -->
<!-- #$DATE:Sat Mar 16 10:56:04 1996 -->
<!-- #$PATH:C:\JavaScript\ -->
<!-- #$GIF:calcbttn.gif -->
<AREA SHAPE=RECT COORDS="10,80,40,106" HREF=javascript:pad('1')>
<AREA SHAPE=RECT COORDS="49,80,78,106" HREF=javascript:pad('2')>
<AREA SHAPE=RECT COORDS="88,79,117,106" HREF=javascript:pad('3')>
<AREA SHAPE=RECT COORDS="128,81,158,105" HREF=javascript:pad('+')>
<AREA SHAPE=RECT COORDS="11,115,39,141" HREF=javascript:pad("0")>
<AREA SHAPE=RECT COORDS="49,115,78,142" HREF=javascript:pad('.')>
<AREA SHAPE=RECT COORDS="89,116,119,141" HREF=javascript:calcit()>
<AREA SHAPE=RECT COORDS="128,116,158,142" HREF=javascript:pad('-')>
<AREA SHAPE=RECT COORDS="167,80,194,105" HREF=javascript:pad('*')>
<AREA SHAPE=RECT COORDS="167,116,196,141" HREF=javascript:pad('/')>
<AREA SHAPE=RECT COORDS="11,43,39,71" HREF=javascript:pad('4')>
<AREA SHAPE=RECT COORDS="50,45,77,69" HREF=javascript:pad('5')>
<AREA SHAPE=RECT COORDS="88,44,117,71" HREF=javascript:pad('6')>
<AREA SHAPE=RECT COORDS="127,44,158,71" HREF=javascript:pad(')')>
<AREA SHAPE=RECT COORDS="165,43,196,70" HREF=javascript:backspace()>
<AREA SHAPE=RECT COORDS="10,7,40,33" HREF=javascript:pad('7')>
<AREA SHAPE=RECT COORDS="48,7,81,35" HREF=javascript:pad('8')>
<AREA SHAPE=RECT COORDS="87,7,117,34" HREF=javascript:pad('9')>
<AREA SHAPE=RECT COORDS="127,7,156,34" HREF=javascript:pad('(')>
<AREA SHAPE=RECT COORDS="166,7,195,35" HREF=javascript:clearit()>
</MAP>
```

The last step was to assign the calcmap map to the calcbttn.gif image. As you can see in the following example, this task simply involved adding a `USEMAP` attribute to the `<IMG SRC>` tag:

```
<IMG SRC="calcbttn.gif" USEMAP = "#calcmap">
```

I haven't explained every line of my little calculator Web page here because there are numerous table (<TR> and <TD>) and other incidentals in the source that tend to clutter things up. Word IA also put all those tags in for me automatically. Figure 28-13 shows how the bottom portion of the alancalc.htm file looks in Notepad. You can see a little bit of the image map (<AREA. . .> tags), as well as the tags for the *calc* form, the table, and the shownum text field.

```
alancalc - Notepad
File  Edit  Search  Help
<AREA SHAPE=RECT COORDS="127,7,156,34" HREF=javascript:pad('(')>
<AREA SHAPE=RECT COORDS="166,7,195,35" HREF=javascript:clearit()>
</MAP>
<H1><CENTER>Alan's JavaScript Calculator</CENTER></H1>
<P>
Here's a simple little calculator that lets you type in, then
evaluate, an expression. For example, you could type 25*34 using
the numbers. Then click = to see the result. Follows the standard
order of precedence. For example 10+5*3 results in 25 (when you
click the = button.) Whereas (10+5)*3 results in 45. Use the C
button to clear the current number, Bk to backspace.

<FORM NAME = "calc"><P>
<CENTER>
        <TABLE BORDER="1">
        <TR><TD WIDTH=213>
        <CENTER>
                <INPUT NAME="shownum" VALUE="" MAXLENGTH="25" SIZE=25>
        </CENTER>
        </TD></TR>
        <TR><TD WIDTH=213>
        <CENTER>
                <IMG SRC="calcbttn.gif" USEMAP = "#calcmap">
        </CENTER>
        </TD></TR>
        </TABLE>
</CENTER>
</FORM>
```

Figure 28-13: The <FORM>, <TABLE>, and <INPUT> tags for alancalc.htm.

If you want to try the calculator yourself and view its complete source, open alancalc.htm from the JavaScript folder on the *HTML Publishing Bible* CD-ROM or from my Web site at `http://www.coolnerds.com`. Don't forget that you must use a JavaScript-capable browser — which means, as I write this chapter, Netscape Navigator 2.0. In Netscape, to view a page's source, you choose View⇨Document Source from Navigator's menu bar.

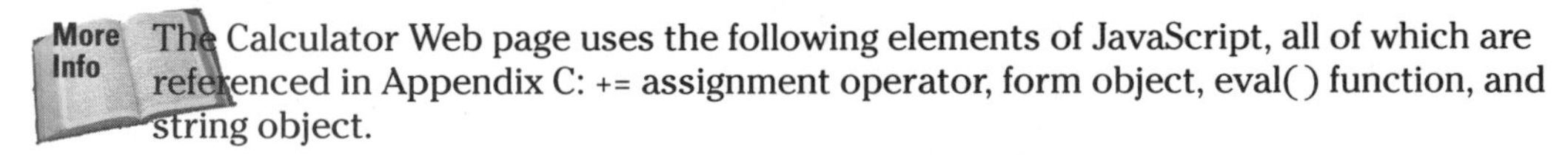

The Calculator Web page uses the following elements of JavaScript, all of which are referenced in Appendix C: += assignment operator, form object, eval( ) function, and string object.

Ticking Clock

Another favorite of JavaScript programmers is the small digital clock that keeps on running right on your Web page. In my JavaScript clock example (Figure 28-14), the clock shows the current time based on the current PC's system clock. The clock is updated every second. To see the clock running on your own screen, use any JavaScript-capable Web browser (Netscape Navigator 2.0) to open alantick.htm in the JavaScript folder of the *HTML Publishing Bible* CD-ROM or in the JavaScript area of `http://www.coolnerds.com`.

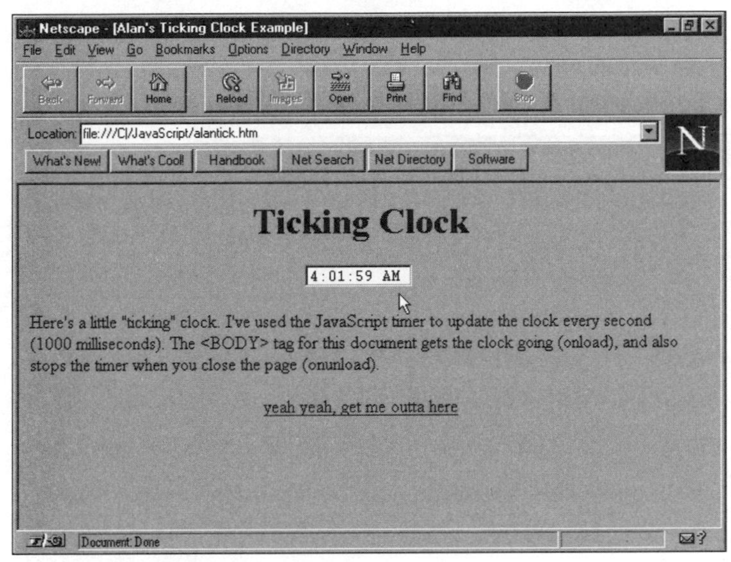

Figure 28-14: A running digital clock.

To keep the clock running, use JavaScript's setTimeout( ) method, which requires the syntax

```
timeoutID=setTimeout(expression, msec)
```

where *timeoutID* is the name of a variable used only to stop the timer later; *expression* is a JavaScript expression, or the name of a JavaScript custom function to run; and *msec* is the number of milliseconds it should pause before executing *expression*. Note that setTimeout( ) doesn't actually execute the expression repeatedly by itself. It just delays the execution. For example, this JavaScript statement

```
timerID = setTimeout("myFunc()",5000)
```

says "Wait five seconds (5,000 milliseconds) and then execute the function named myFunc( )." To get the setTimeout( ) method to keep repeating, you need to use a programming technique called *recursion*, where a function calls itself. Using a timer also requires that you build in some functions to start and stop the timer. Thus, you have some work to do here.

Figure 28-15 shows the start of the source for alantick.htm, where I've created a function to stop the timer [stopTimer()], another to start the timer [startTimer()], and a third function to display the current time in a form field [runClock()]. I'll show you the form field in a moment. For now, take a look at these three custom functions line-by-line.

I often refer to this example as the *ticking clock,* but only because the clock is updated every second. It does not make an actual ticking sound.

```
alantick - Notepad
File  Edit  Search  Help
<HTML><HEAD>
<TITLE>Alan's Ticking Clock Example</TITLE>
<SCRIPT LANGUAGE="JavaScript"> <!-- hide from non JS browsers.

//Define a couple of global variables.
var timerID = null
var timerRunning = false

function stopTimer(){
        //stop the clock
        if(timerRunning) {
                clearTimeout(timerID)
                timerRunning = false
        }
}

function startTimer(){
     // Stop the clock (in case it's running), then make it go.
    stopTimer()
    runClock()
}

function runClock(){
        document.clock.face.value = timeNow()
        //Notice how setTimeout() calls its own calling function, runClock().
        timerID = setTimeout("runClock()",1000)
        timerRunning = true
}
```

Figure 28-15: Some of the source for my ticking clock sample page.

The global variables

The JavaScript code in the head of alantick.htm starts off with these lines:

```
<SCRIPT LANGUAGE="JavaScript"> <!-- hide from non JS browsers.

//Define a couple of global variables.
var timerID = null
var timerRunning = false
```

These lines create two variables. The first is named timerID, which initially has a value of null. (That is, timerID exists as a variable but has not been assigned a value yet.) The second variable is timerRunning, which JavaScript initially assigns a value of false. Creating these variables at the outset makes them *global* — which means that any script or function in the page can call up these variables at any time. As you'll see, some do just that.

Custom stopTimer( ) function

Any page that uses a timer needs some means of stopping the timer when it is no longer needed. But you cannot really stop a timer if it isn't running. As a result, the following stopTimer( ) function first checks to see if the timerRunning variable is true. If timerRunning is true, it turns off the timer by using the JavaScript clearTimeout( ) method. The function then sets the timerRunning variable to false, to indicate that the timer is no longer running as follows:

```
function stopTimer(){
     //stop the clock
     if(timerRunning) {
          clearTimeout(timerID)
          timerRunning = false
     }
}
```

Custom startTimer( ) function

Every script that uses a timer should have some function to get the timer started. However, that function needs to make sure that the timer *isn't* already running before the function makes it start running. The following startTimer( ) custom function does just that:

```
function startTimer(){
     // Stop the clock (in case it's running), then make it go.
    stopTimer()
    runClock()
}
```

The stopTimer( ) statement calls up the stopTimer( ) custom function, which ensures that the timer is indeed stopped. It then calls up the runClock( ) function, which I describe next, to get the clock running and keep it ticking.

Custom runClock( ) function

The real meat of the ticking clock script is in the custom cumClock function that follows. Let's take a look at it line-by-line:

```
function runClock(){
     document.clock.face.value = timeNow()
     //Notice how setTimeout() calls its own calling function,
       runClock().
     timerID = setTimeout("runClock()",1000)
     timerRunning = true
}
```

The statement *document.clock.face.value = timeNow( )* finds a field named face in a form named clock in the current document and then sets the value of the field to timeNow( ). You haven't seen timeNow( ) or the form yet. But you can be confident that when you finish this script and run it, this line will be able to put the current time in a form field named clock.face.

This next line is where the timer actually starts ticking. It tells JavaScript to "start a timer that will execute the function named runClock in one second (1,000 milliseconds)." The timerID gets a value here. The only purpose that timerID serves, however, is to let you stop the timer by using a clearTimeout( ) method (which you used back in the stopTimer( ) custom function). What makes the timer "tick"— keep repeating itself — is the fact that it calls itself every second. That is, this runClock( ) function runs itself over and over again, pausing for one second between each run.

```
        //Notice how setTimeout() calls its own calling function,
          runClock().
        timerID = setTimeout("runClock()",1000)
        timerRunning = true
   }
```

Notice that within this function, you also set the timerRunning variable to true. As you've already seen, the stopTimer( ) custom function uses timerRunning to determine whether or not the timer is running. Setting timerRunning to true here is the JavaScript way of saying "Yes, the timer is running right now."

Custom timeNow() function

You may recall that in order to show the time, the runClock( ) custom function executes the statement *document.clock.face.value = timeNow( ).* It would be handy if timeNow( ) was a built-in JavaScript function that always shows the current time. Unfortunately though, no such function exists in JavaScript, so I had to create one. Like the other custom functions, this function is defined in the head of the page, as you can see in Figure 28-16.

All that timeNow( ) does is grab the system time out of the computer's clock and put it into human-readable form. For your purposes, human-readable form is the standard *hh:mm:ss am/pm* format, where hh is the hour, mm is the minute, ss is the second and am/pm is either a.m. or p.m. For example, you probably know that 12:30:00 p.m. means 12:30 in the afternoon. Let's take a look, line by line, at how timeNow( ) accomplishes this little feat.

The first line under the comment creates a new time object, named now, that contains the current system date and time:

```
   function timeNow() {
        //Grabs the current time and formats it into hh:mm:ss am/pm
          format.
        now = new Date()
```

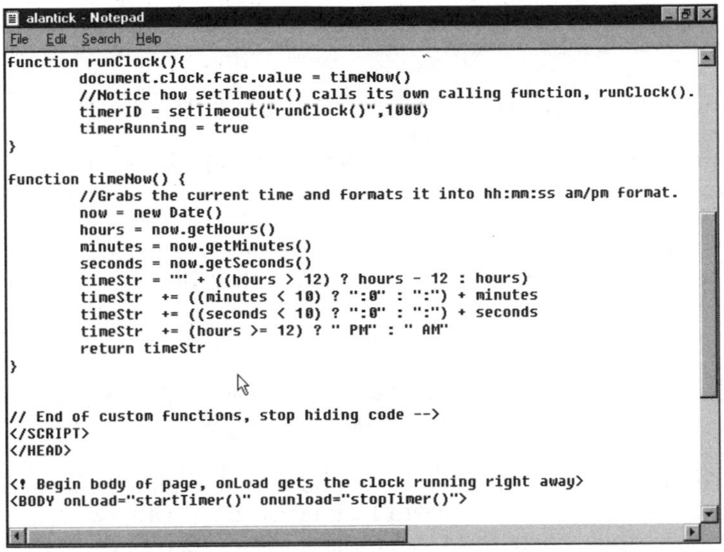

```
alantick - Notepad
File Edit Search Help
function runClock(){
        document.clock.face.value = timeNow()
        //Notice how setTimeout() calls its own calling function, runClock().
        timerID = setTimeout("runClock()",1000)
        timerRunning = true
}

function timeNow() {
        //Grabs the current time and formats it into hh:mm:ss am/pm format.
        now = new Date()
        hours = now.getHours()
        minutes = now.getMinutes()
        seconds = now.getSeconds()
        timeStr = "" + ((hours > 12) ? hours - 12 : hours)
        timeStr  += ((minutes < 10) ? ":0" : ":") + minutes
        timeStr  += ((seconds < 10) ? ":0" : ":") + seconds
        timeStr  += (hours >= 12) ? " PM" : " AM"
        return timeStr
}

// End of custom functions, stop hiding code -->
</SCRIPT>
</HEAD>

<! Begin body of page, onLoad gets the clock running right away>
<BODY onLoad="startTimer()" onunload="stopTimer()">
```

Figure 28-16: More source behind alantick.htm, including the custom timeNow() function.

Using the getHours( ), getMinutes, and getSeconds methods of the JavaScript date object, you pull out the current hour, minutes, and seconds and store those in the variables:

```
hours = now.getHours()
minutes = now.getMinutes()
seconds = now.getSeconds()
```

Suppose that when JavaScript executed the now = newDate( ) statement, the time was 2:30:00 p.m. Right now, the variable hours contains 14 (because getHours returns a value based on a 24-hour "military" clock), the variable minutes contains 30, and the variable seconds contains 0. The lines that appear in the next few examples build a variable named timeStr that contains that information organized into the hh:mm:ss am/pm format you are after.

This first line uses the tricky ? (immediate if) operator to decide what to put into the start of timeStr:

```
timeStr = "" + ((hours > 12) ? hours - 12 : hours)
```

In English, that line says "The variable timeStr contains nothing (to make sure that it starts off as nothing, as in a string) plus if hours is greater than 12, then hours minus 12, otherwise it contains just the hours." In this example, where hours contains 14, timeStr contains 14-12 after JavaScript executes this statement. Or, more specifically, timeStr contains 2.

The next line tacks on a colon and the minutes. It adds a 0 to the front of the minutes if the minutes value is less than 10:

```
timeStr  += ((minutes < 10) ? ":0" : ":") + minutes
```

Looking at the current example, where minutes contains 30 (which is more than 10), the timeStr variable now contains 2:30.

The next line uses a similar technique to tack on a colon and the seconds, again padding the seconds with a leading zero if seconds is less than 10:

```
timeStr  += ((seconds < 10) ? ":0" : ":") + seconds
```

In the current example, seconds contains 0, which is less than 10. As a result, timeStr gets a :00 tacked onto it, so it now contains 2:30:00.

This next line tacks on either AM or PM, depending on the value in the hours variable. If the hours variable is greater than or equal to 12, it tacks on PM. Otherwise, it tacks on AM. In this example, hours contains 14. After this statement executes

```
timeStr  += (hours >= 12) ? " PM" : " AM"
```

then timeStr variable contains 2:30:00 PM. The last lines in the function

```
      return timeStr
}
```

send the timeStr variable back to the call to the timeNow( ) function, replacing timeNow( ) with that returned value.

The body of the ticking clock page

Everything you've defined so far for the ticking clock has been a function. This page needs a body that calls up those functions. Figure 28-17 shows the rest of the source behind alantick.htm, where you can see a little bit of the head and the entire body of that page.

You can find part of the "meat" of alantick.htm right in the <BODY> tag. That tag uses the JavaScript onLoad method to get the clock started as soon as the reader opens the page. It also ensures that the clock shuts down as soon as the reader leaves (unloads) the page:

```
<BODY onLoad="startTimer()" onunload="stopTimer()">
```

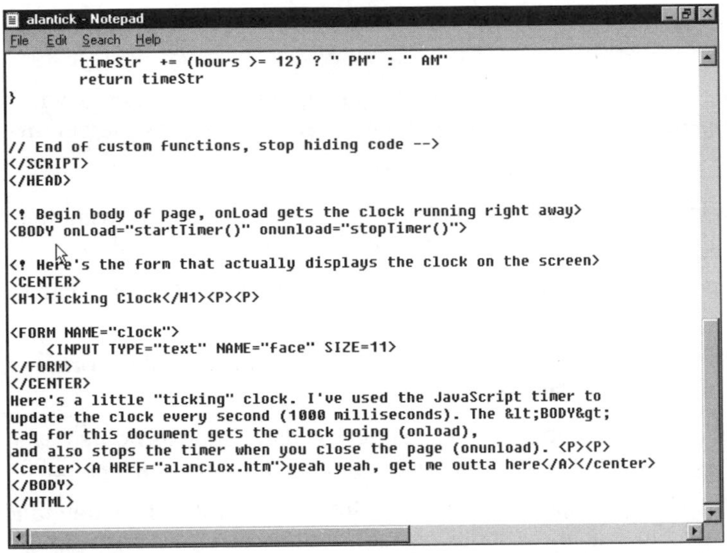

```
alantick - Notepad
File  Edit  Search  Help
        timeStr  += (hours >= 12) ? " PM" : " AM"
        return timeStr
}


// End of custom functions, stop hiding code -->
</SCRIPT>
</HEAD>

<! Begin body of page, onLoad gets the clock running right away>
<BODY onLoad="startTimer()" onunload="stopTimer()">

<! Here's the form that actually displays the clock on the screen>
<CENTER>
<H1>Ticking Clock</H1><P><P>

<FORM NAME="clock">
    <INPUT TYPE="text" NAME="face" SIZE=11>
</FORM>
</CENTER>
Here's a little "ticking" clock. I've used the JavaScript timer to
update the clock every second (1000 milliseconds). The &lt;BODY&gt;
tag for this document gets the clock going (onload),
and also stops the timer when you close the page (onunload). <P><P>
<center><A HREF="alanclox.htm">yeah yeah, get me outta here</A></center>
</BODY>
</HTML>
```

Figure 28-17: The bottom of the source for alantick.htm.

In the runClock( ) function earlier, you told JavaScript to put the current time in a field named document.clock.face. (To do so, you put the statement *document.clock.face.value = timeNow()* in that function.) That function will expect to find that field somewhere on the screen. Here, using standard HTML <FORM> tags, is where you create that field:

```
<FORM NAME="clock">
    <INPUT TYPE="text" NAME="face" SIZE=11>
</FORM>
```

Whew! Quite a hassle just to show a little clock on the screen (especially when you consider that, in Windows 95, the current time is usually displayed right in the taskbar). But the value of this example isn't so much the clock itself. Rather, it's the fact that the script illustrates many programming tricks-of-the-trade. When you can read and understand the source behind the JavaScript scripts presented in this chapter, you'll be able to read and understand many of the scripts you find on the World Wide Web. That's exactly how most programmers become fluent in a programming language — by looking at a working example and then peeking behind the scenes at the source, to see just how that particular script was written.

As I've said, programming is not a skill you can learn overnight. Dawn rises slowly on Marblehead. And when it comes to programming computers, we all start off as marbleheads. Hopefully, these last three chapters have given you enough background information about JavaScript to start seeing a little light on the horizon.

Summary

In this chapter, we've explored some real working scripts to see just how JavaScript scripts are put together. Let's review some of the general techniques used in this chapter:

- Not all JavaScript happens between `<SCRIPT>` tags. The various event handlers can be used right in regular HTML tags such as `<INPUT>` and `<BODY>`.
- JavaScript is closely tied to HTML forms, which can be used to feed data to, and display data from, a JavaScript program.
- The `NAME` attribute of the `<FORM>` and `<INPUT>` tags are critical factors in helping JavaScript interact with data in forms.
- A great deal of programming involves taking raw data (such as hours=12, minutes=30) and organizing it into human-readable formats (such as 12:30).
- Organizing all the jobs that scripts must do into small, isolated custom functions can help turn a big goal into a series of smaller, more easily attained goals.

✦ ✦ ✦

Handy Custom JavaScript Functions

✦ ✦ ✦ ✦

In This Chapter

Custom functions included with this book

Copying the custom functions into your own pages

Using the custom functions in your own Web pages

Custom date functions

Custom math functions

Custom string functions

A custom banner() function for displaying scrolling text

✦ ✦ ✦ ✦

A great deal of programming effort deals with taking the raw data stored in variables and organizing it into some kind of human-readable format. Here's an example: Suppose that you have an on-screen order form that lets readers enter a quantity and a unit price. You can use JavaScript to display an extended price simply by storing those values in a couple of variables and then creating a third variable for the product of the two, such as extprice=qty*unitprice. The only problem is that JavaScript may insist on displaying the result with way too many decimals, such as 1234.5630000003. To make that result more human-readable, you can create a custom function, perhaps named currency( ), that displays the number in the more familiar $1,234.56 format.

Fortunately for you, you don't have to create a currency( ) function because I already have. You can just use mine. In this chapter, I share with you a whole bunch of custom JavaScript functions that I've created. If you're not a programmer already, the usefulness of some of these functions may elude you. But you'll see some examples of their use in later chapters, and you'll no doubt find similar custom functions when you explore other peoples' scripts on the Web.

Summary of Custom Functions

Table 29-1 presents a quick summary of the custom functions presented in this chapter. By the time you read this, I may have come up with more. (I'm also always open to suggestions if you have a good idea for a custom function.) To check out the latest offerings or make a suggestion, stop by my Web site at `http://www.coolnerds.com`.

Table 29-1
My Custom Functions and What They Do

Custom Function	*What It Does*	*Type*
banner(*msg*,*width*)	Displays *msg* as a scrolling marquee in a box that's *width* characters wide	Show
contains(*smstring*, *lrgstring*)	Returns **true** if *lrgstring* contains *smstring*	String
currency(*num*)	Returns number *num* as string in $12,345.67 format	Math
dateObj(*string*)	Returns the date object of a date expressed as a string in mm/dd/yy format	Date
dateStr(*date*)	Returns a string in mm/dd/yy format from date object *date*	Date
daysBetween(*date1*, *date2*)	Returns the number of days between two date objects *date1* and *date2*	Date
decimal(*num*)	Returns the decimal portion of *num* with integer truncated	Math
fixed(*num*)	Returns number *num* as a string in 12,345.67 format	Math
fullYear(*date*)	Returns the year (such as 1996) from any date object *date*	Date
integer(*num*)	Returns just the integer portion of *num* with the decimal portion truncated	Math
isdiv(*num*,*n*)	Returns **true** if *num* is evenly divisible by *n*	Math
iseven(*num*)	Returns **true** if *num* is an even number	Math
isodd(*num*)	Returns **true** if *num* is an odd number	Math
lcase(*str*)	Returns *str* in all lowercase letters	String
left(*str*,*n*)	Returns the leftmost *n* characters from string *str*	String
leftOf(*smstring*, *lrgstring*)	Returns the leftmost characters of *lrgstring* up to character specified in *smstring*	String
mid(*str*,*start*,*n*)	Returns a substring of *str* starting at *start* that's *n* characters long	String
monthAbb(*date*)	Returns the month abbreviation (such as Dec) from any date object *date*	Date
monthDay(*date*)	Returns the day number (1–31) from any date object *date*	Date

Custom Function	What It Does	Type
monthName(*date*)	Returns the month name (for example, December) from any date object *date*	Date
monthNum(*date*)	Returns the month number (1–12) from any date object *date*	Date
now()	Returns the current system date/time as a date object	Date
nowStr()	Returns the current system time as a string in *hh:mm:ss am/pm* format	Date
pcase(*str*)	Returns *str* in proper-noun case (first letter of each word capitalized)	String
rawnum(*str*)	Removes dollar signs and commas from *str* and returns a real number	Math
right(*str,n*)	Returns the rightmost *n* characters of string *str*	String
rightOf(*smstring*, *lrgstring*)	Returns the characters from last *smstring* to the end of *lrgstring*	String
spot(*smstring*, *lrgstring*)	Returns a number indicating the spot where *smstring* appears in *lrgstring*	String
todayStr()	Returns the current system date as a string in mm/dd/yy format	Date
ucase(*str*)	Returns *str* in all uppercase letters	String
weekDay(*date*)	Returns the day name (such as Friday) from any date object *date*	Date
weekDayAbb(*date*)	Returns the day abbreviation (such as Fri) from any date object *date*	Date
weekDayNum(*date*)	Returns the day number (1 = Sunday, 7 = Saturday) from any date object *date*	Date
whenIs(*date*, *n*)	Returns the date that is *n* days from date object *date*	Date
year(*date*)	Returns the two-digit year number (such as 96) from any date object *date*	Date

Where to find these functions

The custom functions presented in this chapter are organized into four files, based on the type of function. Table 29-2 lists the names of the files.

Table 29-2
Location of Custom Functions According to Type

Type	*Filename*
Date	alandate.htm
Math	alanmath.htm
String	alanstr.htm
Show	alanshow.htm

You can find these files in the JavaScript folder of the *HTML Publishing Bible* CD-ROM. You also can find them in the JavaScript section of `http://www.coolnerds.com`.

Copying a function to your page

To use one of these custom functions, you need to type or copy the function into the `<HEAD>...</HEAD>` section of your Web page. I suspect that it will be easier to copy them, so let me show you how to do that.

First, you need to open the file in which the function is stored (as listed in Table 29-2). If you open the page with a Web browser, such as Netscape, you need to view the document source to get to the source. Once there, you can just select the function (or functions) you want to swipe and press Ctrl+C to copy the selection to the Clipboard. Make sure that you copy the entire function, including the last curly brace that ends the function. For example, in Figure 29-1, I've selected the function named daysBetween() from the alandate.htm file.

Optionally, you can open the appropriate page by using Notepad. Select the function(s) you want to copy, as in the example shown in Figure 29-2. Then choose Edit⇨Copy or press Ctrl+C to copy the selection to the Clipboard.

Next, you need to open (or create), using Notepad or some other plain text editor, the page in which you want to use the function. Move the insertion point to somewhere between the `<HEAD>...</HEAD>` tags. Then press Ctrl+V or choose Edit⇨Paste. The custom JavaScript function should appear right in your page.

Don't forget that you also need to define JavaScript functions between a pair of `<SCRIPT Language = "JavaScript">` and `</SCRIPT>` tags. If you haven't already typed those tags into the head of the current page, be sure to do so, as in Figure 29-3.

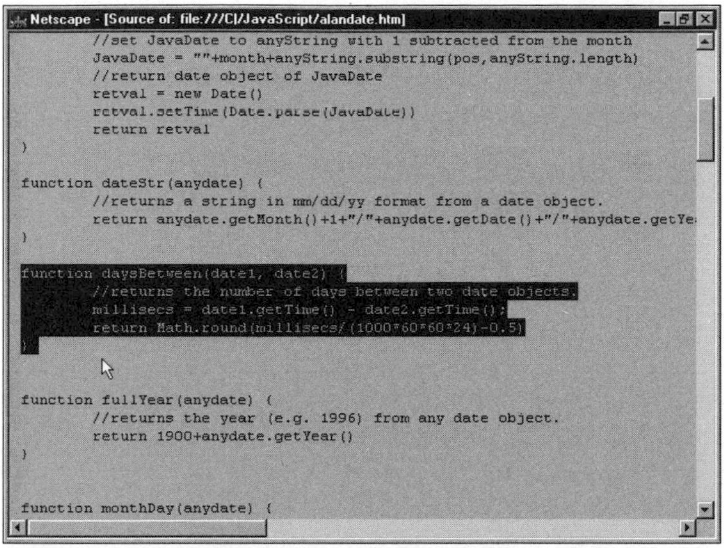

Netscape - [Source of: file:///C|/JavaScript/alandate.htm]

```
        //set JavaDate to anyString with 1 subtracted from the month
        JavaDate = ""+month+anyString.substring(pos,anyString.length)
        //return date object of JavaDate
        retval = new Date()
        retval.setTime(Date.parse(JavaDate))
        return retval
}

function dateStr(anydate) {
        //returns a string in mm/dd/yy format from a date object.
        return anydate.getMonth()+1+"/"+anydate.getDate()+"/"+anydate.getYe
}

function daysBetween(date1, date2) {
        //returns the number of days between two date objects.
        millisecs = date1.getTime() - date2.getTime();
        return Math.round(millisecs/(1000*60*60*24)-0.5)
}

function fullYear(anydate) {
        //returns the year (e.g. 1996) from any date object.
        return 1900+anydate.getYear()
}


function monthDay(anydate) {
```

Figure 29-1: The daysBetween ( ) function selected from alandate.htm in Netscape document source view.

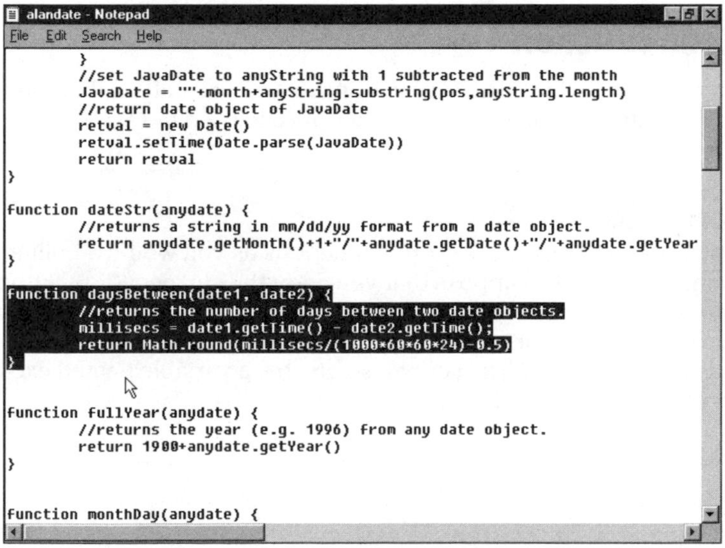

alandate - Notepad

File Edit Search Help

```
        }
        //set JavaDate to anyString with 1 subtracted from the month
        JavaDate = ""+month+anyString.substring(pos,anyString.length)
        //return date object of JavaDate
        retval = new Date()
        retval.setTime(Date.parse(JavaDate))
        return retval
}

function dateStr(anydate) {
        //returns a string in mm/dd/yy format from a date object.
        return anydate.getMonth()+1+"/"+anydate.getDate()+"/"+anydate.getYear
}

function daysBetween(date1, date2) {
        //returns the number of days between two date objects.
        millisecs = date1.getTime() - date2.getTime();
        return Math.round(millisecs/(1000*60*60*24)-0.5)
}

function fullYear(anydate) {
        //returns the year (e.g. 1996) from any date object.
        return 1900+anydate.getYear()
}


function monthDay(anydate) {
```

Figure 29-2: The daysBetween( ) function selected from alandate.htm in Notepad.

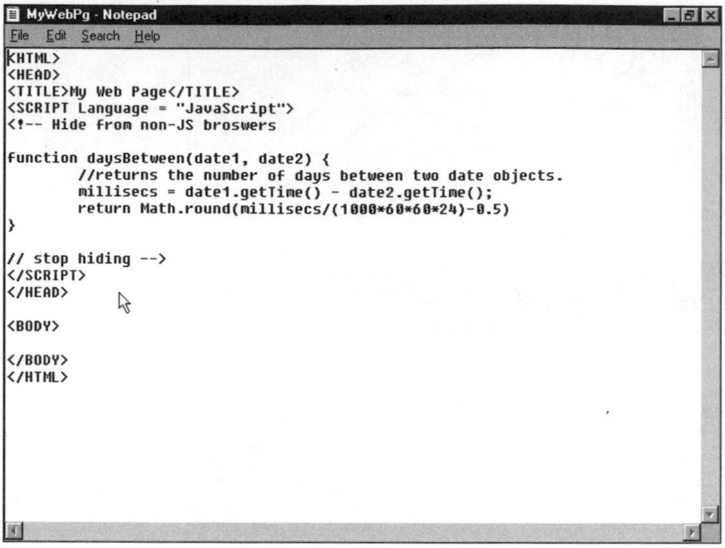

```
<HTML>
<HEAD>
<TITLE>My Web Page</TITLE>
<SCRIPT Language = "JavaScript">
<!-- Hide from non-JS broswers

function daysBetween(date1, date2) {
        //returns the number of days between two date objects.
        millisecs = date1.getTime() - date2.getTime();
        return Math.round(millisecs/(1000*60*60*24)-0.5)
}

// stop hiding -->
</SCRIPT>
</HEAD>

<BODY>

</BODY>
</HTML>
```

Figure 29-3: Custom function pasted in a page head between `<HEAD><SCRIPT>` and `</SCRIPT></HEAD>` tags.

Using a copied function

After you've placed a function in the head of your page, you can call on that function from the body of the page. You can call it from a script (enclosed in `<SCRIPT>` tags) or from an event handler.

Custom functions in scripts

In your own scripts, you can treat these custom functions as you would a built-in JavaScript function. For example, suppose that you copy the currency( ) function from alanmath.htm into the head of your own Web page. You can use the following simple script in that page to multiply a variable named qty by a variable named unitprice to get a new variable named extprice. The script also creates a variable named extstring, using the currency( ) function.

```
<SCRIPT Language = "JavaScript">
var qty = 12
var unitprice = 499.95
var extprice = qty * unitprice
var extstring = currency(extprice)
</SCRIPT>
```

After the script is executed, the extprice variable contains 5999.3999999999996, which is fine for doing additional math. The extstring variable contains $5,999.40, however, which is a better format to display on the reader's screen.

Danger Zone

Don't forget that JavaScript is case-sensitive, even with the names of custom functions. For example, a statement such as *var extstring = Currency(extprice)* produces an error, even if you copied currency( ) into the current document. The reason is that name of the function is *currency(),* not *Currency().*

You also can call one of my custom functions from your own custom functions, provided that you have copied my custom function into a Web page. For example, suppose that you already have copied my leftOf( ) and rightOf( ) functions into your current page. You can then add a new custom function of your own, such as the alphaname( ) function that follows, and have it call up the leftOf( ) and rightOf( ) functions:

```
function alphaname(anystring) {
     var fname = leftOf(" ",anystring)
     var lname = rightOf(" ",anystring)
     return lname+", "+fname
}
```

Within the body of your page, you can call on your own alphaname function as you would any other function. For example, this script

```
<BODY>
<SCRIPT Language = "JavaScript">
fullname = "Wanda Bea Starr"
document.write (alphaname(fullname))
</SCRIPT>
</BODY>
```

displays *Starr, Wanda* on the screen. (It displays the result in this order because your custom alphaname function rearranged the fullname string into *lastname, firstname* order, which is suitable for sorting into alphabetical order.)

Custom functions in event handlers

You can call up any JavaScript function from an event handler in an HTML tag. In fact, this method is one of the most common ways to call JavaScript functions because you often want your scripts to act upon data entered into a form. The following is an example of calling a custom function, pcase( ) here, from an `<INPUT>` tag in a form:

```
<BODY>
text and tags...
<FORM >
<INPUT NAME="fullname" SIZE=50 onchange =
       "this.value=pcase(this.value)">
more text and tags....
</FORM>
more text and tags....
<BODY>
```

The event handler in the <INPUT> tag

```
onchange = "this.value=pcase(this.value)"
```

reads as "Right after the user types something into this field, replace what he or she typed with the proper-case equivalent of that." So, if the reader typed in *WANDA BEA STARR,* that entry would be changed instantly to *Wanda Bea Starr.*

For the rest of this chapter, I talk about each custom function in a little more detail. You'll find it impossible to use any function without knowing what kind of data it expects and what kind of data it returns. Therefore, make sure that you pay careful attention to even the smallest details presented in these sections.

Custom Date Functions

The date functions work on the JavaScript date object. Many date functions duplicate the built-in date object methods. You may find these easier to work with, however, because they use 1–12 as month numbers, instead of 0–11, like JavaScript. Also, these functions use the syntax of other higher-level languages, such as BASIC and xBASE. All of these date functions are stored in my alandate.htm file.

dateObj(string)

This date function takes a date expressed as a string in mm/dd/yy format and creates a new date object with that date. For example,

```
dueDate = dateObj("3/15/97")
document.write (dueDate)
```

displays

```
Sat Mar 15 00:00:00 1997
```

where *dueDate* is a JavaScript date object.

dateStr(date)

This function takes a date object passed as *date* and returns a string in mm/dd/yy format. For example — assuming that today is 12/1/96 — the following script

```
today = new Date()
todayStr = dateStr(today)
document.write (todayStr)
```

displays

```
12/1/96
```

daysBetween(date1, date2)

This custom function returns the number of days between two dates, *date1* and *date2,* where both dates must be date objects. To ensure a positive number in your result, set the later of the two dates as the first argument (*date1*). The following small script example assumes that the current document also contains the custom now( ), dateObj( ) and dateStr( ) functions:

```
<SCRIPT Language = "JavaScript">
var dueDate = dateObj("3/1/97")
days = daysBetween(now(),dueDate)
var msg = "There are <b>"+ days + "</b> days between
       "+dateStr(now())+ " and " +dateStr(dueDate)
document.write (msg)
</SCRIPT>
```

When executed, that script displays

```
There are 106 days between 6/15/97 and 3/1/97
```

You can use the built-in abs (absolute value) method of JavaScript's Math object to ensure a positive result. For example, take a look at this script where earlydate precedes latedate in the daysBetween( ) function:

```
var earlydate = dateObj("3/1/97")
var latedate = dateObj("3/31/97")
days = daysBetween(earlydate,latedate)
document.write ("days = ",days,"<BR>")
document.write ("Math.abs(days) = ",Math.abs(days))
```

When executed, this script displays

```
days = -30
Math.abs(days) = 30
```

fullYear(*date*)

This function returns only the year (such as 1996) from any date object specified in *date*. For example, if the current date is 6/16/97, the following script

```
today = new Date()
document.write (fullYear(today))
```

displays

```
1997
```

monthAbb(*date*)

This function returns the month abbreviation (such as Dec) from any date object passed as *date*. For example, if the current date is 6/15/97, the following script

```
today = new Date()
document.write (monthAbb(today))
```

displays

```
Jun
```

monthDay(*date*)

This function returns the month day number (1–31) from any date object passed as *time*. For example, if today is 6/15/97, then the following script

```
today = new Date()
document.write (monthAbb(today))
```

shows

```
15
```

monthName(*date*)

This function returns the month name (such as December) from any date object passed as *date*. For example, if today is 6/15/97, then this script

```
today = new Date()
document.write (monthName(today))
```

displays

```
June
```

The following larger script, which uses several custom functions from alandate.htm,

```
today = new Date()
fullDate = weekDay(today)+" " +monthName(today)+", " +
       monthDay(today)+ "  " + fullYear(today)
document.write (fullDate)
```

displays

```
Sunday June, 15 1997
```

monthNum(*date*)

This function returns the month number (1–12) from any date object passed as *date*. For example, if today is 6/15/97, thcn thc following script

```
today = new Date()
document.write (monthName(today))
```

displays

```
6
```

now( )

This function returns the current system date/time as a date object. Using this function is identical to setting a variable to new Date(). For example, if today is 6/15/97, then the script

```
todayDate = now()
todayString = dateStr(todayDate)
document.write ("todayDate = ",todayDate,"<BR>")
document.write ("todayString = ",todayString,"<BR>")
```

displays the following when executed:

```
todayDate = Sun Jun 15 14:19:37 1997
todayString = 6/15/97
```

nowStr( )

This function returns the current system clock time as a string in *hh:mm:ss am/pm* format. For example, if you execute the following statement at noon:

```
document.write(nowStr())
```

it displays

```
12:00:00 PM
```

todayStr( )

This function returns the current system date as a string in mm/dd/yy format. For example, if you execute the following statement on June 16, 1997:

```
document.write("Today is ",todayStr())
```

it displays this:

```
Today is 6/16/97
```

weekDay(*date*)

This custom function returns the day name (such as Friday) from any date object passed as *date*. For example, if you run the following JavaScript statement on June 20, 1997 (and the current page contained the weekDay( ), now( ) and todayStr( ) functions as well)

```
document.write("Today is ",weekDay(now()),", ",todayStr())
```

it displays

```
Today is Friday, 6/20/97
```

weekDayAbb(*date*)

This function returns the day abbreviation (such as Fri) from any date object passed as *date:*

```
bday = dateObj("6/18/97")
wday = weekDayAbb(bday)
month=monthName(bday)
day = monthDay(bday)
document.write ("Come to my party on ",wday," ",month,"
       ",day,"!")
```

When you run that script, it displays

```
Come to my party on Wed June 18!
```

weekDayNum(*date*)

This function returns the day number (1 = Sunday, 7 = Saturday) from any date object passed as *date*. For example, if today is March 21, 1996, then the following script

```
today = new Date()
dueDate = whenIs(today,30)
wkday = weekDayNum(dueDate)
if (wkday == 1 || wkday = 7) {
     document.write (dueDate ",is a weekend!")}
else {
     document.write (dueDate ",is a weekday!")}
}
```

displays

```
Sat Apr 20 17:14:56 PDT 1996 is a weekend!
```

The whenIs( ) function used in the preceding example also is a custom function.

whenIs(*date, n*)

This function returns the date that is *n* days from date object passed as *date*. The value *n* can be a positive number to add days to *date* or a negative number to subtract days from *date*. For example, if you execute these statements on 3/21/96

```
orderDate = new Date()
dueDate = whenIs(orderDate,30)
document.write ("This order was placed on ",dateStr(orderDate))
document.write ("<BR>Payment is due on ",dateStr(dueDate))
```

they display

```
This order was placed on 3/21/97
Payment is due on 4/20/97
```

If you execute the following script on 3/21/97:

```
testDate = new Date()
date30ago = whenIs(testDate,-30)
document.write ("testDate = ",dateStr(testDate))
document.write ("<BR>date30ago = ",dateStr(date30ago))
```

the resulting display is

```
testDate = 3/21/97
date30ago = 2/19/97
```

Both scripts also use the custom dateStr( ) function to display dates in mm/dd/yy format.

year(*date*)

This function returns the two-digit year number (such as 96) from any date object passed as *date*. For example, if you execute this script at any time during 1997

```
testDate = new Date()
decade = year(testDate)
document.write ("year = ",decade)
```

the result is as follows:

```
year = 97
```

Custom Math Functions

The math functions work on numeric data.

currency(*num*)

This math function returns a string based on *num* in the U.S. currency format $12,345.67. For example

```
totalSale = 1234567.89
document.write ('Total = ',currency(totalSale))
```

shows this on the screen:

```
Total = $1,234,567.89
```

Negative numbers are shown in parentheses. For example, the following script

```
fee = -12
document.write ('Fee = ',currency(fee))
```

displays

```
Fee = $(12.00)
```

The currency( ) function also can accept an expression as its argument, provided that the expression results in a numeric value. For example, the following script

```
qty = 9
unitprice = 49.95
document.write ("qty = ",qty,"<BR>")
document.write ("unitprice = ",currency(unitprice),"<BR>")
document.write ("extended price = ",currency(qty*unitprice))
```

displays

```
qty = 9
unitprice = $49.95
extended price = $449.55
```

decimal(*num*)

This function returns the decimal portion of *num* with integer truncated. For example, the following script

```
x=1.987654321
document.write ("x = ",x,"<BR>")
```

```
document.write ("integer(x) = ",integer(x),"<BR>")
document.write ("decimal(x) = ",decimal(x),"<BR>")
```

displays

```
x = 1.9876543209999999
integer(x) = 1
decimal(x) = 0.98765432099999995
```

fixed(*num*)

This function returns number *num* as a string in 12,345.67 format. Negative numbers are expressed with a leading minus sign. For example, the following script

```
var x = 12345.67890
var y = -1 * x
document.write ("x = ",fixed(x),"<BR>")
document.write ("y = ",fixed(y))
```

displays

```
x = 12,345.68
y = -12,345.68
```

The fixed() function also can accept an expression as its argument, provided that the expression results in a numeric value. For example, the following script

```
document.write (fixed(123.45/22.7))
```

displays

```
5.44
```

integer(*num*)

This function returns just the integer portion of *num* with the decimal portion truncated. For example, the following script

```
x=-321.98
document.write ("x = ",x,"<BR>")
document.write ("integer(x) = ",integer(x),"<BR>")
document.write ("decimal(x) = ",decimal(x),"<BR>")
```

displays

```
x = -321.98000000000002
integer(x) = -321
decimal(x) = -0.98000000000001819
```

isdiv(*num*,*n*)

This function returns **true** if *num* is evenly divisible by *n*. For example, the following script

```
document.write("15 is evenly divisible by 4: <b>",isdiv(15,4),"
       </b><br>")
document.write("20 is evenly divisible by 4: <b>",isdiv(20,4),"
       </b><br>")
document.write("25 is evenly divisible by 4: <b>",isdiv(25,4),"
       </b>")
```

displays this:

```
15 is evenly divisible by 4: false
20 is evenly divisible by 4: true
25 is evenly divisible by 4: false
```

iseven(*num*)

This function returns **true** if *num* is an even number. For example, the following script

```
for (var i=1;i<=6;i++) {
     document.write (i," is an even number: <b>",iseven(i),"</
       b></br>")
}
```

displays

```
1 is an even number: false
2 is an even number: true
3 is an even number: false
4 is an even number: true
5 is an even number: false
6 is an even number: true
```

isodd(*num*)

This function returns **true** if *num* is an odd number. For example, the following script

```
for (var i=1;i<=6;i++) {
     document.write (i," is an odd number: <b>",isodd(i),"</b></
       br>")
}
```

displays this:

```
1 is an odd number: true
2 is an odd number: false
3 is an odd number: true
4 is an odd number: false
5 is an odd number: true
6 is an odd number: false
```

rawnum(*str*)

This custom math function removes any non-numeric characters, such as dollar signs, parentheses, and commas, from a string and attempts to return the result as a number. You can use it to convert a number stored in currency( ) format (such as $1,234.56) or in fixed( ) format (1,234.56) to a number. The following is an example:

```
currNum = "$1,000.00"
plainNum = 500

document.write (currNum + plainNum,'<p>')
       //displays $1,000.00500
document.write (rawnum(currNum)+plainNum,'<p>')
       //displays 1500
document.write (currency(rawnum(currNum)+plainNum))
       //displays $1,500.00
```

Custom String Functions

The custom string functions operate on string data.

contains(smstring, lrgstring)

This function returns **true** if *smstring* (small string) can be found in *lrgstring* (larger string). The following example

```
taxableStates = "AZ CA OR"
thisState = "CA"
if (contains(thisState,taxableStates)) {
     document.write ("This is a taxable transaction.<p>")}
else {
     document.write ("No tax.<p>")
}
```

displays

```
This is a taxable transaction.
```

But this script

```
taxableStates = "AZ CA OR"
thisState = "NJ"
if (contains(thisState,taxableStates)) {
     document.write ("This is a taxable transaction.<p>")}
else {
     document.write ("No tax.<p>")
}
```

displays

```
No tax.
```

The contains( ) function is case-sensitive. For example, *contains("ca", "AZ CA OR")* returns **false** because the larger string contains *CA* but does not contain *ca*.

lcase(*str*)

This function returns *str* in all lowercase letters. The following example

```
shout = "I LIKE TO SHOUT WHEN I WRITE"
lowered = lcase(shout)
document.write (lowered)
```

displays this when you execute it:

```
i like to shout when i write
```

left(*str,n*)

This function returns the leftmost *n* characters from string *str*. The first character of the string is character number 1. The following example

```
filename = "c:\\index.html"
drive = left(filename,2)
document.write ("drive = ",drive)
```

displays

```
drive = c:
```

leftOf(smstring, lrgstring)

This function returns leftmost characters of *lrgstring* (larger string) up to character specified in *smstring* (smaller string). Example:

```
fullname  = "Wanda Bea Starr"
firstname = leftOf(" ",fullname)
document.write ("firstname = ",firstname)
```

displays

```
firstname = Wanda
```

mid(str,start,n)

This function returns a substring of *str*, starting at number *start* that is *n* characters long. The first character of *str* is character number 1. The following example

```
myString = "Dog eat dog world"
inside = mid(myString,5,7)
document.write(inside)
```

displays

```
eat dog
```

pcase(*str*)

This function returns *str* in proper-noun case (first letter of each word capitalized). The following example

```
badcase = "wAndA bEa StaRR"
propercase = pcase(badcase)
document.write(pcase(badcase))
```

displays

```
Wanda Bea Starr
```

right(*str,n*)

This function returns the rightmost *n* characters of string *str*. For example, this script

```
filename = "c:\\index.htm"
extension = right(filename,4)
document.write ("extension = ",extension)
```

displays

```
extension = .htm
```

rightOf(smstring, lrgstring)

This function returns the characters from last *smstring* (small string) to the end of *lrgstring* (larger string). For example, the following script

```
fullname  = "Wanda Bea Starr"
surname = rightOf(" ",fullname)
document.write ("surname = ",surname)
```

displays

```
surname = Starr
```

spot(smstring, lrgstring)

This function returns a number indicating the spot where *smstring* (small string) appears in *lrgstring* (larger string). The first character in *lrgstring* is character number 1. Take the following example:

```
fullname = "Isabella J. Rossigni"
periodAt = spot (".",fullname)
document.write ("periodAt = ",periodAt,"<p>")
middleInit = mid(fullname,periodAt-1,2)
document.write ("middleInit = ",middleInit)
```

This script displays

```
periodAt = 11
middleInit = J.
```

ucase(*str*)

This function returns *str* in all uppercase letters. For example, the following script

```
myMsg = "i like to shout when i write"
bigMsg = ucase(myMsg)
document.write (bigMsg)
```

displays

```
I LIKE TO SHOUT WHEN I WRITE
```

A Display-Banner Function

The banner( ) function displays text scrolling across a box in a marquee fashion.

banner(msg,width)

This function displays *msg* as a scrolling marquee in a box that's *width* characters widc. For cxamplc, thc following script linc

```
banner("This is a scrolling banner message",50)
```

displays *This is a scrolling banner message* scrolling across an input text box that has a width of 50 characters (Figure 29-4). For a live demo, browse the JavaScript section of the *Web Publishing Uncut* CD-ROM or the `http://www.coolnerds.com site`.

Figure 29-4: The boxed text scrolls because it is displayed with the custom banner( ) function.

To use the banner() function in your own Web page, you must copy both the banner() and the rollmsg( ) functions from alanshow.htm into the head of the page. Be sure to select both functions, as Figure 29-5 illustrates, before copying. Also make sure that you paste both functions between the `<HEAD>` and `</HEAD>` tags (and between `<SCRIPT...>...</SCRIPT>` tags, though you can copy those tags from alanshow.htm if your Web page doesn't already have them).

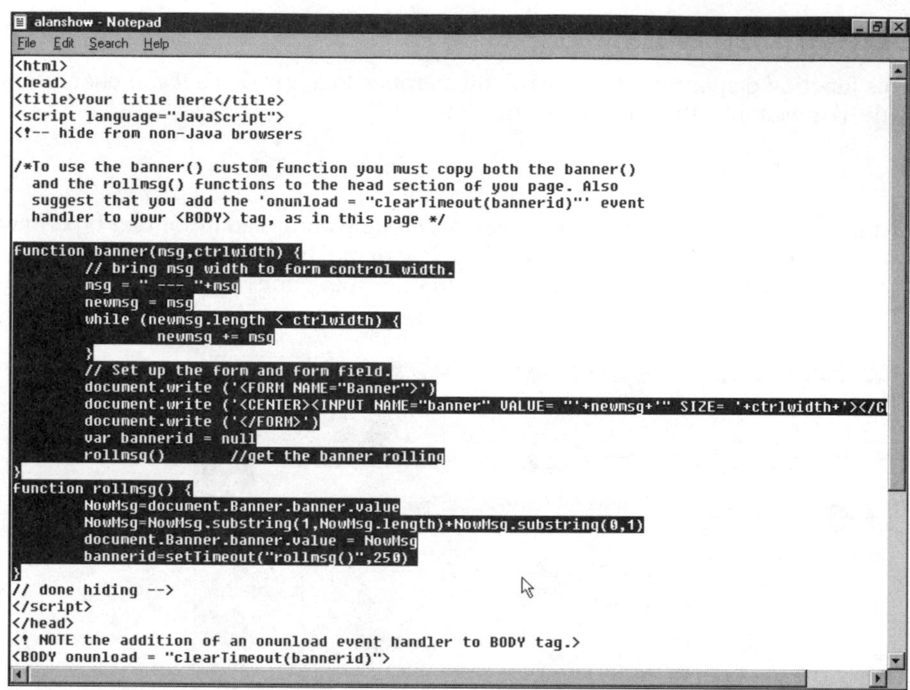


```
<html>
<head>
<title>Your title here</title>
<script language="JavaScript">
<!-- hide from non-Java browsers

/*To use the banner() custom function you must copy both the banner()
  and the rollmsg() functions to the head section of you page. Also
  suggest that you add the 'onunload = "clearTimeout(bannerid)"' event
  handler to your <BODY> tag, as in this page */

function banner(msg,ctrlwidth) {
        // bring msg width to form control width.
        msg = " --- "+msg
        newmsg = msg
        while (newmsg.length < ctrlwidth) {
                newmsg += msg
        }
        // Set up the form and form field.
        document.write ('<FORM NAME="Banner">')
        document.write ('<CENTER><INPUT NAME="banner" VALUE= "'+newmsg+'" SIZE= '+ctrlwidth+'></C
        document.write ('</FORM>')
        var bannerid = null
        rollmsg()       //get the banner rolling
}
function rollmsg() {
        NowMsg=document.Banner.banner.value
        NowMsg=NowMsg.substring(1,NowMsg.length)+NowMsg.substring(0,1)
        document.Banner.banner.value = NowMsg
        bannerid=setTimeout("rollmsg()",250)
}
// done hiding -->
</script>
</head>
<! NOTE the addition of an onunload event handler to BODY tag.>
<BODY onunload = "clearTimeout(bannerid)">
```

Figure 29-5: Copy banner( ) and rollmsg( ) to your page to use the banner( ) function.

You also should add the *onunload = "clearTimeout(bannerid)"* event handler to the <BODY> tag of your page to ensure that the timer stops when the page is unloaded.

If you want to center the banner on the page, enclose the banner( ) message and its <SCRIPT> tags in a pair of <CENTER>...</CENTER> tags, as follows:

```
<BODY onunload = "clearTimeout(bannerid)">
<! Any normal html text and tags....>
<CENTER>
<SCRIPT Language = "JavaScript"><!-- hide
          banner("This is a scrolling banner message",50)
// no hide -->
</SCRIPT>
</CENTER>
<! Any normal html text and tags....>
</BODY>
```

Summary

The custom JavaScript functions presented in this chapter should help you be more productive in your own JavaScript programming. Some important points to remember are as follows:

- These custom functions are stored in the files alandate.htm, alanmath.htm, alanstrg.htm, and alanshow.htm on both the *HTML Publishing Bible* CD-ROM and the `http://www.coolnerds.com` Web site.
- To use a custom function, you must copy it from its source file (one of the preceding alan ... htm files). Make sure that you copy the entire function from the start of the *function(* statement down to, and including, the closing curly brace (*}*).
- When pasting a custom function into your own page, make sure that you put the function between the `<HEAD><SCRIPT Language="JavaScript">` and `</SCRIPT></HEAD>` tags.
- Once you've copied a custom function into your page, you can call it from any script or event handler in the `<BODY>` section of your page. You also can call the custom function from some other custom function you've created.
- If you have any problems with a custom function, make sure that you are passing the correct type of data to it. For example, some functions accept strings, some accept numbers, some accept date objects — whereas others accept some combination thereof. Use this chapter as a guide to using the custom functions correctly.

✦ ✦ ✦

JavaScript and Frames

In This Chapter

Managing frames with JavaScript

A sample framed site

Custom navigation buttons for framed sites

Giving readers a "No Frames" option

Viewing the source documents in framed sites

Before beginning this foray into JavaScript and frames, let me remind you that you can do plenty with frames *without* writing any JavaScript code whatsoever. I cover all the basics of frames in Chapter 25. In this chapter, I review some of the basics of frames, but the main goal is to talk about techniques for manipulating frames and their contents *programmatically.* That is, manipulating frames and their contents from within JavaScript scripts.

How to Refer to Frames in JavaScript

In JavaScript, a frame is an object. Like all objects, it has properties and methods. A frame object is, itself, a property of the larger *window* object in JavaScript. The entire browser window is the window object. That larger object can contain two or more frame objects.

In JavaScript, you are usually faced with the problem of having to say something like "In that other frame over there (not this frame where this code is being executed), do such-and-such." The syntax for making such as statement in JavaScript is as follows:

```
parent.framename.such-and-such
```

where *parent* is a keyword in JavaScript that always means "the larger browser window that contains this frame and others." The *framename* portion of the statement is the actual name of the other frame, as defined in the <FRAME> tag. The other part, *such-and-such,* is some method or an expression that assigns a value to a property. Let's take a look at an example.

Suppose that you have a Web page named index.htm which divides the browser window into two frames — one frame named **toc,** the other frame named **main:**

```
<! Set up the frames >
<! ----- Split into two columns>
<FRAMESET COLS= "130,*">
        <FRAME NAME="toc" SRC = "somedoc1.htm">
    <FRAME NAME="main" SRC = "somedoc2.htm">
</FRAMESET>
```

How would you write JavaScript statements that refer specifically to the frame named “main”? Substituting the actual name “main” for *framename* gives you this:

```
parent.main.such-and-such
```

The *such-and-such* part defines what you want to do. Typically, that action is expressed by using some method of the frame object or by assigning some value to a frame property. The frame object has many of the same properties that the window object has. For example, it has a *location* (the URL of the document displayed in the frame). It also contains a document object. Here are some examples.

Hot Stuff

The parent.*framename* syntax works anywhere that you'd place JavaScript code — in scripts, custom functions, and event handlers.

The statement that follows sets the *location* property of the frame named *main* to home.html. This statement makes the frame display a Web page (from the current Web site) in that frame:

```
parent.main.location = 'home.html'
```

The next JavaScript statement sets the hash property of the location to ‘#Top’. This essentially moves the reader to a bookmark (anchor) named Top within whatever page is being displayed in that frame at the moment (assuming, of course, that the document does indeed contain a bookmark named “Top”).

```
parent.main.location.hash="Top"
```

The following examples use the history( ) method to navigate within the frame named main. This next statement moves the reader back one document in the frame named main (as though the reader had right-clicked the document and chosen “Back in Frame”):

```
parent.main.history.back()
```

This statement moves the reader forward one page in the frame named main:

```
parent.main.history.forward()
```

The document within the frame also has properties and methods. To refer to the document in the frame (as opposed to the frame itself), use the following syntax:

```
parent.framename.document.such-and-such
```

For example, a document has a background color, expressed as the bgColor property in JavaScript. The following JavaScript statements refer to the background color of the document currently displayed in the frame named main:

```
parent.main.document.bgColor
```

This statement changes the background color of the document currently shown in the main frame to hot pink:

```
parent.main.document.bgColor = 'hotpink'
```

One thing that all these statements have in common is that they all refer to the frame named main as *parent.main,* and the document within that frame as *parent.main.document.* Despite the simplicity of the parent.*framename* syntax, however, most people (including myself) find it a bit hard to see how this can be *applied* to creating a highly-interactive, framed Web site. Therefore, let me take you through an in-depth example of a fairly large Web site that uses frames, a clickable image map, and JavaScript to make it easy for the reader to navigate around the site.

A Sample Web Site

We'll need an example to help us along in this chapter. Figure 30-1 shows a sample Web site that uses frames. The frame on the left presents navigation tools — buttons mostly — to the reader. That frame never changes, and the reader can use those buttons at any time to move around within the site.

The larger frame on the right is where regular Web pages are displayed. In the figure, the page titled *Pretend I Am A Home Page* acts as the home page for this hypothetical Web site.

Sample index.html page

When the reader accesses this Web site, the first page that opens is index.html. The source for that index.html page is shown in Figure 30-2. It contains no JavaScript code. Rather, it just contains the HTML `<FRAME...>` tags necessary to define the site's frames. For purposes of this chapter, what is important about index.html are these facts:

- ✦ It creates a frame named toc and puts an HTML document named navbttns.htm in that frame.
- ✦ It creates a frame named main and puts an HTML document named home.htm in that frame.

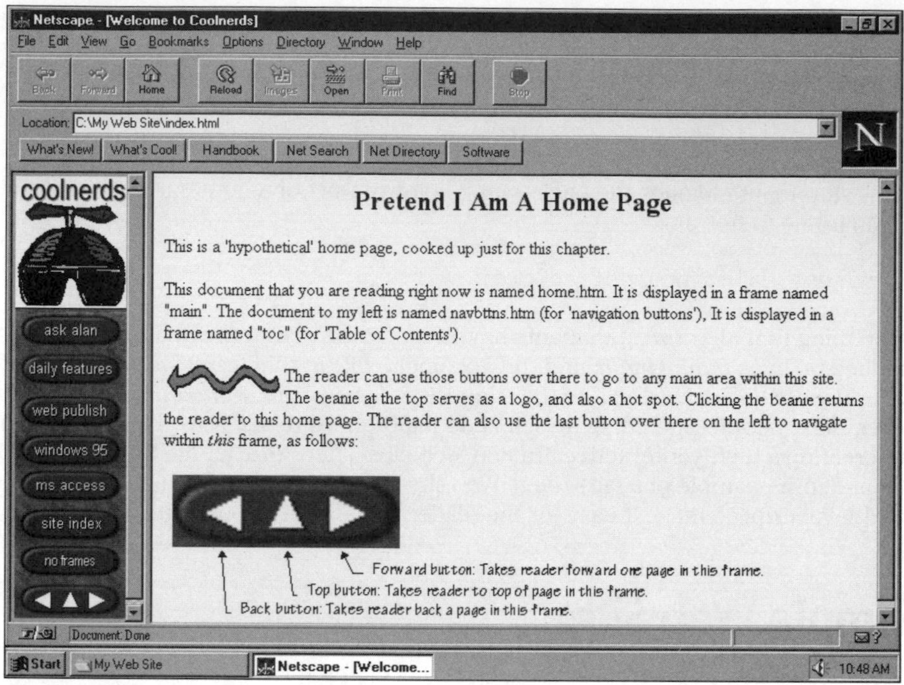

Figure 30-1: Sample Web site discussed in this chapter.

```
<HTML>
<! This is index.html for the sample coolnerds site. >
<! It just defines the sit's frames >
<HEAD>
<TITLE>Welcome to Coolnerds</TITLE>
</HEAD>

<! Set up the frames >
<! ----- Split into two columns>
<FRAMESET COLS= "130,*">
    <FRAME NAME="toc" SRC = "navbttns.htm"
        MARGINWIDTH = "0" MARGINHEIGHT="0">
    <FRAME NAME="main" SRC = "home.htm"
        MARGINWIDTH = "10" MARGINHEIGHT="10">
</FRAMESET>
</HTML>
```

Figure 30-2: Source for sample coolnerds' index.html file.

Let's take a closer look at each of those documents.

Starting on navbttns.htm

The navbttns.htm document, displayed in the thinner frame named toc on the left, is where much of the JavaScript action takes place. The navbttns.htm document contains an `<IMG SRC...>` tag that displays a graphic named navbttns.gif. It also contains a map that makes parts of the image clickable. In addition, it contains some JavaScript code that brings those hot spots to life. Let's take it a step at a time. First, here is navbttns.gif as it appears in Paint Shop Pro. This figure is basically a picture I put together using my own (pathetic) drawing skills in Paint Shop Pro — nothing more than that.

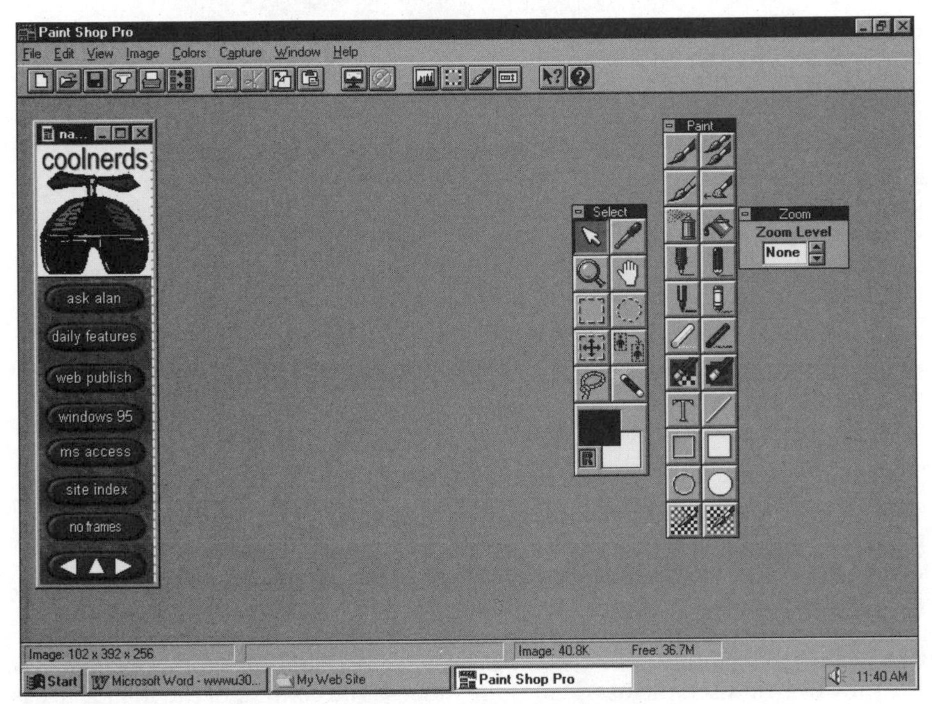

Figure 30-3: The navbttns.gif image viewed in Paint Shop Pro.

To make navbttns.gif into a clickable image map, I used Map This!, which was discussed back in Chapter 24. Truth be told, I wasn't exactly sure what each hot spot in navbttns.gif would actually end up doing. I decided that I would later create a custom JavaScript function named hopto( ) that accepts a filename as a parameter and then displays the document for that filename in the main frame. For example, a call to hopto('askme.htm') would display a page named askme.htm in the larger main frame. Following this method of defining hot spots for navbttns.gif, I just entered the URL for each hot spot as

```
javascript:hopto('wherever.htm')
```

in which *wherever.htm* is the name of the page that I want that hot spot to display in the larger main frame. For example, in Figure 30-4, I've mapped a hot spot around the button labeled *ask alan* and defined the URL for that button as javascript:hopto('askme.htm').

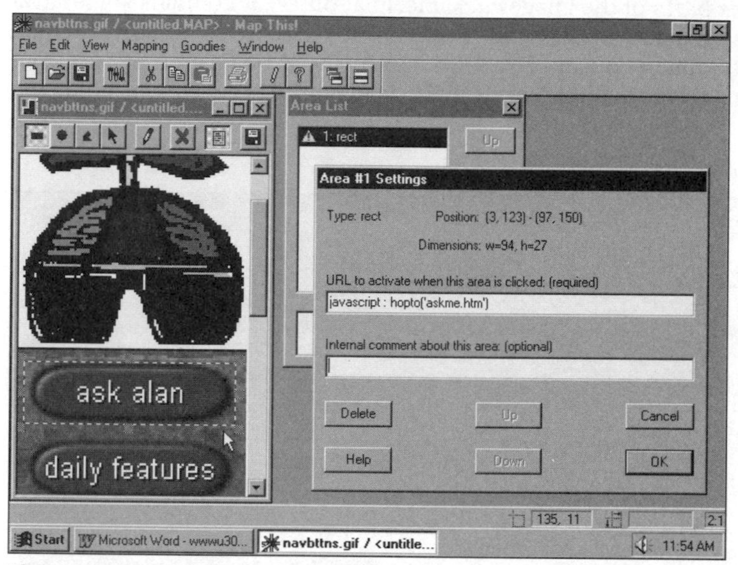

Figure 30-4: Hot spot around the *ask alan* button passes askme.htm to a JavaScript function named hopto().

Within Map This!, I used that same method to map out each button in the graphic image and give it the name of some Web page to display. I even drew a map around the beanie and told it to hop to home.htm when clicked, giving the reader a quick way to jump back to the home page within this site.

Puzzled? You typically might think of index.html as being the home page for a site. In a framed site, however, index.html just defines the frames. The content of the home page is placed in a separate file (home.htm, in my example) and displayed within the main frame that index.html defined.

After mapping out all hot spots, I saved the image map and exited Map This! Then I started creating my navbttns.htm Web page. For starters, I opened a new blank document in Notepad and read in the map that Map This! had created. Next, I added an `<IMG SRC>` tag for the navbttns.gif file, with a USEMAP attribute that defined the map for the hot spots. Thus, the body of my navbttns.htm document started out looking something like Figure 30-5. (However, I've added some comments to help you identify the button to which each `<AREA SHAPE>` tag belongs, as well as some boldface to call your attention to the important stuff I'll be referring to later.)

```
<BODY>
<MAP NAME="navmap">
<!-- #$-: Image Map file created by Map THIS! -->
<!-- #$-: Map THIS! free image map editor by Todd C. Wilson -->
<!-- #$-: Please do not edit lines strating with "#$" -->
<!-- #$-:VERSION: 1.20 -->
<!-- #$-:AUTHOR:Alan Simpson -->
<!-- #$-:DATE:Sun Mar 23 21:27:56 1997 -->
<!-- #$-:PATH:C:\Coolnerds New\ -->
<!-- #$GIF:navbttns.gif -->
<!-- Hotspot for the beanie, which takes the reader to the home page.>
<AREA SHAPE=RECT COORDS="5,17,102,114" HREF=javascript:hopto('home.htm')>
<! Hotspot for the ask alan button..>
<AREA SHAPE=RECT COORDS="6,123,97,150" HREF=javascript:hopto('askme.htm')>
<! Hotspot for the daily features button..>
<AREA SHAPE=RECT COORDS="4,158,97,184" HREF=javascript:hopto('daily.htm')>
<! Hotspot for the web publish button..>
<AREA SHAPE=RECT COORDS="4,193,99,221" HREF=javascript:hopto('webpb.htm')>
<! Hotspot for the windows 95 button..>
<AREA SHAPE=RECT COORDS="5,228,98,255" HREF=javascript:hopto('win95.htm')>
<! Hotspot for the ms access button..>
<AREA SHAPE=RECT COORDS="3,261,99,287" HREF=javascript:hopto('msacc.htm')>
<! Hotspot for the site index button..>
<AREA SHAPE=RECT COORDS="3,294,98,322" HREF=javascript:hopto('sindex.htm')>
<the remaining hotspots are explained later in this chapter
</MAP>
<IMG SRC="mavbttns.gif" USEMAP = "#NAVMAP">
</BODY>
```

Figure 30-5: A map and `<IMG SRC>` tag in the body of navbttns.htm.

The hopto( ) function

With my image and map in place in navbttns.htm, it was time to create the hopto() function that many of the hot spots would be calling. Basically, all this function needed to do was set the location (URL) of the frame named main to whatever file name is passed to it. I just had to add the following tags and codes above the body of navbttns.htm:

```
<HTML>
<HEAD>
<SCRIPT Language = "JavaScript">
function hopto(filename) {
     parent.main.location = filename
}
</SCRIPT>
</HEAD>
```

Now when the reader clicks the ask alan button in the navbttns graphic, the `<AREA SHAPE...>` tag for the hot spot executes the statement javascript:hopto('askme.htm'). This passes *askme.htm* to hopto() as the filename. As a result, the actual statement that gets executed within the function is

```
parent.main.location = 'askme.htm'
```

which makes the page named askme.htm appear in the frame named main. As you can see back in Figure 30-5, quite a few other `<AREA SHAPE...>` tags use hopto() to display other pages in the frame named main.

Back and Forward buttons for frames

If you have navigated around a site that uses frames, you may have noticed that the Back and Forward buttons act strangely. These buttons either appear dimmed or navigate you through other sites when you click them. To navigate within a frame, you have to right-click the frame and choose an option.

An alternative for you, as a Web publisher, is to set up your own navigation buttons in some frame within your site. In my sample coolnerds site, I've added three navigation buttons to the bottom of the thinner navigation frame. Figure 30-6 shows those buttons.

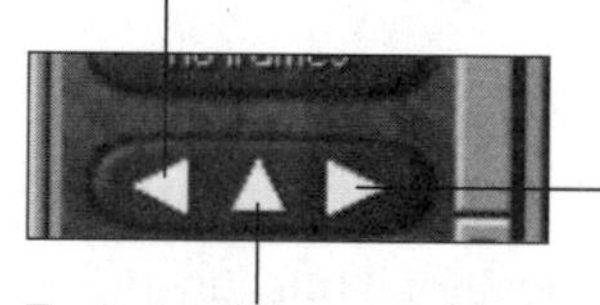
Back button: Moves reader to previous document in the history list over in the main frame.
Forward button: Moves reader to next document in the history list over in the main frame.
Top button: Moves reader to the top of the page over in the main frame.

Figure 30-6: Buttons to navigate within the main frame.

The Back button can use either the back( ) or equivalent go(-1) method, and the Forward button can use the forward( ) or go(1) method, of the history object to move the reader back and forward through the history list. Of course, you want to move the reader through pages in the *main* frame, not those that appear in the skinny little frame that houses the navigation buttons. Thus, you need to apply those methods to the history object for the main frame. Hence, the JavaScript code for the Back button is

```
parent.main.history.go(-1)
```

or the equivalent

```
parent.main.history.back()
```

The JavaScript code for the Forward button is

```
parent.main.history.go(1)
```

or the equivalent

```
parent.main.history.forward()
```

In my sample coolnerds sites, these actions are defined in the <AREA SHAPE...> tags for the image map, as you can see in the code that follows:

```
<! Hotspot for the Back-in-main-frame button>
<AREA SHAPE=RECT COORDS="5,360,38,389"
        HREF=javascript:parent.main.history.back()>

<! Hotspot for the Forward-in-main-frame button>
<AREA SHAPE=RECT COORDS="65,359,98,389"
        HREF=javascript:parent.main.history.forward()>
```

Go to a bookmark in another frame

I like a site that offers a quick way to get back to the top of a lengthy page. In my own Web site, I put this HTML tab just after the <BODY> tag in each page I create, to make a bookmark named Top appear at the top of each page:

```
<A NAME = "Top">
```

As you saw back in Figure 30-6, I then offer a Top button that, when clicked, shoots the reader to the top of whatever page is currently displayed in the main frame. I must confess that I had some problems with this button initially, but I seem to have come up with a solution that works. You need a small custom function to make sure that the current page in the main frame does indeed contain bookmarks (a.k.a. anchors). If so, you then need to have that function jump to anchor[0], the first anchor on the page. To add this feature, use the following code, which goes in the <HEAD> area:

```
function goTop() {
     //Triggered by the "top" button in image map.
     if (parent.main.document.anchors.length > 0) {
          parent.main.location.hash='Top'
     }
     else {
           alert("Page in the main frame has no anchors!")
     }
}
```

The <AREA SHAPE...> tag that calls this function looks like this:

```
<! Hotspot for the Top-of-page-in-main-frame) button>
<AREA SHAPE=RECT COORDS="40,361,63,388" HREF=javascript:goTop()>
```

After you add this feature to your site, making sure that every page in your site has an <A NAME="Top"> tag right next to the <BODY> tag is important. I'm also assuming here that you never show other peoples' sites within your own frames. Therefore, you don't need to worry about whether or not their pages have a Top bookmark.

Puzzled?

I explain why I think you should never show other peoples' sites within your own frames a little later in this chapter.

At this point, the navbttns.htm page is almost done. You haven't done anything with this site yet to accommodate browsers that don't support frames. You also haven't given readers the option to browse frame-free even if their browsers do support frames. I get to those issues next. For now, here is the big picture of the source behind navbttns.htm as it currently stands. The new stuff that was added since I first showed you this page (back in Figure 30-5) appears in boldface.

```
<HTML>
<HEAD>
<SCRIPT Language = "JavaScript">

function hopto(filename) {
     parent.main.location = filename
}

function goTop() {
     //Triggered by the "top" button in image map.
     if (parent.main.document.anchors.length > 0) {
          parent.main.location.hash='Top'
     }
     else {
           alert("Page in the main frame has no anchors!")
     }
}

</SCRIPT>
</HEAD>
<BODY BGCOLOR="#COCOCO" LINK="#COCOCO" VLINK="#COCOCO">
<MAP NAME="navmap">
<!-- #$-:Image Map file created by Map THIS! -->
<!-- #$-:Map THIS! free image map editor by Todd C. Wilson -->
<!-- #$-:Please do not edit lines starting with "#$" -->
<!-- #$VERSION:1.20 -->
<!-- #$AUTHOR:Alan Simpson -->
<!-- #$DATE:Sun Mar 23 21:27:56 1997 -->
```

```
<!-- #$PATH:C:\Coolnerds New\ -->
<!-- #$GIF:navbttns.gif -->
<! Hotspot for the beanie, which takes reader to the home page.>
<AREA SHAPE=RECT COORDS="5,17,102,114"
       HREF=javascript:hopto('home.htm')>
<! Hotspot for the Ask Alan button>
<AREA SHAPE=RECT COORDS="6,123,97,150"
       HREF=javascript:hopto('askme.htm')>
<! Hotspot for the Daily Features button>
<AREA SHAPE=RECT COORDS="4,158,97,184"
       HREF=javascript:hopto('daily.htm')>
<! Hotspot for the Web Publish button>
<AREA SHAPE=RECT COORDS="4,193,99,221"
       HREF=javascript:hopto('webpb.htm')>
<! Hotspot for the Windows 95 button>
<AREA SHAPE=RECT COORDS="5,228,98,255"
       HREF=javascript:hopto('win95.htm')>
<! Hotspot for the MS Access button>
<AREA SHAPE=RECT COORDS="3,261,99,287"
       HREF=javascript:hopto('msacc.htm')>
<! Hotspot for the Site Index button>
<AREA SHAPE=RECT COORDS="3,294,98,322"
       HREF=javascript:hopto('sindex.htm'))>
<! Hotspot for the No Frames button>
<AREA SHAPE=RECT COORDS="0,327,98,353" HREF="homenf.htm" TARGET =
       "_top">
<! Hotspot for the Back-in-main-frame) button>
<AREA SHAPE=RECT COORDS="5,360,38,389"
          HREF=javascript:parent.main.history.back()>
<! Hotspot for the Top-of-page-in-main-frame) button>
<AREA SHAPE=RECT COORDS="40,361,63,388"
          HREF=javascript:goTop()>
<! Hotspot for the Forward-in-main-frame) button>
<AREA SHAPE=RECT COORDS="65,359,98,389"
          HREF=javascript:parent.main.history.forward()>
</MAP>
<IMG SRC="navbttns.gif" USEMAP = "#navmap">
</BODY>
</HTML>
```

Puzzled? The various colors I added to the <BODY . . .> tag are for aesthetics and do not affect how this page functions. Typically, when you define an image as a clickable image map, Navigator displays a blue frame around that map. I didn't want the blue frame in this example, so I set the background color, link color, and visited link colors to gray (C0C0C0).

Accommodating "Old" Browsers

You always need to take into consideration those readers who will be visiting your site with frame-incapable browsers. For example, they won't even see the navigation frame in the sample coolnerds site. Thus, you need to give those visitors some other means of getting around. The simple solution is to use Word IA (or whatever tool you like) to create a home page for such browsers. Figure 30-7 shows a page that I've created for the sample coolnerds site. I named this page homenf.htm (for "home no frames"). I know that it is not a particularly glamorous home page, but it will do for our purposes here.

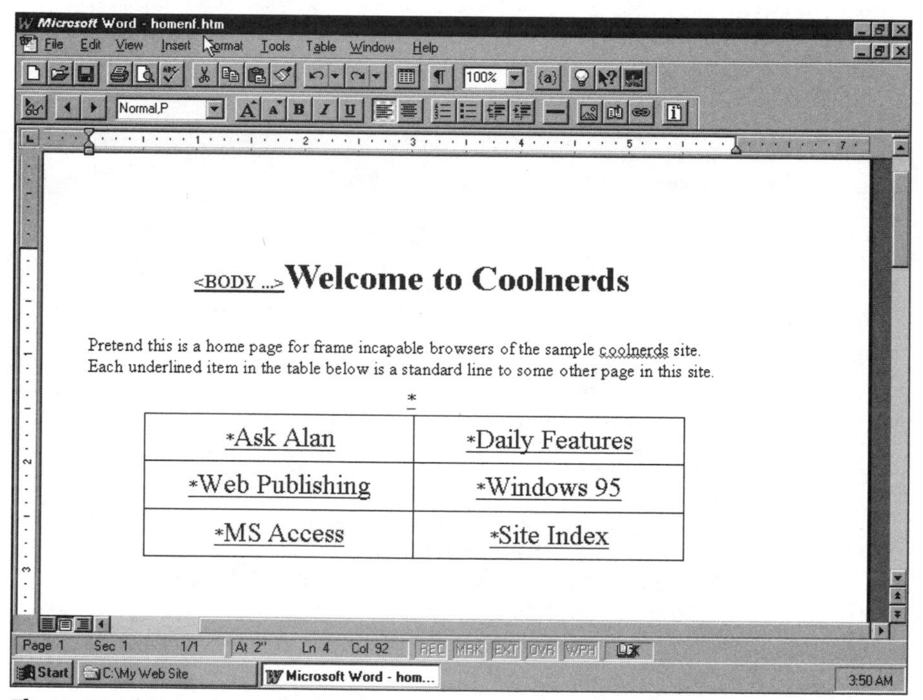

Figure 30-7: Home page for frame-incapable browsers, named homenf.htm in my example.

After you create and save your homenf.htm page, you need to copy and paste the body of that page to the index.html page, between the `<NOFRAMES>...</NOFRAMES>` tags, so that readers who visit the site with frame-incapable browsers see that page right away. In Figure 30-8, I've opened my sample index.html page and added the `<NOFRAMES>...</NOFRAMES>` tags with a little space in between. Then I opened my new homenf.htm page and selected everything between (and including) the `<BODY>...</BODY>` tags. Now all I have to do is press Ctrl+C to copy the selected text, move the insertion point over so that it appears between the `<NOFRAMES>...</NOFRAMES>` tags in index.html, and then press Ctrl+V to paste the copied text into index.html.

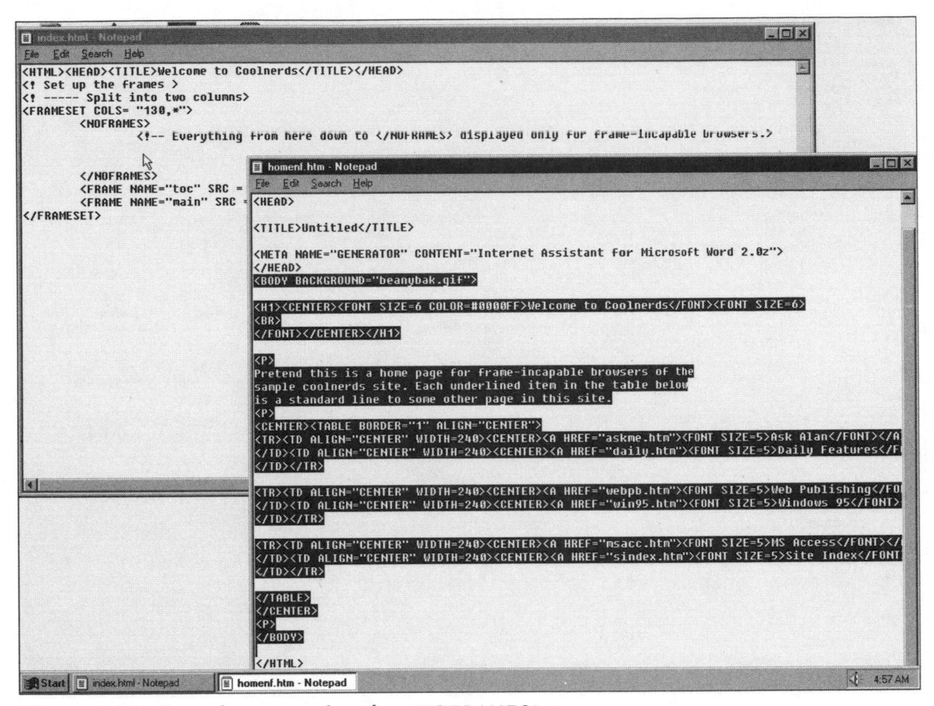

Figure 30-8: Sample page using the <NOFRAMES> tags.

More Info The <NOFRAMES> tags were originally introduced in Chapter 25. In that chapter, I also said that you do not have to copy the actual <BODY> tags into the page that defines the frames. In this example, however, the <BODY> tag specifies a background image for the page being displayed. Here I included the <BODY> tags to make sure that the background image is displayed for frame-incapable browsers.

Once the copy-and-paste process is done, the index.html file will be considerably larger, as you can see in Figure 30-9. But it does accommodate both "new" and "old" browsers, which is what you want!

To test this version of index.html after saving it, you need to open it with a frame-capable browser, such as Netscape Navigator 2.0. Then you need to open it with a frame-incapable browser, such as Internet Explorer 2.0.

Accommodating Voluntary "No Frame" Browsers

You may have noticed way back in Figure 30-1 that my navigation buttons include a No Frames button. This button enables people with frame-capable browsers to browse this site without frames. Why would someone want to do that? I can think of a couple of reasons right off the bat:

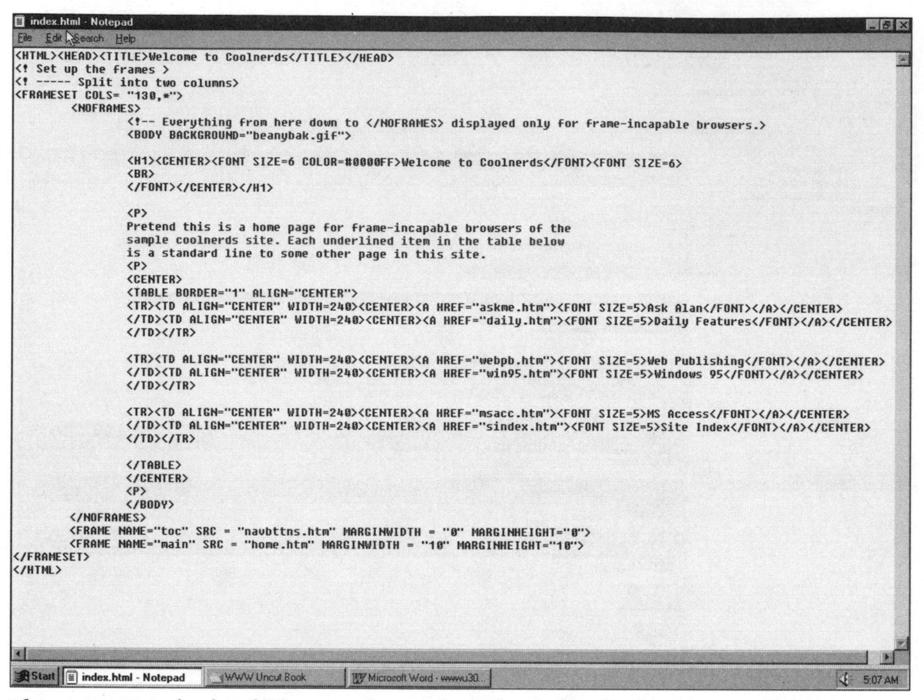

```
<HTML><HEAD><TITLE>Welcome to Coolnerds</TITLE></HEAD>
<! Set up the frames >
<! ----- Split into two columns>
<FRAMESET COLS= "130,*">
        <NOFRAMES>
                <!-- Everything from here down to </NOFRAMES> displayed only for frame-incapable browsers.>
                <BODY BACKGROUND="beanybak.gif">

                <H1><CENTER><FONT SIZE=6 COLOR=#0000FF>Welcome to Coolnerds</FONT><FONT SIZE=6>
                <BR>
                </FONT></CENTER></H1>

                <P>
                Pretend this is a home page for frame-incapable browsers of the
                sample coolnerds site. Each underlined item in the table below
                is a standard line to some other page in this site.
                <P>
                <CENTER>
                <TABLE BORDER="1" ALIGN="CENTER">
                <TR><TD ALIGN="CENTER" WIDTH=240><CENTER><A HREF="askme.htm"><FONT SIZE=5>Ask Alan</FONT></A></CENTER>
                </TD><TD ALIGN="CENTER" WIDTH=240><CENTER><A HREF="daily.htm"><FONT SIZE=5>Daily Features</FONT></A></CENTER>
                </TD></TR>

                <TR><TD ALIGN="CENTER" WIDTH=240><CENTER><A HREF="webpb.htm"><FONT SIZE=5>Web Publishing</FONT></A></CENTER>
                </TD><TD ALIGN="CENTER" WIDTH=240><CENTER><A HREF="win95.htm"><FONT SIZE=5>Windows 95</FONT></A></CENTER>
                </TD></TR>

                <TR><TD ALIGN="CENTER" WIDTH=240><CENTER><A HREF="msacc.htm"><FONT SIZE=5>MS Access</FONT></A></CENTER>
                </TD><TD ALIGN="CENTER" WIDTH=240><CENTER><A HREF="sindex.htm"><FONT SIZE=5>Site Index</FONT></A></CENTER>
                </TD></TR>

                </TABLE>
                </CENTER>
                <P>
                </BODY>
        </NOFRAMES>
        <FRAME NAME="toc" SRC = "navbttns.htm" MARGINWIDTH = "0" MARGINHEIGHT="0">
        <FRAME NAME="main" SRC = "home.htm" MARGINWIDTH = "10" MARGINHEIGHT="10">
</FRAMESET>
</HTML>
```

Figure 30-9: Index.html after copying and pasting in the body of homenf.htm.

- ✦ The reader is more comfortable with the old style of full-page browsing and the normal operation of the Back button.
- ✦ The reader wants the View➪Document Source menu commands to work normally (not always display the source for index.html).

To give the reader the option to browse frame-free, the No Frames button needs to open homenf.htm (the home page for non-frame browsers) in a new Navigator window. The "magic word" for such a window, in JavaScript, is *_top.* As a result, the `<AREA SHAPE ...>` tag for the No Frames button in navbttns.htm looks like this:

```
<! Hotspot for the No Frames button>
<AREA SHAPE=RECT COORDS="0,327,98,353" HREF="homenf.htm" TARGET =
      "_top">
```

Once executed, this tag places the reader in the same view that a frame-incapable browser would see, and the reader can navigate and view the document sources as though he/she were using a frame-incapable browser.

Showing Other Peoples' Sites

While I'm on the topic of showing stuff in a new window by using the _top magic word, I should point out a potential sore spot with this whole frames business. You can display any page within any frame — even pages from other peoples' sites. But I think that we should all agree never to show other peoples' sites within our own frames. There are two reasons why:

✦ If the other person's site has its own frames, those frames will be squeezed into whatever space you've allotted for your own main frame.

✦ If your frame logo appears next to someone else's site, it looks like you're trying to claim authorship for that site. (Tacky, tacky. And also likely to be illegal someday.)

Let me give you an example of the latter, where I'll play the bad guy showing someone else's site in my frames. (I would never do this in real life. And I hope nobody would do it to me.) Figure 30-10 shows the sample coolnerds site after the reader has navigated in quite deeply and is looking at my links to related sites. So far, everything that the reader sees is stuff I've authored.

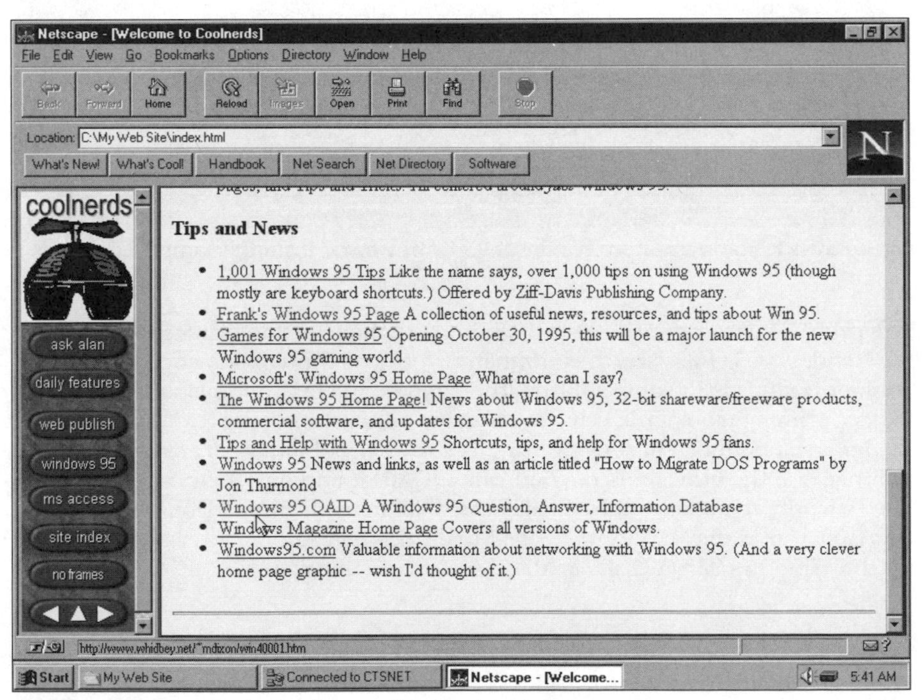

Figure 30-10: Reader is viewing my list of related sites.

Now suppose that the reader clicks on the Windows 95 QAID link and a standard `<A HREF...>` tag in my page opens that site. The reader starts scrolling around in that site and perhaps finds a bit of information that proves very valuable to him or her, as in Figure 30-11.

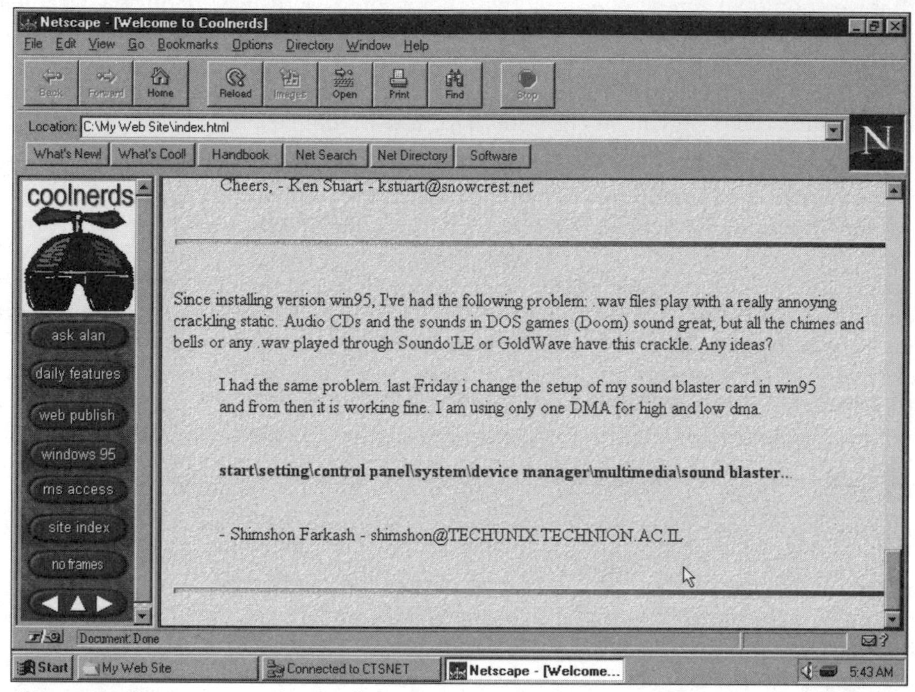

Figure 30-11: Some text from Windows 95 QAID viewed from the sample coolnerds site.

The problem with Figure 30-11 is that although the useful information is coming from the Windows 95 QAID site, the information looks as though it is coming from the coolnerds site. Or, looking at it from the Windows 95 QAID publisher's perspective, it looks as though coolnerds is trying to claim authorship of the text displayed to this reader. As an author, I'm sensitive to this sort of problem. I also assume that if I really did this, and the publishers of Windows 95 QAID found out, their lawyers might e-mail me a friendly reminder not to display their site in my frames. (Don't bother, QAID — this is *just* an example. My site doesn't really do that. And by the way, reader, the URL for the Windows 95 QAID site is `http://www.whidbey.net/~mdixon/win40001.htm`.)

Thus, whenever you put an `<A HREF...>` tag in your own site that points to someone else's site, the trick is to always include the attribute `TARGET='_top'`. For example, in my page, the `<A HREF...>` tag that sends the reader to Windows 95 QAID should look like this:

```
<A HREF="http://www.whidbey.net/~mdixon/win40001.htm"
      TARGET='_top'>

Windows 95 QAID</A>
```

That way, whenever you send the reader to a different site, that site opens in a new Navigator window that appears on top of your own framed site. Your frames will be hidden until the reader comes back to your site by using the Back button in his/her browser. You do lose the "free advertising" of having your own site's logo displayed on the reader's screen no matter where he or she is browsing, but consider the alternative. If we don't nip this problem in the bud right now, we'll all end up trying to browse the Web with a bunch of logos stuck on our screens and the main frame for viewing pages reduced to the size of a postage stamp!

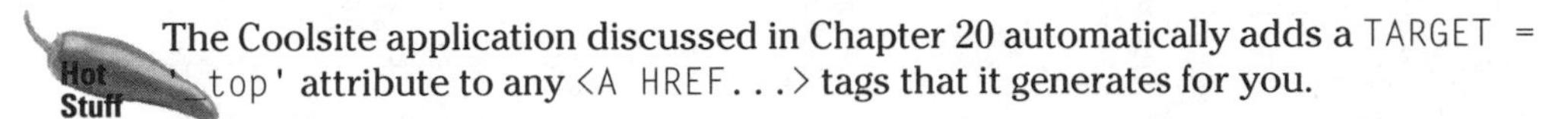

Hot Stuff

The Coolsite application discussed in Chapter 20 automatically adds a `TARGET = '_top'` attribute to any `<A HREF...>` tags that it generates for you.

Viewing the Source in Framed Sites

The sample coolnerds site I presented in this chapter is structurally similar to my real coolnerds site. Of course, my real site is evolving all the time. If you want to see the state-of-the-art in frame browsing, a la yours truly, you're welcome to poke around in the source documents of my coolnerds site.

There is one little catch. (This catch applies to all framed sites, not just coolnerds.) When you choose View⇨Document Source from Navigator's menu bar, you see the source for index.html — as in Figure 30-12 — not the source for whatever page you're actually viewing within a frame.

One simple solution here is to close the Source window and choose No Frames from coolnerds' navigation buttons. Then browse to any page in the site without frames and choose View⇨Document Source when you get to the page you want to explore.

The one page you cannot reach with this approach is the navbttns.htm page because that page only appears when frames are displayed. But a simple way around that problem exists, too. If you look near the bottom of Figure 30-12, you see this tag in index.html.

```
<FRAME NAME="toc" SRC = "navbttns.htm"
        MARGINWIDTH = "0" MARGINHEIGHT="0">
```

This tag actually provides a very useful bit of information (in any framed site, not just coolnerds) because it tells you the name of the document displayed in the smaller toc frame. To get to that document in full-page view, you simply need to specify that document in your Location box. For example, when you're in coolnerds, the Location box in Navigator's window usually shows the following:

```
Location: http://www.coolnerds.com/index.html
```

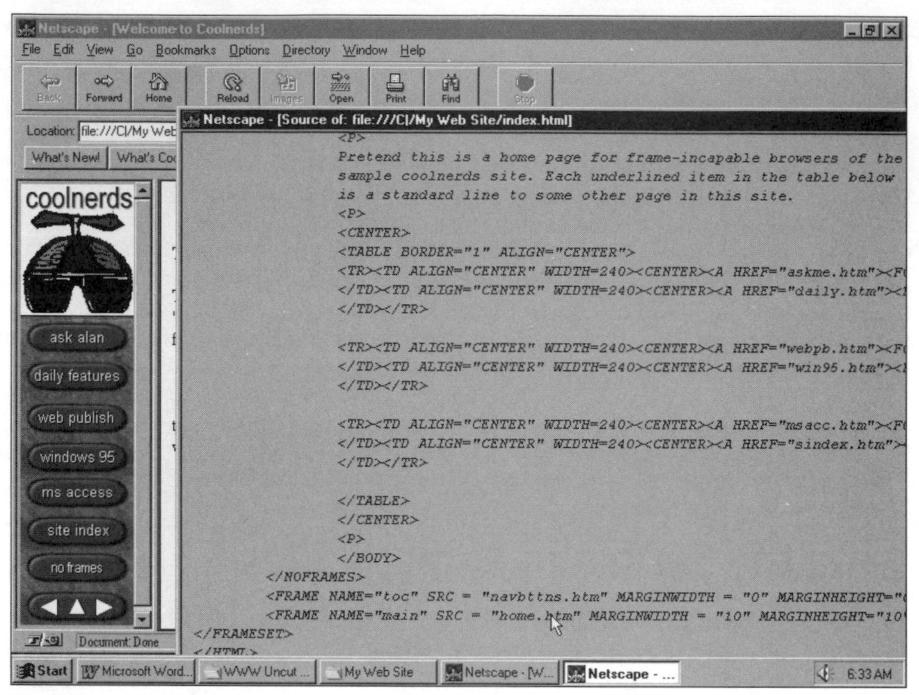

Figure 30-12: The Document Source for a framed site is always the page that defines the frames.

If you just change index.html to the filename pilfered out of the <FRAME NAME...> tag, such as this:

```
Location: http://www.coolnerds.com/navbttns.htm
```

the navbttns.htm page opens in full-screen (non-framed) view. *Then* you can choose View➪Document Source to see the underlying code of the navbttns.htm page, as in Figure 30-13.

Puzzled? The Location box in the figures shown in this chapter show C:\My Web Site\index.html as the document's location because these pages were on my local PC when I wrote this chapter. You'll see the actual URL for the site, http://www.coolnerds.com, when you view the pages from your PC.

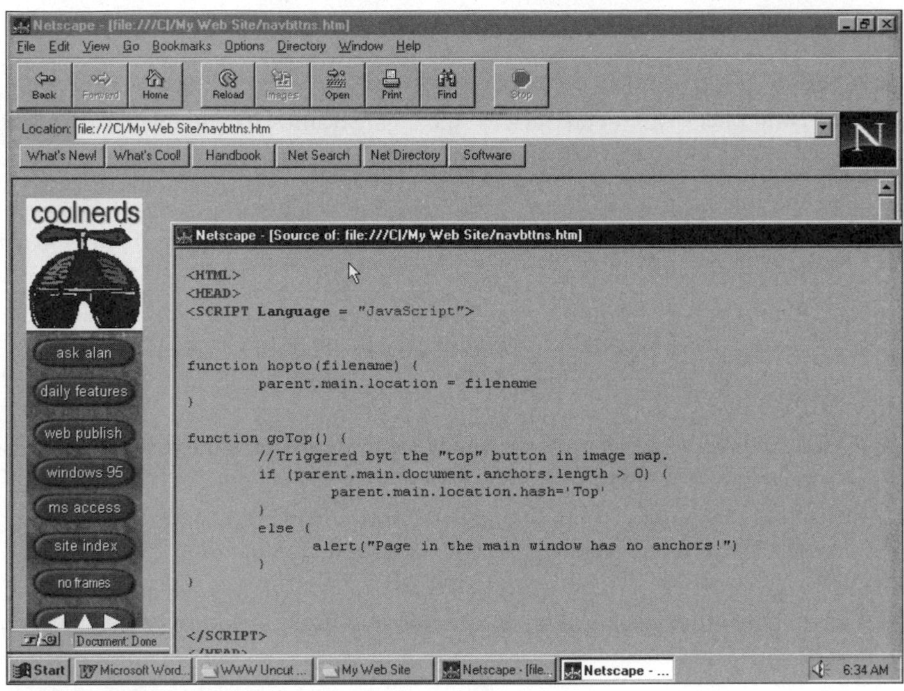

Figure 30-13: The source behind navbttns.htm.

Summary

In this chapter, I expanded on the original discussion of frames (back in Chapter 25) by discussing JavaScript techniques for managing frames. The following are some important points to keep in mind:

- ✦ To refer to a specific frame in a site by using JavaScript, use the general syntax parent.*framename,* where *framename* is the name of the frame defined in the site's <FRAME> tag.
- ✦ To display a page in a frame, use the syntax parent.*framename*.location = "*filenameOrURL,*" where *framename* is the name of the frame that you want to display the page in and *filenameOrURL* is the filename or URL of the page to display.
- ✦ You can use the JavaScript statement parent.*framename*.history.back() to send the reader back one page in the frame named *framename.*
- ✦ Use the JavaScript statement parent.*framename*.history.forward() to send the reader forward one page in the frame named *framename.*
- ✦ Use the TARGET = '_top' attribute in JavaScript code and event handlers to display another person's site or a non-framed page of your own in a new, non-framed Navigator window.

✦ ✦ ✦

Cookies, Arrays, and Custom Objects

✦ ✦ ✦ ✦

In This Chapter

Understanding local variables

Creating global variables

Creating and using persistent cookies

Storing data in arrays

Creating custom objects

Creating an array of custom objects

✦ ✦ ✦ ✦

In this chapter, I want to introduce you to some more advanced JavaScript programming techniques, which you may find useful in developing highly interactive Web sites of your own. In particular, the focus will be on storing and managing *data,* which is likely to be an important element of any interactive Web site you design.

Understanding JavaScript Variables

As I've mentioned in earlier chapters, a variable is a little placeholder in the computer's memory where you can store small bits of data for your script to act upon. Creating a variable is a pretty simple task. You just come up with a name (that starts with a letter and contains no spaces) and put some value in it. For example, the first JavaScript statement that follows creates a variable named *x* and puts the number 10 into it. The second one creates a variable named msg and puts some text (a string) in that variable.

```
x=10
msg = "Hello There"
```

To get a firm grasp of how variables work within a Web site, you need to understand the concept of *scope.* Scope is a fancy way of saying "how long the variable exists" (or, as it is often termed, the *lifetime* of a variable).

Regular variables

For the purposes of this chapter, let's say that a regular variable isonecreatedwithinacustomfunction.Forexample,takealookatthefollowingJavaScriptcode,which contains two custom functions — one called getReaderName() and another called showHelloMsg(). Notice that the getReaderName() function, when executed, *creates* a variable named ReaderName and then *assigns* that variable a value based on the contents of the readername form field (which gets created in the body of this page).

```
<HTML><HEAD>
<SCRIPT Language = "JavaScript">

function getReaderName() {
     //Create a variable named ReaderName then put form content
       into it.
     var ReaderName = null
     ReaderName=document.getname.readername.value
}

function showHelloMsg() {
     //Try to display that ReaderName variable in an "alert"
       message.
     msg = "Hello "+ReaderName
     alert (msg)
}
</SCRIPT></HEAD>

<BODY>
<! Let's create a form named 'getname'>
<FORM Name = "getname">
Please type in your name:
<INPUT Type="text" Name = "readername" onChange =
       "getReaderName()")
<! As soon as user enters name, the onChange event calls upon the
       getReaderName() >
<! custom function to put the reader's entry into a variable
       named ReaderName> <P><P>
Then
<INPUT type="button" Value="Click Me" onClick = 'showHelloMsg()')
<! When reader clicks this button, try to execute the
       showHelloMsg() function >
<! to say hello to this reader.>
</FORM>
</BODY>
</HTML>
```

When I open this page, it displays a prompt for typing in my name and a button to click. Suppose that I type my name and then click the button. What happens? Unfortunately, an error happens, as Figure 31-1 shows. The error message tells me that the variable named ReaderName doesn't exist. But how can this be? I definitely remember creating a variable with that name.

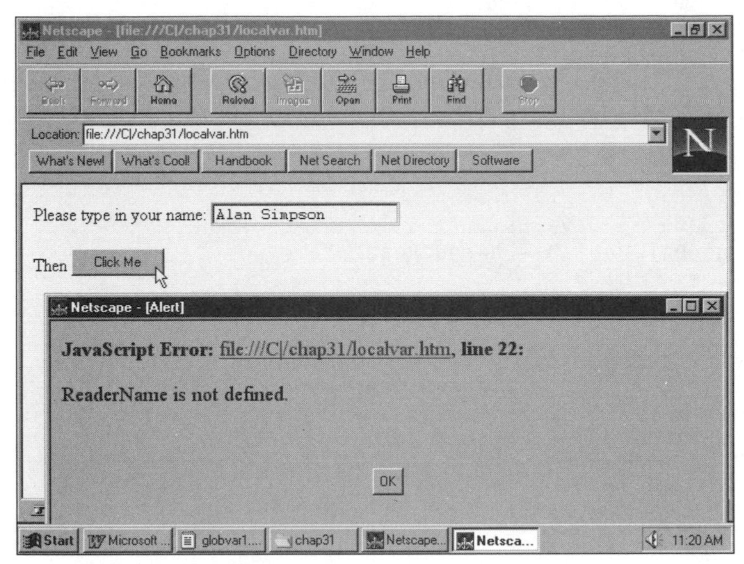

Figure 31-1: The preceding sample script only displays an error message.

The problem here lies in the fact that when you define a variable *inside* a function, that variable becomes local to that function. That is, the variable exists only while the function is being executed (which takes about one zillionth of a second). As soon as the function is finished executing, the variable ceases to exist.

That reason is why the showHelloMsg() function failed to run and instead showed an error message. By the time JavaScript reached the point at which it needed to execute the statement msg = "Hello "+ReaderName, the variable named ReaderName had been killed off. It was killed off because the custom function that created it, getReaderName(), had finished doing its thing, and hence all of its local variables (such as ReaderName in this example) were long dead and forgotten.

Global variables

The solution to this problem of getting two functions to refer to the same variable is to create a *global variable.* As the name somewhat implies, a global variable is one to which all JavaScript code in a page has access. Creating a global variable is simple — you just have to follow two basic rules:

- ✦ Create the variable once, using *var* before any JavaScript code *refers* to the variable.
- ✦ Never recreate the variable with the page (that is, never use *var* in front of the variable name after that initial definition).

What this boils down to is simply defining the variable right off the bat — just under the <SCRIPT> tag in the head of your page — so that it exists right away. In the preceding example, all I needed to do was move the var ReaderName = null statement *out* of the getReaderName( ) function and place it at the top of the initial set of scripts, as shown here:

```
<HTML><HEAD>
<SCRIPT Language = "JavaScript">
//Create a global variable named ReaderName
var ReaderName = null


function getReaderName() {
     //Put whatever the reader entered as his name into the
       global readername variable.
     ReaderName=document.getname.readername.value
}

function showHelloMsg() {
     //Show a message that contains that global ReaderName
       variable.
     msg = "Hello "+ReaderName
     alert (msg)
}
</SCRIPT></HEAD>

<BODY>
<! Let's create a form named 'getname'>
<FORM Name = "getname">
Please type in your name:
<INPUT Type="text" Name = "readername" onChange =
       "getReaderName()")
<! As soon as user enters name, the onChange event calls upon the
       getReaderName() >
<! custom function to put the reader's entry into the global
       variable named ReaderName> <P><P>
Then
<INPUT type="button" Value="Click Me" onClick = 'showHelloMsg()')
<! When reader clicks this button, execute the showHelloMsg()
       function >
<! to say hello to this reader.>
</FORM>
</BODY>
</HTML>
```

I've also changed some comments in the sample code to better explain how this new version of the script works. When I run this version, I can type in my name and click the button. This time, instead of getting an error message, I get a little alert box that says hello and has my name in it, as Figure 31-2 shows.

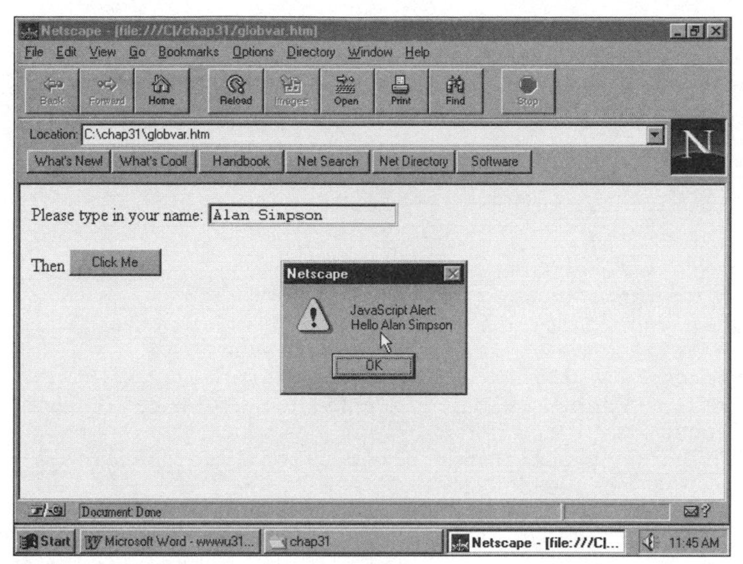

Figure 31-2: The second script doesn't cause an error message.

Puzzled? The alert message looks kind of alarming, but it is not an error message. You can display your own message in an alert box (*Hello Alan Simpson,* in my example). But you cannot make it look less alarming. I've used an alert( ) box in this example because this method provides the simplest way to display a custom JavaScript message.

Just how global is a global variable?

Now that you know a global variable is one accessible to all JavaScript code in the current page, you need to ask this question: "Is it also accessible to other pages in my site?" Unfortunately, the answer is no. Even a global variable's life does not extend beyond the life of the current page. Let me show you what I mean.

In the following script, I have a page named globvar1.htm, which is essentially the same page as the one I just showed you. The only exception is that it includes a hyperlink to a new page named globvar2.htm (shown in boldface):

```
<HTML><HEAD>
<SCRIPT Language = "JavaScript">
//Create a global variable named ReaderName
var ReaderName = null


function getReaderName() {
     //Put whatever the reader entered as his name into the
       global readername variable.
     ReaderName=document.getname.readername.value
}
```

```
function showHelloMsg() {
     //Show a message that contains that global ReaderName vari-
       able.
     msg = "Hello "+ReaderName
     alert (msg)
}
</SCRIPT></HEAD>

<BODY>
<! Let's create a form named 'getname'>
<FORM Name = "getname">
Please type in your name:
<INPUT Type="text" Name = "readername" onChange =
       "getReaderName()")
<! As soon as user enters name, the onChange event calls upon the
       getReaderName() >
<! custom function to put the reader's entry into the global
       variable named ReaderName> <P><P>
Then
<INPUT type="button" Value="Click Me" onClick = 'showHelloMsg()')
<! When reader clicks this button, execute the showHelloMsg()
       function >
<! to say hello to this reader.>
</FORM>

<! When we click to go to another page, will that page still >
<! recognize the global ReaderName variable? >
Then <A HREF="globvar2.htm" >Go To Page 2</A>
</BODY>
</HTML>
```

Here is the content of the globvar2.htm page:

```
<HTML>
<! This is globvar2.htm>
<HEAD></HEAD>
<BODY>
<SCRIPT Language = "JavaScript">
     // Will this new page be able to display the value in
       ReaderName?
     document.write ('Hello ',ReaderName)
</SCRIPT>
<! Unfortunately, the answer is No. The global variable is only
       'global'>
<! to the page in which it was created.
The global ReaderName variable didn't make it to this page. It's
       only
'global' to the JavaScript code within that page.
</BODY>
</HTML>
```

When I open the glob1var.htm page, fill in the blank, and click the button, everything works fine and I get the result shown back in Figure 31-2. But when I click the hyperlink to go to the next page, I get the result shown in Figure 31-3. This new page, globvar2.htm, knows nothing of the variable named ReaderName. Hence, it displays an error message when it tries to execute the document.write ('Hello ',ReaderName) statement.

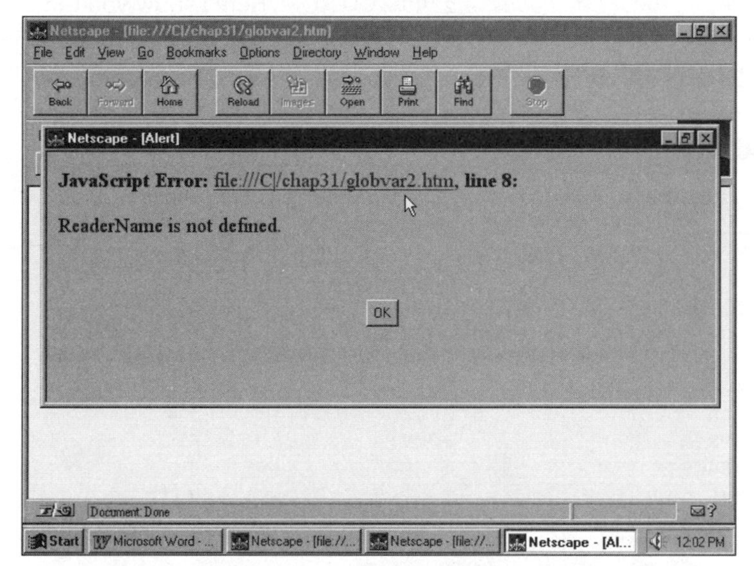

Figure 31-3: The globvar2.htm page knows nothing of the global ReaderName variable created in globvar1.htm.

Hmmmmmm. Okay, but suppose that I *do* want to have a little chunk of data, such as the reader's name, that I can pass around from page to page within my site. Is such a thing possible? The answer is *yes*. But you can't do it with just variables. You need to add a *cookie* to the recipe.

JavaScript Cookies

In JavaScript, a *cookie* is a little chunk of data, such as a variable. However, its lifespan is not limited to the current page. And unlike a variable, which is stored in RAM, a cookie is stored in a disk file named cookies.txt. The normal lifespan of a cookie is the current Web-browsing session. Because the cookie is stored in a disk file, however, you can extend its life to virtually any duration.

The only drawback to cookies is that, despite the cute name, they are fairly complicated to deal with. Also, no official spec for cookies exists, so using them in your JavaScript scripts involves a little danger. But I've found that if you don't try to get *too* fancy, cookies can be simple to use and very useful. I also found some nice custom functions on the Web, written by Bill Dortch of hIdaho Design, that make managing cookies even easier. In this chapter, I share three of those functions with you. The functions are SetCookie( ) (to store a value in a cookie), GetCookie( ) (to pull a value back out of a cookie), and getCookieVal( ), which the GetCookie( ) function needs to do its job.

For the larger set of custom cookie functions written by Mr. Dortch, see dortch.htm in the JavaScpt folder on the *HTML Publishing Bible* CD-ROM. Here I show you the custom functions and how to use them to create variables that last for the duration of the reader's current browsing session.

Function to create a cookie

The SetCookie( ) function follows:

```
//  Cookie Function written by  Bill Dortch, hIdaho Design
       <bdortch@netw.com>
function SetCookie (name, value) {
     var argv = SetCookie.arguments;
     var argc = SetCookie.arguments.length;
     var expires = (argc > 2) ? argv[2] : null;
     var path = (argc > 3) ? argv[3] : null;
     var domain = (argc > 4) ? argv[4] : null;
     var secure = (argc > 5) ? argv[5] : false;
     document.cookie = name + "=" + escape (value) +
     ((expires == null) ? "" : ("; expires=" +
       expires.toGMTString())) +
     ((path == null) ? "" : ("; path=" + path)) +
     ((domain == null) ? "" : ("; domain=" + domain)) +
     ((secure == true) ? "; secure" : "");
}
```

Life Saver

You do not have to type these custom functions from scratch. You can simply copy and paste them from the dortch.htm, alanck1.htm, or alanck2.htm pages in the JavaScpt folder of the *HTML Publishing Bible* CD-ROM or from my coolnerds Web site.

The listing that follows shows an example that uses SetCookie() in a page to store the contents of the variable named *ReaderName* in a cookie named *cookie1*. The name of this page is alanck1.htm. I boldfaced the important elements for you to look at as follows:

```
<html><head>
<! This is alanck1.htm>
<title>JavaScript Cookies Demo</title>
<script language = "JavaScript">

//Create global variable ReaderName
var ReaderName = null
```

```
function setReaderName() {
     //Takes reader's form entry and puts it in a cookie named
       cookie1.
     ReaderName=document.getname.readername.value
     SetCookie('cookie1',ReaderName)
}

//  Cookie Function written by  Bill Dortch, hIdaho Design
       <bdortch@netw.com>
function SetCookie (name, value) {
     var argv = SetCookie.arguments;
     var argc = SetCookie.arguments.length;
     var expires = (argc > 2) ? argv[2] : null;
     var path = (argc > 3) ? argv[3] : null;
     var domain = (argc > 4) ? argv[4] : null;
     var secure = (argc > 5) ? argv[5] : false;
     document.cookie = name + "=" + escape (value) +
     ((expires == null) ? "" : ("; expires=" +
       expires.toGMTString())) +
     ((path == null) ? "" : ("; path=" + path)) +
     ((domain == null) ? "" : ("; domain=" + domain)) +
     ((secure == true) ? "; secure" : "");
}

</script></head>
<body>
<! Let's create a form named 'getname'>
<FORM Name = "getname">
Please type in your name:
<! As soon as user enters name, setReaderName() puts that entry
       in>
<! a global variable named ReaderName, and a cookie named
       cookie1.>
<INPUT Type="text" Name = "readername" onChange =
       "setReaderName()")
<P><P>
</FORM>
<P><P>
<! When we click to go to another page, alanck2.htm, that page>
<! will be able to get ReaderName from cookie1.>
Then <A HREF="alanck2.htm" >Go To Page 2</A>
</body>
</html>
```

Function to retrieve a cookie

It takes two functions to retrieve a cookie: GetCookie() and getCookieVal(). Both functions appear in the following script:

```
//  Cookie Functions written by Bill Dortch, hIdaho Design
      <bdortch@netw.com>
//  Function to return the value of the cookie specified by
      "name".
function GetCookie (name) {
     var arg = name + "="
     var alen = arg.length
     var clen = document.cookie.length
     var i = 0
     while (i < clen) {
          var j = i + alen
          if (document.cookie.substring(i, j) == arg)
               return getCookieVal (j)
                i = document.cookie.indexOf(" ", i) + 1
                if (i == 0) break
          }
     return null;
}

// Called by GetCookie() -- required in any script that uses
      GetCookie().
function getCookieVal (offset) {
     var endstr = document.cookie.indexOf (";", offset)
     if (endstr == -1)
          endstr = document.cookie.length
          return unescape(document.cookie.substring(offset,
      endstr))
}
```

The complete listing that follows is for a sample page named alanck2.htm file, which the reader can open from alanck1.htm. The alanck2.htm file uses the GetCookie( ) function to pull ReaderName out of cookie1 and then display it on the screen. I boldfaced the important parts (for our current interests). This script does not produce any error messages when executed because the second page shown here can use the cookie to define a value for its variable named ReaderName.

```
<html><head>
<!This is alanck2.htm>
<title>JavaScript Cookies Demo, Page 2</title>
<script language = "JavaScript">

//  Cookie Functions written by Bill Dortch, hIdaho Design
      <bdortch@netw.com>
//  Function to return the value of the cookie specified by
      "name".
function GetCookie (name) {
     var arg = name + "="
     var alen = arg.length
```

```
     var clen = document.cookie.length
     var i = 0
     while (i < clen) {
          var j = i + alen
          if (document.cookie.substring(i, j) == arg)
               return getCookieVal (j)
                i = document.cookie.indexOf(" ", i) + 1
                if (i == 0) break
          }
     return null;
}

// Called by GetCookie() -- required in any script that uses
       GetCookie().
function getCookieVal (offset) {
     var endstr = document.cookie.indexOf (";", offset)
     if (endstr == -1)
          endstr = document.cookie.length
          return unescape(document.cookie.substring(offset,
       endstr))
}
</script></head>

<body>
<P><H1><CENTER>
<SCRIPT Language = "JavaScript">
     ReaderName = GetCookie ('cookie1')
     document.write ("Hello ",ReaderName)
</SCRIPT>
</CENTER></H1>
</body>
</html>
```

The bottom line is this: If you want to create a variable that lasts from page to page, you need to store that value in a cookie. The page that creates the cookie must contain the custom SetCookie( ) function. The simple syntax for SetCookie( ) is

```
function SetCookie ("name", "value")
```

where *name* is a name that uniquely identifies the cookie and *value* is the actual string you want to store. If either name or value is a variable name, you should omit the quotation marks.

Any page that retrieves a value from a cookie must contain the custom GetCookie( ) and getCookieVal( ) functions. The basic syntax for GetCookie( ) is

```
variablename = GetCookie ("name")
```

where *variablename* is the name of the variable within the current page that will hold the cookie value and *name* is the name of the cookie as stated in the SetCookie( ) function that created the cookie.

If you want to learn more about cookies, see the official spec at `http://home.netscape.com/newsref/std/`. Alternatively, you can search the Web for sites that talk about *JavaScript.* For now, I want to turn your attention away from this topic and look at other ways to store and manage data within your Web pages — namely *arrays* and custom objects.

JavaScript Arrays

Many programming languages offer arrays. An *array* is a bunch of variables with the same name but different *subscripts.* The subscript is a number that indicates the variable's position in the list. For example, the following list is an array of product names:

product[1] = "Coffee Beans"

product[2] = "Regular Grind"

product[3] = "Drip Grind"

product[4] = "Espresso Grind"

product[5] = "Instant Coffee"

This array contains five *elements,* the first element being product[1] (pronounced *product sub one*). The second element is product[2] (pronounced *product sub two*), and so on. Each element in this particular array contains a string literal — which means that each element contains a little chunk of text.

Function to create an array

JavaScript supports the use of arrays, but it has no specific statements for creating arrays. If you want to create an array, you first need to create a custom function that can build an empty array. To do that, you just need to stick this MakeArray( ) function into the head portion of your Web page, between a pair of `<SCRIPT...>...</SCRIPT>` tags:

```
        <HEAD>
    <SCRIPT Language = "JavaScript">

    function MakeArray(n) {
    this.length = n           // Element zero will contain the
      array's length
    for (var i = 1; i<= n; i++) {
         this[i] = 0 }
         return this
    }
    </SCRIPT>
</HEAD>
```

Creating a new (empty) array

Once you have the MakeArray( ) custom function in your page, you can call upon it to create a new, empty array with whatever variable name you like. You also need to tell it how many items will be in the array. The statement to create the array generally appears in the body, rather than in the head of the current page. It also should have the following general syntax:

```
variablename = new MakeArray(n)
```

where *variablename* is the name of each item in the list (the part before the subscript) and *n* tells how many items will be in the array. For example, this statement

```
product = new MakeArray(5)
```

creates an array with five elements: product[1], product[2], product[3], product[4], and product[5]. Initially, each of these array elements will contain the number zero. But you can *populate* the array with whatever data you wish.

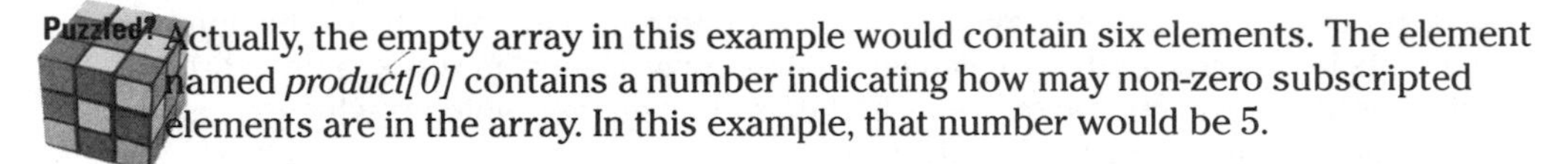

Actually, the empty array in this example would contain six elements. The element named *product[0]* contains a number indicating how may non-zero subscripted elements are in the array. In this example, that number would be 5.

Populating the array

To populate the array, simply assign a value to each array element as you would assign a value to any normal variable. This makes sense because each array element *is* a variable. The only thing that makes these variables different from the regular kind is the name subscript — that is, having *product[1]* rather than *product* as the variable name.

Then how do you (a) create a new array named product and (b) put five product names into that array? Assuming that the MakeArray( ) custom function appears in the head of the current Web page, you need to execute the following script to create the blank array and then fill in the product names:

```
<BODY>

product = new MakeArray(5)

product[1] = "Coffee Beans"
product[2] = "Regular Grind"
product[3] = "Drip Grind"
product[4] = "Espresso Grind"
product[5] = "Instant Coffee"


</BODY>
```

Displaying an array's contents

One of the beauties of using an array is that no matter how many elements exist in the array, you can display them all by using one simple *for* loop. The basic syntax of this loop is

```
for (var i = 1;i <= variablename[0]; i++) {
     document.write ('variablename[',i,'] contains
       <b>'variablename[i],'<br>')
}
```

For the example of creating an array named products, the display loop would look like this:

```
for (var i = 1;i <= product[0]; i++) {
     document.write ('product[',i,'] contains
       <b>'product[i],'<br>')
}
```

Remember that the MakeArray( ) custom function automatically stores the number of elements in an array in the [0] element of that array. Hence, in this example, product[0] contains the number of items in the products array, which is why you can use it in the for( ) loop that prints the array.

Here's an entire Web page that pulls all the different array-producing tricks together. I've added some comments as reminders to what each little routine (chunk of code) is doing. Just like plain English, no? (Yeah, right!)

```
<HTML><HEAD>
<TITLE>My First Array</TITLE>

<SCRIPT Language = "JavaScript">

/*Function to create a new, empty array. Element[0], and
       element.length,
   will both contain a number indicating how many non-zero-
       subscripted
   elements are in the list. That info will come in handy later. */

function MakeArray(n) {
     this.length = n
     for (var i = 1; i<= n; i++) {
          this[i] = 0      //Just stick a zero in each new ele-
       ment for now.
     }
          return this
}
</SCRIPT>
</HEAD>

<BODY><! Out of the head, and into the body>
<SCRIPT Language = "JavaScript">
```

```
//Create a new array named product with five elements.
product = new MakeArray(5)

//Populate that array with these data.
product[1] = "Coffee Beans"
product[2] = "Regular Grind"
product[3] = "Drip Grind"
product[4] = "Espresso Grind"
product[5] = "Instant Coffee"


/* Now let's display the array's contents using product.length
   to determine how many times to repeat a "for" loop. */

document.write ('product.length contains <b>',
          product.length,'</b></br>')

for (var i = 1;i <= product.length; i++) {
     document.write ('product[',i,'] contains <b>',
          product[i],'</b><br>')
}

</SCRIPT>
</BODY></HTML>
```

Opening that page with a JavaScript-capable browser, such as Netscape 2.0, produces the result shown in Figure 31-4. Not too terribly exciting, but trust me, some potentially useful stuff is brewing here (no pun on the product list intended).

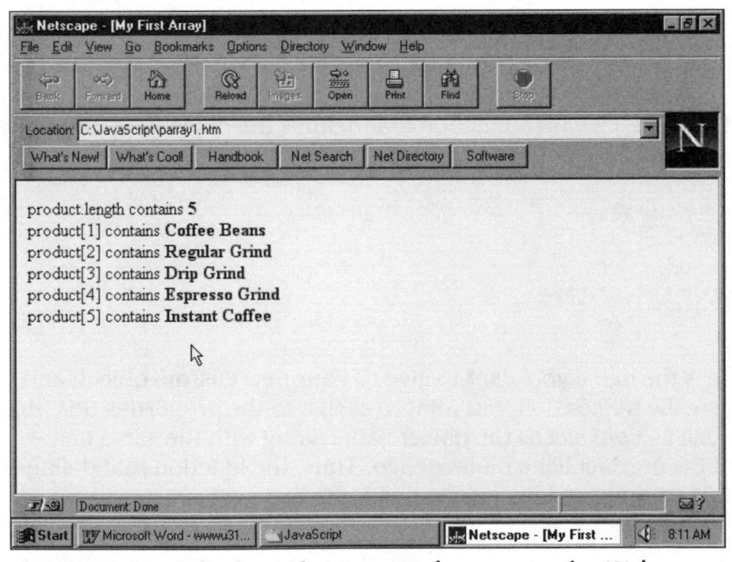

Figure 31-4: Result of opening my sample array-creating Web page.

Creating Custom Objects

As you may recall, JavaScript defines many of the things you see on the screen as objects. JavaScript also can refer to those objects and make those objects do things through properties and methods. As it turns out, JavaScript also lets you create your own custom objects. Like the built-in objects, your custom objects can have their own properties and methods.

Defining a custom object

To define a custom object, you need to do two things:

✦ Create a custom function that defines the object.

✦ Create an instance of the object using the keyword **new.**

Let's take a look at each step by using an example. Forget about the products array you created earlier, and create a new object named product. Give this new object three properties; prodnum, name, and unitprice. Rather than only having a list of product names, you can come up with a list like this:

```
prodnum      name              unitprice
C-111        Coffee Beans      $10.00
C-222        Regular Grind     $10.50
C-333        Drip Grind        $11.00
C-444        Espresso Grind    $11.50
C-555        Instant Coffee    $12.00
```

Custom function to define a new object

Now that you have an idea of the kind of information you want to put into the product object, you need to come up with a function that defines the object and its properties. The general syntax for such an object is

```
function objectname(prop1, prop2,...propN)
     this.prop1 = prop1
     this.prop2 = prop2
     this.propN = propN
}
```

where *objectname* is the name you want to give to your new custom object, and *prop1, prop2, . . . propN* are the names that you want to assign to the properties this object will contain. You can use *product* as the object name along with the same names you used at the top of the product list a moment ago. Thus, the function that defines the custom product object ends up looking like this:

```
function product(prodnum, name, unitprice) {
     this.prodnum = prodnum
     this.name = name
     this.unitprice = unitprice
}
```

Creating one new instance of an object

To create an instance of an object, you need to call up the custom product() function using the **new** keyword. For example, this statement:

```
myprod = new product("C-111","Coffee Beans",10)
```

creates a single product object named *myprod.* After executing that statement, the following statements

```
/* Let's print out myprod's properties */
document.write ("myprod.prodnum = ",myprod.prodnum,"<br>")
document.write ("myprod.name = ",myprod.name,"<br>")
document.write ("myprod.unitprice = ",myprod.unitprice,"<br>")
```

display this:

```
myprod.prodnum = c-111

myprod.name = Coffee Beans

myprod.unitprice = 10
```

This is all well and good, but this still doesn't give you a single product named myprod to deal with. You have several products (five to be exact, in this example) to deal with instead. It might be nice if you could create an array of objects such that you had a list of products. Then you could refer to any property of any product in the list just by using its property name, such as *.name* or *.unitprice.* As it turns out, you *can* create an array of objects by combining JavaScript's capabilities to handle arrays and objects.

Creating an Array of Objects

In the earlier products array, I had you put the names of several products into a list. If you make a product into an object, you can then make a list that contains the product code, product name, and unit price for every product that you carry. This method is potentially a very organized way to handle a product list with JavaScript.

The following listing illustrates a Web page named customob.htm that creates an array of custom product objects. Figure 31-5 shows what happens when you open that page with a JavaScript-capable Web browser.

```
<HTML><HEAD>
<TITLE>My First Array of Custom Objects</TITLE>
<! This is customob.htm>
<SCRIPT Language = "JavaScript">

// Function to create a new, empty array.
function MakeArray(n) {
     this.length = n
     for (var i = 1; i<= n; i++) {
          this[i] = 0      //Just stick a zero in each new ele-
       ment for now.
     }
          return this
}

/* Function to define a new custom object named product.
   This product will have three properties, prodnum (a product
   id), name (a product name), and unitprice.*/
function prodobj(prodnum, name, unitprice) {
     this.prodnum = prodnum
     this.name = name
     this.unitprice = unitprice
}

</SCRIPT>
</HEAD>

<BODY><! Out of the head, and into the body>
<SCRIPT Language = "JavaScript">

//Create a new array named product with five elements.
product = new MakeArray(5)

//Populate that array with these product objects.
product[1] = new prodobj('C-111','Coffee Beans',10.00)
product[2] = new prodobj('C-222','Regular Grind',10.50)
product[3] = new prodobj('C-333','Drip Grind',11.00)
product[4] = new prodobj('C-444','Espresso Grind',11.50)
product[5] = new prodobj('C-555','Instant Coffee',12.00)


/* Now let's display the array's contents using product.length
    to determine how many times to repeat a "for" loop. */

document.write ('product.length contains <B>',
          product.length,'</B><P>')
for (var i=1; i<=product.length; i++) {
     document.write ('product[',i,'].prodnum contains
       <b>',product[i].prodnum,'</b><br>')
     document.write ('product[',i,'].name contains
       <b>',product[i].name,'</b><br>')
```

```
      document.write ('product[',i,'].unitprice contains
        <b>',product[i].unitprice,'</b><p>')
}

</SCRIPT>
</BODY></HTML>
```

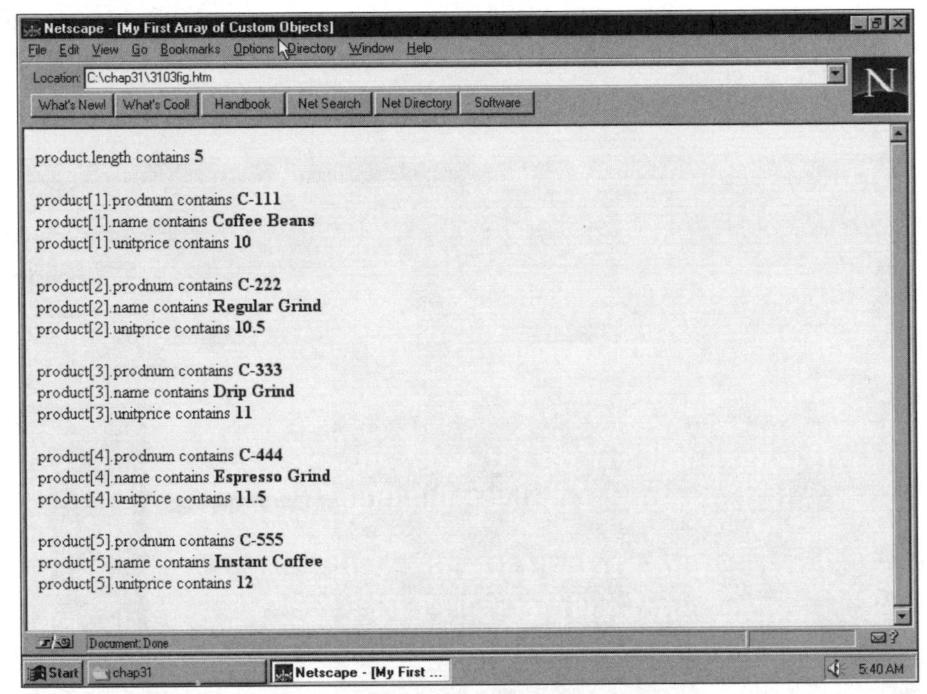

Figure 31-5: Results of opening the customob.htm Web page.

I hope you are now thinking this: "Big deal. If I wanted to show a little table of products, I could have just created the table in Word IA. No need for all this JavaScript code, arrays, and custom objects." You would be absolutely right. The real value of arrays and custom objects isn't apparent until (1) You have a fairly large list to work with and (2) You want to handle the data in the list in many different ways. You see some practical examples of this in the next chapter.

The Color Schemer Page

I thought I'd mention that my Color Schemer page uses an array of custom "color objects" to give the reader a means of trying out different color schemes on the screen. When opened, the Color Schemer presents two simple select boxes. The reader can choose a color from either select box and then click the Apply button to apply the selected colors to the lower frame.

More Info

My Color Schemer Web page is stored in the JavaScpt folder of the *HTML Publishing Bible* CD-ROM and on my Web site at `http://www.coolnerds.com`. It consists of three files: alancolr.htm (the page you actually open), coloropts.htm, and colortrg.htm — all of which are opened automatically in separate frames when you open alancolr.htm.

For example, in Figure 31-6, I've already selected black as the background color and white as the foreground color. However, I'm just about to try out a new color from the foreground color select list. The lower frame currently shows how the black/white color combination looks on-screen, and also shows you the "official" name and color triplet of those colors.

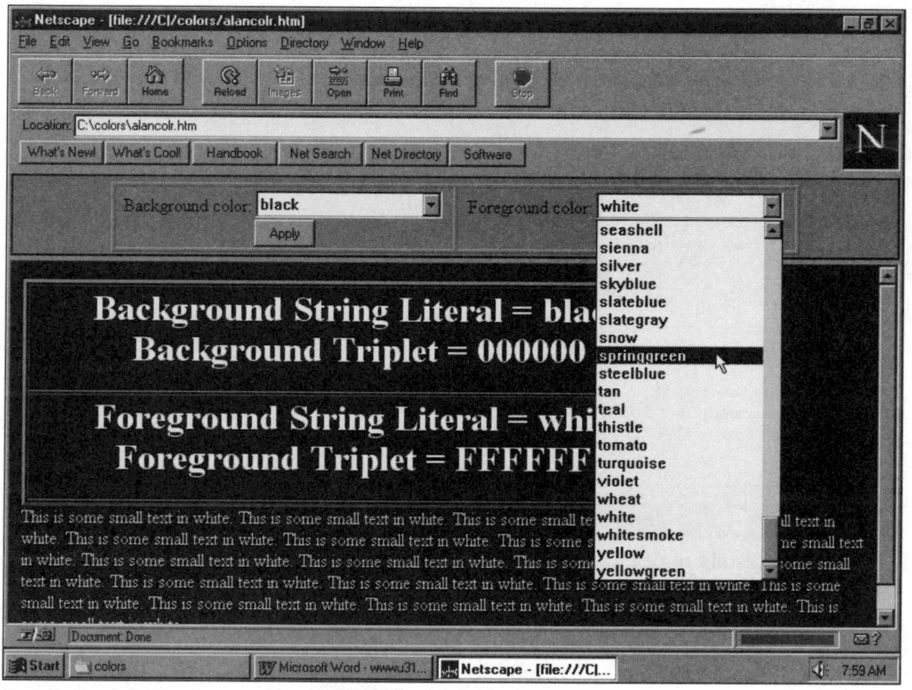

Figure 31-6: Here's the Color Schemer page in action.

If you are interested in exploring the source document for the Color Schemer, you need to open the coloropts.htm file in Notepad or some other simple text editor. The array of custom color objects, named ColorList, is created in that page. That same page creates the little form consisting of two select boxes. And if you really poke around, you see that the select box options are actually created with for loops that pull color names from the ColorList array. We explore this cool trick in more depth in Chapter 32.

Summary

This chapter focused on concepts and techniques for storing and managing data within Web pages. To recap:

- ✦ Any variable created within a function is local to that function and not accessible to any code outside the function.
- ✦ A global variable is one that is accessible to all JavaScript code within a Web page.
- ✦ To create a global variable, make sure that you create the variable outside any custom functions — preferably just under the `<SCRIPT>` tag in the head of the page.
- ✦ If you want a variable to be accessible beyond the current page, you must store that variable in a cookie. Then retrieve the cookie value in any subsequent pages that need the data in the variable.
- ✦ An array is a means of organizing variables into a numbered list where each variable has the same name but a different subscript (such as product[1], product[2], and so on).
- ✦ A custom object is sort of like a variable in that it contains data you specify. But, like a built-in object, your custom object can have specific properties.
- ✦ Setting up an array of custom objects can be a very useful technique for managing fairly large tables of data.

✦ ✦ ✦

The Ultimate Interactive Order Form

In This Chapter

A hyper-interactive online order form

Roughing out an interactive form with Word IA

Tailoring my sample order form to your own business

Learning more about JavaScript

It's time for you to see how some of those obscure programming tricks discussed in the preceding chapter apply to something in the real world. In this chapter, I want to present you with the ultimate online interactive order form. (At least *I* think it's the ultimate. Maybe it's just pretty good.) First, I show you how the form works. Then I take you behind the scenes to see what makes it tick.

A Hyper-Interactive Form

Actually, all Web forms are considered to be interactive. In that case, the type of form discussed in this chapter would have to be considered as *hyper-interactive.* The reason is that it provides immediate feedback as soon as the reader (the person filling out the form) makes a selection. Let me show you what I mean. Figure 32-1 shows how the order details section of the form first appears to the reader.

More Info

If you want to try out the form, open alanform.htm in the JavaScript section of the *HTML Publishing Bible* CD-ROM. You can also go to the JavaScript section in my `http://www.coolnerds.com` site.

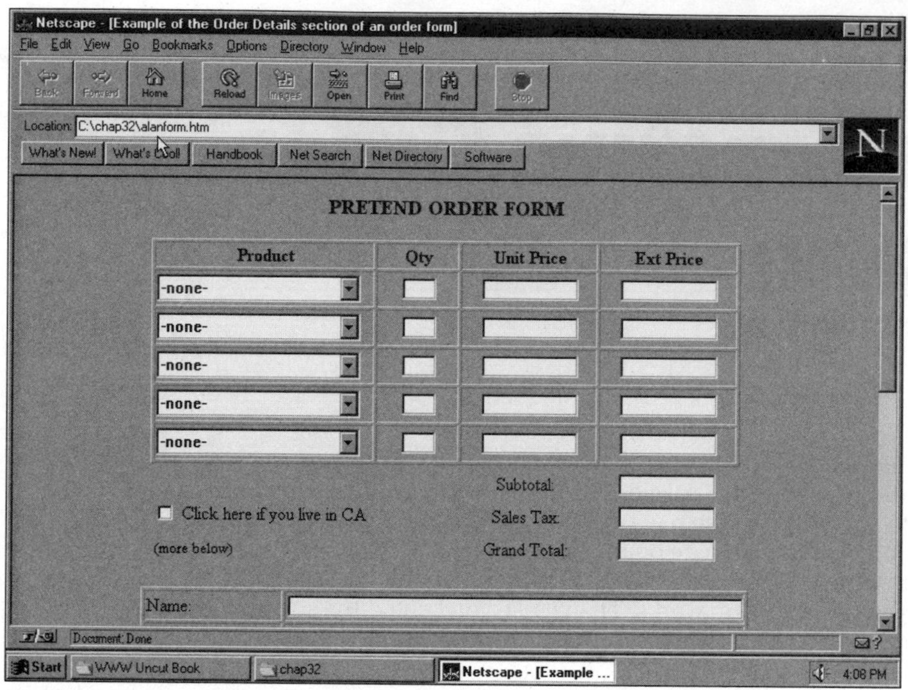

Figure 32-1: How the sample hyper-interactive form appears to the reader.

Every line item in the form contains a drop-down list that shows all products offered by the (hypothetical) business displaying the form. The reader simply needs to click the drop-down arrow and click on a product name, as shown in Figure 32-2.

As soon as the reader makes a selection, the product name appears in the field and the Unit Price column displays the unit price of that product. The reader then can type a quantity into the Qty column. Immediately after the reader completes that entry (by moving to another field), the Unit Price, Extended Price, and various totals are updated on the screen. The reader can choose as many products and enter as many quantities as he or she wants. The form instantly updates with every selection to keep the reader posted of charges incurred so far. The reader also can click the little check box to automatically calculate the sales tax, as Figure 32-3 illustrates.

Now that you see how the form works, let me show you how I created it and explain some of the JavaScript code and concepts used to make it happen.

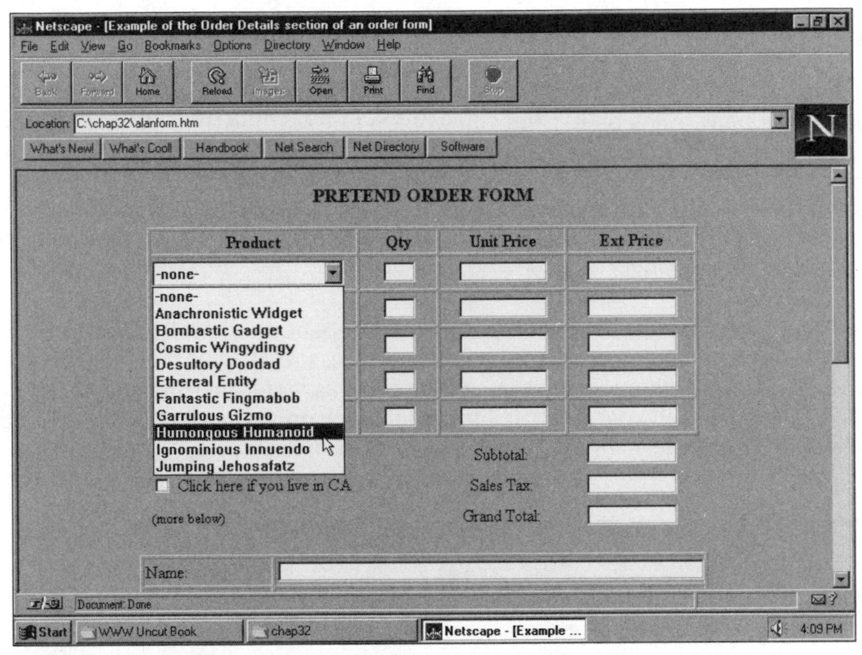

Figure 32-2: Drop-down list of products the reader can order.

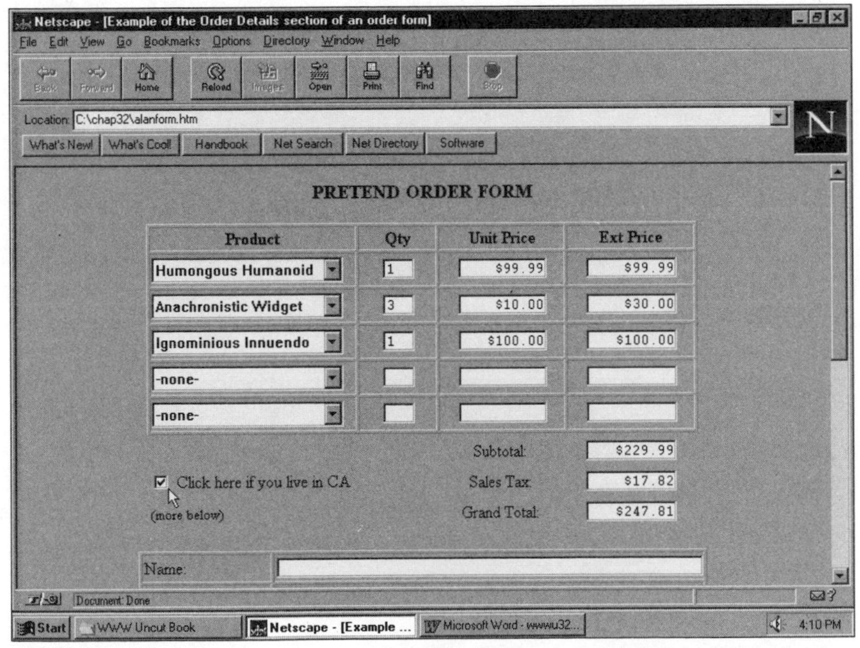

Figure 32-3: Readers need only pick products and quantities. Everything else is calculated automatically.

Roughing Out the Form

If I had attempted to create this form by using only Notepad and HTML tags, I'd probably still be working on it. (And you wouldn't be reading this.) Actually, I gave myself a big head start by sort of roughing out the entire form in Word IA first. Basically, I created a few tables and put some text and form fields into the table cells. I tidied up the column widths so that I wouldn't have to struggle with that once I started working directly with the source tags and JavaScript. Figure 32-4 shows this form's humble beginnings.

I saved that Word IA page as rawform.htm. Then I opened rawform.htm with Notepad, which, of course, gave me immediate access to all the HTML tags that Word IA generated for me. I immediately saved this copy as alanform.htm, so if I made a mess of it, I would still have rawform.htm to fall back on. From this point on though, I'll be talking about the alanform.htm file, not rawform.htm.

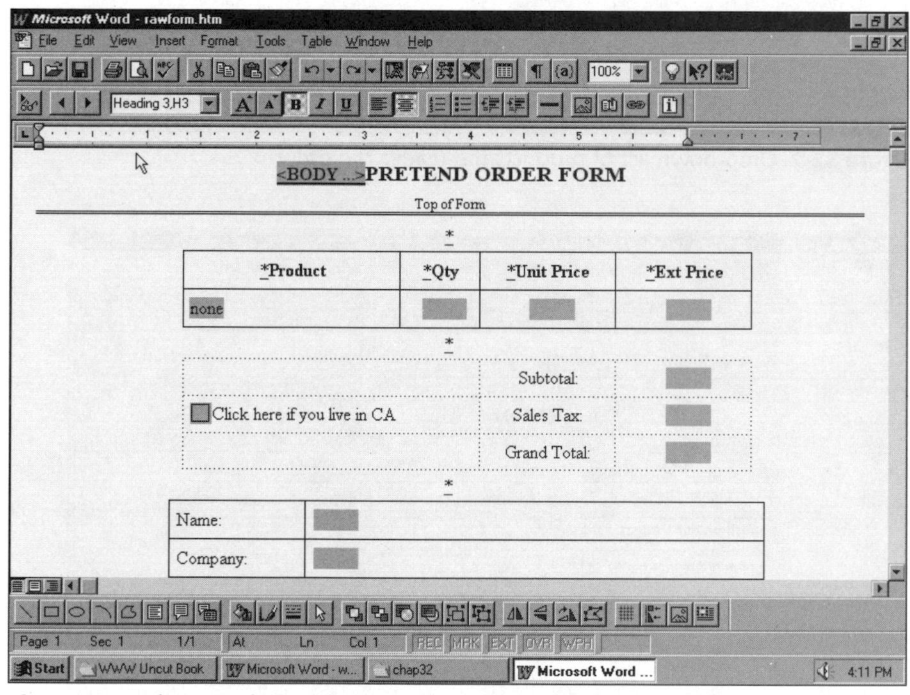

Figure 32-4: The sample form in its embryonic Word IA format.

The Hyper-Form's JavaScript Code

HTML itself doesn't really give you the flexibility to create a form that is as interactive as the one being discussed here. It takes some JavaScript code to make all this happen. Here I want to take you through the code and the concepts to give you a picture of how everything works. Let's start from the top of the alanform.htm Web page.

The global variables

The alanform.htm file begins with some global variables that are used in various places throughout the page. You can see them near the top of Figure 32-5. The following list describes the role that each variable plays:

- ✦ **RowsInForm.** Specifies the number of rows that will appear in the order details section of the form (excluding the heading row). If you customize alanform.htm, you can change this to any value you want.
- ✦ **ProductsInList.** Specifies how many products appear in the product list. I show you the products list a little later in this chapter.

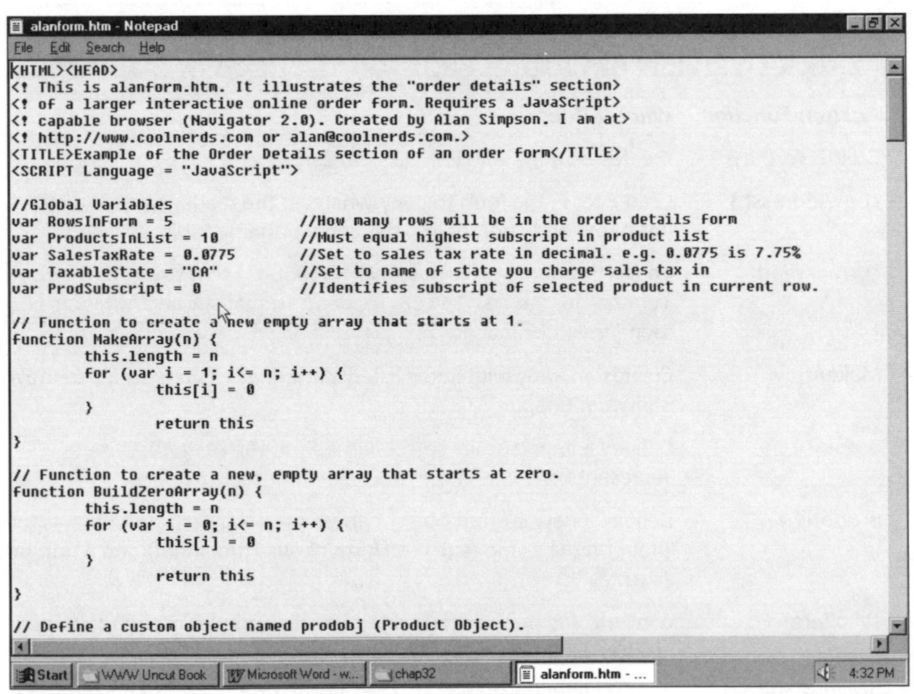

Figure 32-5: The top of alanform.htm, in Notepad, with some JavaScript code already typed in.

✦ **SalesTaxRate.** Specifies the sales tax rate in decimals. For example, 7.75 percent is expressed as 0.0775. If you customize alanform.htm, you can enter your own sales tax rate here. It must be a number less than one.

✦ **TaxableState.** The name of the state in which the sales tax is charged. If you customize alanform.htm, you can set this to your own home state.

✦ **ProdSubscript.** This is a general variable that receives a new value frequently. It should always start out as being equal to zero. Don't change it.

The custom functions

Many custom functions appear in alanform.htm. These functions are all defined in the head, just under the global variables. In fact, you can see a couple of the functions, MakeArray() and BuildZeroArray(), back in Figure 32-5.

Rather than pick through every line of code in every function, I listed their names (in alphabetical order) in Table 32-1 and briefly described what each custom function does. I talk about some of the more important custom functions a bit later in the chapter.

Table 32-1
Quick Overview of Custom Functions Defined in alanform.htm

Custom Function	*What It Does*
BuildZeroArray( )	Creates an array with items listed starting at 0 (zero).
copyAddress( )	Used later in the form to copy whatever the reader types in as the "Bill To" name and address into the corresponding "Ship To" fields.
currencyPad( )	Converts a number (such as 1234.5600043) to a string in American currency format ($1,234.56), padded so that stacked numbers align along their decimal points.
MakeArray( )	Creates an array with items listed starting at 1 (same as MakeArray() shown in Chapter 31).
ordobj( )	Defines a new custom object named ordobj. Each object here represents one line in the order details form.
prodobj( )	Defines a new custom object named prodobj. Each prodobj has two properties: a name (such as Humongous Humanoid) and a unit price (such as 99.99).
strToZero( )	Converts any non-numeric value (such as a letter or null) to 0 (zero). Used to keep math operations from bombing.
updateRow( )	A meaty little function that auto-fills the unit price and extended price fields on the form and more.
updateTotals( )	This little guy calculates and fills in the order subtotal, sales tax, and grand total.

That wraps it up for the <HEAD>. . . </HEAD> section of alanform.htm.

Out of My Head

The <BODY> tag in alanform.htm shows a small title (Pretend Order Form) and then immediately executes some JavaScript code to set up the conceptual framework of the interactive order form. You can see this initial code under the <BODY> tag in Figure 32-6. We need to slow down and talk about what takes place in this area of the page because the interactive form revolves around the custom objects and arrays that are created there.

Puzzled? I'm assuming that you've read Chapter 31 already and that the terms *array* and *custom object* are not totally foreign to you.

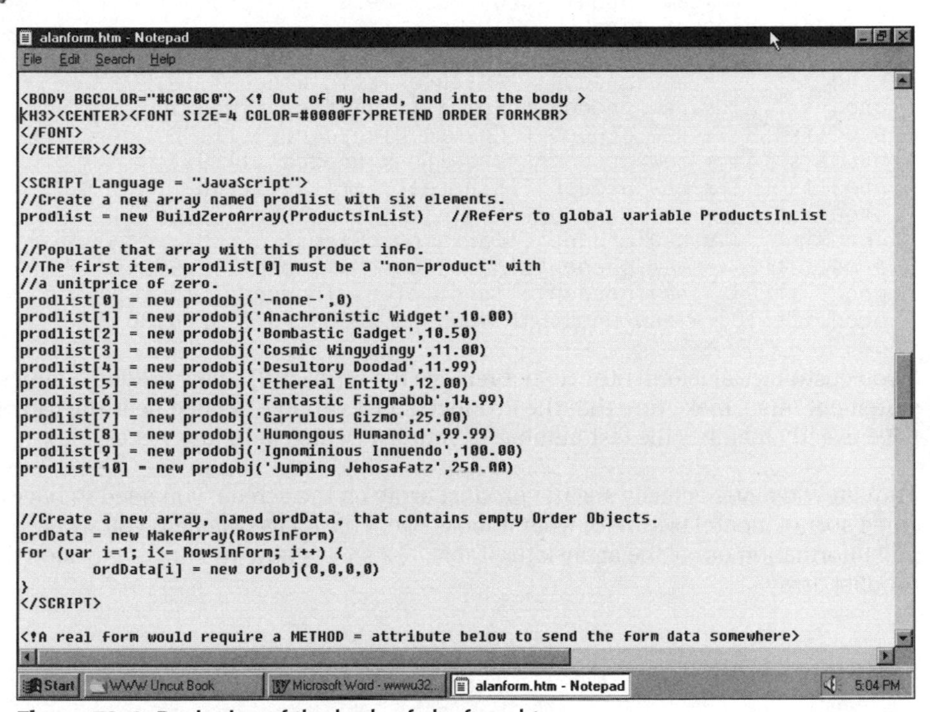

```
<BODY BGCOLOR="#C0C0C0"> <! Out of my head, and into the body >
<H3><CENTER><FONT SIZE=4 COLOR=#0000FF>PRETEND ORDER FORM<BR>
</FONT>
</CENTER></H3>

<SCRIPT Language = "JavaScript">
//Create a new array named prodlist with six elements.
prodlist = new BuildZeroArray(ProductsInList)   //Refers to global variable ProductsInList

//Populate that array with this product info.
//The first item, prodlist[0] must be a "non-product" with
//a unitprice of zero.
prodlist[0] = new prodobj('-none-',0)
prodlist[1] = new prodobj('Anachronistic Widget',10.00)
prodlist[2] = new prodobj('Bombastic Gadget',10.50)
prodlist[3] = new prodobj('Cosmic Wingydingy',11.00)
prodlist[4] = new prodobj('Desultory Doodad',11.99)
prodlist[5] = new prodobj('Ethereal Entity',12.00)
prodlist[6] = new prodobj('Fantastic Fingmabob',14.99)
prodlist[7] = new prodobj('Garrulous Gizmo',25.00)
prodlist[8] = new prodobj('Humongous Humanoid',99.99)
prodlist[9] = new prodobj('Ignominious Innuendo',100.00)
prodlist[10] = new prodobj('Jumping Jehosafatz',250.00)

//Create a new array, named ordData, that contains empty Order Objects.
ordData = new MakeArray(RowsInForm)
for (var i=1; i<= RowsInForm; i++) {
        ordData[i] = new ordobj(0,0,0,0)
}
</SCRIPT>

<!A real form would require a METHOD = attribute below to send the form data somewhere>
```

Figure 32-6: Beginning of the body of alanform.htm.

The prodlist array

The prodlist array in alanform.htm is the product/price list that the form uses. The reader never sees this list directly, but the product names from this list are used to build the drop-down lists in the form, as you'll see later. Here's how the page builds this array. The call to BuildArray( ) creates an empty array that starts with the number 0 (zero):

```
<SCRIPT Language = "JavaScript">
//Create a new array named prodlist with six elements.
prodlist = new BuildZeroArray(ProductsInList)     //Refers to
      global variable ProductsInList
```

The next series of statements populate that array with product objects:

```
//Populate that array with this product info.
//The first item, prodlist[0] must be a "non-product" with
//a unitprice of zero.
prodlist[0] = new prodobj('-none-',0)
prodlist[1] = new prodobj('Anachronistic Widget',10.00)
prodlist[2] = new prodobj('Bombastic Gadget',10.50)
prodlist[3] = new prodobj('Cosmic Wingydingy',11.00)
prodlist[4] = new prodobj('Desultory Doodad',11.99)
prodlist[5] = new prodobj('Ethereal Entity',12.00)
prodlist[6] = new prodobj('Fantastic Fingmabob',14.99)
prodlist[7] = new prodobj('Garrulous Gizmo',25.00)
prodlist[8] = new prodobj('Humongous Humanoid',99.99)
prodlist[9] = new prodobj('Ignominious Innuendo',100.00)
prodlist[10] = new prodobj('Jumping Jehosafatz',250.00)
```

Danger Zone

If you customize alanform.htm, do not remove the prodlist[0] = new prodobj ('-none-',0) statement. Also, make sure that the ProductsInList variable defined near the top of the page exactly matches the last number in your list (which is 10 in my example).

Though you never actually see the prodlist array on the screen, you need to have some sort of mental picture of what it looks like. This image will help you when you pull information out of the array later. Table 32-2 shows how you might envision the prodlist array.

Table 32-2
How to Envision the prodlist Array

Subscript (i)	*prodlist[i].name*	*prodlist[i].unitprice*
0	-none-	0
1	Anachronistic Widget	10.00
2	Bombastic Gadget	10.50

Subscript (i)	*prodlist[i].name*	*prodlist[i].unitprice*
3	Cosmic Wingydingy	11.00
4	Desultory Doodad	11.99
5	Ethereal Entity	12.00
6	Fantastic Fingmabob	14.99
7	Garrulous Gizmo	25.00
8	Humongous Humanoid	99.99
9	Ignominious Innuendo	100.00
10	Jumping Jehosafatz	250.00

The beauty of the prodlist array is that given a simple number, such as 4, you can determine both the name (Desultory Doodad) and unit price (11.99) of that item. In fact, you could say that the entire alanform.htm page revolves around that one simple fact.

The ordData array

In addition to storing product names and prices, this page needs to store information about the order being placed by the customer. The alanform.htm form uses an array, named ordData, of custom ordobj objects to store that information. The following code creates the (initially empty) array:

```
//Create a new array, named ordData, that contains empty Order
      Objects.
ordData = new MakeArray(RowsInForm)
for (var i=1; i<= RowsInForm; i++) {
     ordData[i] = new ordobj(0,0,0,0)
}
</SCRIPT>
```

Note that the RowsInForm variable was originally assigned a value of 5 early in this page. The call to MakeArray( ) creates an empty array named ordData with items listed 1 to 5. The loop then fills that array with order objects. The ordobj( ) custom function, defined in the head, gives each object four properties; .prodsub, .qty, .unitprice, .extprice. The names are somewhat similar to names used in the prodlist array but this ordData array is something completely different. Though you never actually see the array, a good way to envision it is with a row-and-column layout, as in Figure 32-7. Notice how this layout reflects the layout of the fields in the order details portion of the form, also shown in Figure 32-7.

Row Num.	Product (Subscript)	Qty	Unit Price	Ext Price
1	ordData[1].prodsub	ordData[1].qty	ordData[1].unitprice	ordData[1].extprice
2	ordData[2].prodsub	ordData[2].qty	ordData[2].unitprice	ordData[2].extprice
3	ordData[3].prodsub	ordData[3].qty	ordData[3].unitprice	ordData[3].extprice
4	ordData[4].prodsub	ordData[4].qty	ordData[4].unitprice	ordData[4].extprice
5	ordData[5].prodsub	ordData[5].qty	ordData[5].unitprice	ordData[5].extprice

Layout of ordData array parallels arrangement of form fields

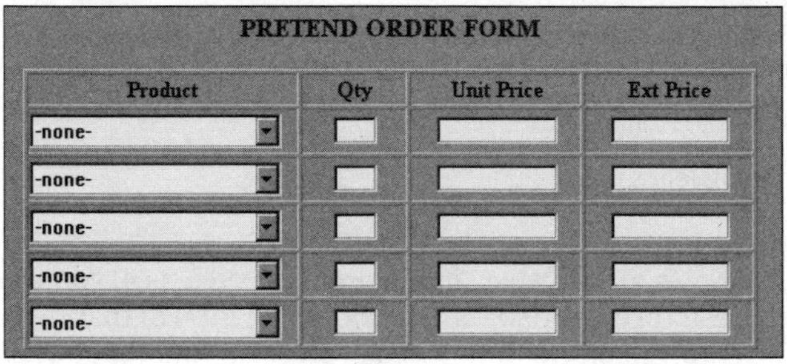

PRETEND ORDER FORM

Product	Qty	Unit Price	Ext Price
-none-			
-none-			
-none-			
-none-			
-none-			

Figure 32-7: How you might envision the ordData array.

Puzzled?

The ordData array doesn't contain the column headings or row numbers shown in Figure 32-7. Those are just there for your information. The concept here is that the name of each variable in the ordData array identifies a specific field in the order details section of the form.

The order details section

Although you've been through a lot of code here, this page still has not displayed any of the actual form on the screen yet! In alanform.htm, I use a combination of HTML tags and JavaScript to create the order details section of the form. You can see the JavaScript code, under the `<FORM>` tag, that creates the form in Figure 32-8.

The first two for loops write all the text and HTML tags required to display the entire order details portion of the form. The table tags (`<TR> <TD>`) are there to place everything in the table. The meat appears in the `<SELECT>` and `<INPUT>` tags that the loop writes. If you ignore the table tags, the first pass through these loops creates the following tags in the reader's Web page:

```
<SELECT NAME="prodchosen1" onChange= "updateRow(1)>
        <OPTION>-none-
        <OPTION>Anachronistic Widget
        <OPTION>Bombastic Gadget
        <OPTION>Cosmic Wingydingy
        <OPTION>Desultory Doodad
        <OPTION>Ethereal Entity
```

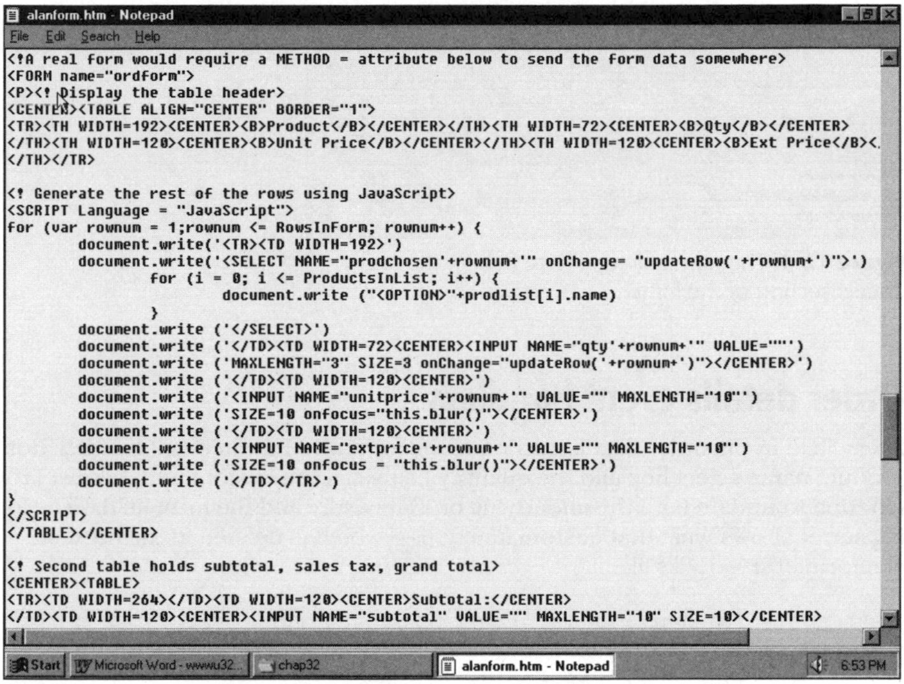

```
alanform.htm - Notepad
File Edit Search Help
<!A real form would require a METHOD = attribute below to send the form data somewhere>
<FORM name="ordform">
<P><! Display the table header>
<CENTER><TABLE ALIGN="CENTER" BORDER="1">
<TR><TH WIDTH=192><CENTER><B>Product</B></CENTER></TH><TH WIDTH=72><CENTER><B>Qty</B></CENTER>
</TH><TH WIDTH=120><CENTER><B>Unit Price</B></CENTER></TH><TH WIDTH=120><CENTER><B>Ext Price</B><
</TH></TR>

<! Generate the rest of the rows using JavaScript>
<SCRIPT Language = "JavaScript">
for (var rownum = 1;rownum <= RowsInForm; rownum++) {
        document.write('<TR><TD WIDTH=192>')
        document.write('<SELECT NAME="prodchosen'+rownum+'" onChange= "updateRow('+rownum+')">')
                for (i = 0; i <= ProductsInList; i++) {
                        document.write ("<OPTION>"+prodlist[i].name)
                }
        document.write ('</SELECT>')
        document.write ('</TD><TD WIDTH=72><CENTER><INPUT NAME="qty'+rownum+'" VALUE=""')
        document.write ('MAXLENGTH="3" SIZE=3 onChange="updateRow('+rownum+')"></CENTER>')
        document.write ('</TD><TD WIDTH=120><CENTER>')
        document.write ('<INPUT NAME="unitprice'+rownum+'" VALUE="" MAXLENGTH="10"')
        document.write ('SIZE=10 onfocus="this.blur()"></CENTER>')
        document.write ('</TD><TD WIDTH=120><CENTER>')
        document.write ('<INPUT NAME="extprice'+rownum+'" VALUE="" MAXLENGTH="10"')
        document.write ('SIZE=10 onfocus = "this.blur()"></CENTER>')
        document.write ('</TD></TR>')
}
</SCRIPT>
</TABLE></CENTER>

<! Second table holds subtotal, sales tax, grand total>
<CENTER><TABLE>
<TR><TD WIDTH=264></TD><TD WIDTH=120><CENTER>Subtotal:</CENTER>
</TD><TD WIDTH=120><CENTER><INPUT NAME="subtotal" VALUE="" MAXLENGTH="10" SIZE=10></CENTER>
```

Start | Microsoft Word - wwwu32... | chap32 | alanform.htm - Notepad | 6:53 PM

Figure 32-8: The <FORM> tag starts the actual form display.

```
                <OPTION>Fantastic Fingmabob
                <OPTION>Garrulous Gizmo
                <OPTION>Humongous Humanoid
                <OPTION>Ignominious Innuendo
                <OPTION>Jumping Jehosafatz
</SELECT>
<INPUT NAME="qty1" VALUE="" MAXLENGTH="3" SIZE=3
        onChange="updateRow(1)">
<INPUT NAME="unitprice1" VALUE="" MAXLENGTH="10" SIZE=10
        onfocus="this.blur()">
<INPUT NAME="extprice1" VALUE="" MAXLENGTH="10" SIZE=10 onfocus =
        "this.blur()">
```

Subsequent passes through these loops generate the same tags but with different field names. For example, on the second pass, the field names are prodchosen2, qty2, unitprice2, extprice2. On the third pass, they are prodchosen3, qty3, unitprice3, extprice3, and so on.

Of course, the reader never sees the tags. Nor do you, because the browser interprets them before it displays them on the screen. If you put the table tags back into the equation, the browser's interpretation of those tags would look something like Figure 32-9. The browser won't show the field names, however — I just typed those in for your information.

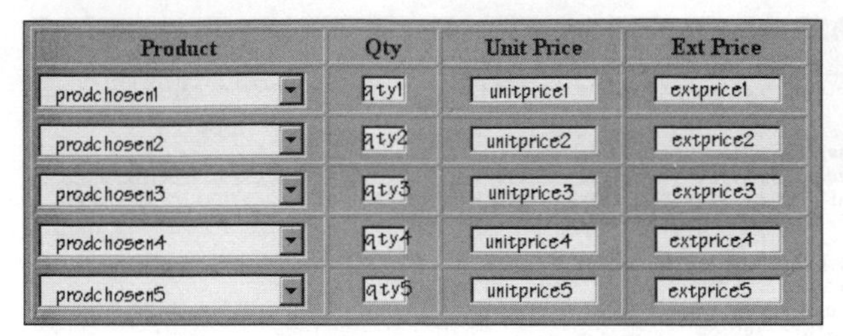

Figure 32-9: The name of each form field in the order details section of the form.

Order details event handlers

Every field in the order details section of the form also has an event handler. Both the product name select box and the quantity fields call the custom updateRow() row function to update both the underlying ordData array and the form fields. The following script shows what that custom function — which is defined in the head of alanform.htm — looks like:

```
//update current row in order array and form.
function updateRow(rownum){
     var exec = 'ProdSubscript =
       document.ordform.prodchosen'+rownum+'.selectedIndex'
     eval (exec)
     ordData[rownum].prodsub=ProdSubscript
     //get qty from the form
     var exec='tempqty=document.ordform.qty'+rownum+'.value'
     eval (exec)
     ordData[rownum].qty = strToZero(tempqty)
     //get unit price from the product price list.
     ordData[rownum].unitprice=prodlist[ProdSubscript].unitprice
     ordData[rownum].extprice = (ordData[rownum].qty) *
       ordData[rownum].unitprice
     var exec = 'document.ordform.unitprice'+rownum+'.value =
       currencyPad(ordData['+rownum+'].unitprice,10)'
     eval (exec)
     var exec = 'document.ordform.extprice'+rownum+'.value =
       currencyPad(ordData['+rownum+'].extprice,10)'
     eval (exec)
     updateTotals()            //update totals at bottom of form
}
```

Let's take a quick peek at what happens when this function is called. Suppose that the reader has just made a selection in the first row of the order detail form (row 1). There the reader has selected Cosmic Wingydingy as the product and has entered 2 as the quantity (qty) to buy. Referring back to Table 32-2, you can see that Cosmic Wingdingy is item number 3 in the prodlist array and that it has a unit price of 11.00. The onChange( ) event handler calls updateRow(1), where the 1 refers to the row number from which the reader has made the selection. Here's what happens in updateRow( ). These following statements

```
var exec = 'ProdSubscript =
  document.ordform.prodchosen'+rownum+'.selectedIndex'
eval (exec)
```

evaluate to and execute as

```
ProdSubscript = document.ordform.prodchosen1.selectedIndex
```

where selectedIndex is a built-in property of select box object. Given that the reader chose the third item in the list, the variable ProdSubscript now contains the value 3.

The next statement updates the prodsub property of the first object in the ordData array:

```
ordData[rownum].prodsub=ProdSubscript
```

These next statements update the qty property of the ordData array, using a custom function named strToZero to ensure that qty is a number. (strToZero() converts any string to the number 0.)

```
//get qty from the form
var exec='tempqty=document.ordform.qty'+rownum+'.value'
eval (exec)
ordData[rownum].qty = strToZero(tempqty)
```

The next statements yank the product unit price out of the prodlist array (based on the value of ProdSubscript) and put that value in the unitprice property of this row in ordData. Then the extprice property of the ordData array is assigned a value that is the product of multiplying the quantity times the unit price as follows:

```
//get unit price from the product price list.
ordData[rownum].unitprice=prodlist[ProdSubscript].unitprice
ordData[rownum].extprice = (ordData[rownum].qty) *
  ordData[rownum].unitprice
```

At this moment in time, then, the ordData array looks something like Table 32-3 (in RAM — we can't see it, of course).

Table 32-3
ordData Array After User Opted to Purchase Two Cosmic Wingydingies (Item 3 in prodlist)

row (i)	*.prodsub*	*.qty*	*.unitprice*	*.extprice*
1	3	2	11.00	22.00
2	0	0	0	0
3	0	0	0	0
4	0	0	0	0
5	0	0	0	0

The rest of the updateRow( ) custom function uses the unitprice and extprice data from the ordData array to fill in the unit price and extended price for fields. We use the custom currencyPad( ) function to format these numbers into American currency format.

```
var exec = 'document.ordform.unitprice'+rownum+'.value =
       currencyPad(ordData['+rownum+'].unitprice,10)'
     eval (exec)
     var exec = 'document.ordform.extprice'+rownum+'.value =
       currencyPad(ordData['+rownum+'].extprice,10)'
     eval (exec)
```

After these statements are executed, the actual form on the screen contains a nicely-formatted copy of the ordData array. In this example, it looks like Figure 32-10.

PRETEND ORDER FORM

Product	Qty	Unit Price	Ext Price
Cosmic Wingydingy	2	$11.00	$22.00
-none-			
-none-			
-none-			
-none-			

Figure 32-10: The order details form after updateRow( ) has been executed.

Down at the end of the updateRow( ) function is a call to another function named updateTotals( ). That function, as you see in a moment, calculates and displays the order subtotal, sales tax, and grand total.

Now you may be wondering why I bothered with the ordData array. After all, the data is visible right in the form. But you need to keep in mind that the form is displaying currency values as strings in the format $x,xxx.xx. You can't do addition and multiplication on those strings, so the ordData array keeps copies of those numbers in their raw form (such as 22.9840000003). All the mathematical work is performed on those raw numbers. In other words, you *use* the data in ordArray to do math, but you *display* the results of that math in a more human-readable $22.98 format.

You also may notice that the unitprice and extprice fields contain the event handler onFocus="this.blur()". This is the technique I described earlier that makes these fields "read-only." You don't want the reader typing over any calculations that the page has performed automatically, so this event immediately blurs the field when the reader tries to focus on it, making it impossible for the reader to change anything in these fields.

That completes the most complex part of this interactive order form. The rest of the stuff is fairly straightforward and requires little JavaScript code.

Subtotal, Sales Tax, and Grand Total

The subtotal, sales tax, and grand total portions of the form are displayed in a separate, borderless table. No JavaScript is required here — the tags are just placed in the page. It's a little easier to see the <INPUT> tags if you remove the table-formatting tags. Let me show you what those tags look like without all the <TR>, <TD>, and <CENTER> tags stuff:

```
<! Second table holds subtotal, sales tax, grand total>
Subtotal:
<INPUT NAME="subtotal" VALUE="" MAXLENGTH="10" SIZE=10
       onfocus="this.blur()">

<INPUT TYPE="CHECKBOX" NAME="Taxable" VALUE="true" onClick =
       "updateTotals()"> Click here if you live in
<SCRIPT Language = "JavaScript">document.write(TaxableState)
       </SCRIPT>
Sales Tax:
<INPUT NAME="salestax" VALUE="" MAXLENGTH="10" SIZE=10
       onfocus="this.blur()">

<FONT SIZE=2 FACE="Arial">(more below)</FONT>
Grand Total:
<INPUT NAME="grandtotal" VALUE="" MAXLENGTH="10" SIZE=10
       onfocus="this.blur()">
```

The fields in this part of the form get their values from the updateTotals() custom function, which is called whenever the reader makes or changes a product selection, quantity, or sales tax field. The following example shows what the updateTotals() custom function looks like:

```
//update the totals in the lower part of order details.
function updateTotals() {
     var subtotal = 0
     for (var i=1; i<=RowsInForm; i++) {
          subtotal = subtotal + ordData[i].extprice
     }
     document.ordform.subtotal.value = currencyPad(subtotal,10)
     salestax = 0
     if (document.ordform.Taxable.checked) {
          salestax = SalesTaxRate * subtotal
     }
     document.ordform.salestax.value = currencyPad(salestax,10)
     document.ordform.grandtotal.value =
       currencyPad(subtotal+salestax,10)
}
```

The first statements, shown in the next example, calculate a variable named subtotal by adding all the ordData.extprice values. These statements then display that result in the currency format in a form field named subtotal:

```
var subtotal = 0
for (var i=1; i<=RowsInForm; i++) {
     subtotal = subtotal + ordData[i].extprice
}
document.ordform.subtotal.value = currencyPad(subtotal,10)
```

The next lines calculate the sales tax as either 0 (if the Taxable check box isn't checked) or as the SalesTaxRate value times the subtotal. (The SalesTaxRate value is defined as a global variable near the top of the page.) The result of the calculation is then displayed in currency format in the form field named salestax, as follows:

```
salestax = 0
if (document.ordform.Taxable.checked) {
    salestax = SalesTaxRate * subtotal
}
document.ordform.salestax.value = currencyPad(salestax,10)
```

The grand total is calculated by adding the subtotal and salestax values and then displayed in currency format in the form field named grandtotal:

```
document.ordform.grandtotal.value =
   currencyPad(subtotal+salestax,10)
```

And that, in a nutshell, is how the order details, subtotal, sales tax, and grand total areas of alanform.htm do their thing.

Billing and Shipping Addresses

The rest of the form lets the reader fill in a billing and shipping address for the order, as shown in Figure 32-11.

The only JavaScript code used here is a script named copyAddress( ) that gets called when the reader clicks the button between the Bill To and Ship To areas. The tag that displays the button looks like this:

```
<INPUT type="button" value="Copy 'Bill To' info to 'Ship To'
      blanks" onclick = "copyAddress()">
```

The copyAddress( ) function is a relatively simple one. It just copies data from the Bill To name and address fields into corresponding Ship To name and address fields. This custom function is defined in the head of the page and looks like the following:

```
//copy the "Bill To" information to the "Ship To" information.
function copyAddress() {
     document.ordform.ShipName.value =
       document.ordform.billName.value
     document.ordform.ShipCompany.value =
       document.ordform.billCompany.value
```

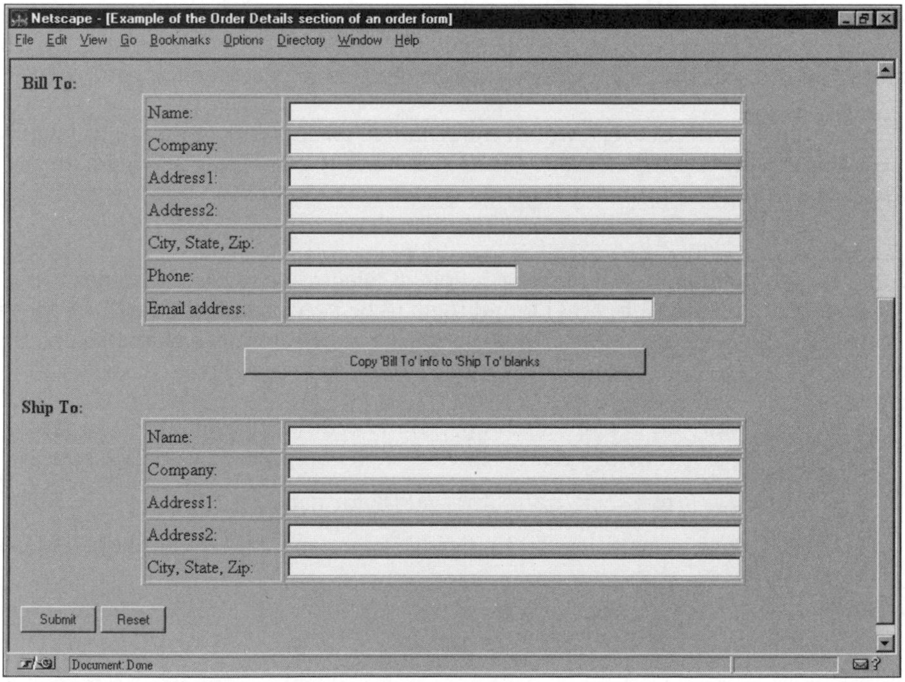

Figure 32-11: The lower half of alanform.htm.

```
        document.ordform.ShipAdd1.value =
          document.ordform.billAdd1.value
        document.ordform.ShipAdd2.value =
          document.ordform.billAdd2.value
        document.ordform.ShipCSZ.value =
          document.ordform.billCSZ.value
}
```

Submit and Reset Buttons

The Submit and Reset buttons are standard fare, as described way back in Chapter 18. In alanform.htm, the Submit button doesn't actually submit the form data because that page is just an example. If I really wanted to submit the data from this form to myself, I'd need to define the appropriate `METHOD` and `ACTION` attributes in the initial `<FORM>` tag. This topic is also covered in Chapter 18.

Where to from Here?

Whew! I guess these last seven chapters have been sort of a crash course in JavaScript, starting from the absolute basics and winding up with some pretty advanced stuff in this chapter. Needless to say, I haven't covered *everything* there is to know about JavaScript. I could write a book as thick as this one just on JavaScript alone! I'm sure many authors will write such books. And if you're interested in learning more about JavaScript, such a book may be the next logical step for you.

The Web itself is, of course, a wonderful resource for learning more about JavaScript. Just search Yahoo! (`http://www.yahoo.com`) or any other search engine for *JavaScript,* and you'll probably find enough information to keep you busy for a month or two.

I also should point out that I found a couple of "electronic reference guides" on JavaScript out on the Web. And I found them to be *very* useful while writing these chapters. They were still under construction when I wrote these chapters but should be pretty clean by the time you read this. I found those references at these URLs:

- `http://www.netscape.com/eng/mozilla/Gold/ handbook/ javascript/ index.html/`. (downloadable zip version decompressed to HTML pages)
- `http://www.ipst.com/docs.htm`. (PDF format)
- `http://www.jchelp.com/javahelp/javahelp.htm`. (Windows Help format)

As for me, that's about all the room I have for JavaScript in this general Web publishing book. I hope these last seven chapters have given you a feel for what JavaScript is all about and the skills required to create, test, and debug JavaScript code. The rest of the chapters that follow this one are sort of generic topics that really didn't fit anywhere else in the book. When you do create your own Web site, you'll definitely want to read the chapter on promoting your site to get that hit count up!

Summary

This chapter pulled together some of the more advanced tools and techniques that JavaScript offers to create a highly interactive online order form. To recap:

- The sample form discussed here is named alanform.htm and is available on the *HTML Publishing Bible* CD-ROM, as well as in my Web site at `http://www.coolnerds.com`.
- When designing your own form, consider using Word IA to lay out the structure of the form before you dive into the nitty-gritty details of writing the JavaScript code.
- If you just want to customize alanform.htm to your own business, you need to change the values assigned to the global variables RowsInForm, ProductsInList, SalesTaxRate, and TaxableState to reflect your own business and form.
- You'll also want to modify the product list defined within alanform.htm. And make sure that the ProductsInList variable near the top of the page matches the largest subscript in your products list.
- The Web itself is a great resource for learning more about JavaScript. Use any search engine to look up the word *JavaScript*.

✦ ✦ ✦

Potpourri

✦ ✦ ✦ ✦

In This Part

✦ ✦ ✦ ✦

Using Netscape Navigator 2

✦ ✦ ✦ ✦

In This Chapter

Getting Netscape 2 up and running

Getting around on the World Wide Web

Keeping track of favorite places

Searching on the World Wide Web

Printing and saving Web pages

Troubleshooting

✦ ✦ ✦ ✦

You might think I'm some kind of Microsoft bigot after reading the bulk of this book, as I so often refer to Microsoft Internet Explorer as your browser. But the reason why I chose Word IA as an authoring tool and Internet Explorer as a browser is because they are tightly integrated not only with each other, but also with Windows 95 and Microsoft Office. That tight integration makes for a very productive Web-authoring environment.

But I am not completely biased towards Microsoft products. In fact, when I browse the Web, I use Netscape Navigator 2 more often than I use Internet Explorer. Why? Because I like the frames and JavaScript features of Navigator. And, like most people, I just find Netscape and its products to be very likable. A newness and freshness surrounds the whole Netscape phenomenon that I find very appealing.

More Info: I should point out that Netscape Navigator Gold has built-in authoring capabilities. However, when I wrote this book, that product was still in beta-testing — not at all ready for prime time usage. But I do discuss that product in Chapter 34.

In this chapter, I want to discuss using Netscape Navigator 2 as your Web browser. Keep in mind that you can have as many Web browsers as you want. You don't have to sacrifice Internet Explorer to use Netscape Navigator, or vice versa.

Getting Netscape Up and Running

As with any Web browser, the first step to using Netscape Navigator 2 is getting some kind of connection to the Internet. If you have not already done that, you can set up an account while you're installing Navigator (you'll see instructions during the installation procedure). If you do already have an Internet

Service Provider, you need to get a hold of your account information, including the passwords, IP address, and so on. Sorry, I can't help you there. The only place to get that information is from your Internet Service Provider.

The second step is to get the Netscape Navigator 2 program. There are two ways to do that: (1) buy it at a retail store or mail-order house or (2) download it from the Internet. If you've been using the Microsoft Internet Explorer or another Web browser, you can download Netscape Navigator 2 right from the Internet. Just point your Web browser to `http://cgi.netscape.com/cgi-bin/123.cgi` and follow the instructions on the download form. Downloading the program takes a while, so be patient.

Individuals, businesses, and government organizations can evaluate Netscape Navigator free for 90 days. Students, faculty, and staff members of an educational institution and employees of charitable non-profit organizations can use it for free. People using freebie copies of Navigator are not entitled to technical support.

You can download various plug-ins for Netscape Navigator, which further enhance using multimedia and virtual reality on the Web. For more information and instructions on downloading the plug-ins, stop by my Web site at `http://www.coolnerds.com` or go straight to `http://www.netscape.com/comprod/products/navigator/version_2.0/plugins/index.html`. You also have a chance to install your favorite plug-ins when you install Netscape itself.

Installing Netscape Navigator

After downloading Netscape Navigator from the Internet, double-click the icon of the file you downloaded and *carefully* follow the installation instructions that appear on your screen. If you've purchased Netscape from a commercial source, carefully follow the installation instructions that come with your package.

When you first install Netscape, a Navigator window containing a shortcut to Netscape Navigator appears on your Windows 95 desktop. To create a desktop shortcut to Navigator, press and hold the Ctrl key and drag that icon to the Windows 95 desktop. You may also want to create a Send To shortcut to Navigator (Netscape.exe), using the same general techniques discussed in Chapter 11.

Starting Netscape Navigator

Starting Netscape Navigator is similar to starting any program in Windows 95. For example, open the window that contains the Netscape Navigator program and double-click the program's icon. If you copied a Netscape Navigator shortcut to the desktop, you can double-click that icon instead. Similarly, if you copied a Netscape shortcut to the Start menu, you can click the Start button on the taskbar and choose Netscape Navigator from the menu.

Why does it want to take me to MSN?

If you have an MSN account, when you first fire up Netscape Navigator, it may offer to connect you to the Internet via MSN. If you have some other ISP and want to use it with Navigator, you need to disable the default to MSN when a program tries to connect to the Internet.

To do that, go to the Windows 95 desktop, click the Start button and choose Settings⇨Control Panel. Double-click the Internet icon, clear the Use AutoDial checkbox, and click OK. To manually connect to the Internet, you need to use the Dial-Up Networking connectoid that the Navigator installation created. The typical scenario is to double-click My Computer on the Windows 95 desktop and double-click the Dial-Up Networking folder icon. Then double-click the icon for the connectoid that connects you to your ISP.

If you can't remember where you installed Netscape or its shortcuts, click the Start button on the taskbar, choose Find⇨Files Or Folders, type **netscape.exe** in the Named box, and click Find Now.

Getting around the World Wide Web

Once you have Navigator on the screen and running, you use it just as you would any other Web browser. In case this is your first browser, I explain the various techniques for getting around in some detail here.

The first thing you need to understand is that every page on the Web has a unique address, called the *URL* (Universal Resource Locator), and most addresses on the Web look something like this:

```
http://www.someplace.com
```

You've probably seen these addresses popping up like mushrooms on billboards, e-mail messages, advertisements, radio spots, and television ads. The addresses can get pretty long. Fortunately, you rarely need to memorize a page's address because Netscape provides many ways to get around on the Web.

Going to a specific site

If you know the URL (address) of the site you want to visit, follow these steps to jump to that site:

1. Click in the Location box in Netscape. Or, if you only want to change part of the address currently shown in the Location box, select the part you want to change by dragging the mouse through it, as shown in Figure 33-1.

The name of the Location box sometimes changes. For example, sometimes it is called the Go To box. Don't let that worry you. If it looks like a place where you can type a URL, it probably is!

2. Type in the new address or the part that needs to be changed. In Figure 33-2, I've changed `www.netscape.com` to `www.benjerry.com`.

3. Press Enter and wait.

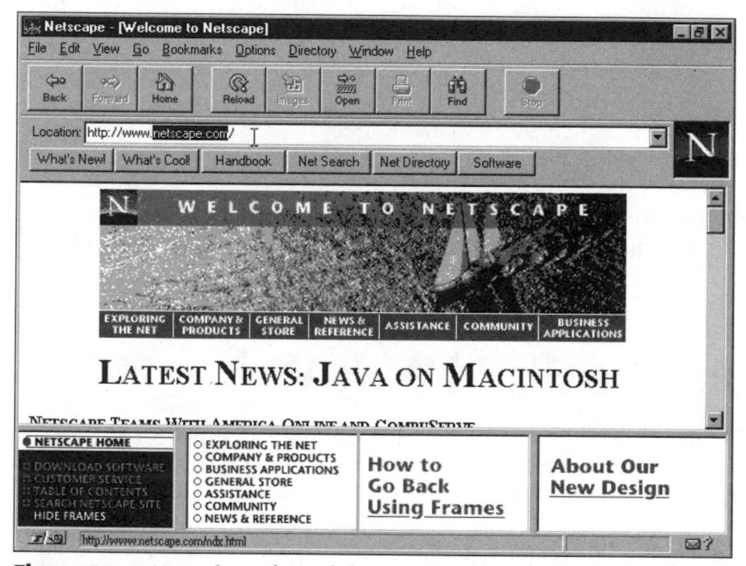

Figure 33-1: Here I've selected the part of the address I want to change.

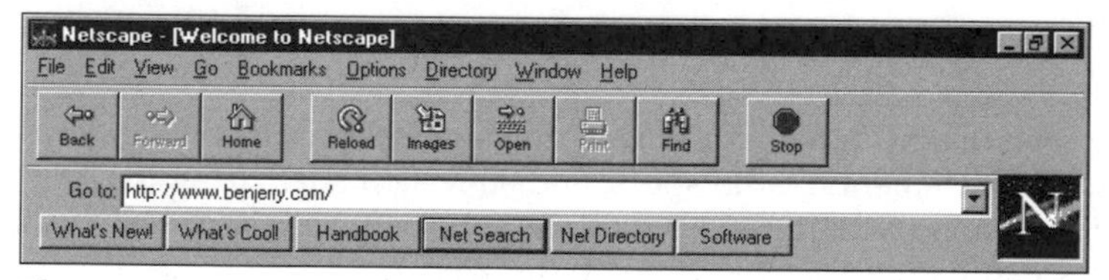

Figure 33-2: Here I've changed `http://www.netscape.com` to `http://www.benjerry.com` by replacing netscape.com.

When typing an address into Netscape, you can omit the `http://`. For example, if you type `www.benjerry.com`, Netscape automatically changes your entry to `http://www.benjerry.com` after you complete Step 3.

While Netscape finds and downloads the site's home page, streaking comets appear in the Netscape logo to the right of the Location box, meaning that you are "going somewhere." When the journey is complete, the comets stop moving in the Netscape logo and you see the requested page. Figure 33-3 shows Ben and Jerry's Web site (`http://www.benjerry.com`) — a great place to get the real scoop on the Web.

Figure 33-3: Now I'm at Ben and Jerry's home page at `http://www.benjerry.com`. Care for some ice cream?

Puzzled?

Remember, when someone tells you to *point your Web browser to* or to *visit* or *go to* some URL, he or she means you should type that URL into the Location box in the Netscape window and press Enter. For example, in the preceding Steps 1–3, I pointed my Web browser to `http://www.benjerry.com`.

Danger Zone

The Internet is based on Unix, which uses forward slashes (/) where DOS used backslashes (\). When typing a URL, be sure to use forward slashes, not backslashes. Also take care to use the correct uppercase and lowercase letters for the URL because Unix treats uppercase and lowercase differently. For example, typing the URL `http://www2.whitehouse.gov/WH/Welcome.html` (with uppercase *WH*) takes you to the White House Welcome page; however, typing `http://www2.whitehouse.gov/wh/Welcome.html` (with lowercase *wh*) takes you to a `Not Found` message instead.

Hot-clicking to another site

Most Web sites contain *hypertext links* and graphic *hot spots* that you can click to go to a related site, without typing its address. Usually the *hypertext link* is colored, underlined, or both. How else can you tell whether text or a graphic image is a hot spot? Just move the mouse pointer to it. If the mouse pointer changes to a pointing hand, the spot is hot. Click the spot to jump to wherever the spot offers to take you.

Hot Stuff

When the mouse pointer is on a hot spot, the lower-left corner of the window shows information about the hot spot, such as `http://benjerry.com/product/sorbet.html` (refer to Figure 33-3).

If a Web page is taller than what your screen can show, use the scroll bars in the window to scroll up and down through the page just as you normally would in a word processor.

Up, down, back, forward, home, stop

You can move around the Web in relation to the current page by using the buttons on the toolbar. If you're not sure which button is which, you can easily discover the name of the button. Just move your mouse pointer so that it touches the toolbar button and wait for the tooltip to appear. You also see a brief description of the button's purpose in the status bar at the bottom of the window, as Figure 33-4 shows.

Figure 33-4: The Netscape Navigator toolbar with the tooltip for the Home button displayed.

The Back and Forward buttons on the toolbar take you forward and backward through pages that you have visited in this session. For example, if you go to a new page and then want to go back to the page you just left, click the Back button.

Hot Stuff

You can customize the toolbar's appearance in Netscape. Choose Options⇨General Preferences from the menu bar and click the Appearance tab. Then choose Pictures, Text, or Pictures And Text and click OK.

The Location box where you type a URL also keeps track of sites you've visited recently. To return to a recently visited site, click the drop-down list button at the right edge of the Location box and choose the address of the site you want to revisit (Figure 33-5).

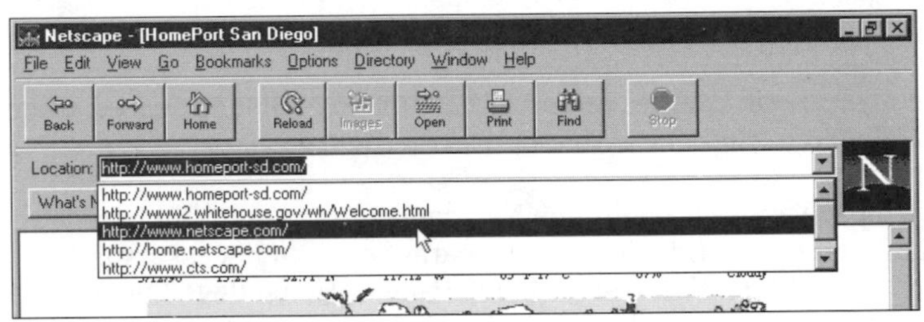

Figure 33-5: The Location box keeps track of the last few Web sites that you've visited.

The Go menu also gives you a list of recently-visited sites during your current session; just open the Go menu and click the site you want to revisit.

For a more detailed list of sites that you have visited during the current session, open the Netscape History window (choose Window⇨History from the menu bar, or press Ctrl+H). Figure 33-6 shows a sample History window after I did quite a bit of Net surfing. To go to a site listed in the history folder, just double-click its name or click its name and then click the Go To button. Close the History window when you are finished using it.

Puzzled?

The History window and Go menu are cleared when you exit Netscape Navigator.

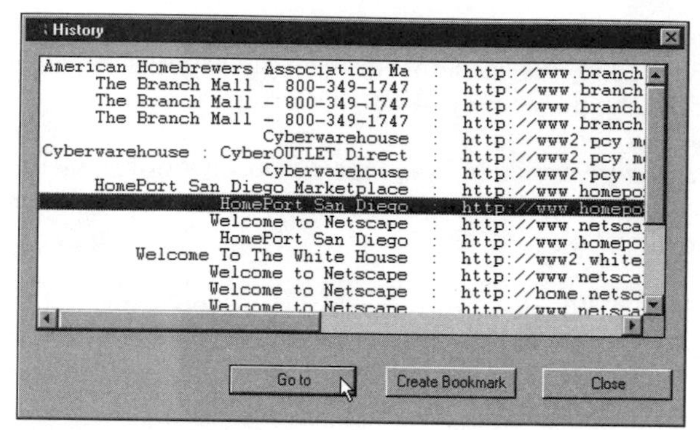

Figure 33-6: The History window keeps track of the many sites you've visited.

If you get completely lost and want to jump back to the page that appeared when you first connected to the Web, click the Home button on the toolbar.

Hot Stuff

You can pick which page appears each time Netscape starts. How? Choose Options⇨General Preferences and click the Appearance tab (if necessary). Next, choose an option next to Start With (either Blank Page or Home Page Location). If you chose Home Page Location, type in the URL for the page you want to start with in the box below Start With. Click OK to save your changes.

If you try to go to another site and it seems to be taking *way* too long to get there, click the Stop button in the toolbar or press the Esc key to stop.

Speeding up your travels on the Net

Pretty pictures and fancy page backgrounds can look great on the Net, but they can take forever to appear, especially if you are using a slow modem. Fortunately, you can speed up your travels through the Net by not loading inline graphic images automatically. The autoload feature is a toggle option on the Options menu that is either checked (turned on) or not checked (turned off). To turn off autoloading, choose Options⇨Auto Load Images (to remove the checkmark). To restore autoloading, choose Options⇨Auto Load Images again (to restore the checkmark). If you want your Auto Load Images settings to stay in effect the next time you start Netscape, choose Options⇨Save Options.

Even if you have turned off autoloading, you can view images on the current page anytime by clicking the Images button on the toolbar or by pressing Ctrl+I. (If images still appear, Netscape probably is looking at a cached copy of the page; click the Reload button on the toolbar or press Ctrl+R to refresh the copy of the page.)

Initially, Netscape displays images incrementally while it downloads pages to your computer's memory. This gives you some feedback during the transmission. However, you may prefer to save a little time by waiting until after the transmission is complete to have Netscape display the images. To control when Netscape displays downloaded images, choose Options⇨General Options and click the Images tab. Then select either While Loading or After Loading and click OK.

Using frames

Frames, a new feature in Netscape Navigator 2, make it easier to understand how a complicated Web site is organized. They also make it easier to navigate a Web site. Figure 33-7 shows frames being used in Netscape Communications' own "Welcome To Netscape" home page.

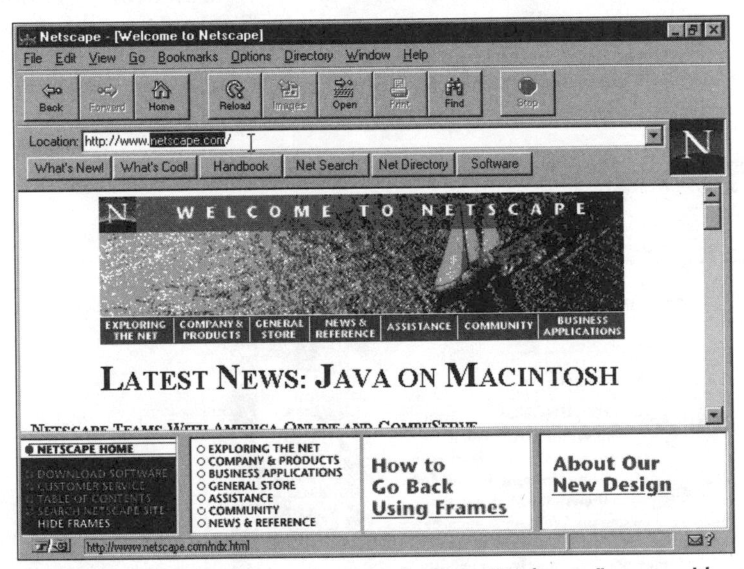

Figure 33-7: The Netscape Communications "Welcome" page, with frames visible.

Puzzled?

Some sites, such as the Welcome page shown in Figure 33-7, let you turn the frames off and on. For the page in Figure 33-7, you can click *HIDE FRAMES* at the bottom of the leftmost frame to redisplay the page without frames. To redisplay the frames, you just scroll down to the very bottom of the frameless Welcome page and click the *Show Frames* button at the lower-right corner of the page.

In Figure 33-7, the page is divided into five frames, something like the panes in a house window. The large top pane displays detailed information like that you'd see in any unframed Web page. The four panes across the bottom of the window serve as the Table of Contents for the top frame. You simply click a link in one of the Table-of-Contents frames, and Netscape displays the information you asked for in the top pane. (If you click a link that takes you to a site that doesn't use frames, the relevant information fills the entire window.)

More Info

Techniques for adding frames to your own Web site are covered in Chapter 25.

Figure 33-8 shows another example of frames — the *PC Magazine* Top 100 Web Sites page. After jumping to the Web page, I clicked the Internet Resources button at the top of the leftmost frame to display the textual Internet Resource information in the center frame. Notice that this page arrangement differs from the example in Figure 33-7. All panes are scrollable, with the first and third panes serving as the Table of Contents for the middle frame. When you click a button in one of the Table-of-Contents frames, the middle pane displays the information you requested. (By the way, this Web site takes a *long* time to download, so be patient.)

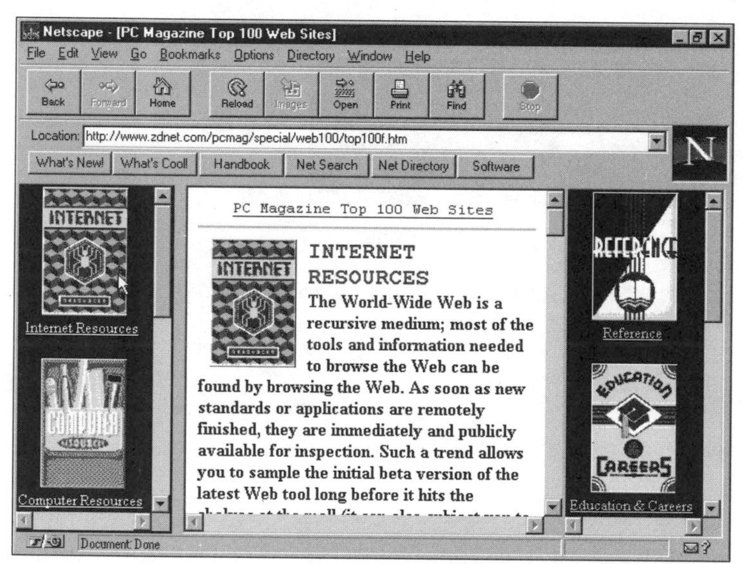

Figure 33-8: PC Magazine's Top 100 Web Sites page uses independently scrollable frames to organize information.

Figure 33-9 shows the Top 100 Web Sites page displayed in Internet Explorer, which doesn't support frames. Notice how much more difficult it is to figure out how this page is organized when it isn't divided into frames. (To give you a better idea of what the page looks like without frames, I've temporarily hidden the status bar, toolbar, and address bar by selecting options on the Internet Explorer View menu.)

Figure 33-9: The Top 100 Web Sites page displayed in Internet Explorer, which doesn't support frames.

Danger Zone

When designing Web pages that include frames, be sure to view them with and without frames. You want them to make sense both ways!

Navigating with frames

Navigating with frames requires you to learn a few new tricks. The first trick involves the Back and Forward buttons. You may expect these buttons to take you back to the previous frame or forward to the next frame when you click them, but that is not what these buttons do. Instead, clicking Back takes you to the URL of the last *entire screen* or *frameset* you viewed; clicking Forward takes you to the URL of the next *entire screen* or *frameset* you viewed.

If you want to back up by one frame, right-click the frame you want to back up in and choose Back In Frame from the shortcut menu. To move forward by one frame, right-click the frame you want to move forward in and choose Forward In Frame. Of course, the Back In Frame and Forward In Frame options will be grayed out if you've backed up or moved forward as far as possible within the frame.

Later, you learn some more tricks for printing frames and marking your favorite frames so you can revisit them later.

Keeping Track of Favorite Places

Remembering long URLs like the one that follows is practically impossible, and typing them accurately into the Location box can be even worse:

```
http://www.zdnet.com/pcmag/special/web100/top100f.htm
```

Fortunately, you can just *bookmark* a site that you are visiting and then easily return to it anytime you want. Use the following techniques:

- ✦ To add a bookmark for a page without frames, go to the site (or page) that you want to return to in the future. Then choose Bookmarks➪Add Bookmark from the menu bar or press Ctrl+D.
- ✦ To add a bookmark for a page that does have frames, turn off the frames (if possible) and then add the bookmark as explained a moment ago. If you cannot turn off the frames, the bookmark you add takes you to the entire frameset (for example, to the Netscape Welcome page shown in Figure 33-7 or to the Top 100 sites page shown in Figure 33-8).
- ✦ To add a bookmark to a specific link on a page or frame, right-click the link you want to bookmark and choose Add Bookmark For This Link from the shortcut menu.

That's all there is to it. Whenever you want to return to that site in the future, choose Bookmarks from the menu bar and click the name of the site you want to visit.

You also can organize your bookmarks into neat categories, insert and delete bookmarks, and do other fun things with bookmarks. To get started, choose Bookmarks➪Go To Bookmarks from the menu bar or press Ctrl+B. You'll see the Bookmarks window, shown in Figure 33-10.

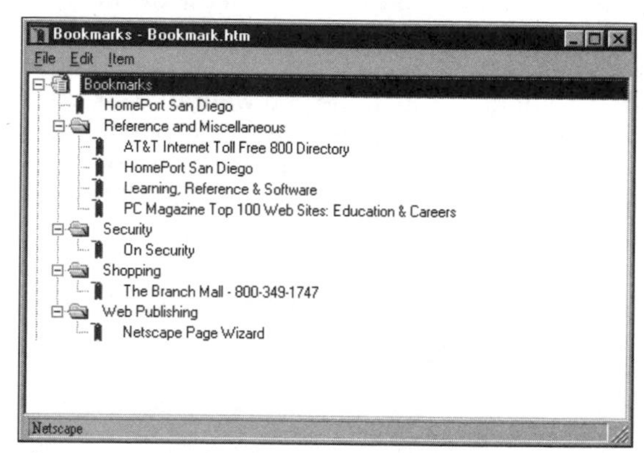

Figure 33-10: The Netscape Bookmarks window after I added several bookmarks and set up folders to organize the bookmarks into categories.

Working with items (bookmarks and folders) in the Bookmarks window is somewhat like using Windows Explorer. You probably could just experiment to get the hang of it, but I'll give you some tips to get you started.

✦ To rename an item or specify a new location or description for the item, right-click the item and choose Properties.

✦ To delete an item, click it and press Delete.

✦ To create a shortcut to an item on the Windows 95 desktop, right-click the item and choose Internet Shortcut.

✦ To return to the site indicated by a bookmark, double-click the bookmark or right-click it and choose Go to Bookmark. (Double-clicking a folder expands or collapses the folder contents.)

✦ To quickly locate and highlight an item in the Bookmarks window, choose Edit⇨Find in the Bookmarks menu bar or press Ctrl+F. Then type any part of the name of the item you're looking for and choose OK.

If your Bookmarks menu gets too crowded, you may want to categorize it into folders like those shown in Figure 33-10. To create a folder while you are in the Bookmarks window, choose Item⇨Insert Folder, type the new folder's name, and choose OK. For example, you can create a folder named *Reference and Miscellaneous* and then move all related bookmarks into that folder just by dragging them there. When you've finished using the Bookmarks window, close it the same way you'd close any window.

Hot Stuff

There is much more that you can do with the Bookmarks window. To explore the possibilities, open the Items menu and point to an option that interests you. A description of the highlighted option will appear on the status bar at the lower-left corner of the Bookmarks window. To choose the option, just click it. If you're unhappy with the result, choose Edit⇨Undo or press Ctrl+Z to undo the change.

Figure 33-11 shows the Bookmarks menu that corresponds to the opened Bookmarks window back in Figure 33-10. Notice how each option marked with a right-pointing triangle in Figure 33-11 corresponds to a folder in Figure 33-10.

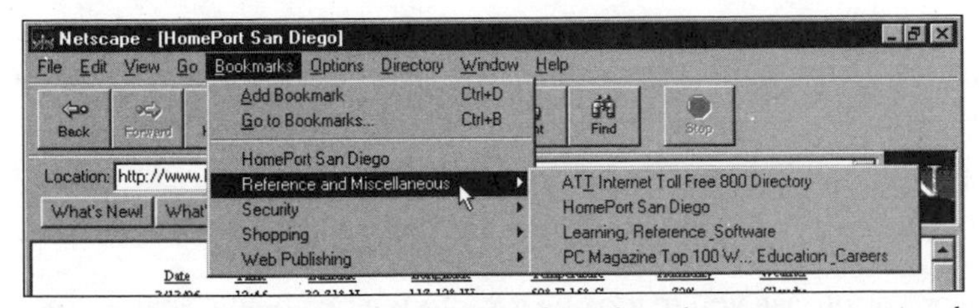

Figure 33-11: Options on this opened Bookmarks menu correspond to folders and bookmarks in the Bookmarks window shown in Figure 33-10.

Searching the Web

Random site-seeing by clicking from one place to the next can be fun, but it may not be the quickest way to find specific information. Consider the Internet as a huge library of books. In a library, you can open each book and scrutinize the Table of Contents and index for the information you seek. Now repeat the steps millions of times and you'll soon appreciate the convenience of using the Web's online *search engines* — sites that do nothing but let you search the Net quickly. Here are two ways to get to and use those search engines:

✦ In Netscape Navigator, click the Net Search button in the bar of directory buttons located below the Location box or choose Directory⇨Internet Search.

✦ Or, go to any one of the addresses listed in Table 33-1. These sites are the same ones listed in Chapter 3, which proves that search engines work no matter which Web browser you're using.

Table 33-1
Some of the Many Popular Internet Search Engines

Search Site	***Address***
Excite	`http://www.excite.com`
Infoseek	`http://www.infoseek.com`
Lycos	`http://www.lycos.com`
Magellan	`http://magellan.mckinley.com`
Microsoft All In One	`http://www.msn.com/access/allinone.htm`
Open Text	`http://www.opentext.com`
WebCrawler	`http://webcrawler.com`
Yahoo!	`http://www.yahoo.com`

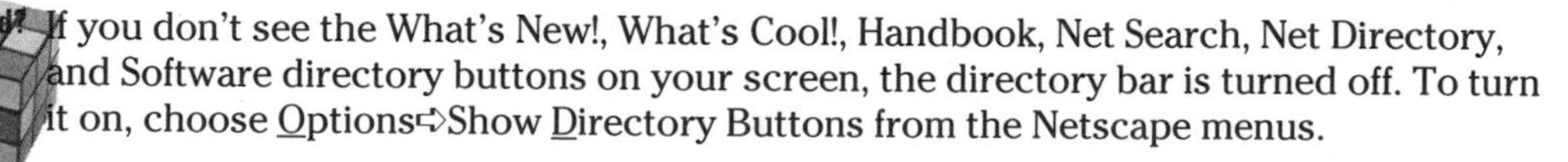

If you don't see the What's New!, What's Cool!, Handbook, Net Search, Net Directory, and Software directory buttons on your screen, the directory bar is turned off. To turn it on, choose Options⇨Show Directory Buttons from the Netscape menus.

If you click the Net Search button or choose Directory⇨Internet Search from the menus, you end up at the Net Search site shown in Figure 33-12. Here's how to use it:

1. Type the word or phrase you're looking for into the box below Search for information about:.

2. Choose the place you want to search from the drop-down list next to <u>in:</u>. Your options are World Wide Web (the default choice), Infoseek Select Sites, Categories of Sites, Usenet newsgroups, and Web FAQs. (*FAQ* is an acronym for Frequently Asked Question.)
3. Click the Search Now button.
4. A list of Web Sites about, or containing references to, that word or phrase then appears. Click on any site name to jump straight to it.

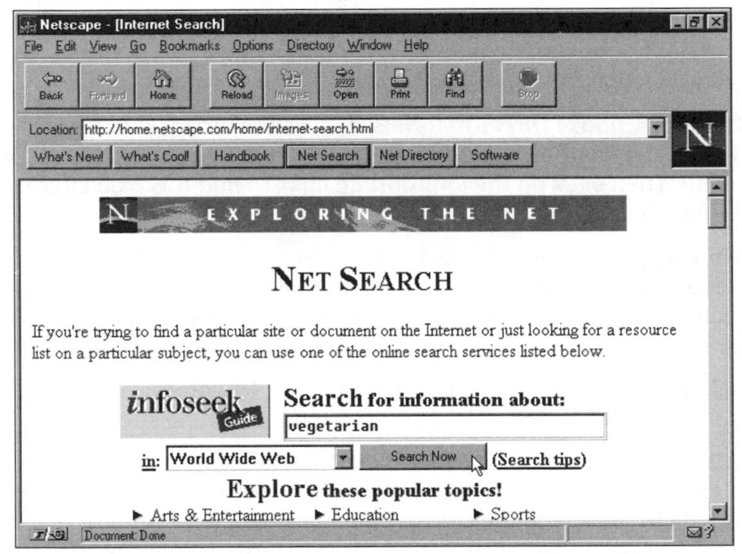

Figure 33-12: The Netscape Net Search page provides quick access to several ways to search the Web.

Every search engine uses a slightly different technique for locating references to your selected word or phrase. If you want to thoroughly track down a particular topic, try using several different search engines.

More Info

Some search engines also offer options for performing complex searches using *and* and *or* logic. When you are in a site that offers searching, look around for information on search tips, search options, or query options.

Searching by category

Another handy way to search the Internet is to start with some broad category, such as Arts & Entertainment or Education, and narrow down the search from there. The Net Search page shown in Figure 33-12 is a great service for that type of searching (so is the Yahoo! engine at `http://www.yahoo.com`).

Scroll down to the broad category you want to search and then click the category to see subcategories within it. Keep on clicking until you see the specific information you want.

Netscape offers many other ways to search for information on the Net, including these methods:

- ✦ **Net Directory.** Click the Net Directory button or choose Directory⇨Internet Directory from the menu bar. You can then search Web sites, Usenet, classifieds, and reviews by keyword or concept, or you can scroll down a bit on the page and click on a broad category. Scroll down even further on the page and you can jump to other directories on the Internet, including A2Z, Infoseek Guide, Yahoo!, Point, Magellan, and Excite.
- ✦ **Netscape Galleria.** Choose Directory⇨Netscape Galleria to view a page that showcases Netscape customers who have built Web sites by using Netscape server software. Then click on the appropriate links to find the Web sites of those customers.
- ✦ **Internet White Pages.** Choose Directory⇨Internet White Pages to find your favorite someone. This page takes you to additional directories, all of which lead to people, companies, universities, e-mail addresses, and other human stuff. Who knows, you may even be able to find your long-lost high-school sweetheart!
- ✦ **What's New!** Click the What's New! button or choose Directory⇨What's New! to find out what's new on the Web. Then jump to any interesting site.
- ✦ **What's Cool!** Click the What's Cool! button or choose Directory⇨What's Cool! to find out which sites Netscape's cool team considers eye-catching, funny, or helpful. Then click on a site name to visit the cool site of your dreams.

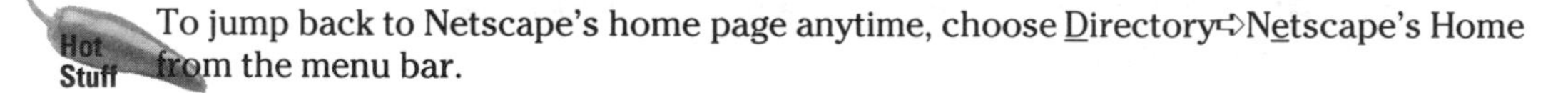

To jump back to Netscape's home page anytime, choose Directory⇨Netscape's Home from the menu bar.

Searching the current page

Once you're on a page, you can search just that page for a particular word or phrase. The technique is identical to using "search" in most word-processing programs:

1. Choose Edit⇨Find from Netscape's menu bar or press Ctrl+F or click the Find button on the toolbar.
2. Type the text you want to find.
3. Change the Match Case and Up or Down options as needed.
4. Click the Find Next button or press Enter. (Repeat this step as needed.)

If Netscape finds a match but the Find dialog box is covering it, just move the Find dialog box out of the way (by dragging its title bar). Or, if you've finished using the dialog box, click its Cancel button or press Esc to remove it.

Printing and Saving Web Pages

The Internet page you are currently viewing on-screen is in your computer's memory. This means you can use everyday Windows techniques to take whatever you see on the screen and print it or save it to your local hard disk for future use.

Printing Web pages

The simplest way to save something from the Web is to print a copy of the document you're viewing. It's easy. Just choose File⇨Print from Netscape's menu bar or click the Print button on the toolbar. You are taken to a standard Print dialog box where you can choose a printer, page range, and number of copies. Click OK in that dialog box to start printing.

If the current page has frames, you can print the contents of any frame. To do so, click in a *neutral part* of the frame you want to print. Then choose File⇨Print Frame or click the Print button on the toolbar.

Puzzled? Finding a neutral part of the frame to click on can be tricky. For best results, click inside the frame but stay away from any buttons or hot spots in the frame or click the outer "molding" of the frame so that a thin black border appears around the frame you clicked.

Saving text from a Web page

You can easily save some text from a Web page to read later or to put in a file somewhere. The following steps describe how to save a chunk of text with the standard Windows copy-and-paste techniques:

1. Select the text you want to save (by dragging the mouse pointer through it). To quickly select the entire page, choose Edit⇨Select All or press Ctrl+A. In Figure 33-13, I've selected some text I want to save for future reference.
2. Choose Edit⇨Copy from the menu bar or press Ctrl+C. A copy of the selection is placed on the (invisible) Windows Clipboard.
3. Open your favorite word processor, such as WordPad or Microsoft Word. Alternatively, open a simple text editor such as Notepad.
4. Click within the document window of the word processor or text editor and press Ctrl+V (or choose Edit⇨Paste from the word processor's menu bar, or click the Paste button in the word processor's toolbar).

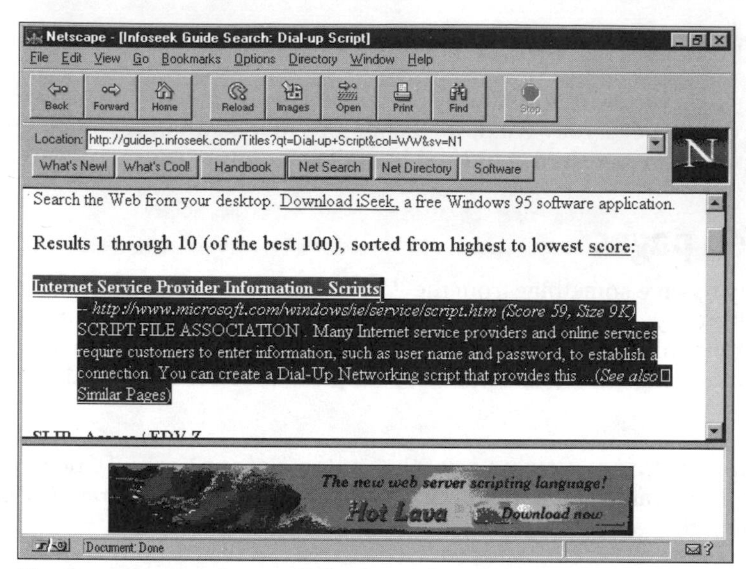

Figure 33-13: Text from a Web page selected for cut and paste.

In Figure 33-14, I opened WordPad with a new, blank document. Then I pasted the selected text and used some basic editing methods to format the pasted text a little. I can now choose File➪Save from the WordPad menu bar to save that copied text as a standard Word document on my own PC.

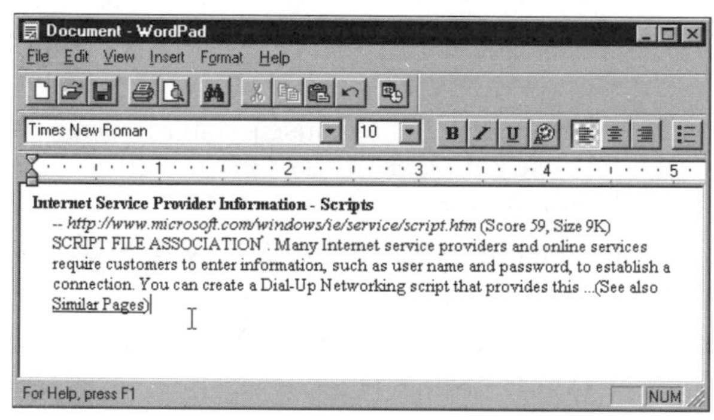

Figure 33-14: Selected text pasted into a WordPad document.

Saving a graphic from a Web page

When you copy and paste text from a Web page, the graphics do not come along for the ride. In Web pages, text and graphics are stored in separate files (see Parts III and IV of this book). If you want to copy a graphic image from a Web page to a file on your own PC, use the following technique:

Danger Zone

Don't swipe copyrighted material, company logos and trademarks, clip art that other people sell, or original art that a site paid for and put it into your own pages! This practice is unethical and can get you into legal hot water. If in doubt about whether you can use copied material, send an e-mail query to the webmaster whose material you want to filch.

1. When you see the graphic image you want to copy, right-click it and choose Save This Image As.
2. In the Save As dialog box that appears, enter a filename (without an extension) and choose a location for the file.
3. Click the Save button.

Most graphic images that you copy from a Web page will be in GIF or JPEG format. Of course, not all graphics programs let you edit and not all word processors let you import images in these formats. But the CD-ROM in this book includes Paint Shop Pro, a great program for working with GIFs and JPEGs (see Chapter 22).

Hot Stuff

Even if you haven't installed programs that can import and edit GIF or JPEG graphics, you certainly can open them in Netscape. Choose File⇨Open File (Ctrl+O). When the Open dialog box appears, type ***.gif; *.jpg** in the File Name box and browse your hard disk until you find the graphic you want to view. After you have found the file, double-click its filename to open it.

Saving a background graphic from a Web page

Saving (or swiping) a Web page background from Netscape Navigator requires a sneak attack from behind, but it's worth a try if you find a background that you especially like. Here's how to do it:

1. Choose View⇨Document Source from Netscape's menu bar.
2. Use your scroll bars as needed until you find a tag like this one:

```
<body background="xxxx.gif">
```

3. Drag your mouse through just the filename portion of the tag. That is, select everything between the quotation marks in the `<body background...>` tag (that is, select *xxxx.gif*).

4. Press Ctrl+V to copy your selection to the Windows Clipboard.
5. Close the source document window (Alt+F4).
6. Click in the Location box to select the URL in the box. Then select only the portion of the URL that contains the filename and press Ctrl+V to paste the text you copied in Step 4 into the Location box. For example, if the Location box currently shows

   ```
   http://www.mypage.com/index.html
   ```

   select index.html and press Ctr+V to change the URL to

   ```
   http://www.mypage.com/xxxx.gif
   ```

7. Press Enter to display the background image.
8. Choose File⇨Save As, and save that pup to your hard disk.

Saving a Web page as an HTML file

A great way to learn HTML is to save copies of Web pages that you especially like. Then you can open the HTML file in a text editor or word processor and see how the author created his or her masterpiece. You also can use the copied HTML file as a basis for your own Web pages. Of course, you should be careful not to plagiarize anyone else's work!

It's easy to save a page or frame as an HTML file:

1. Go to the page or click on a neutral part of the frame you want to save.
2. Choose File⇨Save As (for a page without frames) or File⇨Save Frame As (for a page with frames), or just press Ctrl+S for either type of page.
3. When the Save As dialog box appears, type a name for the file (omit the extension) and choose a disk drive and folder location.
4. Click the Save button.

Netscape saves the page or frame as a file with a .html extension. The following list describes some things you can do with the file after saving it:

- Edit the source in a text editor, such as Notepad.
- Open the page in Netscape Gold, Internet Assistant, or another Web page authoring program, and customize the page as needed.
- Open the file in your Web browser (choose File⇨Open File or press Ctrl+O). It will look like a normal Web page.
- Double-click the icon for the file in any browsing window, such as Windows Explorer or My Computer. The page appears in your favorite Web browser.

Puzzled? When you save the page or frame, Netscape copies the text and HTML tags to your hard disk. But none of the graphics or linked Web pages come along for the ride. Therefore, after opening the page in your browser, don't be surprised if some graphics or links stop working!

Viewing and copying HTML source

Suppose that you want to take a quick peek at the source document behind the page you are currently viewing. This task is easy to do:

1. Go to the page whose source you want to see.
2. Choose View⇨Document Source.

A new window opens with the underlying source visible, as shown in Figure 33-15. In this example, the source document is more complicated than most because this particular page contains frames and a great deal of JavaScript — topics that are discussed in Parts IV and V of this book.

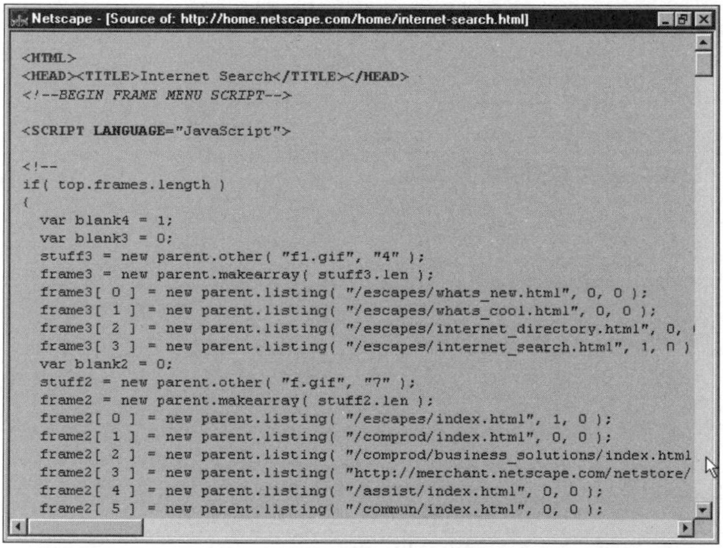

Netscape - [Source of: http://home.netscape.com/home/internet-search.html]

```
<HTML>
<HEAD><TITLE>Internet Search</TITLE></HEAD>
<!--BEGIN FRAME MENU SCRIPT-->

<SCRIPT LANGUAGE="JavaScript">

<!--
if( top.frames.length )
{
  var blank4 = 1;
  var blank3 = 0;
  stuff3 = new parent.other( "f1.gif", "4" );
  frame3 = new parent.makearray( stuff3.len );
  frame3[ 0 ] = new parent.listing( "/escapes/whats_new.html", 0, 0 );
  frame3[ 1 ] = new parent.listing( "/escapes/whats_cool.html", 0, 0 );
  frame3[ 2 ] = new parent.listing( "/escapes/internet_directory.html", 0,
  frame3[ 3 ] = new parent.listing( "/escapes/internet_search.html", 1, 0 )
  var blank2 = 0;
  stuff2 = new parent.other( "f.gif", "7" );
  frame2 = new parent.makearray( stuff2.len );
  frame2[ 0 ] = new parent.listing( "/escapes/index.html", 1, 0 );
  frame2[ 1 ] = new parent.listing( "/comprod/index.html", 0, 0 );
  frame2[ 2 ] = new parent.listing( "/comprod/business_solutions/index.html
  frame2[ 3 ] = new parent.listing( "http://merchant.netscape.com/netstore/
  frame2[ 4 ] = new parent.listing( "/assist/index.html", 0, 0 );
  frame2[ 5 ] = new parent.listing( "/commun/index.html", 0, 0 );
```

Figure 33-15: The source for the page shown back in Figure 33-12.

You can scroll through the window as needed but you can't change the source from here. Of course, you *can* copy any or all of the source to the Windows Clipboard if you want, using either of these two methods:

✦ To copy only part of the source, drag your mouse through the section you want to copy and then press Ctrl+C.

✦ To copy all of the source, press Ctrl+A (select all) and then press Ctrl+C.

With the copy complete, you then can paste the source from the Clipboard into a text editor, such as Notepad, by using standard Windows paste procedures. Simply create or open a text file with Notepad, position the insertion point at the spot where you want the copied material to appear, and press Ctrl+V.

After you've finished using the document source window, close it by pressing Alt+F4 or by clicking the window's Close button.

Troubleshooting

Regardless of which browser you use, things sometimes go wrong. For example, if you see an Error 404 message or a message like the one shown in Figure 33-16 when you try to visit a site, your browser cannot get to the site you've requested. The three most likely causes and solutions are as follows:

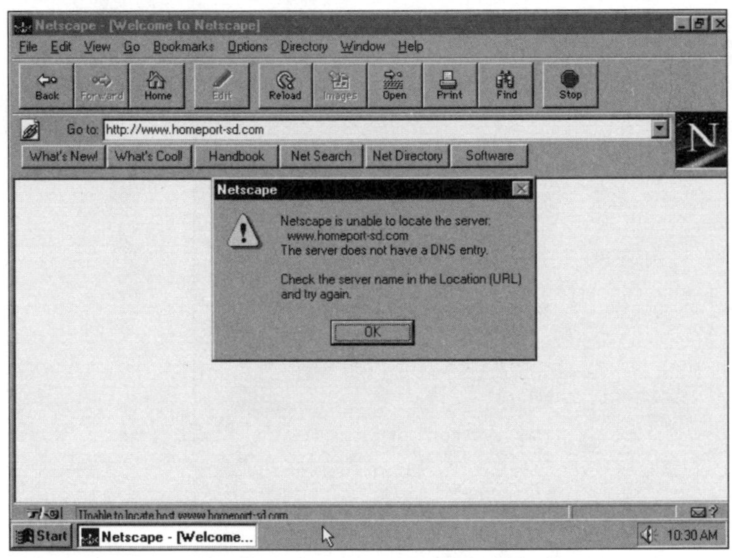

Figure 33-16: Error trying to get to an inaccessible site.

✦ You mistyped the site's URL. Check carefully, and make any necessary corrections.

✦ The site is temporarily offline or has moved to a new address. Try again later, or try using a search engine to find the site's new address.

✦ You're not online. Get back online, and try again.

In Figure 33-16, the problem becomes obvious if you look closely at the screen. Neither the CTSNET button (which appears when my dial-up connection is active) nor the modem indicator appear in the taskbar. Thus, I'm not online and Netscape Navigator cannot find the requested site. The solution here simply is to re-connect to the Internet and try again.

You may be able to visit some sites that you've visited in the past, even when you are not online. Why? Because Navigator automatically saves copies of recently visited sites to your hard disk (in a folder named *cache*). For example, when I clicked OK in the dialog box shown in Figure 33-16, Navigator reloaded the site from my local hard disk rather than retrieving the document from the remote server again. This feature can save a great deal of time!

Summary

In this chapter, you learned how to browse the World Wide Web with Netscape Navigator 2. The topics discussed here included the following:

- When you first connect to the Internet through Netscape Navigator, you are usually taken to a specific start page.
- You can get to any other page on the World Wide Web by typing the page's URL (address) into the Location box and pressing Enter.
- You can use the Back and Forward buttons on the toolbar to navigate through pages you've already visited. To return to Navigator's home page at any time, click the Home button on the toolbar. To stop a download cold, click the Stop toolbar button or press Esc.
- You can use various search engines to locate pages based on some topic or category. To begin your search, try out the What's New!, What's Cool!, Net Search, or Net Directory buttons below the Location box, or choose search options from the Directory menu.
- To make it easy to return to a specific page in the future, you can add the page to the list of favorites on the Bookmarks menu. Just visit the page and press Ctrl+D. To revisit the marked site later, choose a bookmark name from the Bookmarks menu.
- When a Web page appears on your screen, you can print it by choosing File⇨Print from the menu bar or by clicking the Print button on the toolbar.
- You can save whatever is on your screen. To save text, select the text and use standard Windows copy-and-paste techniques.
- To save a graphic from a Web page, right-click the graphic image and choose Save This Image As.

✦ ✦ ✦

Web Authoring with Netscape Navigator Gold

✦ ✦ ✦ ✦

In This Chapter

Getting Netscape Gold up and running

Creating a Web page

Getting your basic skills down pat

Changing the Editor preferences

Try it now!

More handy Netscape Gold tools

✦ ✦ ✦ ✦

In the preceding chapter, you learn how to browse the World Wide Web with Netscape Navigator. In this chapter, you learn how to edit Web pages in Netscape Navigator Gold. Netscape Navigator Gold (or just Netscape Gold for short) includes all the great Netscape Navigator 2.0 browsing features covered in the previous chapter, plus a slew of powerful, yet easy-to-use authoring tools for creating your own Web pages without typing any nasty HTML tags.

If you know how to use a word processor such as Microsoft Word or Windows WordPad and you've been cruising the Net and dipping into various chapters of this book, you'll have no trouble learning how to create Web pages with Netscape Gold.

Hot Stuff

After you install Netscape Navigator Gold, you won't need Netscape Navigator for browsing. Just use Netscape Gold for everything — browsing and editing alike.

Getting Netscape Gold Up and Running

You can buy Netscape Gold at a retail store or mail-order house or download it from the Internet. To download it from the Internet, point your Web browser to `http://cgi.netscape.com/cgi-bin/123.cgi` and follow the instructions on the download form. (Be sure to select the *Gold* version of Netscape Navigator on the download form.) The downloading process takes a few minutes, so grab a cup of coffee (or skim this chapter) while you're waiting.

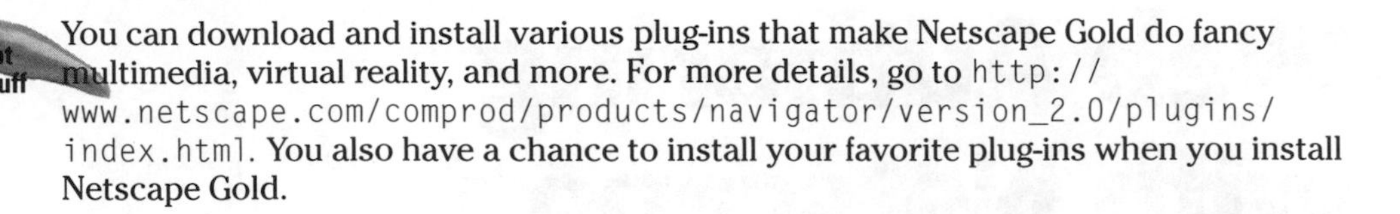

You can download and install various plug-ins that make Netscape Gold do fancy multimedia, virtual reality, and more. For more details, go to `http://www.netscape.com/comprod/products/navigator/version_2.0/plugins/index.html`. You also have a chance to install your favorite plug-ins when you install Netscape Gold.

Installing Netscape Gold

After you download Netscape Gold from the Internet, simply double-click the icon of the file you downloaded and follow the installation instructions on your screen. If you purchase Netscape Gold from a commercial source, follow the installation instructions that came with your package.

Hot Stuff

When you first install Netscape Gold, a Netscape Gold window containing a shortcut to the program appears on your Windows 95 desktop. To make it easier to start Netscape Navigator, press and hold the Ctrl key and drag the Netscape Navigator Gold shortcut from the Netscape Gold window to your desktop. Then add Netscape Gold to your Start menu by pressing and holding the Ctrl key while dragging the Netscape Navigator Gold shortcut to the Start button on the taskbar.

Starting Netscape Gold

You start Netscape Gold the same way you start any Windows 95 program. For example, open the window that contains the Netscape Gold program and double-click the program's icon. If you copied a Netscape Gold shortcut to the desktop, you can double-click that icon instead. Similarly, if you copied a Netscape Gold shortcut to the Start menu, you can click the Start button on the taskbar and choose Netscape Navigator Gold from the menu.

Puzzled?

To look for Netscape Gold or its shortcuts on your hard disk, click the Start button on the taskbar, choose Find⇨Files Or Folders, and type **Netscape Navigator Gold** in the Named box. Then click the Advanced tab, choose Application (or Shortcut) from the Of Type drop-down list, and click Find Now. When the search finishes, double-click the appropriate Netscape Navigator Gold icon in the Find window.

Figure 34-1 shows the Netscape Navigator Gold browser window. If you compare Figure 34-1 with the Netscape Navigator window shown in Figure 34-2, you see just how similar these programs are.

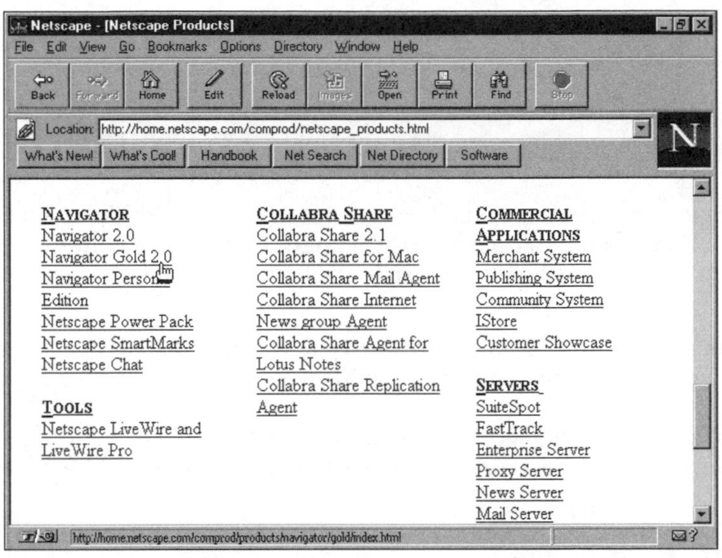

Figure 34-1: The toolbar on the Netscape Navigator Gold browser window features an Edit button and Location icon that are not found in the Netscape Navigator window.

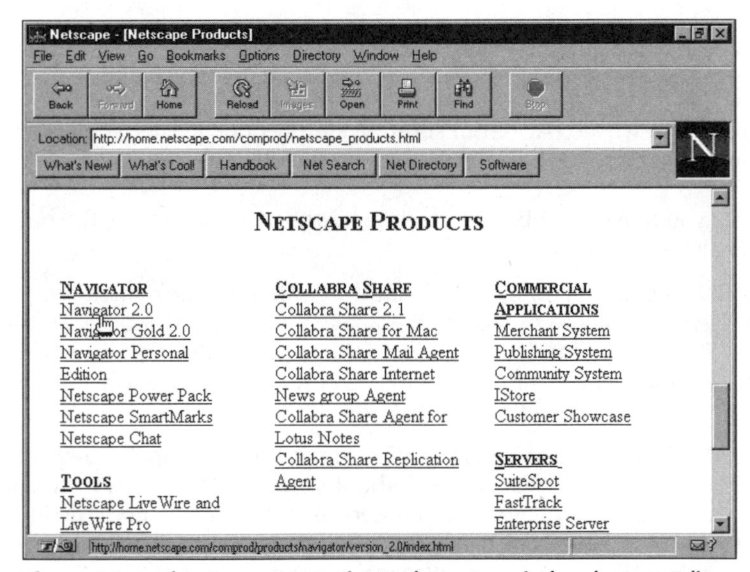

Figure 34-2: The Netscape Navigator browser window has no Edit button or Location icon.

Here are the main differences between the browser windows in Netscape Navigator Gold and Netscape Navigator:

✦ Netscape Gold's browser has an Edit button on the toolbar. This button lets you edit the current Web page by using Netscape Gold's WYSIAWYG (What-You-See-Is-Almost-What-You-Get) editor. Netscape Navigator lacks this button.

✦ Netscape Gold's browser has a little Location icon (which looks like chain links) next to the Location box. You can drag the icon to the Netscape Editor window or double-click it to copy the URL shown in the Location box to the Windows Clipboard.

✦ The File menus in the two browsers are different. Netscape Gold's File menu contains several options that the Netscape Navigator's File menu does not have.

You don't need to sweat the differences between the browsers. In fact, knowing how *similar* the two browser windows are should make you breathe a sigh of relief.

Creating a Web Page

Creating or editing a Web page in Navigator Gold is simply a matter of switching from the browser to the Netscape Editor window. There are several ways to make this switch.

Creating a page from scratch

If you want to create a new Web page from scratch, simply choose File⇨New Document from the browser window. Then choose one of the following options:

✦ **Blank.** Takes you to a new (blank) Netscape Editor window such as the one shown in Figure 34-3.

✦ **From Template.** Opens a new browser window containing the default template page from Netscape's home site or the Web page you set via Options⇨Editor Preferences. If you've opened Netscape's template page, click the hypertext name of the template you want to use and then proceed as I describe in the "Editing the current page" section that follows.

✦ **From Wizard.** Runs the New Document Wizard form at Netscape's home site. Fill in the form with appropriate information about yourself. After you finish, click the Create Page button at the bottom of the form and Netscape uses the information you provided to create a Web page in a new browser window. Now proceed as I describe in the "Editing the current page" section.

Hot Stuff

You also can get to the Netscape New Document Wizard and templates by choosing Help⇨Web Page Starter from the browser or from Editor window's menu bar.

As you see later, the editing window looks and works very much like the editing window in a standard word processor. That similarity is not by accident!

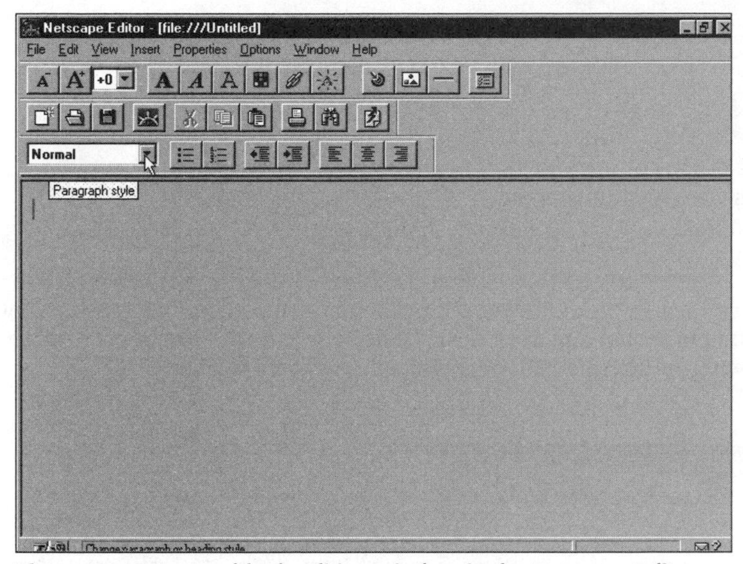

Figure 34-3: A new, blank editing window in the Netscape Editor.

Editing the current page

If you are currently viewing the Web page you want to edit, you can copy it to your hard disk and open it in the Netscape Editor window. Here's how:

1. Click the Edit button on the toolbar or choose File⇨Edit Document from the browser's menu bar. If you are about to edit a page that you have already saved on your hard disk, skip to Step 5.
2. If the page is in a remote document, you see the Save As dialog box shown in Figure 34-4.

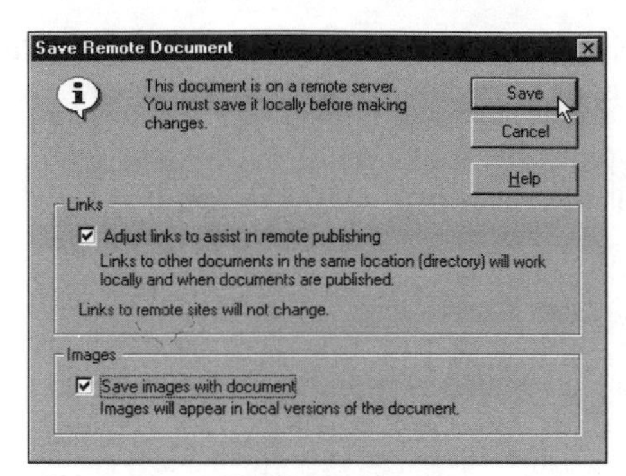

Figure 34-4: This dialog box lets you choose how Netscape copies the remote page to your hard disk.

3. If necessary, change the options in the dialog box shown in Figure 34-4, although the default choices usually work best. Click Save and OK (if necessary) to continue with the standard Save As dialog box shown in Figure 34-5.

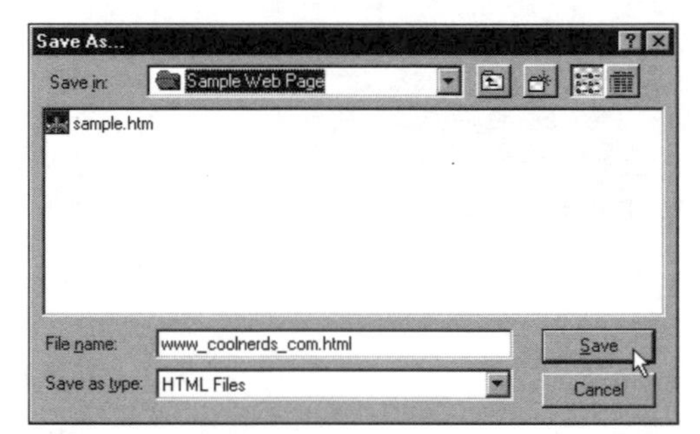

Figure 34-5: The standard Save As dialog box lets you choose a name and location for your Web page.

4. When the standard Save As dialog box appears, type a filename (without an extension) and choose a disk and folder location for your page. Then click the Save button. Netscape copies the page and its images to the folder you specified. (If any of the files being copied already exist in the folder to which you are copying, Netscape will ask for permission to replace the existing files with the new ones.)

Danger Zone

Remember to store your Web page and its associated images in the same folder. Otherwise, your page may not work properly after you install it on the Web server.

5. Your Web page appears in a new Netscape Editor window that resembles Figure 34-6.

Figure 34-6: A Web page ready for editing in Netscape Gold.

Puzzled?

While you are first learning Netscape Gold, it's easy to become confused when trying to determine how many Netscape Gold windows are open and which window is which. Look carefully at the Netscape title bars and toolbars for clues. You also can check out the taskbar to see how many Netscape buttons are available and determine which one is pushed in at the moment. (To view all open Netscape windows simultaneously, right-click an empty spot on the taskbar and choose Cascade, Tile Horizontally, or Tile Vertically.) You also can pull down the Netscape Gold Window menu and choose the window you want to use.

Editing an existing file

You can open and edit any existing HTML file on your hard disk. To do so, start from the browser and choose File⇨Open File In Editor. When the Open dialog box appears, locate and double-click the file you want to edit. Your file opens in a new Netscape Editor window that resembles Figure 34-6.

If you are already in the Netscape Editor window, you can open an existing HTML file by choosing File⇨Open File from the Editor menu bar (or pressing Ctrl+O). The Open dialog box appears, and you can locate and double-click an HTML filename to open that file in a new Editor window.

Getting Your Basic Skills Down Pat

You only need to know a few basic skills — the same ones you use for word processing — to create fabulous Web pages in just a few minutes. Really! Let's take a closer look.

Danger Zone

Pages created in Netscape Gold look great in Netscape Navigator 2.0. They may not look so hot in other browsers, however, so be sure to view your work in several browsers before you unleash those pages on the Net.

The Editor's menus, shortcut menus, and toolbars

The menus, shortcut menus, and toolbars in Netscape Gold work the same as they do in most Windows 95 programs.

For example, to find out what a *menu option* is for, open the menu, point to an option with your mouse, and look at the status bar for a short description of the highlighted option. You then can click the option to select it or press Alt (or click outside the menu) to close the menu without choosing an option.

An appropriate *shortcut menu* appears anytime you right-click selected text, an image or target, or a place where you are about to type new text. You then can click an option on the menu to choose it or press Alt (or click outside the menu) to close the shortcut menu without making a selection.

The *toolbars* offer shortcuts to options on various menus and behave much as they do in any word processor. For example

✦ To find out what a toolbar button does, simply point to the button with your mouse. A tooltip pops up near the mouse pointer, and a descriptive message appears on the status bar.

✦ To activate a button, click it.

✦ To turn the toolbars off or on, choose Options and then select Show File/Edit Toolbar, Show Character Format Toolbar, or Show Paragraph Format Toolbar. Each Show . . . Toolbar option is a toggle. When a Show . . . Toolbar option is checked, the corresponding toolbar is visible; when it is not checked, the toolbar is hidden.

✦ To move a toolbar to a new place on the screen, point to any empty spot between the buttons on the toolbar that you want to move; then drag the toolbar as you'd drag any window. The toolbar displays a title bar anytime you drag the toolbar into the editing area of the window. If the toolbar does have a title bar, you can move the toolbar by dragging its title bar; to hide the toolbar, click the toolbar's Close (X) button.

Easy as 1, 2, 3

As with any word processor, knowing just a few basic steps helps you use the Netscape Gold Editor successfully.

Adding something new

You use these steps to add something new in the Netscape Editor window:

1. Position the insertion point where you want to add new text, an image, or a target.

2. If you want to customize the look of text you are about to type, click appropriate buttons on the Paragraph Format toolbar or Character Format toolbar. Alternatively, you can choose options from the Properties menu.

Life Saver

The buttons on the Paragraph Format toolbar and the options in the Properties➪Paragraph menu affect either the paragraph in which the insertion point is located or any selected paragraphs. Similarly, the buttons on the Character Format toolbar and the options on the Properties➪Character and Properties➪Font Size menus affect the text that you are about to type or the text that you've selected.

3. Do any of the following as needed:

   - Type text using normal word-processing techniques (see Chapter 12 for some tips). Or, paste text from the Clipboard by pressing Ctrl+V.
   - Drag-and-drop an object from a Web page, the desktop, or an Explorer-type window. You learn more about drag-and-drop tricks in a moment.
   - Insert a link, an image, or a target from scratch (you learn how to do so soon).
   - Insert a horizontal line by clicking the Insert Horiz. Line button on the Character Format toolbar (or by choosing Insert➪Horizontal Line from the menu bar). Press Enter after the line appears.
   - Insert various breaks and hard spaces. You can insert a new-line break (choose Insert➪New Line Break or press Shift+Enter), a break below the image just to the left of your insertion point (choose Insert➪Break Below Image(s)), or a nonbreaking space (choose Insert➪Nonbreaking Space or press Shift+Space).

Changing something old

Changing something that already appears on your page is equally easy:

1. Tell Netscape Gold what you want to change by using one of these techniques:

   - Select (highlight) text by dragging your mouse through it or by using standard keyboard selection methods (such as Shift+arrow keys).

- Position the insertion point in a paragraph you want to change.
- Click an image or target that you want to change (a border appears around the selected image or target).

2. If you want to delete your selection, press Delete or Backspace (or type the text that should replace the selection).
3. If you want to customize the selection or paragraph, click the appropriate buttons on the Paragraph Format toolbar or the Character Format toolbar. Alternatively, you can choose options from the Properties menu or right-click the selection and choose options from the shortcut menu that appears.

That's all there is to it!

The basic typing, editing, and selection techniques described in Chapter 12 for Word Internet Assistant are the same ones that work in Netscape Navigator Gold. Check out Chapter 12 if you need a review.

Saving your work

As soon as you make some changes that you are happy with, click the Save button on the File/Edit toolbar or choose File⇨Save or press Ctrl+S. Saving your work frequently is a good idea.

Undoing mistakes

If you make a mistake, you can easily undo the most recent change. Simply choose Edit⇨Undo or press Ctrl+Z; to redo your most recent undo, choose Edit⇨Redo or press Ctrl+Shift+Z. You can undo and redo several levels of changes just as you can in most word processors. If it is too late to undo your changes, click the View In Browser button on the File/Edit toolbar (or close the Netscape Editor window) and answer No when asked about saving your changes.

Viewing and changing the HTML source

You can take a look at the HTML source for your Web page whenever you are in the browser or the Editor by choosing View⇨Document Source. When you finish viewing the source page, close it by clicking its Close button or by pressing Alt+F4.

If you are in the Netscape Editor window, you can go one step further and edit the HTML source directly. With all the great tools that generate and change the HTML for you automatically, you may never need to edit the tags directly. But just in case you do, here is how to do it:

1. Start in the Netscape Editor window and choose View⇨Edit Document Source. If prompted, save or discard your most recent changes.

2. If you have not yet chosen an editor for changing the HTML source, you'll be asked if you want to choose one. Click Yes. When the Editor Preferences dialog box appears, click the Browse button next to the HTML Source box, locate your favorite text editing program (for example, Notepad or Microsoft Word), and double-click its filename. Then click the OK button.

3. Edit the HTML file as needed (be careful). After you finish, close the editing window normally (by pressing Alt+F4) and save your work if prompted to do so.

Hot Stuff

Advanced users can enter a single HTML tag at the insertion point, right from the Netscape Editor window. To get started, position the insertion point where the tag should appear and choose Insert⇨HTML Tag. An HTML Tag dialog box opens. The dialog box explains what to do next and also includes a handy Verify button (which lets you test your entry) and a Help button (which does the obvious).

Viewing your work in the browser

Whenever you want to see your handiwork in the Netscape Gold browser, save your work and then click the View In Browser button on the File/Edit toolbar, or choose File⇨Browse Document. Netscape Gold takes you to a new browser window, where you can work with the page as you'd work with any Web page.

When you are ready to edit some more, close the browser window (press Ctrl+W), and you'll be taken back to the Netscape Editor window.

Changing the page title, colors, and background

If you are in the Netscape Editor window, you can change the title that appears on the title bar when someone views your page in a browser. You also can choose the colors for text on the page and choose the color or image for the page's background.

The following list describes how to change any of these things:

1. Choose Properties⇨Document.

2. Choose the tab you want to use as follows:

   - **General tab.** Lets you change the information shown in Figure 34-7.
   - **Appearance tab.** Lets you change the colors and background of the page. See Figure 34-8 and the "Changing the Colors and Background" section for details.
   - **Advanced tab.** Lets you change advanced technical stuff such as Netscape system variables and user variables.

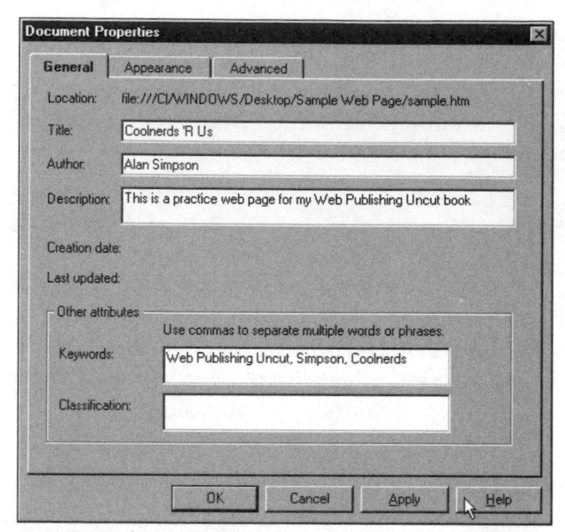

Figure 34-7: The Properties dialog box with the General tab selected.

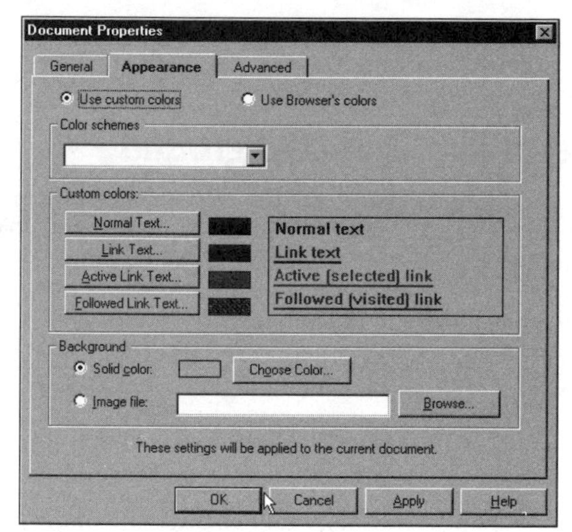

Figure 34-8: The Properties dialog box with the Appearance tab selected.

3. Change whatever options you want.
4. Repeat Steps 2 and 3 as needed. After you finish, click OK to accept your selections and return to the Editor (or click Cancel to discard your changes and return to the Editor).

Netscape Gold provides you with lots of help throughout it. To view it, just click the Help button anytime you see it in a dialog box.

Changing the colors and background

The Appearance tab of the Properties dialog box lets you tweak the text colors and background color or background image used on the page. Getting the right look for your page may take some experimentation, but here are some tips to guide you in this process:

- If you want the page to use whatever colors the user has selected in his or her browser, choose Use Browser's Colors from the top of the Appearance tab. (Choosing this option prevents you from adjusting the color schemes or choosing custom colors and backgrounds for your page.)
- If you want the page to use custom colors and backgrounds, choose Use Custom Colors from the top of the Appearance tab.
- Assuming that you choose Use Custom Colors, you can choose a scheme from the Color Schemes drop-down list. You also can choose custom colors for normal text, link text, active link text, and followed link text. If you want to tweak the background, you can either choose a solid color or a previously saved image file.

Dragging and dropping links and images

You can add links and images to your Web pages in several ways. Because the drag-and-drop technique is so handy (and fun), I show that method to you first. Then I show you some other methods.

The following steps describe how to copy an image or link from a Web page to the page you are currently editing:

1. Open or create your page in the Netscape Editor window. You will be copying the image or hypertext link to this page.
2. From the Netscape Editor menu, choose File⇨New Web Browser to open a new Netscape browser window. (Or, if a Netscape browser window is open already, click its button on the Windows 95 taskbar or choose it from the Window menu.)
3. Go to the Web page that contains the hypertext or image you want to copy to your own Web page.
4. Arrange the Netscape Editor and Netscape browser windows so that you can see them both, as shown in Figure 34-9. To do this task quickly, minimize all windows except the Editor and browser windows, right-click an empty part of the taskbar, and choose Tile Vertically.

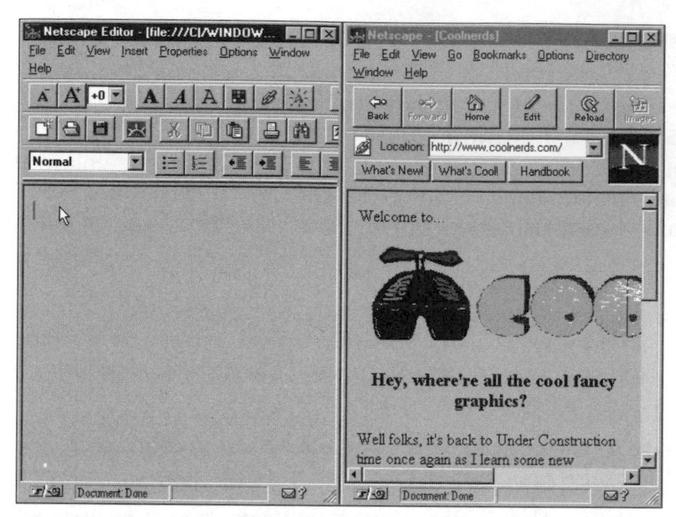

Figure 34-9: A Netscape Editor and Netscape browser window ready for copying.

5. Move your mouse pointer to the image or hypertext link you want to copy. Or, if you want to copy the URL of the page that you are currently viewing, move your mouse pointer to the Location icon next to the browser's Location box.
6. Click and hold the mouse button and drag the image or link to the location where it should appear on your own Web page. When the mouse pointer changes to a little image icon (see Figure 34-10) or a link icon (see Figure 34-11), release the mouse button.

The image or hypertext link pops into place right on your Web page. Easy!

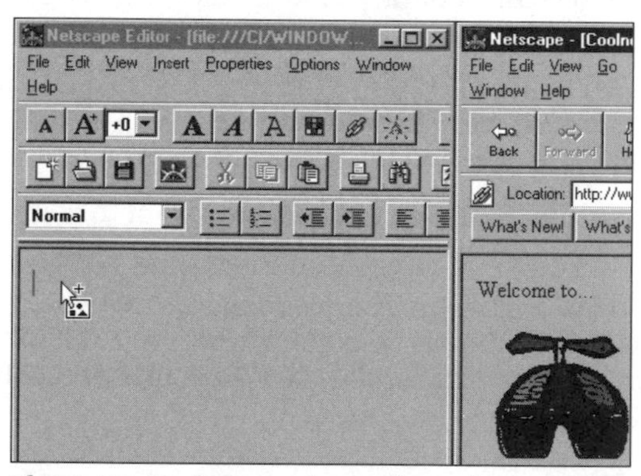

Figure 34-10: Drag an image from the browser to your Web page in the Editor. When the mouse pointer changes to a little image icon, release the mouse button and your image pops into place.

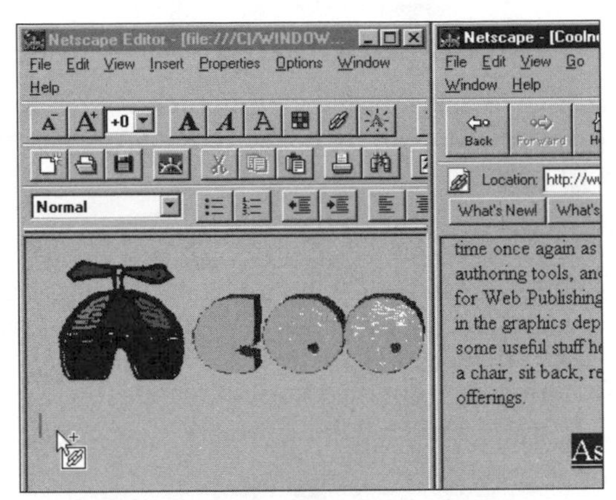

Figure 34-11: Drag a link from the browser to your Web page in the Editor. When the mouse pointer changes to a little link icon, release the mouse button and the entire hypertext link appears on your page.

Hot Stuff

Actually, you can drag and drop stuff from just about any window or from the desktop to the Web page that you are editing. For instance, you can copy links and images from one Netscape Editor window to another. You can even drag and drop Web page filenames and images from Windows Explorer, the desktop, My Computer, and so on. Just experiment! As long as you can see what you want to copy and the place where you want to copy it, the drag-and-drop procedure will probably work just fine.

Inserting targets (named anchors)

Targets (also known as *named anchors*) are places in your document that can be quickly reached through a hyperlink. For example, you can mark a target named Top at the top of a lengthy Web page. Then, to make it easy for readers to jump back to the top of your page, you can create hyperlink text or images that take the reader back to that target. The following steps explain how to create a target on your Web page:

1. In the Netscape Editor window, position the insertion point at the location where you want to place the target. For example, if you want to set up a target at the top of the page, place the insertion point at the top; similarly, to set up a target at the start of a particular section in your page, place the insertion point at the beginning of that section.
2. Click the Insert Target (Named Anchor) button on the Character Format toolbar or choose Insert⇨Target (Named Anchor) from the menu bar.
3. Type a descriptive name for the target (such as **Top**) and click OK.

A little target icon then appears at the insertion point position. To complete the job of setting up a target, simply insert a hyperlink that jumps to the target, as explained in the next section.

Inserting hyperlinks without drag and drop

The following steps provide an alternative to using drag and drop for creating hyperlinks that take you to a specific URL on the Web, to a Web page on your hard disk, or to a particular spot within a Web page:

1. If you don't want to manually type the hyperlink's URL, do one of the following:
   - To copy a URL from an existing link to the Clipboard, go to the page that contains the link that you want to copy. (You can copy a link while you are in the Editor or the browser.) Then right-click the link you want to copy and choose Copy Link To Clipboard from the shortcut menu.
   - To copy the URL of the page you are viewing to the Clipboard, double-click the Location icon next to the browser's Location box.
2. In the Netscape Editor window, type the text for your link (if necessary) and then select the text. Alternatively, click on an image to select it or just position the insertion point where the link should appear (you type in the text in Step 4).
3. Click the Make Link button on the Character Format toolbar. Alternatively, you can choose Insert⇨Link from the menu bar or press Ctrl+L. The dialog box shown in Figure 34-12 appears.

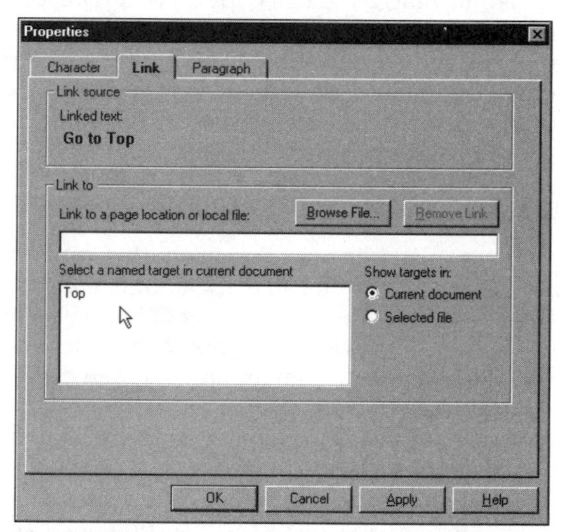

Figure 34-12: The Properties dialog box with the Link tab selected.

4. If you didn't select any text or an image in Step 2, type some descriptive text in the Enter Text box that appears (this box does not appear in Figure 34-12).

5. To specify the link, click in the Link To box (if necessary). Then do one of the following:
   - To link to a specific URL, type the URL you want to link to or paste it from the Clipboard (press Ctrl+V).
   - To link to a file, click the Browse File button and double-click the filename to which you want to link.
   - To link to a target in the current file, choose Current Document under Show Targets In and click the target name shown in the Select A Named Target box near the bottom of the tab. The selected target name (for example, #*Top*) appears in the Link To box.
   - To link to a target in a different file, choose the filename to which you want to link (for example, by using the Browse File button). Then choose Selected File under Show Targets In and click on the target name shown in the Select A Named Target box. Again, the selected target name appears in the Link To box.
6. Click OK.

Your text or image will be transformed into a hyperlink.

Inserting images without drag and drop

Say that you stored an image in the folder along with the Web page you are creating, and now you want to put the image into your Web page. Copying the image to your page is certainly easy to do with drag and drop (as explained earlier), but the manual method that follows works fine, too:

1. In the Netscape Editor window, click at the location where you want the image to appear on your page.

Life Saver If you want your image to appear below the last text or image currently on your page, click at the bottom of the page and then press Shift+Enter as many times as you want.

2. Click the Insert Image button on the Character Format toolbar or choose Insert⇨Image from the menu bar. The Properties dialog box shown in Figure 34-13 pops up.
3. In the Image File Name box, type in the image filename or use the Browse button next to the Image File Name box to locate the image.
4. If you want, choose other options in the Insert Image dialog box to change the appearance of the image.
5. Click OK to return to the Netscape Editor window.

The image now appears on your Web page.

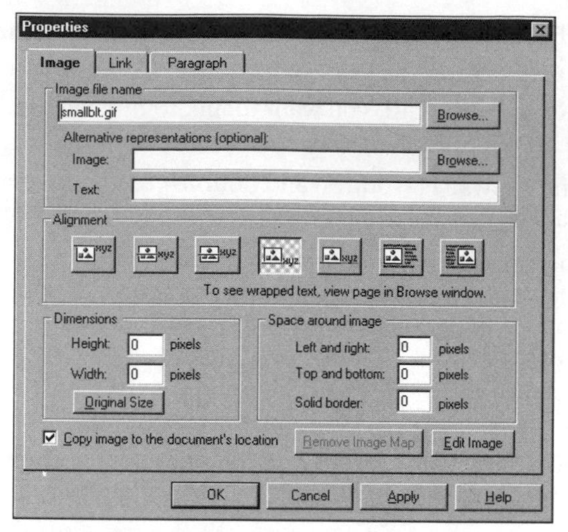

Figure 34-13: The Properties dialog box with the Image tab selected.

Changing hyperlink, image, and target properties

You can change the way a hyperlink, image, or target looks or behaves by changing its *properties*. First, make sure that you are in the Netscape Editor window. Then follow these steps:

1. Click anywhere in the hypertext or click the image or target whose properties you want to change.
2. Click the Object Properties button on the Character Format toolbar. (You also can right-click on the item and choose an appropriate option from the shortcut menu or choose an option from the Properties menu.)

Hot Stuff

As a shortcut, you can double-click an image or target icon to open the Properties dialog box.

3. A Properties dialog box will appear.
4. If necessary, click on a tab to select the type of properties you want to change, adjust the settings as needed, and click OK to return to the Editor.

Life Saver

If you simply want to delete an image or target, go to the Netscape Editor window, click the image or target, and press Delete. Likewise, to delete a link, select the link's text in the Netscape Editor window and press Delete.

Changing the Editor Preferences

Several settings control how the Netscape Editor behaves, and you can, of course, change them. If you want to explore some of these settings, choose Options⇨Editor Preferences. Figure 34-14 shows the Editor Preferences dialog box with the General tab selected. Choose the tab that contains the settings you want to change and change the settings as needed. As usual, you can click the Help button for specific tips about any option on the tab. After you finish making changes, click OK.

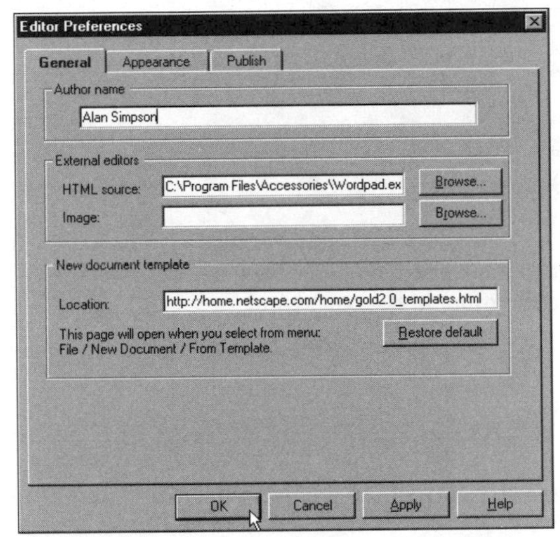

Figure 34-14: The Editor Preferences dialog box with the General tab selected.

Try It Now!

Just so that you can get the hang of using the Netscape Editor, why not try the following steps to build the Web page shown in Figure 34-15? I'll pull some information from my own Web site at `http://www.coolnerds.com` so that you can practice adding a few twists of your own. You'll be amazed at how quickly you can create a great-looking Web page.

Danger Zone

Of course, you should avoid stealing anyone's logos when creating Web pages for real. But this is just an example, so feel free to borrow my coolnerds logo for your make-believe Web page.

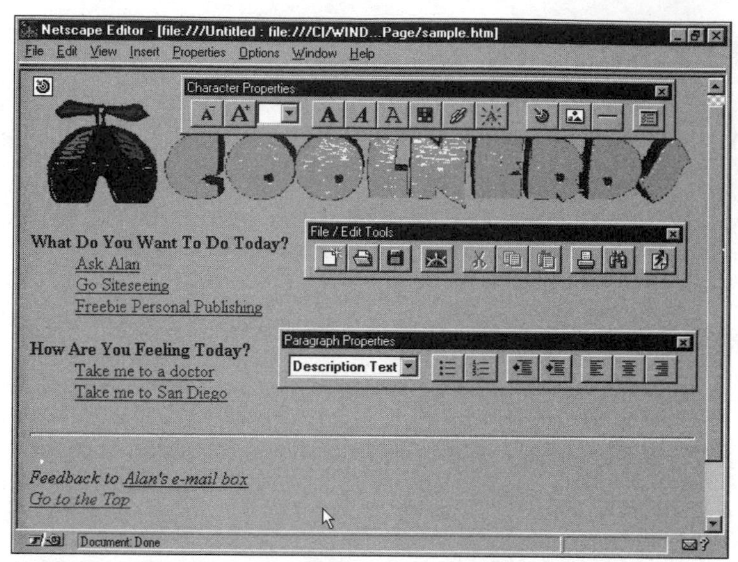

Figure 34-15: The finished Web page in the Netscape Editor. I've moved the toolbars to the editing area so more of the page would be visible.

Getting started

Let's start by creating the new page with a target, an image, and the first section (What Do You Want to Do Today?):

1. Start Netscape Navigator Gold and choose File⇨New Document⇨Blank. If you cannot see all the toolbars, check the appropriate Show Toolbar options in the Options menu.
2. Save your empty Web page by clicking the Save button on the File/Edit toolbar or by pressing Ctrl+S. In the Save As dialog box, type a name (such as **sample**) and choose a disk and folder location for your page. Click Save.
3. Just for fun, insert a target at the top of the page. To do this, click the Insert Target (Named Anchor) button on the Character Formatting toolbar (it looks like a little archery target). Now type the name **Top** and click OK. A target icon appears.
4. Right-click an empty area of the taskbar, and choose Tile Vertically. Your browser and Editor windows appear side by side.
5. Using the *browser* window, go to my Web site at `http://www.coolnerds.com`.
6. Use the drag-and-drop technique to copy the coolnerds image to your own Web page (see Figure 34-10). In the *Editor* window, click just to the right of the image and press Enter to start the next text on a new line.

7. In the Editor window, type **What Do You Want To Do Today?** and press Enter.
8. In the browser window, scroll down until you can see the *Ask Alan, Go Siteseeing,* and *Freebie Personal Publishing* hyperlinks. Then use drag and drop to copy the *Ask Alan* link to your Web page (see Figure 34-11).
9. Click after the *Ask Alan* link in your Web page and press Enter. The insertion point moves to a new line.
10. Using the techniques in Steps 8 and 9, drag and drop *Go Siteseeing* and *Freebie Personal Publishing* onto your page.
11. Save your work (press Ctrl+S).

Making it prettier

Now format the first section of the page to look more like the example in Figure 34-15

1. In the Editor window, select *What Do You Want to Do Today?*
2. Click the Bold button on the Editor's Character Format toolbar or press Ctrl+B.

Hot Stuff

Ctrl+B is a universal shortcut that toggles text between plain and bold and it works in most Windows programs. Likewise, Ctrl+I toggles italics and Ctrl+U toggles underlining.

3. Using the Paragraph Style drop-down list at the left edge of the Editor window's Paragraph Format toolbar, select *Description Title* (it's near the bottom of the drop-down list).
4. Select the *Ask Alan, Go Siteseeing,* and *Freebie Personal Publishing* links on your Web page.
5. Using the Paragraph Style drop-down list on the Paragraph Format toolbar again, select *Description Text* from the bottom of the list.
6. Click at the bottom of the document, making sure that the insertion point appears at the start of a new line (press Enter if you need to).
7. Save your work (Ctrl+S).

Finishing the text

Now your page is starting to look like something! Let's add the rest of the text. This time I'll have you format the text as you type it and then I'll have you add some links manually. Here's what to do:

1. To give yourself more room to work, close the browser window and maximize the Editor window.
2. Click near the bottom of the document and make sure that the insertion point appears at the beginning of a new line.

3. Turn on bold (press Ctrl+B).
4. Choose the *Description Title* style from the Paragraph Style drop-down list on the Paragraph Format toolbar.
5. Type **How Are You Feeling Today?** and press Enter. Press Ctrl+B again to turn off bold.
6. Choose the *Description Text* style from the Paragraph Style drop-down list.
7. Type **Take me to a doctor** and press Enter.
8. Type **Take me to San Diego** and press Enter.
9. Choose the Normal style from the Paragraph Style drop-down list.
10. Add a horizontal line by clicking the Insert Horiz. Line button on the Character Format toolbar. Then press Enter.
11. Choose the *Address* style from the Paragraph Style drop-down list.
12. Type **Feedback to Alan's e-mail box** (or type your own name in place of *Alan*) and press Enter.
13. Type **Go to the Top** and press Enter.
14. If you want to add a blank line before *How Are You Feeling Today?,* click at the beginning of that line and press Shift+Enter.
15. Save your work (Ctrl+S).

Finishing the links

What is left to do? Just to add our remaining links. The following steps explain how:

1. Select *Take me to a doctor* and click the Make Link button on the Character Format toolbar. In the Link To box, type the URL **http://msa2.medsearch.com/pfo/** and click OK.
2. Select *Take me to San Diego* and click the Make Link button on the Character Format toolbar. In the Link To box, type the URL **http://www.homeport-sd.com/** and click OK.
3. Select *Alan's e-mail box* and click the Make Link button on the Character Format toolbar. In the Link To box, type the URL **mailto:alan@coolnerds.com** (or type your own e-mail address in place of `alan@coolnerds.com`). Click OK.
4. Select *Go to the top* and click the Make Link toolbar button again. This time, click the target named *Top* in the Select A Named Target box and click OK.
5. Save your page again (Ctrl+S).

Congratulations! You created a great-looking Web page in about five minutes flat. Now click the View In Browser button on the File/Edit toolbar and test your page. If you need to make any changes, close the browser and tweak the page to perfection.

More Handy Netscape Gold Tools

You just looked at the most important offerings in Netscape Gold, but it provides still more. For example, you can publish your page on your ISP's Web server by clicking the Publish button on the File/Edit toolbar or by choosing File➪Publish. This one-button publish feature automatically FTPs the required files from your local hard drive to a designated directory on the ISP's server.

More Info

To learn more about Netscape Gold's features, just experiment! Or, take a look at the Netscape Gold Data Sheet at `http://cgi.netscape.com/comprod/products/navigator/gold/datasheet.html`.

Summary

Authoring a Web page is easier than ever with Netscape Navigator Gold. The following is a review of the most important points in this chapter:

✦ You can use Netscape Gold to create a Web page from scratch, to edit the page you're currently viewing, and to edit existing pages on your hard disk. To get started, choose an option on the browser's File menu (either New Document, Edit Document, or Open File In Editor).

✦ You work in the Netscape Editor window much as you do in a standard word processor. That is, you position the insertion point or select text or an image or target; then you do something to your selection. What can you do? Type new text, insert a new image or target, delete the selection, or choose an option from the menus, toolbars, or shortcut menus.

✦ To save your work, click the Save button on the File/Edit toolbar or choose File⇨Save or press Ctrl+S. Save often!

✦ To undo mistakes, choose Edit⇨Undo or press Ctrl+Z as needed.

✦ To view your page in the browser, click the View In Browser button on the File/Edit toolbar or choose File⇨Browse.

✦ To return to the Navigator Editor after browsing your page, close the browser window (Ctrl+W).

✦ To change the page title, colors, and background of your page, go to the Netscape Editor window and choose Properties⇨Document.

✦ To quickly copy an image, hyperlink, or other object to your Web page, simply drag the object from its original spot on another Web page, the desktop, or to an Explorer-type window in the Web page you are editing.

✦ To change images, targets, or hyperlinks, click the object that you want to change; then click the Object Properties button on the Character Format toolbar.

✦ ✦ ✦

Doing Money on the Internet

In This Chapter

Protecting your money on the Internet

How secure servers and browsers work

Using Netscape Navigator browser security

Using Internet Explorer browser security

Where to learn more about security

If you want to make money or spend money on the Internet, you probably care about security. As a seller, you want your customers to feel comfortable paying for products and services online. And as a buyer, you want assurance that no hi-tech snoops will be able to intercept sensitive information, such as your credit card account numbers and expiration dates. This chapter helps you understand how to keep money safe on the Internet.

How to Protect Your Money on the Internet

Historically, security on the Internet has been pretty lax, slowing the growth of online commerce. The problem is that virtually anything you send from your computer to another computer can be intercepted by clever crooks and viewed by every computer in between (see Figure 35-1). Yikes!

Today, however, the online commerce picture is rapidly changing. Many companies doing business on the Internet now offer *secure sites,* meaning they have taken some high-tech steps to prevent unauthorized people from grabbing sensitive financial and personal information off the Web. To take advantage of that security, both the Web site's server software and the Web browser must have built-in security. We'll look at how secure sites work in a moment, but first let's explore some of the most common ways to pay for purchases on the Net.

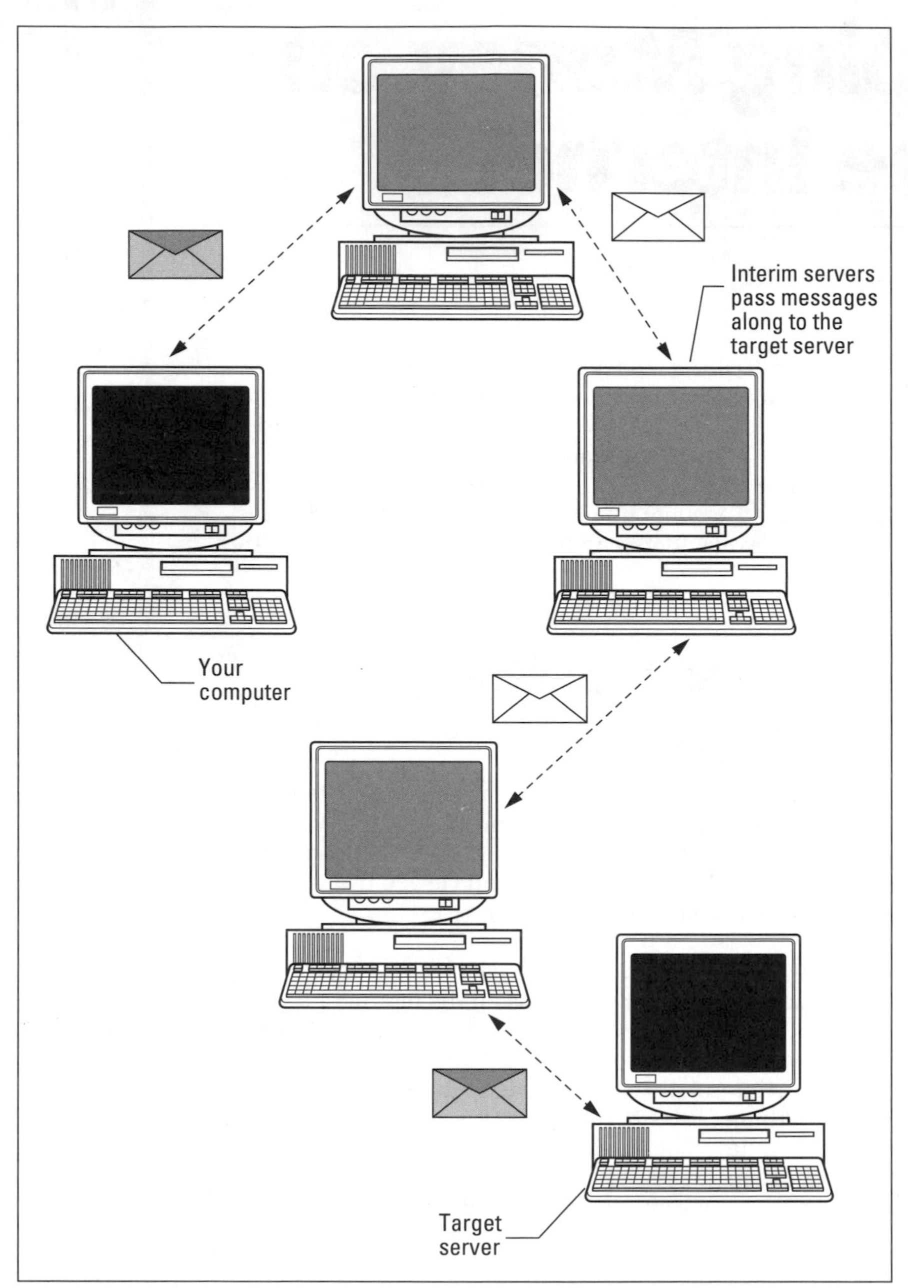

Figure 35-1: Information sent via the Internet can be intercepted by intermediate computers along the path between you and the server with which you are communicating.

Low-tech solutions for paying outside the Net

Whether you do business on or off the Net, you always have the traditional option of billing or being billed for purchases. So, for example, if you sell magazine subscriptions over the Net, you simply mail an invoice to the customer for the subscription price. The customer pays you according to the payment methods you offer (cash, credit card, check, wampum, whatever) — without sending any sensitive information over the Net. You then send the magazine to the reader's electronic (or real) mailbox each month.

In another low-tech solution, customers can call in or fax their orders, charging purchases to their credit cards. It turns out that the telephone company's network is a very safe way to transmit credit card information because it is almost impossible to eavesdrop on conversations that travel through the phone company wires. As you may expect, however, phoning in or faxing credit card information involves a few security risks:

- Someone lurking over your shoulder could overhear your credit card number or see the number on your fax message. You take the same risk when paying for purchases in person.
- The person receiving your credit card information by phone or fax may be dishonest or careless. Of course, you face those same risks anytime you hand your credit card to someone at a restaurant or store or whenever someone carelessly throws your credit card slip into a trash can.

Danger Zone

For utmost safety, *do not* use a cellular phone or cordless phone to send or receive credit card information. Because cellular phone and cordless phone transmissions spend at least part of their time traveling through the air (like radio signals), crooks with the right equipment can intercept them with surprising ease.

High-tech solutions for online payments

Today, people are using the Internet to purchase and pay for all kinds of products and services. As you see later in this chapter, several high-tech, online payment methods are in use today. Many of these methods are still in their infancy, and the coming years are sure to bring refinements and new options.

Sending non-secure payment information

Today, most customers who pay online transmit their credit card numbers and expiration dates to non-secure servers, typically by using online forms or e-mail messages. These non-secure methods pose a slight risk of intercepted messages and stolen credit card information.

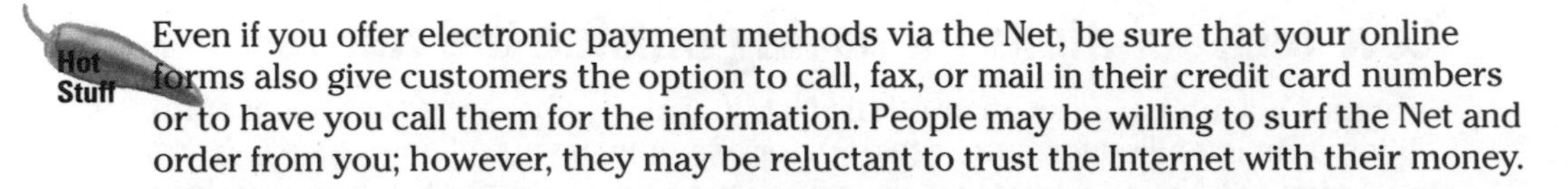

Even if you offer electronic payment methods via the Net, be sure that your online forms also give customers the option to call, fax, or mail in their credit card numbers or to have you call them for the information. People may be willing to surf the Net and order from you; however, they may be reluctant to trust the Internet with their money.

Sending secure payment information

When you use a security-enabled browser or e-mail program to send online forms or e-mail messages to a secure server, little chance exists of anyone stealing sensitive information. These secure systems employ special techniques to protect your transaction. (You see more about this security stuff later in the chapter.)

If your Web pages reside on an Internet Service Provider's server — rather than your own secure server — find out whether your ISP offers secure servers. If the answer is Yes, find out which secure browsers or e-mail programs work with the secure servers offered. You'll certainly want support for the hottest browsers, including Netscape Navigator and Internet Explorer. If the answer is No, your ordering methods definitely should include the option of letting customers call in their credit card information or having you call them for it.

More Info

Lotus Notes and Microsoft Exchange Server are two e-mail systems that offer full security for your e-mail messages. You can learn more about Lotus Notes at `http://www.lotus.com/home/notes.htm`. For details about Microsoft Exchange Server, visit `http://www.microsoft.com/Exchange/exchdata.htm`.

Sending payments through a third party

Credit card companies collect money from buyers on behalf of sellers worldwide, which is a wonderfully convenient arrangement for everyone. Unfortunately, thieves often use both high-tech and low-tech methods to steal credit card numbers and expiration dates. Then they make purchases by phone, using the information they have stolen; they don't even need to have the credit card in hand.

A company named First Virtual has one solution to this credit card security problem. First Virtual issues buyers a Personal Identification Number (PIN) associated with the real MasterCard or Visa credit card number; only the buyer and First Virtual know the connection between the PIN and the real credit card. When buying from a seller that is part of this system, you send your PIN — not your real credit card information — to the seller. First Virtual sends you e-mail asking you to verify each purchase made via the PIN. If you confirm the sale, your credit card is charged (completely off the Internet) and payments go directly into the vendor's checking account. This method is simple, secure, and safe, and it requires no special hardware, software, or encryption. If you want to explore this option further, visit `http://www.fv.com/html/fv_main.html`.

Danger Zone

As you can see, third-party payment methods like First Virtual's put yet another finger in the payment pie. This can be costly for the seller and ultimately for the buyer — especially for low-priced items. For example, according to First Virtual, a product costing $1 yields the seller $.69 after fees are deducted; a product costing $10 yields $9.51; and a product costing $100 yields $97.71.

Paying with electronic cash (ecash)

New on the horizon is electronic cash (ecash), a digital equivalent of cash that lets you make online payments anonymously. In the scheme offered by the Amsterdam-based company, Digicash, you can withdraw digital coins from your Internet bank account and store them on your hard disk. When you want to buy something, you pay for it with these coins. Additional security is included to prevent other users from accessing your ecash, and ecash can be stored in *smart cards* that you can carry with you.

More Info

For more about Digicash, visit `http://www.digicash.com`. To further explore the fascinating topic of electronic money on the Internet, rev up your search engine and look for *ecash, digicash,* or *electronic money.*

How Secure Servers and Browsers Work

Many security measures are available to prevent people from stealing money and information on the Internet. The following discussion won't qualify you to work for the NSA (National Security Agency) as a cryptographer or spy; however, it will familiarize you with some security buzzwords and help you impress people at cocktail parties.

Secure Sockets Layer protocol

Much of today's security-enabled browser and server software uses a standard protocol called Secure Sockets Layer (SSL) to provide advanced security features for data communications on the Internet. SSL incorporates the following features:

- **Authentication** thwarts imposters. That is, it prevents any computer from impersonating the real server and from attempting to appear secure when it isn't. Because of authentication, you can rest assured that the server to which you are connecting is the correct server.
- **Encryption** thwarts eavesdroppers by using sophisticated cryptographic means to scramble transferred data. Even if eavesdroppers can grab the information as it travels the Internet, they cannot understand the information, so having it does them no good.

Puzzled? *Encryption* is a process — similar to that used in a decoder ring but much more sophisticated — in which data is scrambled so that only someone with a specific *key* can unscramble (or decrypt) the message in a readable form.

✦ **Data integrity** thwarts vandals. You are immediately alerted if any person or computer along the public route has altered your data in any way.

Danger Zone The entire communication is secure *only* if both the browser (client) and the server use the same security protocol. For example, both Netscape Navigator and Internet Explorer are SSL-enabled browsers. However, unless you are using them to connect to an SSL-enabled server such as Netscape Commerce Server or Internet Information Server, your sensitive information may not be 100 percent secure.

Secure commercial servers

If you are hot to build your own secure server, consider installing the widely-used Netscape Commerce Server software from Netscape Communications or the Internet Information Server software from Microsoft Corporation.

Netscape Commerce Server (NCS) supports the standard SSL security protocol and SSL-enabled browsers, including Netscape Navigator (of course) and Internet Explorer. It costs about $995. This server runs on many Unix hardware platforms, including

How authentication works

The first step in a secure exchange is for the browser to authenticate the server's identity — that is, to make sure that the server is exactly who it says it is. The following steps describe the general way in which it works:

1. The client asks to connect to the secure server.
2. The server sends a *signed digital certificate* to the client (see the section "Security Certificates").
3. The client decrypts the digital signature and matches it with the certificate information. If the certificate doesn't match, the client ends the connection with the server. If the certificate does match, it's considered the real McCoy.
4. The client generates a *session key* and encrypts it by using the server's public key from the certificate (see the section "Public and Private Keys"). The session key is used to encrypt and decrypt data and ensure data integrity.
5. The client sends the encrypted session key to the server. Only the server's private key can decrypt the session key.

Digital Alpha; Hewlett-Packard PA; IBM RS/6000; Silicon Graphics MIPS; Sun SPARC; and Intel 386, 486, and Pentium. On the Windows NT side, you can run NCS on Digital Alpha and Intel 386, 486, and Pentium computers. For details about NCS, visit `http://home.netscape.com/comprod/netscape_commerce.html`. For up-to-date pricing, descriptions, and ordering information concerning all of Netscape's servers, visit `http://merchant.netscape.com/netstore/soft/serv/items/leaf/product0.html`. (Whew, what a URL!)

Internet Information Server (IIS) is a Windows NT-based server that claims to be powerful enough for the biggest Web sites, yet easy enough for small departments to set up. IIS also supports SSL and can communicate with SSL-enabled browers, including Internet Explorer and Netscape Navigator. If you already have Windows NT Server, IIS costs about $99, or you can download it for free. If you don't have Windows NT Server, you can get Windows NT Server and IIS for about $999. For general information, visit `http://www.microsoft.com/infoserve` and explore the links from there. For a product tour and links to more detailed information, visit `http://www.microsoft.com/infoserve/tourstart.htm`.

Public and private keys

Two types of keys are used during secure communications: *public keys* (which are publicly known) and *private keys* (which are known only to the key's user). You use these keys as follows:

- ✦ Public keys are used to exchange session keys, to verify the authenticity of digital signatures, and to encrypt data.
- ✦ Private keys are used to decrypt session keys that were encrypted using the matching public key and to create a digital signature when setting up a digital certificate.

You only need to worry about public and private keys if you are administering a secure Web site. When you are simply using a security-enabled browser to exchange data with a secure Web site, all this public key and private key stuff happens automatically and you can remain blissfully unaware of it.

Security certificates

Security certificates unequivocally identify a secure server, much like your signed photo ID, driver's license, and Social Security cards identify you. Certificates are sent along with messages so that your security-enabled browser can verify the server's identity.

A server must have a digital certificate before it can use SSL protocol. Only authorized Certification Authority (CA) companies, such as RSA Certificate Services (a division of RSA Data Security, Inc.), can issue digital certificates.

Each signed security certificate contains two groups of security information:

1. The certificate information itself along with the certificate issuer's name, the server's name, the server's public key, and some time stamps that indicate how long the certificate is valid.
2. A secret digital signature that cannot be forged.

As explained later, you can view certificate information in both Netscape and Internet Explorer. For more information about what digital certificates are and how to buy them for your Web site, see your secure server's manual (for example, the Netscape Commerce Server or Internet Information Server manual). You also can check out Netscape's great documentation about security at the following URLs:

✦ `http://www.netscape.com/comprod/server_central/config/secure.html`

✦ `http://www.netscape.com/newsref/ref/internet-security.html`

✦ `http://home.netscape.com/info/security-doc.html`

Other security techniques

Many companies use several other strategies to protect servers from sneaks and vandals on the Internet. These techniques involve using special computers to guard against electronic assaults:

✦ **Firewalls** stand between the server or local area network you want to protect and the big, bad outside world (that is, the Internet). All outside communications are made to the firewall rather than to the "real" computer. The firewall then lets valid communications through to the real computer.

✦ **Filtering routers** verify the source and destination network address of each network packet and determine whether to let each packet through. Filtering routers prevent malicious users on an Internet machine from masquerading as an internal network machine. They also can filter packets to allow network traffic to access specific network services only — thus preventing attacks that flood various services on a machine with meaningless traffic.

✦ **Proxy servers** answer requests intended for another machine that you want to protect from direct contact with the outside world. The proxy, which presumably can be trusted, accepts responsibility for routing packets to the real destination.

Danger Zone

All these fancy technologies only guarantee secure connections between the server and the client. They *cannot* control the security of information once the client or server machine has it nor can they prevent physical access to the machine or its directories and files. That point is where humans must take responsibility for guarding the sensitive information they receive.

Using Netscape Navigator Browser Security

Netscape Navigator offers quite a few security options and also gives you visual feedback about whether a transaction will be secure. Let's take a look at what's available.

Setting Netscape security options

You can set two types of security options in Netscape Navigator — general security and site certificates security.

Setting Netscape's general security options is easy:

1. Choose Options⇨Security Preferences from the Netscape Navigator menu bar and select the General tab (if necessary). You'll see the dialog box shown in Figure 35-2.
2. Enable or disable the use of the Java programming language with Netscape and choose when to display various *security alerts* dialog boxes.
3. Choose OK.

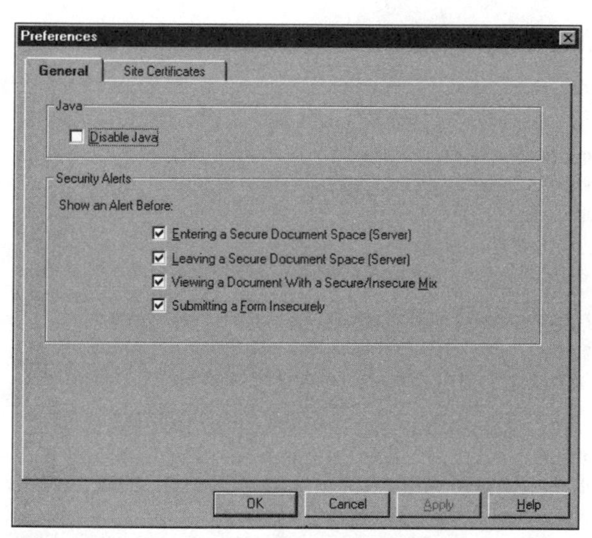

Figure 35-2: The Preferences dialog box for security after choosing Options⇨Security Preferences and clicking the General tab.

Life Saver

For maximum security, check all the boxes in the Security Alerts area of the General tab. You also may want to check Disable Java if you are concerned about non-secure or sneaky Java scripts grabbing sensitive information.

You also can view, edit, or delete the site certificates issued to your server, though you'll seldom need to. To get started, choose Options⇨Security Preferences from the Netscape Navigator menu bar and click the Site Certificates tab (see Figure 35-3). If you want to view or change certificate options, click the name of the certificate that you want to work with and then click the Edit Certificate button (or simply double-click the certificate name). For more details about the Site Certificates tab, click the Help button shown in Figure 35-3. Click OK after you finish.

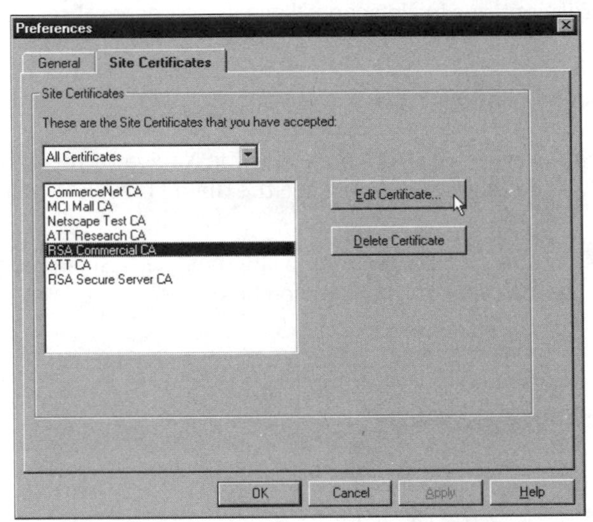

Figure 35-3: The Netscape Navigator Preferences dialog box after choosing Options⇨Security Preferences and choosing the Site Certificates tab.

Is this site secure? How Netscape lets you know

Netscape Navigator uses several techniques to let you know whether transactions are secure:

✦ If you requested alerts in Options⇨Security Preferences, a Security Information dialog box alerts you when you are about to enter or leave a secure space, submit a non-secure form, or view a secure document that contains non-secure inline images. Figure 35-4 shows a typical security alert that appears when you are about to submit non-secure information.

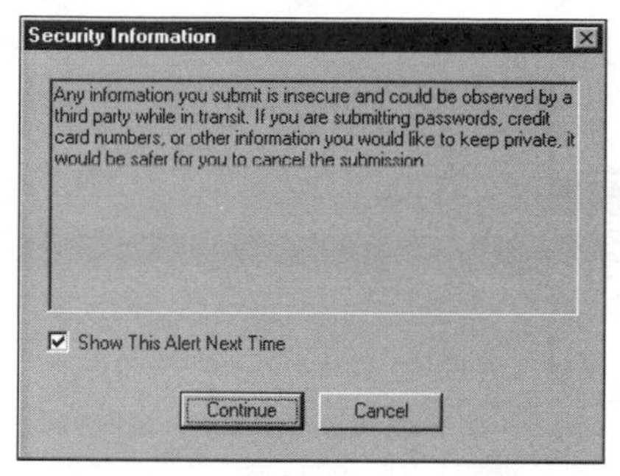

Figure 35-4: This Security Information message appears when you are about to submit non-secure information.

✦ A *security colorbar* appears at the top of each Netscape Navigator window, just above the scrolling document area. It is blue for secure documents and gray (invisible) for non-secure documents.

✦ An icon in the lower-left corner of each Netscape Navigator window indicates the same status as the security colorbar. A broken doorkey icon with a gray background indicates a non-secure document, and a solid doorkey icon over a dark blue background indicates a secure document. Figure 35-5 shows an example of the colorbar and doorkey icon for a secure form. In Figure 35-6, you see the colorbar and doorkey icon for a non-secure form.

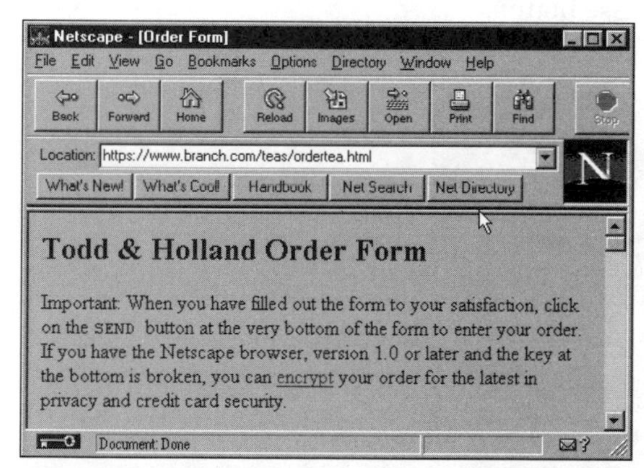

Figure 35-5: The colorbar for a secure Web page is blue (though, of course, it looks black in this book), and its doorkey icon appears unbroken on a blue background.

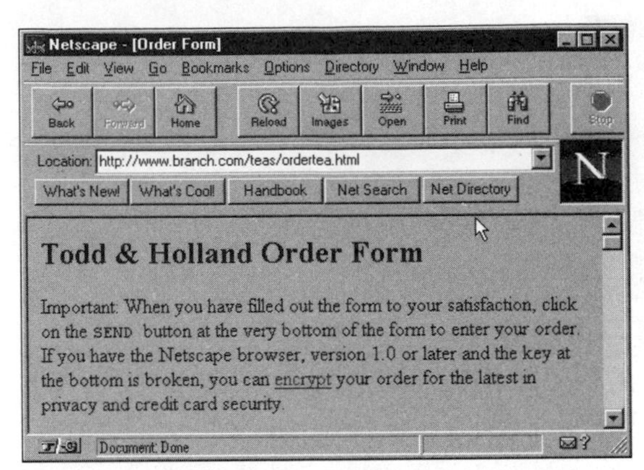

Figure 35-6: The colorbar for a non-secure Web page is gray (and usually invisible), and its doorkey icon appears broken on a gray background.

- ✦ Some sites are *medium security* while others are *high security.* A key icon with one tooth indicates medium security. Two teeth in the key indicates high security.
- ✦ To display the security details for the current Web page, choose View➪ Document Info. A new window opens. As Figure 35-7 shows, the top portion of the window describes the structure of the Web page and the bottom portion displays additional information including the page's security status. After you have finished viewing the Document Info window, close it by pressing Alt+F4 or by clicking the window's Close button.

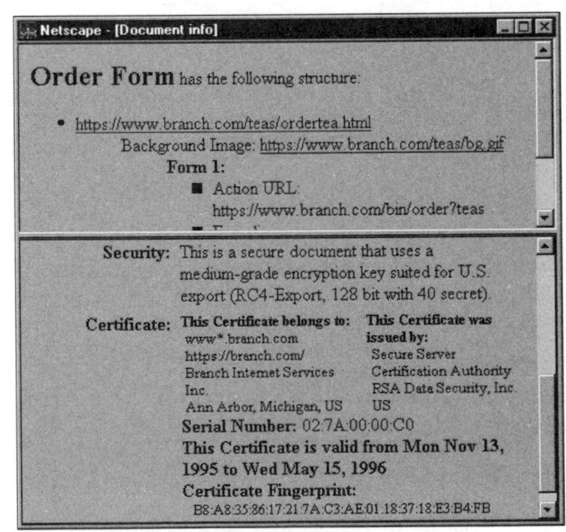

Figure 35-7: The Netscape Navigator Document info page for a secure page.

A different URL access method called *https* is used in place of *http* to connect to secure servers. For example, to connect to the secure site for ordering exotic teas from Todd & Holland, you enter the URL `https://www.branchmall.com/teas/ordertea.html`. The non-secure URL for this order form is `http://www.branch.com/teas/ordertea.html`. (The default https port number is 443, whereas the default `http` port number is 80.)

Using Internet Explorer Browser Security

Like Netscape Navigator, Internet Explorer offers several security options and provides you with visual feedback about whether a transaction will be secure.

Setting Internet Explorer security options

You can choose which security warnings will appear and whether Internet Explorer will check security certificates before you send or view data on the Internet. Here are the steps:

1. Choose View⇨Options from the Internet Explorer menu bar and click the Security tab to open the dialog box shown in Figure 35-8.

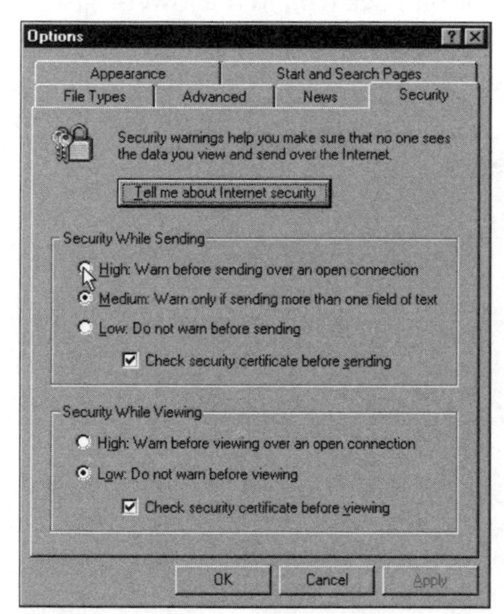

Figure 35-8: The Internet Explorer Options dialog box after choosing View⇨Options and clicking the Security tab.

2. Choose the level of security you want for sending and for viewing.
3. Click OK.

If you need more detailed information about any option, click the question mark (?) button in the upper-right corner of the Options dialog box and then click the option you need help with. Or, click the Tell Me About Internet Security button in the Options dialog box.

Life Saver

For maximum security with minimum inconvenience, choose Medium security while sending, Low security while viewing, and check the security certificate before sending and viewing.

Is this site secure? How Explorer lets you know

Internet Explorer also gives you the following visual feedback to let you know whether your transactions are secure:

✦ Depending on the level of security you've requested on the View➪Options➪ Security tab, a Security Information dialog box alerts you when you are about to send or view a non-secure document. It's similar to the example shown back in Figure 35-4.

✦ An icon in the lower-right corner of each Internet Explorer window indicates whether the current page is secure. A padlock icon indicates a secure page, whereas no padlock icon appears on a non-secure page. Also, the text "(secure Web site)" appears in the status bar when Explorer is opening the secure page and anytime you point to the Explorer or padlock icon in the lower-right corner of the window. Figure 35-9 shows an example of the padlock icon for a secure page.

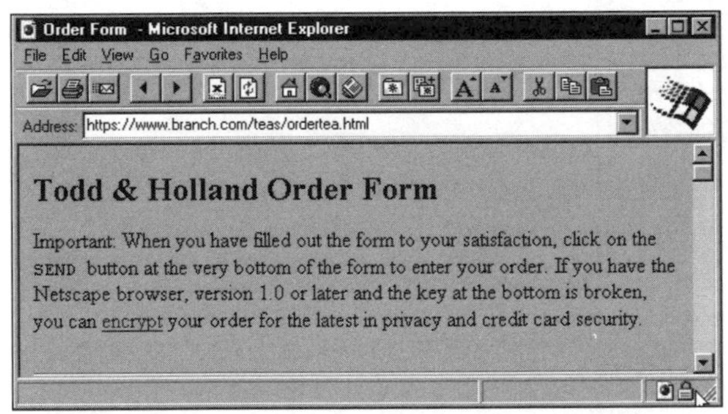

Figure 35-9: A padlock icon appears at the lower-right corner of the window for a secure Web page.

✦ To display security details for the current Web page, choose File➪Properties and click the Security tab. A Properties dialog box similar to Figure 35-10 opens (this information corresponds to the bottom part of the window shown back in Figure 35-7). To see general information about the page (corresponding to the top part of the window shown in Figure 35-7), click the General tab. After you finish viewing the information, choose OK.

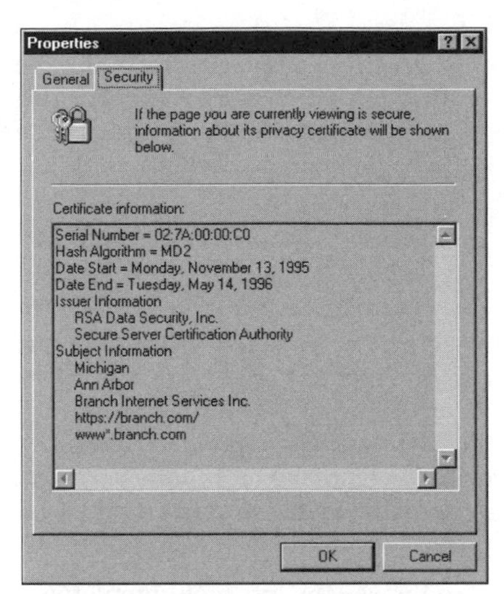

Figure 35-10: The Security tab of the Properties dialog box for a secure page.

Where to Learn More about Security

An enormous amount of information about security is available from the Internet. If you want to explore further, fire up any Internet search engine and search for topics such as *security, credit card,* and *encryption.* You also can check out the following newsgroups: *alt.privacy, alt.security, comp.society.privacy, comp.security.misc,* and *talk.politics.crypto.* Here are some specific URLs to try:

✦ `http://www.alw.nih.gov/Security/security.html`. A useful index with links to general information about computer security.

✦ `http://www.fivepaces.com/product/security.html`. Security solutions being used in online banking. Also provides good definitions of basic security concepts and includes links to other security-related information.

✦ `http://www-genome.wi.mit.edu/WWW/faqs/www-security-faq.html`. A lengthy yet understandable FAQ about World Wide Web security. Many of the questions and answers are Unix-oriented.

✦ `http://www.rsa.com/faq/`. Frequently-asked questions about cryptography, sponsored by RSA Laboratories (a division of RSA Data Security, Inc.). RSA's technologies are the global defacto standard and proposed Internet standard for public-key encryption and digital signatures — in fact, they are used in Netscape's and Microsoft's security-enabled browsers and servers. For information about RSA Data Security, visit `http://www.rsa.com/`.

Finally, you can get a hefty dose of security information from the online handbook on Netscape's server. To get started, choose Help⇨On Security from the Netscape Navigator menu bar. Or, choose Help⇨Frequently Asked Questions; then click the *Netscape Communications and Commerce Servers FAQ* link or the *Netscape Proxy Server FAQ* link.

Summary

You have now learned something about your security options on the Internet and you know how to tell whether any given Internet communication is secure. The following is a summary of this chapter's key points:

- By its nature, the Internet is not secure. However, many techniques are already in place and more are coming to protect sensitive data such as credit card information.
- You can use low-tech security solutions to bypass the Internet completely. For example, call in your credit card information by telephone or send it in a fax message.
- The most widely used, high-tech security solution is to send sensitive information over the Internet via security-enabled browsers to secure servers. Netscape Navigator and Internet Explorer are popular, security-enabled browsers. Netscape Commerce Server and Internet Information Server are examples of secure servers.
- Security-enabled browsers and secure servers work together to protect data by enforcing *authentication* (to thwart electronic impostors), *encryption* (to thwart eavesdroppers), and *data integrity* (to thwart vandals).
- To set security options in Netscape Navigator, choose Options⇨Security Preferences. To set security options in Internet Explorer, choose View⇨Options and click the Security tab in the Options dialog box.
- Netscape Navigator indicates security status with alert dialog boxes, a security colorbar at the top of the scrolling portion of the Web page, and a solid or broken doorkey icon at the lower-left corner of the window. You can choose View⇨Document Info to review general and security certificate information for the current Web page.
- Internet Explorer indicates security status with alert dialog boxes. Secure Web pages appear with a padlock icon at the lower-right corner of the window. No padlock icon appears when you're viewing a non-secure page. You can choose File⇨Properties and then click the Security tab to review security certificate information for the current Web page.

✦ ✦ ✦

Promoting Your Site

In This Chapter

Promoting your site through specialized services

Good search engines to see and be seen on

Promoting through newsgroups and mailing lists

Promoting through your Internet Service Provider

Swapping URLs

Traditional print promotion

A Web site without promotion is hardly a Web site at all. There are tens of thousands of Web sites out there, and people aren't going to be able to find your site unless you tell them where it is. This chapter covers easy, inexpensive resources for promoting your Web site. Make sure that you have your Web site up and running — perfectly — before you start promoting it. You don't want to lead people to a half-baked site that isn't quite working yet.

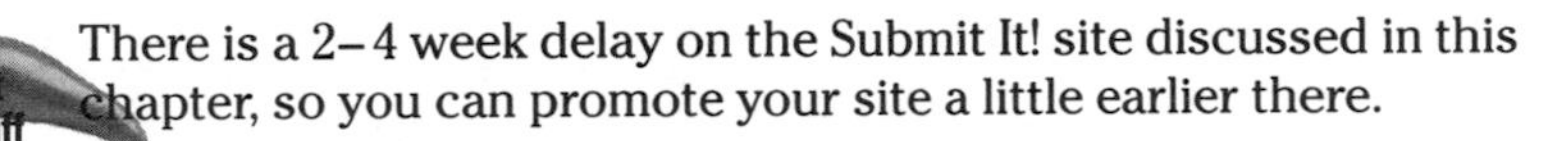

There is a 2–4 week delay on the Submit It! site discussed in this chapter, so you can promote your site a little earlier there.

Think about Keywords

Before you start your promotion, make a list of keywords that best describe your site. Remember that when people go looking for information on the Web, they usually search for a certain word or phrase. You need to think to yourself, "I want my site to show up whenever someone searches for *word or phrase*." Fill in a word or phrase, and repeat this little exercise until you've come up with a good list of words. For example, I might use these words to describe the topics presented in my coolnerds site:

- ✦ Web Publishing
- ✦ JavaScript
- ✦ Windows 95
- ✦ MS Access

Promoting through Submit It!

One of the best ways to get your publicity started is by registering your site with Submit It! This one service submits information about your Web site to all of the following search engines:

- Apollo
- ElNet Galaxy
- Jump Station
- Harvest
- Infoseek
- Lycos
- Open Text Web Index
- New Riders' WWW Yellow Pages
- NetCenter
- Nikos
- Pronet
- Starting Point
- WebCrawler
- What's New Too
- Whole Internet Catalog
- World Wide Web Worm
- Yahoo!
- YellowPages.com

To use Submit It!, point your Web browser to `http://submit-it.com` to get to the site shown in Figure 36-1. There you'll find current instructions for getting your site promoted through this service.

The PostMaster

The PostMaster is another service that will post your URL to 17 sites, for free. Or, for $500, you can have your URL posted to more than 300 electronic and print media. To get to PostMaster, point your Web browser to `http://www.netcreations.com/postmaster` (Figure 36-2).

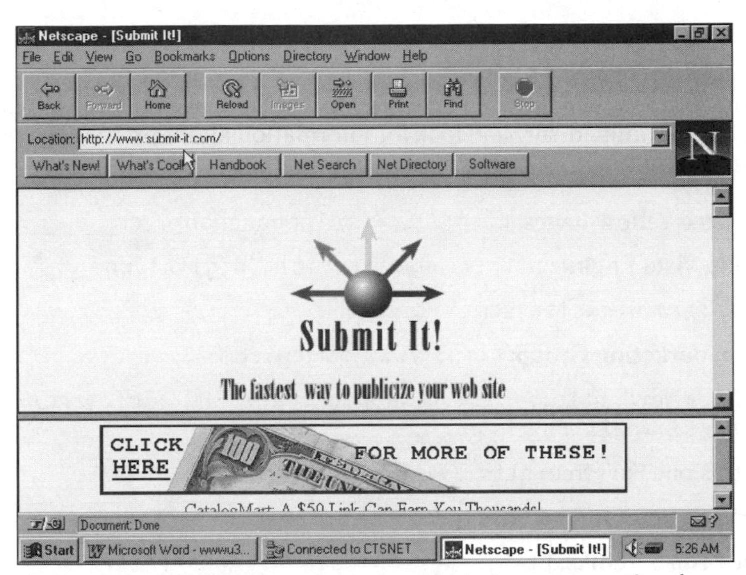

Figure 36-1: Submit It! is a great place to start your promotional campaign.

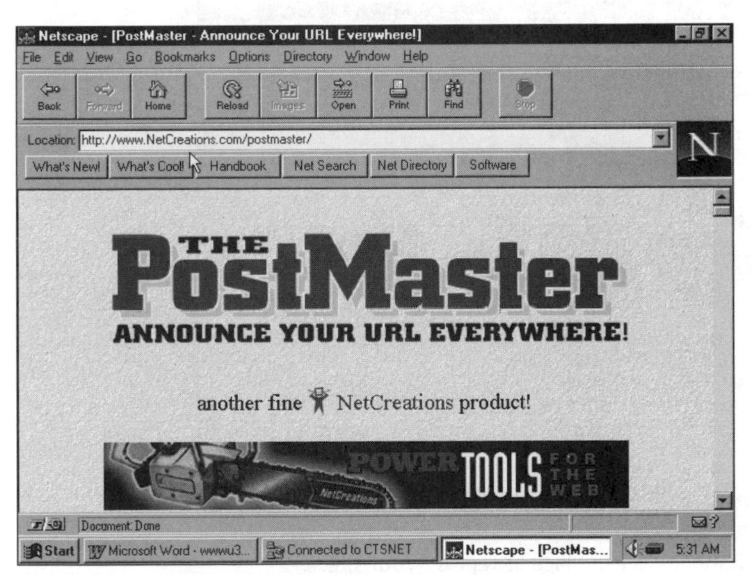

Figure 36-2: The PostMaster site.

Individual Search Engines

Some of the popular search engines aren't covered by the posting services. You may want to visit these sites individually and look for information about promoting your site. These engines include the following:

- **Central Source Yellow Pages:** `http://www.telephonebook.com/`
- **Digital's Alta Vista Engine:** `http://www.altavista.digital.com`
- **Excite:** `http://www.excite.com`
- **Multimedia Marketing Group:** `http://www.mmgco.com`
- **NCSA's What's New!:** `http:// www.ncsa.uiuc.edu/ SDG/ Software/ Mosaic/ Docs/ whats-new.html`
- **NetPost:** (this one isn't free) `http://www.netpost.com`.
- **Open Market's Commercial Sites Index:** `http://www.directory.net`
- **Webaholics Top 50 Links:** `http://www.ohiou.edu/ ~rbarrett/ webaholics/ favlinks/ entries.html` (Figure 36-3)

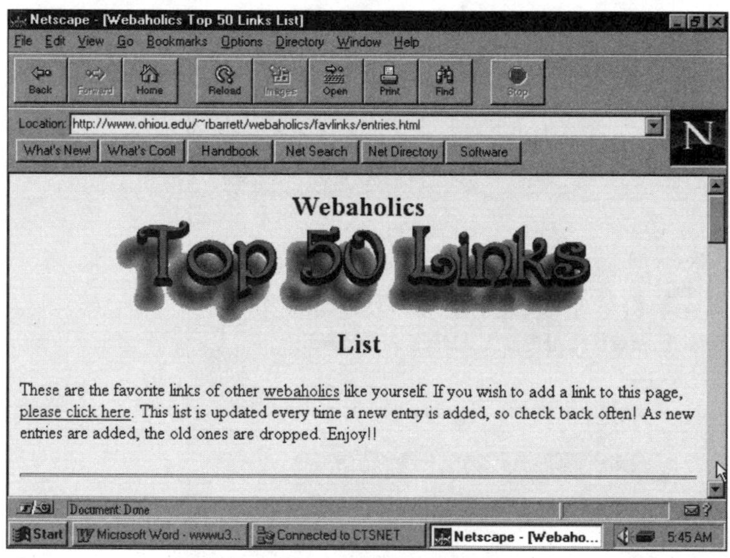

Figure 36-3: Webaholics: a fun place to register your site.

Newsgroups and Mailing Lists

Chances are that many newsgroups exist on the Internet that deal with some topic covered in your Web site. You want to announce your site with the appropriate groups. (Make sure that you read some of the newsgroup postings first, so that you target your promotion accurately.)

More Info

If you haven't tried the Usenet newsgroup service of the Internet yet, see Chapter 38. Or point your Web browser to `http://scwww.ucs.indiana.edu/NetRsc/usenet.html`.

You also may want to take a peek at `news:comp.infosystems.www.announce`, which is a group for making general announcements of new Web sites.

Mailing lists are similar to newsgroups. As with newsgroups, people who subscribe to mailing lists do not appreciate getting junk mail. Before you announce your site through a mailing list, make sure that you subscribe to the list and verify that the content of your Web site will be relevant to the people on that mailing list. (Failure to do so results in a deluge of flame mail from the irritated recipients!) To get a start on using mailing lists, point your Web browser to `http://www.nova.edu/Inter-Links/listserv.html` or `http://tile.net/listserv`.

Danger Zone

Never, ever post an announcement of a commercial Web site to a non-commercial newsgroup or mailing list! Make sure it's an announcement, NOT a sales pitch!

Your Internet Service Provider

The hosting of Web sites is a fiercely competitive industry, and many Internet Service Providers offer lots of free publicity for people who publish on their sites. Be sure to check with your own Internet Service Provider to see what kind of promotional services it offers.

Other Peoples' Sites

Look around the Web for other sites that cover topics similar to your own topics. Maybe you can swap URLs with them (which means they'll point readers to your site if you'll point readers to their site). To find sites that cover topics similar to your own, search Yahoo! or any of the other engines for keywords you plan on using to describe your own site.

Print Media

Lastly, don't forget about print media. Though not often free, this method is an effective means of announcing your site. For starters, always remember to put your Web site address on your company letterhead and business cards. Then just browse through some traditional print magazines to see if other people are advertising sites similar to your own. To find out what it costs to advertise in a magazine, contact the publisher and ask for a rate card.

Electronic versions of print magazines are yet another possible source of promotion. For quick access to tons of online magazines, point your Web browser to the Electronic Newsstand at `http://www.enews.com` (Figure 36-4).

Figure 36-4: The Electronic Newsstand.

Summary

Before you promote your site, make sure that it works perfectly. Then do the following:

- ✦ Jot down a list of keywords that identify your site's main subject(s).
- ✦ For quick, widespread promotion, register with one of the large promotional services like Submit It! and PostMaster.
- ✦ Be sure to register with some of the more popular search engines as well, including Excite and Webaholics Top 50 Links.
- ✦ You also can promote your site through newsgroups and mailing lists, but be very careful to promote your site to interested parties only. And do not promote a commercial site through a clearly non-commercial group or list.
- ✦ Check with your own Internet Service Provider to see what kinds of promotional services they offer.
- ✦ Search for sites that cover the same subject that your site does and then offer to swap URLs with its webmaster.
- ✦ Don't forget traditional print media. At the very least, you want to put your URL on your company letterhead and business cards.

✦ ✦ ✦

Customizing Internet Explorer 2.0

In This Chapter

Changing the font and colors

Changing the default start and search pages

Speeding up Internet Explorer

Balancing speed and disk space

Customizing your Favorites menu

Earlier I mentioned that Web documents are sent to your computer as text, some tags, and pictures. Exactly how that information ends up looking on your screen depends on the Web browser that you use. Furthermore, you can customize how documents look and behave simply by personalizing your Web browser. In this chapter, we look at different ways to personalize Internet Explorer 2.0 — everything from customizing the font and colors shown on Web pages to speeding up your cruises on the Internet and organizing your favorite Web pages so that you can jump to them quickly.

Changing the Font and Colors

Your Web browser (not the server) usually determines which fonts and colors appear on Web pages on your screen, so you can choose whatever colors and fonts you like. Follow these steps to do so:

1. Choose View➪Options from Internet Explorer's menu bar.
2. Click the Appearance tab to open the dialog box shown in Figure 37-1.

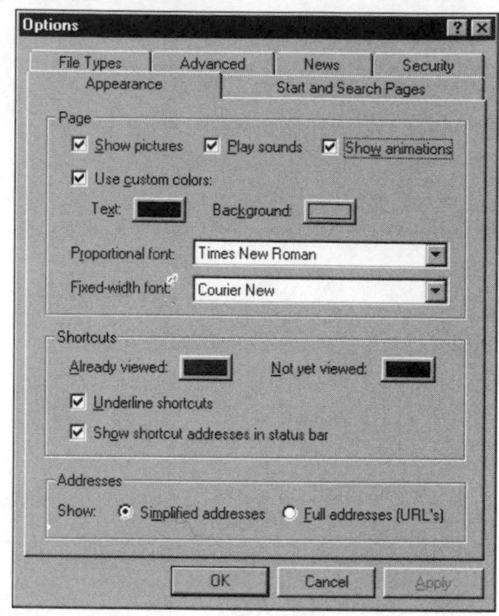

Figure 37-1: The Appearance options in Internet Explorer.

3. Choose whichever options you want. For example, check Use Custom Colors and choose a text color and background color for your Web pages. Or, pick a proportional font such as Comic Sans MS to give the text a funkier look. Or, try different colors and appearances for the hypertext links (or *shortcuts*) on each Web page.

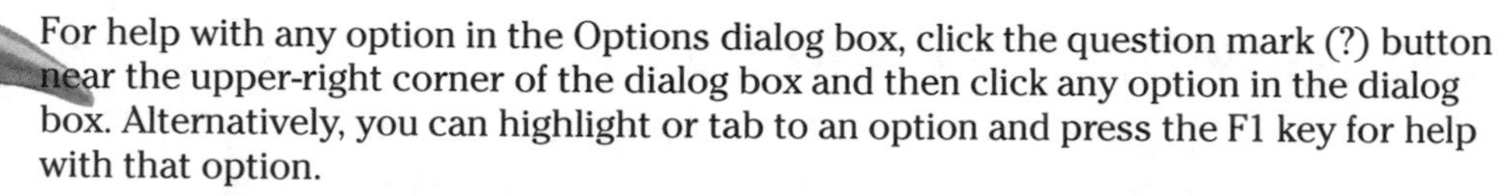

For help with any option in the Options dialog box, click the question mark (?) button near the upper-right corner of the dialog box and then click any option in the dialog box. Alternatively, you can highlight or tab to an option and press the F1 key for help with that option.

4. Click OK.

Your selections won't affect *all* Web pages that you view because some pages have their own, built-in color schemes and fonts. But in general, most Web pages carry only unadorned text and basic formatting codes, so the selections that you make here apply to many of the pages you view.

Changing the Default Start and Search Pages

When you start your Web browser, it needs to jump to *some* page on the Web. With Internet Explorer, the default starting page is Microsoft's own home page. But you can easily change that to any other page on the Web or even to an empty page by following these steps:

1. Using your browser, go to the page you want to use as your start page (for example, `http://www.coolnerds.com`).
2. Choose View➪Options from the Internet Explorer menu bar and click the Start and Search Pages tab to open the dialog box shown in Figure 37-2.

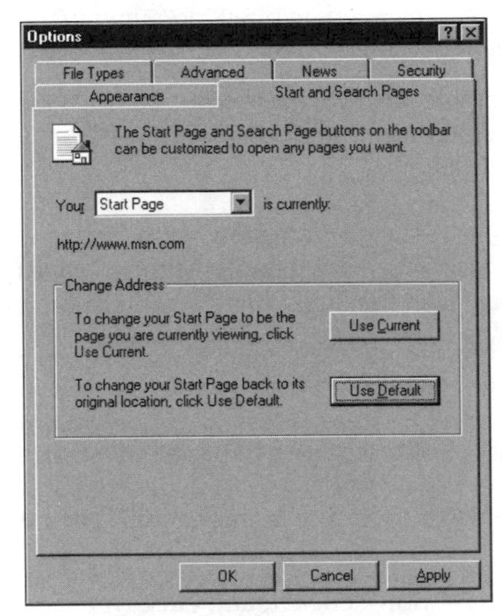

Figure 37-2: Dialog box for changing the default Start and Search pages.

3. From the drop-down list, choose Start Page.
4. Click the Use Current button and click OK.

When you click the Search The Internet button on the toolbar or choose Go➪Search The Internet, Internet Explorer usually takes you to Microsoft's All In One search page. But you can change that default search page if you like:

1. Use your browser to go to your favorite search engine site (such as `http://www.yahoo.com`).
2. Choose View➪Options from the Internet Explorer menu bar and click the Start and Search Pages tab.
3. From the drop-down list, choose Search Page.
4. Click the Use Current button and click OK.

Should you change your mind in the future, you can easily go back to using the original start or search pages. Just choose View➪Options and click the Start and Search Pages tab. Then choose either Start Page or Search Page from the drop-down list, click the Use Default button, and click OK.

Choosing a blank or custom start page

You've already seen how to choose any real page on the Web as the Internet Explorer start page. But you are also free to choose *any* page on your hard disk as the Internet Explorer start page. The first step is to create and save the page you want to use:

1. In Notepad or your favorite HTML editor, create a new blank document (for example, choose File➪New from the Notepad menu bar).

Hot Stuff

You can leave your start page blank or customize it with links to your favorite Web sites, sounds, graphics, and animations. To customize the page, just type in the standard HTML commands discussed in Part III.

2. To save your new start page, choose File➪Save As, enter any valid filename — for example, **startpage.htm** — and choose Save. (By default, Notepad saves files in your \windows folder. Your start page filename must have a *.htm* extension so that Internet Explorer will recognize it as a bona fide HTML Web page.)
3. Exit Notepad or your HTML editor by choosing File➪Exit.

Now you just need to hook up your new start page to Internet Explorer, like this:

1. To start Internet Explorer, choose File➪Open from the menu bar and click the Open File button.
2. Find your start page file (such as startpage.htm), click it, and click Open.
3. Choose View➪Options from the menu bar and click the Start and Search Pages tab.
4. Choose Start Page from the drop-down list, click Use Current, and click OK.

The next time you start Internet Explorer, you are greeted with your blank (or customized) starting page.

Speeding Up Internet Explorer

The amount of time it takes a page to appear on your screen depends mostly on two factors: (1) the speed of your modem and (2) the complexity of the page you're trying to view. Pages with lots of graphics, sound, or animations take much longer than pages that only contain text. If you are in a hurry, you can turn off graphics, sound, and animations and download only the text from each page as follows:

1. Choose View➪Options from the Internet Explorer menu bar.
2. Click the Appearance tab.

3. Clear the Show Pictures, Play Sounds, and Show Animations check boxes to disable any or all of those features.
4. Click OK after making your selections.

After you disable graphics and animations, these features appear as icons on a page. You still can view the picture or play the sound manually, if you like. Just right-click the appropriate icon and choose Show Picture. (If you become impatient while the picture or sound takes its sweet time to materialize, press Esc or click the Stop button on the toolbar to interrupt the process.)

Puzzled? If pictures persist in some pages, you are probably viewing a *cache* copy of the page, which I discuss in a moment. To fix the problem, click the Refresh button on the toolbar or choose View⇨Refresh (or press F5). This downloads the entire page again with the pictures converted to icons.

Balancing Speed and Disk Space

When you visit a page, Internet Explorer usually copies that page to your hard disk (without your even being aware of it). As a result, when you return to that page, Internet Explorer doesn't have to download the entire page again from the Internet. Instead, it just copies that page from your hard disk.

Puzzled? In case you are wondering, Internet Explorer stores the copies of the Web pages you visit in a folder named *cache* (pronounced as *cash*). To peek inside this folder, choose File⇨Open from the Internet Explorer menu bar, click the Open File button, and double-click the cache folder icon. Within the cache folder, the elements of each page are split into text, graphics, and other file types. So if you try to explore them without a Web browser, you'll find a lot of seemingly unrelated pieces of Web sites!

A big advantage to this approach is that the return trip to a page is always much, much faster than the original trip. Unfortunately, however, this fast-return approach does have a couple of disadvantages.

One disadvantage is that if the page has changed since your last visit, you may not see those changes. To make sure that you receive the latest edition of a Web page, click the Refresh button on the toolbar or press F5 while you're viewing the page. Internet Explorer re-downloads the entire page from the Internet.

Another disadvantage is that it takes a good chunk of disk space to store all those pages from previous site visits. You can, however, follow these steps to limit how much space Internet Explorer uses for storing those pages:

1. Choose View⇨Options from the Internet Explorer menu bar.
2. Click the Advanced tab to open the dialog box shown in Figure 37-3.

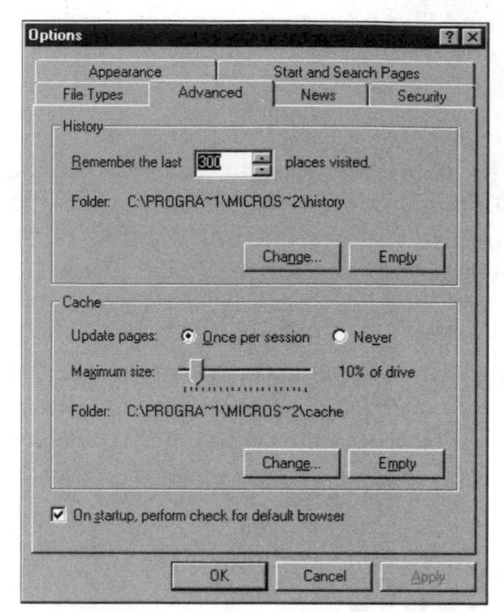

Figure 37-3: The Advanced tab lets you set limits on disk space used for cache and history.

3. Under Cache, set the Maximum Size slider to the amount of disk space you are willing to dedicate to saved Web pages.

As Figure 37-3 shows, the Advanced tab in Options also lets you change other settings. Under History, you can change the number of URLs that Internet Explorer maintains in its history folder. You also can change the location of the history folder or empty it.

Puzzled?

The difference between history and cache is this: History only stores URLs (the addresses of sites you've visited), whereas cache stores the actual Web pages and graphics. Every URL in history takes up just a tiny amount of disk space (approximately 1K). Each page in cache, however, can gobble up several megabytes of disk space.

From the Advanced tab, you can change the location of the cache folder and empty it, if you want. You also can choose to have pages in the cache updated once automatically during each session or never updated. If you choose Never, Internet Explorer only updates the page when you manually view the page and then click the toolbar's Refresh button or press F5.

Hot Stuff

Internet Explorer lists a history of the most recent pages that you have visited at the bottom of the File menu. To quickly revisit one of those pages, open the File menu and click the item you want to visit. For a full listing of all items in the history folder, choose File➪More History.

Customizing Your Favorites Menu

Some Web pages are so cool that you'll want to visit them often. You can easily add your favorite pages to your Internet Explorer Favorites menu and jump to them later with a couple of mouse clicks. For example, I like to check out the weather in various parts of the United States, so I added the Interactive Weather Browser, located at `http://rs560.cl.msu.edu/weather/interactive.html`, to my Favorites menu. Now when I want to laugh about the freezing cold in Montana or snicker over the sizzling heat in Southern Arizona from the comfort of my San Diego office, I simply choose Interactive Weather Browser from the Favorites menu.

Adding an item to your Favorites menu is easy:

1. Using Internet Explorer, go to the page you want to add.
2. Click the Add To Favorites button on the toolbar or choose Favorites➪Add To Favorites from the menu bar. An Add To Favorites dialog box, similar to that shown in Figure 37-4, appears.

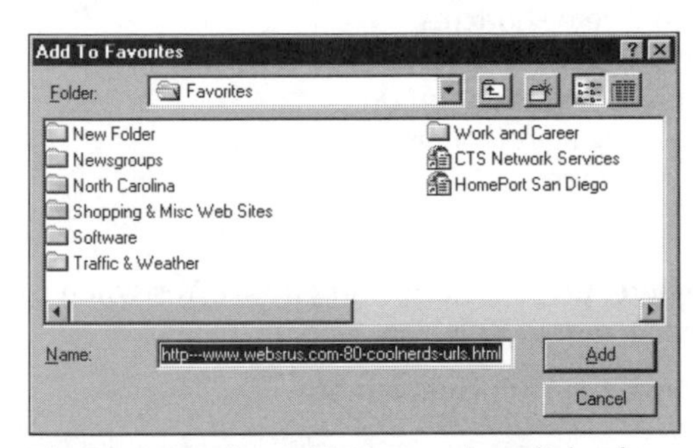

Figure 37-4: The Add To Favorites dialog box lets you add items to your Favorites menu.

3. Optionally, type a name for this item (or just accept the suggested name).
4. Optionally, open the folder where you want to store this Favorites item (more about folders in a moment).
5. Click the Add button.

In the future, you can jump to your favorite Web page by choosing Favorites from the menu bar and clicking the name of the page you want to visit.

Hot Stuff

To quickly add any hypertext link or current Web page to your Favorites menu, right-click the link or an empty part of the page you want to add. Then choose Add To Favorites and click the Add button.

Organizing your Favorites menus

Adding a page to your Favorites menu is so easy that your Favorites menu can become long and unwieldy in a hurry. Fortunately, organizing the Favorites to your liking is an easy task as well.

If you no longer want an entry on the Favorites menu, you can delete it. Here's how:

1. Choose Favorites⇨Open Favorites from the Internet Explorer menu bar. A Favorites window, similar to that shown in Figure 37-5, opens.

Figure 37-5: Use the Favorites window to delete shortcuts, create new folders, and move folders and shortcuts as you do when browsing any standard folder in Windows 95.

2. Click the shortcut you want to delete, press Delete, and choose Yes when asked for confirmation. Repeat this step as needed.
3. After you finish deleting items, close the Favorites window.

Another way to shorten your Favorites menu is to organize it into submenus, which are nothing fancier than standard Windows folders. The basic idea is to create the folders — one for each submenu you want on the Favorites menu — and then drag shortcut icons to the appropriate folders as needed. To set up a Favorites submenu, follow these steps:

1. Choose Favorites⇨Open Favorites from the Internet Explorer menu bar. The Favorites window opens (see Figure 37-5).
2. Choose File⇨New⇨Folder from the Favorites window menu bar.
3. Type a name for the new folder and press Enter. (The new folder becomes a submenu on the Favorites menu.)
4. Drag any shortcuts that should appear on the submenu into your new folder.
5. Close the Favorites window.

Figure 37-6 illustrates the Favorites menu and submenus after I organized them as shown in Figure 37-5.

Figure 37-6: A sample Favorites menu after organizing it into submenus.

Hot Stuff

Internet Explorer opens your Favorites folder in a standard Windows 95 browse window (similar to the windows that appear when you open My Computer and double-click on various disk drive and folder icons). You can move, copy, rename, and drag items in this window just as you would in any standard Windows 95 browse window. In fact, you can use My Computer or Windows Explorer to organize your Favorites submenus, if you prefer. You can find the Favorites folder in \windows\favorites.

Converting Netscape bookmarks for use with Internet Explorer

In Netscape Navigator, you use the Bookmarks menu to jump quickly to your favorite Web pages. If you have already defined some Netscape bookmarks, you can add them to your Favorites menu in Internet Explorer. Follow these steps:

1. Choose File⇨Open from the Internet Explorer menu bar and click the Open File button.
2. Look for the folder that contains your Netscape files (usually C:\netscape) and double-click the Bookmark.htm file. Your Bookmark file then opens as a standard Web page in Internet Explorer.
3. Choose Favorites⇨Open Favorites.
4. Resize the Internet Explorer window on your screen until it fits side by side with the Favorites window. (To do this quickly, right-click a neutral place on the taskbar and choose Tile Vertically.)

5. Drag the bookmarks that you want to add from the Internet Explorer window to the Favorites window.

6. Close the Favorites window.

More Info

You can learn more about fine-tuning Internet Explorer by checking out the Internet Explorer Frequently Asked Questions (FAQ) at `http://www.microsoft.com/windows/ie/ie20faq.htm`. For other cool stuff about Internet Explorer and Microsoft Windows, check out `http://www.microsoft.com/windows`.

Summary

Tweaking Internet Explorer to look prettier, to run faster, and to organize your favorite Web pages can make your travels along the Internet much more fun and efficient.

- ✦ You can customize the look of most Web pages by choosing View⇨Options; clicking the Appearance tab; and choosing text and shortcut colors, proportional and fixed-width fonts, and appearance options for shortcuts.
- ✦ You can choose the default start page and search page for Internet Explorer. First, go to the page that should become your new start page or search page. Then choose View⇨Options, click the Start and Search Pages tab, pick either Start Page or Search Page from the drop-down list, click Use Current, and click OK.
- ✦ To speed your travels along the Internet, choose View⇨Options; click the Appearance tab, clear the Show Pictures Play Sounds and/or Show Animations check boxes, and click OK.
- ✦ Internet Explorer stores the URLs of your recently visited Web pages in a history folder and also stores copies of recently visited Web pages in a cache folder. To control the amount of disk space used for history and cache folders, choose View⇨Options, click the Advanced tab, select options under History and Cache, and click OK.
- ✦ The Favorites menu enables you to jump quickly to your favorite pages on the Web. To add the current Web page to your list of favorites, choose Favorites⇨Add To Favorites and click Add. To organize the Favorites menu into submenus, choose Favorites⇨Open Favorites, then create new folders (File⇨New⇨Folder), and drag shortcuts into the folders as needed.

✦ ✦ ✦

E-Mail, FTP, and Newsgroups

In This Chapter

Beating the postoffice with electronic mail (e-mail)

Downloading files with FTP

Getting the news in cyberspace (newsgroups)

Those of you who get hooked on the Web right away may not get a chance to explore some other great features of the Internet — e-mail, FTP, and newsgroups, to be specific. Though you don't *have* to be an expert in these areas to be a successful Web publisher, it would be a shame not to at least give them a try and see which services may be useful in your work.

Of course, I cannot explore all these features in depth here in *Web Publishing Uncut*. But I would hate to think that I didn't mention them at all. In this chapter, then, I want to introduce the other "biggies" of the Internet and help you get started in using them.

Beating the Postoffice with Electronic Mail

Electronic mail (or *e-mail*) accounts for a huge chunk of traffic on the Internet. Without so much as licking a postage stamp, you can instantly send text, graphics, sound, and video to the electronic mailboxes of your friends, colleagues, and family members. Windows 95 comes with a great e-mail package named Microsoft Exchange, which can manage the following types of electronic communications:

- **Fax.** If you have installed and set up a fax modem as explained in Chapter 1, you can use Exchange to send and receive faxes.
- **Microsoft Network mail and CompuServe mail.** Members of The Microsoft Network (MSN) and CompuServe can use Exchange to send and receive e-mail with other members of those online services.
- **Internet mail.** If you have installed Internet software, you can exchange e-mail with other Internet users.

✦ **Local e-mail.** If you are connected to a local area network (LAN), you can exchange e-mail with other users on your network. The network administrator is responsible for setting up the LAN and will assign you a mailbox name and password.

In the sections that follow, you learn how to set up Microsoft Exchange; then you learn the basics of sending and receiving e-mail messages with Exchange.

Getting set up

Before you can use Microsoft Exchange, you must make sure that it is installed on your PC. If Exchange *has* been installed, an Inbox icon appears on your Windows 95 desktop and you should feel free to skip ahead to the "Using Microsoft Exchange" section. If no Inbox icon appears, you need to install Exchange. The following sections in this chapter help you install Exchange:

✦ **"Creating a postoffice and mailboxes"** tells network administrators how to create a postoffice and mailboxes for LAN users.

✦ **"Installing Microsoft Exchange"** explains how to install Microsoft Exchange.

✦ **"Hooking into MSN mail"** explains how to set up MSN and Exchange so that you can send and receive The Microsoft Network e-mail via Exchange.

✦ **"Hooking into CompuServe mail"** explains how to install the CompuServe drivers that let you send and receive CompuServe e-mail via Exchange.

Creating a postoffice and mailboxes (administrators only)

Before LAN users can exchange network e-mail via Microsoft Exchange, the network administrator must set up a postoffice and create user mailboxes. This process has four steps, in which you set up a shared folder to hold the postoffice and mailboxes, install Microsoft Exchange on the LAN server machine, create the postoffice, and then create the user mailboxes. As you see, each step takes only a few moments.

Puzzled?

Please skip this section if you are not the network administrator!

Step 1: Creating the shared postoffice folder

The following steps describe one easy way to create a shared folder for your LAN's postoffice:

1. On the LAN server machine, start Windows Explorer (choose Start⇨Programs⇨Windows Explorer).
2. Click the drive C icon in the left side of the Explorer window to select drive C.
3. Choose File⇨New⇨Folder, type a name for your postoffice folder (such as **postoffice**), and press Enter.

4. To make the folder shareable, select (click on) the new folder in the right side of the Exploring window and choose File⇨Sharing. Then select Shared As, set the Access Type to Full, and click OK.

Step 2: Installing Microsoft Exchange on the LAN server

After creating the shared postoffice folder, you should install Microsoft Exchange on the LAN server. The steps are almost the same as those for installing Exchange on a workstation (see the "Installing Microsoft Exchange" section that follows for detailed steps). The main difference is that the postoffice does not already exist. Therefore, when the Inbox Setup Wizard asks for a postoffice name during the Exchange setup steps, just click Next and fill in the remaining dialog boxes that appear. When prompted for your postoffice name, mailbox, and password, click the Offline button and click OK. Then exit Microsoft Exchange and continue with "Step 3: Creating the postoffice."

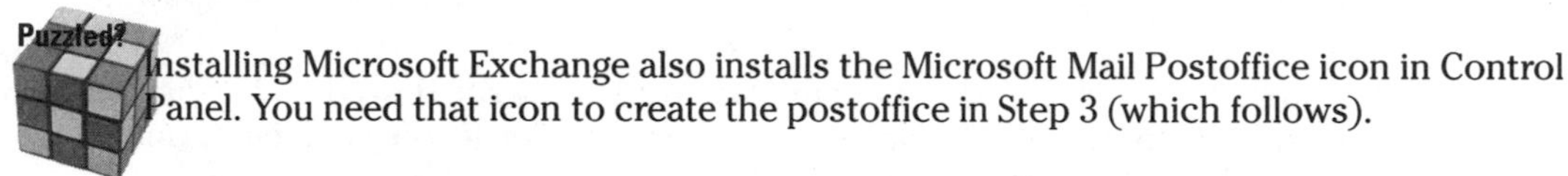

Installing Microsoft Exchange also installs the Microsoft Mail Postoffice icon in Control Panel. You need that icon to create the postoffice in Step 3 (which follows).

Step 3: Creating the postoffice

Creating the postoffice is a piece of cake. Just follow these steps:

1. Open Control Panel (Start⇨Settings⇨Control Panel), double-click the Microsoft Mail Postoffice icon, choose Create A New Workgroup Postoffice, and click Next.
2. Specify the disk and directory location of the postoffice folder you created in the preceding step (such as C:\Postoffice), click Next, and then click OK.
3. Enter your administrator account details, including your name, the name of the administrator's mailbox, and the administrator's password.
4. Click OK as needed to return to Control Panel.

Step 4: Setting up user mailboxes

Each user will need a mailbox and a password in order to exchange e-mail on the LAN. Here's how to set up a user's mailbox (you can set up as many mailboxes as you need):

1. Open Control Panel (Start⇨Settings⇨Control Panel), double-click the Microsoft Mail Postoffice icon, choose Administer An Existing Workgroup Postoffice, and click Next.
2. Specify the workgroup postoffice name (such as C:\Postoffice\wgpo0000) and click Next.
3. Enter your administrator mailbox name and password and click Next.
4. In the Postoffice Manager dialog box (see Figure 38-1), click Add User.

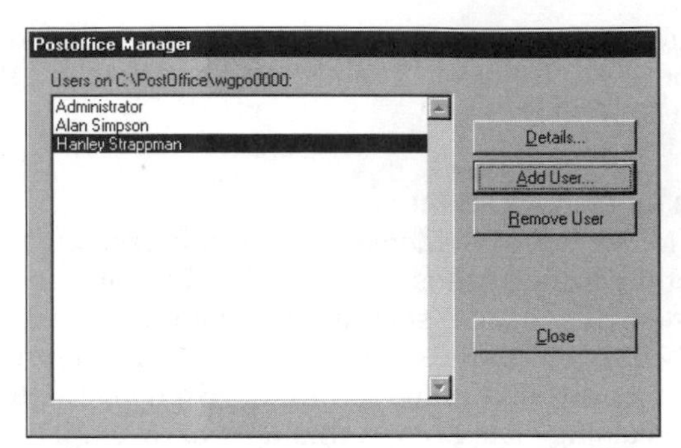

Figure 38-1: Use the Postoffice Manager dialog box to add mailboxes, change details about them, and remove mailboxes.

5. Fill in the user's Name, Mailbox, and Password and write down this information in a safe place so that you can give it to the user later. If you want, enter optional details about the user and click OK.
6. Repeat Steps 4 and 5 as needed. You also can select (click on) any user name and then edit the user's information (click Details) or remove the user's mailbox (click Remove User).
7. When you've finished, click Close.

Installing Microsoft Exchange

Installing Microsoft Exchange on the LAN server or your workstation takes just a few minutes. Follow these steps:

1. Gather your original Windows 95 diskettes or CD-ROM.
2. Open Control Panel (choose Start➪Settings➪Control Panel), double-click the Add/Remove Programs icon, and then click the Windows Setup tab.
3. Select (check) the Microsoft Exchange checkbox. If you also want to use Exchange to send faxes, select the Microsoft Fax checkbox, as shown in Figure 38-2.

Hot Stuff

Initially installing only Microsoft Exchange is usually easier. Later, when you become more comfortable using e-mail, you can install Microsoft Fax (by using Steps 1 through 3) and add Microsoft Fax to your profile (see "Changing Exchange Profiles").

4. Click OK and follow the instructions in the Inbox Setup Wizard dialog boxes.

The Inbox Setup Wizard asks several questions as it configures Microsoft Exchange. For example, it asks whether you have used Microsoft Exchange before (choose Yes or No and click Next). It also asks you to choose the information services you want

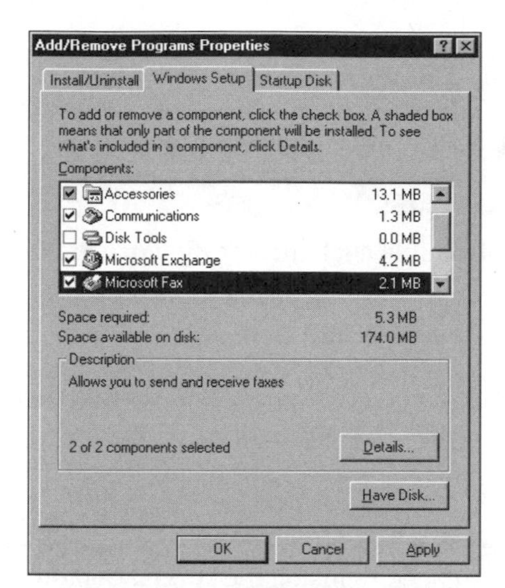

Figure 38-2: The Windows Setup tab of the Add/Remove Programs Properties dialog box after selecting the Microsoft Exchange and Microsoft Fax icons.

to configure. Select (check) the information services that you want to install and deselect (clear) the ones that you don't want to install and then click Next to continue. Your answers to the remaining questions helps the Wizard set up each information service you selected. Answer the prompts that appear, clicking Next or Back as needed. When you get to the last prompt, click Finish.

Puzzled? Don't worry if you make a mistake while setting up an information service and don't feel as though you need to set up all information services at once. If you are not sure how to answer a question, try using the options that the Inbox Setup Wizard suggests. You can always update the settings later, as explained shortly.

Hooking into MSN mail

Exchange can automatically pick up and deliver mail from your Microsoft Network mailbox. Setting up this service involves two main steps.

1. Set up and subscribe to The Microsoft Network (MSN) if you haven't done so already.
2. Pick The Microsoft Network Online Service as one of the available information services anytime you change your profile (see "Changing Exchange Profiles").

Setting up MSN

To set up MSN, simply double-click the Setup The Microsoft Network icon or The Microsoft Network icon on your Windows 95 desktop. If neither of these icons appears on your desktop, you need to install the MSN software by following these steps:

1. Gather your original Windows 95 disks or CD-ROM.
2. Choose Start⇨Settings⇨Control Panel, double-click the Add/Remove Programs icon, and then click the Windows Setup tab.
3. Select (check) The Microsoft Network checkbox and click OK.

After the software is copied to your hard disk, you can set up MSN by double-clicking The Microsoft Network icon on your Windows 95 desktop.

Hooking into CompuServe mail

Members of CompuServe can use Exchange to pick up and deliver CompuServe e-mail automatically. To enable this cool feature, you need to install the special CompuServe *driver* programs squirreled away on your Windows 95 installation CD-ROM. Follow these steps:

1. Insert the Microsoft Windows 95 installation disc into your computer's CD-ROM drive (sorry, these drivers don't come with the Windows 95 floppy disks).
2. Choose Start⇨Run from the Windows 95 taskbar.
3. Click the Browse button to open a Browse dialog box.
4. On the CD-ROM drive (typically drive D), locate and double-click \drivers\other\exchange\compusrv\setup.
5. Click OK to copy files and update system settings.
6. When asked about installing CompuServe in your default profile, click Yes or No. If you choose No, you can add the CompuServe information service to your profile later (see "Changing Exchange profiles").

Changing Exchange profiles

When you install Microsoft Exchange, the Inbox Setup Wizard sets up a *profile* that contains configuration information, such as which information services are available to you, the location for storing incoming mail, and so on. You may never need to change your profile, but if you do, follow these steps:

1. Open Control Panel (choose Start⇨Settings⇨Control Panel) and double-click the Mail And Fax icon; or, right-click the Inbox icon on your desktop and choose Properties. You then see the Properties dialog box shown in Figure 38-3.

Hot Stuff

If you have already started Exchange, you can change your current profile by choosing Tools⇨Services from the Exchange menu bar. The resulting dialog box resembles Figure 38-3, but it does not include a Show Profiles button (skip to Step 3).

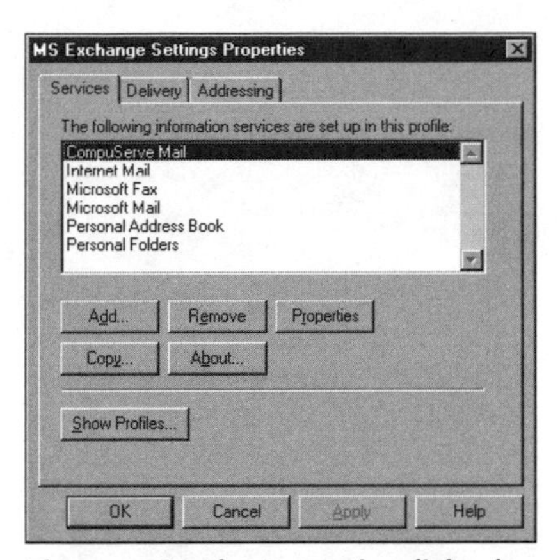

Figure 38-3: The Properties dialog box appears when you double-click the Mail And Fax icon in Control Panel.

2. If you want to add a new profile, change a different profile, or delete a profile, click the Show Profiles button to open the Profiles dialog box shown in Figure 38-4. You can do the following tasks in this dialog box:
   - To add a new profile, click the Add button and let the Inbox Setup Wizard take you through setting up the information services, just as it did when you installed Exchange.
   - To delete an existing profile, click the profile name you want to delete, click Remove, and then click Yes.
   - To copy an existing profile to a new profile, click the profile name you want to copy, click Copy, type a new profile name, and click OK. Often it is easier to copy a profile and then update the copy rather than to create a new profile from scratch.
   - To choose a different profile to use when starting Microsoft Exchange, select the profile you want from the When Starting Microsoft Exchange Use This Profile drop-down list.
   - To change the properties of an existing profile, click the profile name you want to change and choose Properties, or double-click the profile name. You see the dialog box shown back in Figure 38-3.

Figure 38-4: This dialog box appears when you double-click the Mail And Fax icon in Control Panel and click Show Profiles.

3. Whenever you see a dialog box like the one shown in Figure 38-3, you can change the properties of the currently selected profile (typically named MS Exchange Settings). Here are some tips to guide you:

- To add a new service to the profile, click the Add button, double-click an information service in the Add Service To Profile dialog box that appears, and fill in the following dialog boxes with details about the new information service.
- To delete a service, click the name of the service you want to delete, click the Remove button, and click Yes.
- To copy a service to another profile, click the name of the service you want to copy, click the Copy button, and double-click the name of the profile you want to copy it to.
- To change the properties of an existing service (for example, if you made mistakes when setting it up originally), click the name of the service that you want to update and then click the Properties button or just double-click the service name. Make any necessary changes in the dialog box that appears and click OK.
- To control where Exchange delivers new mail and how it processes recipient addresses, click the Delivery tab and change the settings as needed.
- To tell Exchange which address list to show first, where to keep personal addresses, and where to look when checking for valid e-mail addresses, click the Addressing tab and change the settings as needed.

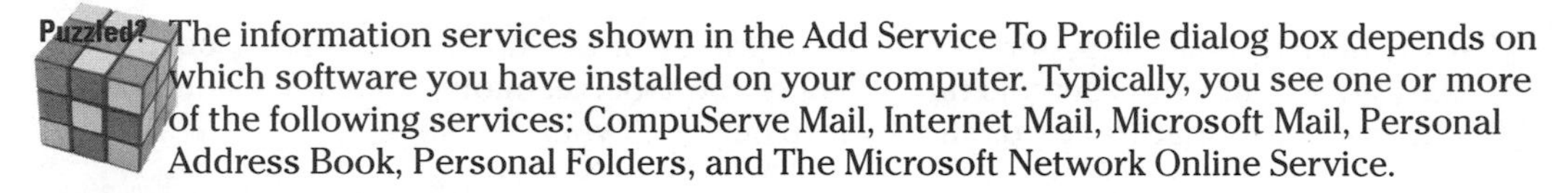

Puzzled? The information services shown in the Add Service To Profile dialog box depends on which software you have installed on your computer. Typically, you see one or more of the following services: CompuServe Mail, Internet Mail, Microsoft Mail, Personal Address Book, Personal Folders, and The Microsoft Network Online Service.

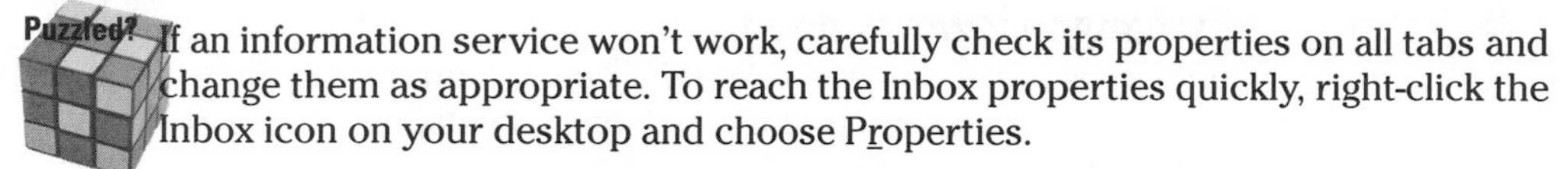

Puzzled? If an information service won't work, carefully check its properties on all tabs and change them as appropriate. To reach the Inbox properties quickly, right-click the Inbox icon on your desktop and choose Properties.

4. After you finish making changes, click OK and Close as needed.

Using Microsoft Exchange

Once you set up Microsoft Exchange, starting it is easy:

1. Double-click the Inbox icon on your desktop.
2. If your computer needs to dial up any information service, some dialog boxes now appear. Just fill them in and click OK as needed.

The Microsoft Exchange window opens, and headers for any messages that you have received now appear within your Inbox in boldface type, as shown in Figure 38-5.

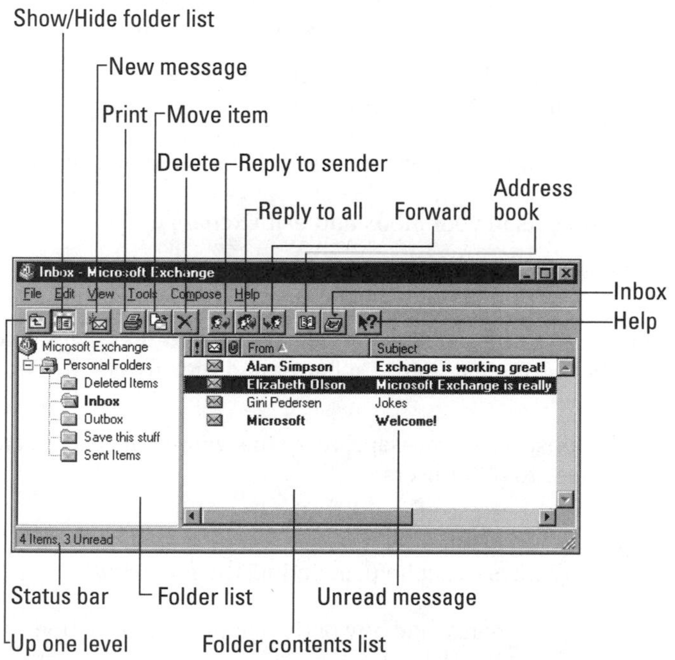

Figure 38-5: The Microsoft Exchange Viewer window with some unread messages in the Inbox.

If you have trouble with your LAN, modem, printer, or dial-up connections, choose Start⇨Help, click the Contents tab, and open the Troubleshooting book. Then double-click the appropriate topic for step-by-step help with your problem.

Navigating the Exchange Viewer window

The main window in Microsoft Exchange is called the *Viewer,* and it is similar to the Windows 95 Explorer window you already know and love. Navigating the Microsoft Exchange Viewer is easy if you know the techniques listed below:

✦ To display or hide the list of folders, choose View⇨Folders or click the Show/Hide Folder List toolbar button. It is best to leave the folders visible, with the Viewer divided into two panes as shown in Figure 38-5. If you hide the folders, only the contents of your Inbox folder are visible.

✦ To display or hide the toolbar or status bar, choose View⇨Toolbar or View Status Bar, respectively. It is best to leave the toolbar and status bar visible.

✦ When folders are visible, the left side of the Viewer window shows the *folder list.* The folder list works like the left side of the Windows Explorer window. For example, to view the contents of a particular folder, click the folder icon in the folder list. To expand or collapse a folder, click the + or - symbol next to the folder icon.

✦ When folders are visible, the right side of the Viewer window shows the *folder contents list.* This list shows the messages in the currently selected folder in the folder list, and it works like the right side of the Windows Explorer window.

✦ After you finish using Microsoft Exchange, close the Viewer window or choose File⇨Exit And Log Off from the Viewer window's menu bar.

Just in case you are wondering what the Viewer menus do, here's a quick summary:

✦ **File.** Lets you manage objects in your Inbox and exit Exchange.

✦ **Edit.** Lets you select all messages and mark selected messages as read or unread.

✦ **Tools.** Lets you connect to an information service and deliver messages, maintain your online address book, customize Exchange and the current profile, find items in a folder, and more.

✦ **Compose.** Lets you compose a new message, reply to selected messages, and forward selected messages to other users.

Getting help with Exchange

Microsoft Exchange offers many ways to get help, including the following:

✦ To get help with Microsoft Exchange and any of the installed information services, choose options from the Help menu.

✦ To find out the purpose of any button on the toolbar, point to the button with your mouse. A descriptive tooltip appears near the mouse pointer. (If you don't see the tooltips, choose Tools⇨Options, click the General tab, select (check) Show ToolTips On Toolbars, and click OK.)

✦ To find out what any menu option does, open the menu and point to the option with your mouse. A brief description of the highlighted option appears in the status bar.

✦ For help anytime, press F1 or click the Help button (if any) in a dialog box. You also can click the Help toolbar button and then click the part of the window that you want to learn more about.

Composing and sending e-mail messages

Composing and sending a new e-mail message is a cinch. To begin, either choose Compose⇨New Message, press Ctrl+N, or click the New Message button on the toolbar. A New Message window opens, as shown in Figure 38-6.

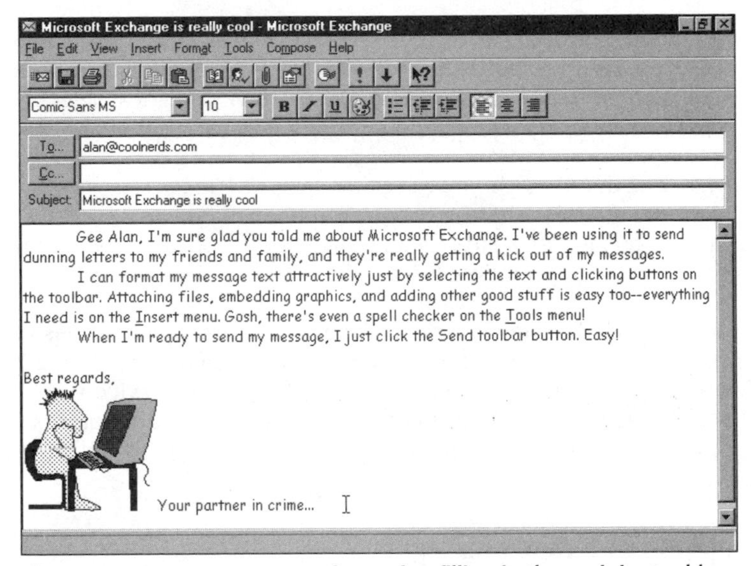

Figure 38-6: A new message form after filling in the recipient address, subject, and message text.

Then follow these steps:

1. Specify your main recipient(s) by clicking in the box next to the To button and typing the recipient's e-mail address. A typical Internet e-mail address appears in the form *name@domain,* as in `alan@coolnerds.com`. If you want to send the message to more than one recipient, separate each recipient's address with a semicolon.

2. Optionally, specify the e-mail addresses of recipients who should receive a copy of the message by clicking in the box next to the Cc button and typing the e-mail address for the copy-to recipient(s).

Hot Stuff

Instead of typing e-mail addresses, you can select them from an online address book. To do so, click the To button (for the main recipient) or the Cc button (for the copy-to recipient). When the Address Book dialog box appears, double-click the recipient name(s) you want and click OK.

3. Type a descriptive subject in the box next to Subject.

4. Type your message text in the big box below the Subject box.

When typing the message text, use standard text-editing and word-processing techniques. You also can use the Formatting toolbar buttons (View⇨Formatting Toolbar) to change the font name and size and dress up the text with boldface, italics, underlining, color, bullets, indents, and various alignments (left, center, and right). If you want to insert a file, message, or other object at the insertion point position, choose an option from the Insert menu.

You also can change various properties of your message. For example, you can request notification when the message is read or delivered and change the importance of the message. To change message properties, choose File⇨Properties, select the properties that you want, and click OK.

When you are ready to send the message, you can either press Ctrl+Enter, choose File⇨Send, or click the Send toolbar button to transmit it. Exchange temporarily places your message in the Outbox folder, sends the message to the specified recipient(s), and then moves the message to your Sent Items folder.

Puzzled?

If you connect to your e-mail system via modem, or if your outgoing messages seem stuck in your Outbox, choose Tools⇨Deliver Now or Tools⇨Deliver Now Using⇨*Service Name* (where *Service Name* is the name of the information service you want to use for sending the messages). Exchange connects to the e-mail system, places any incoming messages in your Inbox, transmits any outgoing messages, and disconnects from the e-mail system.

Reading and replying to e-mail messages

You can open and read any message in your Deleted Items, Inbox, Outbox, or Sent Items folders. Unread messages appear in boldface in the folder contents list; messages that you have already read are not bold. To read a message, open the appropriate folder in the folder list and double-click the message that you want to read. The message appears in a new window.

After opening a message, you can click toolbar buttons to print the message, move or delete it, reply to the sender, reply to the sender and all message recipients, forward the message, read the previous or next message, or get help. (Alternatively, you can use equivalent options on the File, Compose, and Help menus.) Of course, you also are free to close the message window anytime you want by pressing Alt+F4 or by clicking the window's Close button.

Hot Stuff

Remember that you can find out the purpose of any toolbar button by pointing to it with your mouse.

Managing your e-mail messages and folders

The Viewer window provides a handy way to work with messages and folders, and it is especially convenient when you don't feel like opening messages before you print, move, copy, delete, reply to, or forward them. Using the Viewer window is basically the same as using Windows 95 Explorer. The following list gives you the *Cliff's Notes* version of techniques that you can use:

- To view and select messages, click the appropriate folder icon in the folder list (left side of Viewer). Then select the message(s) you want to work with by clicking, Ctrl+clicking, or Shift+clicking items in the folder contents list (right side of Viewer).
- To delete the selected messages, press Delete. You also can drag messages to the Deleted Items folder or click the Delete toolbar button. To permanently delete messages, delete them from the Deleted Items folder.

Hot Stuff

If you want to empty the Deleted Items folder automatically when you exit Microsoft Exchange, choose Tools⇨Options, click the General tab (if necessary), select (check) Empty The 'Deleted Items' Folder Upon Exiting, and click OK.

- To copy the selected messages, hold down the Ctrl key while dragging the selection to a new folder (or to the Windows 95 desktop).
- To move the selected messages, simply drag the selection without holding down the Ctrl key.

There's lots more you can do with messages and folders. If you want to experiment with the possibilities, select the message or folder you want to work with. Then open the File menu or right-click the selection and choose the option you want to use.

Microsoft Fax tips

If you have Microsoft Fax set up, you can print any document to your fax modem instead of to the printer. Choose File⇨Print from your program, select Microsoft Fax as the printer, and click OK. The Compose New Fax Wizard takes over and prompts you through the steps for sending your document as a fax.

Puzzled?

If your faxes are rejected as *undeliverable,* try this trick: Right-click the Inbox icon on the Windows 95 desktop, choose Properties, and then click the Delivery tab. Next, click Microsoft Fax Transport in the list near the bottom of the Properties dialog box and click the ↑ button until you have moved Microsoft Fax Transport to the top of the list. Click OK and try faxing again.

Connecting other programs to Microsoft Exchange

Once you've installed Microsoft Exchange, you can use it to send e-mail and faxes from programs outside of Exchange. For example, many programs (including WordPad, Microsoft Word, and Internet Explorer) offer a File⇨Send command or toolbar button that lets you send the current document via e-mail. Similarly, while browsing in My Computer, Windows Explorer, and other file management windows, you can right-click a filename, choose Send To, and then choose Mail Recipient or Fax Recipient.

Hot Stuff

Netscape Navigator has its own e-mail capabilities. To set up Netscape's e-mail features, choose Options⇨Mail And News Preferences from the Netscape menu bar.

Downloading Files with FTP

File Transfer Protocol (or *FTP*) is the method used to send files over the Internet. For example, you use FTP to download the latest copy of Internet Explorer or some hot new game to your computer. FTP has been around since long before the Web was a gleam in anyone's eye. In the bad old days, using FTP required you to know all the moves of a Unix guru. But not anymore! Now you can fire up FTP and download files right from your favorite Web browser.

There are two ways to use FTP from your browser:

- Type the FTP site's URL in the Address or Location box near the top of the browser window.
- Click Web page hyperlinks that connect you to the FTP site's URL automatically.

More Info

Not surprisingly, dedicated FTP programs are available, and as a Web publisher, you'll probably use one often to upload your Web pages. If you need an FTP program, check out CuteFTP at `http://papa.indstate.edu:8888/CuteFTP` or WS_FTP at `http://www.csra.net/junodj/ws_ftp.htm`.

FTPing by typing URLs

FTP addresses look like most URLs on the Internet — cryptic! But once you understand their format, typing FTP addresses is pretty easy. The URL for a file that you can download via FTP looks like this:

```
ftp://hostname/directory-path/filename
```

For instance, WinZip is a top-notch utility for compressing and uncompressing files. The URL for the Windows 95 evaluation version of this program is

```
ftp://ftp.winzip.com/winzip/winzip95.exe
```

In the preceding example, `ftp://` is the service (FTP), `ftp.winzip.com` is the hostname, `winzip` is the directory-path, and `winzip95.exe` is the filename.

Here's how to download a file by typing its FTP address:

1. Click in the Address box near the top of the Internet Explorer window or the Location box near the top of the Netscape Navigator window.
2. Type the URL of the file and press Enter. For example, to get an evaluation copy of WinZip for Windows 95, type **ftp://ftp.winzip.com/winzip/winzip95.exe** and then press Enter.
3. When the Confirmation File Open dialog box appears, click Save As, specify a disk and folder location for your downloaded file, and click the Save button to start downloading.

Now wait patiently while the file is copied to your computer. When the download is complete, check the file for viruses (see the sidebar "Virus Alert!"). After making sure that the file is virus-free, simply double-click the downloaded file to open it or to launch its installation program.

Virus alert!

Believe it or not, some people on the Internet are not very nice. Such cyber spoil-sports try to ruin your fun by spreading electronic viruses that print nasty messages or unleash malicious mischief on your computer when you open infected files. Although some viruses are benign, many are capable of inflicting major damage to information stored on your disks. For this reason, you should always use a special anti-virus program to scan all downloaded files for the presence of viruses. If the anti-virus program detects any viruses, either clean out the virus or immediately remove the infected files from your disk. Most anti-virus programs can disinfect or delete any infected files quickly and automatically.

Several anti-virus programs are available, including two that you can download from the Internet. These are McAfee's VirusScan (`http://www.mcafee.com/`) and ThunderBYTE's TBAV (`http://www.thunderbyte.com/`). Both come in Windows 95 and Windows 3.1 flavors.

Note that computer viruses, like human viruses, are changing constantly. Therefore, be sure to update your anti-virus software periodically. Check with the anti-virus software manufacturer (or the manufacturer's Web site) to make sure that you are getting the very latest version.

Logging on to an FTP site that requires a user name and password

Millions of files are accessible via FTP just for the asking, and you rarely need an account name or password to download them. The reason is that most hosts follow a standard Internet practice called *anonymous FTP*, which lets any user log onto an FTP host using the name *anonymous* (or no name at all). If such sites do prompt you for a password, try typing your e-mail address as the response.

By contrast, some File Transfer Protocol (FTP) sites require you to log on before you can list or transfer files from that site. To provide the logon information and get connected, click in the Address or Location box at the top of your browser, type the address and logon information for the FTP site using the syntax that follows, and press Enter:

```
ftp:username:password@hostname
```

For example, to connect to an FTP server named `ftp.sneakypete.com` with the user name *nobody* and the password *secret*, you would type this address in the browser's Address or Location box and press Enter:

```
ftp://nobody:secret@ftp.sneakypete.com
```

From there, you could peruse the FTP site by clicking links as explained earlier.

Navigating an FTP site

If you omit the filename of the file you want to download — perhaps because you don't know the filename or you want to explore what's available at the site — you are taken to a list of directories and files on the FTP site (see Figure 38-7). Simply click a directory name to move down to that directory. If you need to jump up a level in the directory tree, click the Up one level link. Once you find the file that you want to download, click that filename in the list and the Confirmation File Open dialog box appears.

You can explore the hierarchy of an FTP site by lopping off directories in the URL, starting from the right. To see what I mean, try typing **ftp://ftp.winzip.com/winzip** in the Address or Location box of your browser to explore the WinZip FTP site.

FTPing with hyperlinks

Now that just about everyone uses Web pages to publicize their downloadable software, you rarely need to know the FTP address of files you want to download. Instead, you just click the hypertext link or graphic that downloads the file. For example, clicking the *winzip95.exe 359kb* link on the Web page shown in Figure 38-8 does exactly the same thing as typing **ftp://ftp.winzip.com/winzip/winzip95.exe** into the browser's Address or Location box — and it's a heckuva lot easier!

For a great list of Internet software that you can download just by clicking on hyperlinks, check out the Consummate Winsock Applications list at `http://cws.wilmington.net/`.

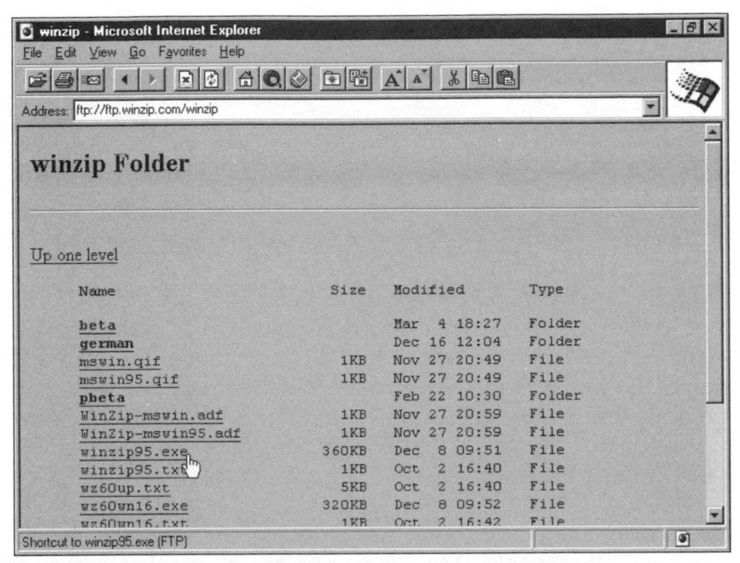

Figure 38-7: A list of available folders and files appears when you omit the filename from an FTP address.

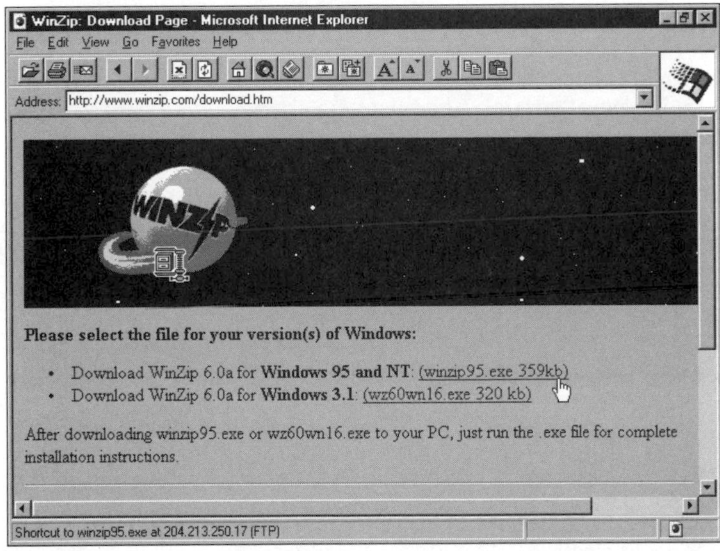

Figure 38-8: It is much easier to download a file by clicking its link on a standard Web page.

Getting the News in Cyberspace

Usenet is a worldwide network on the Internet for exchanging news bulletins that are grouped into subject categories called *newsgroups.* Each newsgroup functions as an online bulletin board where people with common interests post messages that express their opinions, request help from others in the group, and dispense news and information. Most newsgroups are open to everyone, and you should expect to see many uncensored, free-for-all, no-holds-barred discussions. Some newsgroups have a restricted membership or are moderated to keep the discussions under control.

Most Web browsers, including Internet Explorer and Netscape Navigator, include built-in *newsreaders* — special software for posting, reading, and responding to newsgroup articles and navigating the vast array of newsgroups in cyberspace. You also can use special-purpose newsreaders, such as FreeAgent, which make it easy to browse newsgroups online and offline. The following sections look at the basic newsreading capabilities built into Internet Explorer.

Newsgroups reside on computers called *news servers,* which use a protocol called *Network News Transport Protocol* (NNTP) to distribute Usenet bulletins. You need to know the name or IP address of your Internet provider's news server before you can dive into newsgroups.

Setting up Internet Explorer to use newsgroups

Internet Explorer provides basic newsreading features that enable you to read Internet newsgroups, respond to news articles, and post new articles. By default, the newsreading feature is turned off.

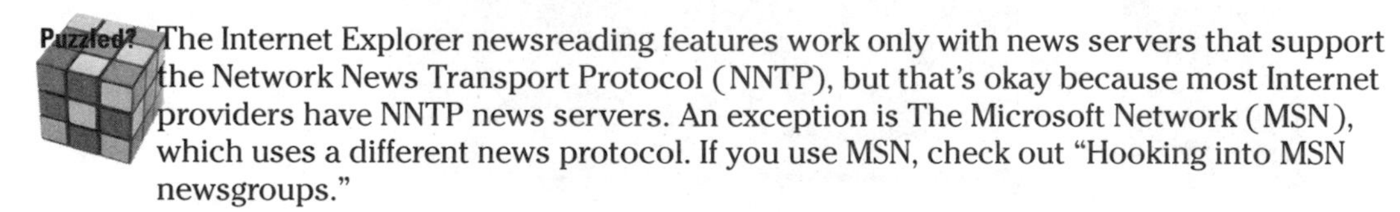

The Internet Explorer newsreading features work only with news servers that support the Network News Transport Protocol (NNTP), but that's okay because most Internet providers have NNTP news servers. An exception is The Microsoft Network (MSN), which uses a different news protocol. If you use MSN, check out "Hooking into MSN newsgroups."

Follow these steps to set up Internet Explorer as your newsreader:

1. Find out the following information from your Internet Service Provider:
   - Your NNTP news server's address
   - The user name and password you should use if your NNTP news server requires authorization
2. From the Internet Explorer menu bar, choose View➪Options and click the News tab of the Options dialog box that appears.
3. Select (check) the Use Internet Explorer To Read Internet Newsgroups checkbox.

4. In the Settings area, fill in the information obtained from your Internet Service Provider. Be sure to enter the News Server Address. If your news server requires authorization to use it, select (check) This Server Requires Authorization and enter your User Name and Password.
5. In the Posting area, supply your full Name and Email Address. This information appears at the top of any articles you post to the newsgroups.
6. Click OK.

Now you are ready to browse newsgroups, as explained in "Reading the news."

Puzzled? If you decide to stop using Internet Explorer as your newsreader, clear the Use Internet Explorer To Read Internet Newsgroups checkbox on the News tab of the Options dialog box. If necessary, re-install any newsreading software that you were using previously.

Hooking into MSN newsgroups

If you are an MSN user and you have upgraded your MSN account to support the Internet, you already have access to Usenet newsgroups. However, Internet Explorer cannot read the newsgroups by itself. Instead, Internet Explorer needs to call upon the MSN newsreader to read newsgroups. Follow these steps to make sure that your current copy of Internet Explorer is configured to call upon the MSN newsreader when you request Usenet news:

1. Set your MSN service type to Internet And MSN. To get started, right-click the MSN icon on your desktop, choose Connection Settings, and click the Access Numbers button. Choose Internet And The Microsoft Network from the Service Type drop-down list, and click OK as needed to return to the Windows 95 desktop.
2. In Internet Explorer, choose View⇨Options and click the News tab in the Options dialog box.
3. Deselect (clear) the Use Internet Explorer To Read Internet Newsgroups box checkbox and click OK.

Now you're ready to use Internet Explorer to explore the newsgroups on MSN.

Choosing a newsgroup

There are two ways to select a newsgroup and find out what's cooking there:

- ✦ If you are not sure which newsgroup you want to join, first list the available newsgroups (as explained next). Once you've found the newsgroup in which you are interested, click its name to jump into the fray. As you will see, there are thousands of newsgroups from which to choose.
- ✦ If you do know which newsgroup you want to join, you can jump directly to it as explained in "Jumping to your favorite newsgroup."

Some good and useful stuff can certainly be found in newsgroups. But a great deal of junk, put-downs, and just plain rude (and worse) stuff is out there as well. Usenet newsgroups represent the closest thing to global anarchy that this planet has ever seen, so keep that in mind before you let your kids loose in a newsgroup.

Getting a list of newsgroups

To get a list of available newsgroups from Internet Explorer, choose Go➪Read Newsgroups or click the Read Newsgroups button on the toolbar and wait patiently. Internet Explorer displays a list of the newsgroups available on your Internet Service Provider's news server, as shown in Figure 38-9.

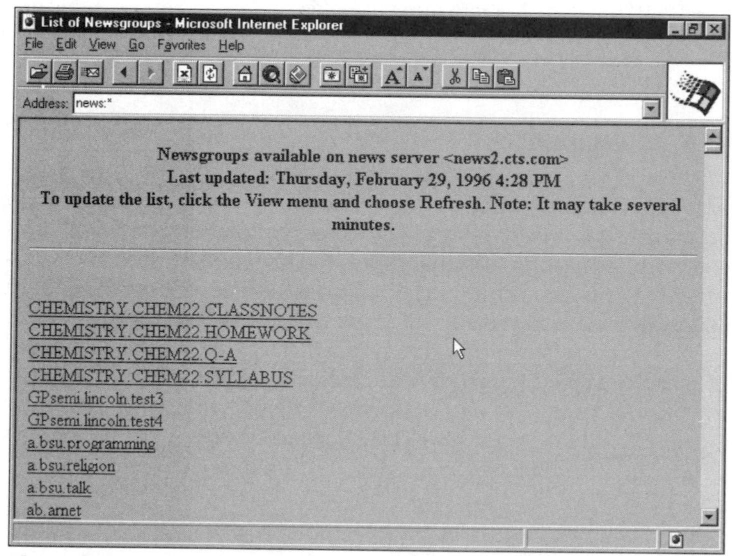

Figure 38-9: A list of newsgroups displayed in Internet Explorer.

If you are denied access to a news server and you are certain that you specified the correct news server name and authorization information, contact your ISP. Some Internet Service Providers allow newsgroup access only if you connect to the Internet via their phone numbers.

Figure 38-9 cannot begin to show the huge number of newsgroups available. You can scroll through the list from A to Z if you have a lot of time to kill or if you are just curious about what's available. But if you are in a hurry, you probably want to search for a keyword that matches all or part of a newsgroup name. To begin your search, choose Edit➪Find or press Ctrl+F. In the Find dialog box that appears, type a word or phrase — for example, **animals** — and click Find Next or press Enter. Continue clicking Find Next or pressing Enter until you find a topic that interests you (say, **clari.living.animals**). After you finish searching, click Cancel or press Esc to close the Find dialog box.

After you find the newsgroup in which you are interested, simply click its name to jump to that newsgroup's list of articles. Figure 38-10 shows the list of articles in the clari.living.animals newsgroup on March 5, 1996.

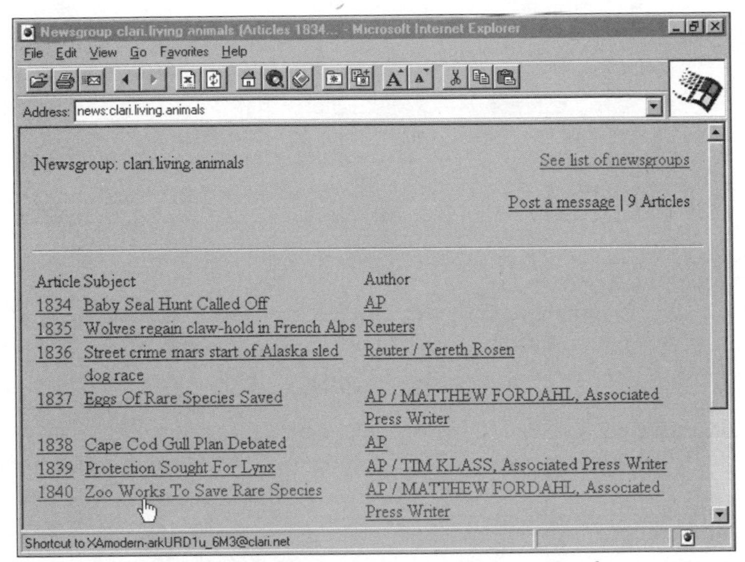

Figure 38-10: The list of articles in the clari.living.animals newsgroup on March 5, 1996.

Jumping to your favorite newsgroup

If you know the URL for the newsgroup that you are interested in, you can jump to the newsgroup in one quick step. Simply type the newsgroup's address in the Address box by using the following syntax and then press Enter:

```
news:newsgroup
```

For example, to jump to the clari.living.animals newsgroup, type **news:clari.living .animals** in the Address box and press Enter.

Hot Stuff

You can create a Favorites menu shortcut for a newsgroup. To do this, use the techniques described earlier to go to your favorite newsgroup and then click the Add To Favorites toolbar button or choose Favorites⇨Add To Favorites from the menu bar. The next time you want to jump to that newsgroup, simply choose its name from the Favorites menu.

Newsgroup names

Each newsgroup has a name indicating the topic or topics of articles posted therein. The names are formed in a hierarchical manner, with the name getting more specific as you move to the right. For example, the name *alt.gossip.royalty* deals with the top category of alt (alternative) and then gets more specific about the topic (*gossip* about *royalty*). Here are some of the major top-level newsgroup categories:

alt: *Alt*ernative views of the world. Watch out! This category often includes pornography, and it may be blocked on your service provider. *Example:* alt.gossip.royalty.

bionet: Biology discussions. *Example:* bionet.mycology.

biz: Business-related discussions. This is the place to post and find announcements about new businesses, products, and books. *Example:* biz.books.technical.

comp: All kinds of computer-related discussions! *Example:* comp.internet.net-happenings.

misc: The obligatory miscellaneous category for discussions that don't fit elsewhere. *Example:* misc.jobs.technical.

news: Newsgroups about the use and discussion of Usenet. *Examples:* news.answers and news.newusers.questions.

rec: Discussions about recreation, artistic activities, and hobbies. *Example:* rec.video.production.

soc: Discussions dealing with social issues and various cultures. *Example:* soc.culture.japan.

Navigating within a newsgroup

Finding the newsgroup that you are interested in is the biggest battle. Once you are there, you can read articles, post responses, send e-mail to an article's author, and post new articles of your own. These tasks are easy and intuitive in Internet Explorer.

✦ To see a list of earlier (or later) articles in the current newsgroup, click the Earlier articles (or Later articles) link at the top or bottom of the page of newsgroup articles (refer to Figure 38-10).

✦ To post a new message to the current newsgroup, click the Post a message link at the top or bottom of the page of newsgroup articles (refer to 38-10).

✦ To return to the list of newsgroups, click the See list of newsgroups link at the top of the page of newsgroup articles (refer to Figure 38-10). Or, click the Back toolbar button (or press the Backspace key) as needed. You also can click the Read Newsgroups toolbar button or choose Go➪Read Newsgroups.

Once you've found an article you're interested in, you can do one of the following:

✦ To read an article, click its name in the list of newsgroup articles. The article text appears, as shown in Figure 38-11.

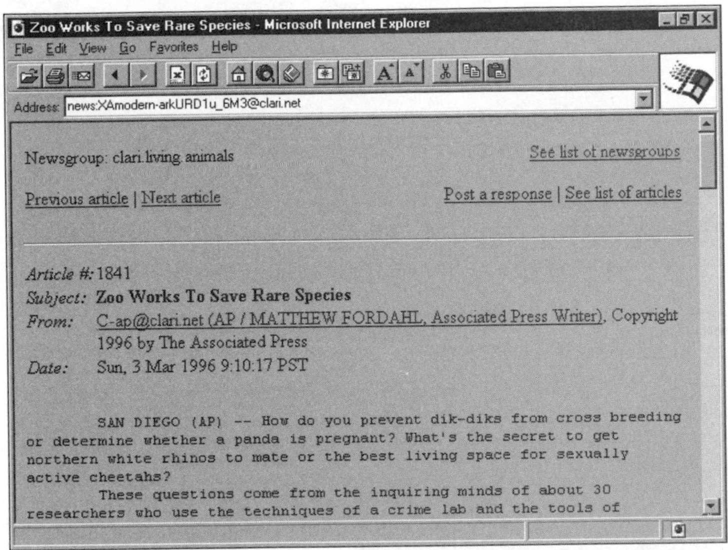

Figure 38-11: This article appeared when I clicked the title "Zoo Works to Save Rare Species" shown back in Figure 38-10.

- To respond to the article that you are reading, click the Post a response link at the top or bottom of the page (see Figure 38-11). Everyone in the newsgroup will be able to read your response.
- To send a personal e-mail message to the article's author, click the author's e-mail address in the From: line of the article and send an e-mail message using the standard Microsoft Exchange techniques given earlier in this chapter. Only the author will see your message.

Danger Zone Be sure to read several messages in the newsgroup before you respond to or post messages. Each newsgroup has its own culture, and you are likely to get flamed (insulted) if you write material that does not fit in.

While reading a message, you also can jump to the previous article or the next article, view the list of articles in the newsgroup, or view the list of newsgroups by clicking the appropriate links at the top or bottom of the current page. You can even click a URL in the article and jump to a Web page (if the author included a URL in the text).

Once you finish exploring newsgroups, you can type a different URL into the Address box, jump to a different page from your Favorites menu, or simply exit the browser.

Other newsgroup readers

Internet Explorer's newsreading capabilities are not fancy, but they certainly do the job for casual news perusing. If you plan to spend a great deal of time reading and contributing to newsgroups, however, you probably want to use the fancier newsreading features found in programs such as Netscape Navigator. Figure 38-12 shows how Netscape Navigator presents the same Zoo article found in the clari.living.animals newsgroup shown back in Figure 38-11.

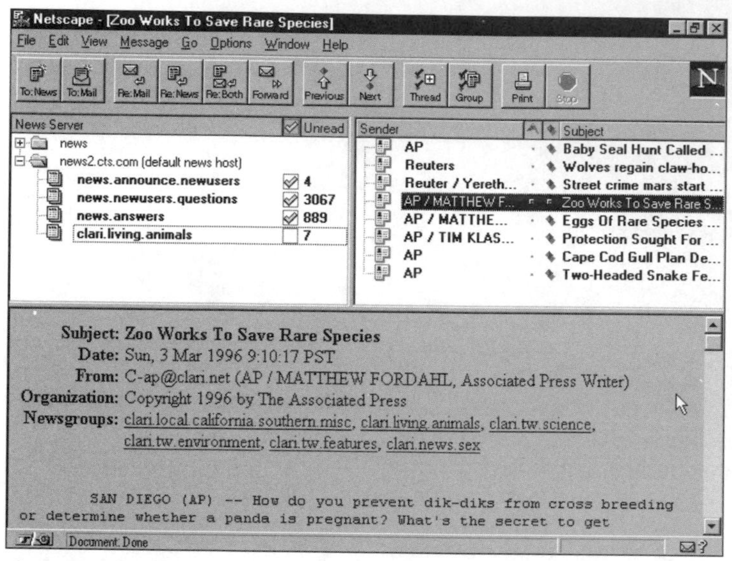

Figure 38-12: The Zoo article in Netscape Navigator.

> **More Info** If you are looking for a dedicated newsreader, consider trying Free Agent — a top-notch newsreader that is free for academic and non-profit use. You can download FreeAgent at `http://www.forteinc.com/forte/agent/freeagent.htm`. For information about other newsreaders on the Net, visit `http://cws.wilmington.net/news.html`.

A crash course on Netscape's newsgroup reader

Netscape Navigator's newsgroup reader is elegant and intuitive. The following list provides the minimal information you need to know to at least get started with it:

- ✦ To get set up, choose Options⇨Mail And News Preferences from Netscape's menu bar and click the Servers tab. Fill in the information about your mail and news servers and directories in the Mail and News areas (of course, you can click the Help button for details). Next, click the Identity tab and fill in your name, e-mail address, and other information. After you finish setting your preferences, choose OK.
- ✦ To open the Netscape newsreader, choose Window⇨Netscape News from Netscape's menu bar. Maximize the window for best results.

- To display the entire list of newsgroups, choose Options➪Show All Newsgroups from the news window's menu bar.
- The left side of the news window shows the available newsgroups and works a great deal like Windows Explorer. To select a newsgroup, click its name.
- The right side of the news window shows articles in the currently selected newsgroup. To read an article, double-click it.

Use the buttons on the News window's toolbar or the options on the Edit, Message, and Go menus to post new articles, send e-mail, reply to or forward an article, and navigate within the newsgroup. After you finish exploring newsgroups, press Ctrl+W or click the Close button to close the News window.

Summary

This chapter introduced three "non-Web" Internet services that you may want to take a peek at when you are not too busy publishing on your own Web site.

- Use electronic mail (or e-mail) to send messages to a specific user anywhere on the Internet. Microsoft Exchange, which comes with Windows 95, offers easy-to-use yet powerful e-mail capabilities. To launch Microsoft Exchange, double-click the Inbox icon on the Windows 95 desktop.
- The File Transfer Protocol (or FTP) enables you to download all types of files to your computer. To download a file from your browser, type a URL — for example, `ftp://ftp.winzip.com/winzip/winzip95.exe` — into the Address or Location box of your browser and press Enter. Alternatively, you can click a Web page hypertext link or graphic that fills in the correct URL automatically.
- After transferring a file to your computer via FTP, be sure to run the file through an anti-virus program that can detect and remove any viruses in the downloaded file.
- Newsgroups are the electronic bulletin boards of the Internet. You can join newsgroups and read articles in Internet Explorer, Netscape Navigator, and various dedicated newsreading programs.

✦ ✦ ✦

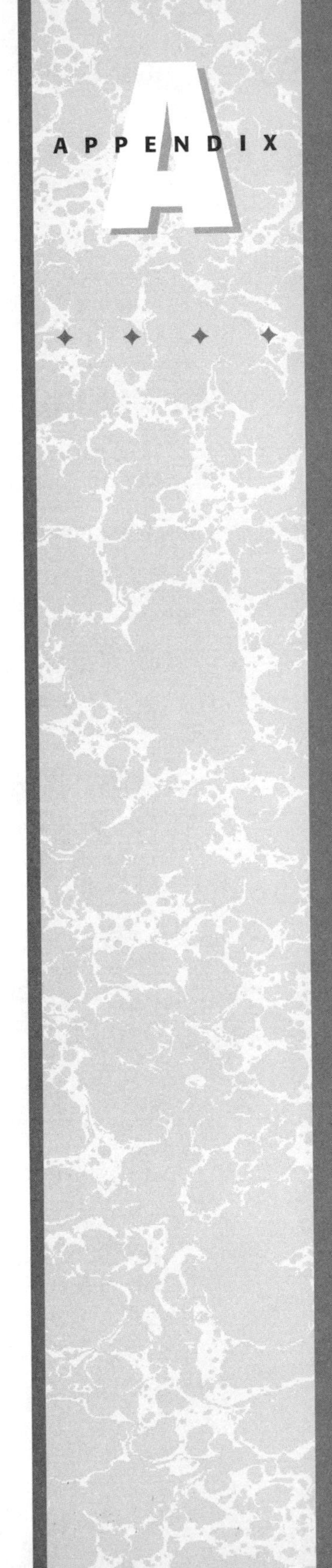

About the CD-ROM

The CD-ROM at the back of this book contains some stuff that you will no doubt find useful in your Web publishing endeavors, including the following:

- **Coolsite.** This is an exclusive shareware app created by yours truly that can manage lists in database form and instantly translate them to HTML documents for publication on the World Wide Web.
- **Microsoft Internet Explorer 2.0.** This is a great Web browser for Windows 95 users that is absolutely free!
- **Microsoft Word Internet Assistant for Windows 95.** This is a must-have tool for all Web authors and publishers. Word IA brings all the power of Microsoft Office 95 — including Microsoft Word, WordArt, Excel Charts, tables, forms, equations, org charts, and much more — to your Web pages.
- **Map This!** Map This! is a terrific tool for creating state-of-the-art, client-side, clickable image maps with Windows 95 ease.
- **Paint Shop Pro.** This new, 32-bit Windows 95 version of Paint Shop Pro offers full-graphics capabilities and supports Internet GIF and JPEG formats, including transparent-background GIFs.
- **WinZip for Windows 95.** This new Windows 95 version of the classic zip-and-unzip utility supports the Internet TAR format.
- **Web Art.** This package contains backgrounds, bullets, buttons, lines, and sound clips ready to be copied and pasted into your own Web pages, plus links to thousands more free images on the World Wide Web.

✦ **Examples.** This contains sample video clips, forms, entire Web sites (with Frames!), and a ton of pre-written, ready-to-use JavaScript code!

The CD-ROM is set up like a Web site so that you can easily browse the CD-ROM as you would a regular Web site. My own coolnerds Web site keeps you up-to-date on all the latest tools and techniques for Web authors and developers.

Browsing the CD-ROM

The easiest way to get around the *HTML Publishing Bible* CD-ROM is to simply browse it with your favorite Web browser. Follow these steps:

1. Put the *HTML Publishing Bible* CD-ROM in your CD-ROM drive.
2. On the Windows 95 desktop, double-click My Computer and then double-click the icon for your CD-ROM drive.
3. Double-click the icon named BrowseMe.htm (Figure A-1) or start your favorite Web browser and use its File➪Open File capabilities to open *D*:\BrowseMe.htm (where *D* is the drive letter for your CD-ROM drive).

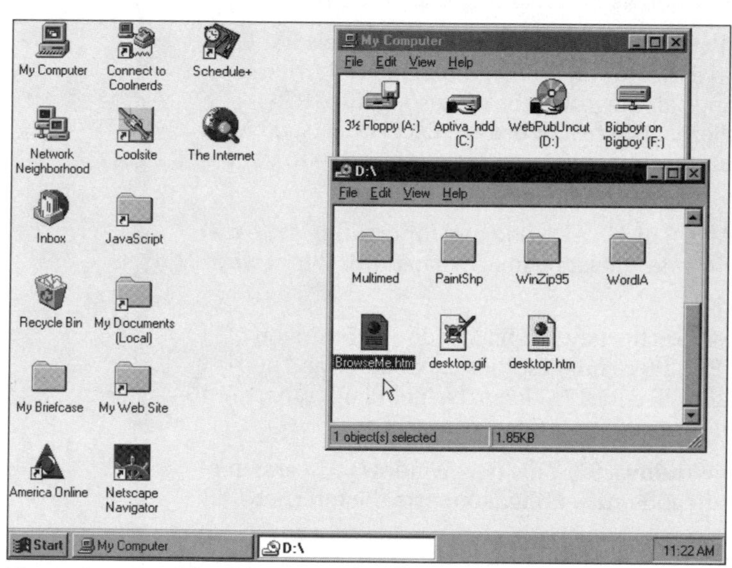

Figure A-1: Double-click BrowseMe.htm to browse the *Web Publishing Uncut* CD-ROM.

The "home page" for the *HTML Publishing Bible* CD-ROM appears (see Figure A-2). From there, you can browse to your heart's content. Here are a couple of pointers in case you have problems:

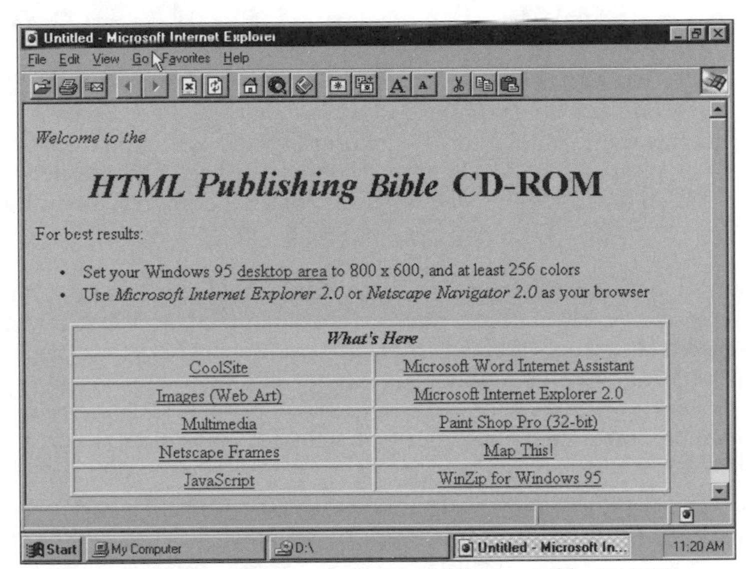

Figure A-2: Home page for the *HTML Publishing Bible* CD-ROM.

✦ If you haven't installed a Web browser on your PC, you cannot browse the CD-ROM. In that case, you should go right to the section titled "Installing Microsoft Internet Explorer 2.0," complete the installation, and then come back here.

✦ If you do have a Web browser installed but don't know how to use it, see Chapter 3 for some Web-browsing basics. But don't worry about all the online stuff yet. You just need to open the BrowseMe.htm file in your Web browser.

You also may want to consider the following when browsing the CD-ROM:

✦ For best results, set your desktop area to 800 × 600 and the color palette to at least 256 colors. If you don't know how to do that, just click the desktop area hotlink on the page.

✦ Video clips look best with 16-bit or higher color palettes and require high-performance hardware to run smoothly.

✦ Inline multimedia examples require Microsoft Internet Explorer 2.0 or a browser with appropriate plug-ins or helper apps.

✦ Frames and JavaScript require modern browsers as well. At the time of this writing, only Netscape Navigator 2.0 (and Gold) support those features.

You can download a trial copy of Netscape Navigator from Netscape's Web site at `http://home.netscape.com`.

Installing Microsoft Word Internet Explorer 2.0

If you don't already have a Web browser, you can install Microsoft's Internet Explorer version 2.0 from the *HTML Publishing Bible* CD-ROM. In fact, even if you *do* have some other browser, you may want to add Internet Explorer to your collection because it has some cool features, such as inline sound and video. I often refer to Internet Explorer in this book, so if you need or want to install Internet Explorer, follow these steps:

Hot Stuff The CD-ROM includes *only* the Windows 95 version of Internet Explorer. If you already have a Web browser and Internet access, you can download the very latest version of Internet Explorer from Microsoft's Web site (`http://www/microsoft.com`). You also can find versions for Windows 3.11 and the Mac there.

1. Close all open programs (including your Web browser if it is open) to get to a clean Windows 95 desktop.
2. Double-click My Computer, double-click the icon for your CD-ROM drive, and then double-click the Explorer folder on the CD-ROM.
3. Point to the icon titled msie20 (or msie20.exe) , press and hold the right mouse button, drag the icon to the Windows 95 desktop, release the right mouse button, and choose Copy Here (Figure A-3).

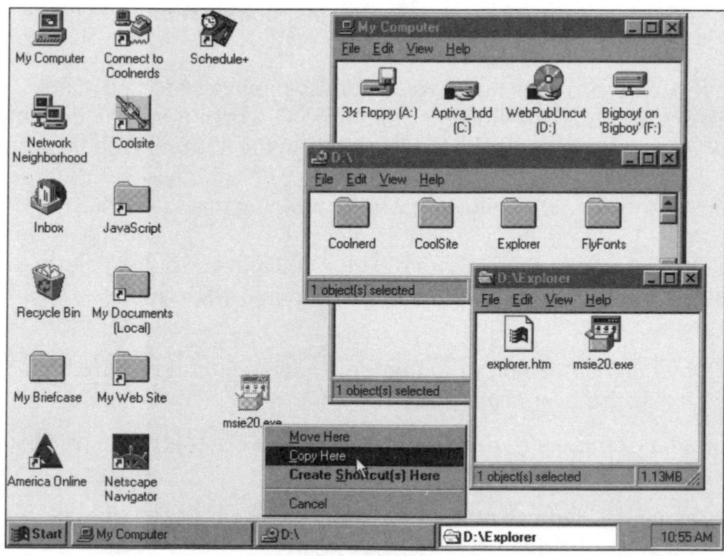

Figure A-3: Copying msie20.exe to the Windows 95 desktop.

4. Now you can close all the windows displaying stuff from the CD-ROM.

Hot Stuff

To close all three open windows with a single click, press and hold Shift and then click the little X in the upper-right corner of the last opened window, D:\Explorer in this example.

5. Double-click the msie20 (or msie20.exe) icon that you dragged to the Windows 95 desktop. You see the following message:

```
This will install Microsoft Internet Explorer Version 2.0. Do
      you wish to continue?
```

6. Click the Yes button and follow the instructions on the screen. If asked to choose a parent directory, I recommend that you click the icon for your C: drive and then click OK.

7. When you see the message

```
Internet Explorer Update Completed Successfully
```

click the OK button.

8. You don't need the msie20.exe icon anymore, so you can click it once, press Delete, and choose Yes to send it to the Recycle Bin.

A new icon titled The Internet should appear on your desktop. Opening (double-clicking) that icon takes you through all the steps involved in setting up an Internet account, as discussed in Chapter 2. If you don't want to sign up for an account just yet, but would like to browse the *HTML Publishing Bible* CD-ROM, leave the icon alone for now. Instead, just double-click the BrowseMe.htm icon as discussed under "Browsing the CD-ROM" earlier in this appendix. The BrowseMe page opens in Microsoft Internet Explorer, as shown back in Figure A-2.

Be aware that installing Internet Explorer does not automatically give you access to the Internet and World Wide Web. You still need to set up an Internet account as discussed in Chapters 1 through 3 of this book.

Installing Word Internet Assistant

The *HTML Publishing Bible* CD-ROM comes with a copy of Microsoft Word Internet Assistant for Word for Windows 95. (Whew, what a mouthful. Let's just refer to it as *Word IA*.) Word for Windows 95 also is referred to as Word 7.0. If you don't have Word 7.0, don't install the copy of Word IA found on the CD-ROM. You can, however, find similar tools for other word processors. For example, you can download Word IA for Word 6.0 from Microsoft's home page (`http://www.microsoft.com`). WordPerfect offers Internet Publisher. Though the site was under construction when I last visited it, you will probably be able to download a copy from `http://www.wordperfect.com`.

Let's assume that you are using Windows 95 and Word for Windows 95 and that you now want to install Word Internet Assistant from the *HTML Publishing Bible* CD-ROM. Here's what you need to do:

1. Close any open windows and programs (including your Web browser).
2. At the Windows 95 desktop, double-click My Computer, double-click the icon for your CD-ROM drive, and then double-click the WordIA folder.
3. Double-click the icon for wrdia20z.exe and choose Yes when prompted for confirmation.
4. Follow the instructions that appear on the screen until you get to the dialog box showing *Internet Assistant for Microsoft Word Setup was completed successfully.* There you can Launch Word or Exit Setup to return to Windows 95.

To learn how to use Word IA to create Web pages, see Chapter 12.

Installing Paint Shop Pro

No Web publisher's PC is complete without a good graphics program capable of handling Internet GIF and JPEG formats. I was fortunate enough to land a shareware version of one of the best for the *HTML Publishing Bible* CD-ROM. You are welcome to install it and give it a try. I *only* have the 32-bit version here, which means you need to be running Windows 95 or Windows NT to install this version. (Other versions are available for downloading from JASC's Web site at `http://www.jasc.com`.) To install Paint Shop Pro from the *Web Publishing Uncut* CD-ROM, follow these steps:

1. Put the *HTML Publishing Bible* CD-ROM in your CD-ROM drive (of course).
2. Close any open windows and programs (including your Web browser).
3. At the Windows 95 desktop, double-click My Computer, double-click the icon for your CD-ROM drive, and then double-click the PaintShp folder.
4. Double-click the Setup (or Setup.exe) icon in the PaintShp folder and choose Yes when prompted for confirmation.
5. Follow the instructions that appear on the screen to complete the installation.

To get started learning how to use Paint Shop Pro, see Chapter 22. For technical support, registration information, new releases, and other JASC products, point your Web browser to `http://www.jasc.com`. For general techniques for putting pictures in your Web pages, see Chapter 15.

Hot Stuff

Be sure to read Chapter 11 to give yourself quick access to all your Web authoring tools!

Installing Map This!

Map This! is a terrific freeware application that makes it a breeze to create clickable image maps for your Web site. Map This! has no custom setup program — you just need to copy its folder from the *HTML Publishing Bible* CD-ROM to your local hard disk (drive C). Here's how to do that:

1. Put the *HTML Publishing Bible* CD-ROM in your CD-ROM drive. If you're already browsing the CD-ROM, close your Web browser.
2. Double-click My Computer and double-click the icon for your CD-ROM drive.
3. Arrange windows and icons on your screen so that you can see both the icon for your local hard disk (C:) and the MapThis folder on the CD-ROM.
4. Drag the MapThis folder to the icon for your hard drive, as in Figure A-4, and release the mouse button.

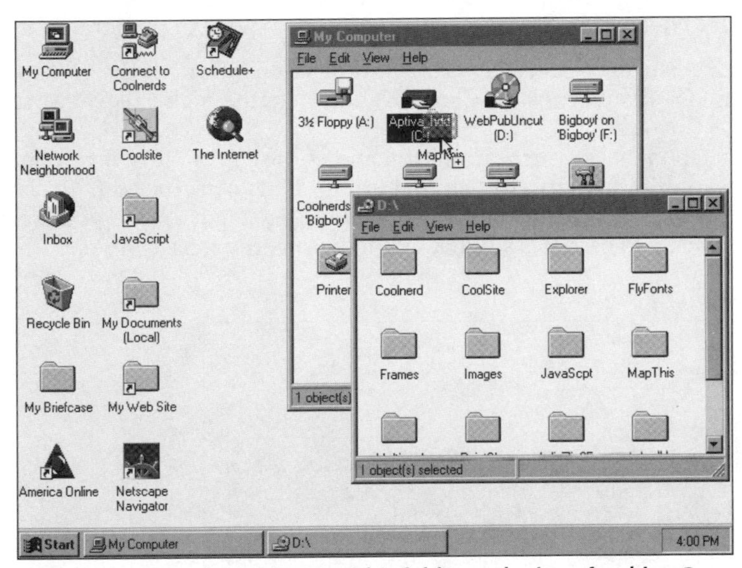

Figure A-4: Drag the entire MapThis folder to the icon for drive C.

A dialog box containing progress odometers appears for a few seconds while Windows copies the MapThis folder from the CD-ROM drive to your hard disk. To verify the copy, open (double-click) the icon for drive C and choose View⇨Arrange Icons⇨by Name. You should then be able to see a folder icon named MapThis included with the rest of your folders on drive C.

To add a startup icon for Map This! to your Programs menu

1. Right-click the Start button and choose Open.
2. Double-click the Programs icon.
3. If you want to put Map This! in with another group of programs, open the folder for that group. Optionally, if you don't go any deeper, Map This! appears on the actual Programs menu (after you complete the remaining steps).
4. Choose File➪New➪Shortcut from whichever folder you opened in Step 3.
5. In the Create Shortcut dialog box, click the Browse button, open the folder named MapThis, and then double-click on MapThis.exe (or MapThis).
6. Click the Next button and type in a name for the shortcut, such as **Map This!**
7. Click Finish.
8. If you also want to create a desktop shortcut icon to Map This!, right-drag the newly created shortcut icon for Map This! out of its current folder and onto the desktop. After you release the right mouse button, choose Copy Here.
9. Now you can close all open windows on your desktop. (To do it the quick way, press and hold Shift and click the Close (X) button in the highest-level window.)

To verify the installation, click your Start button and choose Programs. If you put the Map This! icon into a program group, open that group. Then click the Map This! entry. The Map This! program should open looking something like Figure A-5. If you created a desktop icon as well, you can double-click that icon to verify that it works.

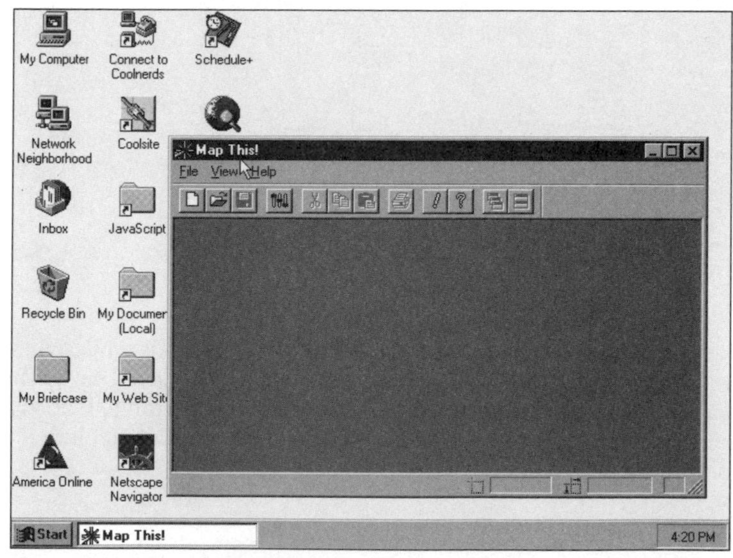

Figure A-5: Map This! as it first appears on the screen.

You learn about clickable image maps and Map This! in Chapter 24. For now, you can close Map This! by clicking its Close (X) button or choosing File⇨Exit from its menu bar.

Installing WinZip for Windows 95

I've also included a copy of the 32-bit WinZip program for Windows 95 and NT. To install it on your PC

1. Close any open windows and programs (including your Web browser) to get to the Windows 95 desktop. Put the *HTML Publishing Bible* CD-ROM in your CD-ROM drive.
2. Double-click your My Computer icon.
3. Double-click the icon for your CD-ROM drive.
4. Double-click the WinZip95 folder.
5. Double-click winzip95.exe (or winzip95) icon and click the Setup button in the dialog box that appears.
6. Follow the instructions that appear on the screen. You can choose Express Setup when given the option.

After the setup is complete, you can close any remaining open windows. Then to start WinZip and verify your installation, click the Start button (in your Windows 95 taskbar), point to Programs⇨WinZip, and click on the WinZip 6.0a 32-bit icon. Click the I agree button, and WinZip opens as shown in Figure A-6.

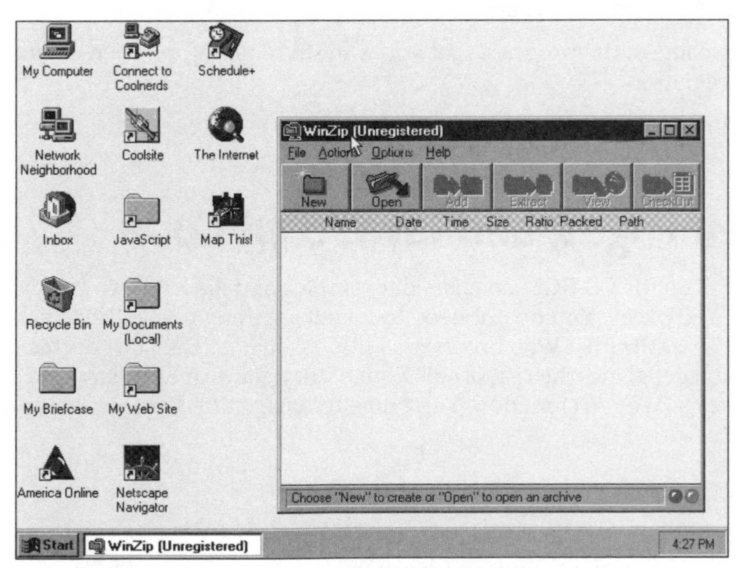

Figure A-6: Shareware version of WinZip installed and open.

To learn about WinZip, choose Help➪Brief Tutorial from its menu bar. For information on registering and purchasing this product, choose Help➪Ordering Information. For information on other great products, WinZip versions for other operating systems, and so on, stop by the WinZip Web site at `http://www.winzip.com`. For the moment, you can close WinZip in the usual manner — click its Close (X) button or choose File➪Exit from its menu bar.

Installing and Using Coolsite

For a complete description of Coolsite, as well as installation and startup instructions, please refer to Chapter 20. For information and support on Coolsite, stop by my Web site at `http://www.coolnerds.com`. You can post questions in the "ask alan" area of that site.

Uninstalling These Programs

Should you decide to remove any of these programs after installing them from the *HTML Publishing Bible* CD-ROM, be sure to use Windows 95's uninstall capabilities. This ensures that all traces, including Windows 95 Registry entries, are deleted. The one exception is for Map This!, which you can remove by simply deleting the MapThis folder from your hard drive. For all the rest, follow these instructions to uninstall:

1. At the Windows 95 desktop, click the Start button and choose Settings➪Control Panel.
2. Double-click Add/Remove Programs.
3. Click on the name of the program that you want to remove, and then click the Add/Remove button.
4. Follow the instructions on the screen to remove the entire program.

Web Art, Web Pages, and JavaScript Code

The rest of the stuff on the CD-ROM consists of examples and materials to help you create your own Web pages. You do not need to install anything to use those items. Just browse the CD-ROM with a Web browser as discussed near the start of this appendix. Once you get going, the rest is self-explanatory. For example, say that you browse to the Images (Web Art) section. You come to a page titled Image Categories, as shown in Figure A-7.

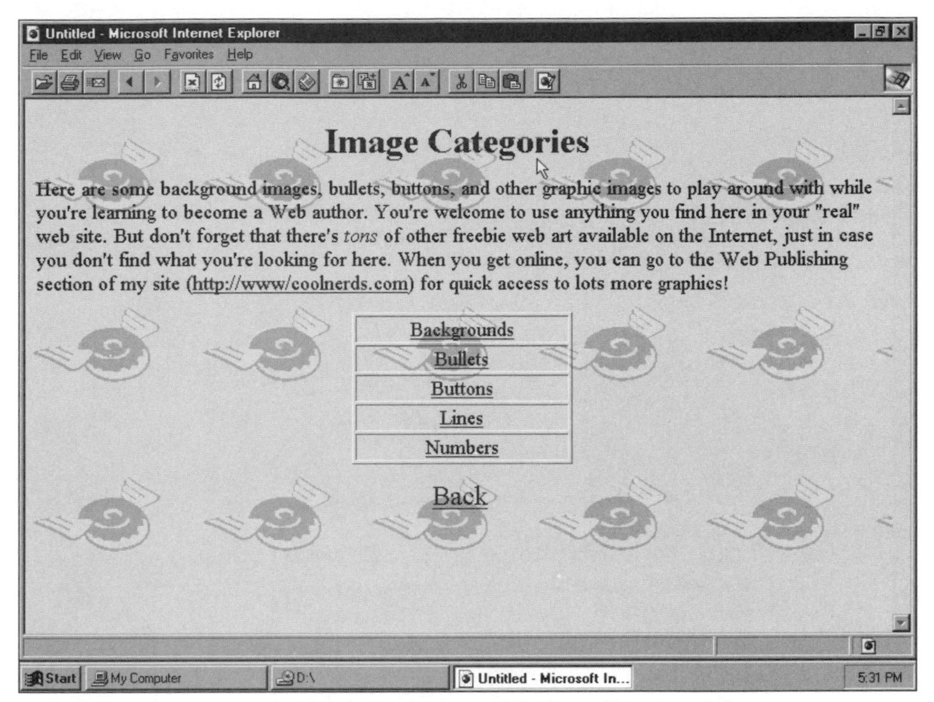

Figure A-7: Image categories on the *HTML Publishing Bible* CD-ROM.

From there, suppose that you choose to view Buttons. When you get to the Buttons page (Figure A-8) you see buttons to choose from. This page also contains a hotlink to instructions on how to copy buttons from this page onto your hard disk and into your Web pages. In addition, you can learn about copying stuff from Web pages in Chapter 3.

Finding a specific file

You also find references to specific files on the CD-ROM, which you can copy by using standard Windows techniques. If you cannot find a particular file on the CD-ROM, try using the Find feature. That is, click the Start button, choose Find➪Files or Folders, and choose your CD-ROM drive next to Look In. Type any part of the name of the file that you are looking for and then click the Find Now button.

A note on read-only files

When you copy a file from a CD-ROM to your hard disk, Windows initially sets that file's Read-Only attribute to on. That may prevent you from modifying or deleting the copied file. To change that situation, turn off the Read-Only attribute for that file. That is, get to the file's icon on your hard disk (C:), right-click that icon, and choose properties. On the General tab (Figure A-9), clear the Read-Only check box and then click OK.

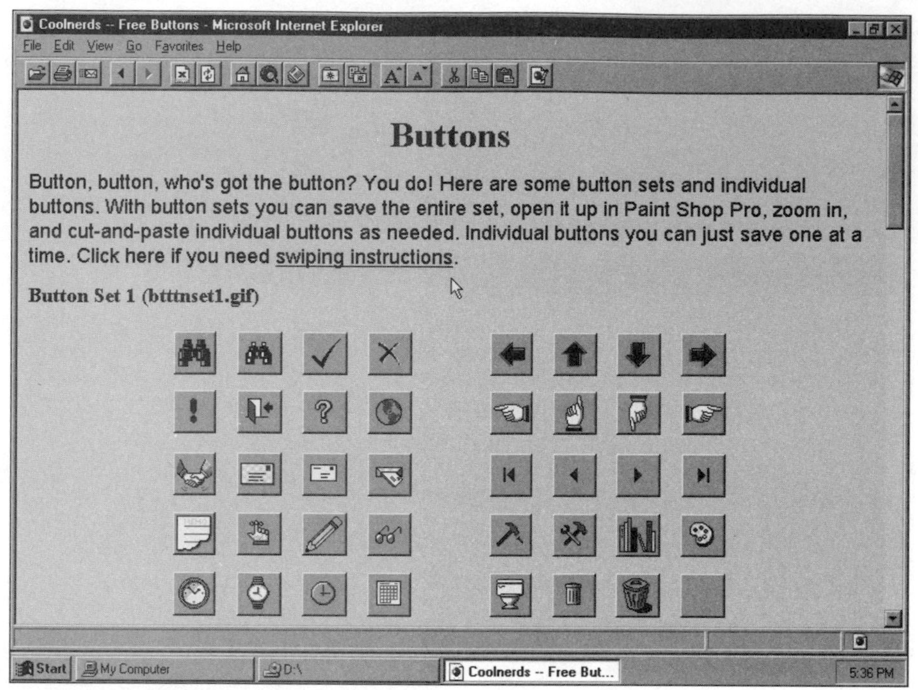

Figure A-8: The buttons page offers buttons that you can put into your own Web pages.

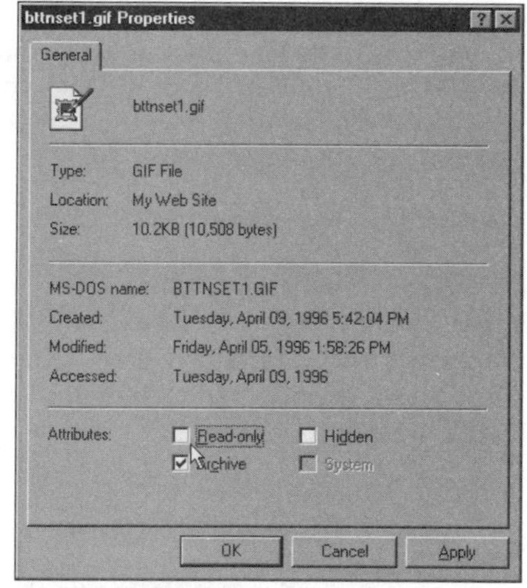

Figure A-9: Any file you copy from a CD-ROM to your hard disk can be made accessible by clearing its Read-Only attribute.

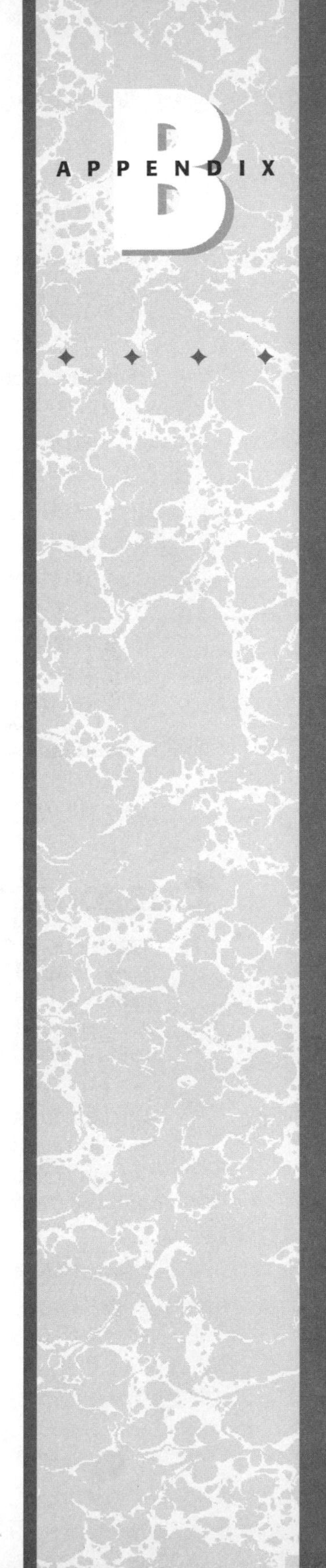

HTML Quick Reference

This appendix provides a quick, categorized summary of every HTML tag available, including those proposed by Netscape Navigator 2.0 and Microsoft Internet Explorer 2.0. More in-depth information about the tags and their attributes is provided on the *HTML Publishing Bible* CD-ROM's Electronic HTML Reference. To use the electronic reference, do one of the following:

- ✦ Open the BrowseMe.htm file on the CD-ROM as discussed in Appendix A. Then click on HTML Reference.
- ✦ Or, double-click on the htmlref.htm filename in Windows 95's My Computer, Windows Explorer, or Find file tools.

The htmlref.htm file is a large Web page. After you open it, you can just click on any hyperlink for more information about a particular tag or topic. To close the reference guide, exit your Web browser.

If you like, you can copy htmlref.htm from the *HTML Publishing Bible* CD-ROM onto your hard disk. Then you can create a shortcut icon to that file for easy access. Once the htmlref.htm file is on your hard disk, you'll be able to use the electronic reference without putting the *HTML Publishing Bible* CD-ROM in your CD-ROM drive.

Other Electronic HTML References

Documenting HTML is a bit of a challenge because different browsers react to tags in different ways: Some tags only work in certain browsers, and HTML itself seems to change everyday. (When you look up *oxymoron* in the dictionary, it could show *HTML Standard* as an example.)

Your best bet is to find an electronic reference that you really like and then update your copy of it periodically to make sure that you have current information. You have lots of options to choose from:

✦ **HTML Publishing Bible Electronic HTML Reference:** `http://www.coolnerds.com`

✦ **EFF Guide to the Internet:** `http:// www.caboose.com/ altopics/ internet/ guides_and_help/EFFGUIDE/`

✦ **HTML Quick Reference (Michael Grobe):** `http://www.cc.ukans.edu/info/HTML_quick.html`

✦ **HTML Quick Reference (Maran Wilson):** `http:// sdcc8.ucsd.edu/ ~mlwilson/ htmlref.html`

✦ **HTML Style Guide & Test Suite:** `http://www.charm.net/~lejeune/styles.html`

✦ **HTML Language Spec:** `http:// www.hp.co.uk/ people/ dsr/ html3/ CoverPage.html`

✦ **W³ Writer:** `http://hake.com/gordon/w3-index.html`

✦ **Windows 95 HTML Help:** Point your browser to `ftp://ftp.swan.ac.uk/ pub/ in.coming/ htmlib` and download the file *htmlib95xx.exe* (where *xx* is the version number, currently *21* for 2.1).

Categorized Tag Summary

The sections that follow organize the HTML tags into handy categories. For example, if you want to know which tags create anchors (hyperlinks), look in the Anchor tags category. Likewise, to find out which tags create tables, look in the Table tags category. After you find a tag that interests you, you can get more information on the tag by using any of the electronic references described earlier in this appendix.

Anchor tags

Anchor tags define hyperlinks and bookmarks (anchors). The `<A HREF=...>` anchor tag lets you define a jump to a new destination; the `<A NAME=...>` anchor tag lets you specify a *bookmark* — a destination within a document that anchor tag can jump to.

Open/Close Tag	***Description***
`<A...>...</A>`	Anchor that defines the jumping-off point (hyperlink) or the landing zone of a hyperlink (sometimes called a target or bookmark).

Block-formatting tags

Use block-formatting tags to format entire blocks of text — for example, paragraphs or quoted material — rather than single characters or chunks of characters. Be sure to place the block formatting tags between the <BODY>...</BODY> tags in the document.

Open/Close Tag	*Description*
<ADDRESS>...</ADDRESS>	Formats the address section of a Web page, usually in italic type that may be indented.
<BASEFONT...>	Specifies the default (base) font size for the document (Netscape Navigator only).
<BLOCKQUOTE>...</BLOCKQUOTE>	Sets text apart by indenting and sometimes italicizing it. Useful for quoting information from another source.
 	Forces a line break.
<CENTER>...</CENTER>	Centers text on the page.
<DIV>...</DIV>	Centers, left aligns, or right aligns text on the page. (Netscape Navigator).
<FONT...>...</FONT>	Sets the font size, font color, and font face of text. (Netscape Navigator and Internet Explorer only. Font face settings are Internet Explorer only.)
<Hn>...</Hn>	Formats any of six levels of heading, where *n* is 1, 2, 3, 4, 5, or 6.
<HR>	Draws a resizable horizontal line on the page.
<NOBR>...</NOBR>	Prevents the browser from word-wrapping any text between the open and close tags. (Netscape Navigator and Internet Explorer only.)
<P>...</P>	Specifies the start and end of a paragraph and its alignment.
<PRE>...</PRE>	Uses text "as is" in fixed-width font.
<WBR>	Allows a word break at the tag position within a <NOBR> section.

Characters (special)

You can type normal text, including spaces and hyphens, in your HTML documents. If you want to use special characters (such as <, >, ", and &) and graphic characters (such as ®, ä, and ©), you must take some special measures.

In the following table, the first column shows the result you want to achieve, the second column shows the text you must type in your HTML editor (for example, Notepad or WordPad), and the third column describes the character in more detail. Each special character must start with an ampersand (&) and end with a semicolon (;).

To Get This Result	*Type This HTML Text*	*Description*
		Non-breaking space. In Netscape Gold Editor, press Shift+Space as a shortcut.
"	"	Double quotation
&	&	Ampersand
<	<	Less than
>	>	Greater than
©	©	Copyright
®	®	Registered trademark
À	À	Capital A, grave accent
à	à	Small a, grave accent
Á	Á	Capital A, acute accent
á	á	Small a, acute accent
Â	Â	Capital A, circumflex accent
â	â	Small a, circumflex accent
Ã	Ã	Capital A, tilde
ã	ã	Small a, tilde
Ä	Ä	Capital A, dieresis or umlaut mark
ä	ä	Small a, dieresis or umlaut mark
Å	Å	Capital A, ring
å	å	Small a, ring
Æ	Æ	Capital AE dipthong (ligature)
æ	æ	Small ae dipthong (ligature)
Ç	Ç	Capital C, cedilla
ç	ç	Small c, cedilla
Ð	Ð	Capital Eth, Icelandic
∂	ð	Small eth, Icelandic
È	È	Capital E, grave accent

To Get This Result	*Type This HTML Text*	*Description*
è	è	Small e, grave accent
É	É	Capital E, acute accent
é	é	Small e, acute accent
Ê	Ê	Capital E, circumflex accent
ê	ê	Small e, circumflex accent
Ë	Ë	Capital E, dieresis or umlaut mark
ë	ë	Small e, dieresis or umlaut mark
Ì	Ì	Capital I, grave accent
ì	ì	Small i, grave accent
Í	Í	Capital I, acute accent
í	í	Small i, acute accent
Î	Î	Capital I, circumflex accent
î	î	Small i, circumflex accent
Ï	Ï	Capital I, dieresis or umlaut mark
ï	ï	Small i, dieresis or umlaut mark
Ñ	Ñ	Capital N, tilde
ñ	ñ	Small n, tilde
Ò	Ò	Capital O, grave accent
ò	ò	Small o, grave accent
Ó	Ó	Capital O, acute accent
ó	ó	Small o, acute accent
Ô	Ô	Capital O, circumflex accent
ô	ô	Small o, circumflex accent
Õ	Õ	Capital O, tilde
õ	õ	Small o, tilde
Ö	Ö	Capital O, dieresis or umlaut mark
ö	ö	Small o, dieresis or umlaut mark
Ø	Ø	Capital O, slash
Ù	Ù	Capital U, grave accent
ù	ù	Small u, grave accent

(continued)

(continued)

To Get This Result	*Type This HTML Text*	*Description*
Ú	Ú	Capital U, acute accent
ú	ú	Small u, acute accent
Û	Û	Capital U, circumflex accent
û	û	Small u, circumflex accent
Ü	Ü	Capital U, dieresis or umlaut mark
ü	ü	Small u, dieresis or umlaut mark
Ý	Ý	Capital Y, acute accent
ý	ý	Small y, acute accent
ÿ	ÿ	Small y, dieresis or umlaut mark
Þ	Þ	Capital THORN, Icelandic
þ	þ	Small thorn, Icelandic

Character formatting tags

Character formatting tags strictly specify the appearance of text in the browser. Text between the open and close tag will have the appearance specified by the tag — for example, **bold**, *italic*, ~~strikethrough~~, or underlined.

Open/Close Tag	*Description*
`<B>...</B>`	Boldface text.
`<BLINK>...</BLINK>`	Blinking text. (Netscape Navigator only.)
`<CITE>...</CITE>`	Citation text; typically appears in italics.
`<CODE>...</CODE>`	Sample code text; typically appears in a monospaced font.
`<EM>...</EM>`	Emphasized text; typically appears in italics.
`<I>...</I>`	Italicized text.
`<KBD>...</KBD>`	User-typed text; typically appears in a monospaced font.
`<S>...</S>`	Strikethrough text.
`<SAMP>...</SAMP>`	Literal characters or sample text; typically appears in a monospaced font.
`<SMALL>...</SMALL>`	Small text.
`<STRIKE>...</STRIKE>`	Strikethrough text.

<STRONG>...</STRONG>	Strongly emphasized text; typically appears in boldface.
_{...}	Subscript text.
^{...}	Superscript text.
<TT>...</TT>	Fixed-width text (also called *Teletype Text*); appears in a monospaced font.
<U>...</U>	Underlined text.
<VAR>...</VAR>	Text used as a variable name; typically appears in italics or fixed-width font.

Document structure tags

The document structure tags define the framework or skeleton of your HTML document. The three required tags are <HTML>...</HTML>, <HEAD>...</HEAD>, and <BODY>...</BODY>.

Open/Close Tag	***Description***
<!-- ... -->	Text between the tags represents comments to yourself and is ignored by the browser. Comments can appear anywhere in the document.
<!DOCTYPE...>	Prologue identifier that describes the level of the HTML document. If present, must appear before the <HTML> tag.
<BASE...>	* Specifies a base address for the document. You can then specify URLs within the document as relative to the base address.
<BODY>...</BODY>	Defines all the text and images that make up the page and all items that provide control and formatting for the page.
<HEAD>...</HEAD>	An unordered collection of information about the document.
<HTML>...</HTML>	Identifies the document as containing HTML tags. Should immediately follow the <!DOCTYPE> prologue identifier, if one is present.
<ISINDEX...>	* Identifies document as an index document that can be searched by keyword.
<LINK...>	Indicates a relationship between this document and some other object.
<META...>	* Specifies miscellaneous document information, which can be extracted by servers and clients.

(continued)

(continued)

Open/Close Tag	*Description*
<NEXTID...>	* Numeric identifier generated by text editing software. Similar to the <A NAME=> tag.
<TITLE>...</TITLE>	* Specifies a descriptive title for the HTML document. Required.

* These tags can appear between the <HEAD> ... </HEAD> tags in any order.

Internet Explorer and Netscape Gold extensions

The following tags are extensions to Internet Explorer and Netscape Gold. They probably won't work in other browsers, so use them with care.

Open/Close Tag	*Description*
<APPLET...>...</APPLET>	Specifies the location and other attributes of a pre-compiled, executable applet that can produce live audio, animation, and other Java applications on the web page. (Netscape Navigator 2.0 and later only.)
<BGSOUND...>	Plays a background sound. (Internet Explorer only.)
<EMBED...>	Specifies the location of an embedded Windows object. (Windows version of Netscape Navigator Version 1.1 and later only.)
<FRAME>	Specifies a single frame in a frameset. (Netscape Navigator 2.0 and later only.)
<FRAMESET>...</FRAMESET>	Provides the main container for a frame. (Netscape Navigator 2.0 and later only.)
<MARQUEE...>...</MARQUEE>	Scrolling marquee. (Internet Explorer only.)
<NOFRAMES>...</NOFRAMES>	Alternative view for browsers that don't support frames. (Netscape Navigator 2.0 and later only.)
<SOUND...>	Background sound. (NCSA Mosaic only.)

Form tags

Form tags let you set up user-input forms right on your HTML document. Great for setting up questionnaires and order forms.

Open/Close Tag	*Description*
<FORM...>...</FORM>	Sets up a data input form within a document.
<INPUT...>...</INPUT>	Sets up a user-editable input field.

<OPTION...>...	Used within a <SELECT> tag to let the user choose an option on the form.
<SELECT...>...</SELECT>	Lets the user choose from a set of alternatives created by <OPTION> tags.
<TEXTAREA...>...</TEXTAREA>	Sets up a user-editable input field that can include multiple lines of text.

List tags

Your HTML document can include five types of lists: definition lists, directory lists, menu lists, ordered lists, and unordered lists. All lists can be nested, and each new level will be indented from the previous level.

Open/Close Tag	*Description*
<DIR>...</DIR>	Defines a directory list in which items can contain up to 20 characters each.
<DD>...</DD>	Specifies a definition item in a definition list.
<DL...>...</DL>	Defines a definition list that typically consists of definition terms and definition items.
<DT>...</DT>	Specifies a definition term in a definition list.
<LI>...</LI>	Specifies a list item in a <DIR>, <MENU>, <OL>, or <UL> list.
<MENU>...</MENU>	Defines a menu list of items that typically appear one line per item. Menu lists are more compact than unordered lists.
<OL...>...</OL>	Defines an ordered list that appears with a sequential number next to each list item.
<UL...>...</UL>	Defines an unordered list that usually appears with a bullet next to each list item.

Image tags

These tags put all those pretty pictures into your Web pages.

Open/Close Tag	*Description*
<IMG...>	Incorporates inline graphics into an HTML document.
<MAP...>	Defines the different regions of a client-side image map and indicates the region to which each links. (See Chapter 24 for details.)

Table tags

Tables present information in a tabular format. Not all browsers support tables and tables are tricky to set up. For best results, use Word IA to set up tables.

Open/Close Tag	***Description***
`<CAPTION...>...</CAPTION>`	Specifies the caption for a table.
`<TABLE...>...</TABLE>`	Specifies the start and end of a table.
`<TD...>...</TD>`	Defines the data for a cell in a table row.
`<TH...>...</TH>`	Defines the data for a cell in a table header. Table header cells appear in boldface and are centered by default.
`<TR...>...</TR>`	Specifies the start and end of a table row.

JavaScript References

This appendix provides a quick summary of JavaScript operators, color values, event handlers, and reserved words. For in-depth information on JavaScript objects, methods, and properties, please refer to one of the electronic references described in the sections that follow.

HTML Publishing Bible Electronic JavaScript Reference

I've included a copy of the *HTML Publishing Bible* Electronic JavaScript Reference on the CD-ROM that comes with this book. This reference is, essentially, a Web page. To get around, just click on any available hypertext links. To open the JavaScript reference, do one of the following:

- Open the BrowseMe.htm file on the CD-ROM as discussed in Appendix A. Then click on JavaScript Reference.
- Or, double-click on the javascpt.htm filename from the Windows 95 My Computer, Windows Explorer, or Find file tools.

If you like, you can copy javascpt.htm from the *HTML Publishing Bible* CD-ROM onto your hard disk. Then you can create a shortcut icon to that file for easy access. Once the javascpt.htm file is on your hard disk, you'll be able to use the electronic reference without putting the CD-ROM in your CD-ROM drive.

Other Electronic References

Like most things on the World Wide Web, JavaScript is evolving and changing all the time. The best way to keep up-to-date with JavaScript is to pick a favorite electronic reference. Then download a copy of that reference to your PC from time to time. Here are some of the references available to you:

✦ ***Web Publishing Uncut* JavaScript Electronic Reference.** The latest version of the JavaScript reference included on the *Web Publishing Uncut* CD-ROM is available at `http://www.coolnerds.com`.

✦ **Netscape's JavaScript Handbook.** A "must have!" Point your browser to `http://home.netscape.com/eng/mozilla/Gold/handbook/javascript/index.html`. For a personal copy, download the Zipped Docs from this site to your own PC.

✦ **JavaScript Docs in PDF.** If you have the Adobe Acrobat Reader, check out the PDF docs at `http://www.ipst.com/docs.htm`.

✦ **Learning JavaScript via Windows Online Help.** Find it at `http://www.jchelp.com/javahelp/javahelp.htm`.

✦ **Woo Woo!** Though still under construction while I was writing this book, this online HTML JavaScript manual shows a great deal of promise. Try `http://colt.mech.utah.edu:6666`.

+ - * / ? % ++ -- && || etc. operators

Operators "operate" on values. You deal with operators every day in your regular life — you've probably just never heard them called that. For example, everyone knows that 1+1=2. In that statement, the + sign is the operator. JavaScript offers many operators beyond the basic ones used in arithmetic.

Arithmetic operators

Arithmetic operators act on numbers. Table C-1 lists the arithmetic operators offered in JavaScript and provides examples of each.

Table C-1
JavaScript's Arithmetic Operators

Operator	*Used For*	*Example*	*Equals*
+	Addition	1+2	3
-	Subtraction	12-10	2
*	Multiplication	2*3	6

Operator	Used For	Example	Equals
/	Division	10/3	3.3333333333
%	Modulus	10%3	1
++	Increment	x=5	x = 5
		x++	now x=6
--	Decrement	x=5	x = 5
		x--	now x=4
-	Unary negation	-20	negative 20

The *modulus* of a number is the remainder after the first division. For example, 10/3 results in 3, remainder 1. The modulo (%) operator returns that remainder, 1.

The increment operator, ++, is just a shortcut way of saying *variable* + 1. For example, the two statements that follow mean exactly the same thing. The latter one is just shorter and quicker to type:

```
x = x + 1
x++
```

The same holds true for the decrement (--) operator.

With the negation operator, if the minus sign is used in front of a value without being part of a larger expression, then JavaScript assumes that it indicates a negative number, just as in day-to-day arithmetic. For example

```
x=5
y=-x
```

results in *x* being equal to 5 and *y* being equal to -5.

Assignment operators

To assign a value to a variable, use the simple = operator with the syntax

```
variablename = value
```

For example

```
x=15
y=20
z=x+y
```

After all three lines have been executed, the variable *x* contains the number 15, the variable *y* contains 20, and the variable *z* contains 35 (the sum of 15+20).

Some shorthand operators exist that you can use to do some arithmetic and assign the result to a value in one fell swoop. Those operators are shown in Table C-2.

Table C-2
JavaScript's Assignment Operators

Operator	*Example*	*Means*
+=	x+=y	x=x+y
-=	x-=y	x=x-y
*=	x*=y	x=x*y
/=	x/=y	x=x/y
%	x%=y	x=x%y

Comparison and logical operators

Comparison and logical operators compare two values and return either *true* or *false*. Table C-3 lists the comparison operators. Table C-4 displays the logical operators.

Table C-3
JavaScript's Comparison Operators

Operator	*Meaning*	*Example*
==	is equal to	10==3 is **false**
!=	does not equal	10!=3 is **true**
>	is greater than	10>3 is **true**
>=	is greater than or equal to	10>=3 is **true**
<	is less than	10<3 is **false**
<=	is less than or equal to	10<=3 is **false**

Table C-4
JavaScript's Logical Operators

Operator	*Meaning*	*Example*
&&	AND	x=10 y=5 (x = 10) && (y < 10) is **true**
||	OR	x=10 y=5 (x=10) || (y=10) is **true**
!	NOT	x=10 y=5 x !=y is **true**

String operators

A string is a chunk of text, such as *hello,* rather than a number, such as 10. Unlike numbers, you cannot add, subtract, multiply, and divide strings. Example: 2*3 = 6 is fine. But what is "Hello" * "There"? The question makes no sense.

You can, however, *concatenate* strings, which is a fancy name for "stick them together." You use the + operator to concatenate strings. Here is an example that creates three variables, *x*, *y*, and *z*, all of which contain strings:

```
x="Hello"
y="There"
z=x+y
```

The result is that *z* now contains *HelloThere.*

Why isn't there a space between the words? Because to a computer, strings are just meaningless strings of characters. The string *hello* is no more meaningful than the string *ghfkredg* to a computer. Both are just strings. If you want to add a space between the words, you can pop a space into the expression. A *literal space* would be a space enclosed in quotation marks (" "). Hence, this series of commands

```
x="Hello"
y="There"
z=x+" "+y
```

results in *z* containing *Hello There*. A shortcut operator also exists for string concatenation +=. For example,

```
x="Hello"
y="There"
x+=y
```

results in *x* containing *HelloThere,* because *x+=y* means "*x* equals itself with *y* tacked onto the end. Alternatively, you can do it like this:

```
x="Hello"
y="There"
x+=" "+y
```

in which case *x* equals itself with a space and *y* tacked on. Ergo, *x* then contains *Hello There.*

Conditional operator

JavaScript also contains a conditional operator that assigns a value to a variable based on some condition. The operators for a conditional expression are ? and :, using this syntax:

myvar = (*condition*) ? *value1* : *value2*

For example, the conditional expression that follows is a shorthand way of saying "If the variable named *gender* contains F, then put the string 'Ms.' in the variable named *salutation.* If the variable named *gender* does not contain F, then put the string 'Mr.' into the variable named *salutation*":

salutation = (gender=="*F*") ? "*Ms.*" : "*Mr.*"

Bitwise operators

Bitwise operators treat their values as binary numbers (1s and 0s) rather than as numeric values. You may never need to use these. I never have. I also have yet to see a JavaScript program that uses them. If I were you, I wouldn't waste any brain cell energy trying to memorize them. But just in case you do come across a bitwise operator, Table C-5 shows what each one does.

Table C-5
The JavaScript Bitwise Operators

Operator	*Action*	*Example*
&	bitwise AND	10&3=2
|	bitwise OR	10|3=11
^	bitwise exclusive OR	10^3=9
<<	left shift	10<<3=80
>>	Sign-propagating right shift	10>>3=1
>>>	Zero-fill right shift	10>>>3=1

Some shortcut operators also exist for bitwise assignments, as listed in Table C-6.

Table C-6
The JavaScript Bitwise Assignment Operators

Operator	*Example*	*Means*
<<=	x<<=y	x=x<<y
>>=	x>>=y	x=x>>y
>>>=	x>>>=y	x=x>>>y
&=	x&=y	x=x&y
^=	x^=y	x=x^y
|=	x|=y	x=x|y

Operator precedence

JavaScript operators follow the standard order of precedence. But you can override natural precedence with parentheses. For example,

```
5+3*10
```

equals 35 because the multiplication is naturally carried out first (according to the rules of precedence). That is, the machine first evaluates 10*3, which equals 30, and then adds 5 to that to get 35. This expression has a different result:

```
(5+3)*10
```

This expression results in 80 because the parentheses force the addition to be carried out first (5+3 equals 8). That result then is multiplied by 10 to result in 80. Table C-7 shows the order of precedence of the operators, from highest to lowest, when you do not use parentheses in an expression. Operators at the same level of precedence within an expression are carried out in left-to-right order.

Table C-7
JavaScript Operators Order of Precedence

Action	*Operator(s)*
call, member	(),[]
negation/increment	! ~- ++ --
multiply/divide	* / %
addition/subtraction	+ -
bitwise shift	<< >> >>>
comparison	< <= > >=
equality	== !=
bitwise AND	&
bitwise XOR	^
bitwise OR	|
logical AND	&&
logical OR	||
conditional	?:
assignment	= += -= *= /= %= <<= >>= >>>= &= ^= |=
comma	,

Color Values

Use the color names in Table C-8 to specify colors in the JavaScript *alinkColor, bgColor, fgColor, linkColor,* and *vlinkColor* properties and the *fontcolor* method. Although you *can* use the string literals in HTML tags, not all browsers can interpret the literals.

Table C-8
JavaScript Color Literals and Triplets

Color String Literal	Triplet	Color String Literal	Triplet
aliceblue	F0F8FF	antiquewhite	FAEBD7
aqua	00FFFF	aquamarine	7FFFD4
azure	F0FFFF	beige	F5F5DC
bisque	FFE4C4	black	000000
blanchedalmond	FFEBCD	blue	0000FF
blueviolet	8A2BE2	brown	A52A2A
burlywood	DEB887	cadetblue	5F9EA0
chartreuse	7FFF00	chocolate	D2691E
coral	FF7F50	cornflowerblue	6495ED
cornsilk	FFF8DC	crimson	DC143C
cyan	00FFFF	darkblue	00008B
darkcyan	008B8B	darkgoldenrod	B8860B
darkgray	A9A9A9	darkgreen	006400
darkkhaki	BDB76B	darkmagenta	8B008B
darkolivegreen	556B2F	darkorange	FF8C00
darkorchid	9932CC	darkred	8B0000
darksalmon	E9967A	darkseagreen	8FBC8F
darkslateblue	483D8B	darkslategray	2F4F4F
darkturquoise	00CED1	darkviolet	9400D3
deeppink	FF1493	deepskyblue	00BFFF
dimgray	696969	dodgerblue	1E900FF
firebrick	B22222	floralwhite	FFFAF0
forestgreen	228B22	fuchsia	FF00FF
gainsboro	DCDCDC	ghostwhite	F8F8FF
gold	FFD700	goldenrod	DAA520
gray	808080	green	008000
greenyellow	ADFF2F	honeydew	F0FFF0
hotpink	FF69B4	indianred	CD5C5C
indigo	4B0082	ivory	FFFFF0

(continued)

Table C-8 (continued)			
Color String Literal	***Triplet***	***Color String Literal***	***Triplet***
khaki	F0E68C	lavender	E6E6FA
lavenderblush	FFF0F5	lawngreen	7CFC00
lemonchiffon	FFFACD	lightblue	ADD8E6
lightcoral	F08080	lightcyan	E0FFFF
lightgoldenrodyellow	FAFAD2	lightgreen	90EE90
lightgrey	D3D3D3	lightpink	FFB6C1
lightsalmon	FFA07A	lightseagreen	200B2AA
lightskyblue	87CEFA	lightslategray	778899
lightsteelblue	B00C4DE	lightyellow	FFFFE0
lime	00FF00	limegreen	32CD32
linen	FAF0E6	magenta	FF00FF
maroon	8000000	mediumaquamarine	66CDAA
mediumblue	0000CD	mediumorchid	BA55D3
mediumpurple	9370DB	mediumseagreen	3CB371
mediumslateblue	7B68EE	mediumspringgreen	00FA9A
mediumturquoise	48D1CC	mediumvioletred	C71585
midnightblue	1919700	mintcream	F5FFFA
mistyrose	FFE4E1	moccasin	FFE4B5
navajowhite	FFDEAD	navy	000080
oldlace	FDF5E6	olive	808000
olivedrab	6B8E23	orange	FFA500
orangered	FF4500	orchid	DA70D6
palegoldenrod	EEE8AA	palegreen	98FB98
paleturquoise	AFEEEE	palevioletred	DB7093
papayawhip	FFEFD5	peachpuff	FFDAB9
peru	CD853F	pink	FFC0CB
plum	DDA0DD	powderblue	B0E0E6
purple	800080	red	FF0000
rosybrown	BC8F8F	royalblue	4169E1
saddlebrown	8B4513	salmon	FA8072
sandybrown	F4A460	seagreen	2E8B57

Color String Literal	Triplet	Color String Literal	Triplet
seashell	FFF5EE	sienna	A0522D
silver	C0C0C0	skyblue	87CEEB
slateblue	6A5ACD	slategray	708090
snow	FFFAFA	springgreen	00FF7F
steelblue	4682B4	tan	D2B48C
teal	008080	thistle	D8BFD8
tomato	FF6347	turquoise	40E0D0
violet	EE82EE	wheat	F5DEB3
white	FFFFFF	whitesmoke	F5F5F5
yellow	FFFF00	yellowgreen	9ACD32

Event Handlers

Event handlers are used in HTML tags, such as `<INPUT>` and `<BODY>`, to execute JavaScript code in response to some event that occurs in the reader's page. Table C-9 summarizes the event handlers, what actions trigger them, and the tags that can use them.

Table C-9
Summary of JavaScript Event Handlers

Event Handler	When Triggered	Used in Tags of These Objects
onBlur	When the reader moves the insertion point out of a field	select, text, textarea
onChange	After the reader changes the contents of a field and moves on to another field	select, text, textarea
onClick	When the reader clicks on an item	button, checkbox, radio, link, reset, submit
onFocus	When the reader moves the insertion point into a field	select, text, textarea
onLoad	When a document is loaded into view	window (`<BODY>`, `<FRAMESET>`)

(continued)

Table C-9 *(continued)*

Event Handler	*When Triggered*	*Used in Tags of These Objects*
onMouseOver	When the reader points to a hyperlink	link (<A> . . . </A>)
onSelect	When the reader selects text within a text or text area field	text, textarea
onSubmit	When the reader submits a form	form (<FORM>)
onUnload	When the reader exits a document	window (<BODY>, <FRAMESET>)

Reserved Words

These words have special meaning in JavaScript and cannot be used as variable names, function names, methods, or object names. Some are not used in current JavaScript but are reserved for future use.

abstract	boolean	break	byte	case	catch
char	class	const	continue	default	do
double	else	extends	false	final	finally
float	for	function	goto	if	implements
import	in	instanceof	int	interface	long
native	new	null	package	private	protected
public	return	short	static	super	switch
synchronized	this	throw	throws	transient	true
try	var	void	while	with	

Index

G

H

(continued)

P

Q

R

S

(continued)

T

U

V

W

(continued)

Y

Z

IDG BOOKS WORLDWIDE, INC. END-USER LICENSE AGREEMENT

<u>Read This</u>. You should carefully read these terms and conditions before opening the software packet(s) included with this book ("Book"). This is a license agreement ("Agreement") between you and IDG Books Worldwide, Inc. ("IDGB"). By opening the accompanying software packet(s), you acknowledge that you have read and accept the following terms and conditions. If you do not agree and do not want to be bound by such terms and conditions, promptly return the Book and the unopened software packet(s) to the place you obtained them for a full refund.

1. **<u>License Grant</u>.** IDGB grants to you (either an individual or entity) a nonexclusive license to use one copy of the enclosed software program(s) (collectively, the "Software") solely for your own personal or business purposes on a single computer (whether a standard computer or a workstation component of a multi-user network). The Software is in use on a computer when it is loaded into temporary memory (that is, RAM) or installed into permanent memory (for example, hard disk, CD-ROM, or other storage device). IDGB reserves all rights not expressly granted herein.

2. **<u>Ownership</u>.** IDGB is the owner of all right, title, and interest, including copyright, in and to the compilation of the Software recorded on the CD-ROM. Copyright to the individual programs on the CD-ROM is owned by the author or other authorized copyright owner of each program. Ownership of the Software and all proprietary rights relating thereto remain with IDGB and its licensors.

3. **<u>Restrictions on Use and Transfer</u>.**

   (a) You may only (i) make one copy of the Software for backup or archival purposes, or (ii) transfer the Software to a single hard disk, provided that you keep the original for backup or archival purposes. You may not (i) rent or lease the Software, (ii) copy or reproduce the Software through a LAN or other network system or through any computer subscriber system or bulletin-board system, or (iii) modify, adapt, or create derivative works based on the Software.

   (b) You may not reverse engineer, decompile, or disassemble the Software. You may transfer the Software and user documentation on a permanent basis, provided that the transferee agrees to accept the terms and conditions of this Agreement and you retain no copies. If the Software is an update or has been updated, any transfer must include the most recent update and all prior versions.

4. **<u>Restrictions on Use of Individual Programs</u>.** You must follow the individual requirements and restrictions detailed for each individual program. These limitations are contained in the individual license agreements recorded on the CD-ROM. These restrictions include a requirement that after using the program for the period of time specified in its text, the user must pay a registration fee or discontinue use. By opening the Software packet(s), you will be agreeing to abide by the licenses and restrictions for these individual programs. None of the material on this disc or listed in this Book may ever be distributed, in original or modified form, for commercial purposes.

5. **<u>Limited Warranty</u>.**

   (a) IDGB warrants that the Software and CD-ROM are free from defects in materials and workmanship under normal use for a period of sixty (60) days from the date of purchase of this Book. If IDGB receives notification within the warranty period of defects in materials or workmanship, IDGB will replace the defective CD-ROM.

   (b) IDGB AND THE AUTHOR OF THE BOOK DISCLAIM ALL OTHER WARRANTIES, EXPRESS OR IMPLIED, INCLUDING WITHOUT LIMITATION IMPLIED WARRANTIES OF MERCHANTABILITY AND FITNESS FOR A PARTICULAR PURPOSE, WITH RESPECT TO THE SOFTWARE, THE PROGRAMS, THE SOURCE CODE CONTAINED THEREIN, AND/OR THE TECHNIQUES DESCRIBED IN THIS BOOK. IDGB DOES NOT WARRANT THAT THE FUNCTIONS CONTAINED IN THE SOFTWARE WILL MEET YOUR REQUIREMENTS OR THAT THE OPERATION OF THE SOFTWARE WILL BE ERROR FREE.

   (c) This limited warranty gives you specific legal rights, and you may have other rights which vary from jurisdiction to jurisdiction.

6. **<u>Remedies</u>.**

   (a) IDGB's entire liability and your exclusive remedy for defects in materials and workmanship shall be limited to replacement of the Software, which is returned to IDGB at the address set forth below with a copy of your receipt. This Limited Warranty is void if failure of the Software has resulted from accident, abuse, or misapplication. Any replacement Software will be warranted for the remainder of the original warranty period or thirty (30) days, whichever is longer.

   (b) In no event shall IDGB or the author be liable for any damages whatsoever (including without limitation damages for loss of business profits, business interruption, loss of business information, or any other pecuniary loss) arising out of the use of or inability to use the Book or the Software, even if IDGB has been advised of the possibility of such damages.

   (c) Because some jurisdictions do not allow the exclusion or limitation of liability for consequential or incidental damages, the above limitation or exclusion may not apply to you.

7. **<u>U.S. Government Restricted Rights</u>.** Use, duplication, or disclosure of the Software by the U.S. Government is subject to restrictions stated in paragraph (c) (1) (ii) of the Rights in Technical Data and Computer Software clause of DFARS 252.227-7013, and in subparagraphs (a) through (d) of the Commercial Computer—Restricted Rights clause at FAR 52.227-19, and in similar clauses in the NASA FAR supplement, when applicable.

8. **<u>General</u>.** This Agreement constitutes the entire understanding of the parties and revokes and supersedes all prior agreements, oral or written, between them and may not be modified or amended except in a writing signed by both parties hereto which specifically refers to this Agreement. This Agreement shall take precedence over any other documents that may be in conflict herewith. If any one or more provisions contained in this Agreement are held by any court or tribunal to be invalid, illegal, or otherwise unenforceable, each and every other provision shall remain in full force and effect.

Installation instructions

Please read Appendix A for complete installation instructions and information about the files on the CD-ROM.

IDG BOOKS WORLDWIDE REGISTRATION CARD

RETURN THIS
REGISTRATION CARD
FOR FREE CATALOG

Title of this book: HTML Publishing Bible, Windows® 95 Edition

My overall rating of this book: ❑ Very good [1] ❑ Good [2] ❑ Satisfactory [3] ❑ Fair [4] ❑ Poor [5]

How I first heard about this book:

❑ Found in bookstore; name: [6] ________

❑ Book review: [7] ________

❑ Advertisement: [8] ________

❑ Catalog: [9] ________

❑ Word of mouth; heard about book from friend, co-worker, etc.: [10] ________

❑ Other: [11] ________

What I liked most about this book: ________

What I would change, add, delete, etc., in future editions of this book: ________

Other comments: ________

Number of computer books I purchase in a year: ❑ 1 [12] ❑ 2-5 [13] ❑ 6-10 [14] ❑ More than 10 [15]

I would characterize my computer skills as: ❑ Beginner [16] ❑ Intermediate [17] ❑ Advanced [18] ❑ Professional [19]

I use ❑ DOS [20] ❑ Windows [21] ❑ OS/2 [22] ❑ Unix [23] ❑ Macintosh [24] ❑ Other: [25] ________ (please specify)

I would be interested in new books on the following subjects:
(please check all that apply, and use the spaces provided to identify specific software)

❑ Word processing: [26] ________

❑ Spreadsheets: [27] ________

❑ Data bases: [28] ________

❑ Desktop publishing: [29] ________

❑ File Utilities: [30] ________

❑ Money management: [31] ________

❑ Networking: [32] ________

❑ Programming languages: [33] ________

❑ Other: [34] ________

I use a PC at (please check all that apply): ❑ home [35] ❑ work [36] ❑ school [37] ❑ other: [38] ________

The disks I prefer to use are ❑ 5.25 [39] ❑ 3.5 [40] ❑ other: [41] ________

I have a CD ROM: ❑ yes [42] ❑ no [43]

I plan to buy or upgrade computer hardware this year: ❑ yes [44] ❑ no [45]

I plan to buy or upgrade computer software this year: ❑ yes [46] ❑ no [47]

Name: ________ Business title: [48] ________ Type of Business: [49] ________

Address (❑ home [50] ❑ work [51]/Company name: ________)

Street/Suite# ________

City [52]/State [53]/Zipcode [54]: ________ Country [55] ________

❑ **I liked this book!** You may quote me by name in future IDG Books Worldwide promotional materials.

My daytime phone number is ________

IDG BOOKS

THE WORLD OF COMPUTER KNOWLEDGE

YES!

Please keep me informed about IDG's World of Computer Knowledge. Send me the latest IDG Books catalog.

NO POSTAGE NECESSARY IF MAILED IN THE UNITED STATES

BUSINESS REPLY MAIL

FIRST CLASS MAIL PERMIT NO. 2605 FOSTER CITY, CALIFORNIA

IDG Books Worldwide
919 E Hillsdale Blvd, STE 400
Foster City, CA 94404-9691